There is substantial disagreement among policy makers about how governments should respond to the problem of high unemployment. Thus far there has been little, if any, systematic attempt to evaluate the strengths and weaknesses of the main unemployment policies available to governments in market economies. Individual policy recommendations are usually made in isolation from one another. This book attempts to provide a balanced assessment of the various policy options, including the following: demand management versus supply-side policy, subsidising employment and training, reforming labour market regulations and unemployment benefit systems, changing the structure of taxation and restructuring various welfare state provisions. The book also examines the political economy of unemployment policy, the policy implications of technological change and international trade, the relation between unemployment and productivity growth, and the significance of job reallocation for unemployment policy.

Unemployment policy

Consorcio de la Zona Franca de Vigo

'El Consorcio de la Zona Franca de Vigo' is a state-run corporation established by law on 20 June 1947 by the Spanish Government. The Consorcio acts as a development agency for the Vigo area, collaborating with public and private organisations to promote entrepreneurial activities.

'El Consorcio' is currently working on different projects to diversify the sites available for industrial location in the area (industrial parks and a technology park). 'El Consorcio' also supports the formation of innovative companies through its participation in a Business Innovation Center and a Venture Capital company and it invests directly in R&D projects. It also coordinates and finances initiatives to improve and rebuild old city districts.

'El Consorcio de la Zona Franca de Vigo' organises seminars, conferences and courses as well as publishing papers on subjects related to its activities.

Executive Committee

Chairman
Francisco López Peña, Special State Delegate

October 1996

Centre for Economic Policy Research

The Centre for Economic Policy Research is a network of over 300 Research Fellows, based primarily in European universities. The Centre coordinates its Fellows' research activities and communicates their results to the public and private sectors. CEPR is an entrepreneur, developing research initiatives with the producers, consumers and sponsors of research. Established in 1983, CEPR is a European economics research organisation with uniquely wide-ranging scope and activities.

CEPR is a registered educational charity. Institutional (core) finance for the Centre is provided by major grants from the Economic and Social Research Council, under which an ESRC Resource Centre operates within CEPR; the Esmée Fairbairn Charitable Trust; the Bank of England; the European Monetary Institute and the Bank for International Settlements; 18 national central banks and 39 companies. None of these organisations gives prior review to the Centre's publications, nor do they necessarily endorse the views expressed therein.

The Centre is pluralist and non-partisan, bringing economic research to bear on the analysis of medium- and long-run policy questions. CEPR research may include views on policy, but the Executive Committee of the Centre does not give prior review to its publications, and the Centre takes no institutional policy positions. The opinions expressed in this volume are those of the authors and not those of the Centre for Economic Policy Research.

Unemployment policy: government options for the labour market

Edited by

DENNIS J. SNOWER

and

GUILLERMO DE LA DEHESA

Published by the Press Syndicate of the University of Cambridge
The Pitt Building, Trumpington Street, Cambridge CB2 1RP, United Kingdom

Cambridge University Press
The Edinburgh Building, Cambridge, CB2 2RU, United Kingdom
40 West 20th Street, New York, NY 10011-4211, USA
10 Stamford Road, Oakleigh, Melbourne 3166, Australia

First published 1997

Printed in Great Britain at the University Press, Cambridge

Typeset in Times Roman

A catalogue record for this book is available from the British Library

Library of Congress Cataloguing in Publication data

Unemployment policy: government options for the labour market / edited by Dennis J. Snower and Guillermo de la Dehesa.
p. cm.
Includes bibliographical references and index.
ISBN 0 521 57139 1
1. Manpower policy – United States.
2. Manpower policy – Great Britain.
3. Manpower policy – Europe
I. Snower, Dennis J. II. Dehesa, Guillermo de la.
HD5724.U613 1997
331.13′77 – dc20 96-43913 CIP

ISBN 0 521 57139 1 hardback
ISBN 0 521 59921 0 paperback

CE

Contents

Figures

Tables

Preface

When it comes to unemployment, economists and policy makers have lost their innocence. There was a time when broad agreement prevailed on what caused unemployment, and what governments should do about it. Since then we have awoken from this comforting dream and have come to recognise that unemployment can have a wide variety of potential causes, matched by a similar variety of policy responses. The trouble is that, in practice, the causes are difficult to identify and the policies difficult to evaluate. This bewildering state of affairs provides the rationale for this book, made possible by the generous financial support of Consorcio de la Zona Franca de Vigo. Its aim is to provide an overview of the available unemployment policies, a rigorous analysis of how they work, and an assessment of their robustness in the face of unemployment's multiple causes.

Before embarking on this undertaking, it is important to be aware from where we have come. The world used to be so simple. In the first two decades of the postwar period, economists were agreed that governments could spend their way out of unemployment. Their diagnosis was straightforward and so was their policy prescription: unemployment was due to an insufficient demand for labour, and firms were not demanding enough labour because there was an insufficient demand for their products. So, if the private sector of the economy was not spending enough, then the government could reduce unemployment by spending more itself. Any type of spending would do the trick – even, as Keynes suggested, spending on pointless things such as pyramids, wars, burying bottles – for it would raise people's income, thereby leading them to demand more goods and services and thus inducing the firms to hire more people.

This Keynesian vision evaporated in the early 1970s, amidst rising inflation and growing government budget deficits. Slowly a new consensus began to emerge, according to which movements in unemployment could be understood as random fluctuations around a 'natural rate of unemployment', determined by supply-side factors such as labour market regulations, union density, and labour mobility. Supply-side policies might reduce the natural rate by mitigating labour market rigidities, but they could do so only gradually and incrementally. Demand-side policies, by contrast, were said to have at most a temporary effect on unemployment, primarily by generating random fluctuations around the natural rate. In this context, Keynesian demand management had little, if any useful role to play. Once again, the policy prescription was straightforward: stop interfering with the forces of competition and free enterprise, perhaps encourage training, investment and other supply-side factors, and otherwise put up with whatever the resulting unemployment rate turns out to be.

The European unemployment experience of the 1980s has posed some difficulties for the natural rate theory. In most European countries during this period, labour market rigidities – measured in terms of job security legislation, union density, labour market regulation, and so on – either declined or remained constant, while unemployment rose for most of the decade. If the European natural rate of unemployment had risen, it was somewhat of a mystery why this had happened. If it hadn't risen, the mystery was why European unemployment had increased anyway.

Since then, there has been a proliferation of unemployment theories and policy prescriptions. Some economists view today's unemployment problem as the result of skill-biased technological change or the expansion of international trade in the presence of labour market frictions. Others focus on the market power of employees, supported by union actions and labour turnover costs. Others concentrate on wage formation under asymmetric information. Yet others argue that, since wages and prices are often sluggish, a drop in spending might create unemployment of the Keynesian variety. And so on.

In view of this fragmentation of perspectives, policy makers appear to have become increasingly disillusioned by unemployment theory. As a result, unemployment policies often rest more heavily on the instincts of politicians and civil servants than on rigorous economic analysis. In turn, many of the academic economists in the field appear to have retreated to their ivory towers. It has become increasingly common for their work to deliver ample analytical bravado, while allowing policy conclusions to degenerate into vague generalisations and afterthoughts in the concluding sections of academic journal articles.

This book is an attempt to swim against this tide. In it, major contributors to the unemployment literature explain their positions in terms easily accessible to the educated layperson, without sacrificing intellectual rigour. The result, hopefully, is a lucid picture of the policy instruments available for combating unemployment, and a reasoned assessment of their effectiveness.

Dennis J. Snower
Guillermo de la Dehesa

October 1996

Acknowledgements

The editors and publishers acknowledge with thanks permission to reproduce the following copyright material.

OECD, for figures D5.1–D5.4 and 11.5, and tables 10.3, 10.4, 10.9, 11.1 and 15.1, from *Economic Survey*, *Economic Outlook*, *Labour Force Survey and Employment Outlook*, various issues.

EUROSTAT, for figure 8.4.

Brookings Papers on Economics, for figure 13.1, and *Brookings Papers on Microeconomics*, for figure 16.4.

ILO Yearbook, for figure 10.1.

UN, *International Trade Statistics* and *International Trade Statistics Yearbook*, for figures 16.2 and 16.3.

NBER, Trade and Immigration Data Base, for figure 16.4.

Economie et Prévision, for figures 8.1 and 8.2, from B. Maillard and H. Sneessens, 'Caractéristiques de l'emploi et du chômage par PCS: France, 1962–1989' (1994).

Journal of Economic Literature, for figure 8.3, from F. Levy and R.J. Murnane, 'US earnings levels and earnings inequality: a review of recent trends and proposed explanations' (1992).

OECD, for figure 11.5.

Boston College, for table 7.1, from P. Gottschalk and M. Joyce, 'Is earning inequality also rising in other industrialized countries?' (1992).

Current Population Survey (1990), for table 7.2 and D9.1.

CERC (1991), for table 8.1 and 8.5.

Oxford University Press, for tables 8.2, 10.1 and 10.8 from P.R.G. Layard *et al.*, *Unemployment: Macroeconomic Performance and the Labour Market* (1991).

Statisches Bundesamt, for table 8.3.

US Bureau of Labour Statistics (1993), for table 8.4.

OECD, for table 8.6, from *Economic Perspectives* (1993).

Oxford University, for table 9.2, from S.J. Nickell and B. Bell, 'Would cutting payroll taxes on the unskilled have a significant effect on unemployment?' (1994).

Statistics Canada, for table D9.1.

Insee, for table D9.1.

OECD (Germany), for table D9.1.

Confindustria, for table D9.1.

Labour Force Survey, for table D9.1.

NBER, for table 10.3, from S.J. Davies, 'Cross-country patterns of change in relative wages' (1992).

General Household Survey, data tapes, for tables 10.6, 10.7 and 10.8.

CBI, *Industrial Trends Survey*, for table 10.9.

Quarterly Journal of Economics, for table 15.1, from S.J. Davis and J. Haltiwanger, 'Gross job creation, gross job destruction, and employment reallocation' (1992).

Economic Policy, for table 15.1, from J. Leonard and M. Van Audenrode, 'Corporatism run amok: job stability and industrial policy in Belgium and the United States' (1993).

Social Security Statistics, various years, for table 10.8.

American Economic Review, for table D8.1, from S.J. Nickell and B. Bell, 'Changes in the distribution of wages and unemployment in OECD countries' (1996).

List of conference participants

George Alogoskoufis *Athens University of Economics and Business and CEPR*
Charles R. Bean *London School of Economics and CEPR*
Brian Bell *Nuffield College, Oxford*
Samuel Bentolila *Centro de Estudios Monetarios y Financieros*
Giuseppe Bertola *Università di Torino and CEPR*
Olivier J. Blanchard *Massachusetts Institute of Technology*
Alison L. Booth *ESRC Research Centre for Micro-social Change, University of Essex, and CEPR*
P. Buitelaar *De Nederlandsche Bank*
Michael Burda *Humboldt Universität zu Berlin and CEPR*
Juan J. R. Calaza *CERPEM, Paris*
David T. Coe *International Monetary Fund*
Daniel Cohen *CEPREMAP, Paris, and CEPR*
Guillermo de la Dehesa *Banco Pastor and CEPR*
Juan José Dolado *Banco de España and CEPR*
Jacques H. Drèze *CORE, Louvain-la-Neuve*
Jeff Frank *Royal Holloway, London*
Robert J. Gordon *Northwestern University and CEPR*
Jonathan Haskel *Queen Mary and Westfield College, London, and CEPR*
Zmira Hornstein *UK Department of Employment*
Richard Jackman *London School of Economics*
Richard Layard *London School of Economics*
Edmond Malinvaud *INSEE-CREST*
Alan Manning *London School of Economics and CEPR*
Patrick Minford *University of Liverpool and CEPR*
Dale T. Mortensen *Northwestern University*
Stephen J. Nickell *Institute of Economics and Statistics, Oxford, and CEPR*
Edmund S. Phelps *Columbia University*

Christopher Pissarides *London School of Economics and CEPR*
Rafael Repullo *CEMFI, Madrid, and CEPR*
Ana L. Revenga *The World Bank*
Gilles Saint-Paul *DELTA, Paris, and CEPR*
Christoph M. Schmidt *SELAPO, Universität München, and CEPR*
Eric Smith *University of Essex*
Dennis J. Snower *Birkbeck College, London, and CEPR*
Romesh Vaitilingam *CEPR*
Pilar Diaz-Vazquez *Birkbeck College, London*
Brendan Walsh *University College Dublin*
Klaus F. Zimmermann *SELAPO, Universität München, and CEPR*

1 Introduction

GUILLERMO DE LA DEHESA and
DENNIS J. SNOWER

1 Purpose of the volume

Large-scale unemployment has become the prime social, economic and political issue in Europe and a number of other OECD regions. It is a colossal waste of human potential and national product; it is responsible for poverty and inequality; it erodes human capital; it creates social and political tensions wherever it strikes. In the last few years a large number of books, reports and papers has been published, most of them attempting to analyse the ascent of European unemployment, but very few have focused on the policies necessary to reduce it. This volume is an attempt to fill this gap.

In most countries where unemployment is a major problem, it is product of several simultaneous causes, each of which interact with the rest: small wonder that unemployment policies are difficult to design. Moreover, many policies that could improve economic efficiency are not politically implementable. The political realities dictate that it is not enough to find policies that give more jobs for those currently unemployed than they take away from those currently employed; it is vital that those who stand to gain are in the political majority.

This volume attempts to deal with these problems head-on, and this requires a break with a hoary academic tradition. The tradition is to write papers that develop detailed theoretical and empirical models of unemployment and to include a short section at the end about vague 'policy implications'. Unemployment theoreticians and econometricians largely ignore the policy makers, and the latter – understandably – return the compliment.

While this book recognises the critical importance of theory and empirical analysis in isolating the sources of unemployment and deriving the associated policy responses, the emphasis is on the policy. Here academics are speaking not only to each other, but to the policy makers. Although the arguments are rigorous, based on formal models, the bulk of the exposition is accessible to readers with little technical background: sections containing formal models can be skipped without loss of continuity or comprehension. To achieve a balanced assessment of the various policy options, the chapters are each followed by critical, evaluative discussions by economists bringing a fresh slant and a different persuasion to the subject.

In many important respects, countries with high unemployment – in Europe and elsewhere in the OECD – face a number of common problems:

- how to create new employment opportunities without reducing existing oncs;
- how to promote more equal employment opportunities for those out of work: the short-term versus the long-term unemployed, the youth entering the labour force versus older employees who have been laid off;
- how to create more skilled, relatively well-paid jobs and to promote the education and training necessary for these jobs;
- how to induce the private sector to adapt its jobs promptly to changes in market conditions; and
- how to avoid the need for large and expensive government provision of employment in order to take people off the unemployment register.

Different countries have dealt with these problems in very different ways. Some have concentrated on supply-side policies in an attempt to improve the productivity of their workforce; others have relied more heavily on demand-management policies in order to create the product demand necessary for the creation of new jobs; others have subsidised the creation of jobs of various sorts; yet others have experimented with a variety of policies aimed at changing labour market institutions with a view to creating more employment opportunities.

Considering the diversity in economic institutions and policy goals from country to country, this disparity in employment policy approaches is hardly surprising. What is surprising, however, is that the existing policies are generally not responses to specific diagnoses of where the prevailing unemployment comes, where the resulting inefficiencies and inequities lie, and which measures can tackle these problems without creating another set of potentially even more serious inefficiencies and inequities. Recently, for example, policy makers in several European countries have shifted their focus of attention to the task of spreading the cost of unemployment across the population, through jobsharing and early retirement programmes. The implicit, underlying assessment is that the existing unemployment is inevitable and that employment policy should be relegated to the distribution of the resulting hardship. Such an assessment is at variance with the analysis of many economists, who have articulated a portfolio of measures for creating more jobs with satisfying career prospects. It is often apparent that policy is formulated and designed in isolation from the best current economic thinking on the subject.

Furthermore, policy makers are often not aware of the full range of policy instruments that can be used to create employment and thereby promote competitiveness, social solidarity, and growth. Different countries have tended to focus attention on different groups of measures, but the policy choice is often not grounded in a full understanding of the complete range of possibilities available. These include demand-management policies, productivity-enhancing supply-side policies, wage subsidies, recruitment vouchers, training subsidies, policies to make more credit available to unskilled workers, reductions in payroll taxes, government employment and training programmes, changes in job security legislation, reform of unemployment benefit and welfare systems, reform of wage-bargaining systems, negative income taxes and basic income guarantees.

Each of these policy options is covered in this volume. After two overviews of the economic and political prerequisites for unemployment policies in Part One, we cover demand-management and supply-side policies in Part Two, a wide variety of subsidies, vouchers and tax breaks in Part Three, and labour market institutions in Part Four. Finally, Part Five examines the relation between unemployment, productivity and job reallocation and Part Six provides a comparative evaluation of different unemployment policies.

Some major causes of unemployment are unemployment policies themselves. Frequently, policies designed to combat unemployment or the effects of unemployment – ranging from unemployment benefits and other welfare state entitlements, to job security legislation, to tax and transfer systems – introduce inefficiencies that serve to increase unemployment. Many informed observers believe that unemployment could be reduced in many countries where it is a serious problem by changing the policy design so as to give firms more incentive to take on employees and unemployed people more incentive to search for jobs – all without necessarily increasing the government's budgetary outlay or ignoring the realities of the political process. This book attempts to provide a balanced, rigorous assessment on how well founded this belief is.

2 An overview of the volume

This volume has a transparent story-line: after two chapters on general policy issues, it examines a wide variety of different policy approaches, then turns to the implications for job reallocation and the unemployment–productivity relation, and concludes with two chapters comparing the effectiveness of alternative policies.

Part One, dealing with general policy issues, begins with a survey, 'Evaluating unemployment policies: what do the underlying theories tell us?', by Dennis J. Snower (chapter 2). This survey is based on a simple idea that has received little attention in the literature on unemployment policy; different unemployment policies are generally based on different theories of unemployment, and our confidence in a policy should depend – at least in part – on the ability of the underlying theory to account for some prominent empirical regularities in unemployment behaviour. Accordingly, chapter 2 evaluates unemployment policies for advanced market economies by examining the predictions of the underlying macroeconomic theories.

Chapter 2 considers four policy types: (1) The *laissez-faire* policy stance implies that the government should do little or nothing to influence unemployment. It is supported by the traditional natural rate theory, the intertemporal substitution theory, and the real business cycle theory. (2) *Demand-management policies*, based on Keynesian and New-Keynesian theories, as well as recent developments concerning transmission mechanisms between labour and product markets, cover both government employment and macroeconomic policies aimed at changing product demand. (3) *Supply-side policies*, designed to raise the productivity of workers across the board, cover a variety of measures ranging from reductions in payroll taxes to government infrastructure investment to improvements in information dissemination. The chapter shows how the influence of these policies may be analysed through search theory, implicit contract theory, and efficiency wage theory. (4) *Institutional policies* aim to change labour market institutions so as to reduce unemployment. Labour union theories, bargaining theories and insider–outsider theories can shed light on how these policies operate. The policies include reform of wage-bargaining systems, measures to reduce labour turnover costs, job search support for the long-term unemployed, worksharing, early retirement, policies to reduce barriers to the creation of new firms, profit sharing, reform of unemployment benefit systems, recruitment subsidies, training subsidies, and benefit transfers.

In chapter 3, 'High unemployment from a political economy perspective', Gilles Saint-Paul addresses the following question: as unemployment is recognised to be a serious problem in many OECD countries, why don't governments do more about it? And why do they often deal with the unemployment problem by implementing policies that make the problem worse? Saint-Paul's answer is that economic policies are the outcome of a political process, and those which benefit primarily the unemployed – who are a poorly organised, heterogeneous voting minority – are unlikely to see the light of day. On the other hand, policies that increase labour market rigidities, such as high firing costs, high minimum wages and high payroll taxes, may find the support of the majority of the voters.

According to Saint-Paul, politically successful policies to reduce unemployment must get the support of the unemployed, and this support will be given more readily, the more the employed people are exposed to unemployment. Such exposure depends less on the level of unemployment than on the rate at which unemployment is changing. Saint-Paul discusses various examples of unemployment policies that are affected by these political constraints, such as the reduction of firing costs, the reduction of minimum wages, the reduction of payroll taxes and the conversion of unemployment benefits into employment subsidies. He concludes that the European unemployment problem is less a problem of deficient understanding than a lack of political concern. From this analysis, he derives political prerequisites for successful employment policy.

Part Two, on demand management and supply-side policy, begins with a chapter on 'The role of demand-management policies in reducing unemployment', by Charles Bean (chapter 4). He argues that while the evidence suggests that contractionary demand shocks are partly to blame for the high levels of European unemployment, the potential effectiveness of activist policies is limited by the presence of mechanisms that make unemployment persistent. In isolation, furthermore, these policies can do nothing to tackle the significant fraction of shocks due to adverse supply or structural developments. However, if appropriate supply-side policies are introduced, Bean argues, supportive demand-management policies can speed the reduction in unemployment. The chapter considers what such supportive demand management policy should look like, and argues that in some cases a mild, although temporary, increase in inflation may be appropriate. The implications of uncertainty about the long-run unemployment rate are also considered. Bean argues that such supportive policies are probably best sustained through monetary rather than fiscal policies and are likely to require changes in intra-European real exchange rates. Consequently, a rapid move to full monetary union may be ill-advised. Finally, a potential role for temporary incomes policies is also identified.

In chapter 5, 'Edmund Phelps' theory of structural slumps and its policy implications', Edmond Malinvaud reviews Phelps' recent work (Phelps, 1994), developing a structuralist theory of how the natural rate of unemployment is disturbed by real demand and supply shocks (foreign and domestic). Malinvaud observes that, of the two traditional macroeconomic instruments, Phelps considers primarily fiscal policy as a medium-run discretionary instrument to stimulate employment. Malinvaud thinks that this view is too extreme and that, to achieve a given path of real interest rates, the interaction of fiscal and monetary policy is essential. More attention, in Malinvaud's view, should also be paid to microeconomic policies in changing the structure of the labour market.

Part Three deals with specific policy proposals centring on various ways to subsidise employment and training.

In chapter 6, 'The simple economics of benefit transfers', Dennis Snower proposes to give long-term unemployed people the option of transferring a fraction of unemployment benefits, which currently impose an implicit tax on work, into employment vouchers for firms that hire them. This Benefit Transfer Programme (BPT) – that has been partially implemented, in Austria, Australia, Germany, France, and the UK – is voluntary, so that the long-term unemployed decide freely to use it only if it is to their advantage, and employers join only if they find it profitable. Another variant of the proposal is to permit the long-term unemployed to transfer a portion of their unemployment benefits plus training entitlements to provide training vouchers for employers.

Snower observes that since the government would not be spending more on the vouchers than it would have spent anyway on unemployment benefits and training, the resulting fall in unemployment can be achieved at no extra budgetary cost. Furthermore, since the long-term unemployed exert no noticeable dampening influence on wages, the programme would not be inflationary. The training vouchers, Snower argues, would not only give firms an incentive to provide training that is maximally appropriate to the available jobs, but could also play a role in tackling regional unemployment problems, since regions of relatively high unemployment would contain a relatively high proportion of subsidised workers, providing an incentive for firms to move there and retrain the local workforce.

In chapter 7, 'Wage subsidy programmes: alternative designs', Edmund Phelps argues that wage subsidies are more transparent and efficient in the short term than compulsory education and training programmes, which have very long-term effects and give no freedom to the low-wage earner to decide what kind of training or education she needs. The cost of the wage subsidy should be shared by the rest of the society that is benefiting from the gains of technological progress or the gains of free trade, the two factors that most severely affect the disadvantaged workers. In principle, everybody can thereby be made better off: the unemployed with higher salaries, the employers with lower labour costs, and the government with more employment creation without substantial increase in spending.

In chapter 8, 'Technological development, competition from low-wage economies and low-skilled unemployment', Jacques Drèze and Henri Sneessens examine the options available to policy makers to reduce unemployment of low-skilled workers, provide them with reasonable incomes, and promote incentives for economic efficiency. The authors argue that, as technological developments and foreign competition by low-wage countries are the main threats to low-skilled workers, policies over the long run should try to promote practical education and training and then proceed to promote the demand and supply of 'proximity services' that are more immune to competition from machines or foreign workers. These services include assistance to elderly, children and the disabled, as well as environmental protection and safety. In the short run, the authors suggest, it is desirable to reduce the wedge between labour costs to employers and net marginal earnings to low-skill employees through reductions or exemptions of employers' social security contributions. Then, a basic policy choice must be made between (i) maintaining minimum wages and unemployment benefits but look for a compensation by introducing employment subsidies concentrated on low-wage earners, and (ii) eliminating minimum wages, reducing the duration of unemployment benefits, and introducing individual transfers to all adult workers independently of their employment status, i.e. the so-called 'participation income' or 'social dividend'.

The advantages of the second option are that it restores labour market efficiency at the low end of the wage scale by letting wages fall to market-clearing levels and eliminating the so-called 'unemployment trap', and that it simplifies social security systems. The drawbacks of the second option are, first, that it produces a relatively high budgetary outlay and a high level of distortive taxes which may interfere with labour market efficiency at high wage levels and, second, that its political feasibility is open to doubt since wage flexibility, even at the low end of the wage scale, is totally opposed by labour unions.

In chapter 9, 'Macroeconomic and policy implications of shifts in the relative demand for skills', Olivier Blanchard argues that the rise in the demand relative to the supply of skilled labour and the opposite movement for unskilled labour has played an important role in generating the rise in long-term non-employment in the Europe and the

USA and the associated rise in European unemployment. The reason is that the supply of unskilled labour is much more responsive to wage changes than the supply of skilled labour. Consequently the rise in the demand for skilled labour does relatively little to stimulate the supply of skilled labour, whereas the fall in the demand for unskilled labour may reduce the supply of unskilled labour significantly. Blanchard suggests that if these supply and demand trends continue, employment rates will continue to fall. Furthermore, Blanchard indicates that unemployment policies aimed at subsidising unskilled labour are too costly to deal with the European unemployment problem as it stands. He suggests, instead, that governments should reduce the credit constraints faced by unskilled workers and subsidise college education for poor students. As for the unemployment that remains, we may have little choice but to tolerate it.

In chapter 10, 'Would cutting payroll taxes on the unskilled have a significant impact on unemployment?', Stephen Nickell and Brian Bell investigate two of the policy proposals to reduce unemployment recommended by the OECD *Jobs Study* (1994). The first is to *reduce non-wage labour costs*, especially in Europe, by reducing taxes on labour. According to Nickell and Bell, there is no relation between the level of social security contributions and the level of unemployment. The reason is that if wages are flexible, non-wage costs are, in the long run, borne by the employees. This is why countries with comparable levels of productivity have comparable labour costs, despite large variations in non-wage labour costs. But not only do the non-wage labour costs tend to be borne by employees, but so do income taxes and excise taxes, so that shifting the tax burden from one type of tax to another has no impact on employment in the long run.

The second recommendation is to *reduce direct taxes* (social security and income taxes) *on those with low earnings*, basically the unskilled, to raise their demand. The advantage of this policy proposal is that although payroll taxes in general are borne by labour, wages at the low end are not flexible because of the wage floor generated by minimum wage laws, unions, or the benefit system. This ensures that payroll taxes are not borne by labour at the bottom end of the pay distribution. This in turn ensures that payroll taxes cuts and subsidies may have a significant long-run employment effect as well as some positive impact on take-home pay. The disadvantage of this proposal is that it reduces the incentive for the unskilled to acquire training, and may require some additional policies to improve training for the unskilled.

In chapter 11, 'Preventing long-term unemployment: an economic analysis', Richard Layard argues that the way to help the long-term unemployed back to work is to stop paying them unemployment benefits after 12 months of unemployment and finding them work for at least six months instead. Work could be offered on a temporary basis in the public sector, or it could be generated through the transfer, for six months, of the unemployment benefits to any private-sector employer who offers jobs to the long-term unemployed. If after six working months the employer does not hire them on a permanent basis, they come back into the unemployment benefit system for another 12 months, and so on. Layard believes that this compulsory job guarantee scheme is more effective than the job creation schemes proposed thus far because, first, the new jobs are regular (not marginal) and thus these jobs make the long-term unemployed become more employable and, second, job subsidies without compulsion to accept an offer tend to be ineffective and encourage fraud.

Part Four, on labour market regulations, begins with a chapter on 'An analysis of firing costs and their implications for unemployment policy', by Alison Booth (chapter 12). She shows that in a competitive 'spot labour market', where there are no advantages to long-term employment relationships, the introduction of mandatory firing costs increases the incidence of short-term employment contracts. But in the long run, when it is in the firm's interest to have continuing employment relationships, firing costs reduce the variance of labour demand across the business cycle.

Booth finds that firing costs bargained by unions and firms have a stabilising impact on employment in bad times, although they reduce hiring in good times by an amount that depends crucially on the firm's discount rate. So mandated firing costs may result in a welfare loss unless they are set at the same level that is determined through bargaining. On this basis, Booth suggests that the level of redundancy pay might best be determined by bargaining rather than being centrally imposed. While there may be market failure arguments for statutory redundancy pay, the case for central determination of an appropriate economy-wide level of redundancy pay remains to be established.

On the opposite side of the policy spectrum, Paul Gregg and Alan Manning, in chapter 13, 'Labour market regulation and unemployment', take the view that complete labour market de-regulation does not lead to efficiency. The authors challenge the idea that government interference in the free working of the labour market is a major cause of unemployment and that unemployment would necessarily be reduced through 'market de-regulation', and show that, on the contrary, de-regulation can sometimes lead to more unemployment. The reason, they argue, is that de-regulated labour markets contain important elements of monopsony, so that to reduce unemployment it is at least as important to make jobs attractive to workers as to encourage job creation by firms. Labour market regulation is necessary to give workers some countervailing power against employers. The important issue, they argue, is to find an optimal degree of market regulation.

In view of the well known danger that unemployment policies which promote employment at the expense of productivity may lead to low-wage, dead-end jobs and high rates of labour turnover, *Part Five* focuses explicitly on the policy implications of the unemployment–productivity relation and job reallocation.

In chapter 14, 'Is there a trade-off between unemployment and productivity growth?', Robert Gordon shows how misleading is the facile contrast of Europe following a path of high productivity growth, high unemployment and relative greater income equality, with the opposite path being pursued by the USA. While structural shocks may initially create a positive trade-off between productivity and unemployment, Gordon contends that they set in motion a dynamic path of adjustment involving capital accumulation or decumulation that in principle can eliminate the trade-off. The main theoretical contributions of the chapter are to show how a productivity–unemployment trade-off might emerge and how it might subsequently disappear, as this dynamic adjustment path is set in motion. On the empirical side, the chapter develops a new data base for levels and growth rates of output per hour, capital per hour, and multi-factor productivity in the G-7 countries, both for the aggregate economy and for nine subsectors. It provides estimates that decompose observed differences in productivity growth across sectors. It finds that much of the productivity growth advantage of the four large European countries over the USA is explained by convergence and by more rapid capital accumulation, and that the only significant effect of higher unemployment is to cause capital accumulation to decelerate, thus reducing the growth rate of output per hour relative to multi-factor productivity.

In chapter 15, 'Gross job reallocation and labour market policy', Pietro Garibaldi, Jozef Konings and Christopher Pissarides look at job reallocation rates for 10 OECD countries, and explore their relation to unemployment and labour market policies. This is a very important issue since job reallocation (the number of jobs closed down and opened up every year) is a clear measure of 'labour market flexibility'. The authors find that gross job reallocation, especially when firm exit and entry are excluded, is positively associated with long-term unemployment. Countries with less job reallocation experience longer duration of unemployment.

Employment protection such as high firing costs and long duration of unemployment benefits slows down the reallocation of jobs and leads to longer duration of unemployment. In contrast, the level of unemployment benefit exerts a positive influence on job reallocation, although a very mild one. Finally, surprisingly, active labour market policies do not appear to have a significant influence on job turnover.

Part Six contains two studies comparing the effectiveness of alternative unemployment policies. In chapter 16, 'Unemployment in the OECD and its remedies', Patrick Minford indicates that the threat of low-wage competition to the living standards of unskilled workers in OECD countries is likely to put strain on those countries' commitments to free trade. How, then, to relieve this strain? Minford discusses three possible options: low-wage job subsidies, a basic income guarantee, and a negative income tax.

The low-wage job subsidies have similar effects to protection of manufacturing in Minford's trade model. While not directly creating labour supply disincentives, they can create distortions between the jobs outside the subsidy and the job inside. The subsidies are also not well targeted on *household* poverty or those who, because their household's work income is low, have the greatest incentive to remain unemployed under the current systems of transfer payments.

The basic income guarantee, by contrast, is a transfer to poor families, not to individuals, irrespective of their working situation; it is not means-tested. This can be very expensive. Although it has the advantage that the marginal tax rate for the poor family is kept down, since any income other than the transfer is taxed in the normal way, the opposite side of the coin is that this needs to be financed by raising the marginal tax rate substantially for the average family, which has to pay for the high cost of the guarantee through higher general income tax, so reducing incentives and efficiency.

The negative income tax is targeted, like the guarantee, on poor families, but it is means-tested and withdrawn gradually as incomes rise. This is less costly to the government and so reduces the marginal tax rate on the average family. Its main disadvantage is that it reduces incentives to work for low-incomes households. Minford argues that this system should be decentralised to local agencies, who closely monitor recipients – in the manner of charities – on the basis of need. Under this 'targeted negative income tax', poor families' disincentives can be minimised.

Finally, in chapter 17, 'The unemployment and welfare effects of labour market policy: a comparison of the USA and the UK', Stephen Millard and Dale Mortensen evaluate the unemployment effects of different labour market policies in the UK and the USA. Their analysis shows that the higher unemployment rate in the UK between 1983 and 1992 was a consequence of much longer unemployment duration and smaller unemployment incidence. They find that these observed differences are explained by different labour market policies and worker market power in these countries. The two major differences in labour policies is that the unemployment benefit period is limited to six months in the USA while there is no limit in the UK, and that firing costs in the UK amount to about two months' of average earnings while in the USA there is not any rule about firing costs. The authors' model predicts that a reduction to six months in the period of unemployment benefits would reduce the unemployment rate in the UK by two points, and that if firing costs were eliminated in the UK unemployment duration would fall but unemployment incidence would almost double. Although the net effect of this last measure would be an increase in unemployment, its positive impact on job creation would improve economic welfare and labour income, mainly through the increase in productivity resulting from a more rapid process of reallocating workers from less to more productive jobs, reflected in the shorter duration and greater incidence of unemployment.

This volume thus covers a wide range of unemployment policies from a wide range of perspectives. The reader thereby gains insight into the way the labour market incentives and institutions may be changed to encouraged job search and employment creation.

REFERENCES

OECD, 1994, *The OECD Jobs Study: Facts, Analysis, Strategies*, Paris: OECD

Phelps, E.S., 1994. *Structural Slumps: The Modern Equilibrium Theory of Unemployment, Interest, and Assets*, Cambridge, MA: Harvard University Press

Part One

General policy issues

2 Evaluating unemployment policies: what do the underlying theories tell us?

DENNIS J. SNOWER

1 Introduction

This chapter is motivated by a simple idea that has received lamentably little attention in the literature on unemployment policy: different unemployment policies are generally based on different theories of unemployment, and our confidence in a policy should depend – at least in part – on the ability of the underlying theory to account for some prominent empirical regularities in unemployment behaviour.

Some theories depict unemployment as the efficient outcome of market activity. These usually serve to rationalise a laissez-faire policy stance. Others depict unemployment as the product of market failures. Here, unemployment must be seen as the symptom of many possible diseases: many different market failures can produce the same problem of joblessness. And just as different diseases require different treatments, so different market failures may call for different government policies.[1] It is because different theories of unemployment focus on different market failures that different policies are generally based on different theories.

It is difficult to evaluate the various unemployment policies by assessing the practical significance of the market failures identified by the underlying theories. After all, market failures arise when people are not fully compensated for the costs and benefits they impose on one another, and uncompensated costs and benefits are inherently difficult to measure. For this reason, it is natural to evaluate unemployment policies by investigating the predictive power of the underlying theories. And a particularly simple first step in this direction is to examine the degree to which these theories are able to account for some generally recognised regularities in the movement of unemployment rates in OECD countries over the postwar period. This would perhaps be too obvious for words were it not so frequently at variance with the standard rationalisations of unemployment policies.

Admittedly, the suggested criterion is highly simplistic. It is reasonable to expect that, in practice, unemployment will arise from several different causes operating simultaneously. It would then be unreasonable to expect any single theory to explain all the salient empirical features of unemployment behaviour in the OECD. But all that this chapter claims is that confronting unemployment policies with these empirical features can be a useful preliminary guide to the potential significance of these policies. It would surely be unwise to have a heavy stake in a policy whose underlying theory explains little of how unemployment has evolved in the postwar period.

The chapter is organised as follows. Section 2 deals with the laissez-faire policy stance, based on theories of voluntary unemployment, section 3 demand-management policies, resting on Keynesian theory. Section 4 turns to supply-side policies, aimed at raising workers' productivity. Section 5 considers institutional policies, designed to change labour market institutions. Section 6 considers contractual policies, aimed at changing the nature of labour market contracts. Finally, section 7 draws some conclusions.

2 Laissez-faire

As already noted, the laissez-faire policy stance – for the government to do little or nothing to influence unemployment – is based primarily on models in which the observed swings in unemployment are viewed as the outcome of the optimising decisions by job-seekers and job-providers in efficient markets. Here, active unemployment policy is generally undesirable since it disturbs the workings of the Invisible Hand, interfering with people's free choices to remain unemployed.

There are two main types of laissez-faire stances. One discourages government interventions aimed at influencing the long-run equilibrium unemployment rate (arguing that such interventions would be ineffective or undesirable), but acknowledges the possible effectiveness and desirability of policies to deal with cyclical swings in unemployment. In particular, it advocates predictable policies, whose effects can be readily foreseen by economic agents. This view receives its most forceful expression in the market-clearing variant of the natural rate theory. The other laissez-faire stance discourages intervention to deal not only with the long-run equilibrium unemployment rate, but also with cyclical unemployment swings. It rests primarily on the intertemporal substitution theory and the real business cycle theory.

2.1 Policy predictability

The *market-clearing variant* of the *natural rate theory*[2] is an obvious vehicle for rationalising the paramount importance of policy predictability. In this theory, unemployment is at its 'natural rate' when people's expectations about wages and prices are correct. Under conditions of perfect competition and perfect information, this natural rate depends only on people's tastes, technologies, and resource endowments. When people's wage–price expectations are out of line with actual wages and prices, then unemployment deviates from its natural rate.

Provided that tastes, technologies, and endowments[3] do not fluctuate cyclically, fluctuations in unemployment – according to this theory – must be explained by fluctuations in expected wages and prices around their actual values. In order for this theory to have predictive power, it needs to be combined with a theory of how expectations are formed. The dominant one is the *rational expectations theory*, which asserts – quite plausibly – that people are not fooled in ways that they themselves could have predicted. To test this hypothesis, we require yet another theory, one that describes people's 'information sets', from which we could then infer what wages and prices they expect. This is, of course, an empirically impossible task; so the empirical models in this area generally assume that everyone has the same information sets as the authors of these models, except that the authors are able to get the data somewhat faster.

The implication of this approach is well known: if people make no systematic expectational errors (errors they could have predicted), then unemployment cannot diverge systematically from its natural rate. Just as expected wages and prices fluctuate randomly around their actual values, so unemployment will fluctuate randomly around the natural rate.

It is not hard to see why policy predictability is advisable in this context. Under well functioning markets, there is clearly no efficiency case to be made for interfering with the natural rate of unemployment. Policies which have no influence on this natural rate – such as monetary policies – can only affect unemployment by driving a wedge between actual and expected wages and prices. This, in turn, can be done through unexpected variations in policy instruments, such as unexpected changes in the money supply. Put simply, demand-management policies are effective only when they are deceptive. But deceptive policies are generally not in the public interest: if people were initially pursuing their own interests under perfect information – and thereby, through the workings of the Invisible Hand, promoting the public interest as well – unexpected changes in policy parameters will just prevent these people from doing this job so well. In short, stabilisation policy is reduced to the limited task of being predictable.

The problem with this theory is that it fails to address many facts of European unemployment over the past decade. With the decline in union density and the moves towards deregulation, privatisation, and liberalisation of labour markets in many OECD countries over the 1980s, no one could argue that the natural rate of unemployment could have risen significantly. Furthermore, given the stable rates of inflation over much of the decade, it could also not be argued that people's wage–price expectations were getting further and further out of line with actual wages and prices. Nevertheless European unemployment rose massively in that decade. There is nothing in the market-clearing variant of the natural rate theory that provides a clue about why this should have happened.

Nor does this theory shed useful light on why unemployment has been so much more persistent in Europe than in the USA, or why European unemployment rose with each major recession of the 1970s, 1980s, and early 1990s while US unemployment has always tended to return to its pre-recession level. Can we honestly believe that Europeans are much slower than Americans to adjust their expectations, so that expectational errors are more persistent in Europe than the USA?

Beyond that, the theory tells us little, if anything, about why unemployment spells tend to be longer in Europe than the USA (for given unemployment rates), why US unemployment rates are more variable than most European ones, why unemployment falls unequally among different population groups, and why labour and product markets move so much more closely in tandem in the USA than in Europe. Expectational errors provide few insights in these domains.

2.2 *Non-interference with business cycles*

The case against stabilisation policies in the labour market is made quite explicit in the intertemporal substitution theory and the real business cycle theory.

As the name implies, the *intertemporal substitution theory*[4] is concerned with workers' desire to engage in intertemporal substitution of work for leisure, and vice versa, in response to various economic incentives. For example, if workers believe that real wages are temporarily depressed and will rise in the future, they may wish to partake of more leisure now and work harder later. The same may be true if they perceive real interest rates to be temporarily low, since that means that their current wage income cannot be transferred into the future at an advantageous rate.

The implication is that cyclical swings in employment may be an optional response – by individual agents and society at large – to temporary shocks to tastes, technologies and endowments.[5] Whereas most economists used to see business cycles as undesirable, needing to be damped through stabilisation policies, the intertemporal substitution theory indicates that this need not be so. Within the analytical framework of this theory, it is not in the public interest to implement counter-cyclical monetary and fiscal policies, since these would prevent people from making the optimal dynamic responses to external shocks.

This theory can be used to generate an empirical account of much of the unemployment persistence and variability observed in the USA and other OECD countries.[6] But it is hard to see intuitively how it can provide a reasonable explanation of European unemployment over the past 25 years. Many millions of Europeans joined the unemployment register in the mid-1970s, early 1980s and early 1990s. Is it believable that these were simply colossal leisure binges, taken because workers were expecting real wages or real interest rates to rise later on? Regarding the upward trend in European unemployment rates since the mid-1970s, is it believable that we are observing a very long-term intertemporal substitution, whereby workers have decided to enjoy a lot of free time for two decades, perhaps with the intention of working very long hours for the next two decades? And even if the monstrous implausibility of these suppositions is put aside, we are still left with the fact that the available empirical evidence indicates that people's hours of work are unresponsive to real wage and real interest rate variations,[7] and that much of these variations tends to be permanent rather than temporary.

The *real business cycle theory*[8] builds on the intertemporal substitution theory and identifies technological shocks as the main source of macroeconomic fluctuations. Perfectly informed individuals, all maximising their utility subject to technological and resource constraints, respond to these technological shocks by intertemporally substituting labour, leisure, and consumption.

Beyond the predictive problems of the intertemporal substitution theory, it is difficult to get a clear picture of what the technological shocks are. Whereas technological advances (that are the source of the booms in the real business cycle theory) are relatively easy to identify, the technological setbacks (that give rise to the recessions) are not.[9] It is hard to see how knowledge and expertise gets lost, particularly on the large scale that is necessary to account for the deep recessions we have witnessed over the past two decades. Some would argue that the negative technological shocks reflect such adverse macroeconomic events as oil price hikes or inappropriate investment (such as machinery that does not work or that produces goods for which the demand did not materialise). But the negative technological shocks of the real business cycle models last much longer than the oil price hikes did, and it would be strange – in the real business cycle world of rational expectations in clearing, perfectly functioning markets – for the exogenous shocks to generate sufficient price misperceptions for the resulting investment fluctuations to pull the massive OECD recessions in their wake.

Finally, it would be difficult, if not impossible, to defend the real business cycle models by de-emphasising the role of technological shocks and concentrating on swings in, say, tastes instead. For then these models would be unable to explain why consumption rises and leisure falls in an economic upturn, and the opposite happens in a downturn. The reason is that a change in tastes does not affect the labour demand curve, and thus in an upturn employment would rise only if the real wage fell; but a fall in the real wage would reduce consumption and increase leisure – the opposite of what actually happens.

3 Demand-management policies

Demand-management policies to reduce unemployment fall into two broad categories: (i) government employment policies, whereby the government stimulates employment directly by hiring people into the public sector, and (ii) product demand policies, which stimulate employment by raising aggregate product demand (e.g. through tax reductions, increases in government spending on goods and services, or increases in the money supply).

3.1 Demand-management policies in the short run

For the 'short run', in which wages and prices respond sluggishly to demand fluctuations, the main underpinning for both types of policies is the *Keynesian theory*.[10] Here recessions are characterised by deficient labour and product demand reinforcing one another: workers are unemployed because firms are not producing enough goods and services; firms are not doing so because there is too little demand; and demand is deficient because people are unemployed. In short, deficient demand in the labour market originates in the product market and deficient demand in the product market originates in the labour market. Activity in these two markets goes up and down together. The mechanism that couples these two markets is wage–price sluggishness. A fall in product demand will reduce labour demand if wages don't fall sufficiently; a fall in labour demand will reduce product demand if prices are sluggish downwards.

This interaction between product and labour markets gives demand-management policy a lot of leverage in the Keynesian theory. A rise in government employment will raise the purchasing power of the people thereby employed. They, in turn, will demand more goods and services, which induces firms to hire more people, and so on. In the same vein, a stimulus to product demand (resulting, say, from a tax reduction) gives firms the incentive to raise employment, which creates more purchasing power, which raises product demand even further, and so on. The more sluggish wages and prices are, the greater these multiplier effects become.

Of course, in practice wages and prices are sluggish only over limited periods, and thus the critically important question is how short this 'short run' really is, Clearly, if it is shorter than the time it takes for most firms to make and implement their employment and production decisions, then we cannot expect the Keynesian employment repercussions of demand-management policies to be significant. Wage–price sluggishness in excess of the relevant production and employment lags is required before Keynesian policies come into their own.

The Keynesian quantity-rationing theory[11] provided no guidance in this respect, since it merely *assumed* wages and prices to be indefinitely rigid. The New Keynesian theories of nominal sluggishness move beyond this primitive assumption. They seek to *explain* why wages and prices don't change sufficiently to obviate the need for substantial output–employment adjustments in response to changes in demand. This approach thereby aims to shed light on the degree of wage–price sluggishness and consequently help determine the length of time over which Keynesian policy effects are operative. The three dominant New Keynesian theories in this area are the 'menu cost' theory,[12] the theory of 'near rationality'[13] and the wage–price staggering theory.[14]

According to the *menu cost theory*, small costs of price change induce firms to adjust quantities instead of prices in response to a sufficiently small change in aggregate demand. The same holds even in the absence of price-adjustment costs when firms are 'nearly rational', changing their prices only if that has a substantial effect on profits. There are, however, a number of obstacles to using these theories to derive the degree of wage–price sluggishness. First, the existing menu cost models show how product demand variations affect employment when the costs of price change are the *only* adjustment costs. In practice, however, employment adjustment costs (such as hiring, training and firing costs) generally exceed the price-adjustment costs by a large margin, and then it is no longer clear why product demand changes should have Keynesian effects on employment. Second, the menu cost theory implies that prices are either rigid or completely responsive to demand shocks, for the cost of small is generally no different from the cost of large price changes. This implication makes the theory unable to explain an important feature of wage–price sluggishness in practice, namely, that many firms change their prices frequently, but not by sufficiently large amounts to obviate the need for significant quantity adjustments. These two difficulties make it difficult for the menu cost theory to predict the degree of wage–price sluggishness and the short-run effectiveness of Keynesian demand-management policy.

The *theory of near rationality* is subject to the first of these two difficulties: to explain the effectiveness of Keynesian demand-management policy, the deviation from complete rationality must be sufficiently large to outweigh the costs of adjusting employment and production. Moreover, since it is hard to see how this deviation could be measured empirically, this theory also does not yield firm quantitative predictions on the degree of wage–price sluggishness.

The *wage–price staggering theory* demonstrates that if wages and prices, once set, are fixed over substantial contract periods and if different wages or prices are staggered (rather than set simultaneously), then a current change in aggregate product demand will affect production, employment and unemployment well beyond the expiry of the current contract period. However, several important lacunae in this theory keep it from providing a firm basis to predict the degree of wage–price sluggishness. First, the staggering theory does not identify the wage–price adjustment costs that keep wages and prices fixed over substantial intervals. Without a handle on these costs, we cannot derive the length of the contract periods that play such an important part in determining the degree of wage–price sluggishness. Second, the theory rests on the assumption that wages and prices are set in advance in nominal terms; it does not explain why wage–price setting rules generally do not involve indexing. If people have no money illusion and if simple indexation schemes (such as making the wage depend on an aggregate price index) are easy to formulate and monitor, it remains an open question why so many wages and prices are set in nominal terms.[15] Third, the theory does not tell us what determines the degree to which wage–price-setting rules are time-dependent (changing as a function of time) versus state-dependent (changing as a function of external contingencies).[16] This is an important issue because these rules have very different implications for the degree of wage–price sluggishness following a change in product demand.[17] Fourth, little attention has been given to the question why wage–price decisions are staggered rather than synchronised. Ball and Romer (1989) attribute it to firm-specific shocks, whereas Ball and Cecchetti (1988) suggest that staggering can arise from firms' incentives to set their prices after they have gained information about their rivals' price changes. As these examples show, different sources of staggering imply radically different staggering structures and also, presumably, radically different degrees of wage–price inertia. And finally, different sectors of the economy are characterised by vastly different periods of nominal adjustment in practice, and the resulting patterns of staggering are enormously complex – perhaps too complex, as the requisite level of disaggregation, to be a convenient predictive tool.

Nevertheless, many economists agree that the Keynesian view sheds *some* light on unemployment behaviour during deep recessions. When economies suffer from high unemployment and low capital utilisation, increases in aggregate demand generally lead to increases in employment, and demand reductions usually lead to declines in employment. But the 1980s have exposed an important shortcoming of the Keynesian theory: for most of that decade, European labour and product markets did not move together at all. Product demand started to pick up towards the end of 1982, but employment did not start to improve until 1986 in the UK and even later in most other EC countries. This gap is simply too large to be explained away by inventory dynamics or lags between inputs and outputs in production processes. The Keynesian vision of tightly linked labour and product demand is called into question here. It turns out that the link was much stronger in the USA than in most European countries over the 1980s. This disparity is simply too large to be rationalised simply in terms of greater wage–price sluggishness in the USA than in Europe.

3.2 Demand-management policies in the longer run

Now turn to the effectiveness of demand-management policies in the 'longer run', a time span long enough to permit full adjustment of wages and prices. A growing number of economists has come to suspect that the effectiveness of demand-management policy is undersold by the Keynesian mechanisms above, whereby the employment effect of demand management policy rests on wage–price sluggishness. Many believe that aggregate demand had a role to play in sustaining the periods of prolonged low European unemployment in the 1960s and prolonged high European unemployment in the 1980s. But for that to be the case, of course, the influence of aggregate demand on employment must extend well beyond the span over which wages and prices can be presumed sluggish.

To understand how aggregate demand could exercise such an influence, it is useful to picture the labour market equilibrium in terms of the intersection between a downward-sloping labour demand curve[18] and an upward-sloping wage-setting curve.[19] In this context, an increase in product demand can stimulate employment by shifting either the wage-setting curve or the labour demand curve outwards in real wage–employment space. If it was only the wage-setting function that shifted (along an unchanged labour demand curve), then the real wage would move counter-cyclically. But since real wage movements are often acyclical or even pro-cyclical (particularly in the USA), it is important to explore how product demand-management policy can shift the labour demand curve, thereby allowing for the possibility of pro-cyclical real wage movements.[20]

Since the labour demand curve is the set of real wage–employment combinations at which the real marginal value product of labour is equal to the real wage, a change in product demand can shift the labour demand curve only if it affects the real marginal value product of labour at any given level of employment. It is easy to show[21] that this occurs whenever the product demand change affects (i) the price elasticity of product demand, (ii) the imperfectly competitive interactions among firms, (iii) the user cost of capital, (iv) the degree of capital utilisation, (v) the number of firms in operation and (vi) the marginal product of labour.

Of these channels whereby product demand changes can be transmitted to employment, the first two do not appear to provide a firm foundation for the effectiveness of product demand management policy:

3.2.1 Price elasticity of product demand

Some authors[22] have suggested that changes in government spending can affect employment by changing the composition of product demand and thereby changing the associated price elasticity of aggregate demand. There are, however, good reasons to believe that this would be a tenuous basis for government policy. First, an increase in government spending would shift the labour demand curve outwards through this channel only when the public-sector price elasticity of demand exceeds the private-sector elasticity, but there is no evidence that in practice this is consistently the case across sectors and through time. Second, this transmission mechanism has the implausible implication that whenever an increase in government expenditures shifts the labour demand curve outwards, then a tax reduction must shift that curve inwards: for whereas the former policy raises public-sector relative to private-sector spending (thereby raising the aggregate price elasticity), the latter policy has the opposite effect. Affecting the price elasticity through changes in the composition of domestic versus foreign expenditures does not put us on firmer ground. In fact, if – as appears plausible – the foreign price elasticity exceeds the domestic one, an increase in domestic demand will *reduce* the aggregate elasticity and thereby move the labour demand curve *inwards*!

3.2.2 Imperfectly competitive interactions among firms

Others[23] have suggested that oligopolists may behave more competitively in a boom, so that a rise in product demand could shift the labour demand curve outwards via its influence on competition. But Rotemberg and Saloner (1986) show this effect to hold only when firms are implicitly colluding oligopolists, and this induced-competition channel is a weak foundation for demand-management policy.

That leaves the other four channels, which appear to be more promising avenues for the transmission of product demand management policies to employment.

3.3 The interaction between demand- and supply-side policies

What these four channels have in common is that they all make the employment impact of demand management policies depend on their supply-side effects. Supply-side policies thereby gain a special role in enhancing the effectiveness of demand management.

3.3.1 The user cost of capital

It is widely recognised that if an increase in product demand reduces the real interest rate, it will thereby reduce the user cost of capital, increasing the size of the capital stock and shifting the labour demand curve outwards, provided that labour and capital are Edgeworth complements in production (so that the marginal product of labour depends positively on the capital stock). This could happen either through expansionary monetary policy, or through a decline in the risk premium on investment[24] brought about by the expansion of demand. Naturally, if the rise in the demand takes the form of an increase in government spending, the real interest rate may rise (rather than fall), shifting the labour demand curve inwards through the above mechanism. Moreover, even if the real interest rate falls, the labour demand curve will still shift inwards when labour and capital are Edgeworth substitutes.

3.3.2 The degree of capital utilisation

It can be shown[25] that when there is excess capital capacity, demand-management policy can affect the marginal product of labour by influencing the degree of capital utilisation. To fix ideas, consider the following sequence of labour market decisions. First, each firm sets its supply of physical capital and determines, from the range of its available technologies, those that are to become accessible through its capital stock (where, say, the range of accessible technologies may be characterised by an interval of capital–labour ratios within its *ex ante* production function). Next, the nominal wage is determined (say, through bargaining between the firm and its employees). Then the firms observe the position of their product demand curves, and finally they make their employment decisions. Under these circumstances, an unanticipated, adverse product demand shock could make it unprofitable for firms to operate at full capacity.[26] A subsequent, favourable demand shock would induce firms not only to hire more labour at the existing level of capital services, but also to raise the degree of capital utilisation. When economies emerge from recessions in this way, with workers recalled to operate vacant machines and re-start idle assembly lines, the capital brought back into use is often highly complementary to labour. Through this channel expansionary demand management policy may raise the marginal value product of labour, leading to pro-cyclical movements of the real wage.

3.3.3 Entry and exit of firms

Increases in product demand can induce entry of new firms, which shifts the labour demand curve outwards – both directly, and indirectly by increasing the degree of product market competition.[27] Specifically, if nominal wages are temporarily rigid, a rise in product demand can reduce the real wage by raising prices, leading to the entry of new firms. Once nominal wages adjust, this entry ceases, but the recently entered firms remain operative. In this way, a temporary nominal wage rigidity can give product demand-management policy an influence on employment in the longer run.[28]

3.3.4 The marginal product of labour

If the increase in government spending takes the form of industrial infrastructure investment, there may obviously be a direct stimulus to the marginal product of labour. In this case, expansionary demand management policy shifts the labour demand curve outwards through its effect on the capital stock.

The policy implication regarding these four channels are potentially of considerable significance: The longer-term influence of product demand-management policy on employment depends on the *availability of a limited number of supply-side channels of transmission.* Supply-side policies – such as those which reduce the barriers to the entry of new firms,[29] or those which augment industrial infrastructure – can help open these supply-side channels and thereby improve the long-term effectiveness of demand management. In the long run, therefore, demand- and supply-side policies are interdependent.

4 Supply-side policies

4.1 Policies centring on physical capital formation

These policies – which range from government infrastructure investment to policies that raise the rate of capital utilisation, stimulate the entry of firms, or promote physical capital formation by reducing the user cost of capital – have already been discussed in section 3. What they all have in common is that they raise the level of capital services provided in the economy and consequently, if labour and capital are complementary in the production process, increase the marginal product of labour.

4.2 Policies centring on human capital formation

Policies which focus on human capital formation include government training programmes, training subsidies to firms or workers,[30] and – more broadly – also policies that reduce the rate of interest and thereby reduce the rate at which future returns to human capital formation are discounted.

Many of the market failures addressed by these policies can be analysed effectively through the *theory of search and matching*.[31] In this theory, workers are not perfectly informed about the available jobs and firms are not perfectly informed about the available workers. Thus both sides of the market engage in search. Each agent acquires information up to the point at which the cost of searching for an additional job (or worker) is equal to the discounted stream of expected future returns from that job (or worker). Unemployment arises because jobless workers know that there are vacant jobs with wages sufficiently high to make the return from search exceed the cost, but since they don't know precisely where these jobs are, they may not find them right away. The result is 'frictional unemployment'. This unemployment does not go away since there are always some workers getting fired, some entering the labour force, and some retiring from it. At centre-stage in all search models lies a 'matching function', which specifies how the expected number of matches is related to the number of unemployed workers and the number of vacant jobs.

It is not possible, of course, to attribute the rise in European unemployment to a deterioration of this matching technology, because the dissemination of labour market information has, if anything, improved with the passage of time. Nor are the recent periods of high unemployment related to comparatively high degrees of labour market 'turbulence', i.e. sectoral imbalances responsible for job creation and job destruction.[32]

But search and matching models can be used to explain how unemployment can arise on account of market failures in the demand for and supply of training.[33] First of all, since unemployed people have relatively few firm-specific skills, training them may involve a relatively large poaching externality. Specifically, if unemployed people were given training, a relatively large share of the benefits from that training, in imperfectly competitive labour markets, would fall neither on the firms supplying the training nor on the workers receiving it, but on third parties – namely, the firms that may poach the workers after they have been trained. In that event, the social benefit from training will exceed the private benefit, regardless of how the costs of training are distributed between the trainer and trainee. Then the free market will generate too few matches between firms and currently unemployed workers, whereby the workers are made productive and profitable through training. As a result, an inefficiently large number of these workers remains jobless.[34] This problem may become magnified considerably through the 'low-skill, bad-job trap':[35] a deficient supply of trained job-seekers induces firms to create an excessive number of unskilled vacancies, and these in turn further reduce workers' incentives to acquire training: this leads to even more unskilled vacancies, and so on. It could be argued that these market failures are particularly pronounced with regard to the long-term unemployed. They are likely to be particularly poorly endowed with firm-specific skills and thus particularly prone to the poaching externality and the low-skill, bad-job trap.

In response, government training programmes or training subsidies to the unemployed – particularly the long-term unemployed – may have a role to play in combating unemployment. Many government training programmes, however, are ill-suited to firms' needs. This is scarcely surprising, since these needs are extremely diverse while government training programmes are inevitably standardised and limited in variety. In this regard, training subsidies granted to firms appear preferable, for the firms then have the incentive to make the resulting training maximally appropriate to their available jobs. To keep firms from illicitly diverting the training funds to other purposes, it may be necessary to provide the training subsidies only for programmes leading to nationally recognised qualifications, granted by institutions independent of the firms receiving the subsidies.[36]

To assess the theory underlying this policy approach, it is worth noting that some of the rise in European unemployment over the past two decades might arguably be due to the interaction between the market failures above (on the one hand) and the joint pull of skill-biased technological change and international trade (on the other). Both technological developments that raise the productivity of the skilled relative to the unskilled workers, as well as rising trade with countries that have a comparative advantage in producing goods which are relatively intense in unskilled labour, pull in the same direction, in that they reduce the demand for unskilled relative to the demand for skilled labour. And if the market failures above are responsible for a deficiency in the acquisition of skills and an excessive number of unskilled workers without jobs, then that technological change and trade could lead to a rise in unemployment.

In addition, an expansion of trade or an increased rate of technological change could generate unemployment by raising the amount of labour market 'turbulence', particularly by increasing the rate of job creation and destruction.[37] This, of course, is not an argument for policies limiting the degree of technological change or trade, for – as is well known – the latter generally permit a given amount of goods and services to be produced with less labour input, and thereby could improve everyone's material standard of living, provided that the appropriate redistributions from the winners to the losers can be made without substantial loss of efficiency. Rather, the above diagnosis is an argument for job search support in order to improve the effectiveness of the matching process.

Moreover, according to the Keynesian theory, technological improvements and specialisation in skill-intensive goods both enable the economy to satisfy a given (deficient) aggregate product demand with less labour input. Hence, employment will fall and unemployment will rise. This may strengthen the need for expansionary demand management policy.

4.3 Job search support and information dissemination

This general policy approach covers such measures as counselling the unemployed, assisting them with personal problems such as alcoholism and drug addiction, and alerting them to available training opportunities.[38] It also involves disseminating information about available labour services to firms and about available vacancies to workers.

If imperfect information about vacant jobs and unemployed workers were the only problem for this policy approach to overcome, its potential would be quite limited for the simple reason that frictional unemployment accounts for only a small fraction of the European unemployment problem. However, the same strategy may also be useful in overcoming the discouragement and demoralisation that prevents many long-term unemployed people from seeking jobs effectively. The search and matching theory views this problem as the consequence of a decline in unemployed people's returns from job search as their unemployment spells lengthen. The declining returns may, in turn, be due to the depreciation or obsolescence of their skills and to a resulting fall in firms' efforts to attract these workers.

Another reason why workers' search intensity may decline as their period of unemployment proceeds is that their preferences gradually change. In particular, the long-term unemployed can become accustomed and reconciled to remaining jobless, adopt it as a way of life, and stop searching seriously at all.[39] Counselling and personal assistance may help to mitigate these problems by restoring the attitudes and expectations necessary for successful job search strategies.

The potential importance of this policy approach may be highlighted by the recognition that the decline of search intensity with unemployment duration undoubtedly plays a significant role in explaining unemployment persistence (the dependence of current unemployment rates on past unemployment rates).[40] It also helps explain why the burden of unemployment is distributed unequally. If people's search intensity falls the longer they remain unemployed, and if the corresponding search intensity of potential employers falls as well, then the expected future length of these workers' unemployment spells will depend positively on how long they have been unemployed already.

Aside from the search and matching theory, another rationale for policies to improve information dissemination – as well as various other policies to be discussed below – come from the *efficiency wage theory*. Here firms are assumed to have imperfect information about individual employees' productivities and are thus unable to make their wage offer contingent on their employees' performance. The firms, as wage-setters, observe that by raising their wage offers they are able to stimulate the average productivity of their workforce. The reason is that higher wage offers enable a firm to recruit more highly qualified employees or motivate employees to work harder.[41] In other variants of the theory, higher wages discourage workers from quitting the firm, thereby reducing the firm's labour turnover costs.[42] Consequently firms may have an incentive to keep the wage above the level that would be necessary to ensure full employment. The unemployed are unable to get jobs by offering to work for less than the prevailing wage, because it is not in the firms' interests to allow the wage to fall.

In this context, policies that improve the dissemination of information about workers' ability, motivation, and quit behaviour would enable firms to base their wage offers more closely on workers' individual productivities and potential labour turnover costs, thereby reducing the role of wages as an incentive mechanism and bringing down the associated level of unemployment.

The great strength of the efficiency wage theory is that it provides one conceivable explanation for why, even under perfectly flexible wages, people may be unemployed even though they would prefer to do the jobs of the current job-holders at less than the prevailing wage. Beyond that, however, it is not clear that the theory can shed much light on why EC unemployment has risen over the past two decades, why US and Japanese unemployment has fared better, why the average duration of unemployment in Europe has significantly exceeded that in the USA and Japan since the mid-1970s, why labour and product market activities tend to move together in the USA but not in Europe, or why unemployment in many countries varies less within a business cycle than from one cycle to the next. These phenomena clearly cannot be ascribed to differences in monitoring technologies through time and across countries. For instance, it is quite implausible that EC unemployment should have risen because firms have become worse at monitoring their employees' performance; nor is it plausible that US unemployment recovered more quickly from the recent recessions than EC unemployment because US firms had more information about their employees than EC firms.[43]

4.4 Policies to stimulate worker mobility

Some policies that are meant to reduce the burden of housing costs to the poor – such as rent control or low-cost public housing – reduce worker mobility and, by inhibiting workers from moving to the available jobs, create unemployment. This is a potentially significant problem in a number of OECD countries containing both booming and slumping regions and large house-price and rent differentials across these regions.[44] These differentials can become an especially serious impediment to matching in the labour market, since they often expand with the mismatch between vacancies in the booming regions and unemployment in the slumping ones. The reason, of course, is that the greater is the regional mismatch, the greater will the house-price and rent differentials be as well. Rent control and housing subsidies that are tied to the current place of residence give leverage to this obstacle to matching. Replacing these policy interventions by more efficient ways of redistributing income (such as conditional negative income taxes, discussed in section 5.3) could therefore help reduce unemployment. A similar argument can be made for policies that increase the portability of health insurance and pensions between firms.

5 Institutional policies

Institutional policies, as their name suggests, aim to change labour market institutions so as to reduce unemployment. These policies come in many guises, of which only the most prominent will be considered here.

5.1 Policies to reduce the power of labour unions

Policies to reduce the power of labour unions range from restrictions on secondary picketing, to laws prohibiting closed shop agreements, to regulations restricting the coverage of union wage agreements, and much more. These policies may be analysed straightforwardly through the theory of labour unions. In the traditional variants of this theory,[45] all union members are assumed to have identical preferences and an equal share in the available work. Then the union represents the interest of its members by exerting its monopoly power in wage-setting, much like sellers of goods or services exert their monopoly power in price-setting. The resulting wages will be higher and employment will be lower than it would have been in the absence of the union's influence on the wage. If all workers in the economy belong to unions, then aggregate employment will be less than it would have been under full employment. The difference is unemployment (or under-employment).

More recent union theories recognise that unions take greater account of the interests of their employed members than of the unemployed and that the employed workers have greater access to work than the unemployed do. The unemployment arising in this setting may be voluntary from the vantage point of the employed union members, but is generally involuntary from the vantage point of the unemployed, since the latter could be made better off by a wage reduction associated with a rise in employment.

The main theoretical weakness of this theory lies not in what it tells us, but in what it doesn't. It doesn't tell us why the unemployed don't leave unions that don't represent their interests, and start new unions making lower wage claims. Nor does it tell us what gives unions their clout. Since union coverage in most market economies is far under 100 per cent, why don't employers simply throw out high-wage union members and hire low-wage non-members instead?[46]

On the empirical front, there is some evidence of an inverse relation between inter-country differences in unemployment rates (on the one hand) and inter-country differences in indexes of union power and union coverage (on the other) over the postwar period. Yet the union theories have not performed well over the past decade in predicting movements of unemployment through time. In the first part of the 1980s, for example, union membership in the UK and several other European countries fell while unemployment rose. For this reason, it is certainly premature to say that unemployment policies designed to reduce union power are on a firm predictive foundation.

5.2 *Reforming the wage-bargaining system*

In recent years there has been a growing call to strengthen firm-level and national-level bargaining at the expense of bargaining at the sectoral level.[47] This policy strategy is based on the analysis of Calmfors and Driffill (1988), who explore how the economic efficiency of wage bargaining depends on the number of independent agents engaged in bargaining. They argue that when there is a high degree of centralisation in bargaining – with few unions confronting few employers' confederations, such as in Austria and Sweden – the negotiating partners internalise most of the effects of their claims: in particular, the unions take account of the price increases associated with their wage claims, and the employers take account of the wage increases associated with their employment and pricing decisions. The resulting wage–employment outcome is therefore reasonably efficient. On the other hand, when there are large numbers of negotiating workers and firms, each occupying a small portion of the market, the resulting activity is efficient for the standard competitive reasons. The USA approximates this setup. Calmfors and Driffill claim that it is only in the intermediate range, where the independent negotiators are sufficiently few in number to have market power, but sufficiently numerous to ignore the external effects of their decisions, that gross inefficiencies arise. Calmfors and Driffill (1988) adduce some empirical evidence in favour of this thesis, and Layard, Nickell and Jackman (1991, p.55) provide cross-section evidence that the unemployment rates in 20 OECD countries tend to be inversely related to the degrees of union and employer coordination.

On this account, it has been argued, wage-bargaining systems need to be either highly centralised or highly decentralised.[48] Policies that reduce the power of labour unions, reduce labour turnover costs and promote international trade are all likely to strengthen decentralised, firm-level bargaining. Government sponsorship of 'social pacts' – whereby unions accept targets for nominal wage growth (based on productivity growth and price inflation), firms accept targets for price increases (based on wage inflation), the central bank sets the growth of the money supply with a view to non-inflationary growth, and the fiscal authority aims to control unemployment – encourages centralised, national-level bargaining. As a practical matter, however, wage-bargaining systems are very difficult to reform and thus this structural policy should be seen more as a long-term desideratum than as a short-term tool.

5.3 Reforming the unemployment benefit system

The main deficiency of all unemployment benefit systems is that, in helping to cushion the blow of unemployment, they make the underlying problem worse. The reasons are that unemployment benefits (i) discourage job search (because when an unemployed person finds a job, the unemployment benefits are withdrawn and taxes are imposed) and (ii) put upward pressure on wages (by improving incumbent workers' negotiating positions). The first effect lies in the domain of search and matching theory, the second is the province of bargaining theory. Together, these effects make unemployment benefit systems inherently inefficient and inequitable.

In reforming unemployment benefit systems, it is important to distinguish carefully between the equity and efficiency objectives of these systems. The equity goal is simply to redistribute income from the rich to the poor. The efficiency goal is to respond to market failures in the provision of unemployment insurance.[49] But unemployment benefits are generally a very poor tool to accomplish these objectives.

With regard to equity, it is worth keeping in mind that, for most poor people, employment is the best – and often the only – way to overcome poverty. Thus it is particularly unfortunate that unemployment benefits discourage employment, since they thereby make the distribution of employment opportunities more unequal. Clearly, a more effective way to redistribute income from rich to poor is to use income as the criterion of redistribution; the employment criterion is obviously a blunt instrument for this purpose since some employed people are poor while some unemployed people are well-off.

With regard to efficiency, the gains from provision of unemployment insurance must be set against the efficiency losses that arise when unemployment benefits discourage employment and encourage unemployment. It is by no means a forgone conclusion that the efficiency gains will invariably exceed the associated losses. In any case, the unemployment benefit schemes that predominate in Europe – characterised by either flat-rate components or ceilings on benefits that depend on past wages – have much less in common with optimal unemployment insurance schedules than with standard redistributive schemes. In short, the unemployment benefits encountered in practice are not designed to yield major efficiency gains in correcting for failures in the unemployment insurance market.

But that is nowhere near the end of the problem. The efficiency wage, labour union, and insider–outsider[50] theories identify market failures that give free market activity a tendency to yield excessively high wages and excessively low employment. Unemployment benefit systems exacerbate these market failures by driving wages up further and discouraging employment even more. Furthermore, these market failures are perpetuated through various dynamic effects. As noted above, the longer people are unemployed, (i) the more their skills depreciate and become obsolescent, (ii) the more discouraged and ineffective they become in the process of job search, and (iii) the more wary firms become of hiring them. When the government rewards unemployment (through unemployment benefits) and penalises employment (through income taxes), it unwittingly amplifies these dynamic effects by keeping unemployed people from competing for jobs and becoming 'enfranchised' in the wage determination process. As result, their unemployment becomes less effective in moderating wages or raising firms' return from searching for new recruits. In this way, unemployment benefit systems make unemployment more persistent, and put the long-term unemployed at a greater disadvantage in competing for jobs.

For all these reasons, unemployment benefit reform has become a topic of growing policy interest throughout Europe. But while it is relatively easy to recognise the need for reform, it is frightfully difficult to agree on its content. The critical question is how to provide a safety net for the disadvantaged and the unfortunates without dramatically reducing people's incentives to fend for themselves, thereby creating more disadvantaged and unfortunates in the process.

A growing number of European economists[51] argue that unemployment benefit should be generous, but for a limited period of time. The generosity is allegedly required to give people the opportunity to make judicious job matches, which credit constraints may keep them from doing. Limited benefit duration, it is claimed, is necessary to induce people to find work quickly, before they become discouraged, stigmatised, and deskilled. This advice sounds eminently sensible to the uninitiated public, but little attempt has been made thus far to explore whether the theory that keeps this advice afloat captures empirically important determinants of unemployment. It seems doubtful, to put it mildly, that workers' credit constraints are an important aspect of the

European unemployment problem. If they were, then the problem would be that unemployment durations are too short, resulting in over-full employment. This, it appears, is the least of Europe's worries.

Beyond that, the prescription to shorten benefit duration characteristically becomes vague once we ask what happens to people who remain jobless after their unemployment benefits have expired. Some recommend that they be given training, others put more emphasis on job counselling. But that still leaves us with the question of how to treat those who are left unemployed even after the training and counselling. At that point, many European economists revert to the popular European opinion that the social safety net cannot be withdrawn from these hapless individuals; income support and a range of welfare state benefits are then required to keep them from destitution. Then, however, a short benefit duration may cease to give unemployed people an effective incentive to find jobs promptly.

This is in fact the problem that the current, unreformed European benefit systems face. Many European countries – such as Germany, France, Greece, Ireland and the Netherlands – grant some form of unemployment insurance of limited duration, followed by unemployment assistance that is frequently unlimited. It is hard to see how the disincentive effects generated by these systems could be overcome simply by shortening the time span for unemployment insurance and inserting a period of training and counselling prior to the receipt of the unemployment assistance.

Overall, it is safe to say that unemployment benefit reform should be guided by the objective to overcome its two biggest deficiencies, namely, the disincentive effects and the imperfections in targeting the poor. It is arguable that both could be mitigated by simply *replacing* unemployment benefit systems by a conditional negative income tax (NIT) programme,[52] whereby people's receipt of negative income taxes is made to depend on their ability to pass stringent tests on their willingness and readiness to work.[53]

Another policy proposal, concerned with *redirecting* unemployment benefits to provide employment vouchers, is discussed below.

6 Contractual policies

'Contractual policies' are ones designed to change the nature or provisions of labour market contracts, with a view to reducing unemployment. Here, too, we find a wealth of candidates and, in the interest of brevity, I shall be highly selective.

6.1 *Worksharing and early retirement*

Worksharing and early retirement has begun to look attractive to an increasing number of European policy makers, particularly in Germany. It is based on the view that there is a fixed amount of work to be done in an economy in any given period of time, and thus it is the job of the policy makers to decide how this work is to be distributed across the available workforce. If it is currently distributed unequally, with most people in the workforce working full-time and some remaining unemployed for prolonged periods, worksharing and early retirement could spread the job opportunities more equitably.

But to call this a 'theory' is an over-statement. Most economists would rather call it the 'lump-of-labour fallacy', since it is well understood that the amount of work to be done in an economy is not a fixed number of hours, beyond the influence of the policy makers.[54] The Keynesian theory drives this point home particularly forcefully: the more people are employed, the more they earn, the greater their purchasing power, the more they spend, and the more people firms will seek to employ.

Moving beyond their non-existent theoretical foundation, jobsharing and early retirement schemes suffer from a number of serious problems. First, they tend, in practice, to increase non-wage labour costs, particularly those associated with hiring, screening, training and administration. Thus they may be expected to discourage employment and create more unemployment. Second, insofar as they are successful in reducing the pain from unemployment by distributing it among more people, they lessen the political pressure on governments to address the unemployment problem through more promising means. Third, in reducing the number of unemployed people competing for jobs, they may well drive up wages and stimulate price inflation. This may induce governments to implement restrictive macroeconomic policies, which would raise unemployment, possibly creating a further perceived need to redistribute job opportunities through yet more worksharing and early retirement. The main advantage of worksharing and early retirement schemes is that they may 'enfranchise' a larger number of people in the wage determination process and thereby moderate the insiders' wage demands. It appears unlikely, however, that this advantage would dominate the disadvantages above.

6.2 *Policies centred on labour turnover costs*

Policies that aim to reduce unemployment by mitigating the harmful effects of labour turnover costs are as varied as the turnover costs themselves. Some involve dismantling job security legislation (such as laws reducing statutory severance pay or simplifying mandated firing procedures); others reduce the ability of incumbent workers to exploit existing labour turnover costs in order to boost their wages (such as legal restrictions on strikes and picketing); yet others help the unemployed surmount the obstacles created by turnover costs (such as training subsidies, recruitment subsidies, profitsharing schemes, policies to reduce the barriers to the entry of new firms and reform of wage bargaining systems). This section focuses attention on the first two groups of policies; policies in the third group are discussed in sections 3.3, 4.2, 5.2 and 6.3–6.6.

What the first two groups of policies have in common is that they reduce the market power of the 'insiders' (incumbent employees whose jobs are protected by significant labour turnover costs) and thereby strengthen the position of the 'outsiders' (who are either unemployed or have jobs that are not protected in this way). In the process, insiders become less insulated from the forces of labour demand and supply and firms find it easier to hire and fire employees. The upshot is (i) insider wages face downward pressure, since insiders now face greater competition from outsiders and (ii) employment becomes more responsive to variations in revenue and cost conditions. The first effect stimulates employment,[55] for as insiders become more profitable, firms have a greater demand for new recruits, who eventually turn into insiders. The second effect reduces the degree of employment and unemployment persistence.

This policy approach lies in the domain of the insider–outsider theory.[56] Here labour turnover costs, falling at least in part on the firms, give market power to the insiders, who know that their employers would find it costly to replace them. The insiders are assumed to use this power to pursue their own interests in the wage-setting process. Although the resulting insider wages are higher than they would otherwise have been, the labour turnover costs discourage firms from firing the insiders. Of course the excessive insider wages also discourage the hiring of new entrants.

Some of the labour turnover costs (such as training costs) are an intrinsic part of the production process: others (like severance payments) are primarily associated with rent-seeking activities. The rent-related turnover costs give the insiders preferential conditions of employment over the outsiders. Unemployment can then arise on account of the outsiders' inferior employment opportunities. In this context, policies that reduce labour turnover costs, or ones that check the insiders' ability to exploit them in wage-setting, will generally lead to a reduction in unemployment.

The insider–outsider theory is able to account for a variety of empirical regularities in unemployment behaviour. The relatively high labour turnover costs in Europe – both in their own right and through their influence on insiders' wages – play a role in making European unemployment more persistent (serially correlated) than US unemployment. Since high labour turnover costs make firms reluctant both to hire and to fire employees, they thereby raise the duration of unemployment. In this way, Europe's relatively high labour turnover costs can lead to its relatively high unemployment durations and relatively low unemployment variability, in comparison with the USA. Furthermore, since labour turnover costs raise insiders' job retention rates relative to the outsiders' job acquisition rates, they imply that unemployment falls relatively heavily on population groups with relatively unstable work patterns (i.e. relatively high entry and exit rates in the job market), such as young people.

Insofar as many of the full-time unskilled jobs in the traditional industrial sectors are associated with significant labour turnover costs, the insider–outsider theory also gives an account of why wages in these sectors have refused to fall with falling demand. It also helps explain why much service-sector employment and temporary employment – associated with relatively low turnover costs – has been buoyant in comparison with industrial employment in the OECD.

When business cycles are short-lived and mild, most European countries – facing comparatively high labour turnover costs – may be expected to do relatively little hiring or firing, hoarding labour in the slumps and bringing it back into use in the booms. But in the face of deep, prolonged recessions, those countries will stop hoarding and start firing labour. In the subsequent recovery, firms will then be comparatively slow to re-hire this labour, fearing that they may incur further firing costs should the recovery not materialise, and thus investment in labour-saving capital equipment may then take the place of new employment. This helps explain why unemployment rates in Europe were significantly lower than in the USA in the 1950s and 1960s (when business cycles were short-lived and mild), but significantly higher since the mid-1970s, why US unemployment has been more variable than European unemployment, and why production and employment move together to a greater degree in the USA than in Europe.

6.3 Profitsharing

Under profitsharing contracts, a part of workers' remuneration is paid as a fraction of the profits earned by their firms (or specific teams within those firms).[57] For any given level of remuneration, it is clear that a firm's marginal cost of employment is lower under profitsharing than under a fixed wage, since (under diminishing returns to labour) the profit share declines as employment rises, whereas a fixed wage, by definition, does not. Consequently, it is alleged, profitsharing contracts lead to lower unemployment than wage contracts do. Weitzman has suggested that, in a world where wages seldom involve profitsharing, firms have deficient incentives to offer profitsharing contracts, and thus government subsidies for profitsharing are called for.

The claim that profitsharing contracts reduce unemployment is less general than it may appear at first sight. It turns out that the effectiveness of profitsharing depends crucially on what is generating the unemployment. If, for instance, the unemployment is an efficiency-wage phenomenon, the switch from wage contracts to profitsharing ones will do little, if anything, to reduce unemployment, since workers' incentives to shirk and quit depend on the total amount of remuneration, but not on how this amount is divided between wages and profit shares. The same may be said of firms' ability to attract workers of relatively high productivity.

Yet if the unemployment is predominantly generated by insider–outsider considerations, profitsharing may have an effective role to play. In the insider–outsider theory, the outsiders are unable to 'bribe' insiders to forgo the rent-seeking activities that keep the outsiders from getting jobs. The insiders may, for example, boost their wages and protect themselves from competition with outsiders by refusing to cooperate with them in the process of production, thereby creating an insider–outsider productivity differential; or they may harass outsiders who offer to work for less than the prevailing wages and thereby make the available jobs more disagreeable for those outsiders than for the insiders. Alternatively, the insiders may be involved in determining the wages of new entrants, and may use their market power to drive entrant wages up, thereby discouraging the employment of entrants that would drive down the insiders' marginal products.

In this context, profitsharing contracts may be construed as a device that may permit the outsiders to bribe the insiders to stop these activities, so that everyone – the insiders, the outsiders and their employers – can be made better off. In particular, if insiders were given a bonus for consenting to profitsharing contracts for new entrants, the firm's marginal cost of hiring new entrants would fall, the entrants would receive more than they did when they were unemployed, and the firm's profits would rise. In the process, of course, unemployment would fall.

But while profitsharing schemes are indeed promising in this context, it is important to be aware of some potential difficulties. First, it may be impossible to induce the insiders to consent because the insiders' rent-seeking activities – like their harassment activities – may not be objectively monitorable. Second, to make profitsharing operational may require implementing costly monitoring procedures that enable workers to gain access to profit information.[58] Third, the extra profit generated through the introduction of profitsharing may be insufficient to compensate the insiders for their loss of market power resulting from the inflow of new entrants. Fourth, the extra profit generated may be insufficient to pay the premium that the new entrants would require to induce them to bear the income risk associated with profit-sharing. And finally, the insiders may refuse to be bribed because that would create a two-tier remuneration system that would give firms an incentive to lay off the insiders and retain the entrants, once the latter had been fully trained.

6.4 Low-wage subsidies and payroll tax reductions

This set of policies[59] is meant to address the problem that, in many OECD countries, the relative position of workers at the bottom of the earnings distribution has worsened over the past two decades. This worsening has taken the form of lower relative real wages in the USA (and, to a lesser degree, in the UK) and higher relative unemployment rates in many continental European countries. Providing subsidies or payroll tax reductions to low-wage workers is meant to raise firms' demand for these workers, thereby reducing their unemployment rates and raising their take-home pay.[60] It has been suggested that these policy measures be financed through a rise in VAT or the CO_2 tax. Econometric simulations[61] suggest that the expansionary employment effect of a drop in the payroll tax on low-wage earners may substantially outweigh the contractionary effect of a corresponding rise in the VAT.

Since these policies reduce unemployment by reducing employers' labour costs at the bottom of the wage spectrum, their effectiveness does not appear to be very sensitive to the precise underlying cause of the unemployment (in contrast to profitsharing subsidies). For example, regardless of whether the unemployment is generated by union pressures, efficiency wage considerations, or insider–outsider conflict, a drop in labour costs is bound to raise employment, since it permits firms to substitute labour for capital and enables them to reduce product prices and thereby create more demand.

There are three major factors limiting the effectiveness of these policies: (i) 'deadweight' (subsidies or tax reductions received by workers who would have become employed anyway), (ii) 'displacement' (incumbent employees displaced by the subsidised new recruits) and (iii) 'substitution' (firms that benefit from the policies driving firms that don't benefit out of business). Clearly, the more closely the subsidies and the payroll tax reductions are targeted at the low-wage workers, the smaller the deadweight and substitutions, but the larger the displacement.

Aside from this, a potential drawback of these policies is that, by raising the take-home pay of unskilled workers relative to skilled workers, they reduce the returns to training. Insofar as labour and capital are complementary in production, the resulting fall in human capital acquisition may also lead to a fall in physical capital formation. For this reason, it appears desirable that these policies be supplemented by subsidies to education and training. This additional element, however, would substantially increase the cost of the intervention. Another drawback is that these policies may encourage excessive creation of unsatisfying, dead-end jobs, providing little potential for advancement. In that event, the unemployment trap would be replaced by the 'trap of the working poor'. But even in that event, workers would experience a rise in their living standards: since the take-up is voluntary, workers and firms will avail themselves of these policy measures only if it is to their advantage.

6.5 Recruitment subsidies

The case for recruitment subsidies is similar to that for low-wage subsidies and payroll tax reductions:[62] they bring down labour costs and thereby promote employment and reduce unemployment. In fact, they are better targeted, since they are granted only to new recruits.

Once again, deadweight, displacement and substitution limit the employment effect of recruitment subsidies. Obviously, the deadweight is generally lower for recruitment subsidies than for low-wage subsidies or payroll tax reductions, but the displacement and substitution effects are likely to be higher. In any event, the aggregate employment impact of recruitment subsidies is invariably less than the number of jobs subsidised. Beyond that, their effectiveness is likely to be further reduced by the ways in which they are financed. If employer-based taxes are used for this purpose, these taxes will directly discourage employment; if income taxes are used, they will reduce product demand and thus discourage employment indirectly. In either case, the positive effect of the recruitment subsidies on employment will generally outweigh the negative effect of the taxes.

It is sometimes alleged that another deficiency of recruitment subsidies – once again shared by low-wage subsidies and payroll tax reductions – is that they distort firms' decisions concerning factor composition, encouraging labour at the expense of capital, for example. This matter is quite unlikely to be of macroeconomic significance: the inefficiencies resulting from a distorted labour–capital mix are generally insignificant in comparison with the inefficiencies associated with long-term unemployment. Besides, as the efficiency wage, insider–outsider and union theories suggest, free market activity may often be associated with market failures that give rise to excessive wages and deficient unemployment. In this context, recruitment subsidies may correct for an existing distortion, rather than create a distortion themselves.

6.6 *Benefit transfers*

The 'benefit transfers programme' (BTP) involves giving long-term unemployed people the opportunity to use part of their unemployment benefits to provide vouchers for firms that hire them.[63] The longer a person is unemployed, the greater is the voucher. Larger vouchers are also granted to firms that use them entirely on training. Once the worker finds a job, the voucher gradually falls as the period of employment proceeds.

In this way, benefit transfers are a combination of several different structural policies: the vouchers are equivalent to a special type of recruitment subsidy; the voucher supplement for training is a special type of training subsidy; and the transfer of unemployment benefit amounts to a reform of the unemployment benefit system.

The rationale for benefit transfers are various. (i) They permit people to transfer funds out of a system that discourages employment in order to give firms an incentive to create employment. (ii) They extend the choice sets of workers and firms. Workers offer the vouchers to potential employers when their expected wage offers are sufficiently high; the employers accept the vouchers when the resulting labour costs are sufficiently low. Thus the scheme is used only when both parties are made better off. (iii) The scheme is costless to the government, since the vouchers are financed through the unemployment benefits forgone benefits. (iv) The scheme is not inflationary, since the long-term unemployed have no significant effect on wage inflation, and since the vouchers reduce labour costs and thereby exert downward pressure on prices. (v) The scheme functions as an automatic stabiliser, since a fall in unemployment reduces the amount spent on unemployment benefits, which in turn reduces the funds available for the employment vouchers. (vi) By providing generous vouchers to firms that use them for training, the scheme gives these firms an incentive to maximise the productivity-enhancing effect of this training. (vii) Finally, the scheme could help overcome regional unemployment problems. Regions of high unemployment would become ones in which a large proportion of the workforce commanded training subsidies. This may give firms an incentive to relocate there and give the unemployed people the requisite skills.

Since benefit transfers are voluntary, non-inflationary, costless to the government and would doubtless increase employment, countries have little, if anything, to lose from adopting them. They therefore appear desirable as a first line of attack against long-term unemployment. Once the employment-creating potential of unemployment benefits has been exploited in this way, further measures may well be necessary to bring European unemployment down to socially acceptable levels.

7 Concluding remarks

It has become a platitude to say that every sensible piece of economic policy advice rests on a reasoned analysis of the underlying policy problem, and every reasoned analysis is based on a theory of how the economy functions. Politicians may believe that their policy proposals rest simply on 'common sense'; but if there is any sense underlying this common sense, it exists in the form of a coherent, self-contained theory. As Keynes (1936) put it,

> The idea of economists and political philosophers, both when they are right and when they are wrong, are more powerful than is commonly understood. Indeed, the world is ruled by little else. Practical men, who believe themselves to be quite exempt from any intellectual influences, are usually slaves of some defunct economist.

But given that this is obvious, it is surprising that so little is done to explore the predictive power of a theory, before that theory is used as basis for policy formulation. This survey is a tentative first step towards evaluating unemployment policies in this light.

It goes without saying that such an evaluation alone is not sufficient for the design of unemployment policies but – as we have seen – it can provide a variety of useful insights about where promising policy approaches are to be found. For example, we have examined how differences in labour turnover costs across sectors (e.g. services versus manufacturing) and regions (e.g. the EC versus the USA) may help account for differences in levels, variability, duration, persistence and distribution of unemployment. This analysis suggests that policies to reduce the harmful effects of these labour turnover costs – such as reductions in statutory severance pay, training and recruitment subsidies, benefit transfers and policies to lower the barriers to the entry of new firms – may have a significant role to play in combating unemployment. These and the variety of other insights adduced above show why it is important to evaluate employment policies through the predictions of the underlying theories.

NOTES

This chapter was written while I was a Visiting Scholar at the Research Department of the International Monetary Fund. The views expressed in this chapter do not necessarily represent those of the IMF or its member countries. I am deeply indebted to David Coe, Bob Ford and Bert Hickman for their perceptive comments and suggestions.

1 It may, but need not, call for government intervention at all since (i) it may not be feasible to correct some market failures through government unemployment policy and (ii) even when it is possible to do so, the gains from correcting the market failures may fall short of the losses from the 'government failures' (policy-induced inefficiencies).

2 See, for example, Lucas (1972, 1975). Some economists use the term 'natural rate of unemployment' more broadly, letting it stand for any short-term equilibrium unemployment rate, regardless of whether the labour market clears (e.g. Phelps, 1970, 1994) and regardless of the underlying institutional structure (e.g. Friedman, 1968). In that view, the natural rate clearly rests on much more than tastes, technologies and endowments; it could also depend on the existence of credit constraints, degree of competition in labour and product markets, the nature of wage-bargaining institutions, the level of labour turnover costs, and the size of the incumbent workforces, to give just a few examples. Then, however, the natural rate theory becomes so all-inclusive that it can no longer be distinguished from labour union, insider–outsider, efficiency wage and other theories.

3 Taking a wider view of the natural rate theory, it is worth noting that the degree of competition and the economic institutions governing behaviour in the labour, product, credit, and international markets are generally not subject to cyclical fluctuations either. Thus cyclical fluctuations in unemployment remain to be explained by fluctuations in expectational errors.

4 See, for example, Barro (1981), Lucas and Rapping (1969).

5 The real business cycle theory, discussed below, makes much of this implication, particularly with respect to technological shocks.

6 Inter-country differences in persistence and variability are motivated by differences in preferences and technological opportunities.

7 Some claim that the standard measures of the elasticity of labour supply are irrelevant because the choice between work and inactivity is often a discrete one. In that event, the theory requires that people's decisions about whether or not to participate in the labour force be very sensitive to variations in real wages and real interest rates.

8 See, for example, King and Plosser (1984), King, Plosser and Rebelo (1988a, 1988b), Kydland and Prescott (1982) and Long and Plosser (1983).

9 In the real business cycle models, the technological shocks are measured by 'Solow residuals', which are the differences through time between the growth

rate of output and a weighted average of the growth rates of factor inputs. But given the difficulty of interpreting negative Solow residuals as technological regress, it is perhaps more plausible to see them as reflecting labour and capital hoarding.

10 See Keynes (1936). A microeconomic rationale for these effects, based on exogenously given wages and prices, was proposed by Barro and Grossman (1976) and others.

11 For example, Barro and Grossman (1976), Malinvaud (1977) and Muellbauer and Portes (1978).

12 For example, Mankiw (1985).

13 Akerlof and Yellen (1985).

14 For example, Blanchard (1983), Calvo (1983) and Taylor (1979).

15 See, for example, Carlton (1986), who finds significant price rigidities in manufacturing. Gordon (1990) has argued that, in the context of a complex input–output system, complete indexation may be difficult due to 'the informational problem of trying to anticipate the effect of a currently perceived nominal demand change on the weighted average costs'; but it is hard to see why some (albeit imperfect) indexing should not be better than none.

16 In practice, some wage–price-setting rules appear to involve both time- and state-dependence, such as the provision in wage contracts to renegotiate at specified intervals but only under specified conditions, such as the inflation rate exceeding a certain magnitude. It has been suggested that if the major cost is that of learning the state, a time-dependent rule is desirable; whereas if the major cost is a menu cost, a state-dependent rule will be chosen. However, menu costs and learning costs are notoriously difficult to measure.

17 Compare, for example, the non-neutrality of money under the time-dependent contracts of Taylor (1979) with the neutrality under the state-dependent contracts of Caplin and Spulber (1986).

18 This depicts the horizontal sum of firms' profit-maximising relations between labour demand and the real wage, under perfect or imperfect competition.

19 This could represent either a labour supply curve or the real wage that emerges, at any given level of employment, from wage bargaining or efficiency wage minimisation. Strictly speaking, the wage-setting curve need not necessarily be upward-sloping, just larger in slope than the labour demand curve. Under some bargaining and efficiency wage conditions, the wage-setting curve may be upward-sloping and this is clearly also the case when the curve represents a labour supply curve in a range where the income effect exceeds the substitution effect.

20 There are, of course, a number of other ways whereby changes in product demand could affect employment, such as income effects on labour supply (e.g. Dixon, 1987; Mankiw, 1988, Startz, 1989), increasing returns (e.g. Cooper and John, 1988 and Chatterji and Cooper, 1989), search with strategic complementarities (e.g. Howitt, 1985 and Pissarides, 1985), union-induced labour immobilities which make the employment level sensitive to the allocation of government spending across sectors (Dixon, 1988), and unemployment persistence mechanisms in operation after a change in product demand temporarily reduces the real wage due to a temporary nominal wage rigidity (e.g. Lindbeck and Snower, 1989).

21 Formally, the labour demand curve is given by $F(1m) \cdot h_n = w$, where the left-

hand term is the real marginal revenue product of labour and w is the real wage. Specifically, F is the number of firms, $h_n = h_n(n, k)$ is the marginal product of labour (where n and k are each firm's use of labour and capital, respectively) and $m = c(\eta \cdot F)$ is the Lerner's index of monopoly power (where c is the conjectural variations coefficient and u is the price elasticity of product demand). Thus channels (i) and (ii) work through the degree of monopoly power, channels (iii) and (iv) work through the effect of the capital stock on the marginal product of labour, channel (v) deals with shifts of the labour demand curve due to changes in the number of firms (which also affects the degree of monopoly power) and channel (vi) is concerned with the direct effect of product demand on the marginal product of labour. Lindbeck and Snower (1994) provide a formal analysis of all these channels of transmission.

22 A useful survey is contained in Dixon and Rankin (1994).

23 See, in particular, Rotemberg and Saloner (1986). This approach is in line with a long-standing tradition, characterised by Pigou (1927), Kalecki (1983) and Keynes (1939), who asserted that firms' market power may vary countercyclically.

24 See Greenwald and Stiglitz (1988).

25 See Lindbeck and Snower (1994).

26 In other words, the real marginal revenue product of labour at full capacity may fall short of the real wage.

27 See, for example, Pagano (1990), Snower (1983b).

28 See Lindbeck and Snower (1989).

29 These policies involve measures to dismantle government regulations restricting the creation of new firms, reforming the system of profit, income, capital gains and wealth taxes to put new firms at less of a disadvantage in comparison with established firms, increasing competition among financial institutions so as to reduce credit constraints on new firms, and reducing the coverage of collective bargaining wage agreements so as to permit new firms to hire new recruits on competitive terms.

30 In general, training programmes, whether in the public or private sector, may be divided into two broad categories: vocational training and 'employability training'. The latter focuses on a limited number of basic skills that enable people to adjust to a worker environment and adapt to the requirement of semi-skilled jobs. In some countries Germany in particular, vocational training is integrated within a formal system of basic education.

31 See, for example, Blanchard and Diamond (1989), Diamond (1982), Mortensen (1986) and Pissarides (1986).

32 The turbulence hypothesis has been formalised by Lilien (1982), but has found no significant empirical support, for example Abraham and Katz (1986).

33 There are a variety of market failures in training provision that apply to all classes of workers. See, for example, Becker, Murphy and Tamura (1990) and Booth and Snower (1994). Some of these market failures fall with particular severity on the unemployed. It is these latter failures that make the case for using training subsidies as an instrument for combating unemployment.

34 See Snower (1994b).

35 See Snower (1994a).

36 The German apprenticeship system has both of these ingredients.

37 As noted, however, there is little evidence that this has actually happened in advanced industrialised countries over the past two decades.

38 The EC Commission has laid stress on these measures in combating European unemployment. For example, the Council Resolution of 29 May 1990 recommended that counselling interviews be made available to all long-term unemployed people. There is also wide recognition that these measures will have a chance of being particularly effective only if they are combined with other active labour market policies, such as training programmes.

39 They have been said to become 'addicted' to being unemployed. The theory of addiction provides some useful insights here. See, for example, Becker and Murphy (1988).

40 This is, of course, not the only conceivable explanation of unemployment persistence. Other, comparably important, causes are employment adjustment costs, wage–price staggering effects, insider membership effects and labour force participation adjustment costs.

41 In Weiss (1980) a higher wage offer encourages workers of high skill, who were previously self-employed, to join the firm. In Shapiro and Stiglitz (1984) the firm randomly samples workers' effort and fires those who shirk; thus a higher wage offer raises effort by raising the expected penalty for shirking. In Snower (1983a) a higher wage offer discourages workers from searching on the job and thereby promotes productivity. In Akerlof (1982) workers agree to work more than what is specified in their contract and firms, in return, pay more than the minimum amount that would be necessary to attract them.

42 See, for example, Salop (1979) and Stiglitz (1985).

43 Of course many efficiency wage models also explain how unemployment may rise in response to a drop in labour productivity, a rise in the real interest rate, or a rise in the unemployment benefit. But as with the search models, the efficiency wage models cannot lay unique claim to these predictions. The efficiency wage models do not add much to what other theories have to say in this respect. Similarly, the inclusion of labour turnover costs in an efficiency wage-setting can provide an explanation of why unemployment rates tend to be serially correlated, and differences in the magnitude of these costs can help account for inter-country differences in such serial correlation as well as inter-country differences in unemployment durations. But labour turnover costs are not an intrinsic building-block of efficiency wage models. These models can rationalise the existence of unemployment even in the absence of labour turnover costs, and the addition of these costs to a wide variety of other theories would yield equal insights into unemployment dynamics.

44 See, for example, Bover, Muellbauer and Murphy (1989).

45 See, for example, McDonald and Solow (1981) and Oswald (1982, 1985).

46 This question is answered by the insider–outsider theory, discussed below. But if the answer of the insider–outsider theory is accepted – namely, that it is labour turnover costs that prevent firms from replacing union members by non-members – the traditional union theories must undergo substantial revision. (See, for example, Lindbeck and Snower, 1987b.)

47 This issue can be addressed through labour market bargaining theory, which deals with the question of how employers and employees split the economic rent from employment activity. There are two broad approaches: in one, employers and employees bargain over wages and, once the wages have been set, the employers make the employment decisions unilaterally; in the other, the employers and employees bargain over wages and employment simultaneously. (There are also models that straddle these two extremes, e.g.

Manning, 1987.) The former are called 'right-to-manage models' (since the firms make the employment decisions by themselves). It can be shown that the bargaining outcome here is inefficient, in the sense that it is possible to find wage–employment combinations that make one party to the negotiations better off without making the other party worse off. This is a common feature of institutional setups in which the price and quantity decisions are made by different agents. The inefficiency of course does not arise in the latter models, which are therefore called 'efficient bargain models'.

48 However, in a more recent article (Calmfors, 1993), Calmfors distances himself somewhat from this simple policy conclusion. He acknowledges that centralisation is a multi-faceted feature of bargaining systems and that labour market performance is likely to respond quite differently to changes in the degree of centralisation across occupations, sectors, unions, employers' confederations, and geographic regions. He also notes that the degree of centralisation is likely to be particularly significant for labour market performance only in the non-tradeable sectors, where foreign competition is weak.

49 Under free market conditions, the private sector generally has deficient incentives to provide unemployment insurance, due to moral hazard and adverse selection problems (giving people unemployment insurance increases their chances of being unemployed) and credit constraints (which prevent workers from purchasing their optimal amounts of insurance).

50 This theory is discussed below.

51 See, for example, Layard, Nickell and Jackman (1991).

52 See, for example, Coe and Snower (1994) and Snower (1994e) for more detail on this policy approach.

53 Handicapped people and those who are likely to be more productive in the household sector than in the labour market (like single mothers with several infants) would be exempted from this condition. (See Snower, 1994c.)

54 Of course, economies may generate something like a 'lump of labour' over the very short run, that is, over a time span short enough to preclude readjustments in the size of firms' workforces. But this time span is of little interest for the design of unemployment policy.

55 Of course, a reduction in labour turnover costs also has a direct effect on unemployment. This effect could be either positive (as when a reduction in hiring costs stimulates hiring) or negative (as when a reduction in firing costs leads to more firing). (See, for example, Bentolila and Bertola, 1990.)

56 See, for example, Lindbeck and Snower (1986, 1988).

57 See Weitzman (1983, 1984).

58 Firms may not wish to disclose this information in order to preserve the confidentiality of their business strategies.

59 See, for example, Drèze, Malinvaud *et al.* (1994) and Phelps (1994).

60 The effectiveness of these policies on these variables clearly depends on the elasticity of labour demand. The greater the elasticity, the more the unemployment rates of the low-wage workers will fall and the less their take-home pay will rise.

61 Such as those reported in Drèze, Malinvaud *et al.* (1994).

62 See, for example, Bishop and Haveman (1979), Kaldor (1936) and Layard and Nickell (1980).

63 See Snower (1994d, 1994e).

REFERENCES

Abraham, K. and L.F. Katz, 1986. 'Cyclical unemployment: sectoral shifts or aggregate disturbances?' *Journal of Political Economy*, **94**, 507–22

Akerlof, G.A., 1982. 'Labor contracts as partial gift exchange', *Quarterly Journal of Economics*, **97**, 543–69

Akerlof, G.A. and J.L. Yellen, 1985. 'A near-rational model of the business cycle, with wage and price inertia', *Quarterly Journal of Economics*, **100**, (Supplement), 823–38

Ball, L. and S.G. Cecchetti, 1988. 'Imperfect information and staggered price setting', *American Economic Review*, **78**, 999–1018

Ball, L. and D. Romer, 1989. 'The equilibrium and optimal timing of price changes', *Review of Economic Studies*, **56**, 179–98

Barro, R., 1981. 'Intertemporal substitution and the business cycle', *Carnegie–Rochester Conference Series on Public Policy*, **14**, 237–68

Barro, R.J. and H. Grossman, 1976. *Money, Employment and Inflation*, Cambridge: Cambridge University Press

Becker, G. and K.M. Murphy, 1988. 'A theory of rational addiction', *Journal of Political Economy*, **96**, 675–700

Becker, G., K.M. Murphy and R. Tamura, 1990. 'Human capital, fertility, and economic growth', *Journal of Political Economy*, **98**, S12–S37

Bentolila, S. and G. Bertola, 1990. 'Firing costs and labour demand in Europe: how bad is Eurosclerosis?, *Review of Economic Studies*, **57**, 381–401

Bishop, J. and R. Haveman, 1979. 'Selective employment subsidies: can Okun's Law be repealed?', *American Economic Review, Papers and Proceedings*, **69**, 124–30

Blanchard, O., 1983. 'Price asynchronization and price level inertia', in R. Dornbusch and M.H. Simonsen (eds.), *Inflation, Debt, and Indexation*, Cambridge, MA: MIT Press

Blanchard, O. and P. Diamond, 1989. 'The Beveridge curve', *Brookings Papers on Economic Activity*, **1**, 1–60

Blanchard, O. and L. Summers, 1986. 'Hysteresis and the European unemployment problem', in S. Fischer (ed.), *NBER Macroeconomics Annual*, **1**, Cambridge, MA: MIT Press, 15–77

Booth, A. and D.J. Snower (eds.), 1994. *Acquiring Skills: Market Failures, their Symptoms, and Policy Responses*, Cambridge: Cambridge University Press

Bover, O., J. Muellbauer and A. Murphy, 1989. 'Housing, wages, and UK labour markets', *Oxford Bulletin of Economics and Statistics*, **51**, 97–136

Calmfors, L., 1993. 'Centralization of wage bargaining and macroeconomic performance: a survey', *OECD Economic Studies*, **21**, 161–91

Calmfors, L. and J. Driffill, 1988. 'Centralization of wage bargaining and macroeconomic performance', *Economic Policy*, **6**, 13–61

Calvo, G.A., 1983. 'Staggered prices in a utility-maximizing framework', *Journal of Monetary Economics*, 12 (November), 383–98

Caplin, A. and D. Spulber, 1987. 'Menu costs and the neutrality of money', *Quarterly Journal of Economics*, **102**, 703–26

Carlton, D. 1986. 'The rigidity of prices', *American Economic Review*, **76**, 637–58

Chatterji, S. and R. Cooper, 1989. 'Multiplicity of equilibria and fluctuations in dynamic imperfectly competitive economies', *American Economic Review*, **79**, 353–7

Coe, D. and D.J. Snower, 1994. 'Fundamental labor market reform', Washington, DC: IMF, mimeo

Cooper, R. and A. John, 1988. 'Coordinating coordination failures in Keynesian models', *Quarterly Journal of Economics*, **103**, 441–64

Diamond, P., 1982. 'Aggregate demands management in search equilibrium', *Journal of Political Economy*, **90**, 881–94

Dixon, H., 1987. 'A simple model of imperfect competition with Walrasian features', *Oxford Economic Papers*, **39**, 134–60

1988. 'Unions, oligopoly and the natural range of employment', *Economic Journal*, **98**, 1127–47

Dixon, H. and N. Rankin, 1994. 'Imperfect competition and macroeconomics: a survey', *Oxford Economic Papers*, **46**, 171–99

Drèze, J., E. Malinvaud *et al.*, 1994. 'Growth and employment: the scope of an European initiative', *European Economic Review*, **38**

Friedman, M., 1968. 'The role of monetary policy', *American Economic Review*, **58**, 1–17

Greenwald, B. and J.E. Stiglitz, 1988. 'Examining alternative macroeconomic theories', *Brookings Papers on Economic Activity*, **1**, 207–60

Gordon, R., 1990. 'What is New-Keynesian economics?', *Journal of Economic Literature*, **28**, 1115–71

Howitt, P., 1985. 'Transactions costs in the theory of unemployment', *American Economic Review*, **75**, 88–100

Kaldor, N., 1936. 'Wage subsidies as a remedy for unemployment', *Journal of Political Economy*, **44**

Kalecki, M., 1938. 'The determinants of the distribution of the national income', *Econometrica*, **6**, 97–112

Keynes, J.M., 1936. *The General Theory of Employment, Interest, and Money*, London: Macmillan

1939. 'Relative movements of real wages and output', *Economic Journal*, **49**, 34–51

King, R.G. and C. Plosser, 1984. 'Money, credit and prices in a real business cycle', *American Economic Review*, **74**, 363–80

King, R., C. Plosser and S. Rebelo, 1988a. 'Production, growth and business cycles I: the basic neoclassical model', *Journal of Monetary Economics*, **21**, 195–232

1988b. 'Production, growth and business cycles II: new directions', *Journal of Monetary Economics*, **21**, 309–41

Kydland, F. and E.C. Prescott, 1982. 'Time to build and aggregate fluctuations', *Econometrica*, **50**, 1345–70

Layard, P.R.G. and S.J. Nickell, 1980. 'The case for subsidizing extra jobs', *Economic Journal*, **90**, 51–73

Layard, P.R.G., S.J. Nickell and R.A. Jackman, 1991. *Unemployment: Macroeconomic Performance and the Labour Market*, Oxford: Oxford University Press

Lilien, D.M., 1982. 'Sectoral shifts and cyclical unemployment', *Journal of Political Economy*, **90**, 777–93

Lindbeck, A., 1994, 'The welfare state and the employment problem', *American Economic Review*, **84**

Lindbeck, A. and D.J. Snower, 1986. 'Wage setting, unemployment and insider–outsider relations', *American Economic Review*, **76**, 235–9

1987a. 'Union activity, unemployment persistence and wage–employment ratchets', *European Economic Review*, **31**, 157–67

1987b. 'Strike and lock-out threats and fiscal policy', *Oxford Economic Papers*, **39**, 760–84

1988a. 'Cooperation, harassment, and involuntary unemployment', *American Economic Review*, **78**, 167–88

1988b. 'Long-term unemployment and macroeconomic policy', *American Economic Review*, **78**, 38–43

1989. 'Transmission mechanisms from the product to the labour market', *Discussion Paper*, Institute for International Economic Studies, University of Stockholm

1994. 'How are product demand changes transmitted to the labor market?', *Economic Journal*, **104**, 386–98

Long, J.B. and C. Plosser, 1983. 'Real business cycles', *Journal of Political Economy*, **91**, 1345–70

Lucas, R.E., 1972. 'Expectation and the neutrality of money', *Journal of Economic Theory*, **4**, 103–24

1975. 'An equilibrium model of the business cycle', *Journal of Political Economic*, **83**, 1113–44

Lucas, R.E. and L.A. Rapping, 1969. 'Real wages, employment, and inflation', *Journal of Political Economy*, **77**, 721–54

Malinvaud, E., 1977. *The Theory of Unemployment Reconsidered*, Oxford: Oxford University Press

Mankiw, N.G., 1985. 'Small menu costs and large business cycles: a macroeconomic model of monopoly', *Quarterly Journal of Economics*, **100**, 529–39

1988. 'Imperfect competition and the Keynesian Cross', *Economics Letters*, **26**, 7–13

Manning, A., 1987. 'An integration of trade union models in a sequential bargaining framework', *Economic Journal*, **97**, 121–39

McDonald, I.M. and R.M. Solow, 1981. 'Wage bargaining and employment', *American Economic Review*, **71**, 896–908

Mortensen, D.T., 1986. 'Job search and labor market analysis', in O.C. Ashenfalter and R. Layard (eds.), *Handbook of Labor Economics*, vol. 2, Amsterdam: North-Holland, 849–919

Muellbauer, J. and R. Portes, 1978. 'Macroeconomic models with quantity rationing', *Economic Journal*, **88**, 788–821

Nickell, S., 1978. 'Fixed costs, employment and labor demand over the cycle', *Economica*, **46**, 329–45

Oswald, A., 1982. 'The microeconomic theory of the trade union', *Economic Journal*, **92**, 576–95

1985. 'The economic theory of trade unions: an introductory survey', *Scandinavian Journal of Economics*, **82**, 160–93

1987. 'Efficient contracts are on the labor demand curve: theory and facts', London School of Economics Centre for Labour Economics, *Discussion Paper*, 284

Pagano, M., 1990. 'Imperfect competition, under-employment equilibria and fiscal policy', *Economic Journal*, **100**, 440–63

Phelps, E.S., 1970. 'Money wage dynamics and labor market equilibrium', in E. Phelps (ed.), *Microeconomic Foundation of Employment and Inflation Theory*, New York: Norton

1994a. *Structural Slumps: The Modern Equilibrium Theory of Unemployment, Interest, and Assets*: Cambridge, MA: Harvard University Press

1994b. 'Wage subsidy programs: alternative designs', chapter 7 in this volume

Pigou, A.C., 1927. *Industrial Fluctuations*, London: Macmillan

Pissarides, C., 1985. 'Short run equilibrium dynamics of unemployment, vacancies, and real wages', *American Economic Review*, **75**

1986. 'Unemployment and vacancies in Britain', *Economic Policy*, **3**, 499–559

Rotemberg, J. and G. Saloner, 1986. 'A supergame-theoretic model of price wars during booms', *American Economic Review*, **76**, 390–407

Salop, S., 1979. 'A model of the natural rate of unemployment', *American Economic Review*, **69**, 117–25

Shapiro, C. and J.E. Stiglitz, 1984. 'Equilibrium unemployment as a worker discipline device', *American Economic Review*, **74**, 433–44

Snower, D.J., 1983a. 'Search, flexible wages and involuntary unemployment', *Discussion Paper*, **132**, Birkbeck College, University of London

1983b. 'Imperfect competition, under-employment and crowding-out', *Oxford Economic Papers*, **35**, 245–70

1994a. 'The low-skill, bad-job trap', *Working Paper*, Washington, DC: IMF

1994b. 'Poaching and unemployment', Department of Economics, Birkbeck College, University of London, mimeo

1994c. 'Converting unemployment benefits into employment subsidies', *American Economic Review Paper and Proceedings*, **84**, 65–70

1994d. 'The simple economics of benefit transfers', chapter 6 in this volume

1994e. 'Unemployment benefits versus conditional negative income taxes', *Working Paper*, Washington, DC: IMF

Startz, R., 1989. 'Monopolistic competition as a foundation for Keynesian macroeconomic models', *Quarterly Journal of Economics*, **104**, 737–52

Stiglitz, J.E., 1985. 'Equilibrium wage distributions', *Economic Journal*, **95**, 595–618

Taylor, J.B., 1979. 'Staggered wage setting in a macro model', *American Economic Review*, **69**, 108–13

Weiss, A., 1980. 'Job queues and layoffs in labor markets with flexible wages', *Journal of Political Economy*, **88**, 526–38

Weitzman, M., 1983. 'Some macroeconomic implications of alternative compensation systems', *Economic Journal*, **93**, 763–83

1984. *The Share Economy*, Cambridge, MA: Harvard University Press

3 High unemployment from a political economy perspective

GILLES SAINT-PAUL

1 Introduction

Unemployment in Europe has now been abnormally high for almost 20 years. Yet this has generated no major disruption in the way society is organised or in the political system: it seems that many people have learned to live with it. An article in the *Financial Times* (17 May 1994) acknowledged that

> given the intractability of the jobless problem, and the universal political commitment to resolving it, unemployment may have surprisingly little impact on voting patterns ... In most large European countries the electorate has lived with persistently high unemployment for nearly two decades and any party offering a quick-fix solution would face a large credibility gap.

Yet we see countries which for years have avoided high unemployment: the USA, Switzerland, Sweden, Japan, Portugal. So maybe it is not the problem which is intractable but the political commitment to resolving it which is not as universal as it may seem.

In this chapter we study the problem of (European) unemployment from a political economy perspective. That is, we study how the policies that are conducive to high unemployment are the outcome of the political process and thus reflect the balance of power in society. We also analyse how policies aimed at curing unemployment must pass the test of political viability.

The chapter is organised as follows. Section 2 ('Theory') discusses some general principles that are useful in understanding the political aspects of labour market policy. Section 3 (labelled 'Implications') tries to illustrate how these principles may help to analyse the viability of (good or bad) policies, and hence why the good ones are not implemented and the bad ones not removed. We shall take standard views about the way these policies work, even though the theoretical and empirical support for these views is often weak.

2 Theory

In this section we analyse different mechanisms through which the interplay between political and economic considerations may lead to high unemployment. We first study the nature of the distributive conflicts in the labour market. We then study how coordination failures may lead to too many labour market rigidities. Then we discuss how the employed's exposure to unemployment is a crucial determinant in shaping labour market policy. Last, we analyse the relevance of time-consistency issues for the problem of unemployment.

2.1 Distributive conflicts in the labour market

In this section we start from the simple observation that if labour market rigidities exist, it must be the case that they benefit some politically powerful groups (meaning either a majority of the people or a strongly organised minority). Yet this must be true only in a relative sense, since to the extent that these rigidities reduce economic efficiency and lead to an under-utilisation of resources, there should exist some side-payments schemes which would make everybody strictly better off when associated with a removal of rigidities. However, this is a rather theoretical possibility, for at least two reasons. First, the computational difficulties in designing such schemes are considerable, and lead to uncertainty with respect to the precise outcome of the reform (as in Fernandez and Rodrik, 1989), this uncertainty itself may be enough to block the reform. Second, and more importantly, after rigidities are removed the political system will deliver a system of transfers and taxes of its own, which has no reason to pertain to the set of taxes and transfers which would make everybody better off (we return to these issues below).

The question we ask in this section is therefore: what is the margin of manoeuvre for a group in the labour market to increase its welfare at the expense of others, and how can this lead to 'rigidity'?

If there were constant returns to scale and labour were the only factor of production, the answer would be simple. The income of any worker would be dictated by the marginal product of labour, which would be constant; labour would reap all the surplus from production and there is nothing more it could appropriate. Therefore, in such a world, workers would not be in favour of rigidities. Redistribution across workers would be feasible, but would not arise as long as labour was homogeneous.

2.1.1 Labour versus capital

What happens, now, when labour is not the only factor of production? Suppose capital is the other factor, and assume first that it is fixed. Then the marginal product of labour is decreasing in the amount of labour employed. In competitive equilibrium the marginal product of labour must equate the wage rate. Figure 3.1 illustrates this by plotting a labour demand curve and a labour supply curve. The surplus from production is equal to the surface between the two curves, with *A* the workers' surplus and *B* the firms' surplus. Now, it is clear that by either restricting employment or setting a wage floor, labour can increase its surplus at the expense of capital (figure 3.2). The surplus of labour moves to area *A'* which is greater than *A*, while the capitalist's surplus shrinks to *B'*. There are various real-world institutions which resemble such wage floors, such as the minimum wage, unemployment benefits, etc. Furthermore, it seems that this is a pretty efficient way of redistributing income from capital to labour! The wage floor (figure 3.2) allows us to redistribute a full rectangle *LMPQ* from capital to labour at the cost of a (traditionally small) triangle while economising on the costs of state intervention such as affecting the tax system, etc. I do not mean that this is the most efficient redistributive tool, but at a first-order approximation it looks satisfactory.

Of course, in the long run the story is quite different. The wage floor reduces the return on capital, so that its supply will actually shrink. The labour demand curve will shift downwards, as will the size of the cake and accordingly the surplus of labour. In many models the capital stock will collapse to zero unless the return to capital goes back to some required level (which typically depends on the saver's preferences or the international interest rate). This will force the real wage back to its previous level (this argument is hardly new, see Bean, 1988, 1994). In other words, in the long run, the capital–labour ratio is dictated by the required rate of return so that the reduced form production function has constant returns to labour, which consequently cannot increase its surplus.

Unless unions are very myopic (or very stupid), or capital adjusts very slowly, it is therefore unlikely that labour market rigidities can be used to redistribute income from capital to labour.

2.1.2 Skilled versus unskilled

Assume now that the two factors of production, instead of labour and capital, are skilled labour and unskilled labour. The argument we developed above is still valid, with 'capital' replaced by 'skilled labour'. The unskilled, by pushing up their wages, can increase their income while

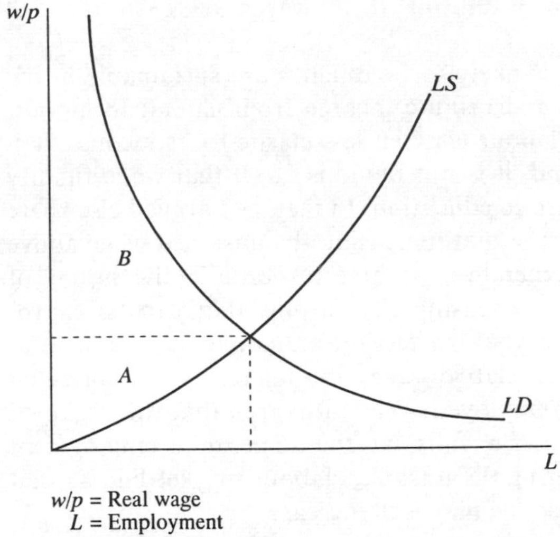

Figure 3.1 Labour demand and labour supply curve

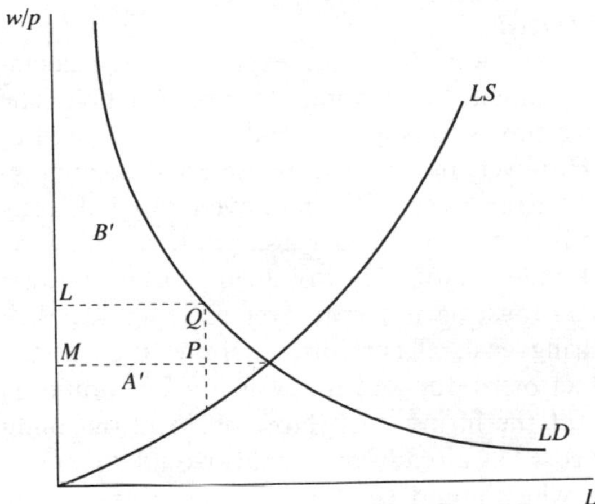

Figure 3.2 Increase in labour surplus at expense of capital

reducing the marginal product of the skilled and the skilled wage. A wage push will therefore redistribute income from the skilled to the unskilled, but also from those unskilled who are unlucky enough to lose their job to those who keep it. Once the policy is in place, the unskilled employed have little incentive to remove it, even though in principle they could be compensated for a fall of their wages back to the full employment level.

Moreover, such a scheme is likely to be much more sustainable in the long run than those which redistribute income from capital to labour. First, the supply of skilled labour is much less elastic to its income than the supply of capital. Second, it is not obvious at all that wage rigidity will actually reduce the return to education. In fact, as I argued elsewhere (1994a), it may well be the case that increasing the unskilled wage above the equilibrium level will generate a positive response in the supply of skilled labour, thus further increasing the surplus that can be expropriated away. This is because what matters for an individual's decision to invest in human capital is not relative wages, but relative wages corrected for the probability of being employed. While it is true that the unskilled wage rises and the skilled wage falls, at the same time employment prospects for a worker entering the unskilled labour market fall, so that the net return to becoming skilled may well increase.

Therefore, while attempts to expropriate capital are likely to be defeated in the long run as its supply shrinks, the unskilled may successfully expropriate the skilled and avoid a negative supply response.

2.1.3 Employed versus unemployed

Can the employed increase their welfare at the expense of the unemployed? At face value, one might be tempted to answer 'no'. The unemployed do not produce any surplus that could easily be expropriated by the employed.[1] However, in a model of frictional unemployment with costly search and recruitment, the employed can indirectly expropriate the unemployed by increasing their wages while reducing the unemployed's probability of finding a job. The argument runs as follows: in equilibrium, the employers must earn a rent over each worker they employ to recoup their hiring costs. Therefore, there will be a gap between the marginal product of labour and the wage, which would be equal to the annuity value of the hiring cost. Now, insiders (meaning workers for who the hiring cost has already been paid) would support a general increase in wages – which could be the outcome of any policy change associated with an increase in the insider's bargaining power or alternative wage – provided they remained below the marginal product of labour. Such an increase would protect their jobs but reduce the rent earned by firms, thus reducing the amount of hiring costs they are willing to pay. Hirings and vacancies would then fall, so that the unemployed would find jobs less often and therefore would be worse off. The employed have thus managed indirectly to expropriate the unemployed. Even though there are constant returns to scale in the production function, there is an indirect factor of production, 'vacancies', which is complementary with unemployment in the process of producing new hires. The surplus is split between labour and this indirect factor and there is room for redistributing it between these two factors. By raising wages, the employed reduce the return to vacancies and therefore the supply of vacancies, which reduces hirings and therefore the welfare of the unemployed.

2.1.4 Conclusion

We have examined how labour market rigidities may be the outcome of distributional conflicts among heterogeneous social groups. The 'marxist' view that this might be the outcome of 'class struggle' between labour and capital is incorrect. If there are constant returns and capital is a fully flexible factor in the long run, there is no scope for labour expropriating capital. Furthermore, in many instances labour will side with capital as sectoral or regional interests are at stake. Instead, we have seen that there is scope for redistributive conflicts within the labour market, in particular between skilled and unskilled workers and between the employed and the unemployed. These conflicts may help to explain where labour market rigidities come from, even though they are not likely to be the most appropriate weapon.

2.2 Coordination failures and the spreading of rigidities

In this section we study how the lack of coordination among various decision makers may lead to too many 'rigidities'. Although this is a frequently used word, it lacks a precise meaning. By 'rigidity' we mean any device that prevents the adjustment of prices and/or quantities in response to a shock. Such device may benefit the agents which will bear the burden of adjustment. A simple example to keep in mind is firing costs, which will protect jobs in declining industries and at the same time increase the bargaining power of insiders. Another example is subsidies, which slow re-allocation from declining to productive sectors.

Rigidities may be decided by society as a whole as thc outcome of some political mechanism of aggregating preferences. For example, if the employed are a majority, they could increase wages and firing costs at the expense of the unemployed; if the unskilled are more numerous than the skilled, they could impose a minimum wage which would help them and harm the skilled. Alternatively, rigidities may be imposed by a particular sector or agent on some variable which is especially relevant for that sector or agent, regardless of what happens in the rest of society. This could be done through lobbying at the legal or government level, or simply because the variable we consider is entirely controlled by the agent we consider. In all societies, decision making is actually a mixture of coordinated, democratic mechanisms and uncoordinated mechanisms such as lobbying or local (or sectoral) bargaining.

Now, the uncoordinated mechanisms are likely to lead to a 'sclerotic' society with too much rigidity. Mancur Olson (1965, 1982) has written extensively on that. I want to insist on two phenomena which would lead to excess rigidity and which are particularly relevant in order to understand where it comes from.

The first phenomenon is the well known 'prisoner's dilemma'. When some agent takes a decision it ignores the impact of its decision on other agents. When all agents do this, the outcome is likely to be inefficient. Unions (or sometimes firms) in a particular sector or region may create rigidities to insulate themselves from competition. By doing so they reduce opportunities in the rest of society. In equilibrium, all sectors are rigid and the economy is blocked by an inefficient equilibrium. Societies with a higher degree of centralisation in decision making will tend to be better off (see Calmfors and Driffill, 1988), although centralisation may create problems of its own (Calmfors and Horn, 1986).

The second phenomenon is related to the first. It is the propensity of rigidities to spread like a disease across sectors and markets. The virus is called 'opportunity cost'. When a sector (or region) is hit by a negative shock, it can elect to adjust to the shock or to resist it by establishing rigidities (provided it has some degree of collective action). The choice it will make will depend on the relative costs and benefits of these two alternatives. Now, if the rest of the economy is more rigid, adjusting will be more costly because it will be more difficult to relocate in a new region or sector. For example, if firing costs are high in those sectors which hire, there will be fewer hirings in these sectors. Thus the sector will have more incentive to choose the rigid option. In other words, the opportunity cost of establishing a rigidity falls when the rest of the economy is more rigid. Along the same lines, rigidity may also spread across markets. For example, if the housing market is heavily regulated geographical mobility will be very costly to workers, so that they will have more incentive to support policies which prevent such geographical mobility.

To summarise: if X decides to be more 'rigid', not only will this exert a negative spillover on Y (the prisoner's dilemma), but Y is more likely to also become rigid (the opportunity cost virus).

These coordination failures have an important policy implication: *a gradual reform of the labour market may be impossible*. Consider, for example, an economy with two sectors. Each sector may elect to be either 'rigid' or 'flexible'. The payoffs are given by the following matrix:

	R	F
R	0,0	2,-1
F	-1,2	1,1

This is a standard prisoner's dilemma situation: each sector will elect to be rigid regardless of the other's choice. The Nash equilibrium outcome is therefore (R, R), which yields a payoff inferior to the Pareto-superior outcome (F, F). Such a situation could arise in many real-world problems of interest to us, for example if sectors are competing for subsidies or if unions try to raise their bargaining power. Suppose now that one votes sequentially over removing rigidities in one sector and then the other. Assume that any sector can block a reform.[2] Then clearly both reforms would be rejected. If one were to vote once and for all over a policy package of removing all rigidities at the same time, the reform would pass.

We will discover below, however, that a quite different type of gradualism may be useful to implement labour market reform.

2.3 *Exposure and politico–economic complementarities*

The social group who presumably benefits most from policies to cure unemployment is the unemployed themselves. The problem is that, by their nature, it is unlikely that they could impose such policies. First, even in situations where unemployment is considered as 'large', they are a minority. Second, they are poorly organised and few political parties are interested in getting support from them. One may ask why this is so. There are at least two reasons. First, this is quite a heterogeneous group. Hence they are likely to support different policies: an 18-year-old male unemployed would, for example, support a reduction in the minimum wage or social security taxes, while a 47-year-old long-term unemployed would be in favour of training programmes; women might have a preference for increases in flexibility and part-time work, etc. Second, this is a transient category: even with the low turnover rates which prevail in European societies, people get out of unemployment at a speed which is large compared to the political cycle. When they exit unemployment, their interests change. So addressing the problems faced by the unemployed is probably not a good way to establish a stable constituency.

Therefore, policies which cure unemployment must get the support of the employed. Such support will be easier to obtain when the employed are less different from the unemployed, i.e. when they are more exposed to unemployment. The next question is then: what are the economic ingredients which may lead to such a favourable situation?

One element of the answer is that the employed will be more exposed, and reform will be easier, if the labour market is not too 'rigid' to start with (for example, if firing costs are not too high). Therefore, there is a 'politico–economic complementarity' between the functioning of the labour market and the political incentives to change its regulation. This complementarity may lead to multiple equilibria: the economy may be stuck at a rigid equilibrium where the employed are not exposed enough to unemployment to support a reform of the labour market. The policy implication is that the more reform is needed (the higher the rigidities), the harder it is to get it through. Mild rigidities are easier to dispose of.

Another element of the answer is that some times are more appropriate than others to implement the reform. For example, when unemployment is sharply rising the employed are likely to be more exposed. Here it is not so much the level as the rate of change of unemployment that matters. A steady state with a high level of unemployment but low exposure is conceivable, if hirings are low. In such a situation, the employed will not bother much about unemployment.

It should also be noted that the distribution of exposure across employed workers matters. What is important is typically the exposure of the median voter, not the average exposure of the employed. Hence, in a 'dual economy' where 80 per cent of the employed have a 5 per cent separation rate and the remaining 20 per cent a 100 per cent separation rate, there will be less support for labour market flexibility than in a society where all employed workers have a 24 per cent separation rate. Yet average turnover is the same in both cases.

One piece of evidence which corroborates the view that the employed's exposure is an important determinant of whether unemployment is of political concern is the correlation between election results and unemployment. In Saint-Paul (1993), I have shown that the incumbent was more likely to lose an election when unemployment was rising, but not when it was high. It is the rate of change of unemployment, not its level, which is significant. Similar results are traditionally obtained when one looks at popularity polls. A natural interpretation of this regularity is that the rate of change of unemployment is a good proxy of the flow of job destruction, which is what matters for the employed.

2.4 *The issue of time-consistency*

Time-consistency is, like the prisoner's dilemma, another economist's workhorse. In a situation of strategic interaction between a policy maker and other agents, the course of events may differ from the one which was originally planned. This is because the policy maker will have an incentive to renege on its commitments once the agents have taken irreversible actions on the basis of those commitments. A popular example is capital taxation: it is optimal to promise to tax capital at a zero rate, but once it is installed there will be an incentive to tax it at a 100 per cent rate.

Time-consistency issues may help to explain why rigidities are persistent and difficult to remove. These issues may arise at two levels. First there is the standard commitment failure problem, as in the example of capital taxation. The government would like to commit itself not to adopt a policy which increases unemployment, but once firms and workers have made their choices on the basis of that expectation, it will actually have an incentive (for example, for tax revenue purposes) to adopt the policy. Of course, in equilibrium that will be anticipated by agents when they make their decisions, so that the outcome will be worse than under commitment. The implication is that some policies should be outlawed by a constitutional rule. The commitment problem will be worse when the actions taken by the agents are more irreversible. Interestingly, this irreversibility is itself affected by previous regulatory decisions, and we expect that in general a more 'rigid' regulation will also lead to more irreversibility (for example, firing costs make hiring decisions more irreversible), and hence a more severe time-consistency problem. Here we again have an example of politico–economic complementarities: an initially more rigid society is more likely to adopt wrong policies.

The second level at which time-consistency issues arise is more subtle: the incentive to deviate from the original plan arises because the first steps that have been undertaken have altered the balance of power in such a way that the original policy will be abandoned. Here, the problem is not so much the policy maker's lack of commitment as the fact that its 'preferences' are the outcome of a political process and therefore change with the balance of power. Of course, the recognition by the initial voters of the political consequences of the reform may induce them to actually oppose the reform. This may help to explain why apparently inefficient redistributive schemes such as the minimum wage are difficult to remove (see below).

3 Implications for economic policy

In section 2 we discussed some theoretical ideas which might help explain where 'rigidities' come from and why they do not go away. We now discuss some examples of policies which illustrate these ideas.

3.1 Reducing firing costs

Although the theoretical literature does not deliver a clear-cut message over this issue,[3] firing costs are often blamed as creating unemployment. What is less controversial, however, is that they certainly increase the duration of unemployment, thus making unemployment a more severe problem. So why not reduce them? Here, we take the view that firing costs benefit the employed by lowering their probability of losing their job and increasing their bargaining power in wage determination.

Therefore, to the extent that existing policy is shaped by the interests of the employed rather than the unemployed, reducing firing costs is bound to be a difficult task: one should design the reduction in firing costs in order to avoid making those currently employed worse off. One way to do it is to specify that the reform will only apply to new hires, leaving firing costs unaffected for those already employed. This will generate a two-tier system where 'rigid', high-firing cost contracts will coexist with 'flexible', low-firing cost contracts. This two-tier system has been used to reduce firing costs in many countries, including France, Portugal and Spain. In these countries, 'determined duration contracts' (DDCs) have been introduced which last for a short period of time and have a low firing cost. Such a two-tier system is likely to be favoured by the employed because they have the best of both worlds – high job protection now, higher probability of finding a job if they are fired – due to the existence of new contracts. It will also be favoured by the unemployed, so that the two-tier system generates consensus between the employed and the unemployed.

The two-tier system is therefore a politically realistic, gradual way of reducing firing costs: while generating consensus, it eventually achieves a complete reform of the labour market since in the long run all contracts will have reduced firing costs. Furthermore, it is almost as efficient as a full reform since flexible contracts are likely to be used 'on the margin': the next worker to be hired or fired is likely to have a flexible contract, so that the marginal cost of labour is determined by flexible contracts, so that aggregate employment will be the same as if all contracts were flexible. A second look, however, suggests that it might not be that easy to implement.

First, although designed to protect the interests of the incumbents, it will be costly to them to some extent. There is the simple practical problem that firms will be tempted to 'cheat' by closing a unit and reopening one with flexible contracts. More importantly, as discussed in Saint-Paul (1993), the interests of 'flexible' workers are different from those of 'rigid' workers. As time passes, flexible workers are more and more numerous and may be used by the government as political support for further reforms. So the two-tier system has costs for the incumbents. Note that if the government could commit on the path of reform following the adoption of the two-tier system, for example ensuring that there will be no further increases in flexibility, these costs would be reduced, thus increasing the likelihood of adoption.

Second, the benefits to the incumbents are lower when they are less exposed to unemployment, since they will benefit from flexible contracts only if they end up losing their jobs. Hence the lower is exposure initially, the more difficult it is to implement the reform. If the labour market is very rigid to start with, there will be very little support for the reform, and the economy will be locked in a trap where reducing firing costs is politically impossible, even through a two-tier system. If rigidity is not too big, then there will be more support for the reform and further increases in flexibility are politically viable.

The model can also be used to analyse which environment is more favourable to reform. We have seen that exposure must be relatively high, but reform will be also easier if job creation is very sensitive to a drop in firing costs. Therefore, periods of restructuring are likely to be more favourable than demand-driven recessions.

We have thus an example where issues of time-consistency and exposure interact with each other to make reform impossible if turnover is initially too low. Note that the time-consistency issue is closely linked with the dynamics of the political process, rather than the outcome of a mere commitment failure.

The above argument helps to explain why unions have tended to oppose such marginal liberalisation, even though their interests seemed protected. They realised that their support would gradually be eroded and accordingly managed to limit the use of flexible contracts. The Spanish experience, in that respect, is revealing (but similar issues arose in France, too). The government managed to liberalise the use of DDCs in 1984, when the economy had experienced an unprecedented period of massive job destruction. In order to prevent the use of these contracts being too widespread, the unions managed to restrict their renewal to two occasions, after which they had to be converted to rigid contracts. Nevertheless as much as 95 per cent of new hires were under flexible contracts, and the proportion of the workforce under DDCs quickly rose to 30 per cent in the early 1990s. At that time the government was in a situation where it could use these workers and the unemployment as a coalition to back further increases in labour market flexibility – even if consensus had to be reached to avoid a social explosion, it could strike a deal with the unions to trade the removal of temporary contracts against increases in flexibility. This is actually what happened as a reform of the labour market was engineered in 1994, but the reform turned out to be very timid. Although temporary contracts were maintained for a while, their phasing out was agreed. The government has therefore lost an opportunity which may not be available again.

That two-tier systems are clever politically does not necessarily imply that they are a good idea economically. Although it is the author's opinion that they are a pretty efficient way of increasing flexibility at the margin (that is, where it is needed), a study of Bentolila and Dolado (1994) argues that they can have negative side-effects on wage formation because they further insulate permanent workers from outside competition. However, what matters is the wage of the marginal worker, who is a temporary one, so that if this effect does not push up wages for temporary workers there will be no adverse effect on employment. In practice, however, there is some indexation of temporary wages on permanent ones, so that the Bentolila–Dolado effect may lower employment, at least relative to a fully flexible world.

3.2 Reducing the minimum wage

It is not necessarily those who seem to benefit from a measure who will most strongly oppose it. Consider the case, already mentioned above, where skilled and unskilled workers are complements in production and where an increase of the unskilled wage above its equilibrium level creates unskilled unemployment and reduces the skilled wage. Various measures would lead to such a wage push, but let us assume for simplicity that it comes from a minimum wage. In the absence of taxes and transfers, the skilled and the unemployed would favour a removal of the minimum wage legislation, while the unskilled would oppose it. However, because there is an efficiency gain associated with such a move, it is possible to design a transfer scheme that would compensate the unskilled employed while leaving other categories strictly better off. The simulations I have run in Saint-Paul (1994b) suggest that even if taxation is quite distortionary such a scheme is feasible. In that case everybody would support a reform package such that the minimum wage has been removed and replaced with transfers.

So why does this not happen? Because the story is different when taxes and transfers, instead of being designed so as to enforce agreement on the reform, are collectively decided at regular intervals through some political process. Suppose that in this process the unskilled employed are the decisive voters, which is a plausible assumption given that in Europe the unskilled are more numerous than the skilled. Then theory predicts that taxes will be higher when the employed unskilled are poorer relative to the skilled (for example Meltzer and Richard, 1981). This is simply because the unskilled, who effectively decide on the tax rate, have more to gain from an increase in the tax rate when the skilled are richer relative to them. Therefore, the wage compression induced by the minimum wage will lead to lower taxes. *The skilled may therefore oppose a lowering of the minimum wage if they expect that this will have a large effect on the tax rate.*[4] The minimum wage can therefore be interpreted as a device for the skilled to limit the incentives for the unskilled to expropriate them. It does so by indirectly taking money away from a minority of unskilled workers (the unemployed) and giving it to the remaining majority, thus generating convergence between the interests of the unskilled and those of the skilled employed. Such convergence will make actual decision making closer to the skilled's interests, not only with respect to tax rates but with respect to any issue for which preferences are correlated with pre-tax income, such as public education, child care, etc.

The logic of this example is more general than the particular issue of the minimum wage, and it yields an interesting insight about the nature of European labour market rigidities: they are not the outcome of a greater care for equality as a whole since, as we have argued, they favour exclusion and unemployment among the poorest. Rather, their role is to increase consensus within the middle class (or between the middle class and the 'upper working class') by making it more homogeneous. This makes collective decision making less controversial and political platforms less polarised.[5] It is striking to see how the degree of political polarisation has been reduced in many European societies such as France, Italy, or Portugal. It is not surprising, in light of the above argument, that this process started in the late 1970s/early 1980s, at the apex of the welfare state and 'eurosclerosis'. Rigidities do not eliminate dissent, but ensure that dissenters are a politically unimportant minority. Furthermore, they are kept out of the workforce, which makes collective action more difficult for them.

There is therefore more consensus than one might think on at least some aspects of the 'European model'. A recent illustration is the considerable protest that France experienced as a reaction to a rather timid attempt to lower the minimum wage for the young. Many people, not all of them young, opposed the scheme even though one would have expected them to earn more than the minimum wage over most of their life cycle. And among those who expected to earn the minimum wage, many of those did not have a job yet and therefore were supposed to benefit from a higher probability of finding a job.

Minimum wages may also benefit incumbent employers in a world of imperfect competition, by preventing entry from less efficient rivals.[6] This is another example of labour siding with capital, at the expense of the unemployed.

3.3 Interactions between firing costs and labour taxes

Almost everybody complains about the heavy burden of payroll taxes in many European countries (especially France and Germany). Yet it seems that they are invariably augmented whenever one has to adjust to an increase in social security expenses. Widening the tax base of these expenses and making them less distortionary (not to mention reducing them) is a painful task which has been undertaken only recently and marginally by the French government.

Why is this so? Why is it that employment is such a heavily taxed activity at the time everybody cries out for jobs? Here we want to emphasise one contributing factor, although there are probably others.

The idea is that taxing employment is associated with a time-consistency issue. This is because labour is 'like capital' to the extent that adjusting the labour force is costly. Once labour is hired, a moderate increase in the payroll tax will not induce firms to fire because they are not willing to pay the firing cost. Of course, in equilibrium firms will properly anticipate the tax rates and refrain from hiring before the tax increase. If the government could make a firm commitment not to raise the tax rate then employment would be higher. The lack of commitment leads to too high taxes and unemployment. Not only will the level of payroll taxes be too high, but they will be too sensitive to changes in social security expenditures.

The argument is identical to the usual one about capital taxation, with the complication that the degree of irreversibility in the hiring decision is itself a policy variable. When firing restrictions are higher, there will be more incentives for the government to increase payroll taxes. We again have an example of 'politico–economic complementarities'.

Firing costs therefore not only affect employment and wage determination through the usual economic mechanisms, but they also alter decision making. In the example we consider, the government has an interest in reducing firing costs because by making labour more sensitive to taxes, it

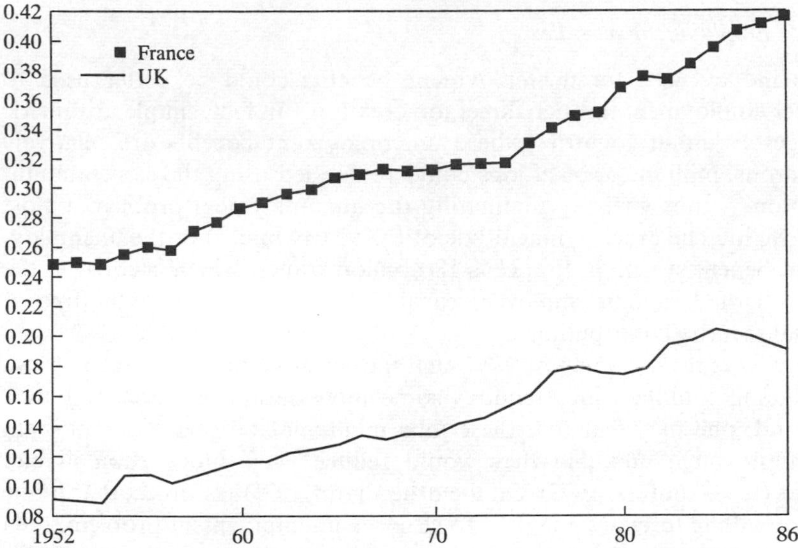

Figure 3.3 France and Britain: payroll taxes, 1952–86, per cent gross wages

reduces its incentives to increase payroll taxes in the future.[7] Low firing costs therefore act as a commitment device. However, the government loses the option of using such taxes, which might be desirable if some unfavourable shock which requires large tax rates hits the economy.[8] If such an option is valued, perhaps because uncertainty is large, the government will be willing to increase firing costs to reduce the elasticity of employment with respect to payroll taxes, thus keeping the option of using them in the future.

A glance at the French and British experiences seems to validate the above arguments. Figure 3.3 shows the path of payroll taxes in both countries between 1952 and 1986. Demographic evolutions are similar in both countries. It is clear, however, that the evolutions of payroll taxes are different. They have increased less in the UK, which has lower firing costs than France.

Before we proceed to the next example, however, we should keep in mind two things: first, payroll taxes create unemployment only if there is another rigidity which prevents wages net of these taxes falling to restore equilibrium. Second, everything which is taxable is more or less mobile, so that it is not easy to find an alternative tax to increase to compensate for a reduction in payroll taxes. In particular, it may well be the case that one of the culprits in high wage taxes is the increase in capital mobility.

3.4 *Employment subsidies*

The money used for unemployment benefits could be better used to foster employment through direct job creation.[9] In fact, simple arithmetic suggests that in countries where unemployment benefits are relatively generous, millions of relief jobs could be funded using the same amount of money, thus virtually eliminating the unemployment problem almost overnight! The order of magnitude of the yearly budget of the unemployment benefit system in France is 180 billion francs, which is equal to the payroll of 3 million employees earning 5000 francs a month (free of social security contributions)!

So why is it that we do not see such measures being undertaken? First, designing 3 million jobs requires some imagination, a scarce resource. Second, one may fear that these jobs might not be that different from unemployment and that they would reduce wage moderation in bad times (see Calmfors, 1993). On the other hand, one may object that if one is not willing to take some risks to cure the unemployment problem, then it is not that much of a problem. Following the general line of this chapter, let us examine the political obstacles that such a policy would encounter.

It is not difficult to imagine that many unemployed workers would prefer earning 90 per cent or so of their previous salary doing nothing than 5000 francs ($1000) cleaning graffiti. In particular, long-term unemployment is not a serious threat for many unemployed people, who presumably prefer the current system to the one I outlined above. On the contrary, long-term unemployed who ran out of benefits and are excluded from the labour market would find a real opportunity in relief jobs. So some unemployed, but not all, would support the scheme. However, the unemployed are not likely to be numerous enough to block the scheme. Let us now turn to the employed. At first glance, one could think that they do not care about the issue, since in both cases they contribute the same amount of money. However, the system which is eventually adopted will affect them for (at least) two reasons. First, they might lose their jobs. If they expect to be unemployed for only a short time, they would probably prefer the benefit system. If they expect to be unemployed for long periods, they might prefer relief jobs. In the end, this ultimately depends on their age, skills, the sector where they are working, etc. If long-term unemployment is very concentrated among specific age groups or skills or sectors, then it is unlikely that the 'median employed' will favour relief jobs. Second, which system prevails affect wage formation. If relief jobs bring the unemployed back into the labour market, thus making them more likely to apply for jobs and under-bid the insiders, they would increase wage flexibility relative to the benefit system. The employed might then support the benefit system because it shelters them more from competition. If relief jobs reduce the unemployed's incentives to find a job, then the employed might support them.

The perverse aspect of this is that the employed are more likely to support such jobs when they are a bad idea! This is why relief jobs in the public sector are more likely to be supported than subsidies to employment in the private sector, which are more likely to increase competition and wage flexibility.

So we conclude that:

- the reform is more viable when the employed are more likely to experience long-term, but not short-term, unemployment;
- it is more likely to succeed if relief jobs are less efficient in increasing wage flexibility, a depressing conclusion;
- however, if the employed are less exposed to unemployment, either long-term or short-term, they will care less about the reform, which in some instances may make it more viable; so there is an opportunity for a very rigid society to implement such a reform.

4 Conclusion

In this chapter we have not tried to 'solve' the European unemployment problem: we have not proposed new policies and have not made claims about the quantitative impact of any policy on the level of unemployment. Rather, we have tried to organise the discussion about European unemployment from a political economy perspective. One may conclude from this exercise that it is not so much lack of knowledge which explains the lack of political response to unemployment, as lack of concern.

NOTES

I thank my discussants Samuel Bentolila and Richard Jackman, as well as Dennis Snower and Zmira Hornstein, for helpful comments and suggestions.

1 Clearly, there are conflicts of interest between the employed and the unemployed over the level of unemployment insurance, but this conflict would tend to limit rigidities rather than increase them since it is likely to lead to a suboptimal level of insurance (see Wright, 1986).

2 This will happen in a society where some degree of consensus is required to implement a reform. For example, one could assume that each sector has equal weight and that a majority of more than 50 per cent is required to defeat the status quo.

3 See Bertola (1990), Bentolila and Bertola (1990), Bentolila and Saint-Paul (1992).
4 There is a slight logical difficulty with this argument: if the unskilled employed are the decisive voters, why could the skilled block the reform? We assume that removing the minimum wage is a more serious issue than deciding on the current tax rate, so that it requires a larger majority.
5 Social conflicts then occur only at the margin of society and not within the political sphere, because those who are excluded are not numerous nor organised enough to participate in the political system. These marginal conflicts take the form of petty crime, drug addiction, and so forth.
6 I am indebted to Zmira Hornstein for this point.
7 This argument is very similar to the one used in the debate about monetary policy credibility that increases in the cost of inflation can increase efficiency by reducing the incentives to inflate (see Rogoff, 1985; Giavazzi and Pagano, 1988). One way to increase the cost of inflation is to appoint an independent, conservative central banker. Another is to belong to a fixed exchange rate system. Here reducing firing costs increases the cost of payroll taxes.
8 See Calvo and Guidotti (1993) for the monetary policy equivalent of this argument.
9 See Snower (1994), for example.

REFERENCES

Bean, C., 1988. 'Capital shortage', *Economic Policy*, **18**

Bentolila, S. and G. Bertola, 1990. 'Firing costs and labour demand in Europe: how bad is Eurosclerosis?', *Review of Economic Studies*, **57**, 381–402

Bentolila, S. and J.J. Dolado, 1994. 'Labor flexibility and wages: lessons from Spain', *Economic Policy*, **18**, 53–100

Bentolila, S. and G. Saint-Paul, 1992. 'The macroeconomic impact of flexible labour contracts, an application to Spain', *European Economic Review*, **36(5)**, 1013–47

Calmfors, L., 1993. 'Lessons from the macroeconomic experience of Sweden', *European Journal of Political Economy*, **9(1)**

Calmfors, L. and J. Driffill, 1988. 'Bargaining structure, corporatism and macroeconomic performance', *Economic Policy*, **6**, 14–47

Calmfors, L. and H. Horn, 1986. 'Employment policy and centralized wage setting', *Economica*, **53(211)**, 281–302

Calvo, G. and P. Guidotti, 1993. 'The flexibility of monetary policy', *Review of Economic Studies* **60(204)**, 667–87

Fernandez, R. and D. Rodrik, 1989. 'Resistance to reform', *American Economic Review*, **81(5)**, 1146–55

Giavazzi, F. and M. Pagano, 1988. 'The advantage of tying one's hands', *European Economic Review*, **32(5)**, 1055–74

Meltzer, A. and S.F. Richard, 1981. 'A rational theory of government size', *Journal of Political Economy*, **89(5)**, 914–27

Olson, M., 1965. *The Logic of Collective Action*, Cambridge, MA: Harvard University Press

1982. *The Rise and Decline of Nations*, New Haven: Yale University Press

Rogoff, K., 1985. 'The optimal degree of commitment to an intermediate momentary target', *Quarterly Journal of Economics*, **100(4)**, 1169–90

Saint-Paul, G., 1993. 'On the political economy of labor market flexibility', *NBER Macroeconomics Annual*, 8, Cambridge, MA: MIT Press

1994a. 'Unemployment, wage rigidity, and the returns to education', *European Economic Review*, **38(3/4)**, 535–44

1994b. 'Do labor market rigidities fulfill redistributive roles?: searching for the virtues of the European Model', *IMF Staff Papers*, **41(4)**, 624–42

Snower, D., 1994. 'The simple economics of benefit transfers', chapter 6 in this volume

Wright, R., 1986. 'The redistributive role of unemployment insurance and the dynamic of voting', *Journal of Public Economics*, **31**, 377–99

Discussion

SAMUEL BENTOLILA

Gilles Saint-Paul has written an intriguing chapter on the political economy of labour market policies. The chapter is full of new ideas, breaking new ground in political economy, an exciting field with potentially valuable insights into the interaction of economics and politics. Since unemployment policy is an area where political calculations are clearly very important, the chapter addresses a very relevant issue from a useful viewpoint. In my discussion, I will make a couple of general remarks and then go on to more detailed points.

My first remark has to do with labour market rigidities as the culprits for high European unemployment. We should realise that, apart from what one may believe on this issue, the evidence produced by economists concerning the blame that can be put on these rigidities is weak. For example, in his 1994 survey on the research about European unemployment in the *Journal of Economic Literature*, Charles Bean (p. 614) states: 'So what have we learned from this decade-long research effort? A cynic might reply: not much.' More to the point, referring to flexibility-enhancing measures (p. 615) he adds: 'The UK has probably gone furthest in enacting such structural policies, although so far with rather little beneficial effect on unemployment.' The chapters and discussions in the present volume also reflect, in my opinion, the deep controversy on the causes of European unemployment, which translates into conflicting views on the best policies to reduce it.

Saint-Paul recognises this when he writes, '[w]e shall take standard views about the way these policies work, even though the theoretical and empirical support for these views is often weak'. But then he concludes the chapter by stating that 'it is not so much lack of knowledge which explains the lack of political response to unemployment, as lack of concern'. In the light of the uncertainties mentioned above, can we really state so emphatically that it is lack of concern? Could it not be, at least partly, caution on the part of society and politicians, who are weary of acting based on the weak and/or conflicting advice that policy makers often get from economists?

My second general remark refers to the current state of the political economy field. Chapter 3 reveals a few weaknesses in the current approach. The first one is the lack of a historical perspective. Little information is given in this chapter on when these labour market institutions were established (I think it was mostly in the 1950s and 1960s) and on what was the prevailing environment at the time and also at the time when some reforms of labour market regulations were implemented (since the early 1980s). A second weakness is the lack of cross-country comparisons. Questions that naturally come to mind in this respect are: why were these regulations never instituted in the USA, or why were they implemented more strongly in some countries than in others? While in standard economic analysis we would take institutions as given, political economy is *the* field where the latter have to be explained. The third and last issue is the lack of reference in the chapter to seemingly important institutions – like political parties – for the issues at hand, and to the place of these issues in the current debate on the reform of the welfare state. I view these three points as crucial ways to test the predictions arising from the political economy approach.

I now turn to more specific points, starting with section 2.1 on distributive conflicts. One interesting point made in the chapter is the following. We normally focus on the distributive conflict between capital and labour. Recent theories of so-called insider wage-setting have underlined the existence of conflicts among workers themselves, between the employed and the unemployed. This chapter goes one step further, by explaining that there are also conflicts between skilled and unskilled workers, and that, by affecting the setting up and the reform of labour market institutions, they can affect the level of unemployment. I hope that more empirical evidence can be provided in the future in order to ascertain the relevance of this conflict.

On section 2.2, about coordination failures, I have several comments relating to the chapter's implicit objective of enlightening policy-makers on recent economic concepts. First, Saint-Paul states that a prisoner's dilemma is a situation in which agents ignore the impact of their decisions on other agents. In fact, this feature is what economists have always called an 'externality'. Secondly, externalities may be positive or negative (for example, if I invest in my own education and ignore the positive effect of this action on the overall productivity of the economy, the externality is a positive one). Saint-Paul is implicitly assuming that labour market rigidities always lead to negative externalities and never to positive ones, an assumption which could be challenged.

Thirdly, the presence of a negative externality is a necessary but not a sufficient condition for the game being a prisoner's dilemma. The latter happens only if the payoffs are of a specific form, which is given by the payoff matrix presented in the chapter for a rigid (*R*) or a flexible (*F*) economy:

	R	*F*
R	0,0	2,-1
F	-1,2	1,1

Lastly, a prisoner's dilemma gives rise to *cooperation failures*, not to *coordination failures* as stated in the chapter. Since this may be a subtle difference, let me explain why this matters. In the above matrix, the only outcome which is an equilibrium (the rigid economy with payoffs (0,0)) is Pareto-dominated (by the flexible economy with payoffs (1,1)). But the three other outcomes do not dominate each other (both agents do not simultaneously gain by moving from one case to another); in other words, they lie in the so-called 'Pareto-efficient frontier'. So, if a given outcome is to be achieved (say, the flexible economy), the agents will need to *cooperate* with each other.

This is a different situation from that arising in coordination failure games, when the payoffs are of the type:

	R	*F*
R	1,1	0,0
F	0,0	2,2

Since there is more than one equilibrium, the agents' actions need to act in a *coordinated* way so as to reach the best outcome (in this case, the flexible economy). Note that the externality here is a positive one.

Designing institutions in order to solve coordination failures is normally easier – everybody gains by internalising a positive externality – than to solve cooperation failures – the externality is negative. In this sense, if labour market rigidities do in fact lead to prisoner's dilemma type of situations, talking about coordination failures is actually under-stating the problems they create.

On section 2.3 about exposure and politico–economic complementarities, Saint-Paul argues that the unemployed are a small, heterogeneous, and poorly organised group, and that these features do not allow them to lobby for reforms that would benefit them. What is ignored is that there are links between different groups in society. For example, if I am employed but my wife or children are unemployed, I may support measures that increase their likelihood of finding a job, even if such measures weaken my own position as an employee. In other words, family links weaken selfish interests. This type of consideration has been explored in the so-called 'Ricardian equivalence' literature on taxes, and it may prove more appropriate in the area of labour market policies than in the original one.

On section 3 of the chapter, dealing with implications for policy, I will take each labour market regulation in turn. On fixed-term contracts, I would like to mention the two main lessons that I think have been learned from the 10-year-long Spanish experience with this type of contract. The first one is that having a two-tier labour market, with one tier of permanent workers protected by very high firing costs and a sizable second tier of temporary workers with very low firing costs, is not a desirable permanent feature of a labour market. This is true on social fairness grounds but also on the basis of the perverse effects on wage formation that occur when wage-setting is kept in the hands of the first tier of workers. This suggests that any policy change should take into account how the reformed institution can be expected to interact with the remaining (unchanged) institutions in the labour market.

The second lesson is that the use of fixed-term contracts as a sort of Trojan horse strategy for increasing labour market flexibility has been of only limited effectiveness. The strategy of aligning the interests of a fraction of the employed workers (the temporary ones) with those of the unemployed has not, at least in Spain, been powerful enough to yield a significant reduction in firing costs, and explaining this is a challenge for a political economy approach.

My last comments are about the few instances in which the chapter tries to illustrate the argument with empirical evidence. In these cases, the arguments seem to fly in the face of some empirical stylised facts.

In section 3.2 on minimum wages, Saint-Paul recalls that the theory shows that 'taxes will be higher when the employed unskilled are poorer relative to the skilled', and builds an argument on this prediction. But a rough cross-country comparison seems to belie this theoretical implication. In particular, the USA or the UK, countries with high wage dispersion (so that the unskilled are poorer relative to the skilled), do not show a higher but a lower tax burden than countries with low wage dispersion, like Germany or Sweden.

Secondly, on the interaction of firing costs and labour taxes (section 3.3), Saint-Paul stresses the role of low firing costs as a commitment device for not raising labour taxes, and provides figure 3.3 as alleged supportive evidence. I cannot see this graph as strong evidence for this point, since what I read from the picture is that the UK, with low firing costs, starts from a lower level of labour tax rate than France, with a higher initial level of firing costs, but that the rate of increase of that tax rate (the slope of the line) is very similar in both countries.

Lastly, there is a section discussing why large-scale public employment programmes are not politically viable (section 3.4). The political economy view then needs to explain one important exception to the rule – the case of Sweden, where exactly that kind of programme has existed during most of the postwar period.

REFERENCE

Bean, C., 1994. 'European unemployment: a survey', *Journal of Economic Literature*, **32**, 573–619

Discussion

RICHARD JACKMAN

Gilles Saint-Paul's chapter 3 presents an important and interesting perspective on unemployment policy. It addresses the problem of why it should be that governments often appear to take policy actions which seem likely to make matters worse and are sometimes reluctant to adopt policies which might be expected to reduce unemployment. The argument is that governments adopt policies not on the basis of overall social benefit (or economic efficiency) but in response to pressure from politically powerful groups.

While, in very general terms, this is not a new idea, there are a number of less familiar implications developed in the chapter. One of the most interesting is an application of the time-consistency problem. The idea is that governments cannot commit themselves to addressing policy objectives through the tax system, since whatever they may promise *ex ante* they have an incentive *ex post* to adjust tax rates in response to immediate electoral or other advantage. Hence governments prefer laws and regulations, which cannot as easily be revoked, as methods of delivering policy objectives. Minimum wages may have greater efficiency costs than the tax system as a means of assisting the low paid but, because they become entrenched in the economic structure in a way the particular tax parameters cannot be, they provide a continuing means of support which redistributive taxation does not.

In this comment I wish to ask, however, whether this approach can explain observations other than those which led to its formulation. On p. 56 of the chapter we are reminded of a couple of very significant observations: that unemployment in Europe has risen very sharply over the past 20 years, and that there remain very significant differences in unemployment rates across OECD countries. But the political economy approach appears to offer no very obvious insights towards explaining these phenomena, and one wonders what exactly is the empirical content of the approach.

In introducing the theory (section 2 of the chapter), Saint-Paul starts (p. 55) 'from the simple observation that, if labour market rigidities exist, it must be the case that they benefit some politically powerful groups (meaning either a majority of the people or a strongly organised minority)'. The assumption that rigidities necessarily benefit politically powerful groups is not self-evidently true (they may be the result of inertia, ignorance or incompetence), nor is it clear that the assumption has empirical content in that there are presumably many politically powerful groups in the economy and there can be few decisions that do not benefit some at the expense of others. A simply 'majority rules' view of the policy process can explain some rigidities (rent controls to benefit tenants at the expense of landlords, employment protection to benefit workers at the expense of employers), but much of the concern of the chapter is with narrower sectional interests (typically producer interest groups as against consumers). Clearly some minorities have more political power than others, but is there any *a priori* method of distinguishing those that are powerful (farmers) from those that are not (schoolteachers)?

Turning from assumptions to outcomes, one might think that, if politics matter, the political system might also be expected to matter, in that it might affect the power of interest groups to influence elected bodies or the executive. In the OECD context, the sharpest difference in political systems is between the USA and European countries. In the USA, with Congressional elections every two years, and the constitutional system of checks and balances, the executive is exceptionally weak and the power of sectional interests exceptionally strong. While as a result the legislative systems is endlessly clogged up, the economy does not appear to suffer particularly from rigidities and in particular the labour market is exceptionally flexible. Are there any types of systematic prediction from the theoretical approach as to how political structure may influence economic outcomes, and in particular labour market performance?

An interesting type of natural experiment might be if a country experienced a regime change in terms of political arrangements – for example, a new constitution, affecting the relative power of different parts of the government, the frequency of elections or whatever. There appear, however, to be few examples within recent years, at least in terms of changes within democratic structures. What in many respects appears more remarkable is the extent of changes in policy regime which appeared to have occurred independently of any change in political structure or external shock affecting the interests of different groups in society. Why should the political process in Britain, for example, have delivered such very different outcomes in terms of economic policy in 1979, with the election of a Conservative government with Mrs Thatcher as Prime Minister, than it had in 1978?

This is a very interesting and thought-provoking chapter, but there appears to be a long way to go before we can add any political variables to our econometric models of the determinants of unemployment.

Part Two

Demand management and supply-side policy

4 The role of demand-management policies in reducing unemployment

CHARLES R. BEAN

> Macroeconomic policy has two roles in reducing unemployment: over the short term it limits cyclical fluctuations in output and employment; and over the longer term it should provide a framework, based on sound public finances and price stability, to ensure that growth of output and employment is sustainable, *inter alia* through adequate levels of savings and investment.

This quotation appears at the beginning of the Policy Recommendations section of the OECD's Jobs Study (OECD, 1994a). However of the 59 separate recommendations only three concern macroeconomic policies, and only 10 per cent of the background analysis is concerned with macroeconomic issues. The three specific macroeconomic recommendations are: (i) maintaining demand at a level appropriate for achieving non-inflationary growth, (ii) fiscal consolidation, (iii) improving the mix of public spending and taxation (as much a microeconomic measure in any case). Likewise most of the contributions in this volume concentrate on structural issues connected with labour markets rather than traditional macroeconomic questions.

Let me state clearly at the outset that I do not wish to argue that this emphasis on the supply side is mistaken. While it is almost certainly the case that adverse demand shocks have played at least some role in pushing European unemployment to its present levels, the scope for more expansionary macroeconomic policies alone to reverse the trend are distinctly limited, for reasons that will be discussed below. Rather, reducing unemployment levels to something that is socially acceptable will surely require the implementation of various structural measures to improve the functioning of labour markets. One, rather Classical, view would be to argue that this is *all* that is required: if the supply side is put right then the demand side will take care of itself through appropriate adjustments in wages and prices. I think that the presence of various rigidities in the economy make this too sanguine a view and that the likelihood of the labour market measures being successful will be enhanced if accompanied by suitably expansionary macroeconomic policies – in the words of Blanchard *et al.* (1985), a 'two-handed' approach. Apart from leading to further unnecessary output losses, a Classical strategy of allowing the demand side to adjust automatically through downward wage and price adjustment runs the risk of leading to an early reversal of what may be quite painful supply-side reforms if their benefits are not immediately apparent to the electorate. However, saying that policies towards aggregate demand should be complementary to supply-side policies still leaves many questions unanswered.

In this chapter I shall try to address some of these. I shall start by presenting some evidence on the role of demand factors in the movements in US and European unemployment, and then review the mechanisms by which macroeconomic policies affect unemployment, paying particular attention to persistence mechanisms that lead demand shocks to have supply-side consequences. I conclude that the scope for demand-management policies alone to reduce the present very high levels of European unemployment is limited. I shall then go on to consider how macroeconomic policy should be set to complement appropriate unemployment-reducing supply-side measures, taking cognisance of the uncertainty surrounding the equilibrium unemployment rate and the constraints on fiscal and monetary policies. Finally I shall consider the desirability of other policies that might enhance the effectiveness of macroeconomic policies.

1 Macroeconomic policy and unemployment

1.1 Cyclical unemployment

Figure 4.1 depicts the conventional framework for thinking about unemployment. Figure 4.1a drawn in employment–real wage space, is a straightforward generalisation of the usual competitive labour market diagram to allow for imperfections in both labour and product markets. *LL* is the competitive labour supply schedule, for simplicity drawn assuming a common reservation wage across the whole labour force and inelastic labour supply above that level. *WW* is a wage-setting schedule (or in Phelps', 1994, terminology a 'surrogate labour supply schedule') describing how wages are set. This could represent the outcome of bilateral bargaining between firms and workers or the operation of efficiency wage considerations. In either case, the premium of the wage over the reservation wage is increasing in the employment rate. *NN* is a 'medium-run' labour demand schedule (or more accurately a price–employment schedule) depicting firms' optimal price and employment

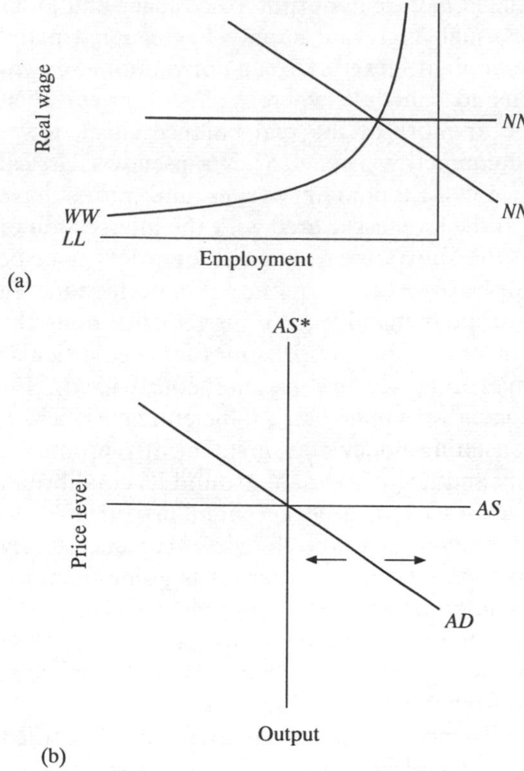

Figure 4.1 Cyclical unemployment
(a) The labour market
(b) The product market

decisions, given the nominal wage they face and their existing stock of capital. Equilibrium employment, and by residual also unemployment, is then given by the intersection of *WW* and *NN*. In the long run capital can be adjusted, leading the *NN* schedule to shift outwards (inwards) as capital accumulates (decumulates) towards its optimal level. We can then also construct a long-run labour demand schedule which allows for this endogeneity of capital; this schedule will be horizontal if there is constant returns to scale, as in *NN**. Note that this implies that in the long run an upward shift in the wage-setting schedule will ultimately show up entirely in unemployment with no change in the real wage or productivity; looking at the evolution of real wages or labour shares – as in the old 'wage gap' literature – may thus tell us rather little about the ultimate causes of movements in unemployment.

Figure 4.1b gives the associated picture in output–price space and looks (and behaves) just like the usual aggregate supply–aggregate demand model of introductory undergraduate texts. *AD* is a conventional downward-sloping aggregate demand schedule whereby lower prices elicit higher demand through one or more of the real balance effect, lower interest rates, and improved competitiveness. *AS** is a pseudo-Classical aggregate supply schedule in which nominal wages and prices have adjusted fully and output is at the level associated with the intersection of *NN* and *WW*. However, in the short run wages and/or prices may be sticky because of contracts or because of informational imperfections. In this case fluctuations in aggregate demand lead to movements along the short-run aggregate supply curve *AS* (drawn horizontal for the particular case where both nominal wages and prices are instantaneously fixed).[1]

If policy makers observe fluctuations in demand sufficiently early and *if* they can take appropriate offsetting policy action sufficiently promptly, then they can stabilise activity and unemployment around its equilibrium level. However, while this analysis might be accepted in principle, in practice most policy makers today would take the view that uncertainty about where the economy is today, let alone where it is going, coupled with uncertainty about the timing and impact of any policy action makes activist policies to eliminate such cyclical fluctuations hazardous. While this suggests that 'fine-tuning' is impossible, it does not rule out the scope for modest attempts to 'coarse-tune' the level of activity.

In this simple framework movements in unemployment can be caused by shifts in aggregate demand which lead to cyclical unemployment, and by movements in the price- or wage-setting schedules which are associated with a change in equilibrium unemployment (defined as the level of unemployment associated with full wage and price adjustment). How much of the movements in unemployment is attributable to each sort or disturbance? If we can answer this, then we might also get some idea about the scope for activist macroeconomic policies. Studying the causes of the rise in unemployment has, of course, been a huge academic industry in the last decade or so and demand movements have been one of the factors extensively studied. Rather than survey this literature in detail (see Bean, 1994b, for such a survey) I instead report the results of a simple exercise using vector autoregressive techniques which conveys the flavour of this literature. This has the virtue of imposing relatively little in the way of additional untested conditioning assumptions and of obviating the need for objective measures of supply-side variables like union power. However, it turns out that the end results are consonant with those obtained using more traditional structural econometric approaches.

My vector autoregressions contain just three variables: inflation; capacity utilisation; and the (logarithm of the) unemployment rate.[2] The data is annual, the sample period (after allowing for lags) runs from 1964 to 1995 (OECD projections are employed for 1994 and 1995), and the two regions studied are the USA and the EU. In addition to two lags of each variable and a constant, each equation contains dummies for the aftermath of the two oil price shocks, the first taking the value of unity from 1974 to 1976, the second from 1980 to 1983. These are added in recognition of the fact that this sample is dominated by adverse shocks, concentrated particularly in these periods. However, in subsequent analysis the contributions of the dummies are treated as though they are part of the equation error, i.e. as part of the exogenous driving shocks.

As is well known, the estimated residuals from a vector autoregression will in general be a linear combination of the underlying, and economically interesting, disturbances. Thus the residual in the unemployment equation will generally reflect the impact of both demand and supply shocks. In order to recover these underlying disturbances some additional assumptions must therefore be made. Here I assume that contemporaneously disturbances to the wage- and/or price-setting schedules impinge entirely on inflation and their effect on activity only comes through with a lag. Since the residuals to the inflation and capacity utilisation equations are virtually uncorrelated this provides virtually the same identification as assuming that disturbances to demand impinge only on activity in the short run, with the effects on inflation only coming through later. In effect it means that in figure 4.1b the short-run aggregate demand schedule is rather steep and the short-run aggregate supply schedule is rather flat. In addition to these supply and demand disturbances, the model implicitly contains a third disturbance, most reasonably thought of as a labour force shock which is assumed in the short run to impinge on neither inflation nor capacity utilisation.[3]

Figures 4.2a and 4.2b display the time series for US and EU unemployment respectively, together with counterfactual simulations from the model in which there are assumed to have been no demand shocks. It is clear that the USA fits the conventional picture beloved of macroeconomic textbooks quite well, namely movements in unemployment are primarily cyclical fluctuations around a relatively constant equilibrium, or natural, rate of unemployment. In the EU, by contrast, while the contribution of demand shocks is not negligible, it is supply-side disturbances that appear to be the dominant cause of the recent rise in unemployment. Although the precise details of this analysis may not be completely robust to changes in the identifying assumptions, it is in line with the vast bulk of existing empirical work using more traditional

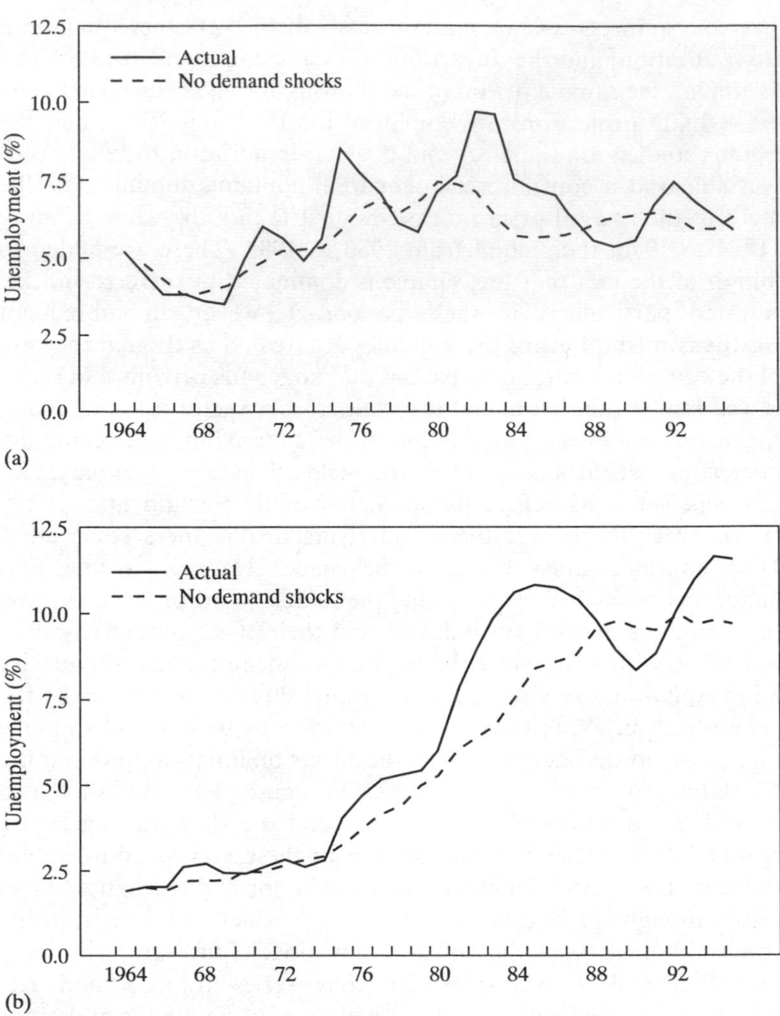

Figure 4.2 Effect of demand shocks on unemployment, 1964–92
(a) USA
(b) EU

econometric methods. For instance Layard, Nickell and Jackman (1991) find that, in the absence of nominal demand shocks, unemployment in the EU would have averaged about 2.3 per cent in the 1960s and 6.8 per cent in the 1980s (based on Layard *et al.*, table 14, p. 436); the corresponding number from the vector autoregressive analysis are 2.1 per cent and 7.5 per cent. These simulations would appear to suggest that,

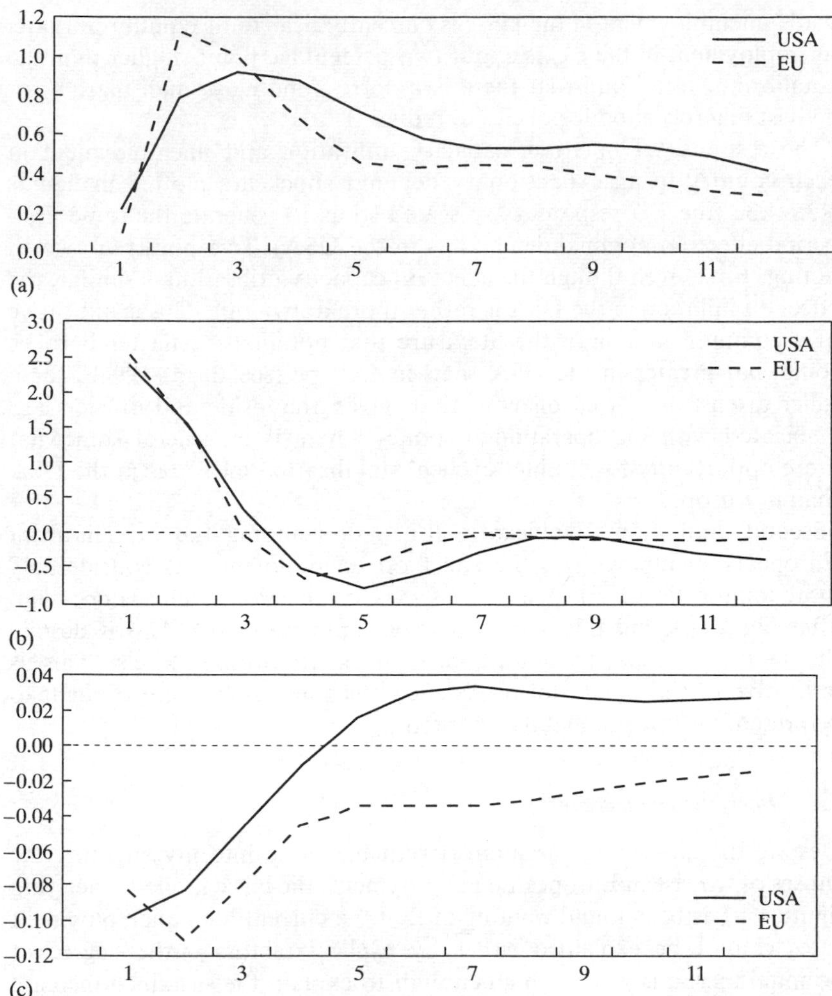

Figure 4.3 Response to demand shock
(a) Inflation
(b) Capacity utilisation
(c) Unemployment

while unemployment in the USA is currently near to its equilibrium rate, unemployment in the EU is about two percentage points higher than the equilibrium rate,[4] and that there is a correspondingly small margin for activist macroeconomic policies to reduce it.

The response of inflation, capacity utilisation and unemployment in each country to an expansionary demand shock are plotted in figures 4.3a–4.3c (the EU responses are scaled so as to generate the same first-period effect on nominal demand as in the USA). Two points are worth noting. First, even though the effect on capacity utilisation is similar, the effect on inflation in the USA is rather more drawn out. This is indicative of a common finding in the literature that nominal inertia tends to be somewhat greater in the USA than in Europe (see Bean, 1994b, for a fuller discussion). A corollary is that, given the inside and outside lags associated with the operation of policy, there is in general somewhat more opportunity for counter-cyclical stabilisation measures in the USA than in Europe.

Second, and more significantly for understanding the behaviour of European unemployment, the effect on unemployment is considerably more long-lasting in Europe (the response in the USA even switches sign after five years, but this may simply be sampling error). This is despite the fact that capacity utilisation is back to normal levels. This is indicative of the significant persistence mechanisms that are thought to be present in European labour markets.

1.2 Persistence mechanisms

Despite the massive research effort that has gone into investigating the causes of the rise in European unemployment, the basic model underlying figure 4.1 has been found wanting in that the current high unemployment rates cannot be explained either by cyclical factors – the degree of nominal inertia is just not high enough to explain the sustained increase in unemployment – or by exogenous shifts on the supply side. In regard to the latter the effects of the deterioration in the terms of trade following the two oil price shocks, changes in tax rates, the productivity growth slowdown, benefit levels, minimum wages, union power, high real interest rates, increased mismatch, demographics and a host of other factors have all figured. While some of these have been found helpful in explaining particular episodes, neither singly nor as a group do they seem to be able to account for the continuous high unemployment levels. Rather in addition there appears to be persistence mechanisms present that lead today's equilibrium unemployment rate to be positively related to yesterday's realisation of unemployment. As a consequence temporary disturbances, to either demand or supply, can have long-lasting (or even permanent) effects. The presence of these mechanisms blurs the simple-minded distinction between demand and supply factors because demand shocks end up having longer-term supply consequences.

These persistence mechanisms are usually introduced into macroeconomic work and policy analysis by adding into the Phillips curve or wage equation a term in the change,[5] as well as the level, of unemployment (in the case of full hysteresis it is *only* the change that appears). Assuming that these mechanisms operate in a symmetric fashion, the implication for both disinflation and stabilisation policy is that it pays to keep unemployment closer to its long-run equilibrium rate than in the absence of the persistence mechanism (see Layard, Nickell and Jackman, 1991, p. 525). Consequently, it pushes one towards favouring a gradualist strategy to disinflation and a more aggressive attitude to stabilising unemployment in the face of shocks, essentially because allowing unemployment to rise a lot today has adverse effects on the short-run equilibrium unemployment rate in subsequent periods.

The presence of these persistence mechanisms, which are embedded into the equations of the vector autoregressions, implies that one cannot simply identify the gap between actual and the 'no-demand-shock' unemployment rates in the EU as indicating the margin of unemployment that can be eliminated through demand-management policies alone. This is because adverse demand shocks *have* occurred in the past and this will have acted to raise the equilibrium unemployment that prevails in the short run today. (The underlying long-run equilibrium unemployment rate that obtains once all the persistence mechanisms have worked their way out will not be affected unless full hysteresis is present.) Consequently, there will be a limit to the speed at which the gap between the actual unemployment rate and the 'no-demand shock' unemployment rate in Europe can be eliminated though more expansionary macroeconomic policies without re-igniting inflation. Furthermore this approach is overly mechanistic in assuming that the persistence mechanisms are symmetric in the sense of operating in the same way in the face of expansionary shocks as in contractionary ones. In practice they are quite likely to be either asymmetric and/or non-linear, depending on the source of the persistence.

There are four main classes of persistence mechanisms that have been proposed in the literature, two of which operate on the supply (wage-setting) side of the labour market and two on the demand side. The first of the supply-side persistence mechanisms relies on insider membership dynamics and is due to Blanchard and Summers (1986) and Lindbeck and Snower (1988). They argue that the presence of hiring and firing costs gives the existing workforce at a firm bargaining power and an ability to push wages above market-clearing levels. The existing workforce will then try to push up wages, subject to not pricing themselves out of a job. However, if there is an unexpected contradiction in demand, and wages and prices do not respond immediately, then employment will fall. The key assumption is that only those left – the 'insiders' – will have a say in subsequent wage negotiations. If demand subsequently recovers they will prefer to push for higher real wages than in the *status quo ante* rather than allowing employment to return to its initial position (subject to the constraint that if wages get *too* high a firm might find it profitable to sack all its workforce and start anew). The key to whether this mechanism operates in reverse or not would seem to rely on whether the insiders are aware of the reversal of the demand shock. If they are, then other policies would be required alongside a recovery in demand to ensure that it was simultaneously associated with an increase in employment and thus in insider membership (see section 3 on incomes policies).

The second supply-side persistence mechanism operates through the characteristics and behaviour of the unemployed rather than the employed. Phelps (1972) was one of the first to cite the possibility of such a mechanism when he suggested that unemployment leads to reduced rates of skill formation and weakens work habits. On the face of it, it is not clear why such a reduction in worker productivity should lead to higher unemployment, rather than lower wages. However Blanchard and Diamond (1994) have developed a more subtle version of the story in which firms are assumed to use the unemployment history of potential workers in order to rank them in order of desirability. Because the newly unemployed will have a better chance of being re-employed than the long-term unemployed, other things being equal, wages tend to be higher when ranking occurs because the bargaining position of those with jobs is enhanced. Furthermore, and more importantly, persistence can be quite long because the reduction in the perceived average quality of the unemployed that occurs in the face of a contractionary shock will also lead firms to open fewer vacancies so perpetuating the problem (Pissarides, 1992). The mechanisms in operation here seem to be entirely reversible and there is no reason for expecting asymmetries in the response to contractionary and expansionary shocks.

A different explanation of persistence that also focuses on outsider behaviour emphasises the job-seeking behaviour of the long-term unemployed, rather than their skill characteristics and the attitudes of employers (Layard and Nickell, 1987). Prolonged lack of success in finding a job leads the long-term unemployed to give up searching, believing that it is a futile exercise, while at the same time they adjust to living on unemployment benefits and earnings from the 'black' economy. As a result the 'effective' labour force shrinks. However, a recovery in the demand for labour will not automatically lead to these discouraged workers re-entering the effective labour force, unless it is accompanied by active labour market policies that keep the long-term unemployed in touch with the labour market. So here again asymmetries are a possibility.

Turning to the demand side of the labour market, the presence of hiring and firing costs means that firms will only take on extra labour if they expect the demand for it to be long lived. Consequently if firms are unsure of the permanence of any recovery then they will be disinclined to expand employment. It is often asserted that high levels of firing costs are to blame for the increase in European unemployment. This cannot be correct on average because firing costs should *reduce* the variability of employment, but should not greatly affect its average level. But the presence of firing costs can explain why employment gets stuck around a particular level for some while (Bentolila and Bertola, 1990). This is because hiring and firing costs create a 'zone of inaction' within which the firm is neither hiring nor firing. Thus if firms have generally been shedding labour in response to a contraction in demand or an increase in labour costs, they will not immediately start taking labour back on as soon as demand starts expanding or labour costs begin to fall, but wait until the recovery has proceeded beyond a threshold level that amongst other things depends upon the degree of uncertainty. This zone of inaction thus generates both non-linearities and asymmetries in the behaviour of unemployment.

The final persistence mechanism operates through the capital stock. Consider figure 4.1a, and suppose there is an increase in wage pressure that shifts the wage-setting schedule, *WW*, up. Equilibrium employment falls. However the intersection of medium-run labour demand, *NN*, with *WW* now lies above the long-run labour demand schedule, *NN**, along which capital is also allowed to vary. The mechanism that brings the economy back to long-run equilibrium is capital decumulation which shifts *NN* in until *NN*, *NN**, and the new *WW* curves all intersect at the same point. This process of capital decumulation is associated with further increases in unemployment. As stated, there is no reason for this process to be either irreversible or asymmetric. However an extra dimension is added if the possibilities for substituting capital for labour are limited.[6] The effect of an increase in wage pressure, or a negative demand shock, is to lead to a fall in unemployment and capital being left idle. If the adverse shock is maintained capital decumulation will set in. However, when the shock is reversed employment possibilities will be limited by the availability of capital, however low wages may fall. Employment may thus fall rapidly in the downswing, but the speed of recovery in the upswing will be governed by how quickly the capital stock is built up. There is again an asymmetry in behaviour.

The various persistence mechanisms thus have rather different implications for the extent and speed to which the gap between actual unemployment and 'no-demand-shock' unemployment can be eliminated, and thus also for the short-run room for manoeuvre for macroeconomic policies. In my view the empirical evidence tends to favour outsider disenfranchisement ahead of insider membership dynamics; for instance, the degree of unemployment persistence across countries seems to be positively related to the duration for which benefits are payable, but not to the degree of unionisation (Layard, Nickell and Jackman, 1991, pp. 433–4; Bean, 1994a) – but there certainly may be some instances where insider membership effects are important e.g. in Spain (Bentolila and Dolado, 1994). The same cross-country evidence also points to the importance of firing costs. Capital constraints seem not to have been an important persistence mechanism in the past – business surveys do not suggest that firms have been constrained by a shortage of capital in recent years – but this might no longer be the case if a sustained and rapid growth in demand were to occur. The bottom line seems to be that, even if appropriate labour market measures are introduced, it is going to be very difficult for policy makers to judge what the current short-run equilibrium unemployment level is. I shall return to this issue later.

1.3 Supply effects of macroeconomic policies

We have just considered the possible mechanisms whereby shifts in aggregate demand have longer-term effects on the equilibrium unemployment rate. However, macroeconomic policy instruments can also have more immediate effects upon supply. Aside from the obvious channels whereby government spending on infrastructure and training affects the demand for, and supply of, labour, there are a number of other routes worth mentioning briefly. First, the level of taxes will affect the wedge between the cost of labour to the firm and the consumption value of the worker's wage after tax. In terms of figure 4.1a, if we identify the real wage on the vertical axis with the real value of the wage to the worker, or consumption wage, an increase in any of payroll, income or consumption taxes would result in an increase in labour costs at a given consumption wage and thus a downward shift in the labour demand schedule, *NN*, and a decline in employment. Second, movements in the terms of trade will also affect this wedge because what matters to the firm is the cost of labour relative to the price at which it can sell its product, whereas what matters to the worker is the purchasing power of the wage which includes, presumably, imported goods. A depreciation of the currency thus raises the product wage at an unchanged consumption wage. In terms of figure 4.1a there is thus again a downward shift in the labour demand schedule and a decline in employment. Since a fiscal expansion can be expected to lead to a real appreciation as net exports are crowded out, it will simultaneously reduce the size of the wedge and thus expand employment.

The impact of the wedge – particularly taxes – has received quite a lot of attention in the unemployment literature. However, in my view its role tends to be over-stated. What matters crucially in the two experiments just considered is whether the reservation wage is also affected. Now the reservation wage will be determined not only by the level and availability of unemployment benefits but also by the level of existing savings, by the worker's expected future earnings against which borrowing may be possible, and by the possibility of support from other members of the household. A permanent deterioration in the terms of trade or a permanent increase in consumption taxes should also reduce the real value of the reservation wage by an equal amount. As a consequence the wage-setting schedule will also shift downwards, nullifying the effect on employment. A permanent increase in income or payroll taxes would have some effect because neither of them affects the consumption value of past savings and current unemployment benefits (assuming these are not taxed), but the consumption value of future earnings – which are arguably the most significant component of the reservation wage – would still be reduced.[7] Furthermore if we are in a region where the wage-setting schedule is fairly steep most of the effect will be shifted onto wages rather than employment anyway.

The other mechanism whereby macroeconomic policies have supply-side effects is through the real interest rate. An increase in the real (post-tax) interest rate raises the cost of capital and leads to capital decumulation and declining employment demand. (In figure 4.1a *NN** shifts down and *NN* shifts inwards over time.) In addition Phelps (1994) has pointed to a number of other channels whereby increases in real interest rates can shift both the labour demand schedule down and the wage-setting schedule up, in both cases increasing unemployment. Thus macroeconomic policies associated with increased real interest rates, such as higher budget deficits and debt, can have adverse consequences on employment. Such considerations are obviously of less concern to a small economy with a negligible effect on world interest rates than to a large economy like the USA. These real interest rate effects may be an important part of the unemployment jigsaw, but more research here would be useful.

2 Macroeconomic policies to support supply reforms

2.1 What is an accommodating policy stance?

The presence of persistence mechanisms which are not easily put into reverse limits the scope for macroeconomic policy to reduce unemployment in Europe even though demand shocks may have played some part in creating it in the first place, it is not a trivial matter to put Humpty-Dumpty back together again. However, as I indicated at the outset I am in favour of a 'two-handed' approach in which expansionary aggregate demand policies are adopted *alongside* the necessary improvements to supply – in other words a broadly accommodating approach. However, this begs the question of what exactly constitutes an 'accommodating' policy in this context.

On the face of it 'accommodating' might seem to imply keeping the inflation rate steady at its present relatively low levels. Certainly such a definition would appeal to many central bankers. Faster demand growth when there is economic slack, coupled with the prompt adjustment of policies to avoid any rekindling of inflation once recovery is under way – the first policy recommendation of the OECD jobs study – also seems to amount to much the same thing. Is there anything more to be said? I think the answer is 'yes'.

By way of providing a benchmark, let us start by looking at the historical experience after the Great Depression. In the USA between 1933 and 1939 real output rose at an average annual rate of 6.2 per cent while civilian unemployment declined from 24.9 per cent of the workforce to 9.9 per cent. The annual inflation rate averaged 3.8 per cent over this period, compared to 6.4 per cent over 1929–33. In the UK, where unemployment levels peaked at something nearer that currently seen in Europe today, real output grew at an annual rate of 3.8 per cent between 1932 and 1939 while unemployment fell from 15.6 per cent of the workforce to 5.8 per cent. Inflation averaged an annual 1.5 per cent compared to 2.2 per cent over 1929–32. Assuming that current labour force trends continue, a reduction in unemployment in Europe to around 5–6 per cent by the end of the decade would seem to require an average annual growth rate in the region of 4 per cent. Conditional on the implementation of appropriate labour market reforms such a rate of growth is more likely to materialise if policy is appropriately accommodating. The historical experience suggests that 'accommodating' in this context might actually involve some acceleration in inflation. Now, of course, both the causes of the unemployment and the inflationary background are both rather different from that of the interwar years so direct extrapolation is inappropriate. But does theory suggest anything on this score?

Over the years there has been considerable discussion over the appropriate targets for macroeconomic policy, especially monetary policy. There is a sizable group of economists who have advocated explicitly targeting nominal income (including Meade, 1978; Tobin, 1981; Brittan, 1981), and those who favour the use of monetary targets would presumably argue that in the absence of precise knowledge of movements in the velocity of circulation this is what they are trying to achieve in any case. The good operating properties of a nominal income rule in the face of shocks to private spending and portfolio shifts is well known, something it shares with a policy of targeting the price level (or inflation). In Bean (1983) I argued that a nominal income rule also has good operating properties against supply (technology) shocks in an environment where money wages move sluggishly and the wage-setting schedule is relatively steep. This is because under nominal income targets an unanticipated beneficial technology shock is associated with lower prices than would otherwise have been the case, and thus also higher real wages than would otherwise have been the case. This rise in real wages is something that is required in equilibrium and when wages are sticky it is most efficient to let it happen through a somewhat lower price level. By contrast a price or inflation target would not allow this to occur and so lead to an excessively large boom.

This might seem to suggest that supply-side improvements to the labour market ought to be accompanied if anything by a rather more restrictive policy stance than implied by stabilising forces or inflation. However supply-side reforms that improve the functioning of the labour market are not the same as a technology shock. Most of the measures discussed in this volume can loosely be thought of as ways of shifting the wage-setting schedule downwards and to the right. The new level of equilibrium unemployment must then be associated with *lower* real wages than would obtain without the supply reform.[8] If money wages are at all sticky this could nevertheless be swiftly brought about through an *increase* in prices (relative to what was anticipated when the money wage was set). Thus beneficial supply-side developments within the labour market might best be accompanied by an increase in inflation in order to generate a positive price 'surprise'; an appendix (p. 107) spells out the analysis more formally. Note, importantly, that this increase in inflation should not gender higher subsequent wage inflation because while inflation is faster than expected by wage bargainers it is offset by the beneficial effects of the supply-side reform.

In case readers think I have lost leave of my senses in advocating more inflation, it is useful to put some ball park numbers on the quantitative magnitudes involved. A reasonable estimate for the short-run wage elasticity of the demand for labour is around unity.[9] Consequently in order to generate extra employment of 5 per cent, the real wage would need to be 5 per cent lower than otherwise. With a predetermined money wage this would require a price level 5 per cent higher. However, in practice any beneficial effects from labour market reforms are likely to come through only gradually. A reduction in wage pressure corresponding to a decline in equilibrium unemployment at the rate of one percentage point a year seems around the best that can be hoped for. Assuming the implications of these reforms for the path of real wages are not built into nominal wages at the outset – and if they *are* then no special action is called for anyway – then the required change in real wages could be accomplished by an inflation rate just one percentage point higher than otherwise would have occurred. This is fairly small beer, and well within the likely control error for any inflation target. So in practical terms governments and/or central banks may not go far wrong in following the objective of stabilising the inflation rate, although they might do well to err on the side of laxity.

2.2 Uncertainty about the equilibrium rate of unemployment

We have seen that there is still considerable uncertainty about the quantitative importance of the various possible causes of the rise in European unemployment. As a consequence the quantitative impact of labour market policies on the equilibrium unemployment rate is also rather uncertain. This uncertainty is greatly compounded by the operation of the various persistence mechanisms, which may or may not be easily reversible. Consequently during any recovery policy makers are likely to be faced with considerable uncertainty as to the prevailing equilibrium rate of unemployment, and therefore also to the appropriate rate of expansion of nominal demand to secure their inflation target. How should policy makers take cognisance of this?

If the world were nice and linear so that a one percentage point reduction in unemployment produced the same absolute change in inflation as did a one percentage point increase in unemployment, and the authorities were indifferent as to the direction of any policy error,[10] then the answer is that it would not matter much. Policy should simply be set according to the 'certainty-equivalent' rule whereby the equilibrium unemployment rate is treated as though it is known and equal to the policy maker's best guess of its magnitude, i.e. to its expected value. It is not obvious why the authorities' objective function should be locally asymmetric, but the world certainly may not be linear. In particular, many economists and policy makers probably take the view that a given fall in unemployment tends to have a stronger upward effect on inflation than the downward effect of an equivalent increase in unemployment. The old-fashioned Keynesian view that nominal wages were upwardly flexible but downwardly rigid is a particular variant on this. The wording of the first policy recommendation of the OECD jobs study, namely that

> policy should focus on assisting recovery through faster non-inflationary growth of domestic demand where there is substantial economic slack, while policies should be adjusted promptly to avoid a rekindling of inflation when recovery is well under way

could for instance be construed as subscribing to the doctrine of a non-linear response of inflation to the amount of economic slack in the economy. From an empirical perspective there are also good reasons for suspecting that such a non-linear response as wage equations or Phillips curves with a non-linear transformation of the unemployment rate (such as the logarithm or the reciprocal) frequently outperform models that just contain the level.

Uncertainty now can have important consequences for the setting of policy because any temporary reduction in unemployment below the equilibrium rate, and with it any increase in inflation, may have to be followed in due course by an even larger increase in unemployment above the equilibrium rate to squeeze the extra inflation out of the system. It is reasonable to believe that this uncertainty about the equilibrium rate will diminish with time and experience. As a consequence an optimising policy maker concerned to minimise the total cumulative unemployment associated with maintaining the existing inflation rate will tend to err on the side of caution now by setting a somewhat tighter policy in which the unemployment rate is higher than her best guess (i.e. conditional expectation) of the underlying, but presently unobservable, equilibrium unemployment rate. This is a straightforward application of Jensen's inequality and is discussed more formally in an extended footnote.[11]

Just as with the appropriate definition of what is an 'accommodating' policy, it is helpful to have some idea of orders of magnitude. This depends very heavily on the degree of non-linearity involved in the response of inflation to activity. Since a number of studies suggest that the level of wages is quite well explained by the logarithm of the unemployment rate (e.g. Blanchflower and Oswald, 1994), this seems a natural benchmark to take. Suppose the authorities' conditional expectation on the equilibrium unemployment rate is 8 per cent with a standard deviation of 2 per cent, which seems a reasonable value for the extent of policy makers' uncertainty. Then the optimal setting of policy today should generate an unemployment rate of 8.25 per cent (see n. 11 for details). So just as with our discussion of defining an accommodating policy to complement a set of labour market reforms, the practical implications of uncertainty about the equilibrium rate are fairly modest. (This would not be the case if the wage-setting equation involved a very highly non-linear response of wage inflation to the unemployment rate.)

There is, however, a caveat to this argument. The story above relies on the assumption that the policy maker's knowledge about the value of the equilibrium unemployment rate is not affected by her particular choice of policy action today; over time she learns more about the state of the economy, but the speed at which that knowledge accrues is not related to her own decisions. In practice, given the imprecision with which econometric relationships are formulated and estimated, it will be difficult to infer the equilibrium unemployment rate associated with relatively stable inflation if the economy is operating with unemployment a long way above that level. Indeed in the extreme case where unemployment above the equilibrium rate exerts no downward pressure whatsoever on inflation, a high unemployment rate would tell the policy maker nothing about the equilibrium rate (other than that it is not even higher). The only way to learn about the limits to demand expansion in this case would be to punish unemployment down until the point at which inflation starts to take off. In other words a more expansionary policy may have a payoff in generating experimental knowledge about the limits to such policy.

2.3 *Fiscal constraints*

I now turn to a consideration of the potential sources of demand growth and the limitations on fiscal and monetary policies. The first thing to be noted is that the introduction in Europe of effective labour market policies susceptible of reducing unemployment by five percentage points by the end of the decade would, at unchanged real interest rates, imply an equiproportionate increase in the capital stock. With a capital–output ratio of around four this implies a total increase in investment of roughly 20 per cent of one year's output, or assuming it is spread over five years a boost to investment of about four percentage points of output per annum. This is simply the converse of the adverse effects of the decline in investment in the late 1970s and early 1908s and would more than absorb the extra output resulting from the supply-side reforms. In practice, one might expect the increase in investment to be somewhat smaller than this, both because of some upward pressure on global interest rates and because the extra jobs created may be of rather low capital intensity, e.g. in the services sector.

This raises the attractive prospect of a recovery that is, on the demand side, investment-led. However, it would be imprudent to rely on this, especially in the early stages when the impact of any reforms may not yet be clear to producers. Likewise although permanent income should rise as a result of reforms, it may not be immediately reflected in higher consumption. In that case, is there any scope for fiscal action? Here the room for manoeuvre does not look very wide with all OECD countries, except Japan, presently running not only a budget deficit (amounting to 4 per cent of GDP across the OECD as a whole and 6.1 per cent for Europe) but also a structural budget deficit, i.e. correcting for the automatic effects of the cycle on taxes and spending (amount to 2.8 per cent of GDP for the OECD and 4.1 per cent for Europe). However, the room for manoeuvre depends critically on not only the current level of potential output, but also the prospective rate of growth. Simple reorganisation of the government's budget identity tells us that the rate of growth of the debt–output ratio, b, is just

$$\hat{b} = r - n + d/b$$

where d is the government's primary deficit (including seigniorage revenue) as a fraction of output, r is the real interest rate, n is the rate of growth, and a hat denotes a growth rate. The latest OECD forecasts (OECD, 1994b) include medium-term projections for OECD public-sector debt and deficits (incorporating some near-term fiscal consolidation). The basic reference path involves an average growth rate until the end of the decade in the rage 2.5–3 per cent. Under this scenario the OECD debt–GDP ratio stabilises around 73 per cent. But a slightly less optimistic projection of growth at a rate 0.5 per cent less per cent produces a debt–GDP ratio that is rising steadily and is about 10 percentage points higher by the end of the decade. This reflects both the slower growth of the denominator of the debt–GDP ratio and the fact that slower growth tends to lead to a more pessimistic outlook for the primary deficit itself because taxes are lower and transfers higher.

Now a successful programme of structural reforms should be compatible with a medium-term growth rate significantly faster than the

OECD's reference scenario. Other things being equal faster growth should thus not only see debt–GDP ratios stabilising, but actually declining quite rapidly. If a modest fiscal expansion today is required to achieve this growth, then surely it ought to be nothing to worry about? The difficult is that there may in effect be multiple expectational equilibria present. On the one hand there is a virtuous equilibrium with a temporary fiscal expansion and buoyant medium-term growth. On the other hand if the financial markets are pessimistic about the effects of the structural reforms on the medium-term growth prospects they may regard the fiscal action as unsustainable and inevitably associated with yet higher debt–output levels in the medium term. This will push up long-term interest rates and have adverse effects on the level of aggregate demand today. This in turn will postpone – perhaps indefinitely – reaping the benefits of the structural reforms. In the present context there is a good chance that the latter case is the relevant one. This suggests (i) that the scope for fiscal action to expand demand is limited in the short term and (ii) that any fiscal action is more likely to be successful if it is explicitly temporary.

2.4 Exchange rates and monetary policy

If budgetary positions leave little scope for fiscal action,[12] in the short term at least, the burden of maintaining an appropriate level of aggregate demand must rely on monetary policy. In the EU, however, the scope for independent national monetary policies is limited by the operation of the ERM of the EMS. As a result of the exchange market turmoil of 1992–3 the previously tight 2.25 per cent fluctuation bands have been broadened to 15 per cent for all except Germany and the Netherlands, while sterling has left the mechanism altogether. This gives countries considerable *de jure* national monetary autonomy even without resorting to realignments. However *de facto* a number of countries – especially France – have not used the new-found monetary freedom to the full and instead kept exchange rates close to the central parities. One view is that maintaining a zone of exchange rate stability in this way will help to put the EMS back on the road to monetary union, as envisaged in the Maastricht Treaty.

Is this altogether wise, or in other words is exchange rate flexibility a desirable feature of the transition back to reasonable levels of unemployment? Suppose appropriate supply-side reforms are implemented in a particular country, what should happen to monetary policy and the exchange rate? Certainly the supply of goods and services should expand as a result of these measures. As these measures are presumably supposed to be permanent in their effect, permanent income and consumption should also rise, so that private saving should not be much affected. However higher activity should reduce budget deficits so that national saving will probably increase somewhat. But on the other side of the fence we have seen that we should probably also expect an investment boom to materialise in due course. During the early phases of a recovery one would expect the savings effect to dominate. Given the lack of scope for fiscal action, maintaining an appropriate level of aggregate demand will thus tend to require a loosening of monetary policy and with it a nominal and real depreciation.

Since member countries of the EU are likely to proceed with labour market reforms at differing speeds, there seems to be good reason for permitting fluctuations in nominal rates as an efficient way of achieving the appropriate movements in real rates. However, the size of these required movements should be kept in perspective. Nothing that is contemplated here rivals the effects on equilibrium real exchange rates of German reunification, and all of them should be readily achievable within the wide 15 per cent fluctuation band. The danger arises if policy makers seek to confine European monetary policies to a straitjacket by pressing for an early return to formal narrow fluctuation bands – although it is doubtful whether such bands would be sustainable in any case – or by pushing ahead to premature monetary unification.

3 Enhancing the effectiveness of macroeconomic policies

3.1 Policy coordination

I conclude with a brief discussion of other actions that may enhance the effectiveness of macroeconomic policies, specifically policy coordination and incomes policies. On the first of these the OECD jobs study suggests that

> countries should use the policy coordination process to ensure that the setting of macroeconomic policy is more consistent across countries ... At times this may involve a common strategy, but in the current situation ... international cooperation does not require them all to be pushing in the same direction ... at the same time.

It is not entirely clear what is meant by 'consistent' in this context ('coherence' appears in a similar context somewhat later in the same paragraph) and as it stands it seems difficult to imagine anything more vacuous!

During the early 1980s a burgeoning literature appeared on international policy coordination (see, for example, Buiter and Marston, 1985). This literature focused on the international externalities of macroeconomic policies in the form of demand and terms of trade spillovers. Despite the elegance of some of the theoretical developments, however, the quantitative magnitude of the spillovers that policy coordination was supposed to internalise appears to be negligible between the major trading blocs. Worse, even where the spillovers are quantitatively more important, e.g. within Europe, there is ambiguity over even the sign of the impact of the spillovers on the value of the policy maker's objective function (Bryant *et al.*, 1988). Consequently it may be difficult to know whether the effect on uncoordinated policy making is to lead to policies that are over- or under-expansionary. Given that policy makers are as uncertain over the way the world works as academic economists, the prospects for meaningful practical policy coordination do not look good (Frankel and Rockett, 1988).

Are there any obvious reasons for thinking that active macroeconomic policy coordination is likely to be an important ingredient in any strategy to lower OECD unemployment? Certainly it cannot be an issue as far as the major trading blocs are concerned because most trade is within blocs rather than between them. Even within Europe I am doubtful that policy coordination is anything other than a rather marginal issue, provided that countries have freedom of manoeuvre with respect to monetary policy. The only potential problem comes in the short run, if the appropriate supply reforms in one country are not swiftly accompanied by increased domestic consumption and investment. In that case, an increase in net exports is required, and with it a real depreciation, most easily brought about through a monetary relaxation. Since this will in the short run also reduce the demand for foreign goods, and hence employment abroad, it may prompt other countries to level charges of 'social dumping', especially if the supply-side reforms lead to a redirection of foreign direct investment away from them and into the reforming country. But the biggest danger here is that 'policy coordination', in the guise of inflexible exchange rates, may actually prevent the desirable policies from being undertaken in the first place.

3.2 Incomes policy

Traditionally incomes policies have been thought of as a counter-inflationary strategy, but it is perhaps more correct to think of them as a particular supply-side policy that reduces wage pressure and thus also reduces the equilibrium rate of unemployment. The role for a reform of the wage-setting process in achieving a lasting reduction in equilibrium unemployment will be considered by other contributors to this volume. Here I want to briefly note the possible role for a temporary incomes policy to enhance the effectiveness of any expansion in aggregate demand.

Incomes policies, particularly those of a rather *dirigiste* nature, have a bad reputation amongst both academic economists and policy makers. There are two reasons for this. On the one hand, they limit the action of market forces in directing labour from declining to expanding sectors of the economy, and thus reduce economic efficiency. On the other hand, they have usually proven difficult to enforce for more than a short period as individual groups of workers find ways around the controls. When the policy collapses the economy is no better off than before. Only in small economies, such as the Nordic countries and Switzerland, have centralised forms of wage-setting shown any durability, presumably because in such economies it is easier to discourage individual groups from seeking to free ride on the restraint of others.

In the past incomes policies have often been invoked when unemployment has been at historically relatively low levels. A temporary incomes policy may however be useful in economies where unemployment persistence due to insider membership dynamics is important. The key here is somehow to increase the pool of insiders who are responsible for wage negotiation. An incomes policy can prevent the existing pool of insiders from pushing up wages in the face of an expansion in demand, and instead lead to an increase in employment. Provided the new hirees become part of the group of insiders, then subsequent wage pressure will be reduced and the increase in employment should be self-sustaining without the continual application of incomes policy and absent further unanticipated shocks.

It could be objected that this is an inferior policy to removing the features that give the insiders bargaining power in the first place. However while some of these, such as firing costs, may be susceptible to government regulation others, such as the presence of firm-specific skills and the ability of the insiders to harass or refuse cooperation to new hires, are not. Furthermore even when government action can attack the source of insider power directly it may be politically difficult to do so. In such circumstances temporary controls on incomes may be a useful second-best policy.

A country where I think this may prove useful is Spain. There administrative approval is required for collective dismissals affecting more than 10 per cent of the workforce and severance payments of 20 days' wages per year of service (45 days' wages in the case of 'unfair' dismissals) are required. These firing costs give the incumbent workforce considerable bargaining power, which is further underpinned by the system of collective bargaining under which agreements at the sectoral level provide a floor for subsequent negotiations at the firm level. From 1984 firms were, however, allowed to hire workers on fixed-term contracts of six months' duration (renewable up to five times) which were not subject to the same restrictions. By 1993 roughly a third of those in employment were engaged under this sort of temporary contract.

On the face of it these temporary contracts are the sort of thing that the OECD jobs study endorses, and indeed they have led to increased labour market flexibility in the sense that total employment is now more variable than before. However, as Bentolila and Dolado (1994) document, the effects on unemployment have not been as straightforward as one might expect. One might expect the presence of workers on temporary contracts to undermine the position of permanent workers, who are effectively the insiders in this economy. However, by providing a buffer of variable employment at the margin and thus reducing the layoff probability for permanent workers they in fact seem to have had the effect of enhancing the bargaining position of the insiders. And unemployment in Spain has remained the highest in the EU.

The latest (1994) reforms have done away with temporary contracts except for apprentices. However severance pay requirements remain at their existing levels. Reducing these to more reasonable levels would probably help to reduce unemployment in the medium term – not by making employment more flexible, but by reducing worker bargaining power. However, this is politically difficult to implement when unemployment is high, because its immediate impact would probably be to increase unemployment further. Instead a temporary incomes policy – probably in the form of a floor and a ceiling on wage settlements in order to give some local flexibility – coupled with a demand expansion and a credible commitment to reduce firing costs once unemployment was falling, could make the transition to an economically preferable outcome politically feasible as well.

4 Conclusions

Despite the fact that adverse demand shocks share part of the blame for the rise in European unemployment, macroeconomic policies alone can carry only a little of the burden in reducing it. The most difficult task facing policy makers now is devising and implementing appropriate, and possibly politically difficult, supply-side reforms. Once this is done, however, macroeconomic policies can play a useful supporting and cementing role by ensuring that the full benefits of structural reform materialise quickly. Such a supporting macroeconomic strategy will involve sustained robust growth and should aim at maintaining existing inflation rates, or even permitting a mild, but temporary, acceleration. Politicians and central bankers should therefore not be unduly alarmed by continuing strong growth in the wake of structural reform. Although such robust growth would help to solve many of the current fiscal difficulties, there seems little room for fiscal action to support demand in the short run. Instead monetary policy must bear most of the burden. Given that successful reforms will tend to become self-sustaining in due course via their effect on investment, the appropriate monetary policy is likely to involve initial loosening and subsequent tightening. Finally in some countries a temporary incomes policy may prove a useful adjunct in overcoming unemployment persistence due to insider membership effects.

Appendix

Aggregate demand policies with a labour market reform

Output is given by the technology

$$y_t = (1 - a)\ell_t + u_t \tag{1}$$

where y_t is the logarithm of output, ℓ_t is the logarithm of employment and u_t indexes the level of technology. Competitive labour demand is then

$$w_t - p_t = b - a\ell_t + u_t \tag{2}$$

where w_t is the logarithm of the wage, p_t is the logarithm of the price level and $b = (1 - a)$. The wage-setting schedule is

$$w_t - p_t = c + d\ell_t + v_t \tag{3}$$

where v_t indexes the degree of wage pressure. The money wage is set at the start of the period to equilibrate labour demand and wage-setting in expectation

$$w_t = Ep_t + \phi_0 + \phi Eu_t + (1 - \phi)Ev_t \tag{4}$$

where Ex_t denotes wage-setters' expectation of x_t at the start of the period (which may, but need not necessarily, be rational), $\phi_0 = (ac + bd)/(a + d)$ and $\phi = d/(a + d)$. Substituting the wage into (2) and then the resulting employment level into (1) gives output as

$$y_t = \beta[(p_t - Ep_t) + b - \phi_0 - \phi Eu_t - (1 - \phi)Ev_t] + (1 + \beta)u_t \tag{5}$$

where $\beta = (1 - a)/a$. Equilibrium output under full information, y_t^*, is

$$y_t^* = \beta(b - \phi_0) + [1 + \beta(1 - \phi)]u_t - \beta(1 - \phi)v_t \tag{6}$$

Hence the deviation of output from equilibrium is

$$(y_t - y_t^*) = \beta[(p_t - Ep_t) + \phi(u_t - Eu_t) + (1 - \phi)(v_t - Ev_t). \tag{7}$$

Hence in order to stabilise output the authorities would need to respond to a reduction in wage pressure (a fall in v_t) by increasing the price level through expansionary policies.

NOTES

This chapter was originally prepared for the Annual Symposium of the Federal Reserve Bank of Kansas City, Jackson Hole, Wyoming (26–27 August 1994), and has appeared in the volume *Policies to Reduce Unemployment* (Federal Reserve Bank of Kansas City, 1994). The opinions expressed in this chapter are personal and should not be taken as indicative of any official position. I am grateful for the comments of my discussant, Stanley Fischer. The Centre for Economic Performance is financed by the Economic and Social Research Council.

1 Since the real wage exceeds the reservation wage and price exceeds marginal cost if firms have some market power, both workers and firms will be jointly willing to supply the required increase in output so long as wages and prices cannot be adjusted.

2 The reason for using the logarithm is the likely convexity of the wage-setting schedule, and reflects the fact that in Europe a given movement in capacity utilisation in the 1960s was associated with a much smaller movement in the unemployment rate than during the 1980s.

3 These assumptions correspond to the contemporaneous recursive ordering: capacity utilisation; inflation; unemployment. With demand shocks assumed to have no contemporaneous effect on inflation the ordering becomes: inflation; capacity utilisation; unemployment. Other, non-recursive decompositions have been investigated without altering the main message.

4 The 'no-demand-shock' unemployment rate is not strictly the same as the equilibrium unemployment rate, because sluggish wage and price adjustment will mean that supply-side disturbances do not have their full impact on unemployment immediately. However, the general tenor of the results is not affected by this caveat.

5 Suppose the Phillips curve is

$$\pi_t = \alpha(u_t^* - u_t) + \pi_t^e \tag{1}$$

where u_t is unemployment u_t^* is equilibrium unemployment, π_t is inflation and π_t^e is expected inflation. The equilibrium unemployment rate follows the process

$$u_t^* = B\bar{u} + (1 - \beta)u_{t-1} \tag{2}$$

where $\bar{u}$ is the long-run equilibrium unemployment rate. Substituting into the Phillips curve gives

$$\pi_t = \alpha\beta(\bar{u} - u_t) - \alpha(1 - \beta)(u_t - u_{t-1}) + \pi_t^e \tag{3}$$

6 In the context of figure 4.1a the labour demand schedule, instead of being downward-sloping, is an upside-down and backwards-facing L.

7 Empirical evidence also suggests that it is the change, rather than the level, of the wedge (or its components) that matter. See for instance Newell and

Symons (1986) who in a cross-country study of 16 OECD countries report that 43 per cent of any tax or terms of trade change is shifted onto product wages in the short run, but an average long-run effect of almost exactly zero.

8 One might object that our earlier analysis demonstrates that in the long run, when capital is variable, no fall in real wages need occur. However, in the short run, capital is *not* variable, and furthermore the increase in profitability associated with the decline in real wages will probably be necessary to elicit the extra investment that should occur subsequently.

9 The wage elasticity conditional on the capital stock is actually the ratio of the elasticity of substitution between capital and labour to capital's income share. For a Cobb–Douglas technology this should be in the range 3–4. With adjustment costs to labour present, a somewhat smaller value would be appropriate for evaluating a short-run elasticity. Much of the empirical work on the aggregate demand for labour actually suggests a *long-run* wage elasticity of around unity; in Bean (1994b), however, I argue that these studies are unlikely to have uncovered the true wage elasticity and instead estimate a combination of the labour and capital demand schedules.

10 For instance if preferences were quadratic in inflation and unemployment.

11 As a simple example suppose that inflation, π_t, is generated by the accelerationist Phillips curve

$$\pi_{t+1} = \pi_t + f(u_t, u^*), \tag{1}$$

where u_t is unemployment, u^* is equilibrium unemployment, $f_1 > 0, f_{11} < 0$ and $f(u^*, u^*) = 0$. There are two periods ($t = 1,2$), inflation starts at zero (i.e. $\pi_0 = 0$) and must also end at zero ($\pi_2 = 0$). Thus

$$f(u_1,\ u^*) + f(u_2,\ u^*) = 0. \tag{2}$$

The equilibrium rate, u^*, is uncertain during period $t = 1$, but that uncertainty is resolved before the start of period $t = 2$. The authorities then pick current unemployment, u_1, in order to minimise the expected cumulative level of unemployment, $u_1 + u_2$, subject to (2). The associated optimality condition is

$$E[f_1(u_1, u^*)/f_1(u_2 u^*)] = 1 \tag{3}$$

where E denotes the expectation operator. In the absence of uncertainty about u^* this is satisfied at u_1-$u_2 = u^*$. However with uncertainty $u_1 > u^*$ is generally optimal.

As a particular (relevant) example let $f(u,u^*) = \alpha \ell n(u^*/u)$. Then (2) implies that $u_2 = (u^*)^2/u_1$ while (3) becomes $E[u_2/u_1] = 1$. Hence

$$u_1^2 = E[u^2] = \{E[u^*]\}^2 + var[u^*]. \tag{4}$$

12 But I certainly do *not* rule out the possibility of deficit-neutral actions to improve the structure of the tax and spending system. In particular, moving towards an income support system that subsidises work rather than idleness is highly desirable.

REFERENCES

Bean, C.R., 1983. 'Targeting nominal income: an appraisal', *Economic Journal*, **93**, 806–19

1994a. 'European unemployment: a retrospective', *European Economic Review*, **38**, 523–34

1994b. 'European employment: a survey', *Journal of Economic Literature*, **32**, 573–619

Bentolila, S. and G. Bertola, 1990. 'Firing costs and labour demand in Europe: how bad is Eurosclerosis?', *Review of Economic Studies*, **57**, 381–402

Bentolila, S. and J.J. Dolado, 1994. 'Labor flexibility and wages: lessons from Spain', *Economic Policy*, **18**, 53–100

Blanchard, O. and P.A. Diamond, 1994. 'Ranking employment duration and wages', *Review of Economic Studies*, **61**, 417–34

Blanchard, O. and L.H. Summers, 1986. 'Hysteresis and the European employment problem', in S. Fischer (ed.), *NBER Macroeconomics Annual*, **1** Cambridge, MA: MIT Press, 15–77

Blanchard, O., R. Dornbusch, J.H. Drèze, H. Giersch, P.R.G. Layard and M. Monti, 1985. *Employment and Growth in Europe: A Two-handed Approach*, Brussels: Centre for European Policy Studies

Blanchflower, D. and A.J. Oswald, 1994. *The Wage Curve*, Cambridge, MA: MIT Press.

Brittan, S., 1981. 'How to end the monetary controversy', *Hobart,* **90**, London: Institute of Economic Affairs

Bryant, R., D. Henderson, G. Holtham, P. Hooper and S. Symansky (eds.), 1988. *Empirical Macroeconomics for Interdependent Economies*, Washington, DC: Brookings Institution

Buiter, W. and R.C. Marston (eds.), 1985. *International Economic Policy Coordination*, Cambridge: Cambridge University Press

Frankel, J.S. and K. Rockett, 1988. 'International monetary policy coordination when policymakers do not agree on the true model', *American Economic Review*, **78**, 318–40

Layard, P.R.G. and S.J. Nickell, 1987. 'The labour market', in R. Dornbusch and P.R.G. Layard (eds.), *The Performance of the British Economy*, Oxford: Clarendon Press, 131–79

Layard, P.R.G., S.J. Nickell and R.A. Jackman, 1991. *Unemployment: Macroeconomic Performance and the Labour Market*, Oxford: Oxford University Press

Lindbeck, A. and D.J. Snower, 1988. *The Insider–Outsider Theory of Employment and Unemployment*, Cambridge, MA: MIT Press

Meade, J.E., 1978. 'The meaning of internal balance', *Economic Journal*, **88**, 423–35

Newell, A. and J.S.V. Symons, 1986. 'The Phillips curve is a real wage equation', *Discussion Paper*, **246**, London School of Economics Centre for Labour Economics

OECD, 1994a. *The OECD Jobs Study: Facts, Analysis, Strategies*, Paris: OECD

1994b. *Economic Outlook*, **55** (June), Paris: OECD

Phelps, E.S., 1972. *Inflation Policy and Unemployment Theory*, London: Macmillan

1994. *Structural Slumps: The Modern Equilibrium Theory of Unemployment, Interest, and Assets*, Cambridge, MA: Harvard University Press

Pissarides, C.A., 1992. 'Loss of skill during unemployment and the persistence of employment shocks', *Quarterly Journal of Economics*, **107**, 1371–91
Tobin, J., 1981. 'Stabilisation policy ten years after', *Brookings Papers on Economic Activity*, **1**, 19–72

Discussion

STANLEY FISCHER

Charles Bean has written an interesting and thought-provoking chapter on two topics: the first is whether demand-management policies have a role in stabilising unemployment; and the second is on the potential role of demand-management policies in reducing European unemployment in the remainder of the 1990s.

1 Is there a role for stabilisation policy?

Bean is sceptical about the ability of policy makers to stabilise unemployment. He argues that while in principle policy makers *could* stabilise output and unemployment around their equilibrium values, in practice all the familiar obstacles to perfect stabilisation – especially lags and uncertainty about the structure of the economy and the way individuals form expectations – lead them to believe that 'activist policies to eliminate such cyclical fluctuations [are] hazardous'.

Of course, no one proposes policies that would attempt to eliminate rather than moderate business cycle fluctuations. We need also to recognise that policy makers try to keep both employment and inflation close to their target levels. If one then asks whether policy makers *can* and *should* attempt to stabilise the business cycle, the answer is 'yes'.

That is what central banks try to do, often quite successfully. No central bank should be inactive in the face of a major disturbance; indeed, it is even difficult to know how to define 'inactivity'. Even if fine-tuning is out, coarse-tuning is not. In fact, Bean discusses such activity policies in Section 2 of the chapter.

Bean's discussion of stabilisation policy raises three issues that I would like to pursue. First, in several places he analyses the implications of the non-linearity of the Phillips curve. This is a worthwhile question, because the evidence suggests that the short-run Phillips curve is non-linear: a one percentage point reduction in an already low unemployment rate will push up inflation more than a one percentage point increase in a higher unemployment rate will reduce inflation.

How should this affect policy? Bean shows in an interesting note that in the presence of a non-linear trade off, the authorities should aim for a higher unemployment rate than the natural rate, because a positive shock that reduced unemployment will have a larger effect on inflation than a negative shock of the same size. Bean shows for a logarithmic example that the effect is quantitatively insignificant – but that, of course, depends on the extent of the non-linearity.

Bean's discussion opens up a way for the quality of macroeconomic policy to affect the average rate of unemployment. Suppose that the Phillips curve is non-linear, for example that the inflation rate is driven by the divergence between the log of unemployment and the log of the natural rate. Then, even if the log of unemployment is on average equal to the log of the natural rate, the average level of unemployment will be larger the greater the variance of unemployment. This result thus produces the intuitively appealing result that countries that conduct stabilisation policy better will have a lower average unemployment rate.

Second, Chapter 4 raises, but does not settle, the important question of what the presence of persistence mechanisms implies for stabilisation policy. Suppose that an adverse shock increases unemployment, and that any short-run increase in unemployment translates in part and gradually into an increase in the NAIRU – the non-accelerating inflation rate of unemployment. Suppose that the monetary authority can reduce unemployment in the short run through expansionary monetary policy, at the expense of an increase in inflation. Then I conjecture that optimal monetary policy will be more expansionary in response to a given unemployment increase when there is persistence than when there is not. The argument is that by moving more aggressively, the monetary authority can cut off the higher long-term unemployment that would otherwise result. But that is just a conjecture, and the answer must depend in part on non-linearities in the Phillips curve and on the formation of expectations.

Third, Bean emphasises that uncertainty about the natural rate or the NAIRU severely complicates policy. This argument is put into perspective if we focus on the NAIRU rather than the natural rate, and realise that the policy makers can judge where they are by watching for early signs of increasing inflation. It is thus not clear that the shifting NAIRU poses a special problem for macro policy makers.

2 The role of demand management in Europe in the 1990s

Chapter 4's main focus is on what should be done now to reduce European unemployment. Bean accepts with little discussion the argument put forward in the June 1994 OECD *Economic Outlook* that policy should be vigorously expansionary until the economy comes within reach of the NAIRU.

The chapter seems to give an indication of the excess of the actual over the natural rate of unemployment in figure 4.2, which suggests about 1.5 per cent. However, the 'no-demand-shock' locus in figure 4.2 does not in fact correspond to the NAIRU. Other estimates suggest that European unemployment is currently about 2.5–3 per cent above the NAIRU, which gives ample room for more expansion in Europe.

Bean's main interest is in aggregate demand policies as unemployment reaches the NAIRU. He accepts the diagnosis that the NAIRU can be brought down through supply-side policies; these are discussed briefly but the details are not important for the purposes of this chapter. The major recommendation of the chapter is that monetary policy should accommodate the increased growth and declining unemployment that the supply-side measures should produce.

In discussing these issues, Bean very usefully takes us back to the literature of the early 1980s on European stagflation. The diagnosis then was that Europe suffered from real-wage resistance, that European real wages were too high, and that there was a wage gap that had to be cut to restore full employment. We can interpret the modern discussion of supply-side reforms as explaining why there may be real wage resistance and what policies can be adopted to reduce it.

Bean calculates that real wages would have to drop 5 per cent to reduce the unemployment rate by five percentage points. If that is all it takes, then Europe will not have to go too far down the road of increasing inequality which several chapters in this volume warn is the result of a US approach to the labour markets.

Bean's preferred strategy is to move as fast as possible on labour market reforms, while recognising that they are politically difficult and will therefore take time to implement. At the same time, macroeconomic policy should be expansionary. Ideally, fiscal expansion should help power the recovery; it would then be throttled back as growth picked up and investment took over. Monetary policy would be sufficiently accommodating, not only to allow for the more rapid growth of real income, but also to produce a bit more inflation so that the real wage could decline. But this strategy is ruled out, because there is no room for fiscal expansion. Full employment deficits are too large in Europe, and most European governments are rightly planning to reduce them over the next few years. So expansionary fiscal policy is not available.

That leaves monetary policy as the only other aggregate demand policy. There would be no dispute that monetary policy should accommodate the increased growth that comes through the expansion of supply. Bean calculates that output would grow about 1 per cent per year more rapidly, implying that money growth should be that much faster.

But should monetary policy also be used to try to reduce the real wage, by permitting more inflation? Before answering that question, let me diverge to discuss the two different approaches that chapter 4 takes to the likely behaviour of the real wage. The argument for inflation assumes that the real wage should decline. But in another part of the chapter, Bean argues that with the real interest rate unchanged, investment will grow massively; the same argument would imply that the real wage would not change at all. In that case, there would be no need for the inflation.

I believe that lower real wages – compared with what they would otherwise have been – will be needed in Europe. Nonetheless, I doubt that the slightly higher inflation policy makes sense. The same labour market reforms that are designed to reduce unemployment should also increase wage flexibility – they should reduce European real wage resistance, and presumably also make nominal wages more flexible.

Since the adjustment that is being considered is not one that will cut real or nominal wages, but only require them to grow more slowly than they otherwise would have, it hardly seems necessary to ask for more inflation. Nor is Bean very firm in arguing for inflation, for he concedes that an extra 1 per cent would probably not make much difference to employment.

In the end, Bean's discussion of macroeconomic policy in Europe for the remainder of the decade is an appeal to the central bankers to avoid cutting off the recovery prematurely. It is not a request for higher inflation, but rather an argument that the growth potential of Europe enjoying a supply-side recovery may be as high as 4 per cent a year.

If the supply-side measures are undertaken, central banks should not be alarmed by growth that looks high by the standards of the last decade. Rapid growth by itself would not be a good reason to reduce money growth or raise interest rates. Rather central bankers should judge the supply potential of the economy by the behaviour of the inflation rate – and they should be prepared to tighten policy when inflation threatens. They will surely be prepared to do that.

NOTES

This Discussion was originally prepared for the Annual Symposium of the Federal Reserve Bank of Kansas City, Jackson Hole, Wyoming (26–27 August 1994).

REFERENCE

OECD, 1994. *Economic Outlook*, **55** (June), Paris: OECD

5 Edmund Phelps' theory of structural slumps and its policy implications

EDMOND MALINVAUD

1 Introduction

For most of Western Europe present unemployment is undoubtedly a medium-term phenomenon and requires medium-term policies. Public opinion has well perceived the problem but has lost confidence in economists, precisely because they have proved unable to produce a clear common proposal on what ought to be done. Indeed, a suitable macroeconomic theory for the analysis of the medium-term unemployment phenomenon is not yet recognised to exist. When considering the policy challenge, we economists rely on our intuition as much as on objective science. It is then not surprising that we do not agree.

Some of us draw on the theory of temporary equilibrium with the market imbalances that were found to hold in the short run; the successive temporary equilibria are linked by macroeconomic adjustment laws, which also were found to hold in the short run, but become more and more questionable as the horizon is extended further into the future. Others among us start from the opposite end, namely from the growth theory, which was initially meant to be appropriate for long-term trends; the theory, enriched by the introduction of uncertainty and random shocks, is now taken by some as appropriate for the study of business cycles, real or not, with no market imbalances, even the most obvious ones. Many feel uneasy with the resulting theoretical split, particularly when they consider the medium run, for which they do not know where to turn. Building a valid medium-term theory has become urgent.

Some economists believe, as I do, that the required theory need not trace the evolution of the price level, so that it might be said to be non-monetary, even if it should permit the study of real consequences of monetary policies. These economists ought to be particularly interested in the book of Edmund Phelps (1994a), which aims (p. 1) at uncovering 'the nonmonetary mechanisms through which various nonmonetary forces are capable of propagating slumps and booms in the contemporary world economy'.

There is some ambiguity about the policy claims of the book. On the one hand (p. xi), it is cautiously and modestly presented as offering a valuable addition to the set of economic theories: 'The structuralist theory propounded here will, if it succeeds, push back the domain of some of the other theories, not eliminate any of them.' On the other hand, the subtitle, 'The modern equilibrium theory of unemployment, interest and assets', and many statements in the book present it as being essentially appropriate for the explanation of observed changes in unemployment and for the characterisation of the effects of contemplated economic policies; when the conclusions differ from those derived from the Keynesian or the neoclassical theory, no hesitation is expressed about which is right. Here, I am going to accept the ambitious interpretation of the claims.

Besides being eager to discover new fundamental models for the medium-run study of unemployment, I have two reasons for closely considering the book: a fair degree of agreement on methodological issues and the intuition that Phelps is essentially right in stressing the role of real interest rates. But I also have my reservations. A comment of minor importance consists in stating that the analytical treatment looks to me as unduly sophisticated at the present stage, when the basic ideas have not yet been much tested. More importantly, by focusing on efficiency wages and on almost perfect market adjustments, the theory makes a crucial preliminary choice, which I find to be not yet substantiated, and unlikely ever to be so. When saying (p. vii) 'long swings in unemployment are an equilibrium phenomenon, not a matter of misperceptions or misforecasts and consequent wage–price misalignments', Phelps is also ruling out a number of factors that, according to my belief, a correct diagnosis has to take into account, even for the medium term. I believe this preliminary choice tends to bias analysis and policy recommendations.

My discussion will be incomplete and tentative. Incomplete, because I shall neglect all the theoretical analysis of open economies (part III), in order to concentrate on the new features of the proposed framework. Tentative, because I may unduly resist revising my own ideas when confronted with an unfamiliar vision (not to speak of my difficulty in understanding some details of the argument).

In section 2 I shall try to suggest why fundamental reconstructions, such as the one proposed by Phelps, are needed. Section 3 will briefly discuss other methodological preliminaries. Section 4 will be devoted to the models presented in the book. Section 5 will consider empirical proofs.

Section 6 will comment on chapter 18, which pretends to explain the history of postwar economic activity. In section 7 I shall try and assess the value of Phelps' policy recommendations.

2 In search of a fundamental model

2.1 The operation of the labour market

It seems to be widely perceived that the discussion of medium-term macroproblems, particularly those concerning unemployment, requires a fuller set of theories than that of those now in common use; the aim of a new theory should be to assess, less ambiguously than can objectively be done now, the comparative statics properties that are relevant for effects after five–10 years. Recently published books reflect this perception; but it would be difficult to derive from them a common fundamental theory, which could serve in the same way as does the Keynesian or neoclassical one for other purposes.

These books agree in one respect, namely that the labour market should not be assumed to clear. They also agree on the idea that a useful way for looking at the determination of unemployment is to consider two relations between employment and the real wage rate. The operation of the labour market is viewed as implying a positive relation between the two variables (curve *EW* in figure 5.1 where the employment rate $1u$ is plotted on the horizontal axis). This is called 'the equilibrium wage curve' by Phelps and 'the wage-setting function' by Layard, Nickell and Jackman (1991) or Lindbeck (1993). Authors differ somewhat as to the exact justification of this relation and as to the factors that are likely to explain its shifts (Phelps argues mainly in terms of efficiency wages, others in terms of wage bargaining). But the main differences and uncertainties concern the rest of the model. The simplest formalisations introduce just another relationship linking the real wage rate with employment; otherwise such a relationship may be derived from a set of structural equations. It is grounded, at least partly, in labour demand behaviour of employers; but is it exactly *the* labour demand function?

2.2 Changes in the real interest rate

This is where macroeconomists part from each other: some give an affirmative answer and draw the 'demand wage curve' (to use the term chosen by Phelps) as curve DW_1 in figure 5.1; they indeed consider that markets on which employers are selling their products or services are cleared. If this last postulate is not accepted, then the second relationship

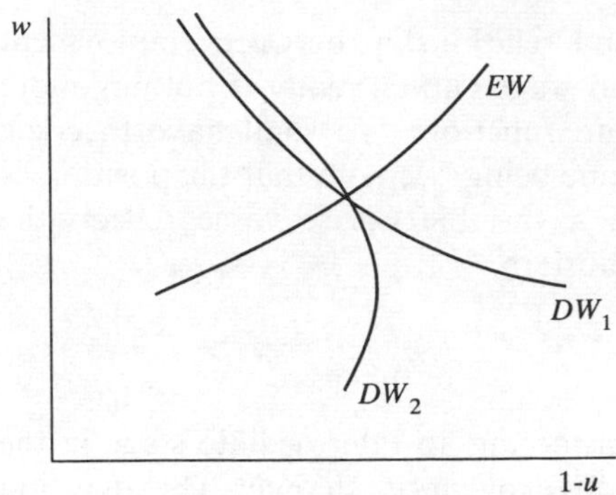

Figure 5.1 The macroeconomic equilibrium

is a more complex concept because it involves much more than the behaviour of employers. The difference becomes particularly significant when the transmission of demand shocks to the labour market is discussed. Then the second curve may have a different shape from what is usually exhibited (see DW_2 in figure 5.1).

I believe that a realistic and simple medium-run macroeconomic theory has to allow for a variable excess supply of goods, in other words has to reject the hypothesis that the market for goods exactly clears (hence also, if one cares for 'foundations', to reject the hypothesis of full price flexibility). The main objection against this view comes from what I think to be a too literal interpretation of the non-market-clearing assumption and from the observation that actual changes in the rate of capacity utilisation are quite small in the medium run. But the growth of capacities is largely induced by increases in product demand; hence, the same rate of capacity utilisation may result in the medium run from quite different levels of product demand, which have quite different implications for employment. If one accepts this remark, one must conclude that the second function relating employment to the real wage ought to depend on a variable capturing the product market slack.

Since in the medium run changes in employment and in productive capital are related to each other, account should be taken of changes in the real interest rate, which may react both on productive capacity building and on the labour requirement by unit of output. This is unfortunately not stressed, or even not considered in most unemployment models. An attractive feature of Phelps' theory is precisely the role given to the real interest rate, which is moreover endogenously determined. On the other hand, in his theory the product market is assumed to clear and so the second relationship between employment and the real wage rate, the 'demand wage curve', really is nothing more than the employers' labour demand function. We shall have to come back later to this feature. For the time being, we note that the position of the curve is shown to depend on a variable whose value reflects the requirement of capital market equilibrium.

2.3 Medium-term effects

Speaking of the medium run is considering an intermediate stage in the unfolding of effects initiated by an exogenous change. The question naturally comes to mind of knowing whether, and how, medium-run analysis ought to be related to both short-run and long-run analyses, and whether, and how, this should appear in theories and models.

One should then not be surprised to realise that less agreement prevails about medium-term effects than about either short-term or very long-term ones, for which disputes among scientists should not be exaggerated. When faced with an actual question about long-term effects most economists rely on neoclassical theory. About short-term effects the analytical apparatuses do not vary so much; most of them involve similar combinations of imperfect competition, quantitative constraints and market imbalances – the policy recommendations may differ, but for strategic reasons that stand beyond positive economics narrowly understood. For medium-term effects, on the contrary, opinions fundamentally differ as to their importance, their special characteristics and the best way to approach them.

Some envisage an ideal dynamic model that would link the short run to the very long run and also be appropriate throughout in order to describe the path of reactions to shocks. 'Real-business-cycle' models have the attraction of seeming to offer precisely such an integrated description. But they can hardly be realistic in their assumptions about the dynamics of phenomena, which are much more complex than any model can be. The description is of course particularly unreliable when full market clearing in the short run is assumed. Alternatives that rely on econometric dynamic equations fitted on quarterly series are certainly to be preferred for dealing with the main reactions up to two years or so; but they are also likely to miss those reactions that need longer time-spans in order to mature, precisely those reactions that give their special features to medium-term phenomena.

When closely examined, most heuristic arguments about the latter phenomena are recognised to have the nature of static equilibrium arguments. In order to give them more rigor and to study whether they fit the facts, one is naturally led to specify corresponding equilibrium models and it is to such models that reference was made at the beginning of this section. I indeed believe that so considering well chosen static models may be sufficient at the present stage. In Malinvaud (1991) I tried to present my line of reasoning for doing so.

Phelps' models are dynamic, but they have asymptotic static solutions that are meant to be appropriate for the medium run and are the focus of attention in comparative analysis. It seems to me that discussion ought indeed to concentrate at present on these static solutions and on the main features of the models that generate them. (If looked at closely, the dynamic specifications used in Phelps' book could be subject to reservations; but I do not think this to be an important issue at this stage.)

2.4 Financial markets

When considered as aiming at providing relevant static solutions, Phelps' models appear to give a large role to adaptations of the price system and to perfect foresight. One might say that, in this respect, there is just one main difference from the neoclassical model, namely that, because of efficiency wages, adaptations of the real wage rate do not lead to full employment (another difference, which plays a less crucial role, comes from the assumption of 'customer markets', implying deviation from perfect competition on the market for goods). Similarly, the dynamic path toward equilibrium would belong to the class of those studied by the real-business-cycle literature, except for a number of differences, mainly efficiency wages and a special analysis of the household sector, to which I shall return.

Systematic considerations of reactions in real factor returns and asset prices is an attractive feature of the models. The formal treatment again uses the assumption of perfect foresight and clearing of capital markets. Is this appropriate for a theory of the medium run? On the one hand, one must say that financial markets are apparently very flexible, so that the neoclassical assumptions not only make analysis easy and well determined, but also look realistic at first sight.

On the other hand, one also recognises on closer scrutiny that shortsightedness of operators and the information asymmetry leading to credit rationing mean important deviations from the neoclassical assumptions. When making such assumptions one should be aware of neglecting important features of actual medium-term evolutions. Erroneous anticipations may prevail and long speculative bubbles of some prices may develop. Credit conditions may be easy in some periods, when solvency tends to be taken for granted and indebtedness of non-financial agents increases; but other periods experience the difficulties of debt deflation.

There is thus a theoretical dilemma. The best way to face it may be to remain eclectic in this respect in medium-term macroeconomic analysis. For the building of formal models there is probably no other way than using assumptions of perfect foresight and clearing of capital markets. But one should then reflect on how the formal models ought to be used when neglected phenomena such as speculative bubbles or debt deflation occur. How should such price or quantity disequilibria be taken into account in applications? If they are not, when is policy analysis unreliable?

3 Further methodological remarks

At this point I shall briefly pause in order to be a little more explicit about the questions that are disturbing me when I reflect on the structure to be given to the fundamental medium-term macromodel. I should like this structure to be such as to: (i) permit a proper representation of the macroeconomy and of the causal relations it contains, (ii) provide easy ways for the introduction of all significant shocks or more progressive exogenous changes, and for the study of their effects, (iii) facilitate confrontation between observed data and abstract theory.

Models proposed by the real-business-cycle movement are definitely attractive with respect to (ii). As long as empirical evidence is meant to be found only in aggregate macroeconomic time series, they stand well with respect to (iii) also. The main difficulty concerns (i), because of the discrepancy between the hypotheses of the formal models and what can be judged from factual information available to economists about behaviours and market institutions.

Here, I should like to insist on requirement (iii). Essentially, macroeconomics is an empirical science. We indulge in a lot of formal analysis in order to build it; and we are right to do so, but only as long as it is necessary for drawing the macroeconomic consequences of all the available factual information, a large part of which is microeconomic. It will appear later that I am not quite satisfied with the place given by Phelps to empirical evidence and with the difficulty of confronting his formal theory with available data.

In comparison with the short-term macromodels, which were obtained in the 1960s and are still essentially appropriate for horizons up to two years or so, the main challenge appears to be the proper modelling of investment, which is the first determinant of the evolutions of capacities and labour requirements. Real prices and remuneration rates have an important part to play in explanations of investment; and one must also account for the fact that investment is decided in a context full of uncertainties, which concern not only future relative prices but also the volume of demand at those prices.

Already at this stage one realises the difficulty of a fully consistent model that would not only explain adaptations in the price system but, when so doing, also capture uncertainties, and anticipations about more or less favourable future market imbalances. The challenge becomes still harder when one wants to allow for bubbles in asset prices and interest rates, as well as for periods of unusually high or low business profitability that last a number of years and for occasional perception of excessive indebtedness.

The difficulty is such that one may wonder whether one ought not to limit modelling ambitions. One possibility of doing so would be to accept going only part of the way toward a fully closed model: some variables could be taken as exogenous by the model even though one would be aware that the corresponding magnitudes interact with others taken as endogenous and simultaneously determined. Such incomplete models have often proved to be useful, even if in applications one has to pay attention to the reflected interactions.

Accepting such a device, for lack of a better workable alternative, of course requires a good deal of common sense: the neglected but truly not negligible interactions ought probably to be those about which one is most uncertain, either because the phenomenon is poorly known or because it is subject to important irregularities. I cannot pretend to be better than others in seeing what to do. I may, however, report that my past behaviour often led me to accept more exogeneity in the price system than I truly believed to be the case. For instance assuming an exogenous real wage rate looked to me as justified when there were special factors that kept the wage away from what would otherwise have been its equilibrium value.

4 Phelps' models discussed

It is now the place to consider the hard core of Phelps' theory and models. To begin with, let us look at efficiency wages. Most readers are now familiar with the way in which they enter models of the economy. But a brief reference to it, given its importance in the present case, may be appropriate. It will also help in exhibiting the role attributed by Phelps to wealth effects on incentives.

4.1 Efficiency wages

Efficiency wages are determined by consideration of three ingredients: the behaviour of employees, the reaction of employers and an equilibrium requirement. Firms have an incomplete control over the behaviour of workers, whether it concerns effort at the work place ('shirking') or separation from the firm ('turnover'); but this behaviour, which matters for the performance of the firm, depends on the wage given by the firm, in such a way that a higher wage elicits a more favourable behaviour from the employer's viewpoint.

Consider for instance the effort e of a worker. It depends positively on the wage because of the risk of losing the job, a risk whose cost is all the higher as the lost wage w is higher. The cost of being fired also depends on the wage w^e that is expected to be earned with another employer, on the chance of remaining long unemployed and on the level of unemployment compensation. Phelps makes the point that one must not forget either the income y^w coming from the wealth of the employee.

We may then consider the behaviour as being represented by:

$$e = \varepsilon(w, w^e, y^w, u) \tag{1}$$

where u is the unemployment rate in the economy, and other determinants such as the level of unemployment compensation are not made explicit. The function ϵ is increasing in w and u; it is decreasing in w^e and y^w.

Knowing this behaviour of its employees, and how effort and the wage rate affect its performance, the firm chooses the optimal rate w, which then is a function of many variables, in particular those listed above. But equilibrium requires that, all firms on the market similarly deciding and employees having correct expectations, the expected wage w^e to be earned elsewhere will finally be equal to the actual wage w.

Since a higher unemployment rate stimulates a higher level of effort and does not otherwise directly affect the profit of the firm, one intuitively understands that, subject to natural hypotheses, a lower optimal wage rate will result. For a similar reason a higher level of capital incomes y^w or a better unemployment compensation will lead to a higher wage rate. To sum up, the argument will determine the 'equilibrium wage curve', which will indeed be increasing with $1 - u$ and shift upwards when y^w or unemployment compensation increases.

4.2 *The context of the firm*

The exact formalisation of the above argument depends on a more precise specification of the context in which the firms operate. Phelps carefully looks at it for three cases, which are introduced in chapters 3 and 4, then fully specified, respectively, in chapters 7, 8 and 9.

In the 'turnover–training model' the behaviour of employees concerns whether or not to quit one's job. The firm aims at preventing quits because it has to invest, once and for all, in the training of each newly hired employee. The analytics of this combination is somewhat complex, which explains why the rest of the model is kept simple. In particular, output depends only on labour input; no productive capital appears. In the other two models the behaviour of employees concerns effort at the workplace, with the risk of being caught and fired when shirking. The analytics is simpler because no training fixed cost occurs. So, the rest of the model may be developed in other respects.

The 'customer–market model' introduces a second incentive consideration in the profit maximisation of the firm, namely to maintain attachment of its customers, who occasionally hear about the prices charged by other firms. So, competition on the product market is not perfect in this model, as opposed to what is assumed in the other two: each firm can choose a price that differs somewhat from the one prevailing in the rest of the market, without losing all its customers or gaining all those of competitors; more precisely, the firm's market share and its rate of change are functions of the ratio of its price to the market price. Equilibrium requires equality between the two but leaves a positive mark-up. Again there is no productive capital.

The third model introduces productive capital, with actually two sectors, respectively producing the consumer good and the capital good. The real price of the capital good then plays an important role that Phelps exhibits, paying particular attention to the case in which the capital-producing sector is the more labour-intensive.

Actually, real assets appear in the two other models also. In the first one it is the stock of trained employees which is valuable for the firms, and leads them to offer an incentive wage leading to the optimally low level of turnover. In the second case it is the stock of customers that the firms succeeded in attracting thanks to their pricing policy. In each of the three cases a capital market equilibrium imposes consistency between the real interest rate and the asset price (a shadow price in the two first cases). In each case the labour demand function resulting from the firm optimisation problem must be indexed by the real price of the asset. General equilibrium may be viewed as resulting from the simultaneous operation of the three markets for labour, product and capital.

Such constructs are claimed by Phelps to belong to 'modern equilibrium theory'. The distinction from neoclassical equilibrium theory (p. 9) follows from 'a radically novel perspective on individual behaviour' that began to invade economics 25 years ago:

> This quintessentially modern outlook brought into play assumptions about the costliness or existence of information quite foreign to (neo) classical theory ... This book, if successful, will help to carry that development toward maturity in the area of macroeconomics.

4.3 Changes in the environment

Beyond this theoretical ambition, the book is also intended to prove the validity of a 'structuralist doctrine', which is made up of a number of theses on the working of the economy and, above all, on the effects of changes in its environment. But these theses do not seem to all have the same level of importance for the author. I shall quote here only the three that I find to be particularly stressed.

An increase in time preference, i.e. an increase in consumption and a decrease in thrift, leads to a drop in the price of real assets, hence to an increase in real interest and to a downward shift of the demand wage curve. The equilibrium wage curve then implies a decrease in employment.

The same kind of effect is to be expected from the creation of public debt through a period of tax cuts. There is then a wealth effect (as we shall see, Phelps rejects the Ricardian equivalence assumption). Not only does this effect stimulate consumption demand in the same way as does an increase in time preference; but also workers' incentives are changed so that the equilibrium wage curve shifts to the left.

Such anti-Keynesian conclusions, which of course have to do with the assumption that product markets clear are, however, overturned if there is a permanent increase in public expenditure for the purchase of capital goods rather than consumption goods. The reason comes from the fact that the increase sets in motion an increase in real asset prices as well as an increase in the derived demand for labour (the production of capital goods is assumed to be more labour-intensive than that of consumption goods).

Confronted with these 'structuralist theses' and with their derivation from theoretical models, we have to wonder whether all relevant 'modern' features of market economies are taken into account. Certainly, incentive wage and job rationing belong to those features, as well as investment in customers. But are there no others? A small section at the end of chapter 5 mentions rationing features on the capital market and briefly speculates on their effects. But, all in all, I find the book considers a too narrow range of 'modern' features. My reasons are apparent in the discussion of the preceding sections. Other readers will correctly find that their favourite subjects of attention are granted too little role (insider–outsider behaviour, union wage bargaining, social norms . . .).

The above comment would not matter if we were only concerned here with the value of a new theoretical exploration; restricting attention is unavoidable for anyone going into a new field of inquiry. But Phelps also claims to reach policy conclusions and we have to wonder whether the models proposed in the book are not biased in important respects. This is also why we must look carefully at other assumptions made in these models, particularly for the enterprise and household sectors.

4.4 Investment

Considering the crucial role I am giving to investment for medium-term evolution, I remain somewhat uncertain about the treatment it receives. First, at the first of being old-fashioned, I must report that I still tend to focus on investment in physical capital, more than on investment in such intangible assets as trained employees or customers, about the change in which we know very little. Second, and more importantly, I notice that investment is analysed in the same way as in neoclassical theory, namely as a progressive change in the capital stock along an equilibrium path with no excess capacity and with a perfectly adapted competitive price system (implying in particular a pure profit rate that is independent of the product market slack and subject to no exogenous shock); I have difficulty in believing that such an equilibrium vision can be appropriate for dealing with actual slumps and booms. The neoclassical representation of firms was often criticised as being too simplistic (a production function *plus* a price-taking profit-maximizing agent); modifying this representation in just one or two respects, choice of incentive wages and monopolistic competition on customer markets, can hardly suffice for the macroeconomics of the medium run.

The two-sector model, with both a capital good and a consumption good, is the only one of the three models to allow for physical capital; it makes an assumption on factor intensities that is crucial for one of the policy theses of the book. The assumption is introduced on p. 46 by the following curious sentence:

> Upon making the conventional specification that the capital-producing activity is the more labour-intensive, the model replicates all the main insights of the Austrian approach.

Considering the policy implications of the assumption, many readers will wonder whether it is realistic and will then probably share my doubts. I have read in the past a few studies about the relative factor intensities of the two aggregate sectors respectively producing capital and consumption goods: the difference was found to be small; if there was a slight indication in favour of 'the conventional specification', this was because of the building industry, the rest of the capital good-producing sector being on the contrary capital-intensive.

The representation of the household sector plays a larger role than might be first realised. It is indeed such that Ricardian equivalence does not hold, notwithstanding the assumptions otherwise made about equilibrium and expectations. Instead of Ricardian equivalence the models accept as fully reliable a formalisation[1] that was introduced in Blanchard (1985).[2] The formalisation is referred to at several places but not so well explained (the best place for understanding it and its role is the beginning of chapter 16, pp. 272–81, where, along the lines of Blanchard, 1985, a one-sector neoclassical model with a competitive wage and no effort or incentive consideration is studied). For me, the realism of this representation of the household sector is open to question.

There is no inheritance. People are subject to a constant instantaneous probability μ of death. When they die their wealth goes to 'the insurance company'. On the other hand as long as they do not die, they receive from the company a flow of transfer μw proportional to their current wealth w; the flow therefore comes on top of interest income. With a large number of individuals 'the insurance company' breaks even. Except for the occurrence of death there is no exogenous life cycle feature. I find it difficult to believe that specialists in the study of household saving could take such a representation as a valid first approximation.

4.5 *Wealth effects and fiscal policy*

At the end of this examination of Phelps' theoretical models two features should be stressed because they play an important role in policy conclusions. First, the wealth effects operate in the opposite direction from the one found in Keynesian analysis. An increase in consumers' wealth is contractionary. Since the product market is assumed to be permanently cleared, no stimulation of employment comes from an increase in aggregate demand, which on the contrary leads to a higher interest rate, in accordance with what the real-business–cycle models would predict. Moreover, a given level of the real wage rate is made less effective to counteract workers' incentives to quit or shirk, unless employment decreases.

Second, analysis of fiscal policy has to take into account not only the global perceived household income and wealth effects, but also the kind of tax being used. In particular, payroll taxes imply a wedge between the after-tax wage, which matters for employees' behaviour, and labour cost, which enters employers profit maximisation. Hence, an increase in this wedge has a specific contractionary effect, to which I shall return in section 7.

5 Empirical evidence

Chapter 17 has the title: 'Econometric tests of the theory: a postwar cross-country time-series study'. It discusses the estimate of a 'reduced-form econometric model' aimed at being adequate for testing 'the main conclusions of the structuralist theory'. Of central interest are: first, the proposition that changes that drive up the world real interest rate have a contractionary effect on employment; second, the role of a number of factors that should raise the interest rate, such as public debt or government expenditures on consumption goods. Hence, the model to be tested has two equations, respectively explaining the unemployment rate and the world real interest rate (the first equation does not exactly belong to the reduced form of the system since it contains as regressor the endogenous interest rate).

The sample is made up of annual data of 17 OECD countries for the period 1955–89 and of corresponding data for world variables. The equation explaining the real interest rate contains only the latter variables. The other equation explains differences in the unemployment rate through both time and space; it contains a country dummy on the unemployment level and a country sensitivity coefficient applying simultaneously to all explanatory variables, whose respective forces are then meant to apply uniformly to all countries and all years.

The main findings in support of the structuralist doctrine are the positive quite significant effects of public debt and public expenditures on the world real rate of interest and of the latter on the unemployment rates. Also, in the unemployment equation independent significant positive effects are found for the capital–output ratio and the rate of direct taxation, which again are claimed to fit with the doctrine. Less satisfactory is the attempt at testing the expansionary effect of public expenditures on capital goods: the proxy variable, military expenditures, has a still more depressing effect than non-military expenditures. The comments of Phelps on this 'surprising' result at the top of p. 317 are worth reading; finally it is said to be 'in no way troubling' because in the two models without physical capital public expenditures do drive up interest rates. It is not clear to me, however, whether this means a revision of one of the propositions 'that are important for structuralist theory'.

Quite naturally this chapter is more eclectic than the rest of the book. In particular, dealing with annual data, the econometric equations have to allow for short-term and monetary effects; those are captured by an additional explanatory variable in both equations: the change in the inflation rate. The transitory component of oil prices, which appears in raising the world real interest rate, should belong to the same category of variables that a theory focused on the medium run has to neglect. However, the same cannot be said about the quite significant independent depressing role of a real price of oil in the unemployment equation. I did not find in the book sufficient information for knowing whether this effect is explained by the structuralist doctrine (does it shift the equilibrium wage curve ?).

Incidentally noteworthy is also the result of a third regression explaining by national characteristics the cross-country differences in the sensitivity coefficient of the unemployment equation. This coefficient can perhaps be interpreted as a measure of unemployment flexibility. If so, one finds that this flexibility is low where labour market programmes for the unemployed are important, where wage-bargaining is centralised and where unemployment benefits are low (on this last effect, at least, I guess that most people would predict the reverse).

This chapter is, of course, interesting. In particular the apparent anti-Keynesian medium-term effect of fiscal policy through the real interest rate is worth remembering.[3] But the chapter falls very much short of what I should like to know about empirical evidence in favour of the structuralist theses. Testing a theory just on some of its consequences is not powerful enough, since many theories could explain the same consequences, as is recognised by Phelps. In particular the depressing effect of high interest rates is also predicted by theories in which the product market slack varies and reacts on investment.

We need a much more deep and thorough confrontation of the theoretical construct with the facts. For instance, am I factually wrong in the reservations I expressed in sections 2 and 3 above? On the opposite front, is Phelps more factually right than are pure neoclassical economists? The answer to this question mainly depends, as we saw, on those given to two other questions: do efficiency wages deviate much, and to a variable degree, from competitive wages? Is the theory used by Phelps for household saving better than the one incorporated in neoclassical growth models with its Ricardian equivalence? No empirical evidence is given in the chapter or in the book about these issues; it is as if real wages and household savings were latent variables of the theory with no real counterpart. If the structuralist doctrine is to be taken seriously, as I do think it ought to be, a whole research programme on its empirical foundations is required before anything else.

6 Explanation of postwar trends

Chapter 18 has the title 'A concise nonmonetary history of postwar economic activity'. Its object is perfectly given by the following quotations from pp. 335 and 336:

> To account for the long swings in unemployment one needs the causal relationships provided by a theory ... The structuralist framework here provides such a theory [and] Can the highlights of the postwar fluctuations in employment be explained to a large or important degree by those causal factors and mechanisms portrayed by the theory?

In principle, trying to answer the question fits very well within the search for an appropriate new theory, because it stimulates thinking about the explanatory power of various causal factors. But it does not provide a true test, because too much flexibility exists for introducing subsidiary factors and for reconciling history with prior ideas. I shall not discuss here the content of the interesting chapter 18, but simply report two general queries related to the main subject of the book: are the structuralist theses referred to in the chapter perfectly congruent with those established in the rest of the book? Should the explanation of trends in postwar activity attribute significant roles to factors that do not appear in the proposed theory?

About the first query, the chapter stresses again changes in oil prices; but the theoretical parts do not contain a neat analysis of the effects of these changes, so far as I can see. Similarly, I do not find in the book a persuasive and unambiguous proof of the following proposition stated at the beginning of the chapter and used in the study of historical trends (p. 335): 'if the world capital stock goes up the employment rate is ultimately increased'.

About the second query, I may list three important potential explanatory factors that might fit within a medium-term theory: financial deregulation, increased uncertainty after the end of the Bretton Woods era and exogenous changes in wage bargaining (at least in Western Europe). In many parts of the world, financial operations were tightly controlled during the immediate postwar period, both within countries and with the rest of the world; this meant extensive capital rationing. Throughout the following decades at various times controls were lifted and the role of market interest rates increased. It is very likely that, when borrowing was restricted, particularly in the first one or two decades after the war but also up to the early 1980s, real interest rates were lower than they would otherwise have been. During the long period of progressive financial liberalisation, a transitory decrease in aggregate saving took place, as previously credit-rationed private agents were increasing their debts; so interest rates were boosted above their long run equilibrium value, not to speak of a bubble that may have magnified the phenomenon. Considering the central position of interest rates in Phelps' theory, should not this exogenous change be taken into account? (It may be the explanation of the postwar puzzle posed at the bottom of p. 337: a low real interest rate in the immediate postwar period.) Intuition and a good deal of microeconomic evidence suggest that, when instability of the economic environment increases, as it did in the early 1970s, business investment decreases unless risk premia (i.e. profit margins) sufficiently increase. A full treatment of uncertainty would be difficult in a realistic macroeconomic model; but the difficulty should not lead to a complete neglect of uncertainty in the theory, still less in empirical applications.

In the early 1970s social unrest and malaise weakened the position of Western European employers in wage bargaining; real wages kept drifting upward quickly while productivity increases were slowing down; profitability greatly decreased. Collective attitudes completely changed in the 1980s, so that firms regained power in wage negotiations. Such changes in bargaining power are easily introduced in a framework similar to the one of the book: they simply mean shifts of the equilibrium wage curve, at first upwards, then downwards. Notice that awareness of the presence of factors such as the three foregoing ones lay behind the position taken in sections 2 and 3 above.

7 Policy implications

Chapter 20 has the modest title 'Economic policies to which the structuralist theory might lead'. It is relegated in a part of 'concluding notes' and presented as 'an informal reconnaissance of the terrain'. But this comes after many pages referring to effects of fiscal policies. No doubt, the policy implications receive major importance in the author's reflections: the second sentence of the chapter indeed is: 'What should countries do when some of them or all of them find themselves in a structural slump or boom?'

The chapter begins with a very welcome section intended to take care of a misunderstanding, which leads to 'the passivist fallacy'. I may reformulate this misunderstanding somewhat by saying that the phrase 'equilibrium unemployment' conveys to many people the idea that one has to accept the corresponding unemployment rate as unescapable in the medium run (this is precisely why, by the way, I am not using the phrase). Here I simply quote Phelps' answers (pp. 360, 361).

> The fallacy in this view is that, although the structuralist perspective assumes that the equilibrium path of unemployment is determined by the economy's current structure, however good an approximation that assumption may be, it does not follow that interventions by the government do not alter this structure. The government is part of the structure.

Clearly, this sentence means that, in the present context, government policy should also be understood to be 'part of the structure'.

> It would be a new fallacy . . . to conclude that, when the structure of the economy shifts unfavorably by a discrete amount, pushing up non-negligibly the equilibrium unemployment, [the policy of] no response by the government is perfectly optimal. Large shocks require correspondingly large policy responses'.

7.1 *Market flexibility*

Reading the question posed by the second sentence of the chapter, one expects the author to take positions in current policy debates and to place the policy conclusions of his book within the broader spectrum of guidelines currently proposed to policy makers. This is not explicitly done. So, the text seems to mean that the answer to the question has to be found mainly in fiscal policies and that other kinds of action will not much matter. At the risk of being provocative I shall expand this comment a little.

The latest expression of wisdom for and by governments on employment problems was published by OECD in 1994. The proposed strategy for coping with the present slump is made up of nine main elements, one of them only concerning macroeconomic policy; 'increasing flexibility' explicitly appears in the denomination of two elements and implicitly in three others.

The word 'flexibility' is not listed in the index of Phelps' book. According to one interpretation of this fact, the author thinks that flexibility should not be a serious matter for concern; indeed, the positive analysis accepts the idea that markets have such a high degree of flexibility as to operate close to equilibrium. A second interpretation would be that flexibility-enhancing measures are not discussed because they would not interfere with the macroeconomic policies, which provide a more interesting subject matter for a macroeconomic theory.

Clearly, some measures, such as those concerning the regulation of job security, would seem to be likely to affect shirking incentives, and hence to shift the equilibrium wage curve (at least if shirking is a real problem). The book itself briefly discusses on p. 156 (together with the effects of the structure of taxation and transfers) the possible role of unemployment compensation; it then admits that 'both the propensity to quit and to shirk may be aggravated by the operation of the welfare system'. But even there labour market flexibility does not appear as an important consideration; the conclusion of the section reads: 'Throughout this section on taxation and entitlements . . . the crucial indicator is the effect . . . on nonwage income'.

Discussing the pros and cons of various components of market flexibility is out of question here, considering the complexity of the subject and the abundance of the literature about it. However, it must be noted that a full discussion needs to take into account much more than effects on incentive wages. A challenging question is precisely to know how the medium-term macroeconomic theory ought to count in other effects.

7.2 Monetary policy

Except for marginal comments on short-term action and on exchange rate stabilisation, chapter 20 says little about monetary policy. The fact may be explained either by the idea that there is no such thing as a medium-term monetary policy or by the premise that a non-monetary theory is unsuited for the analysis of any effect of any monetary policy. I am not so sure of this premise. Would it be unrealistic to consider the case of a monetary authority that would stick to a strategy aiming at a given level of the real interest rate? If feasible, this strategy would be a medium-term monetary policy with real consequences, which could be analysed in a non-monetary model.

To the feasibility of such a strategy one may object that monetary authorities could only control some nominal rates, not real rates which would be determined by market equilibria. Again, I am not so sure of the validity of the argument. I rather see monetary policy, assisted by price and income policy, acting not only on the rate of inflation but also on real interest rates within a corridor left open by the tolerable degree of market imbalance; the corridor is fairly large for short-term rates, much more narrow for long-term ones and the interactions between the two categories of rates complicate the matter.[4] But deliberate policies of low interest rates were consistently adopted during some rather long periods in order to stimulate economic activity.

Of course, the effect of a given medium-term monetary policy, both on inflation and on employment, depends on which fiscal policy is simultaneously adopted. But this is precisely the important aspect of the macroeconomic policy problem. To repeat: of the two familiar macroeconomic instruments, the fiscal and monetary ones, Phelps sees the first one only as available for 'medium-run discretionary action on employment'. This vision looks to me as being too extreme.

7.3 *Fiscal policy*

As for fiscal policy, one must distinguish between the macroeconomic stance, implied by the values of government aggregate expenditures and receipts, and the structures of the tax system. To begin with macroeconomic aspects, I must first make a brief reference to the international dimension, which plays a large part in the chapter as well as in the book, but not in this discussion.

The main point is the interest effect of Keynesian expansionary policies. With free international movement of capital this effect concerns the world rate of interest. Unilateral fiscal expansion by a large country (or a large collection of small countries) may boost employment in the area, but it has a beggar-thy-neighbour effect causing employment contraction abroad because of the increase in interest. This is the argument developed in Fitoussi and Phelps (1988). What, then, should be recommended either to a country that wants to avoid aggravating employment problems abroad or for multilateral international policy coordination? The book discusses a number of alternative proposals, some among which follow from the analysis of a closed economy, to which I now turn.

First, I cannot refrain from reporting on this occasion my embarrassment in debates about medium-term effects of macroeconomic fiscal policy. My own theoretical framework incorporates an essentially Keynesian system of aggregate demand analysis. But I have the uneasy feeling that too many observed facts do not seem to be easy to reconcile with this system and with the comparative statics propositions it usually conveys with respect to the effects of fiscal policies. On this topic still more than on others, I am open-minded and would not like to appear dogmatic.

Of course, one must remember that the implications of Keynesian theory about medium-term effects are not perfectly clear, when this theory is closely examined. These implications were studied by Blinder and Solow (1973), for instance, and a little later in Tobin and Buiter (1976); even under the simplifying assumptions of permanent excess capacity, nominal price rigidity and full incorporation of government bonds with private wealth, the results appeared to be somewhat dependent on the exact specifications of behaviours and policies.

Ricardian equivalence naturally comes to mind in this respect. The theoretical analysis showed it to be quite implausible as an exact property, because private agents often have finite horizons, as considered by Blanchard (1985), but also for a number of other reasons, among which we should not forget the following: if the slack in the goods market varies as a consequence of fiscal policies, the rational expectations of agents take account of the increase in national wealth that result from expansionary policies. However, empirical evidence seems to suggest that there is a good deal of truth in the idea that private saving increases when government debt does (see Seater, 1993 in this respect).

The reason may have to do more with the diffuse pessimism (or optimism) conveyed by the word 'confidence' than with a fully rational evaluation of future economic and fiscal conditions. For an instance along this line, Hellwig and Neumann (1987) argued that, given the budget deficits and rising public debt inherited by the Kohl administration, not only was fiscal consolidation at the time wise, but also it increased private-sector confidence to such an extent that, in this instance at least, it may actually have increased aggregate demand. It is worth remembering that in *The General Theory*, Keynes gave a role to 'the state of confidence' and recognised in particular (1936, p. 120) that, 'with the confused psychology that often prevails', a programme of public works might deteriorate confidence, an effect which would counteract, at least to some degree, the expansionary impact.

7.4 The wealth effect

Rejection of Ricardian equivalence matters for Phelps' theory because of the increase in perceived private wealth which follows from an increase in government debt. But, as we saw above, the wealth effect ends up depressing the demand for labour, the opposite consequence from the one derived by usual Keynesian analysis. I am ready to accept the idea that the incentive effect may contribute to the lack of a clear-cut correlation between the stance of fiscal policy and the change in employment. But by how much?

The same kind of opposition to Keynesian analysis is claimed in chapter 20 to exist about a policy that introduces equal changes in government expenditures and receipts ('the balanced budget fiscal policy'). Here, the theoretical analysis does not conclude about the sign of the net effect, but the empirical evidence is accepted by Phelps as strong enough: the expansionary effect of a tax cut would be sufficient to outweigh whatever contractionary effect the corresponding decrease in government spending could have. Moreover such a policy would induce a decrease in the world interest rate; if the country is large enough for the decrease to be non-negligible, foreign employment would be stimulated. Such a national policy would be internationally favourable, the reverse of beggar-thy-neighbour policies. The only difficulty would be that the short-term domestic effect would work in the opposite direction because of the Keynesian mechanism; Phelps recommends a temporary monetary stimulus in order to counteract the initial deflationary impact.

It seems to me that a systematic investigation of medium-term effects of macroeconomic fiscal policies should consider the full range of theoretical candidates for the explanation of empirical evidence. Some of these candidates do not assume that the market for good clears. For instance Picard (1993) has a chapter 7 entitled 'Efficiency wages, employment fluctuations and fiscal policy', which should deserve serious consideration, particularly for comparison with Phelps' theory (there is in Picard's book not only the recognition of more widespread market disequilibria, but also a different general equilibrium setup for consumption–saving behaviour).

Similarly, the 'anti-Keynesian balanced budget' prediction is also empirically supported, but derived from a different analysis, in the writings of Knoester (for references and some recent results, see Knoester, 1993). A wage bargaining model implies that the tax cut leads to a lower real wage rate, hence to a higher pure profit rate (prices are sluggish, *pace* the assumption made by Phelps); this stimulates investment and hirings.

7.5 Public expenditures and the tax system

A structural theory should be particularly suited for studying how the composition of public expenditures and the structure of the tax system matter. Indeed, Phelps pays much attention to them in his policy analyses.

His recommendation to favour labour-intensive expenditures in case of slump will not seem surprising; it was indeed followed, probably even too much in some countries, wherever the number of government employees increased and public services were developed. I pointed out earlier that labour-intensive expenditures should not be identified with expenditure on capital goods, as is too often done in the book; but this is a minor comment.

Departing somewhat from Phelps' analysis, one may indeed argue for productive public investments, which will sustain aggregate demand in the short run, and will also increase productive capacity and competitiveness in the medium run. Even more generally slumps should be good times for expenditures on long-lived infrastructures, which will have to be repaired or built before long in any case.

The book deserves particular attention for the discussion of the structure of taxes. Indeed, to quote Atkinson and Stiglitz (1980, p. 222),

> the general equilibrium analysis of tax incidence has to date been undertaken largely independently of the literature on macroeconomics. Thus competitive equilibrium models, with all markets clearing, have been used to investigate the incidence of different taxes.

Enlarging the scope of the analysis, which is indeed required can, however, be done in many directions, as many as there are realistic deviations from the competitive equilibrium paradigm. For instance, Atkinson and Stiglitz consider two questions: the incidence of the corporate tax (meant to be levied on the capital input) when wages are rigid and there is a non-corporate sector and the effort of the same tax on employment when there is involuntary unemployment.

Similarly, Picard (1993), chapter 8, considers optimal taxation in an economy with a dual labour market, jobs being rationed in the primary sector and efficiency wages prevailing there. Readers familiar with the taxation literature know that many cases exist for which conclusions are ambiguous. This unpleasant feature does not disappear when one moves away from competitive equilibrium models.

However, in the case of large market disequilibria, intuition often suggests tax reforms that are likely to be favourable; theoretical analysis may then very well support intuition. Particularly noteworthy now is the diagnosis of an increasing skill mismatch in Western Europe between the supply of labour and the demand for labour. The diagnostic also is that this mismatch results in part from a too narrow difference between labour costs of unskilled and skilled workers. Such a diagnosis leads to the now often heard proposal of a decrease in payroll tax on unskilled labour. The proposal is briefly mentioned on p. 366 of the book and is supported in a separate article by Phelps (1994b).

7.6 Employment subsidies

Even without any skill breakdown, the book proposes employment subsidies financed by 'across-the-board increases in tax rates'. The argument for this policy is given in chapter 10 (pp. 154–6); it is worth considering. We must look at the implications, first, of an increase in the value added tax or in the consumption-expenditure tax (meant to be equivalent to the across-the-board increase), second, of a decrease in the payroll or labour-income tax (equivalent to an employment subsidy).

Starting from an equilibrium, an increase in the value added tax leads to a new equilibrium with exactly the same unemployment rate, the same effort and the same nominal values, except for the increase in the price of consumption goods. Indeed, the new equilibrium is equivalent to the old one from the point of view of the firms; it implies in particular the same nominal demand wage curve and the same distribution of non-labour income. There is no change either in the nominal equilibrium wage curve, since (1) still holds with the same values of all variables.[5]

On the contrary a decrease in the payroll tax implies shifts of the two curves of figure 5.1, which is now maintained as applying to the real wage rate. Consider first the demand wage curve. Writing $f(eL)$ for the production function and τ for the rate of the payroll tax, the demand wage curve is such as to satisfy:

$$ef'(eL) = (1 + \tau)w \tag{2}$$

Taking (1) into account, one may see that, with L and u unchanged, a decrease in τ would lead to an increase in w and a decrease in e. Real non-labour income would also increase, but relatively less than w. So, after a decrease in the payroll tax, the demand wage curve shifts upward. Close examination shows that the equilibrium wage curve also shifts upward, but less than the demand wage curve, so that equilibrium employment increases.

The same change in taxes was often claimed to be favourable to employment, but for a different reason, namely that the impact on relative cost of labour with respect to capital would counteract substitution of capital for labour. Such substitution may happen either because of the input mix chosen in production units or because of the output mix induced by the relative prices of labour-intensive with respect to capital-intensive goods and services. It is now well known that a number of conditions are required for the favourable factor-substitution effect and that, in any case, it is slow to appear. Would the (more modern) favourable incentive effect fare better under both theoretical and empirical scrutiny? This is to be seen.

Perhaps a conclusion ought here to be singled out from the many which have been suggested in this chapter. If so, I shall select the following.

When used for extensively testing macroeconomic propositions about the employment effect of fiscal policies, econometric models have to contain some significant intermediate variables. With the recent work of Edmund Phelps in front of us, we should not forget to place the real interest rate among those variables.

NOTES

This version of the chapter has benefited from the comments of my discussants and of R. Calaza.

1 The importance of this formalisation is recognised in n. 19 to chapter 15, where reference is made to the Danthine–Donaldson (1990) work in which the real-business-cycle methodology was used in order to study the role of efficiency wage. Phelps writes:

> This model *is* worth having, but it would seem that it must suffer from Ricardian equivalence, and hence not deliver the interesting implications with regard to the employment effects of public debt and government expenditures which are important to structuralist theory.

2 Blanchard's article was meant to be a theoretical exploration motivated by the claim that many issues in macroeconomics, for instance the effects of government deficits, depend crucially on the horizon of the agents. In the model this (random) horizon was specified except for a parameter, which could be chosen arbitrarily (see parameter μ below). Recognising that Blanchard made his theoretical point thanks to a convenient specification is quite a different thing from admitting that the specification should serve for all other purposes.

3 A natural empirical question to ask is whether the global results exhibited in the book also stand for earlier periods than 1955–89. I was surprised that the book makes no reference to evidence concerning 1900–87 and supporting one of its propositions, namely the correlation between the real interest rate and unemployment. The finding that this correlation is the only one to clearly stand in fits of the US and French unemployment rates was made at OFCE, to which Phelps is associated (Reichlin and Guillemineau, 1989).

4 Incidentally, I was surprised to see that the econometric chapter 17 used series of a short-term interest rate (three-month treasury bills). Since the theory refers to capital market equilibrium and to the prices of such long-term assets as trained employees, customers or physical capital, I had expected to find a long-term rate in the empirical evidence.

5 This simple argument clearly assumes that (1), which was posed with the real wage rates and real non-labour income, also holds with nominal values of the same variables; this is the case for instance if only the ratios w^e/w and y^w/w of these variables matter. A test of the hypothesis would be welcome. Implicitly, the argument also assumes that all transfers, for instance unemployment benefits, remain unchanged in nominal values and that the same kind of homogeneity applies to their effect on effort e.

REFERENCES

Atkinson, A. and J. Stiglitz, 1980. *Lectures on Public Economics*, Maidenhead: McGraw-Hill

Blanchard, O., 1985. 'Debts, deficits and finite horizons', *Journal of Political Economy*, **93**, 223–47

Blinder, A. and R. Solow, 1973. 'Does fiscal policy matter?', *Journal of Public Economics*,

Danthine, J.P. and J. Donaldson, 1990. 'Efficiency wage and the business cycle puzzle', *European Economic Review*, **34**, 1275–1301

Drèze, J. and C. Bean (eds.), 1990. *Europe's Unemployment Problem*, Cambridge, MA: MIT Press

Fitoussi, J.P. and E. Phelps, 1988. *The Slump in Europe*, Oxford: Basil Blackwell

Hellwig, M. and M. Neumann, 1987. 'Economic policy in Germany: was there a turnround?', *Economic Policy*, **5**, 103–40

Keynes, J.M., 1936. *The General Theory of Employment, Interest, and Money*, London: Macmillan

Knoester, A., 1993. 'The inverted Havelmo effect and the effects of fiscal policy in the United States, the United Kingdom, Germany and the Netherlands', in A. Knoester (ed.), *Taxation in the United States and Europe: Theory and Practice*, London and New York: Macmillan and St Martin's Press

Layard, P.R.G., S.J. Nickell and R.A. Jackman, *Unemployment: Macroeconomic Performance and the Labour Market*, Oxford: Oxford University Press

Lindbeck, A., 1993. *Unemployment and Macroeconomics*, Cambridge, MA: MIT Press

Malinvaud, E., 1991. 'A medium-term employment equilibrium', in W. Barnett, B. Cornet, C. d'Aspremont, J. Gabszewicz and A. Mas-Colell (eds.), *Equilibrium Theory and Applications*, Cambridge: Cambridge University Press

OECD, 1994. *The OECD Jobs Study: Facts, Analysis, Strategies*, Paris: OECD

Phelps, E.S., 1994a. *Structural Slumps: The Modern Equilibrium Theory of Unemployment, Interest, and Assets*, Cambridge, MA: Harvard University Press

1994b. 'A program of low-wage employment credits', Russell Sage Foundation, *Working Paper*, **55** and Confindustria, *CSC Ricerche*, **93** (May)

Picard, P., 1993. *Wages and Unemployment*, Cambridge: Cambridge University Press

Reichlin, L. and C. Guillemineau, 1989. 'Chômage et croissance en France et aux Etats-Unis. Une analyse de longue période', Observations et diagnostics économiques, *Revue de l'OFCE*, **29**, pp. 161–84

Seater, J., 1993. 'Ricardian equivalence', *Journal of Economic Literature*, **31**, 142–90

Tobin, J. and W. Buiter, 1976. 'Long-run effects of fiscal and monetary policy on aggregate demand', in J. Stein (ed.), *Monetarism*, Amsterdam: North-Holland

Discussion

EDMUND S. PHELPS

In chapter 5, Edmond Malinvaud has produced a sympathetic and thoughtful review of my (1994) book. Let me begin by restating the book's intention, since some false impressions on that score have appeared here and there. The aim is to understand the causal forces and mechanisms behind lasting shifts and long swings in national unemployment rates. The impetus for this study, of course, is the rise over the 1970s and 1980s of joblessness to new plateaux in one Western country after another.

The approach taken begins with a theoretical study of the path of the general unemployment rate; an empirical section and a policy discussion follow. The vehicles for this study are a selection of what are termed 'modern equilibrium' models. By that term I mean models reflecting some of the *imperfect information* present in real-world markets (thus *modern* theory, not neoclassical theory such as the real-business-cycle or RBC models use) and postulating that the belief of firms and households about wages and prices are correct (until the next unforeseeable shock) – hence *equilibrium* theory, unlike the monetary employment theory of Keynes and Friedman in which agents have to do a lot of guessing. Hence the theory part of the book endogenises the path of the natural unemployment rate – a path to which the equilibrium unemployment rate is always tending. Such an approach is attractive if we are willing to bet that real-life economies, after the confusion following any shock or sea-change, tend toward their new equilibrium path.

This modelling requires attention to the interrelations between wages, prices and the rentals and yields on assets. The 'value added' of the theorising in the book is mainly to have shown how the three basic markets of any economy – labour, product and asset markets – can be hooked up to provide a *general equilibrium* system for analysing the unemployment effects of certain shocks and policy shifts. This is done using the example of the Phelps–Salop incentive-wage model based on quitting or the parallel Calvo–Solow–Stiglitz efficiency wage model based on shirking combined with the customer market model of Phelps–Winter or else the familiar two-sector model of production. Of course it would have been impractical to give equal treatment or indeed any treatment to *all* modern models. But I feel that the results are adequate clues to the results that would have been obtained had other – or additional –

modern models been used. Thus my subtitle, '*The* modern theory of unemployment, interest and assets', (emphasis added) was meant to convey that the book is broadly about some basic conclusions derivable from the interaction of any one of the entire family of modern labour market models of unemployment – including the Zeuthen–Layard–Nickell union model, the Diamond–Mortensen–Pissarides bargaining model and the Lindbeck–Snower–Oswald insider model – with a wide range of models (some modern, some not) of the product market and of the capital and credit markets.

Two interrelations between markets play an important role in these general systems: first, the propensity to quit and to shirk, and thus the required incentive (or efficiency) wage – the wage required to motivate employee performance to the cost-effective degree – are made a function of the worker's degree of financial dependence on holding a job: this depends (inversely) on the amount of non-wage income they have, some of it contingent on circumstances, relative to the wage paid in the jobs they can hold. This consists of the income from their private wealth (home, car, securities, etc.) and what they can draw from their so-called social capital – their relationships to friends and kin and, above all, their entitlements to welfare benefits. Second, in all the general equilibrium examples constructed, the demand for labour is a function of the interest rate – either through Austrian channels or because production involves marketing or labour hiring, which are investments by firms in their future.[1]

It should be obvious, then, that the book does not pretend to present *the new prevailing paradigm* of macroeconomics – only (if fortune smiles) *a* new paradigm case. It would be absurd to think that so special a theory could put Keynesians and Monetarists out of business. They will remain supreme in their domain, as far as I can see. (Besides, there are others tilling the same field, and someone else's formulation may become the standard.) Still, I have come to have far more confidence in the adequacy of my approach for understanding medium-term and long-term developments than I could possibly have had when I started work on it. That is because as one's understanding of the determination of the natural rate improves, the natural rate framework becomes more powerful and thus more nearly self-sufficient as a theory of shifts and long swings in unemployment.

The theoretical studies have yielded some rather appealing implications. A one-time technological advance of the Harrod-neutral type in a country is neutral for its natural unemployment rate – from day 1 in a very special case, but rather generally in the long run. An across-the-board cut in the value added tax occasioned by a reduction in foreign aid sent overseas, say, is neutral from day 1. Most other shocks are not neutral. (Certainly an oil shock is not neutral insofar as nationals own the oil, and is unlikely to be neutral even if they own it all.)

Looking back on the book, I see two main findings. One concerns the unemployment effect of what is called *capital shortage*. The decade-old Fitoussi–Phelps proposition (heretofore based in part on monetary models) carries over to the non-monetary models of the new book: one country's fiscal stimulus – I mean a boost to the demand for domestic output in excess of any boost to domestic supply also resulting – contracts employment in the rest of the world by driving up the world real interest rate and (in one model) by sheltering overseas producers from import competition with the umbrella of real exchange rate depreciation. The stimulus may be expansionary for the home country, but when all countries apply such a stimulus the result is a world-wide contraction. The empirical findings bear out the applicability of this theoretical result. For me, at least, this is an ominous theme. The resumption of steep increases in the world public debt in the past few years together with the new efficiency and dynamism of the 'emerging market economies' to the east and to the south are bracing us for a return of world-wide real interest rates to very high levels over the second half of the 1990s, and this prospect bodes ill for the natural unemployment rates in the mature Western economies.

The other main finding concerns the unemployment effects of the *welfare state* – both through the level and mix of taxes traditionally adopted to finance it and through the inherent impact of the reduced dependency on employment it promotes. The tax channel is becoming understood. Payroll tax rates are devastating for job creation, not just for the wage rates received by workers. They are theoretically non-neutral because they hit wages without evenhandedly striking non-wage incomes (the income from private wealth and welfare entitlements), so the wage required by considerations of incentives for the purpose of minimising costs does not falling accommodatingly by the whole of the drop in the wage that firms can afford to pay (after tax). Empirically, this contractionary effect comes through the regression study loud and clear. Somewhat more controversially, perhaps, it is also found that the personal income tax is contractionary for natural employment. The theoretical rationalisation is that, in practice, that tax is somehow escaped by a great deal of non-wage income. The second channel is less well understood. Knowing that nearly steady employment is not required for medical care, raising children, eating, shelter and so forth not only erodes labour force participation; it undermines the work ethic, thus worsening the employee performance of those who do participate in the labour market, with the result that labour costs are increased and employment contracted.

To sum up: the theory says the natural unemployment rate path is sensitive to the *structure* of real demands and supplies, external real prices, and incentives affecting costs. For that reason, and because some name for it is needed, I have dubbed it the 'structuralist' theory of unemployment.

Now to some of Edmond Malinvaud's reservations and disagreements. My discussion will follow his sequence: theory, evidence, policy.

With respect to the theory, he is most uneasy about the use in all my general equilibrium structures of market-clearing prices in the product market – in contrast to the non-clearing portrayed in the labour market. (Even the customer market treatment I use, the Phelps–Winter model, portrays firms as operating on their demand curves.) Malinvaud suspects that this feature is responsible for those implications of the models that could be regarded as anti-Keynesian. He seems to want a model in which a world-wide increase of public expenditure or public debt would somehow generate a world-wide expansion of output and employment. This despite his willingness to stipulate the neutrality of money, at least in the medium term we are talking about.

Suppose we enrich the theory by treating as stochastic the demand of customers or perhaps the growth of customers at the individual firm. In the enriched structure, there would often be spare, or unused, capacity at most or all firms – idle employees standing by in case there is a call for them and, perhaps, idle machines ready to be switched on. A firm does not want to be unable to serve a customer, though it would cost too much to ensure capacity in worst-case scenarios.

Malinvaud's perplexity, I believe, is over what happens in a (closed) economy having that added product market feature if, starting from a stationary equilibrium at the natural rate, everyone wants suddenly to consume less in the present in order to consume more in the future – that is, there is a general increase in the rate of time preference. Is there a structural expansion, thanks to a reduction of interest rates, as my book concludes from models without spare capacity; or is there a sort of Keynesian contraction, driven by deficient demand? In considering the matter, let us exclude fixed capital as well as inventories from the scene. Let us also assume that the economy was initially in a stationary-state equilibrium – the unemployment rate thus at the old natural rate.

Two questions then arise. If there exists a new stationary-state equilibrium corresponding to the new and lower rate of time preference, what does it look like? The answer, I believe, is that the rate of interest will be reduced accordingly and firms in response will find additional standby capacity (a precautionary reserve of employees) more attractive than before, since its benefits will be less heavily discounted than before. So on this account the demand for labour is increased. In addition, the customer market mechanism already incorporated in the book's analysis – firms will be driven to accept lower mark-ups at the lower interest rate – also implies an increase in labour demand. For these reasons it is pretty clear that the new equilibrium has a higher employment level and a higher wage than the old equilibrium. So it seems to me that the introduction of spare capacity, arising from the stochastic behaviour of customer demands or customer flows, only strengthens the 'anti-Keynesian' conclusion that increased thriftiness is good for jobs.

The other question, which I cannot do justice to here, is the matter of the equilibration process: how does the economy get from the old equilibrium to the new equilibrium just described? Or is it the case that, as an old joke concludes, 'you can't get there from here'? Even without bringing money into the picture we can see that equilibration is not instantaneous. When all persons suddenly start paying out per unit of time from their stock of shares with their left hand, so to speak, they will find that there is an equal decrease in the inflow of shares into their right hand, which they receive as owners of the firms. (There is the analogy to the game of Old Maid that so fascinated Keynes.) Thus there is a *fall* in what is bought and produced – though not a fall of employment – as the average idleness of employees is increased, while there is no sign of any excess in the capital market: no rise of share prices in terms of product, no fall of interest rates.[2] But the matter cannot be left there. With enough space and time, I would try to develop an argument along the following lines. Once a manager detects that customers are buying at a generally reduced rate, it is optimal under conditions for the individual firm to cut its real price (which is its relative price), though not by so much as to have the prospect of restoring sales to the original level. (This cut would not be optimal if the firm believed that the reduction in consumer purchases was general and permanent and that the cost curve would not be lowered by the reduced consumption and thus production at other firms – two rather contradictory expectations, generally speaking; then the firm would plan to keep its old relative price and 'think small'.) This implies that firms begin offering more product per unit of proceeds measured in shares; that is, the real share price rises. The eventual discovery that all firms are doing the same will lead to further declines of the product price in terms of shares, thus rises in the real price of shares, and hence declines in real interest rates. How far does this process go? I believe it will go until the real share price is sufficiently high, and thus the corresponding interest rate sufficiently reduced, that consumer purchases will regain their old level. But in that recovered state, the reduced real interest rate should make firms want to supply more than they were doing in the old equilibrium, because the present discounted value of finding an additional customer is thereby increased, and to demand even more labour since the present discounted value of the benefits of a small addition to the stock of spare employees is also thereby increased.

I would make four remarks about this equilibration. One is that, conceivably, equilibration in a monetary economy is less thorny and no harder to analyse. Another is that a sanguine rational expectations believer would predict a boom in the share market as soon as signs of the general weakness in the goods market came to be reported in the press. (In fact, the stock market seems usually to drop sharply on reports of increased orders.) The third comment is that the problematic character of the equilibration process, as I have just envisioned it (however dimly), appears to emerge in, say, the customer market economy even without the further complication of spare capacity. As soon as the economy contains mostly *price-setting firms*, a drop of consumer demand appears to put the economy in a kind of Keynesian jeopardy – and this *without* the presence of money, usually considered the *sine qua non* of Keynes' theory. But – the last remark – the economy's equilibration does not seem to be theoretically impossible. And it had better not since most economies somehow mange to do it, and I doubt that those which do it owe their success to governmental guidance. If so, the question of equilibration is ultimately empirical: do the advanced market economies manage somehow to equilibrate fairly reliably or not? I have been impressed by the evidence from the econometric section of my book suggesting that the actual unemployment rate path seldom diverges from the estimated natural rate path, though it sometimes crashes through the path and must circle back.

Some of Malinvaud's other worries arise from the empirical results. Let me respond to several of his points.

1 I am not troubled by the finding that military expenditure as a whole is not more expansionary than non-military public expenditure, since the expectation to the contrary rested on the subsidiary hypothesis that the former expenditures are more labour-intensive on the whole than the latter expenditures. The possibility is open that the fault lies with this subsidiary hypothesis rather than the basic premise that the more labour-intensive expenditures reduce the natural rate by pulling up wages relative to many (if not all) non-wage incomes.

2 An increase in the price of oil may push down the equilibrium wage curve. But there is every reason to think that the demand curve will be

pushed down too. So, if the oil price is contractionary for the natural level of employment, as the econometric estimate has it, I do not see that this is a challenge.

3 The effect of the world capital stock on the *world* employment level is a bit ambiguous in theory, since increased capital may mean (as tends to be the case in a two-sector model) increased non-wage income relative to wage rates, which is contractionary for employment, and that effect would outweigh the expansionary effect via the world real interest rate. But the effect on employment in any one country of an increase in the world capital stock, if most of that increment is owned by persons or governments abroad, is clearly expansionary.

4 As I see it, the finding of a positive, statistically significant and non-negligible effect of the world real interest rate on a country's natural rate is a bit more noteworthy than one would think from Malinvaud's reading. The majority of econometric studies have missed it, although the trend is toward greater attention to this factor.

5 Likewise, it is surprising that Malinvaud does not take note of the arresting findings that a country's value added tax is essentially neutral for its natural rate while a payroll tax and the personal income tax operate to increase the natural rate.

I must also register my disagreement with Malinvaud's position that we dare not act on these findings (even taken with those findings of others that are supportive, I suppose) but must instead engage in a major and perhaps lengthy research programme aimed at testing the thrust of the theory. Needless to say, such a research programme will be most welcome to me. And I do not feel so inspired by the three regressions reported in the book to want to lead a crusade to remake the world according to them. Nevertheless, to quote Keynes on this matter as I find myself doing so often, 'finally it is necessary to act'. There are social and economic problems that governments will and do feel impelled to address and to do something about. The question then becomes whether we want to act on the basis of older theories found increasingly inadequate by the younger generations (and myself), simply because we feel it would be risky to jump to another, necessarily less tested theory, or instead to take the chance of acting on a new set of insights, recognising that some or even all of them are all wrong. I want governments to act on the basis of what I think is the most plausible model, based on *a priori* theorising and fortified by such supporting empirical results as have been found to date.

Lastly there is the subject of the economic policies that my unemployment theory suggests. The theory in my book points – not always alone – to three remedies or therapies for high unemployment.

- According to my analysis, modifications of the tax structure in the direction of lessening the burden on labour relative to non-wage incomes – a move away from payroll taxation toward (increased) value added taxation – would be all to the good. In simplistic terms, we would be moving from a tax that is markedly non-neutral for the natural rate to one that is neutral. It is clear that such a move would entail a political cost, as it would raise the cost of living faced by retired persons (unless money wage rates could be reduced through some national bargain). Such a reform of the tax mix is not explicitly mentioned in the policy chapter, probably because that chapter is largely concerned with 'anti-cyclical' policies – with actions to be turned on or off – aimed at dampening the secular rise or fall of the natural rate, while tax reform is a step that, once taken, does not need to be reversed or repeated.
- The policy chapter advocates the use of a wage subsidy, one concentrated at the low end of the wage scale, as the prime weapon to combat increases of the natural rate to unacceptable levels. In the US context, where I first envisaged their use, their main function would be to pull up the wage rates received by low-wage workers, though in fact the stimulus to the demand for labour would end up generating some increase of low-wage employment and, to that extent, a lesser increase of low-end wage rates than would otherwise occur. On the European continent, the effect would fall more heavily on employment and less on wages insofar as wage restrictions enforced by minimum-wage laws or by union legislation has artificially pushed up low-end wage rates relative to wages farther up the scale. When one considers the gulf between bottom wage rates and median wage rates in the US and the wide disparity in many European countries between the unemployment rates of disadvantaged workers – a disproportionate number of them immigrants, but by no means all of them, – and the general unemployment rate, it is surprising to see the reflex reaction of so many economists: that there would be a heavy cost from the resulting distortion in the incentives of low-wage workers to see additional training. It would be good to have Malinvaud's views on wagc, or employment, subsidies.
- Finally, the book concludes with a vision of a world made better for having restored work to its former place of importance not only through wage subsidies but also by pruning the welfare system of the excessive undergrowth of entitlement programmes that, in making the prospect of unemployment more viable, make employees – that remnant of working-age people still driven to participate in the labour force, if only as an unemployed worker – less dependent upon long

employment for their economic support. Once wage subsidies have lifted wage rate and lowered joblessness among the disadvantaged, there will be less reason to treat 'welfare' as a matter of life or death, as jobs will be obtainable with much less wait or effort and their pay rates will permit the jobholders to earn a normal living, even to save a bit and pay back loans, like other people. Welfare will go only to those who demonstrably cannot work, not for those who are not working. The increased self-sufficiency and, as careers are made, the increased self-realisation of the disadvantaged will turn their lives around. When the disadvantaged are in better shape, society can then pursue the opportunities presented by events in the global economy in recent years without being hamstrung by the need to adopt costly third-best policies to shelter disadvantaged workers from every wage cut or lost job. Operation of a genuine market economy becomes morally acceptable and perhaps even politically feasible. I am not sure, however, to what extent my European friends, Edmond Malinvaud among them, are ready for this new day!

NOTES

1 Therefore it seems an exaggeration when Malinvaud, complaining that there are not more modern elements in the framework, characterises the book at one point as just the standard neoclassical model 'plus efficiency wages'. The models featuring a customer market view of the product market receive major attention. Even the two-sector model of production is richer than the standard models of RBC theory.

2 In a continuous time model in which one can speak only of the probability of the arrival of a customer, the elapse of some small interval of time without an actual arrival cannot really said to be unexpected at all. But a drop of that probability unbeknownst to the supplier normally amounts to a reduction of the actual probability relative to the unexpected probability, which is very much like the reduction of actual demand relative to expected demand discussed in discrete-time terms in the text above.

REFERENCES

Fitoussi, J.P. and E.S. Phelps, 1988. *The Slump in Europe*, Oxford: Basil Blackwell

Layard, P.R.G., S.J. Nickell and R.A. Jackman, 1991. *Unemployment: Macro-economic Performance and the Labour Market*, Oxford University Press

Phelps, E.S., 1994. *Structural Slumps: The Modern Equilibrium Theory of Unemployment, Interest, and Assets*, Cambridge, MA: Harvard University Press

Discussion

KLAUS F. ZIMMERMANN

The debate between Edmond Malinvaud and Edmund Phelps provides a significant contribution to the arguments on the unemployment problem, one of the most pressing social issues of our time. Naturally, it is demanding to discuss the review in chapter 5 of Phelps' *Structural Slumps: The Modern Equilibrium Theory of Unemployment, Interests and Assets* that pushes for a new line of (macroeconomic) thinking. Phelps' work has already been widely appraised by others (for instance, see Woodford, 1994). Hence, I can only be selective, and will discuss Phelps' book directly where appropriate. First, I deal with the general approach to the unemployment problem. Second, I explain where I follow Malinvaud's evaluation and where I depart from it. And finally, I examine more closely the central hypotheses behind the new theory of structural slumps.

Phelps' book and Malinvaud's chapter 5 aim at the understanding of unemployment in a rather general context. This is quite a demanding job – also on a macro level. As we have just learned from Charles Bean's survey on European unemployment (1994, p. 615), there seems to be no lack of hypotheses, but an insufficient ability of the data; we have to confess:

> I doubt that more can be learned from analysis of the same data using existing techniques and methodology. There is simply not enough information in the data to give clear signals on the relative merits of the competing hypotheses. The only hope is, I think, to try to develop specifications that are more tightly constrained by theoretical considera- tion than is presently the case.

In Bean's view, there is currently no convincing macroeconomic story at hand (and no single cause) that explains the unemployment problem.

As Bean (1994) wants us to believe, the EU countries (as of 1994) are significantly different from the USA, the Northern (Nordic) European countries (and also Austria and Switzerland), and Japan in that they have experienced a strong increase in the unemployment rate since the early 1970s. This reflects popular beliefs. In Bean's analysis, this is due to a decline in the outflow rate from unemployment in these EU countries. Bean's view was questioned in CEPR (1995). This study provides a more mixed statistical picture of inflow and outflow rates in the USA and Europe, and the differences no longer look so convincing. Furthermore, as an update of the numbers (see figure D5.1) shows, the 'Nordic Model' has disappeared in the meanwhile – unemployment rates there are just as high as in other parts of the OECD Europe.

Anyway, the US model was never a unique model of Northern America: Canadian unemployment rates were also increasing together with the European ones in recent decades (see figure D5.1). And the USA has experienced a significantly widening of inequality and a rise in the working poor (see Blank, 1995). Furthermore, even Japan is not innocent: there is substantial labour-hoarding in large Japanese firms and considerable measurement problems of unemployment. Therefore, 'true' unemployment seems to be much higher, and there is a prospect of rising unemployment rates in the near future.

This all suggests a different explanation: there seem to be fundamental shifts in labour demand within the Western countries that caused a decline in unskilled workers. Consequently, countries with regulated labour markets reacted with rising unemployment while more flexible labour markets experienced rising wage inequality. So Phelps and Malinvaud are right, there is a general problem that calls for a common explanation, but not necessarily a common cause. While Malinvaud points at demand, Phelps suggests a too-high world real interest rate. (Among other potential causes discussed in the recent literature are trade from LDCs and technological change, but these issues find no concern in Malinvaud's discussion nor Phelps' book.)

Phelps makes an attempt to provide a coherent model from various recent contributions to the literature, and Malinvaud presents a clear introduction of the basic issues that helps where Phelps' book is difficult to follow. My concern is that the notion of a medium-term model still remains unsatisfactory. There seems to be not much agreement about the short run and the long run. But, if the short run is too short, and in the long run, 'we are all dead', it is clear why '[b]uilding a valid medium-term theory has become urgent'. Perhaps it is inherent in the notion of a medium term that the time-horizon is unclear. Is it five–10 years, as Malinvaud seems to suggest? But then it is puzzling that he argues that goods markets do not necessarily clear (which I like) in the medium-run (which seems less probable to me in periods of five–10 years) and that Phelps' book uses yearly data and short-run interest rates to test the theory. It is also open how such a medium-term model evolves from a short-run model to the long-run neoclassical framework.

I share Malinvaud's view that the assumptions of Phelps' book of (i) perfect foresight, (ii) clearing of capital markets and (iii) a more labour-intensive capital goods-producing sector (in contrast to the consumption goods-producing sector) are somewhat problematic on empirical

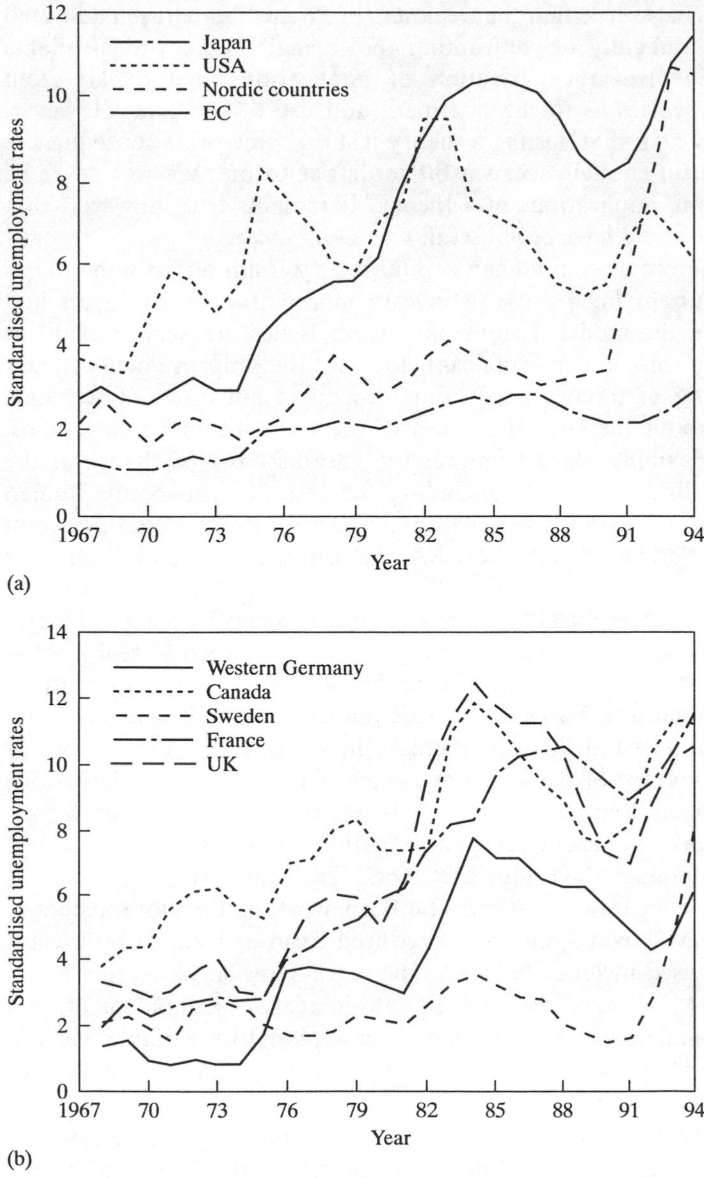

Figure D5.1 Standardised unemployment rates, 1967–94
Source: OECD *Unemployment Outlook*

grounds. It is also true that the weakness of Phelps' book (even admitted there) is its difficulty in confronting the formal theory with available data: this involves the derivation of implications that depart from competing theories as to the treatment and use of the data. However, Malinvaud's cavil that 'testing a theory just on some of its consequences is not powerful enough' seems a bit too strict to me. We will never be able to test *all* implications of a theory. It remains true, however, that more testing would have been useful.

With all the progress in human capital theory, I am not as unhappy as Malinvaud about Phelps' use of investments in trained employees and customers in the model. I think that these issues are very relevant in practice and provide a significant tool in the improvement of our understanding of today's production process. I am also not so much concerned about the lack of the use of the term 'flexibility' in Phelps' book. The flexibility debate ignores the various costs of change at the level of the firm or worker, including the loss of firm-specific human capital that this flexibility may cause. Also, job turnover does not seem to be too different between the USA and Europe and stable over time (OECD, 1994).

Let me finally concentrate on a few empirical issues. Among the major hypotheses from Phelps' theory are: (i) A rise in the world real interest rate has caused the increase in unemployment in the various countries. The world interest rate affects domestic interest rates and asset rates and hence labour demand. (ii) The increase in world-wide public debt has caused the increase of the world real interest rate. Hence, a world-wide fiscal stimulus is contractionary. This is tested in a two-equation framework whereas the unemployment equation contains many country-specific components but also the world real interest rate, which is modelled in a separate equation. The framework is, therefore, recursive as noted by Malinvaud, and not a reduced form as claimed by Phelps. The sample used includes 1955–89. The regressions show, as the theory predicts, that the world real interest rate increases unemployment, and world government spending (among other explanatory variables such as the world capital stock, and the world stock of public debt) increases the world real interest rate.

A few things that I find puzzling with this evidence are now discussed.

Global inspection of Phelps' data provide only partial support for the interest rate effect on unemployment. The world real interest rate as shown in Phelps (p. 320) marks three distinctive periods: a medium-level rate in the 1950s and 1960s, a low level in the 1970s and a high level in the 1980s. The *decline* in the 1970s was *not* associated with a decline in unemployment. Instead, unemployment was rising in the 1980s, when the world real interest rate was also rising. Hence, there is *one* real observation that supports the conjecture – perhaps not too much. It is also true that US unemployment has remained relatively constant. Hence, real world real interest cannot be the dominant cause of unemployment.

World output and the world real stock of money plays no role in the Phelps' regressions. When monetary policy was as tight as in recent decades, it should be tested that the presumption that money has no impact on real interest rates really is correct. It could well be that monetary policy is responsible for the higher interest rates in the 1980s. Also, it seems that demand should have a direct potential impact on unemployment. Hence, the model seems misspecified from an empirical point of view.

As Malinvaud (n. 4) has also noted, it is surprising that Phelps is using short-term interest rates where long-run rates seem to be appropriate. Does this matter much? Figure D5.2 exhibits long-run (solid line) and short-run (dashed line) interest rates for five countries (USA, Japan, Western Germany, Sweden and France) for the period 1970–94. The findings are mixed. Perhaps the difference matters most in the case of Germany. In all countries, however, there is a significant increase in real interest rates from the 1970s to the 1980s. Surprisingly, it is strongest in the US case where unemployment was stable.

It is instructive to study the basic hypotheses in some simple graphs for these key countries (USA, Japan, Western Germany, Sweden and France). Figure D5.3 examines the relationships between the total outlays of government in percent of gross national product (GNP) and the long-run interest rates in the respective countries. The evolution is indicated by connecting the observations over time. Again, the weakest correspondence is found for the USA. While the figures for Japan and Western Germany are also not very supportive for the hypothesis that government spending causes increases in real interest rates. France and Sweden, however, provide better support for this conjecture. Figure D5.4 relates unemployment and real interest rates. Again, France and Sweden provide the most supportive picture for the hypothesis that real interest rates are causing unemployment. The other countries are much less convincing.

Finally, table D5.1 contains the results from a simple cointegration exercise. First, the stationarity of the individual series unemployment, long-run real interest rate and government outlay (as percentage of GNP) were examined, and the results are given in column (1). Then cointegrating regressions containing a time trend were employed, and the findings provided in columns (2)–(4). Here only the effect parameters,

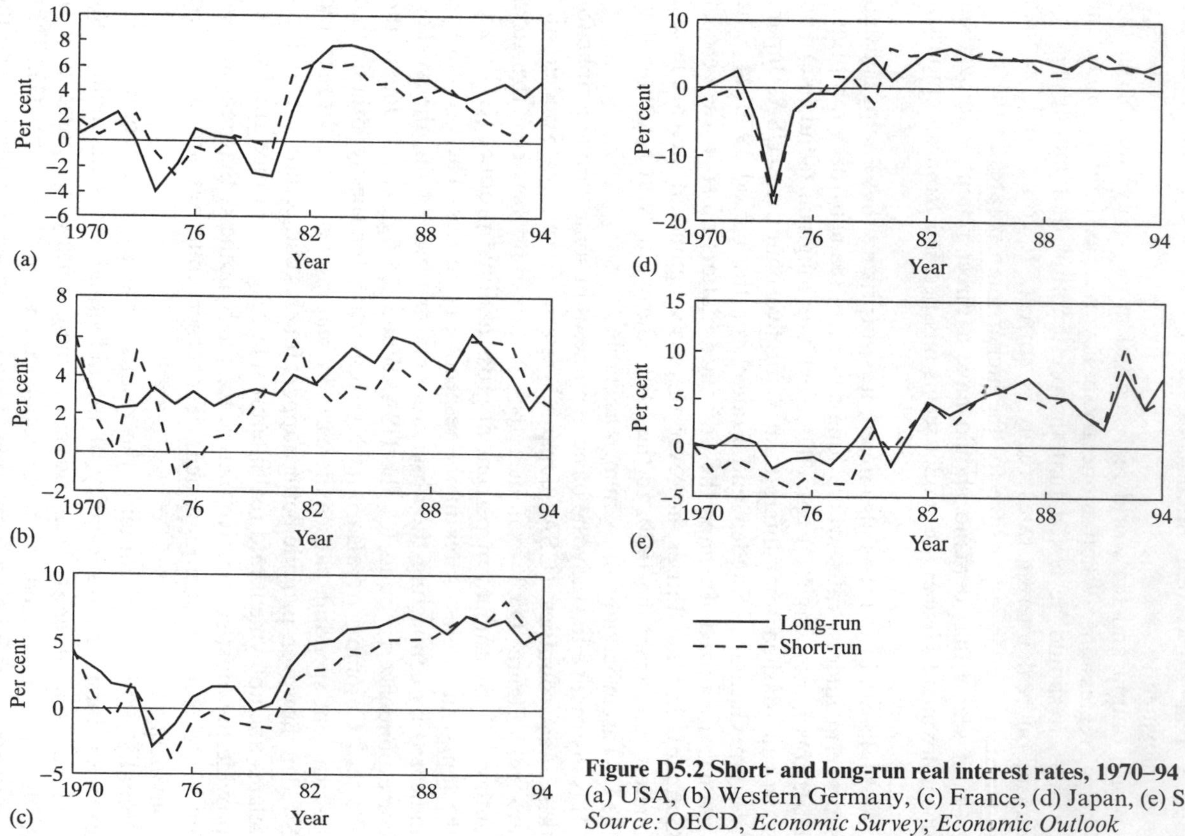

Figure D5.2 Short- and long-run real interest rates, 1970–94
(a) USA, (b) Western Germany, (c) France, (d) Japan, (e) Sweden
Source: OECD, *Economic Survey*; *Economic Outlook*

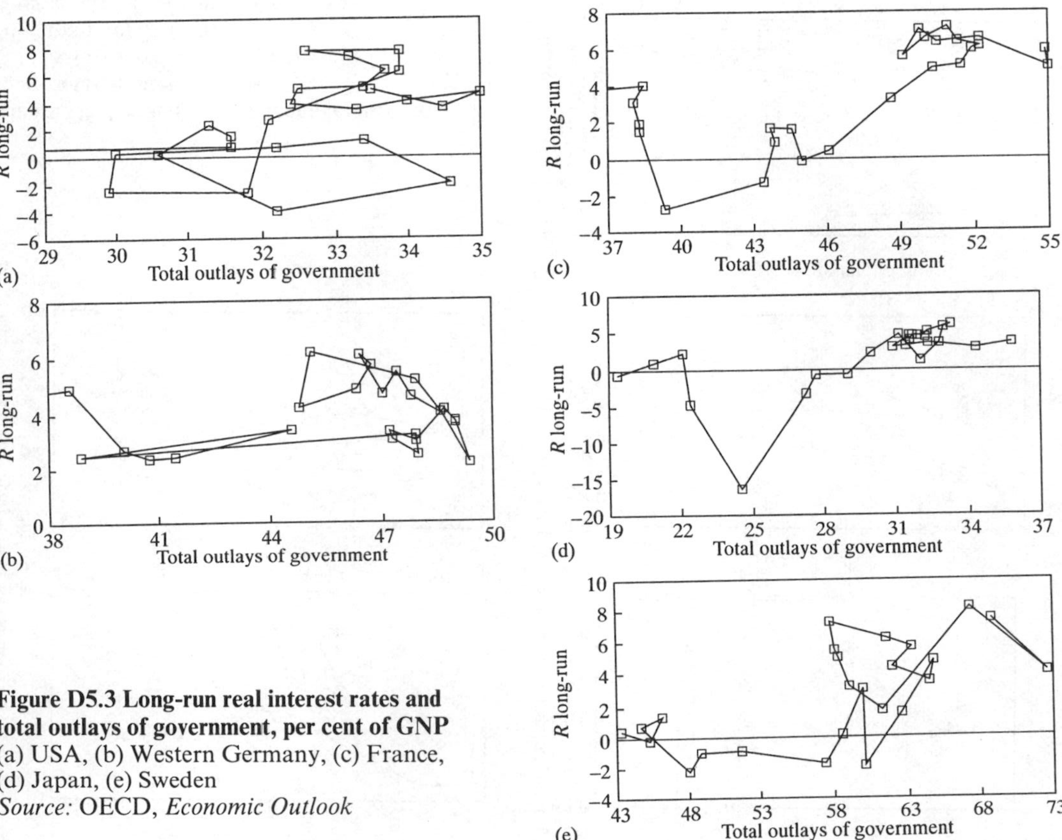

Figure D5.3 Long-run real interest rates and total outlays of government, per cent of GNP
(a) USA, (b) Western Germany, (c) France, (d) Japan, (e) Sweden
Source: OECD, *Economic Outlook*

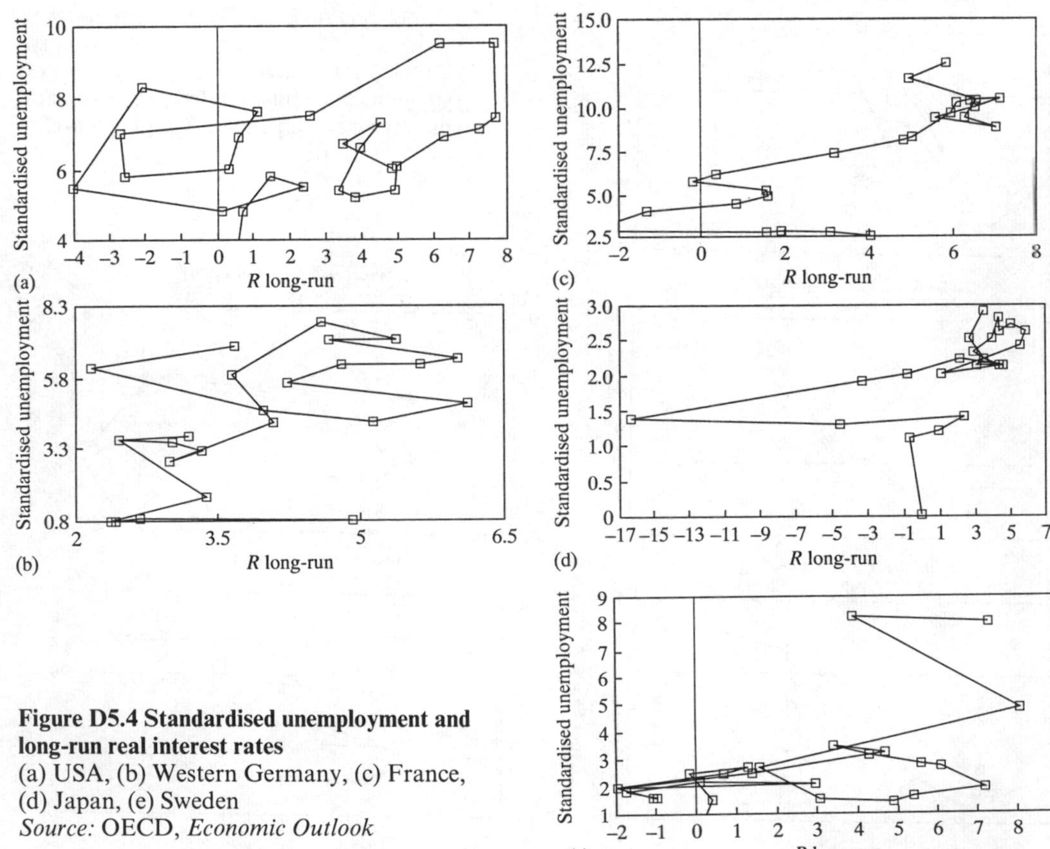

Figure D5.4 Standardised unemployment and long-run real interest rates
(a) USA, (b) Western Germany, (c) France, (d) Japan, (e) Sweden
Source: OECD, *Economic Outlook*

Table D5.1 *Integration and cointegration*

	ADF[a] U R G	*Co-integrating regressions*[b] U←R	R←G	U←R*	R←G*	U←G*
	(1)	(2)	(3)	(4)	(5)	(6)
USA	−2.8	0.19	0.52	–	–	–
	−3.1	(2.1)	(1.0)			
	−4.5	[−4.0]	[−2.9]			
Japan	−2.4	0.04	0.86	0.06	−0.66	0.01
	−3.0	(2.6)	(2.3)	(2.8)	(−0.9)	(0.1)
	−1.9	[−3.1]	[−4.8]	[−3.8]	[−2.9]	[−2.4]
Western	−2.7	0.49	−0.04	0.35	−0.01	0.30
Germany	−1.8	(1.7)	(−0.4)	(4.1)	(−0.0)	(1.2)
	−2.1	[−2.9]	[−1.1]	[−4.9]	[−1.2]	[−2.6]
Sweden	−3.7	0.04	0.00	−0.01	−0.07	0.17
	−2.5	(0.3)	(0.0)	(−0.1)	(−0.2)	(0.6)
	−2.0	[−2.7]	[−2.7]	[−3.7]	[−2.7]	[−3.2]
France	−2.5	0.27	0.20	0.23	0.03	0.07
	−2.9	(2.4)	(1.2)	(4.0)	(0.1)	(0.4)
	−2.2	[−2.9]	[−3.6]	[−3.3]	[−2.9]	[−2.4]

Notes:

[a] U: unemployment rate; R: long-run interest rate; G: government outlay in per cent of GNP; R*: R of USA; G*: G of USA. ADF are the augmented Dickey–Fuller test statistics from a regression including a constant and time trend.

[b] Number of observations: 25. Numbers are coefficients, *t*-values (in parentheses) and ADF [residuals, in brackets]. The co-integrating regression contains a constant and trend. The ADF refers to the residuals of this equation.

their *t*-values as the stationarity tests for the residuals are given. From columns (2) and (3), there is some support that real interest rates cause unemployment (USA, Japan, France), but only evidence from Japan suggests that interest rates are affected by government outlays. If one accepts the US interest rate and government outlays as proxies for the world variables, columns (4)–(6) apply. Here, the unemployment effect of interest rates is stronger, while the impact of government outlays completely disappears either indirectly (on interest rates) or directly (on unemployment).

Hence, some evidence is found that unemployment–employment and interest rates are related. However, this is no direct test on the structuralist view. Similar implication may arise from other theories. Also, the evidence is not overly convincing. Therefore, more empirical work has to be done before the theoretical framework will find wider acceptance.

REFERENCES

Bean, C.R., 1994. 'European unemployment, a survey', *Journal of Economic Literature*, **32**, 573–619

Blank, R.M., 1995. 'Changes in inequality and unemployment over the 1980s: comparative cross-national responses', *Journal of Population Economics*, **8**, 1–21

CEPR, 1995. *Unemployment: Choices for Europe, Monitoring European Integration*, 5, London: CEPR

OECD, 1994. *The OECD Jobs Study: Evidence and Explanations, Part I and II*, Paris: OECD

Phelps, E.S., 1994. *Structural Slumps: The Modern Equilibrium Theory of Unemployment, Interest, and Assets*, Cambridge, MA: Harvard University Press

Woodford, M., 1994. 'Structural slumps', *Journal of Economic Literature*, **32**, 1784–1815

Part Three

Subsidising employment and training

6 The simple economics of benefit transfers

DENNIS J. SNOWER

1 Introduction

> Having plowed the field, the farmer and his son maneuver the tractor across the adjoining road. Suddenly they see a Jaguar speeding towards them at 100 mph. A second before expected impact, the Jaguar veers into the field, skids through a cloud of dust, regains the road and flies off into the distance. The farmer turns to the boy and says, 'Son, we left that field just in time.'

The spirit of this tale goes a long way towards explaining the evolution of unemployment policy in many EC countries and elsewhere. The policy is to pay people when they are unemployed and tax them when they find jobs. So, far from inducing workers to seek employment and firms to take them on, the policy in fact discourages them from doing so and thereby contributes to the unemployment problem. Having done so, the unemployment benefit system is then seen as particularly essential in providing a safety net for those out of work. This is not the only occasion on which economic policy creates the problem it is meant to solve, but it is particularly unconscionable in times of recession, when unemployment becomes a flagrant waste of human resources.

If the money governments spend on unemployment benefit could be redirected so as to provide an incentive, rather than a disincentive, for employment, many countries struggling with the twin burdens of high unemployment and costly unemployment benefits might reap a substantial benefit. This is the purpose of my 'Benefit Transfer Programme' (BTP), on which the UK Workstart schemes are based. A related scheme, called Job Compact, has been introduced on a national level in Australia.[1] The basic idea is to give the unemployed – particularly those who have been unemployed for a long time – a new option: to use a portion of their unemployment benefit *as vouchers for employers that hire them*. In this way, unemployment benefit systems, which currently impose an implicit tax on work, could become a source of employment subsidies for the people who need these subsidies most, namely, the long-term unemployed.

1.1 General description and motivation

In market economies there generally 'ain't no such thing as a free lunch'. But this is an exception, since unemployment benefit systems create inefficiencies that the BTP is designed to mitigate. When an inefficiency is reduced, fewer resources are wasted and society gets a free lunch. The unemployment benefit systems are notoriously inefficient since they keep the unemployed from competing effectively for jobs. They do so by (i) raising the return from remaining unemployed, (ii) reducing the return from finding a job (via the taxes necessary to finance the unemployment benefits) and (iii) putting upward pressure on wages (since they improve workers' fallback positions when their wage claims are rejected). These inefficiencies are magnified by other market failures, such as those that arise when insiders (incumbent employees whose positions are protected by labour turnover costs) exercise their market power in the wage negotiation process[2] or when firms use their wage offers to motivate their workforce and attract high-quality newcomers.[3] Furthermore, these inefficiencies are perpetuated through a wide variety of inertial forces in the labour market, such as labour turnover costs that keep employment from adjusting readily or the tendency for people to reduce their job-search effort as their unemployment spell lengthens. All these inefficiencies tend to pull in the same direction, in the sense that they keep wages undesirably high and employment undesirably low. The BTP is aimed at undoing some of these harmful effects.

Beyond that, it is common knowledge that unemployment benefit systems are not only inefficient, but also inequitable, in that they magnify existing inequities in people's job opportunities. The longer people are unemployed, the more their skills erode, the more discouraged they become in searching for jobs, and the more wary employers become of hiring them. For these various reasons, the long-term unemployed are disadvantaged in the labour market. The equitable policy response to this problem is to make it more profitable for firms to take on the long-term unemployed and for these people to find jobs, rather than merely to provide limited support when people are unemployed.

The BTP has five salient features, that distinguish it from the standard wage subsidy programmes attempted heretofore:

(1) It is voluntary; only those unemployed people and potential employers who wish to take advantage of it need do so. The unemployed retain the option of remaining on unemployment benefit.
(2) The size of each person's employment voucher is linked to the size of her existing unemployment benefits, so that the amount the government spends on employment vouchers is no greater than what it would have spent on unemployment benefits. ('Unemployment benefits' are to be interpreted widely to include forgone taxes and the full spectrum of welfare state benefits falling on the unemployed.)
(3) The longer a person is unemployed (up to a limit), the larger is the stream of employment vouchers to which she is entitled.
(4) Once a person has found a job through the BTP, the size of the voucher gradually falls the longer the person remains employed.
(5) Larger vouchers are given to employers who can prove that they are devoting these funds to training their new recruits.

1.2 An illustrative example of BTP design

There are many ways in which the BTP could be implemented in practice. Here is a specific example. Every person who has been unemployed for over six months would be mailed an employment voucher. This is meant to signal that this individual's employment prospects have improved and thereby to reduce the discouragement – and the associated decline in effort to search for new jobs – that people frequently experience after having sought jobs unsuccessfully for half a year. If the person does not find a job within the period over which the voucher is valid (one month), the voucher expires and the person continues to collect his unemployment benefits. But if he finds a job, he turns the voucher over to his new employer, who can then claim a subsidy from the government.[4] The voucher specifies the size of the subsidy per weekly hours of work; so if the job is part-time, rather than full-time, the subsidy to the employer is scaled down pro rata.

Employers can use the voucher in two ways, as a recruitment voucher or as a training voucher. To cash the voucher as a recruitment voucher, the employer need only show that a worker entitled to a voucher has been hired (possibly subject to some anti-displacement conditions, specified below). To cash the voucher as a training voucher, the employer is also required to prove that the proceeds of the voucher have been spent exclusively on training the new recruit. In order to avoid the danger that firms may divert some of their training budgets to other uses, the subsidised training is to be provided by independent private-sector agencies. To avoid the danger that firms may attempt to retain their new recruits by requiring the training to be excessively firm-specific, the subsidised training must lead to nationally certified qualifications. For any given employee, the training voucher is larger than the recruitment voucher.

On the basis of the voucher, the employer and employee are free to come to any wage agreement they choose. The only restriction is that the recruitment voucher must be less than the wage and the training voucher must be less than the wage *plus* training expenditures.[5] By giving the employer and employee this latitude regarding remuneration, they gain the incentive to maximise the potential gains from productive exchange. Of course, unemployed people will accept employment only if the wage is sufficiently high to compensate them for the loss of their unemployment benefit *plus* the value of their leisure;[6] and the employers will accept only if it is profitable for them to do so. The voucher is meant to create such mutually advantageous deals: some of the unemployed people, who initially would not have been willing to work at the maximal wage that potential employers would have been willing to offer, may now find work, since employers will be able to make higher wage offers upon receipt of the vouchers.

The longer the unemployment spell a person has been through (up to a maximum attained after, say, 2.5 years of unemployment), the greater the size of the initial voucher the person receives upon becoming employed.[7] Once the person is employed, her vouchers decline steadily, month by month, as her job tenure extends. After two years of employment, the voucher is phased out entirely.

Within this general framework, the size of each person's recruitment employment voucher is to be kept approximately in line with the size of the unemployment benefits she would otherwise have received.[8] This means that in the month in which the person becomes employed, the size of the voucher should be roughly equal to the unemployment benefit multiplied by the probability of remaining unemployed in that month. The size of the voucher in the following month of employment should be roughly equal to the unemployment benefit times the probability of still being unemployed after two months, and so on.

In practice, of course, these probabilities are difficult to assess with any accuracy, and thus some population-wide averages would have to suffice. But since unemployment benefits generally vary with people's personal circumstances, this arrangement does imply that different people with equal employment durations will receive different employment vouchers. In this sense, the BTP simply reproduces the unequal treatment of individuals through the unemployment benefit system. Whatever equity considerations underlie this unequal treatment (such as granting higher unemployment benefits to married people with children than to single people), these features are retained through the BTP. In this way, the incentive to find jobs is spread more or less equally across the long-term unemployed, who are entitled to the largest unemployment benefits (and who consequently have the strongest incentive to remain unemployed) receiving the largest employment vouchers.[9]

Similarly, the size of each person's training voucher is to be approximately in line with the unemployment benefits *plus* training subsidies she would otherwise have incurred.

To illustrate the relation of the recruitment and training vouchers to unemployment durations, it may be useful to consider the specific example of a person, with a particular set of benefit-relevant characteristics, receiving a recruitment voucher of

$$v_R = \max[0, (-1 + \tfrac{1}{6}D)]$$

and a training voucher of

$$v_t = \max[0, (-2 + \tfrac{1}{3}D)],$$

where D is the duration of unemployment. This means that a person who has been unemployed for six months or less receives nothing; one who has been unemployed for 12 months receives a recruitment voucher of \$1 (declining at the rate of \$1/6 per month of employment) or a training voucher of \$2 (declining at the rate of \$1/3 per month of employment); one who has been unemployed for 18 months receives a recruitment voucher of \$2, or a training voucher of \$4 (declining at the same monthly rates given above); and so on, up to maximal recruitment voucher of \$4 or a maximal training voucher of \$8, achieved after 30 months of unemployment.

1.3 Economic implications of the BTP

It is a common experience of economic policy makers that wage subsidies are expensive and, given their cost, their employment impact is often disappointingly small. But the BTP is not just another wage subsidy scheme. Whereas the standard wage subsidy schemes is a burden on the tax payer, the BTP is not. Whereas the alternative to the standard wage subsidy scheme is to stop paying employers to take on workers they would otherwise have found unprofitable, the alternative to the BTP is to support people who are idle. Whereas standard wage subsidy schemes are wasteful, both in terms of deadweight (providing subsidies to some workers who would have found jobs anyway) and displacement (including firms to replace incumbent employees with subsidised recruits), the BTP is much less so: it is targeted at the long-term unemployed, and these workers have relatively low chances of finding jobs anyway and they are often very imperfect substitutes for incumbent employees (particularly in jobs that require experience and skill), so that they are in a correspondingly poor position to displace them.[10]

I will argue below (in section 7) that in a good number of OECD countries, the BTP might turn out to have a surprisingly large effect in promoting employment and reducing unemployment. The reason is not that labour demand is generally very responsive to changes in labour costs – standard estimates of aggregate short-run labour demand elasticities are well under a half in most OECD countries – but that many countries spend a lot on unemployment benefits, particularly if these benefits are broadly defined to include not only the cash payments to the unemployed, but also all the associated welfare state benefits and the forgone tax revenues. Replacement ratios – the ratios of unemployment benefits (broadly defined) to the average wage – exceed 50 per cent in most OECD countries. It is because so much is spent on unemployment benefits and related expenditures that, when a substantial fraction of these funds is offered to employers in the form of employment vouchers, the resulting impact on employment may be substantial.

Basically, what the BTP is designed to do is to *raise* the take-home pay of the new recruits, while at the same time *reducing* their cost to the employers. In short, employees could wind up receiving substantially more than their unemployment benefits, and many employers could find themselves paying substantially less than the prevailing wages. The difference between what the employees receive and what the employers pay is the portion of unemployment support that has been transferred to employment vouchers.

When people draw unemployment benefits, the government bears the cost of supporting them single-handedly. But when they transfer their benefits to employment vouchers, the government shares this cost with the firms that hire them. The reason is that once people are employed, they become productive, making goods and service that are sold to consumers and investors. The revenue that is generated in the process is what permits firms to pay wages substantially in excess of the employment vouchers. In effect, when unemployment benefits are used as employment vouchers, the firms and their customers have an automatic incentive to help the government in bearing the cost of bringing the unemployed back to work.

Since the amount that the government spends on the employment vouchers is set so as not to exceed what it would have spent anyway on unemployment support, *the reduction in unemployment can be achieved at no extra budgetary cost*. All that has happened is that the funds that previously encouraged unemployment are now encouraging employment.

If the employment vouchers are appropriately targeted at the long-term unemployed, the reduction in long-term unemployment could be achieved *without stimulating inflation*, since the long-term unemployed exert little if any dampening influence on wage inflation.

By linking employment vouchers to existing unemployment benefits, the BTP becomes an *automatic stabiliser*, providing most employment vouchers when unemployment is highest. Once the recession is over, unemployment falls and, with it, the unemployment benefits transferable into employment vouchers. Thus the BTP would automatically shrink as unemployment fell.

By linking the vouchers to training, the BTP could become the *basis for national training programmes*. Clearly, firms that qualify for training vouchers (by spending them on nationally accredited training programmes at independent agencies) generally have an incentive to retain their recruits after the vouchers have expired. After all there is little to be gained from training someone, even at subsidised rates, if the firm does not intend to use that worker once she has acquired the training. Thus the training for the unemployed would generally come with longer-term career prospects. This is something that existing government training schemes do not offer. Many current schemes also run the risk of being ill-suited to firms' diverse job requirements and workers' diverse productive potentials, whereas under the BTP firms would naturally initiate the training that was most appropriate to the available jobs. And it is worth recalling that, whereas the existing training schemes are costly to run, this one would impose no additional cost to the government.[11]

The BTP could also play an important role in *tackling regional unemployment problems*. If it were adopted on a national level, regions of high unemployment would become ones containing relatively high proportions of subsidised workers, giving the agents that find it least costly to move – either the firms or the currently unemployed workers – an incentive to relocate and retrain.[12]

The case for implementing the BTP is particularly strong where unemployment benefits are generous and employment is responsive to variations in labour costs. As shown in section 7, many countries in the EU and elsewhere fall into this category. The purpose of the intervening sections 2–6 is to provide a simple diagrammatic overview of the basic

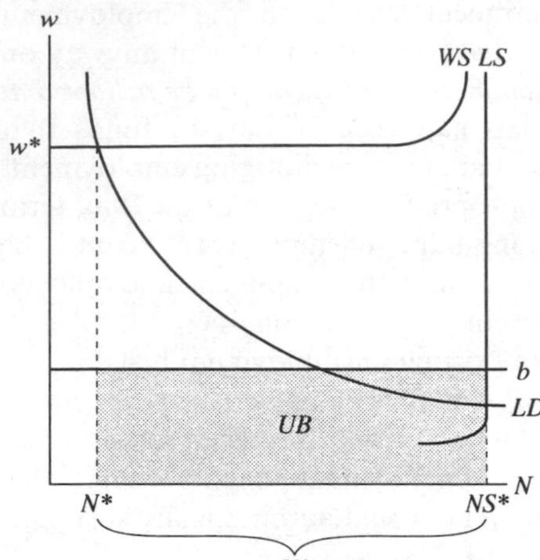

Figure 6.1 The labour market equilibrium

features of the BTP and their salient effects on employment and unemployment.

2 The underlying framework

Let me begin with a simple account of labour market behaviour that provides a convenient background for understanding the role of the BTP in reducing unemployment. Figure 6.1 pictures unemployment as the outcome of an employment and wage-setting process. The labour demand curve is denoted by *LD*. Under perfectly competitive conditions, it shows how much labour firms will employ at any given real wage. Under imperfect competition, it describes the profit-maximising relation between employment and the real wage, when firms make employment and pricing decisions in response to predetermined nominal wages. In either case, the labour demand curve is downward-sloping when there are diminishing returns to labour.

The wage-setting curve, given by *WS* in figure 6.1, shows how the wage is set at any given level of aggregate employment. This curve can be interpreted in a wide variety of ways. If, for example, firms set wages with a view to discouraging their employees from shirking, *WS* traces out the minimum wage (at any given level of aggregate employment) that firms must pay to keep their workers motivated, i.e. *WS* becomes the no-shirking constraint.[13] Whereas if firms set wages so as to discourage quitting, *WS* gives the minimum wage (at each employment level) that firms must pay to retain their workers, i.e. *WS* is the no-quitting constraint.[14] Moreover, if firms' wage offers are made with a view to attracting particularly productive employees, *WS* traces out the minimum wage (for given employment) of attracting workers at a particular level of productivity.[15] Finally, the *WS* curve may also be interpreted as the outcome of wage negotiations between individual employers and employees (at any given level of aggregate employment) or it could be the upshot of union activity.[16]

The wage-setting curve may be upward-sloping, downward-sloping, or flat. There are two countervailing effects on slope. (i) The greater the level of employment, the smaller will be the marginal product of labour and consequently the weaker will be the bargaining position of the marginal employees.[17] On this account, an increase in employment puts downward pressure on the negotiated wage. (ii) The greater the level of employment, the easier it is for employees to supplement their income during a breakdown of negotiations, and the more favourable their fallback positions become. In addition, employers' fallback positions become less favourable, since they have a smaller pool of unemployed workers to draw from. On this account, an increase in employment puts upward pressure on the negotiated wage. The latter tendency may be reinforced when firms use their wage offers to discourage quitting or shirking. The greater is the level of employment, the more likely is a worker to find another job once he quits or has been fired. Thus the more the firm's offered wages may have to exceed the reservation wage in order to discourage quitting and shirking.[18] For simplicity, the wage-setting curve in figure 6.1 is pictured as flat over the relevant range.

The equilibrium level of employment (N^*) and the equilibrium real wage (w^*) are given by the intersection between the labour demand curve (*LD*) and the wage-setting curve (*WS*). The labour supply curve *LS* describes the aggregate amount of labour that workers, each acting on their own and in the absence of unemployment benefits, would be willing to supply at any given real wage. The difference between labour supply (NS^*) and labour demand (N^*) at the equilibrium real wage is the equilibrium level of unemployment (U^*).

The size of the unemployment benefit is denoted by b. Thus the aggregate amount that the government spends on unemployment benefits is bU^*, given by the shaded area *UB* in figure 6.1. As shown below, the BTP uses these unemployment benefits as a resource to promote employment.

Each of the following sections deals with a different aspect of the BTP. Section 3 begins with an elementary finger-exercise, in which the

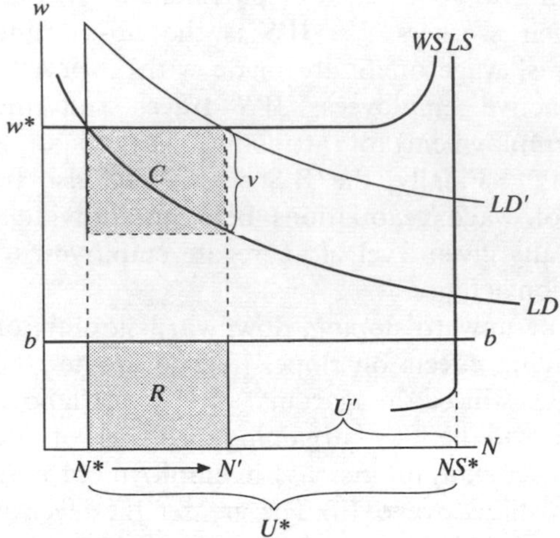

Figure 6.2 The effect of the recruitment voucher

unemployment benefits pay for recruitment vouchers, in a simple world where vouchers are targeted perfectly at net increases in employment and no incumbent workers are displaced. Section 4 examines the implications of directing the vouchers to the long-term unemployed. Section 5 considers the problems of 'deadweight' (people receiving vouchers who would have become employed anyway) and 'displacement' (the subsidised new recruits replacing the incumbents). Section 6 explores the effects of using the unemployment benefits to provide training vouchers. Then section 7 provides some preliminary empirical estimates of how the BTP might affect unemployment in various OECD countries. Section 8 draws some conclusions.

3 Self-financing recruitment vouchers

As a first step toward depicting the influence of the BTP in this setting, consider a hypothetical policy experiment, in which a recruitment voucher v is given to firms for each additional employee they hire. To keep the exposition simple for the moment, let us suppose that the government is actually able to confine its voucher payments only to the net increase in the aggregate employment level, and that no incumbent employees are replaced by the new recruits.

The labour demand curve then moves upwards by the amount v, as shown by the shift from LD to LD' in figure 6.2.[19] For simplicity, suppose that the wage-setting curve remains unchanged.[20] Consequently, the equilibrium level of employment rises from N^* to N', unemployment falls from U^* to U', and spending on unemployment benefits falls correspondingly from bU^* to bU.

Provided that incumbent employees are not displaced, the amount the government saves on unemployment benefits is $bU^* - bU'$. This may be interpreted as the 'revenue' (denoted by the shaded area R in figure 6.2) available to finance the cost of the recruitment vouchers. The cost of the voucher scheme is the size of the voucher (v) times the number of additional employees hired ($N' - N^*$). It is given by the shaded area C in figure 6.2

If the amount of voucher revenue (area R) is greater than or equal to the cost of the vouchers (area C), then the scheme pays for itself. Since the voucher revenue is $b(N' - N^*)$ while the cost is $v(N' - N^*)$, the scheme will be self-financing as long as $v \leq b$, namely, as long as the recruitment voucher does not exceed the unemployment benefit.

Clearly, the highest voucher that the government can afford to offer, without running a deficit on the scheme, is $v^* = b$. The resulting employment level is the maximum amount of employment that can be generated through the self-financing voucher scheme.

4 Targeting the long-term unemployed

We now extend the framework above to take account of another salient feature of the BTP, namely, targeting the long-term unemployed.

As noted, when people remain unemployed, their skills depreciate and become obsolescent, and they lose useful work habits such as reliability, punctuality, conscientiousness, initiative, adaptability, and so on. The simplest way of summarising these regularities in the framework above is to assume that people's potential marginal products fall with their unemployment duration, *ceteris paribus*.

To incorporate this assumption into the labour demand curve, suppose that all the unemployed, U^* in figure 6.3, are ordered in terms of their unemployment durations, so that as we move along the horizontal axis from N^* to NS^*, we include people who have been unemployed for longer and longer periods of time. Then if the marginal product of labour falls not only due to diminishing returns to labour, but also because people with progressively longer unemployment durations are drawn into the workforce, then that portion of the labour demand curve lying to the right of the equilibrium level of employment is no longer LD (corresponding to the labour demand curve in figures 6.1 and 6.2), but may be depicted by LD_u.

In this context, the government can reduce the cost of the recruitment

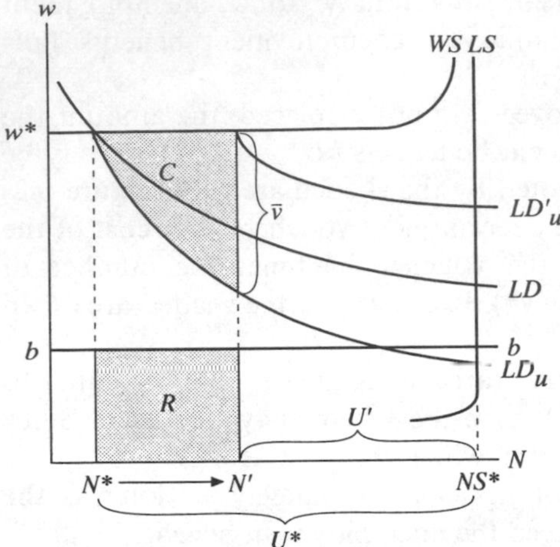

Figure 6.3 Targeting the long-term unemployed

voucher scheme by offering vouchers of different magnitudes to workers with different unemployment durations. Clearly, this cost is minimised when workers with successively higher unemployment durations are each given a voucher amounting to the successively larger differences between their marginal products and the marginal product of the last worker hired without a voucher. For vouchers ranging from zero to $\bar{v}$, the cost is then given by the shaded area *C* in figure 6.3.[21] This cost-minimising way of targeting the long-term unemployed permits the self-financing recruitment vouchers to have a larger employment effect than the uniform voucher scheme in section 3, since it reduces the cost of the scheme relative to the voucher revenue for any given level of employment.

5 Deadweight and displacement

Even if optimal targeting of the long-term unemployed were possible, the framework above would over-state the effectiveness of the self-financing recruitment vouchers. One reason is that we assumed the vouchers could be targeted exclusively at additional employees. In practice, this is generally unachievable. The net increase in aggregate employment is defined as the actual (post-voucher) level of employment *minus* what the employment level would have been in the absence of the voucher. But since the labour market is continually subject to external shocks, it is difficult to assess the latter employment level. Since firms have a clear incentive to under-state this employment level (in order to receive large

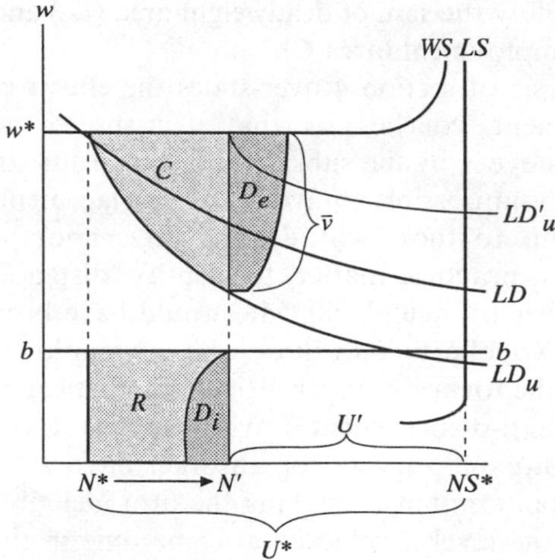

Figure 6.4 Deadweight and displacement

voucher payments) and since the government generally has too little information to correct such claims, it is inevitable that some vouchers would be paid for employees who would have been employed in any case.

In an attempt to get around this problem, recruitment subsidies may be granted for employment in excess of the level achieved at some time in the past (rather than the level that would have been achieved without the voucher). For example, employers could get subsidies for any additions to their workforce over the past year. Thus expanding firms would receive subsidies while contracting firms would not. But since the subsidies to the expanding firms are not balanced by payments from the contracting firms, more than the net increase in aggregate employment would be subsidised. The same holds true of firms that come into existence *vis-à-vis* those that close. Thus it is impossible in practice to avoid spending some vouchers on people who would have found employment even in the absence of the vouchers, i.e. some 'deadweight' is inevitable.

Empirical studies[22] show that the longer people are unemployed, the lower are their chances of becoming employed.[23] Consequently, the magnitude of deadweight falls as the duration of unemployment rises. This is illustrated by the area D_e in figure 6.4, where the wide upper portion of the area corresponds to the upper part of the LD_u curve (underneath the *WS* curve) and, as we move downwards along the LD_u curve, the width of the D_e area declines.

The total cost of the scheme is now the sum of deadweight area (D_e) and the cost of the net increases in employment (area C).

Another reason why the analysis of section 4 over-states the effectiveness of self-financing recruitment vouchers is that it assumed no displacement of incumbent employees by the subsidised new recruits. In practice, of course, it is virtually impossible to avoid any displacement, on account of factors analogous to those why deadweight cannot be avoided. It is very difficult, as a practical matter, to identify 'displacement'. It is defined as the number of incumbents who would have been employed in the absence of the vouchers *minus* those who are employed under the voucher scheme. But the former number, being hypothetical, is hard to assess. For this reason, anti-displacement provisions may make a firm ineligible to receive a recruitment voucher for a worker hired after an incumbent has left. This is tantamount to making the firm ineligible unless its employment exceeds the level it achieved at some time in the past – which is the same as the above-mentioned provisions to avoid deadweight. But as in the case of deadweight, the vouchers received by the expanding or newly created firms are not balanced by payments from the contracting or closing firms and thus inter-firm displacement is still possible. Besides, it is quite easy for firms to circumvent such anti-displacement provisions (such as inducing the incumbent to leave *after* the new entrant has been hired). This is particularly true in sectors where the costs of hiring, training, and firing are low.

In practice, the greater is the employment generated by the vouchers, the greater the number of incumbents that will be displaced. But as recruits with progressively longer unemployment durations are hired, they generally become less and less substitutable for the incumbents. Thus displacement rises less than proportionately with employment. This is illustrated by the area D, in figure 6.4.

Obviously, the greater is the amount of displacement, the smaller will be the voucher revenue, since displaced incumbents frequently join the unemployment pool.[24] Consequently the amount of voucher revenue is now given by the area R in figure 6.4.

Once again, the vouchers are self-financing as long as their total cost (the sum of areas C and D_e) does not exceed the voucher revenue (area R). In response to the voucher scheme depicted in figure 6.4, employment rises from N^* to N'.

Figure 6.4 can also be used to understand the employment effect of the voucher scheme through time for each cohort of workers, where cohorts are defined in terms of the duration of the previous unemployment spell. The last cohort of workers to be employed under the voucher scheme (the ones with the longest previous unemployment spell) generate a direct

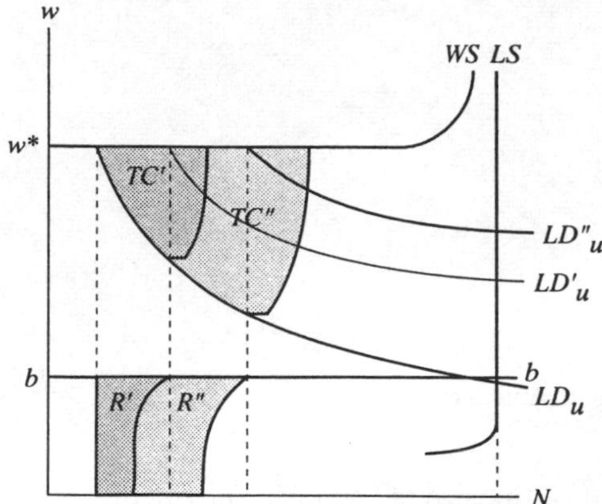

Figure 6.5 The effect of an increase in the voucher

cost given by the rightmost vertical slice of the area *C* in figure 6.4, and a voucher revenue given by the rightmost slice of the area *R*. In becoming employed they make up for the depreciation and obsolescence of their skills that took place during their period of unemployment, and thus their productivity rises from the relevant portion on the LD_u curve to that on the *LD* curve in figure 6.4. With the passage of time, these workers gain employment experience and cease to be the marginal workers in terms of their productivity; this marginal status is taken on by subsequent recruits. Thus the direct costs and revenues associated with the above cohort of workers may be visualised as a succession of vertical slices of the areas *C* and *R* (respectively), each lying progressively further to the left. In this process, the size of the voucher gradually falls as the workers' period of employment proceeds, until eventually the voucher phases itself out of existence and the workers become unemployed again.[25]

Now suppose that the size of the maximal voucher ($\bar{v}$) is gradually increased from an initial level of zero, causing employment to rise. As result, the area of total cost (the sum of the areas *C* and D_e) and the area of voucher revenue (area *R*) both increase, as illustrated by the movement from *TC*′ to *TC*″ and from *R*′ to *R*″ respectively) in figure 6.5.

Clearly, when the maximum voucher is very small, the voucher revenue will exceed the total cost of the scheme,[26] so that the scheme is self-financing. The reason is that as the voucher falls to zero, both the width and the height of the total cost area (*TC*) shrinks to zero, but only the width of the voucher revenue area (*R*) shrinks to zero; the height of the

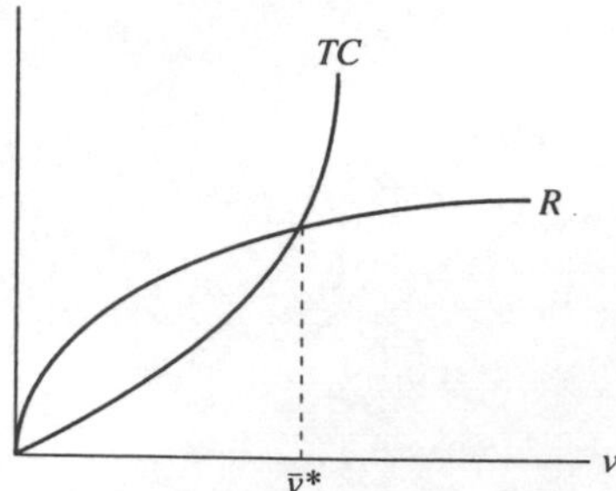

Figure 6.6 The maximal employment voucher

voucher revenue area remains at b, the size of the unemployment benefit. However, as the voucher is increased, the total cost may rise faster than the voucher revenue,[27] so that there may be some maximal level of the maximum voucher ($\bar{v}^*$) beyond which the scheme ceases to be self-financing. This is illustrated in figure 6.6. The maximum level of employment that can be generated through the scheme is then given by the employment level corresponding to $\bar{v}^*$.

6 Training vouchers

The BTP gives unemployed people the opportunity to use not only a part of their unemployment benefits, but also a portion of their existing training budgets to provide training vouchers for firms that are willing to hire them and train them while employed. As above, the training vouchers may be specially targeted at the long-term unemployed. Assuming that the longer people are unemployed, the lower their productivity and the more costly they are to train, the long-term unemployed require larger training vouchers to achieve a given level of productivity than do the short-term unemployed. The cost of the training voucher scheme is then minimised when the size of the training vouchers rises gradually with unemployment duration, as illustrated in figure 6.7. Here the vertical distance between the wage-setting curve WS and the labour demand curve LD_u is the minimum amount by which productivity must be raised in order to make the unemployed employable. The corresponding shaded area c is the cost of increasing net employment by $N'-N^*$ in this way. The maximum voucher required for this purpose is $\bar{v}^*$.

The area d_e represents 'training deadweight', i.e. the amount of training voucher expenditures that are made on people who would have received

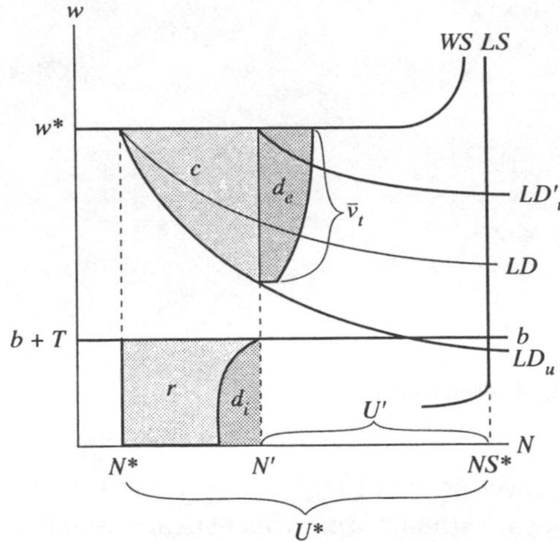

Figure 6.7 Training vouchers

the training even in the absence of these vouchers. Thus the total cost of the training voucher scheme is the sum of the areas c and d_e.

Given that the unemployment benefit is b and the average training expenditure per unemployed person is T, the corresponding voucher revenue is given by the area r. The area d_i stands for 'training displacement', the amount of training voucher funds that are wasted because the newly trained people displace current incumbent employees. The training vouchers pay for themselves provided that their total cost $(c + d_e)$ is less than or equal to the voucher revenue r.

Clearly, the intertemporal effects of the training vouchers differ from those of the recruitment vouchers. As above, the direct costs associated with the marginal recruits (those with the longest previous unemployment spell) may be pictured by the rightmost vertical slice of the area c in figure 6.7 and the corresponding voucher revenue is given by the rightmost slice of the area r. The training vouchers, however, may usually be expected to raisc workers' *long-term* productivity to the level w^*, so that – barring any external shocks to labour demand – these workers will remain employed once their training period is over and their training vouchers have expired. Thus whereas a continuous stream of recruitment vouchers is necessary to maintain the level of employment above its initial level N^*, only a finite stream of training vouchers is sufficient for this purpose.

Figure 6.8 pictures the total cost and revenue from both the recruitment and the training vouchers in terms of the maximal magnitude of these

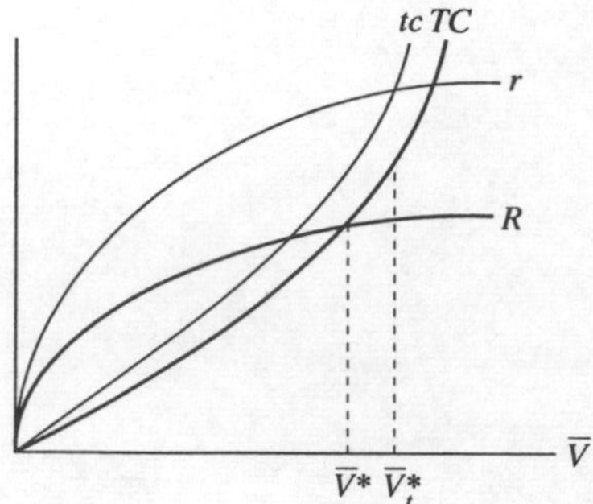

Figure 6.8 The maximum training and recruitment vouchers

vouchers. The training voucher revenue curve (r) lies above the recruitment voucher revenue curve (R), since the training vouchers are financed by both unemployment benefits and the existing training expenditures while the recruitment vouchers are financed by unemployment benefits alone. The total cost curve for the training voucher scheme (tc) lies above that of the recruitment voucher scheme (TC) provided that the cost of making an unemployed person employable through raising her productivity exceeds the cost of doing so through recruitment subsidies. Provided that the r curve lies above the R curve by more than the tc curve lies above the TC curve, the maximum level of the highest training voucher ($\bar{v}_t^*$), i.e. the maximum level of the training voucher allocated to the marginal recruit (namely, the recruit who previously had the highest duration of unemployment) will exceed the maximum level of the highest recruitment voucher ($\bar{v}^*$).[28]

7 Estimating the unemployment effects of the BTP

We now derive some preliminary empirical estimates of how the BTP may affect unemployment in various OECD countries. The analysis is based on very simple calculations of deadweight, displacement, and voucher effectiveness.[29] Since the emphasis is on simplicity, the results are clearly not definitive, but rather illustrative of a method of assessing the possible unemployment effects of the programme. We focus attention exclusively on employment vouchers and ignore training vouchers. Moreover, let the targeted group comprise all the unemployed, and let the vouchers be granted for a one-year period, which will be our period of analysis.

Let us call employment of the target group 'target employment', and let

N_T and N_T^0 be target employment in the presence and absence of the employment vouchers, respectively. By definition,

$$N_T = N_T^0 + \Delta N_T. \tag{1}$$

i.e. target employment with the vouchers is equal to target employment without the vouchers *plus* the additional employment induced by the vouchers (ΔN_T).

The N_T^0 people in the economy, who would claim vouchers under the BTP but who would have found jobs anyway, represent deadweight. To model this in a simple way, we consider an 'initial equilibrium', before the vouchers are introduced, and ask how many employees vacate their jobs each period and how many people who have previously been unemployed fill these vacancies. Let N^0 be aggregate employment in the initial equilibrium, and σ_I be the incumbent workers' separation rate. Then, assuming employment to be stationary in the original equilibrium, the number of vacancies is $\sigma_I N^0$. Suppose that a constant proportion γ of these vacancies is filled, in the initial equilibrium, by those who were previously unemployed. Then the deadweight is

$$N_T^0 = \gamma \sigma_I N^0. \tag{2}$$

By definition, the change in aggregate employment induced by the vouchers (ΔN) is equal to the change in target employment (ΔN_T) *plus* the induced change in the employment of the incumbent workers (ΔN_I):

$$\Delta N = \Delta N_T + \Delta N_I. \tag{3}$$

When the induced change in the employment of incumbents is negative, it represents displacement. For simplicity, let us assume that the number of incumbents displaced by the target group is a constant proportion of the increase in target employment:

$$\Delta N_I = -\alpha_I \Delta N_T \tag{4}$$

where the incumbent displacement coefficient α_I is a constant ($0 < \alpha_I < 1$).

Substituting (4) into (3),

$$\Delta N = (1 - \alpha_I) \Delta N_T \tag{5}$$

and substituting (5) and (2) into (1), we obtain

$$(N_T/N^0) = \gamma\sigma_I + \frac{1}{1-\sigma_I}(\Delta N/N^0). \tag{6}$$

In other words, the aggregate rise in employment is linearly related to the level of target employment.

It is convenient to think of the employment effect of the voucher as related to the percentage by which employment would increase in response to an equivalent wage reduction, since the latter can be summarised by the elasticity of labour demand. Specifically, the effect of a proportional real wage reduction $(\Delta w/w^0)$ on employment $(\Delta N/N^0)$ is

$$\Delta N/N^0 = \eta(\Delta w/w^0) \tag{7}$$

where η is the labour demand elasticity.

In general, an employment voucher may be expected to be less effective in stimulating employment than an equal fall in the real product wage, for several reasons:

(i) We have already taken account of deadweight and the displacement. Our analysis also recognises that the vouchers are aimed at the unemployed, whereas the hypothesised wage reduction falls on all workers.

(ii) Another reason is the potential displacement of those currently out of the labour force ('inactive' people). Whereas vouchers targeted at the unemployed are likely to reduce the job prospects of the inactive workers, a real wage reduction may be expected to have the opposite effect.

(iii) Beyond that, vouchers might conceivably drive up the real wages paid by firms, in which case their labour costs would fall by less than the size of the vouchers. In practice, however, this appears unlikely, since the vouchers have the following countervailing effects on wage negotiations: (a) they improve the employers' fallback positions (since they are now able to find cheaper replacements for their incumbent employees when negotiations fail), thereby reducing the negotiated wages, (b) insofar as they lead to the displacement of incumbents, they put further downward pressure on wages, and (c) they improve the employees' fallback positions (since the voucher-induced fall in unemployment means that employees have an easier time finding alternative jobs when wage negotiations break down), thereby putting upward pressure on wages. When the employment vouchers are introduced, the first two effects will precede the latter, since the vouchers make the unemployed immediately cheaper to employer and immediately raise incumbents' chances of displacement, whereas the fall in unemployment takes some time to unfold. As for the third effect, econometric studies[30] show that in OECD countries real wages are generally not very sensitive to changes in the unemployment rate.

(iv) But probably the most important reason why vouchers tend to have weaker employment effects than equivalent wage reductions is that the vouchers are temporary whereas the wage reductions – at least those which are relevant to the standard estimates of labour demand elasticities – are permanent.

Let us take a closer look at what point (iv) implies. As a first approximation, the employment effect of a one-period voucher relative to be employment effect of an infinite stream of such vouchers may be captured by the ratio of the voucher to the present value of the infinite stream.[31] Let the size of the voucher be v, the firms' discount factor be δ, the separation rate relevant to the new recruits be σ_T and the cost of a future separation from these workers (e.g. the cost of firing them) be Φ. Then the present value of the infinite stream is[32]

$$R = v + [(1\sigma_T)\delta v + (1-\sigma_T)^2\delta^2 v + (1-\sigma_T)^3\delta^3 v + \ldots] \\ - [\sigma\delta\Phi + (1-\sigma_T)\delta^2\sigma_T\Phi + (1-\sigma_T)^2\delta^3\sigma\Phi + \ldots].$$

In other words, in the first period each firm receives the voucher v for a new recruit. With probability $(1-\sigma_T)$ this worker remains at the firm in the second period, when the discounted value of the voucher is δv; whereas with probability σ_T the worker leaves the firm, incurring a separation cost whose present value is $\delta\Phi$. Along these lines, it is easy to see that the first bracketed expression is the value of all the vouchers received by the firm, discounted by the retention probability and the discount factor, and that the second bracketed expression is the value of the separation costs, similarly discounted. Simplifying, we find

$$R = \frac{v}{1-(1-\sigma_T)\delta} - \frac{\sigma_T\Phi\delta}{1-(1-\sigma_T)\delta}. \tag{8a}$$

Thus the ratio of the infinite stream to the size of the one-period voucher is

$$\varsigma = \frac{R}{v} = \frac{1}{1-(1-\sigma_T)\delta} - \frac{\sigma_T\delta}{1-(1-\sigma_T)\delta}\phi \tag{8b}$$

where $\phi = \Phi/v$.

Define the 'voucher ratio' as the ratio of the voucher to the original wage: $\rho = v/w^0$. Furthermore, let

$$\theta = \beta\varsigma \tag{8c}$$

be the 'voucher effectiveness coefficient', where ς takes into account that the voucher is temporary and β is a constant $(0 < \beta < 1)$ that captures the other factors that may reduce the employment effect of the voucher relative to that of an equivalent wage reduction. Then we can move from the employment effect of a proportional wage reduction $(\Delta w/w^0)$, as given in (7), to the employment effect of an equivalent voucher ratio $(\rho = \Delta w/w^0)$ as follows:

$$\Delta N/N^0 = \theta\eta\rho. \tag{8d}$$

In short, the effectiveness of the voucher is taken to be a fraction of the effectiveness of an equivalent wage reduction.

Substituting (8d) into (6)

$$\frac{N_T}{N^0} = \gamma\sigma_I + \frac{\theta\eta\rho}{1-\alpha_I}. \tag{9}$$

This equation tells us that the ratio of target employment to aggregate initial employment depends positively (and linearly) on the voucher ratio. The equation summarises our description of labour market activity and is depicted by the labour market equilibrium curve (*LE*) in figure 6.9.

The government budget constraint (GBC) for the BTP ensures that the cost of the employment vouchers does not exceed the associated reduction in unemployment benefits. Letting the unemployment benefit be constant at b, the GBC is

$$b\Delta N \geq vN_T. \tag{10}$$

Define the replacement ratio as the ratio of the unemployment benefit

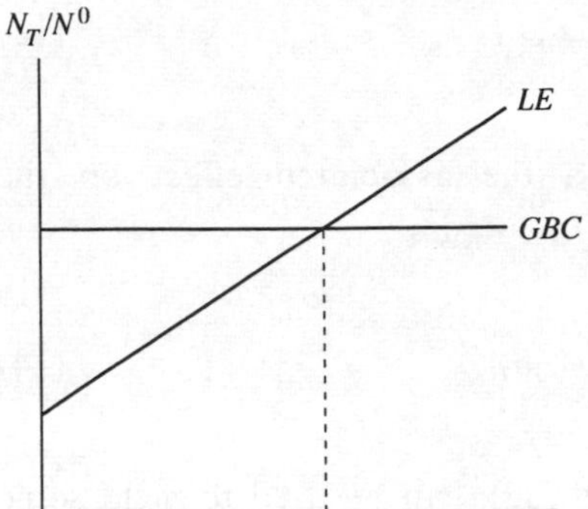

Figure 6.9 The maximum voucher ratio and the maximum employment effect

to the real product wage: $r = b/w$. Recalling that $\rho = v/w$, the GBC becomes

$$r\frac{\Delta N}{N^0} \geq \rho\frac{N_T}{N^0}. \tag{10a}$$

Substituting (8d) into (10a) yields

$$\frac{N_T}{N^0} \leq r\theta\eta. \tag{11}$$

The employment effect of the BTP is maximised when this constraint holds as equality, so that $N_T/N^0 = \rho\theta\eta$ is the maximum level of target employment permitted by the GBC. This equation is pictured by the GBC line in figure 6.9.

Substituting the government budget constraint (11), as an equality, into the labour market equilibrium equation (9) yields the maximum level of the voucher ratio ρ^*:

$$\rho^* = (1 - \alpha_I)\left[r - \frac{\gamma\sigma_I}{\theta\eta}\right]. \tag{12}$$

Inserting this value into (8d) gives us the corresponding effect on employment:

$$\frac{\Delta N}{N^0} = \theta\eta(1 - \alpha_I)\left[r - \frac{\gamma\sigma_i}{\theta\eta}\right]. \tag{13}$$

Assuming a constant labour supply, the associated effect on the unemployment rate (u) is

$$-\frac{\Delta u}{u^0} = -\frac{1 - u^0}{u^0}(1 - \alpha_I)[r\theta\eta - \gamma\sigma_I]. \tag{14}$$

This equation, together with (8b) and (8d), can be used to yield some provisional estimates of how the BTP may affect unemployment in the short run (a year). Take the estimates of the short-run labour demand elasticities[33] (η) and the replacement ratios (r) from Layard, Nickell and Jackman (1991).[34] Let u^0 be represented by the unemployment rates of July 1994. Set the displacement coefficient conservatively at $\alpha_I = 0.4$, i.e. the voucher-induced rise in the number of jobs to the long-term unemployed is assumed to lead to 40 per cent of that number of jobs being lost to the incumbents. Furthermore, set the incumbent separation rate at $\sigma_I = 0.2$ and the fraction of vacancies filled by the long-term unemployed at $\gamma = 0.2$. Assuming that the discount factor is $\delta = 0.9$, the separation rate associated with the new recruits is $\sigma_T = 0.4$, and that the ratio of the firing cost to the voucher is $\phi = 0.5$, we find that $R = 0.56$, and thus we set the voucher effectiveness coefficient at $\theta = 0.5$. The resulting effects of the BTP on unemployment are given in table 6.1.

Table 6.1 *Short-run effects of the BTP*

Country	*U* rate (%)	SR elasticity	Repl. ratio	*N* effect (%)	*U* effect (%)
Austria	5.2	−0.37	0.6	2.8	−51.8
Belgium	14.0	−0.3	0.6	3.0	−18.4
Canada	10.2	−0.35	0.6	3.9	−34.3
Denmark	12.3	−0.49	0.9	10.8	−77.2
France	12.0	−0.17	0.57	0.5	−3.7
Germany	8.3	−0.53	0.63	7.6	−84.2
Netherlands	7.3	−0.18	0.7	1.4	−17.5
Spain	24.6	−0.71	0.8	14.6	−44.9
Sweden	8.8	−0.12	0.8	0.5	−5.0
UK	9.3	−0.4	0.36	1.9	−19.0
USA	6.7	−0.2	0.5	0.6	−8.4

Needless to say, these figures are merely suggestive of rough orders of magnitude. The above estimates of labour demand elasticities and replacement ratios are subject to considerable uncertainty, and different investigators have achieved different results.[35] Setting higher values for the displacement coefficients or the voucher effectiveness coefficient, or allowing for a positive labour supply response to the vouchers would obviously lead to smaller predicted effects on unemployment. However, many of these effects are large enough to remain substantial even once generous allowance has been made for uncertainty.

For most OECD countries, of course, the long-run labour demand elasticities exceed the short-run ones by a considerable margin. Thus the BTP may be expected to remain effective over the longer haul even if the displacement coefficients are substantially higher in the long run than in the short run and the subsidy effectiveness coefficient is substantially lower. Table 6.2 provides an illustrative example.[36] The displacement coefficients are now set $\alpha_I = 0.6$, so that 60 per cent of the additional jobs created through the vouchers are lost through displacement of incumbents and short-term unemployed people.[37] The voucher effectiveness coefficient is now set at $\theta = 0.3$, so that the vouchers are assumed to be only 30 per cent as effective as an equivalent wage reduction. We leave the parameters $\sigma_I = 0.2$ and $\gamma = 0.2$.

As above, it is important to keep in mind that these are just very rough ballpark figures; but it is undeniable that their overall thrust is to suggest that the BTP may be a powerful took for combating unemployment even in the longer run.

Table 6.2 *Long-run effects of the BTP*

Country	LR elasticity	*N* effect (%)	*U* effect (%)
Austria	−0.267	0.3	−5.8
Belgium	−0.589	2.6	−16.2
Canada	−0.42	1.4	−12.5
Denmark	−0.692	5.8	−41.9
France	−0.61	2.6	−18.9
Germany	−0.83	4.7	−51.6
Netherlands	−0.6	3.4	−43.9
Spain	−1.382	11.7	−35.8
Sweden	−0.25	0.8	−8.3
UK	0.63	1.1	10.9
USA	−0.32	0.3	−4.7

8 Concluding thoughts

In concluding, it is important to keep in mind not only the employment potential of the BTP, but also the potential objections and pitfalls that need to be overcome.

Objection 1

The first pitfall is a political economy problem. The political process whereby economic theory is transformed into economic policy is certainly not a matter of faithful, literal translation. Policy makers have an understandable tendency to fit new ideas into old pigeon holes; in so doing, they instinctively, often inadvertently, shy away from the novel insights and concentrate on those features of a proposal that lie in the well-trodden terrain of their past policy experience. If this experience contains a long sequence of unsuccessful measures – and the battle against unemployment is replete with this – then the new ideas, once implemented, are frequently doomed to repeat old failures.

Along these lines it could be argued that implementing the BTP may do more harm than good, since it may turn out that the policy makers will stay clear of its distinctive features (linking the employment vouchers to unemployment benefits, letting the vouchers rise gradually with unemployment durations and fall gradually with subsequent employment durations, and letting potential employers and employees choose freely between recruitment and training vouchers). Instead, they may interpret the programme as yet another attempt at wage subsidies, or as a call to eliminate employers' national insurance contributions for workers who have been unemployed for more than a year, or as an effort to subsidise training programmes run in the private sector, or as an initiative to offer long-term unemployed people extra assistance when they accept work in the public or private sectors, or any number of other possibilities. These latter measures may suffer from well known and well tried deficiencies; they may, for instance, require significant increases in government expenditures or they may create more unemployment than they remove, for instance. The case against the BTP, then, is that it could become an excuse for implementing other policies that share the shortcomings of past policy experiments.

This argument is a bit similar to the argument that no new medical drugs should be approved, because if doctors do not prescribe them properly, they kill more people than they save. The reason that this argument looks peculiar is not that doctors don't make mistakes – misprescriptions of new drugs are virtually inevitable. Rather, it is that we ought to be able to rely on the doctors to learn enough about these drugs to apply them appropriately. Similarly, we ought to be able to rely on economic policy makers to take note of the BTP's distinctive features and learn how to implement them, so that they don't wind up repeating past policy mistakes. Admittedly, it would be naive to believe that the learning process is simple; but it would be foolish to veto new employment policies merely as a vote of no confidence in politicians and civil servants.

The only case in which such a vote of no confidence may be warranted is when a proposal makes impossible demands on the policy makers. To take a well known macroeconomic example, if there are long and variable lags between changes in the money supply and changes in nominal GNP, then monetary stabilisation policy requires central bankers to predict the future course of the business cycle and the future delays in the GNP response to monetary shocks, and central bankers simply cannot be expected to do this. The BTP, however, makes no analogous demands on policy makers. Once it is in place, they need to make no further discretionary decisions on how much to stimulate employment. After all, the BTP is an automatic stabiliser, which necessarily provides the greatest stimulus when unemployment is highest.

Objection 2

The second objection concerns targeting. Some may argue that it is a mistake to target the long-term unemployed – as the BTP does – because targeting usually creates special disincentives to work. For example, the greater the employment vouchers received by the long-term unemployed, the smaller the job-seeking incentives of the short-term unemployed become. In fact, if the vouchers of the long-term unemployed are sufficiently large relative to those of the short-term unemployed, the latter group may find it worthwhile actually to stop seeking jobs, thereby economising on job search costs now and qualifying for higher vouchers in the future. Clearly, if all unemployed workers received the same subsidy, such disincentives could not arise.

This objection – which could be used as an argument for favouring broad-based employment schemes, such as reducing social insurance contributions for low-wage workers – needs to be taken very seriously, since the various major employment policies that have been proposed in recent years differ dramatically in their targeting. Several issues are relevant here. First, the disincentive effects for the short-term unemployment can of course be mitigated through the enforcement of rules requiring people to accept available job offers in order to qualify for unemployment benefits. If the short-term unemployed lose their unemployment benefits when they stop seeking jobs, they may lose their incentive to 'invest in long-term unemployment'.

Second, whatever remains of the disincentive effect for the short-term unemployed must be set against the advantages of targeting. One major advantage is that it economises on the government outlay necessary to achieve a given reduction in unemployment. If we accept the widespread view that long-term unemployment is the most serious problem posed by unemployment, then targeting the employment stimulus at the long-term unemployed is bound to be an efficient way of dealing with this problem.[38]

Third, another advantage of targeting is that it reduces the upward pressure on wages from a given level of subsidy expenditure. A non-targeted employment subsidy or payroll tax reduction improves the re-employment prospects of current jobholders, who then have less to lose by making higher wage claims. Targeting the stimulus at the long-term unemployed largely avoids this danger, since the current employees generally face a much greater likelihood of becoming short-term unemployed, in response to an excessive wage claim, than of becoming long-term unemployed after that.[39] In fact, the targeting of the BTP may actually lead to a reduction, rather than an increase, in real wages[40] since the vouchers may increase the search efforts of the long-term unemployed and thereby increase the degree of competition for the available jobs.

Fourth, as noted, the long-term unemployed are disadvantaged in the labour market and non-targeting policies clearly do nothing to improve their employment opportunities relative to the short-term unemployed and currently employed workers. In short, targeting serves equity objectives that are important in their own right.

Finally, when we examine the full range of prominent employment policy proposals, we find that choice is not between those targeted at the long-term unemployed and those that are not targeted at all. Rather, the choice is between targeting one group of workers or another. For example, reducing social insurance contributions for low-wage workers is obviously another form of targeting, which introduces disincentives of its own, namely, a disincentive to acquire training and thereby earn higher wages. And insofar as this proposal subsidises the employment of a larger group of workers, it is inevitably associated with more deadweight.

Objection 3

A third objection is that the employment impact of the recruitment and training vouchers becomes seriously eroded through deadweight and displacement. It is a fact of life that no practicable voucher scheme can wholly eradicate these twin evils. But that would be a poor argument for not trying to contain them. As we have seen, the BTP seeks to do so by letting the size of the voucher rise with the duration of unemployment and fall with the duration of subsequent employment. Most wage subsidy schemes that have been implemented thus far do not have these features.

Policy makers may wish, in addition, to impose an explicit anti-displacement provision, such as not granting vouchers to firms who are merely replacing employees that have left. The advantage of this approach is that, in refusing to reward displacement, it helps keep the BTP from endangering the jobs of incumbent workers and thereby becoming a socially divisive policy. This may well help gain political acceptance for the policy. It also may avoid inducing incumbents to engage in a variety of rent-seeking activities to restore their job security. The disadvantage is that it substantially weakens the capacity of the BTP to function as an automatic stabiliser, for in times of recession many firms shed labour and none of these firms would qualify for recruitment or training vouchers (unless their subsequent hiring exceeded their firing and quits). Thus the vouchers would not be offered when the need for them is greatest.

Different anti-displacement provisions – such as giving displaced incumbents the right of complaint and imposing fines on firms for which the complaints are substantiated – do not share this disadvantage, at least not to the same degree. Beyond that, of course, displacement is unlikely to be a serious problem in sectors of the economy where labour turnover costs are high.[41]

In any event, the presence or absence of anti-displacement provisions will help determine the main channels through which the BTP influences employment. In the presence of such provisions, the main effect of the BTP may be expected to fall directly on new recruits to the active workforce, whose labour costs on the firms will fall. In the absence of these provisions, however, the BTP may well generate substantial displacement in sectors with low turnover costs. In exposing insiders to greater competition with the outsiders, this displacement may be expected to put downward pressure on wages, which in turn will stimulate employment. But even without this wage effect, the replacement of incumbent employees by people who were previously long-term unemployed may be expected to raise employment, for the simple reason that the incumbents tend to be more skilled, motivated, and in tune with employers' needs than the long-term unemployed, and thus the incumbents generally have much better chances of finding new jobs.

Objection 4

Another potential pitfall of the BTP, briefly alluded to in section 7, is that it might be far less effective in the long run than in the short run. The extreme theoretical form of this argument is what may be termed the 'wage subsidy ineffectiveness proposition', according to which any wage subsidy leads to an equal rise in workers' take-home pay over the long run, so that labour costs remain unchanged. The underlying argument appears to lie more in the realm of theory than practice, but since the proposition has had significant influence among some economists, it deserves to be addressed here. In brief, the argument is that, when the wages paid by firms are the outcome of Nash bargaining, a wage subsidy that falls in equal proportions on both the employee's negotiated take-home pay wage and on her fallback income (her income when negotiations break down) will raise the take-home pay by the amount of the subsidy.[42]

There is, however, little if any reason to expect this argument to hold in practice, particularly with regard to subsidies targeted at the long-term unemployed, such as those of the BTP. First, there is no reason why a wage subsidy should affect the fallback income of a previously long-term unemployed person by as much as her take-home pay. After all, the fallback income of a previously unemployed person may be expected to depend heavily on wage floors determined by the minimum wage and unemployment benefits, and there is no reason for the latter to rise by the amount of the subsidy. But if, over the long run, the subsidy raises take-home pay relative to fallback income, then the firm's long-run labour costs will fall and its employment will rise.

Second, the BTP's training voucher – and, to a lesser degree, its recruitment voucher – may be expected to reduce the labour turnover rate (i.e. the rate of entry and exit from the workforce) of people at the bottom end of the wage distribution (the previously unskilled, disadvantaged workers). This will generally raise their long-run employment level, since people's probability of retaining employment generally exceeds the probability of gaining employment.

Third, the vouchers may be expected to induce people to move from inactivity to active job search, thereby increasing the economy's effective supply of labour, putting downward pressure on wages and thereby raising employment.

Finally, the BTP would also promote employment when wages are set by firms with a view to motivating employees, to attracting and retaining the particularly productive ones, and to discourage quits (in line with the efficiency wage theory). To see why, suppose that employees' take-home pay rose proportionately to the voucher, leaving labour costs unchanged. Then the resulting rise in take-home pay relative to non-wage income would induce these employees to work harder, shirk less, and quit less. Consequently, firms would no longer need to rely as much as previously on wages as an incentive device. So the wages firms pay would fall and thus employment would rise.

Objection 5

Yet another potential pitfall of the BTP is that the vouchers would stigmatise workers in the eyes of their prospective employers, thereby undoing the employment-creating effect of the fall in labour costs. There is some limited evidence of such stigmatisation in US experiments with bonuses to the employers of previously unemployed people.[43] Here workers often failed to reveal that their employers were entitled to bonuses in order to avoid being classified as unproductive.

There is, however, little reason to believe that this stigma effect, if present in the USA, would be equally evident in Europe. The reason is straightforward. The USA has little long-term employment, since employment benefits and most associated forms of support run out after a limited period of time (about half a year) and thus people who fail to get jobs within that period often tend to become inactive. In many European countries, by contrast, a variety of welfare state benefits are conditional on being unemployed and long-term unemployment is a serious problem, particularly in the aftermath of recessions. The difference is important, because long-term unemployment is a far better sign of low productivity than is inactivity: people who have been engaged in prolonged, unsuccessful job search are more likely to be unproductive than people who have simply been out of the labour force. Thus a European employer who knows a job applicant's unemployment duration has more information about the applicant's productivity than an American employer who knows the applicant's duration of inactivity. Consequently, whereas an employment voucher may be able to stigmatise an American worker, it is most unlikely to do so for a European worker, since people's unemployment histories are public knowledge and vouchers for the European long-term unemployed cannot impose any stigma beyond that arising from these unemployment histories.

So, to conclude, the bottom line on benefit transfers is this: in view of the various new features that differentiate benefit transfers from previous wage subsidies, it is difficult to assess what the precise employment effect of the BTP is likely to be. But one thing is clear: as long as unemployment benefits are positive, the BTP will undoubtedly reduce labour costs. Thus it will clearly have *some* positive effect on employment and training. And since it is voluntary, not inflationary and costs the government nothing, what is there to lose?

NOTES

I am grateful to Charles Bean, Alison Booth, David Coe, and Jacques Drèze for their insightful comments. I am also very thankful for the policy feedback I received at a seminar organised by Alan Budd at the UK Treasury. I am particularly indebted to Michael Orszac for his penetrating suggestions. The chapter is part of the Labour Market Imperfections Programme, organised by the CEPR and financed by the UK Employment Department. The initial version of the chapter was written while the author was at the Research Department of the International Monetary Fund. The views expressed in this chapter are those of the author and do not necessarily reflect those of the CEPR, the UK Employment Department, the IMF or its member countries.

1 Other experiments in this vein have been conducted in the USA, Germany, Italy, Canada and elsewhere. See, for example, Byrne (1993), Felli and Ichino (1988) and Woodbury and Spiegelman (1987).

2 This market failure is analysed in the insider–outsider theory. See, for example, Lindbeck and Snower (1988).

3 This failure is the theme of the efficiency wage theory. See, for example, Calvo (1979), Shapiro and Stiglitz (1984) and Weiss (1980).

4 Alternatively, when a job is found, the subsidy could be divided between the employer and the employee. If wages are perfectly flexible over the long run, then the relative shares of the voucher claimed by the employer and employee may be expected to have no effect on employment, since the wage agreement depends on these relative shares: if the employee is allotted more of the voucher, the wage will turn out to be correspondingly lower. In practice, wage scales across employees are often standardised, so that even in the long run wages may not adjust to compensate for vouchers whose magnitude is related to unemployment durations. In any case, in the short run (before all wages in the economy have adjusted fully to the vouchers) the relative shares may have an effect that depends on the relative returns to job search by workers versus the returns to employee search by firms: if the employee gets more of the voucher, her job-search effort will rise, but the search intensity of potential employers will fall.

5 Clearly, if these conditions were violated, employers would find it worthwhile to hire the subsidised workers without requiring any productive effort on the workers' part. That would obviously defeat the purpose of the BTP, namely, to get unemployed people back into productive pursuits.

6 An unemployed person's valuation of her leisure may be either positive or negative.

7 It is desirable that the initial voucher rise gradually with unemployment duration, in order to keep small the size of the 'notches' by which the successive vouchers rise with the length of the jobless spell. Clearly, the greater are these notches, the greater will be the disincentive to work for

people with unemployment spells just under the critical level entitling them to a higher voucher.

8 In those countries where the size of unemployment benefits, *plus* all the related welfare state support, eventually falls with unemployment duration, there is a tension between (i) the requirement that the present value of each person's employment vouchers is approximately equal to the present value of the unemployment benefits that person would otherwise have received and (ii) the requirement that the size of the initial voucher rise with the length of the person's previous unemployment spell (up to a certain limit). In case of such conflict, it may be necessary to meet the second requirement through some redistribution of funds towards those people with the longest unemployment durations.

9 If all individuals with a given unemployment duration were given the same voucher, those receiving relatively large unemployment benefits would have no incentive to take advantage of the BTP, whereas those receiving relatively small ones would have a great incentive to do so. Then, clearly, the employment incentives would fall very unequally on the long-term unemployed.

10 Ways to further reduce deadweight and displacement are discussed in section 5.

11 Another way in which the BTP could encourage training is by encouraging long-term employment relative to temporary employment. The reason, of course, is that the size of the employment vouchers depends on the duration of the previous spell of unemployment In accepting employment, a person therefore loses her voucher entitlement and must go through another unemployment spell before regaining that entitlement. Consequently, people would have a greater incentive to relinquish their voucher entitlement in return for long-term career prospects, yielding a substantial present value of wage incomes, than for temporary jobs. Should policy makers deem this bias to be undesirable, however, they could make the size of the employment vouchers depend on the amount of time a person has been unemployed over, say, the past two years.

12 Specifically, if it is cheaper for firms to relocate, they would move into the area and retrain the local unemployed workforce. If, on the other hand, the workers have lower moving costs, they will leave the area and retrain elsewhere.

13 See, for example, Shapiro and Stiglitz (1984). The underlying idea is that firms are unable to monitor perfectly whether their employees are shirking. Thus they offer a wage above the minimum wage necessary to induce people to work (the reservation wage) and they fire any employee whom they catch shirking. The greater the difference between the offered wage and the reservation wage, the greater is the employee's penalty for shirking. The *WS* curve then traces out the wage the firms need to offer in order to keep workers from shirking.

14 See, for example, Calvo (1979) and Stiglitz 1985). If workers who quit their firms have some likelihood of going through a period of unemployment before finding new employers, the cost of quitting will depend on the difference between their current wage and what they receive when unemployed. Thus, firms can discourage quitting by raising their wage offers.

15 See, for example, Weiss (1980).

16 See, for example, McDonald and Solow (1981), where the wage-setting curve

is portrayed as a contract curve, and Lindbeck and Snower (1990), where it is the outcome of Nash bargaining between firms and their insiders. Furthermore, if unions set the wage unilaterally, then the wage-setting curve can trace out the unions' most preferred points on a family of labour demand curves.

17 The smaller the marginal product of labour, the smaller will be the workers' bargaining surplus (given their fallback position) and thus the lower will be the negotiated wage, *ceteris paribus*.

18 This argument ignores the income effect. It is of course conceivable that the income effect be so strong that a rise in the offered wage *raises* workers' propensity to quit and shirk.

19 Since firms were previously willing to employ N^* workers at wage w^*, they are now prepared to provide the same employment at wage $w^* + v$.

20 If the wage-setting curve represents the no-shirking or no-quitting constraint, it will in fact remain unchanged, since the voucher does not affect the employees' incentives to shirk or quit at any given level of employment. Similarly, the wage-setting curve is unchanged if it is the outcome of union wage-setting. But if it is the outcome of wage negotiations between employers and employees, the vouchers have several countervailing effects on the position of the wage-setting curve. On the one hand, the vouchers raise firms' profits, and employees are able to capture some of this added profit through higher negotiated wages. On the other, the vouchers improve firms' fallback position, since it is now cheaper to hire alternative labour during breakdown in negotiations; this puts downward pressure on the negotiated wage.

21 In practice, of course, such optimal targeting is not achievable since people's potential productivities and the position of the wage-setting curve cannot be known with certainty.

22 See, for example, Layard, Nickell and Jackman (1991).

23 In the UK, for instance, this is the case up to unemployment durations of about 2.5 years, beyond which the employment probabilities flatten out.

24 However, since they join it as short-term unemployed, they also have a relatively high chance of regaining employment.

25 Not only do the voucher costs fall as time proceeds; the voucher revenue falls as well. The voucher revenue associated with each cohort of workers in each period of time is equal to the unemployment benefit associated with the unemployment duration which the cohort would have in that period, multiplied by the probability of still being unemployed in that period. Since the probability that a person remains unemployed falls as time proceeds, the voucher revenue must fall as well. Clearly, workers will remain unemployed until their recruitment subsidies have entirely disappeared only if the slope of the labour demand curve and the evolution of unemployment probabilities is such that the voucher revenue does not decline faster than the associated cost.

26 The reason is that as the voucher falls to zero, both the width and the height of the total cost area (TC) shrink to zero, but only the width of the voucher revenue area (R) shrinks to zero; the height of the voucher revenue area remains at b, the size of the unemployment benefit.

27 This is merely a possibility. There is nothing in our analysis that inevitably makes this happen.

28 Clearly, the positions of the TC and tc curves are interdependent. The greater the number of workers receiving the recruitment voucher, the greater is the

unemployment duration of the workers available to receive the training voucher (*ceteris paribus*). Thus the lower is the marginal revenue product of the workers receiving the training voucher and the lower is the training deadweight. Given that the former effect dominates the latter, this will raise the cost of the training voucher scheme for any given level of induced employment. In addition, training displacement will be lower as well, and this will raise the revenue from the training voucher scheme. In figure 6.8, the positions of the *R* and *TC* curves correspond to the optimal maximal training voucher and the positions of the *r* and *tc* curves correspond to the optimal maximal recruitment voucher.

29 The calculations build on the general approach outlined in Snower (1994).

30 See, for example, Layard, Nickell and Jackman (1991).

31 When firms are credit-constrained, this will under-state the effect of the voucher, since these firms do not have immediate access to the present value of the infinite stream.

32 This expression in fact over-states the present value, since we have ignored hiring and training costs.

33 The underlying regressions are run on annual data and the short-run elasticities thus cover the span of a year.

34 The elasticities for Canada, France, Germany, and the UK are taken from Bean, Layard and Nickell (1986).

35 See, for example, Alogoskoufis and Manning (1988) and Newell and Symons (1985).

36 As in the short-run exercise, the long-run labour demand elasticities are taken from Layard, Nickell and Jackman (1991), except for those of Canada, France, Germany and the UK, which are taken from Bean, Layard and Nickell (1986).

37 As in the short-run exercise, we set the displacement coefficients higher – at 0.9 – in the two countries in our sample (Austria and Switzerland). In contrast to the short-run exercise, however, the degree of nominal wage rigidity is not relevant to displacement in the long run.

38 The act of targeting, of course, may well create other difficulties, such as a rise in short-term unemployment or a displacement of current employees. In that case, we are replacing a serious social problem by a number of less serious problems.

39 In addition, if current employees would take the employment opportunities of the long-term unemployed into account at all, the value of these opportunities to them would be heavily discounted through time. For a formal case in favour of targeting, see, for example, Calmfors (1993).

40 I have argued that this is a particularly likely outcome in the short run.

41 In those countries (such as Spain) in which large segments of the labour market have extremely low labour turnover costs and where the costs of creating and closing firms is very low as well, there is a danger that employers may seek to exploit the voucher scheme by closing existing firms and creating new ones with subsidised employees. To avoid this form of displacement, it may be necessary to restrict the vouchers to firms that have already been in existence for a limited period of time (say, two years).

42 Specifically, let the Nash maximand be the product of (i) the difference between the employee's take-home pay and her fallback income, both of which are proportionately related to the subsidy (by assumption) and (ii) the difference

between the firm's profit and its fallback returns, both of which depend on the product wage. Then the subsidy can be factored out of the Nash maximand, leaving the negotiated wage paid by the firm (the solution to the Nash maximisation problem) unchanged. A form of this argument, applied to taxes on labour, is found in Layard, Nickell and Jackman (1991, p. 108).

43 Three large-scale experiments have been undertaken in Illinois, New Jersey and Washington State. See, for example, Woodbury and Spiegelman (1987).

REFERENCES

Alogoskoufis, G. and A. Manning, 1988. 'On the persistence of unemployment', *Economic Policy*, 7, 427–69

Bean, C.R., P.R.G. Layard and S.J. Nickell, 1986. 'The rise in unemployment: a multi-country study', *Economica*, **53**, S1–S22

Byrne, A., 1993. 'An evaluation of JOBSTART', *EMB Report*, 7/93 Canberra: Department of Employment, Education and Training (November)

Calmfors, L. 1993. 'Macroeconomic effects of active labour market programs – the basic theory', *Seminar Paper*, **541**, Institute for International Economic Studies, Stockholm

Calvo, G., 1979. 'Quasi-Walrasian theory of unemployment', *American Economic Review, Papers and Proceedings*, **69**, 102–7

Felli, L. and A. Ichino, 1988. 'Do marginal employment subsidies increase re-employment probabilities?', *Labour*, **2**, 63–89

Layard, P.R.G., S.J. Nickell and R.A. Jackman, *Unemployment: Macroeconomic Performance and the Labour Market*, Oxford: Oxford University Press

Lindbeck, A. and D.J. Snower, 1988. *The Insider–Outsider Theory of Employment and Unemployment*, Cambridge, MA: MIT Press

1990. 'Demand- and supply-side policies and unemployment: policy implications of the insider–outsider approach', *Scandinavian Journal of Economics*, **92**, 279–305

McDonald, I.M. and R. Solow, 1981. 'Wage bargaining and employment', *American Economic Review*, **71**, 896–908

Newell, A. and J. Symons, 1985. 'Wages and unemployment in OECD countries', *Discussion Paper*, **219**, London School of Economics, Centre for Labour Economics

Shapiro, C. and J.E. Stiglitz, 1984. 'Equilibrium unemployment as a worker discipline device', *American Economic Review*, **74**, 433–44

Snower, D.J., 1994. 'Converting unemployment benefits into employment subsidies', *American Economic Review, Papers and Proceedings*, **84**, 65–70

Stiglitz, J.E., 1985. 'Equilibrium wage distributions', *Economic Journal*, **95**, 595–618

Weiss, A., 1980. 'Job queues and layoffs in labour markets with flexible wages', *Journal of Political Economy*, **88**, 526–38

Woodbury, S.A. and R.G. Spiegelman, 1987. 'Bonuses to workers and employers to reduce unemployment: randomized trials in Illinois', *American Economic Review*, **77**, 513–30

Discussion

DAVID T. COE

Dennis Snower has written a very useful chapter, one that should be studied carefully by policy makers searching for practical measures to reduce high levels of unemployment. The chapter presents a concrete proposal that takes seriously the problem of policy design. The proposed Benefit Transfer Programme (BTP) is voluntary and relatively simple. The programme aims to reduce long-duration unemployment by allowing individuals who have been unemployed for a minimum period of time to convert their unemployment insurance benefits into either recruitment or training vouchers. In this way, it would remove disincentives to job search in unemployment insurance schemes and replace them with incentives for hiring and training. Moreover, the programme is designed to be neutral with respect to government expenditures; and to the extent that the programme reduces unemployment and thereby enlarges the tax base, it will increase government revenues. These are all attractive features that suggest that the programme would be political viable.

Although I see no fundamental problems with the proposed programme, there are a number of issues that could be usefully clarified. It is not clear, for example, how one ensures that the total cost of the voucher scheme is the same as the cost of benefits it replaces. This is because the voucher is not linked to the individual's actual unemployment benefits, the value of which is readily calculated, but rather to benefits broadly interpreted 'to include forgone taxes and the full spectrum of welfare state benefits falling on the unemployed', which are difficult if not impossible to calculate *ex ante*. Linking the vouchers to actual unemployment benefits would make it easy to control costs. But in this case there is a risk that the value of the voucher would be too small to have much of an impact, since benefits generally taper off as unemployment duration increases and since the programme is targeted at the long-duration unemployed.

If the value of the voucher is not linked directly to the benefits the individual long-term unemployed person would otherwise be entitled to, it will be much more difficult to monitor the costs of the programme, partly because it is voluntary. In this case the programme would necessarily involve a redistribution of benefits among those receiving benefits, which would not necessarily be a bad thing. In 1993–4, European governments spent more than 3 per cent of GDP – roughly the size of structural budget deficits – on labour market programmes, about two-thirds of which were on passive income support to the unemployed (OECD, 1994: IMF, 1995). This suggests ample scope for redirecting some of these expenditures to programmes that might be more effective in terms of reducing unemployment. Changes to other benefit programmes or levels of benefits might, however, have implications for the political viability of the programme if, for example, the unemployment benefits of the short-duration unemployed had to be reduced to finance the programme.

Defining the relevant benefits broadly also raises the issue of which elements from the full spectrum of welfare benefits an individual would have to forgo in order to receive the vouchers. Here there may be a trade-off: transferring too few benefits may reduce the funds available to finance the programme, while transferring too many benefits might create important disincentives to participate.

The value of the voucher gradually falls with job tenure, which raises the question of the long-run effects. It seems clear that the long-run effectiveness of the programme will be greater the more participants acquire skills through on-the-job training or through participation in training programmes. For this reason, Dennis Snower proposes that employers would receive large vouchers if they could prove that the funds were devoted to training new recruits. Although all would agree that expanded training and training programmes have the *potential* to increase skills and employability, it is difficult to find many examples where government-sponsored training programmes have had much of an impact. The proposal, however, would have enterprises themselves actively involved in the provision of the training, as in the German apprenticeship system, and this increases the likelihood that the training aspect of the programme would be successful.

The cyclical features of the programme are attractive, but it may be an over-statement to say that the programme would phase itself out at full employment. For this to be true, *all* long-duration unemployment would have to be cyclical, whereas the bulk of long-duration unemployment is likely to be structural. The programme is meant to correct some of the existing policy distortions that are reflected in long-duration unemployment, and thereby lower the equilibrium level of unemployment. But as long as there remains some structural long-duration unemployment, the policy would continue to operate even at full employment.

An inevitable aspect of the programme is that there will be a ‘notch’ at the unemployment duration at which the employment or training voucher kicks in. As unemployment approaches this point, workers will reduce their search intensity. This is another part of the deadweight loss, since with greater search intensity at below-the-threshold level of unemployment duration, some workers who receive the subsidy would have obtained a job in the absence of the programme.

There is a potential problem of acceptance of the programme by the unemployed and by employers because of signalling or stigma considerations. This issue has been very important in US experiments with wage subsidies, although Dennis Snower argues that it is likely to be much less important in Europe. Even if an individual's unemployment history is, in principle, public knowledge in Europe, employers nevertheless do not know the actual unemployment duration of an applicant. This may be particularly the case for unskilled or semi-skilled hires, and providing a subsidy or a voucher may thereby communicate undesirable information. In this case, the programme may not be taken up by a significant proportion of the unemployed, and those who do use the vouchers may face a reduce probability of being hired for signalling or stigma reasons.

All industrial countries have the problem of a large stock of low-skilled, one-skilled, or 'old-technology-skilled' workers that are unemployed. In the long run, the solution, of course, is better education, training and retraining. But education and training systems can only be changed or reformed slowly, and these reforms are unlikely to affect greatly the stock of low-skilled workers in the short run. Given that there is no easy way to transform low-skill, low-productivity workers into high-skill, high-productivity workers, it must be better to have policies that provide incentives for the unemployed to search, for employers to hire, and for training, as does Dennis Snower's BTP, than to have policies that passively provide income support for the unemployed. It is easier to achieve the objective of getting people into good-paying jobs from a starting position of a low-paying job than from a starting position of unemployment.

Having said this, the ballpark estimates of the impact on unemployment of BTPs given in tables 6.1 and 6.2 seem very large for many countries. Although I suspect that the impacts of a BTP are likely to be considerably smaller, such a programme could be an important component of the more broad-based, fundamental labour market reform that I believe is needed to reduce structural unemployment by substantial amounts, especially in Europe, but also in North America and Oceania. One of the reasons that broad-based, fundamental labour market reform is needed is because there has been no single cause of the rise in unemployment in Europe over the past two decades, suggesting that actions may be needed in a number of areas. Moreover, complementarities across rigidities suggest that a piecemeal approach to reform, such as the reforms that have been enacted in most European countries during the 1980s and early 1990s, may fail. High levels of structural unemployment and long-duration unemployment have now existed for so long and become such a common feature of the economic landscape in Europe, that a fundamental break – a regime change – is needed to change attitudes to work and unemployment.

REFERENCES

IMF, 1995. *World Economic Outlook* (October), Washington, DC: IMF, 38–42
OECD, 1994. *Employment Outlook*, **55** (June), Paris: OECD

Discussion

JACQUES H. DREZE

In July 1993, a bright girl graduated from the Business School at Louvain-la-Neuve and set off to spend the summer in Santander, expecting to upgrade her knowledge of Spanish and thereby her career prospects. Before departure, she routinely registered as a job seeker. Upon her return, she was offered a three-month job as research assistant, with an understanding that she could simultaneously prospect the job market. She accepted and reported at the local employment office. To her surprise, a well-meaning counsellor told her:

- 'You should not take that temporary job. Please think about your future!'
- What about my future?'
- 'It hinges on unemployment benefits. If you do not find another job within three months, you will lose your entitlement.[1] Besides you need to remain unemployed for six consecutive months in order to qualify for the latest Benefits Transfer Programme – which is fast becoming a prerequisite for the first job.'

Unlike the fable about 'the farmer, his son and the Jaguar', this is a true anecdote – down to the words 'think about your future'. The Youth Employment Programme of the Belgian government very much resembles the Snower BTP proposal in chapter 6, on a targeted basis. Firms hiring a worker of less than 26 years of age who has been unemployed for six months or more is exempted from employers' social insurance contributions for $2\frac{1}{4}$ years.[2] This amounts to roughly two-thirds of one year's wage costs. Actually the programme is suggestive of what the Snower proposal might look like after the transition from an academic paper to administrative guidelines. The sophisticated fine-tuning would be pruned out – leaving us with an employment subsidy to any firm hiring a long-term unemployed (below 26 years of age in the Belgian case).

The Belgian 'Youth Employment Programme' has been in effect 18 months, and has covered some 73,000 young workers. This is roughly half the eligible stock. The impact on youth unemployment is unquestionably positive. The number of young unemployed has decreased by some 6000 units, which is small in relation to the 73,000 hirings. This suggests that many of these hirings would have taken place anyhow, i.e. 'deadweight' (in Snower's terminology) is probably substantial. But it is recognised that youth unemployment would have increased, in the absence of the programme. Also, it is interesting to note that outflow from unemployment into employment has not decreased, for young workers not eligible under the programme (because they had not been unemployed for six months or more). This suggests limited 'displacement' among the young.

These bits of information bear loosely on some of the open issues connected with the proposals by Dennis Snower in chapter 6 or by Richard Layard in chapter 11 in this volume. A major issue is the evaluation of the extent to which subsidised jobs displace existing or potential jobs instead of being net additions. Snower is less fanciful than Layard, who asserts that displacement is nil on theoretical grounds, or the discussant Minford, who posits a 300 per cent displacement effect. It is too early to conclude about the overall displacement associated with the Belgian Youth Unemployment Programme – but there is scope for a detailed study. The data exist – but need to be assembled and processed. And this Belgian programme is definitely not a unique instance. Empirical research should be encouraged on these issues, for which theory is of limited usefulness.

The quantitative assessment of potential employment effects in Snower's tables 6.1 and 6.2 follow from (13) (pp. 186–7), which is reasonably well approximated by

$$\frac{\Delta N}{N} = \frac{\eta}{u}$$

where η is the wage-elasticity of employment and the factor $\frac{1}{8}$ is the product of an adjusted replacement ratio, close to $\frac{1}{2}$, reflecting the size of the subsidies; an adjustment for displacement, set at $\frac{1}{2}$; and a coefficient θ called 'voucher effectiveness', set at $\frac{1}{2}$, and discussed in the paragraph following (7) (p. 182).

My main reservation about these calculations concerns the 'voucher effectiveness' coefficient θ. In the discussion following (7), Snower lists four reasons why vouchers may be less effective than wage reductions in stimulating employment. In a preliminary version of the chapter, the impact of the first three had been summarised in a coefficient equal to 1/2. The fourth reason, however, is recognised as the most important, namely the fact that vouchers are temporary, whereas wage elasticities of employment are meant to capture the impact of permanent reductions. Snower then attempts to compare the effectiveness of temporary ('one-period') and permanent wage reductions, and concludes from (8) (pp. 183–4) that the effect of a one-period reduction is equivalent to some 56 per cent of the effect of a permanent reduction. I do not regard that figure as plausible, and would rather use myself a figure like 15 per cent. The reason for the disagreement is that Snower's calculations bear on the effectiveness of wage reductions in general, not on the reduced effectiveness associated with the temporary aspect. I would thus suggest discounting the figures in tables 6.1 and 6.2 by a factor of three or so. Under that correction, the effects are still there – but their size seems more realistic.

Dennis Snower concludes his chapter with the question 'what is there to lose'? I do agree that there is much to gain, and little to lose by narrowing the gap between the cost of labour to firms and the opportunity cost to workers and society. I do, however, feel duty bound to echo the objection against the targeting of employment subsidies on long-term unemployed raised by our son Benoit, who runs a group of non-profit firms providing on-the-job training to young dropouts. The objection is simply that such targeted subsidies are not available to his trainees, who find themselves priced out of employment. The suggestion is to keep away from subtle targeting, which inevitably entails some undesired discrimination.

Targeting is bound to have mixed effects. On the one hand, it improves the efficiency of given expenditures; on the other, it introduces new distortions at the margin of the targeted groups. Because the proposed measures fall so much short of the objectives, I think that we need more ambitious programmes, that will naturally involve broader targeting. For instance, the proposal to eliminate social insurance contributions on low wages (see Drèze and Sneessens, chapter 8 in this volume) is a very broad form of targeting, with obvious advantages.

In the last resort, most employment subsidy programmes boil down to this: governments are aware of the existence of a sizable wedge between the private and social cost of specific types of labour; so they devise subsidies to reduce that wedge, and offer these subsidies on terms that contain the budgetary implications. One untested but intriguing approach would consist in creating a market for targeted subsidised jobs. A government could identify the target group: for instance, long-term unemployed, or young unemployed, but possibly also workers employed by non-profit organisations, or workers offering specific services like assistance to the elderly or urban maintenance. The government could then adjust the subsidy levels to reach a specified quantitative goal. A perfect illustration is the provision of temporary jobs for long-term unemployed, advocated by Layard in chapter 11. The level of the subsidies would need to be adjusted so as to create a suitable number of vacancies. If such a market could be made to function, we would learn about the opportunity cost of specific types of labour (the targeted ones), and about the elasticity of employment with respect to subsidies. The idea of a market is to avoid any kind of side-constraints other than the eligible types of labour and to aim for maximal transparency. No doubt, that is also the aim of proponents of the various schemes under discussion – a discussion that must be welcomed and encouraged.

NOTES

1 A Belgian student who registers as a job-seeker upon leaving school becomes entitled to benefits (at a reduced rate) after a waiting period of six months, with no requirement of previous employment. A person leaving a temporary job (hence not dismissed) of less than six months' duration is not entitled to benefits.

2 The exemption rate is 100 per cent in year 1, 75 per cent in year 2 and 50 per cent in year 3.

7 Wage subsidy programmes: alternative designs

EDMUND S. PHELPS

The *equilibrium* volume of joblessness in the advanced economies, though it has in some countries receded a little from its high in the 1980s, far exceeds the accustomed level of the early postwar decades. In the USA and the UK, for example, the natural unemployment rate has been estimated to be around $6\frac{1}{2}$ per cent in the mid 1990s. In France and Italy it stands around 8 per cent.[1] The bulk of this equilibrium rise in aggregate unemployment is adequately explained in terms of a broad-based slowdown in the demand for labour in the face of a lesser slowdown in the general wage level required for effective worker performance as the income from private wealth and especially social entitlements barely slackened; the increased tax wedge between employers' cost of labour and employees' net wage falls into a third category, as do restrictions on hiring and firing.[2]

As usually happens in slumps of macroeconomic origins, the *relative* position of disadvantaged workers – those who, for whatever reason, have poor earnings prospects over their entire lives, not just in their youth – has worsened alongside the aggregates. Joblessness is always heaviest among those workers at the lowest rungs of the labour market ladder, of course. (Although the disadvantaged, which are heavily drawn from racial minorities and recent immigrants, account for little of the unemployment in countries where they are a small proportion of the labour force, the unemployment *rate* among generally disadvantaged subpopulations tends to be much higher than the general unemployment rate in Europe as well as elsewhere.[3]) But when the general unemployment rate rises, even if the relative unemployment rate of disadvantaged workers falls a little or holds steady, which may be the normal pattern, a disproportionate share of the increased joblessness is piled onto those low-wage workers.[4] That is, the excess of the unemployment rate among the disadvantaged over the general unemployment rate is further increased. Also, when a structural decline in general labour demand contracts employment, the accompanying tendency toward reduced wage rates is apt to be more critical for disadvantaged workers, even if all wage rates fall equiproportionately. A great many of the very disadvantaged workers have so tenuous a connection with the labour market that the same small deterioration in wages (relative to wealth and welfare entitlements) or in job openings results in their abandoning the competition for jobs and wages in the market economy on a relatively large scale.

In addition, there is evidence to suggest that the disadvantaged have suffered a decline in the *relative* demand for low-wage labour and a rise in the *relative* tax wedge faced by low-wage workers.[5] Over the 1980s, the relative unemployment rate of disadvantaged workers (as defined by schooling) rose to a higher plateau in nearly every country, and the relative wage rates of low-wage workers declined markedly in all countries – severely in the USA and UK.[6]

In these same market economies, however, the government has open to it a range of means to achieve quickly a major improvement in the employment opportunities of the disadvantaged. A programme of subsidies – best offered in the form of tax credits, or allowances – to business enterprises for their employment of low-wage workers is one of the conspicuous market-based methods available to improve their lot. These subsidies may be called *employment subsidies* or *wage subsidies*. The latter term, though odd (we don't speak of 'price subsidies'), has the merit of suggesting that they would be geared to low-wage workers and would apply to the whole stock of such employees, not merely the inflow of new employees. Whatever we call these subsidies, they would supplement the total pecuniary benefit that enterprises derive from employing disadvantaged workers, thus compensating to a degree for their relatively low productivity.

The consequent stimulus to the demand for low-wage labour worker would have a combination of beneficial effects, pulling up the wage rate *and* driving down the unemployment rate of the lowest-paid workers in society – their unemployment shrinking more the less their wages responded to the tightened labour market. Hence the programme would *increase* the number of jobs open to the least advantaged, not decrease them as minimum-wage restraints tend to do. And the programme would increase the wage rates of *all* disadvantaged workers, not, as wage supplements to targeted workers do, increase them for workers covered by the programme while decreasing them for uncovered workers. By entering the labour market in this way, rather than interfering with it as wage restraints do, the government would be acting to solve simultaneously the *twin* problem of the least productive workers – the paucity of jobs available to them and the low wage rates those jobs pay.[7] Hence an unambiguous expansion in every disadvantaged person's choice set would result. Instituted on a serious scale, these subsidies would reverse the lost ground of those who have suffered most from the increased unemployment–wage slowdown syndrome rather than embark on programmes aimed at lowering joblessness and raising wages in general. Yet further argument is required if governments are to be persuaded to take this action.

This chapter addresses the two outstanding questions that this possibility raises. Section 1 takes up the question of principle: on what grounds should the government adopt any market-based demand-side method to raise the opportunities of the disadvantaged in this way – and why (design details aside) low-wage employment subsidies rather than some other government device to raise low-end labour demand? Section 2 takes up the question of design: is the subsidy best designed as an exemption from all or some payroll taxes up to some threshold level of the hourly wage rate, say, or is it better than the hourly subsidy be graduated, tapering off as the hourly wage increases?

1 The argument for a low-wage employment subsidy[8]

The general argument for a wage subsidy system can be founded on the notion of its external benefits.[9] A subsidy to employment of low-wage workers at enterprises would, of course, supplement the benefit to the enterprise using the low-wage labour, which is the labour's private marginal revenue productivity. The size of the subsidy would reflect society's implicit or explicit estimate of the social benefit from the extra employment of low-wage workers not already measured by the direct benefit to the enterprise making direct use of that labour – in short, the estimated gap between the social and the private benefit from increased employment of disadvantaged workers. With such a subsidy, society would be boosting the benefit to enterprises from employing a less productive worker by an amount that, to a degree, 'fills in' the deficiency in his or her ability, skill or attitude. Any argument for appreciably expanding the job prospects of the least productive workers and thus lifting their wage rates in the process can be translated into a dual argument showing the existence of a gap – a serious gap – between these two benefit levels, the social and the private.[10]

1.1 Three grounds for boosting low-wage labour demand

The main sources of an external benefit from higher demand for disadvantaged workers are readily identified.

1.1.1 Neighbourhood, or community, effects

The dismal wage rates of very disadvantaged workers and acute shortage of jobs have harmful effects on others – external diseconomies. A subsidy or other measure serving to increase the demand for disadvantaged labour in legitimate enterprises, in reversing these effects, would generate external economies.

The plight of very disadvantaged workers may spread like a contagion to others, nullifying advantages and worsening disadvantages. A culture quite distant from that of commercial enterprise may develop in which norms of responsibility and self-reliance are not passed along. When parents and older relatives are frequently unemployed, and hence often dependent on welfare, a child is not provided with the role models from which to acquire the habits of initiative and responsibility needed for realising his or her potential in legitimate business. Disadvantaged workers lacking access to business enterprises are unable to transmit to their children any knowledge of the ways of the economic mainstream.

A drug culture may also develop out of these conditions. Curiously, this effect may be stimulated by the welfare state. To be very disadvantaged in a society rich enough to put up a comfortable safety net means that there is rather little distance between the outcome you can hope for by knocking yourself out and the average expectation for people in your situation; so a sense of powerlessness – little power to do better – must overtake many of the disadvantaged. In any case, drug use is apt to be high in communities heavily populated by the disadvantaged and to spread to those who might not succumb to it or be introduced to it were it not already widespread. (Drug addiction turns some users into suppliers recruiting new addicts to support the addiction.)

A culture of criminality may result as well. Then incidents of violence become common. As the bleak prospect of the disadvantaged reduces the value they put on their own lives, it also reduces the value they place on others' lives as well. It would be surprising if some of the disadvantaged, feeling they were being shown a lack of respect by society, did not seek 'respect' through the use of guns.

1.1.2 Widely held notions of equity

Another external benefit that would be conferred by a wage subsidy is the increased self-respect that people generally would derive from taking collective action through the government to remove or lessen a condition that violates their sense of justice. Virtually nowhere in the philosophical literature is it deemed just that those with only a meagre labour input to offer should receive as their reward only their marginal product – no matter how low. Most notions of fairness in the rewards to workers from their cooperation in the economy suggest that a 'fair shake' requires allocating to the disadvantaged a larger reward. Boosting the wage of the very disadvantaged by means of a wage subsidy, financed by a tax on the wages of high-wage workers or by a value added tax, appears to be the least inefficient – the most cost-effective – means of doing that.

In some conceptions of justice, the more fortunate will not want economic cooperation with others at terms that would (beyond some point at any rate) bring them a gain at the expense of the less fortunate. Ayn Rand, the novelist-philosopher usually placed far to the right, offers the image of a bus in which the less fortunate are given a free ride.[11] The more fortunate pass up any part of the gains from cooperation with the less fortunate, content with the same benefit net of cost obtainable without cooperation. By analogy, a society that reflected on the matter would want somehow to ensure that the disadvantaged as a whole, to the extent practicable at any rate, were rewarded with the 'marginal products' of all the *infra-marginal* persons, whom we can conceive as arriving serially – the first one contributing a lot, the next less, until the last one adds only the marginal product of the less fortunate, which in a perfect competition equilibrium would be the before-tax-subsidy wage.[12]

In John Rawls' world of collaborative production, the incentive effects of taxes and subsidies are taken into account.[13] Starting from a reference point of misguided over-taxation in the service of equality, Rawls' theory of justice would reform the tax structure, generally lowering rates and using the enlarged tax base to subsidise more heavily the wage of the least advantaged, to the point where the reward of the most disadvantaged workers is as large as possible; the accompanying gain to the advantaged is morally acceptable since it does not come at the expense of the disadvantaged. Less uncompromising moral observers than Rawls may be satisfied with *some* subsidy, but not one lifting the bottom wage rate as far as it can be made to go.

1.1.3 The waste of excessive unemployment

The third externality arises from the presence – even under equilibrium conditions – of job rationing, which creates a pool of involuntarily unemployed workers.[14] (The worker's unemployment is 'involuntary' in the sense that offering to work in one's normal sort of job at a lower wage would not help to obtain such a job; if the employer had wanted to pay her employees less she would have done it already – and the same applies to the labour union if it is the party setting the wage.) Low-wage workers are just as vulnerable to this unemployment as higher-wage employees, indeed perhaps more so. As a result, boosting the demand for low-wage employees – up to a point at any rate – yields a gain in the allocative efficiency of the economy, as involuntary unemployment is reduced.

Modern theory argues that firms report to above market-clearing wages (thus rationing the supply of jobs) in response to certain personnel problems. Various modern models determine an equilibrium volume of involuntary unemployment – more generally, an equilibrium path of unemployment, which may be moving (as foreseen) over time. The standard analysis refers to the special case in which all workers are homogeneous with respect to their ability and their job performance. The analysis shows that equilibrium entails a positive level of involuntary unemployment.[15] The argument begins by considering the possibility that, initially, wage rates have somehow been set by firms at just sufficiently low a level that there is no involuntary unemployment – the number of employees demanded at that wage is just large enough to take up all the workers who want to work, namely those in the labour force. In this initial situation, the firms will find a variety of problems with the performance of their employees: quitting before the cost of training can be recouped, shirking their duties, absenteeism and lateness, and so forth. The threat of dismissal for malfeasance would be ineffective since, in the favourable labour market situation, an employee can at once find a job somewhere else at the same wage (two such workers quitting or being fired can trade places at an unchanged wage). A contract involving the employee's payment of a deposit as a sort of bond indemnifying the firm in the event of quitting or non-performance would be problematic.[16] The only incentive-compatible solution is a decision by the individual firm to raise its wages on the theory that, if its employees enjoy a premium wage over what the market offers generally, they will then have something to lose in the event that they quit, are caught shirking, and so forth. The wage that is dictated by the necessity to provide employees with incentives (in a cost-effective dosage) may be called the *required* wage – as opposed to the wage the firms can afford to pay if they are to go on employing the current stock of employees, generally called the *demand* wage, or *affordable* wage.

Unemployment is generated as an equilibrium phenomenon as all firms hit upon the device of using wages as an incentive device. Then they cancel the beneficial effect – the average firm cannot succeed in paying wages above the average. Further, since each firm now must offer a higher wage just to stay as competitive as it was originally – to pay as much as the others – it must regrettably conclude that the cost of hiring employees has gone up. The side-effect of the wage escalation, then, is that firms must cut back their employment, thus creating a pool of unemployed workers who cannot find work at the elevated wage. This reaction has an equilibrating effect on the labour market. At a sufficiently enlarged unemployment rate, the behavioural problems facing the firms will have moderated enough that firms are no longer driven to set a wage above the level at which they can afford to keep all of their current employees. At this equilibrium volume of unemployment, the unemployed workers can only wait for their 'lucky number' to be drawn by chance, as firms hire new employees to replace those who die or move or are fired.

The heterogeneity of workers' earning power enriches the picture considerably. The unemployment rate of disadvantaged workers will tend to be higher – perhaps much higher – than the general unemployment rate. One factor operating to raise the relative unemployment rate of the more disadvantaged workers is the *comparatively* large cushion provided for the low-wage worker by family, friends, the community, and government-supplied entitlements – all elements of what sociologists call social capital – since these sources tend to meet minimum needs, not wants that are in proportion to a worker's normal wage.[17] The greater quitting and shirking by the disadvantaged that this situation causes will drive each enterprise to raise its wage further as an additional inducement to improve the low-wage employees' performance, and the resulting escalation of the going wage will in turn induce employers to cut back further their unemployment of these workers. The equilibrium unemployment rate of the disadvantaged is therefore increased, making it higher than the unemployment rate of the advantaged workers.[18] A second factor is the asymmetric position of workers in the bottom rungs of the ladder. When a high-wage worker is observed shirking or absent or late, the employer can punish him in myriad ways – by cancelling a promotion or by a demotion. There is a cost in lost job satisfaction whether or not there is any pecuniary penalty. But when a permanently very-low-wage worker is caught shirking or absent or late, the employer does not have credible ways to make an object lesson out of his behaviour other than to dismiss him. This suggests that the firm, in its moves to give its employees something to lose if caught performing badly, is driven to offer the low-skill employees a higher wage relative to the market-clearing level than the corresponding wage that is optimal to offer the high-skilled employees.[19] Third, an employee who for whatever reason loses his job can make himself available over the entire range of job openings from the previous level on down, which means that an unemployed worker who had a high wage has a wider range of job prospects and hence is likely to spend a shorter time in the unemployment pool than a worker whose previous jobs have only been at the low end.

This view accords with the impressions of social observers who see in disadvantaged workers a low attachment to jobs, hence an above-average turnover rate and above-average rates of absenteeism and other indicators of poor performance. In the present model, however, this behaviour is not the result of a difference of culture. It is a function of the low wage they are offered relative to the non-wage income, pecuniary and in-kind, available to them from a variety of sources – their own assets and, more important in most cases, the social capital and welfare entitlements to which they have access. One could also say that the 'pathology' of the poor here is a result of the ballooning of non-wage income relative to the wage available to the disadvantaged. This factor intensified in the 1980s when, in a great many countries, there was an absolute decline in the real wage rates of low-wage workers without any accompanying decline in non-wage income.

1.2 Low-wage subsidies versus other measures

Of course, employment subsidies are not the only instrument for reducing the unemployment of disadvantaged workers (and reducing their non-participation in the labour force). Let us review some of the possibilities. Two of them are supply-side approaches.

In countries where low-end wage rates have been forced up by minimum-wage legislation, a simple step to that end would be to lower or abolish the wage restraint, thus causing fewer low-end workers to be 'priced out of the market'.[20] We need not debate whether this would be moral progress or regress. The main point must be that, upon doing such a thing, only the guise of the programme would be altered: it would still be necessary to raise the demand for low-wage labour in order to remedy the external diseconomies left by the other source sources – neighbourhood effects of very low rewards from work and the inequity in rewards for those best-rewarded beyond what could be defended by the 'trickle down' effect on wages at the low end. (To put the matter even-handedly: it is not an acceptable solution of the wage problem to restrict employment opportunitics, as the Europeans tend to do, just as it is not an acceptable solution of the unemployment problem to let wages drop to their free market level, as the Americans have done.)

A not greatly dissimilar approach is to prune the welfare system.[21] A welfare reform can expand employment most strongly if it is directed at those points where it undermines the employability of disadvantaged workers. Reducing the size or duration of unemployment insurance benefits is a conspicuous candidate. Such measures would operate through the ratio of non-wage income to the wage to bolster the incentives of the less advantaged employees to resist temptations to quit, shirk, and the rest. An evident drawback of relying exclusively on shrinking or dismantling the welfare system is that the influx of workers into the labour force (and the greater eagerness of unemployed workers to find work in a hurry) would tend to reduce low-end wage rates in absolute size. Another difficulty is that persuading the electorate to accept large cutbacks in their cherished welfare programmes will require voters to look at these programmes from a new perspective, and that could take several years. For both these reasons it would be prudent to seek a policy mix containing a 'carrot', not simply a 'stick'.

There are three broad classes of demand-side measures that, each in its own way, would operate to raise *both* wage rates and job openings for disadvantaged workers. These measures work by elevating the importance of work and overcoming the attractions of 'welfare'. But not all of them are very attractive or very powerful.

- One demand-side method of raising both the employment and wages of low-wage workers is to make use of *indirect* subsidies to low-wage labour in the form of public expenditure programmes to redirect labour demand toward the disadvantaged. Today, no trained economist imagines that the government can contrive to reduce unemployment to any desired (positive) number, as Keynesian analysis used to hold. However, it is a standard neoclassical exercise to sift out some grains of truth in the old Keynesian dogma. Insofar as the government contrives to step up spending on comparatively labour-intensive goods, such as street sweeping and national park monitoring, there surely is a positive real wage effect; and in some models there would also result as a side-effect an increase of the employment rate as well. By tilting the extra public expenditure more toward the least skilled, and hence the lowest earners, the government can ensure that the wages pulled up are disproportionately those at the bottom end of the distribution.

  The weightiest objection to that method of driving up the wage rates and employment rates of the very disadvantaged, however, is its poor cost-effectiveness. Another objection is that it would not be acceptable simply to hire disadvantaged people and 'warehouse' them in make-work activities aimed simply at removing them from unemployment and non-employment, with whatever upward pull of their wage rates occurs as a by-product. The objective is to integrate disadvantaged workers more fully and intensively into the same world of work that the advantaged workers inhabit, not to draw them off into reservations or camps. But if the projects for which disadvantaged workers are to be employed have the look of normal public-sector activities, these projects will hire capital and land as well as labour, and hire advantaged workers as well as disadvantaged workers. The efficaciousness of these activities for the relative employment and wage levels of disadvantaged workers could turn out to be very nearly nil.

Another objection to such a method of driving up wages at the bottom of the distribution is that, absent some suitable mechanism for doing it, the additional public expenditure would not be apt to have a very high value. It is not so much that the marginal utility of an additional dollar of expenditure in the public sector, even if optimally directed, would not be as high as the corresponding marginal utility of a dollar of expenditure in the private sector; the situation may well be the reverse precisely because there is so much inefficiency in the allocation of public resources. (Consider an extra dollar of gun control.) The question is whether the appropriate average of the marginal utilities of the various goods provided by the public sector would be up to the level of the corresponding average marginal utility in the private sector. On the pork-barrel theory of over-taxation and over-expenditure on vested-interest groups, perfected by the Scandinavians, we must take the *actual* marginal utility of public expenditure (when the extra dollar of expenditure is divided up as it would actually be) to be a good deal lower than that of private expenditure. So public expenditure as an instrument for higher real wages at the bottom of the distribution would require increasing an expenditure level that is already too high for economic efficiency. To put it simply, the legislators have already bloated the public sector with army bases and shipyards and the like, with a view to pulling up the lowest wages and thus buying votes at a low price; doing still more of that kind of thing would be quite expensive in terms of the inefficiency added, so one wants to find another instrument not already in heavy use.

The final objection is that it is not clear that an institutional mechanism could be put in place that would cause legislators systematically to upgrade in their evaluation those projects that a board of economists rated high in labour-intensiveness and to downgrade those projects scoring low on this criterion. It could not ever be demonstrated that the national legislature was duly weighing the board's adjustment allowance in its final decisions.

- Another method is to make across-the-board reductions in the tax burden on employment, particularly that part in the form of payroll taxes (and income taxes which in practice fall disproportionately on labour income), through the substitution of increased value added taxation. This method works by pulling up the demand wage in real terms – the real wage that firms can afford to offer. (If such a stimulus to the demand wage were engineered through a cut in the value added tax, neglecting how the revenue loss is to be made up, the real value of non-wage incomes would be lifted in the same proportion; then, in some models, the real wage required for a cost-effective level of performance by employees would be increased by as much as the demand wage, and there would be no salutary effect on unemployment. In contrast, the wage subsidy would not pull up non-wage incomes, so it would not push up the required wage; thus the equilibrium unemployment rate would be reduced.) The subsidy can be financed by a tax on consumption and thus on wealth, or non-wage income. Such a tax will not entirely undo the benefits of the subsidy, since some of the consumption tax – in the form of a value added tax with exemptions for production for investment or for export – will fall on the existing non-wage incomes of retired persons and of workers who have accumulated some assets but are still working.

This is a policy option of comparatively great appeal on the European continent where the burden of taxation on employment is extraordinarily high and where the value added tax mechanism is already in place. yet the power of this fiscal switch from payroll to value added taxes is not likely to be enormous, since it depends on how far the value added tax shrinks that part of workers' real non-wage income not exempt from the value added tax – not a 'base' of great size.

- The demand-side action that can meet the problem with the greatest precision is to subsidise the employment of *low-wage* workers. In stimulating the demand for disadvantaged workers the subsidies would reduce the unemployment rate of those workers in conditions of labour market equilibrium. In tightening the market for low-wage labour it would tend to push up the lower wage rates – but not by so much as to undo the expansion of employment.

It is right to place the emphasis on encouraging the employment of the less advantaged, since that is where the greatest inefficiency seems to lie and also where the problem of lagging wage rates in recent decades is greatest. This emphasis on low-wage employment is crucial in the USA where the more disadvantaged workers are now suffering from a huge disadvantage in comparison to that in other countries, and are becoming increasingly marginalised from the legitimate market economy. It seems that this is also the locus of the problem in Europe as well, though minimum-wage legislation and union scales operating to force up wage rates at the low end serve to disguise it – with Italy being a seeming exception, since much of its joblessness is 'youth unemployment' and this unemployment is rather broadly based over the population.

1.3 Financing low-wage employment subsidies

One or more ways of financing low-wage employment subsidies must be specified if we are to be able to assess a complete picture of the idea. One possible means of finance is a tax on the employment of high-wage workers. Then pay rates would be increased in that part of the labour market where the unemployment rate is highest and therefore where the level of inefficiency is greatest. The decrease in the pay rates of the more advantaged workers would generate little or no increase in the unemployment of those workers, since their employer is able to encourage their attachment and performance through the establishment of selection criteria for promotion that motivate employees rather than through high wages. Furthermore, any increase in the unemployment rate of the more advantaged is likely to weigh less in efficiency terms that the decrease in the unemployment rate of the less advantaged since the latter (the unemployment rate of the less advantaged) was initially far more excessive than the former (the unemployment rate of the more advantaged).

The other leading possibility is to finance the wage subsidy through a value added tax. That tax, taking as hypothetically given the subsidies and the many other sorts of government outlays that this tax and the other taxes finance, is neutral for the aggregate unemployment rate and for its components. (At least that tends to be more nearly the result the more nearly the tax falls on non-wage income – but free hospital treatments, fire brigade rescues of the cat, and other non-wage income in kind evidently escape such a tax.) The reason is that the expenditure tax lowers the real value of wages and of non-wage incomes in equal proportion, thus not lowering the ratio of wage income to non-wage incomes in equal proportion, thus not lowering the ratio of wage income to non-wage income of the more advantaged workers as the tax on their employment would do and hence not pushing up their unemployment.

2 Employment subsidy schemes

Economists have long been temperamentally inclined to entertain the idea of subsidies to improve the terms obtained by the working poor. But there has been astoundingly little systematic analysis of the concrete forms that subsidisation might take. What to subsidise, and how to design that subsidy? This section will illustrate the design of graduated subsidy schemes and it will take up a relatively realistic programme of this kind in order to get a sense of how much it would cost to achieve a specified increase in the lowest wage rates, leaving aside the supply side responses and consequent effects that would result. We will then go on to examine some alternative schemes in less detail, reflecting on their relative merits and drawbacks.

2.1 The graduated subsidy scheme

The most direct public subsidy to pull up the rewards of disadvantaged workers, of course, is a payment that subsidises the *employment* of low-wage workers in the enterprise sector of the economy – private enterprises and perhaps state-owned enterprises. A firm that has low-paid workers in its employ would then benefit both from the productivity of those workers, as before, and from the subsidy payment which each of those employees would entitle the firm to receive. Hence the after-subsidy marginal revenue productivity of low-wage labour would be increased at the firm. If, contrary to the spirit of our model of unemployment just summarised, we were to take the amount of unemployment and labour-force participation as invariant to (or, in the jargon, perfectly inelastic with respect to) the demand wage – the wage rate that firms can afford at a given employment level – the market wage rate would be bid up by precisely the increase in the after-subsidy marginal revenue productivity; if instead employment exhibits some elasticity, though a finite elasticity, the result will be some increase of the wage rate and some increase in the level of employment of the working poor. Purely for purposes of calculation, I will take employment to be constant at all wage-rate levels in the analysis below. (Calculating the effect on subsidy outlays and the effect on tax revenues of the induced change of employment does not raise any conceptual questions that would need addressing.)

How might such a wage-subsidy scheme be designed? This is an interesting question as it raises the not-unfamiliar problem of incentives to evade the intent of the subsidy law through false reports on the books, much as the income tax creates incentives to earn unreported income. The design task of the government is to achieve the desired effect of the subsidy programme at a cost that is tolerably close to the minimum possible, making some allowance for additional bookkeeping costs at firms and additional monitoring costs of the government.

2.1.1 Two purely pedagogical examples[22]

Let us first work with hypothetical data. For illustrative purposes let us take \$7 an hour as the level to which we wish to drive the wage of the bottom group. (We might imagine that a minimum wage law survives and that it forbids firms from paying less than $7 an hour.) If the government provides a subsidy of $4 an hour, then no worker will be hired (under full compliance) whose marginal revenue productivity excluding the subsidy is less than $3 an hour. So the relevant population of workers here is those with a productivity of $3 an hour or higher. Having in mind that the employment of such workers in the USA at the time of writing (1990) is around 120 million, and putting together odd bits of information on the distribution of the labour force by wage, I will suppose there to be about 5 million workers in the $3–4 an hour category, another 5 million in the $4–5 dollar an hour category, and so forth – a more or less flat distribution at the low end of the scale.

It is instructive to begin with an example of a design that is badly flawed. Imagine a subsidy scheme in which the government stands ready to make up the difference between $7 an hour and the amount the firm pays out of its pocket to those of its employees receiving less than $7; that is, an employee costing the firm $3 an hour would cause the government to contribute $4 an hour, an employee whom the firm pays $4 out of its own pocket would produce a subsidy payment of $3, an employee that costs the firm $5 would occasion a $2 subsidy, and so forth. Then these low-paid workers would all find their wage rates jumping to $7. *If* it were true that firms would not cheat in response to the temptations created by such a scheme, its cost would be minimal: a $4 subsidy per hour times 5 million workers times 2000 hours a year, hence $40 billion per year, for the workers in the bottom wage interval; plus $3 per hour times 5 million workers times 2000 hours, hence $30 billion per year, for the workers in the next wage interval, and so forth. This series of $40, $30, $20, and $10 adds up to a bill of $100 billion per year. Not much in a $6 trillion economy! But there is a design flaw. A firm will now have an incentive to reclassify a $4 worker as a $3 worker and put in a claim for an extra dollar of subsidy to be able to continue the employee's wage at $7. The employee will not be hurt, and might not even be informed, and the firm will go on enjoying the employee's services, but for an increased profit at the expense of the government and hence the taxpayer. So this programme is not incentive-compatible and therefore must be presumed infeasible.

The optimal wage-subsidy scheme must be compatible with the incentive of firms to abuse it by false claims of large numbers of workers in their employ who are not worth paying much out of their own pockets. If it cannot be cheat-proof it must at least compromise with first-best principles in order to dampen the degree of cheating. It will illustrate the form that an optimal wage subsidy scheme takes, I believe, to consider the example in which, descending to lower and lower paid employees, with each decrease of \$1 in the out-of-pocket pay per hour to a worker the government responds with an increase of only \$½. Since the government is not making up the whole of the difference in the firm's out-of-pocket expenditure, the firm does not gain an addition to profit (per hour of this category of workers) equal to the whole of the reduction in its expense; the firm gains only the \$½ paid by the government. (Had the government responded instead with \$¾, the firm would have gained that much instead.) But to achieve a genuine gain the firm will have to claim that its out-of-pocket expense is less \$1 an hour, to obtain the increased subsidy, while at the same time it will have to have to make some manoeuvre to benefit the employee if, as I suppose, it continues to be necessary to ensure that the employee receives the same total compensation (including what comes indirectly from the government) as before. One such manoeuvre is an under-the-table wage payment to the employee to make up the shortfall in total compensation that would otherwise result since the government itself has not made up the whole of the \$1 reduction claimed; while claiming to be paying \$1 less the firm would actually be paying \$½ less and defrauding the government of \$½ in order to come up with the same total wage to the employee as before. It may be supposed that sufficiently strong penalties, taken with the fact that the gain is only \$½ for a whole dollar of misstatement, would be sufficient to deter all or most such cheating. The other manoeuvre that the firm could make would be to create non-pecuniary benefits worth precisely the missing \$½ of wages to the workers involved in the reclassification. 'I am being paid less, but the improved choice of lunches and the new flexible hours makes up for it,' workers might say. This manoeuvre has the advantage of legality, but if the firms were already offering the optimal package of pecuniary and non-pecuniary benefits to employees, the cost of a \$½ of benefits per hour might considerably exceed \$½; the distortions thus introduced would serve to limit the reclassification of workers.

How much would this hypothetically optimal plan cost the government per year? I will confine my calculations to the limiting case in which the deterrents to reclassification of employees just discussed, the penalties and the distortionary costs, actually serve to block all such reclassification. Then there will still be 5 million workers in the \$3 category and they will still occasion a subsidy of \$4 an hour for 2000 hours a year to sustain their new target wage of \$7; the annual cost to the government is \$40 billion, as in the previous calculation. The next tranche of wage earners, those costing the firms \$4 an hour, will now receive a subsidy of \$3.50 per hour, not \$3 as under the unworkable scheme; the annual cost to the government here is $35 billion. The next category will receive a subsidy of $3 an hour, not the $2 called for by the incentive-incompatible scheme; the annual cost is $30. The series is $40, $35, $30, $25, $20, $15, $5. The total cost per annum to the government is $180 billion. That is hardly a daunting figure in a $6 trillion economy, either. But it has to be remembered that it is a lower bound on the true cost in one respect because it assumed that firms did not find it optimal to reclassify workers in view of the penalties and other costs of doing so. On the other hand, wage earners receiving as much as $9 an hour occasion some subsidy to their employers and hence receive some increase in their wage under this graduated subsidy scheme, so the nation's taxable income would be significantly increased and as a result some of the government subsidy outlay would find its way back in the treasury as tax revenue.

In one obvious respect a scheme making the subsidy rate taper off less gradually with higher and higher wage rates would, on a calculation such as the above, cost less. But that cost reduction has to be weighed against the cost increase that would come about from the consequently increased incentive of firms to reclassify employees into lower-paying categories. I am supposing the latter cost to outweigh the aforementioned cost reduction.

2.1.2 A realistic plan

A subsidy plan based on hourly wage rates is peculiarly vulnerable to employer fraud. In an effort to collect a larger subsidy, firms may report their part-time employees as having worked a larger number of hours than was the case in order to represent their hourly wage rate as correspondingly lower.[23]

Another observation about part-time work is pertinent here. Receiving a less low wage rate is less important to those who currently want only a small amount of earnings than it is to those who are at a stage where they depend on their current earnings for much of their current living expenses. A college student facing a low hourly wage rate has a lifetime of good earnings to look forward to, and a retired person facing a low wage rate may have accumulated a level of wealth sufficient to meet most ordinary expenses. In fact, most part-time employees at any given point in time soon move on to a full-time job.

Accordingly, it would seem to make sense to restrict the graduated employment subsidy to *full-time employees*. A worker the firm has paid would be recognised as a full-time employee only on evidence that the firm has paid into an employee pension plan for the worker and has paid medical insurance for the worker in the same way it has paid for the insurance of its employees generally. A part-time worker, in lacking these credentials, would not make the firm eligible for the employment subsidy.

Note also that there is a compelling reason for putting the employment subsidies in the form of a tax credit. We would not want to encourage the establishment of enterprises that produce nothing, and whose payrolls are nothing more than a pass-through, after administrative expenses and mark-ups reflecting frictions of entry, of the wage subsidies. The fundamental purpose of the employment subsidy programme proposed here is to draw disadvantaged workers into the mainstream of society, which must mean for the overwhelming majority of workers the enterprise sector of the market economy. The emergence of 'subsidy mills' whose only function is to pass through the subsidies, not to produce anything, would make a mockery of the programme. Furthermore, it is the enterprise sector – private enterprises and state-owned public enterprises – that has been hit with burdensome payroll taxes and which, in most countries, has exhibited the cutback of jobs over the past decade or two, not general government and the armed forces. For reasons of data availability, however, we will analyse the model plan with employment figures from *private* enterprise only. Of course, employment in public enterprises (such as the University of California) is quite small in the USA compared with that in private enterprises.

Let us now 'cost' the graduated subsidy plan, with the same 50 per cent of graduation, but stripped down to full-time private-enterprise workers. In the USA, according to estimates from the March 1990 *Current Population Survey*, among workers who were in a full-time private-sector job over the previous week, 3.6 million reported that they earned between \$4 and \$3.01. That amounts to wages of about \$7000 per year if the mean hourly earnings rate of these workers was at the mid-point of \$3.50. A subsidy to these workers at the hourly rate of \$3 amounts to \$6000 per year. The budget outlay for such subsidies to this group of workers is therefore \$21.6 billion per year. Table 7.1 tabulates this budget outlay and the outlays for the workers in the higher earnings rate levels in 1990. The total budget outlay is shown to be \$109.2 billion.

That estimate might appear to be a high cost. However, it must be viewed in proper perspective. It is about 1.6 per cent of the nearly \$6 billion dollar GDP around that time, and less than 2 per cent of the national income. It is only about *one-half* of the welfare system, and only *one-third* of government military outlays in 1990.

Furthermore, this figure is an estimate of the gross cost. We have not netted out the many savings in welfare outlays and in law enforcement expenditures that might reasonably be guessed to result from so transformative a change in the labour market conditions of the

Table 7.1 *Percentage differentials in real annual wages and salaries, males, 25–57, 1979–87, selected years*

Full-time workers		
Australia	*10–50*	*20–50*
1981	0.621	0.751
1985	0.605	0.748
Netherlands	*10–50*	*20–50*
1983	0.721	0.790
1987	0.704	0.792
Sweden	*10–50*	*20–50*
1981	0.733	0.829
1987	0.723	0.822
UK	*10–50*	*20–50*
1979	0.656	0.766
1986	0.594	0.714
USA	*10–50*	*20–50*
1979	0.446	0.608
1986	0.436	0.600
All workers		
Canada	*10–50*	*20–50*
1981	0.421	0.641
1987	0.353	0.600
France	*10–50*	*20–50*
1979	0.616	0.736
1984	0.567	0.698
USA	*10–50*	*20–50*
1979	0.409	0.589
1986	0.354	0.542

Source: Calculated from Gottschalk and Joyce (1992).

disadvantaged. In addition, this programme would – and should – be accompanied by cutbacks in several welfare programmes, since large numbers of the remaining beneficiaries of the system, though preferring on balance to stay a beneficiary, could afford to leave the programme without suffering the same increased hardship as would now be the case.

2.1.3 The excess-over-base employment variant

There may seem to be some unnecessary 'fat' in the model plan since it would subsidise some workers who would have survived on their previous wages and who would have remained employees until the normal retirement age. In the interest of cost-effectiveness it is natural to explore the merits and drawbacks of a variant of the above plan in which the subsidy is paid only for employment of low-wage workers in *excess* of the historical level in some base year, presumably the initial year of operation.

The advantage of this variant is that it can be expected to induce a wide number of enterprises to endure losses on infra-marginal employment up to some level in order to obtain the profit on the incremental employment that generates the subsidy and, taken alone, generates a profit as a result. A major drawback, in the judgement of some experts, is the hazard that a great many enterprises will set up new corporate units, whose base employment would be zero at all levels, that would hire away employees from previously existing corporate units within the broad enterprise. Levying a graduated tax on disemployment of low-wage workers would solve the problem if it were not that an enterprise may need to downsize in order to regain profitability, and if it must pay a tax to do so it may be forced to close, causing costly disruptions to resource allocation.

2.2 *A non-graduated subsidy scheme*

Here I want to discuss a wage-subsidy scheme having a somewhat different design principle. I had thought, judging from second-hand accounts, that this was the proposal made recently by Drèze and Malinvaud.[24] I had thought they were proposing simply to exempt all low-wage workers below a certain threshold from collection of social insurance contribution – thus, effectively, a tax credit that firms can apply against the sums they must pay in various payroll contributions. In fact, their proposal also calls for a linear tapering off, just as my example described. Nevertheless, the economics – and politics – of such a blunt instrument is very much worth discussing, even if it lacks illustrious paternity. Besides, it would not be surprising if eventually some government considered such a scheme.

One rationale for the graduation of the subsidy in my scheme was the supposition that *some* tapering off of the hourly subsidy rate rather than an abrupt fall-off might actually be efficient in the sense that the same subsidy to the lowest-paid could be achieved with a smaller aggregate subsidy outlay through a gradual decline of the subsidy rate than through a sudden cut-off. The reasoning was that by making concessions to higher-paid workers the government would dampen the incentive of firms to reclassify workers at lower wage rates (a sort of downgrading from the imperfect vantage point of the treasury agents) and might do so sufficiently to produce a net saving in the subsidy outlay. (Loosely put, the government would be paying a positive subsidy to more workers, but fewer workers would receive large subsidies.) There seems to be a presumption, in the present author's mind at any rate, that the optimal schedule of subsidies exhibits some graduation – some tapering.

There is, however, another possible rationale for graduation. It could be that without graduation there could arise the anomaly that over some range the higher-paid workers would not only suffer a reduction of their wage – more precisely, the pecuniary part of the compensation, which forms the base for calculating the hourly subsidy – as their employer reclassified them in a lower-wage category in order to reap the higher corresponding subsidy; the workers would fail to receive a sufficiently large increase in non-pecuniary benefits to compensate them for the reduction in pay. This anomaly appears to be theoretically impossible as long as the marginal revenue product of these workers is undiminished! Then they should always be able to do at least as well in the job market as they could prior to the subsidy which left them unbenefited. However, the increased employment of lower-wage workers, insofar as that is indeed the general equilibrium outcome, may have a 'substitution effect', *reducing* the marginal product of some workers at higher wage rates. In that event, there is no possibility that competition will keep up the wage rates of these higher-wage workers. Thus some workers could suffer absolute losses – perhaps quite a lot of workers, and perhaps significant losses at that. There is the further point that, even if there are no absolute losses, there is a political calculus that suggests the need to enlarge the set of workers who would benefit from the subsidy programme if it is to have the voter appeal that politicians would look for in a programme with significant budgetary implications. For this reason too, then, it seems to make sense that the subsidy rate be graduated, tapering off only at a deliberate rate.

Notwithstanding these points, which seem valid as far as they go, there is considerable attractiveness in the idea of an exemption from payroll taxes before a critical wage-rate threshold. First, regarding the optimality of graduation from a budgetary standpoint, there is the point that the optimal gradient may be very steep. If the subsidy optimally goes to zero very quickly, the greater administrative simplicity of an abrupt cut-off may weigh in the balance against graduation. Second, the notion that an increase in employment of very low-wage workers would reduce the marginal productivity of higher wage workers is just a theoretical possibility – one that is a favourite of opponents of wage subsidies. Theoretically it is just as possible that the marginal productivity of higher-wage workers will be *increased*.

The choice between a graduated scheme and a non-graduated one may be important – and, then, it may turn out not to be all that important. In any case, the matter deserves some further attention by interested economists.

2.3 *Other schemes*

A few other wage-subsidy schemes exist. A proposal was made some years ago by the American economist Robert Aliber for auctions through which to distribute employment subsidies.[25]

2.3.1 The subsidies auction scheme

The idea is to auction to the qualified enterprise making the highest bid a lump-sum grant – say, $1 million – to be used to finance employment subsidies. The enterprise winning the bidding is the one committing to subsidise equally the largest number of jobs out of the money provided by the grant. A firm willing to hire 500 new workers, hence to allocate the grant at the rate of $2000 per employee hired, would win over a firm committing to spread the grant over a lesser number of new workers. The ideal bid, not feasible in the presence of administrative costs, would create as much demand for labour as is consistent with prevailing minimum wage legislation or with trade union agreements over minimum pay.

The great advantage of this scheme is its simplicity. The rather important disadvantage is that the bids are expressed, operationally enough, in terms of new hiring. That leaves it open to the successful bidder to fire other people, using the subsidised recruits to substitute for them – a problem introduced earlier. Evidently there must be accompanying restrictions (rather like those envisaged in Snower's unemployment benefit transfer scheme (BTP), discussed below) to ensure that an enterprise winning a grant loses the stipend (the next year) in proportion to employment losses through firing. As Aliber recognised, the cost of administering such a programme would not be negligible, therefore, and would have to be weighed against the benefit.

Since there would be a temptation for the employer to induce her pre-existing employees to quit, so that she could substitute for them the new subsidised recruits and thus not add to the number of employees to be paid, it would seem necessary that employers also be required to deduct cumulative voluntary separations (net of hirees outside the subsidy programme) from cumulative subsidised hirees to arrive at the net hiring amount eligible for the subsidy. But, as noted earlier, such a netting of separations from hires could be evaded by the device of setting up a new corporate unit that does the hiring, the downsizing in the old unit presumably going untaxed.

This would mean that if, to take a simple case, just one group of new employees is hired under the subsidy programme, the net increase in eligible employment will steadily erode, as separations mount up, with time approaching zero. But the remaining stock of those recruited will not be approaching zero so fast, since their separations are drawn solely from among themselves while the firm's separations figuring in the net employment amount are the aggregate separations. Thus the amount of the effective subsidy is attenuated by normal dismissals and separations. Maybe this is a good feature, so that the budgetary outlay is gradually self-extinguishing. However, the feature suggests that the subsidy would have to be several times larger at first than its desired average size.

A number of other problems of this kind must be thought through before it can be concluded that this kind of scheme, by virtue of its apparent simplicity, is at all preferable to the graduated scheme, which, despite its own administratively awkward features, possesses a great deal of transparency: you know rather exactly what you are getting in terms of an elevation of the demand price for the least-productive labour.

2.3.2 The fixed-subsidy scheme

This brief glance at alternative designs of a wage subsidy would not be complete without acknowledging what is, from the standpoint of simplicity at least, the most attractive scheme of all: a fixed subsidy paid for every employee in the firm's ongoing workforce to be financed by a proportional tax on the firm's wage bill. As in the case of the graduated wage subsidy discussed above, if financed by a tax on high-wage employment, the *net* addition to payroll taxes is equal to zero, but the tax/subsidy redistributes the gross taxes collected in favour of the low end of the distribution.

Some effects of this scheme have been studied by Richard Jackman and Richard Layard, using a model largely derived from that by Steven Salop.[26] In this model, the effect of the proportional tax on firms' wage bills, taken alone, is neutral for the natural rate, the pay firms offer dropping by just enough to finance the tax without any need to reduce the number of jobs offered; the absence of income from wealth accounts for this result. On the other hand, the *per capita* subsidy to workers that the revenues collected serve to finance operates to reduce the relative wage that firms desire at a given unemployment rate to dampen the quit rate. The effect is to reduce the natural rate of unemployment and reduce also the wage. It is good to have this analysis since one's intuition might not have led to this finding with regard to the wage. (Note that in this model there is only one type of labour from the standpoint of productivity and most profitable wage.)

Until faced with this piece of analysis, I would have said that a major drawback of such a scheme was that it is not very cost-effective, since it spreads the subsidy over all the employed workers. Of course, in the world of the present chapter in which workers are heterogeneous with respect to productivity and thus wages, such an objection could be addressed by making the tax rate on wages progressive according to the hourly wage rate. We end up with a scheme like the one discussed above in which the subsidy is progressive, in the sense that it tapers off with higher wage rates. However, the finding that the wage is actually reduced, unless overturned by introducing worker heterogeneity, suggests that the more serious problem is the tendency of the wage to fall – more generally, the tendency of the scheme to produce a reduction in the required wage at the low end that might compete in size with the rise in the demand wage at the low end. In my view, it is important that the scheme adopted produce *both* more jobs and better pay for low-wage workers. (Better pay without any improvement in job availability could present some serious 'negatives', and more jobs without any improvement in their attractiveness would be far less than what is needed in those countries where relative wages at the low end have suffered a severe decline.)

2.3.3 The unemployment benefit transfer scheme

Under what Dennis Snower has named the unemployment benefit transfer programme (BTP, see chapter 6 in this volume), the unemployed worker would have the discretion over whether her employment was to be subsidised – by deciding whether to assign her unemployment benefit to an employer in return for being hired.[27] Of course, the employer would lose the transferred entitlement were she to fire as many employees as she hired under these terms (so firms in the process of downsizing would not benefit from the plan), and possibly a similar offset would be extended to voluntary separations (exits other than for reasons of death or mandatory retirement) since there would otherwise be a temptation for the employer to induce employees to exit (perhaps even by sharing the gain with them from doing so); the net increase of employment, suitably defined, is what finally counts.

If the scheme were designed that way, the exchange by two firms of their existing workforces would *not* allow them to obtain all their workers with accompanying subsidies. A drawback, then, is that if the workforces would naturally like to trade places over time, the subsidy will be extinguished. It is regenerated only if the workers are transfused by going first through the unemployment state on their way to their new employer, thus becoming qualified in the process for a replenishment of their 'benefit'. In some versions of the scheme, long-term unemployment is required.

A more serious limitation at the practical level, however, comes from the truncation of unemployment benefits. In the USA, for example, the benefit normally runs for only six months – hardly a long-lasting subsidy from the viewpoint of a firm deciding whether to incur the many set-up costs of hiring and training a new employee. In some countries, such as Italy, there is no unemployment compensation at all – the limiting case of a zero-duration horizon. Even in Britain, the entitlement is not for life, so the subsidy will likewise run out with time.

Once again the matter of stock versus flow must be addressed. While the graduated wage subsidy scheme, discussed above, is applied to the current stock of employees rather than to the flow hired in the current period – gross or net of job separations – the transfer scheme under discussion is applied to the net employment inflow. The outlay per year of each of these other two schemes appears to be smaller in relation to the reduction of unemployment first achieved since the government is only subsidising at the margin. But with time, as old workers retired or quit, employment would begin sliding back down since mere replacement hiring is not eligible for a subsidy. Let us assume that the subsidy scheme establishes a series of accounting periods – successive years, most likely – in which the net employment increase is to be computed at each firm.[28] Then, once the firm's stock of employees has fallen back sufficiently far, it has the same incentive it had initially – to take advantage of the subsidy by engaging in a rush of net hiring with the current accounting period. Thus the individual firm will find it optimal to bunch its replacement hiring, at the cost of a 'saw-tooth' pattern in its workforce. Ultimately, however, all current employees will have benefited from the subsidy, and it does not seem that the average unemployment rate attainable with the given annual subsidy outlay could be lower than the unemployment rate finally attained with the same aggregate subsidy outlay applied to the stock of employees. We should keep our minds open to both of these kinds of programmes until the balance of merits and demerits has become clear, as best we can judge it.

3 Conclusions and objections

This century was, until the past couple of decades, a time of widespread disaffection with the norms of hard work and self-reliance and with the institutions of the market and private ownership. Keynes was among the very few who appreciated the importance of jobs and of capitalism. Over the decades, any stubborn problem of joblessness or poverty-level wage rates was addressed with the methods of the dole – ultimately refined into a system of welfare entitlements. That institutional response may have been the path requiring the least economic and social innovation, since it did not require any radical rethinking of the relationship between the government and the economy beyond what had gained recognition with the prototype welfare programmes of the last half of the nineteenth century.

Two forces have now combined to call into question the appropriateness of the welfare system as a solution to unemployment and low wages. By chance, some shocks that are entirely exogenous to the welfare system have come to magnify considerably the scale of joblessness and poverty among disadvantaged workers. And the welfare system has grown to have such a pervasive influence on the calculations of low-wage workers or potential workers that it must be judged a further factor (both from the benefits side and the fiscal side) in the decline in the number of jobs for low-wage workers and in the orientation toward work in poor communities. The possibility cannot be excluded that exogenous forces will bring more bad news or that the ill-effects of the welfare system are not all in yet.

Paradoxically, then, a curtailment of the welfare system now appears to be a reasonable policy step in the interest of reducing joblessness and poverty among disadvantaged workers. The near-term effects of such a curtailment, however, would surely bring considerable hardship and turmoil. And if the resulting budgetary saving were not translated into reductions in payroll and income taxation, the ensuing decline of low-end wage rates might be deemed to offset, or more than offset, whatever reductions of unemployment resulted.

As argued in this chapter, the institution of low-wage employment subsidies – best applied in the form of tax credits for use by employers against payroll taxes – would be a new and extraordinarily effective means to reduce joblessness and poverty. Unlike the welfare system and, for that matter, the institution of the minimum wage, such subsidies would pull up *both* the pay rates *and* the number of jobs available to low-wage workers (see table 7.2).

Three grounds for collective action of that kind have been identified in this chapter. One is equity. Most people would agree that the more advantaged workers should be willing to reconfigure net wage rates (net of taxes and subsidies) in such a way as to relinquish to the disadvantaged at least *some* of the gain in their own wage rates that comes from access to the inputs of the disadvantaged. Another argument is based on the opportunity for gains in economic efficiency: the understandably little attachment to jobs of disadvantaged workers drives

Table 7.2 *Cost of a model tax credit plan for US private-sector full-time employees*

	Full-time workers				
Hourly Wage	Annual wages	Planned subsidy	Number (%)	Number (million)	Outlay (billion)
$1 or less	–	–	0.1	0.061	–
2–1.01	–	–	0.2	0.122	–
3–2.01	–	–	0.8	0.488	–
4–3.01	$7000	$6000	5.9	3.599	$21.594
5–4.01	9000	5000	10.4	6.344	31.720
6–5.01	11000	4000	9.4	5.734	22.936
7–6.01	13000	3000	9.6	5.856	17.568
8–7.01	15000	2000	9.1	5.551	11.102
9–8.01	17000	1000	7.0	4.270	4.270
10–9.01	19000	0	8.1	4.941	0
11–10.01	21000	0	4.2	2.562	0
12–11.01	23000	0	5.3	3.233	0
13	25000	0	4.6	2.806	0
14	27000	0	3.4	2.074	0
15	29000	0	3.7	2.257	0
20	35000	0	10.4	6.344	0
25	45000	0	4.3	2.623	0
25	–	0	3.5	2.135	0
Total			100.0	61.000	109.196

Sources: Percentage distribution from the *Current Population Survey* (March 1990); number of employees from US Census (1990).

up the wages employers need to offer for cost-effective services from disadvantaged employees at the same time that it reduces the worth of having such employees, both effects leading to wastefully high (involuntary) unemployment and a consequent loss of real income. Still another ground refers to practical communitarian concerns: Other people's prosperity and their very safety are threatened – both advantaged persons and the disadvantaged themselves – and the life prospects for career and self-realisation of everyone's children are endangered when they grow up in a society not impelled to place the normal value on work and even human life.

Of course, the general public has not been altogether indifferent to the earning power and employment opportunities of the disadvantaged. And the reasons why it is willing to support various government remedies may be similar to the grounds given here for wage subsidies. But the public and its political representatives have come to view the disadvantaged worker problem as best approached through programmes of education and training targeted at the disadvantaged and aimed to offset or lessen the scale of their disadvantage. Many economists would also favour raising the demand for the labour of the disadvantaged by subsidising their further education and training. There are two difficulties with that approach.

The first is that, as its proponents themselves clearly imply, the benefits from the increased education envisioned would accrue to future generations of the working poor. The middle-aged and older persons among the working poor, and indeed the entire stock of working poor already in the labour force but now beyond the years of education, would not benefit. The education approach does not speak to the desire for economic justice here and now or in the simple self-interest of city-dwellers in their safety and the viability of their city.

The second difficulty with the education approach is its assumption either that the best feasible allocation of resources from the point of view of the working poor must depart from the neoclassical principle that social welfare is best served by efficiency in production and efficiency in the allocation of capital expenditure over investment *or* that the working poor are under-investing in their education in relation to their earnings possibilities. The more usual approach in economics would be to attack the rewards of the working poor directly, pulling up their wages rates thereby, and leave it to the judgement of the poor to decide whether to respond to their improved potential with increased investment of their own financing in their education and training.

It is widely felt that disadvantaged workers have missed out on the optimum level of skills owing to the ineffectiveness of the education system. Undoubtedly there are particular areas of under-investment in education in the USA, for example. However, it may also be that the school children in the inner cities are inefficient at learning in school because of the distractions and disturbances of family and social life they suffer as a result of the poverty of their communities and the absence of attractive earning possibilities other than criminal activities that are risky or degrading. In that case, the returns to further investment per year in education or training may turn out to be not very high, especially once the mis-investments are averaged in with the outstanding ones. If, on the whole, the rate of return to investment in education and training is in some medium range – higher than the long-term real rate on publicly traded corporate shares but lower than the prospective rate on R&D –

then the costs of the education–training approach are quite high. Working with a rate of return of 10 per cent, James Heckman calculated that in the USA a $2 trillion investment would be needed to bring low-wage workers' earnings back to their relative levels at the end of the 1970s.[29] The annual interest and amortisation on that capital would exceed $200 billion.

A good deal of the appeal of the low-wage employment subsidy approach derives from its transparency and in its promise that it will get results here and now: it will either bid up low-end wage rates by a readily calculable amount *or* have a rather substantial effect on employment *or* produce some net resultant between these two extremes. And these short-run impacts would be almost fully realised in a very few years – not just in a few decades.[30] The money will not disappear down a rat hole except insofar as employers find it worth the risks to defraud the government of the subsidies. To the extent that firms see it as profitable to bump employees to lower rungs of the job ladder (if only by delaying their promotion up the ladder) in order to increase the receivable subsidy, more subsidy outlays will end up going for the employment of workers whose wage rates are above the bottom level; if there is a fixed budget, therefore, less of that budget will be left to raise the demand wage of the lowest-paid workers.

It is crucial for further progress with our economic and social problems in the West that the public and the economics profession acknowledge and insist on the importance of decoupling rewards from the marginal productivities of the various kinds of labour. When the benefits of free trade operate to lower wage rates, it is necessary to understand that the gains from trade can be widely shared through the device of a wage subsidy to restore or increase wage rates, the taxes to pay for it being justified by gains to the other factors of production. When real interest rates rises in the world capital market, as investment opportunities spread to east Asia and to Latin America, it is necessary to understand that the gains of outward foreign investment can be widely shared through wage subsidies to shore up wage rates or even increase them, the taxes to do so coming out of the gains of savers and investors. Finally, when the vagaries of technological change dictate a decline of some wage rates, it is necessary to grasp that the gains of technological progress can be widely shared through wage subsidies. Unless we succeed in instituting some mechanism for introducing employment subsidies, and regulating them up and down, we face a future in which there is not only the possibility of high unemployment but, as a result of that experience, a threat to free trade, international capital flows and technical change as well.

No doubt further analysis of the various kinds of employment subsidy will be required before any persuasive judgements about the balance of benefit over costs can be made. But on the strength of the arguments developed in this paper, and the preliminary calculation of some of the benefits and costs, the present author remains of the view that this approach holds out the hope of large social gains.

Having made my case, let me now respond to some of the comments made at the conference, beginning with those of the discussants.

When Jeff Frank makes the objection that concentrating on meeting the needs of low-wage workers with dependants, thus sparing outlays that might otherwise have gone to those who did not need help, is a more cost-effective measure than my wage-subsidy proposal. I know that I have failed miserably to get across my views. To arrest the growing marginalisation of the lower class – a downward spiral of joblessness, drugs, and social dysfunction in the older slums – Western nations must change their culture from one in which society *meets needs* to one in which society *rewards contribution* – not equally, since that would pull everyone's wage down, but in a way strongly tilted toward the reward of those whose rewards are necessarily least. Our statutory minimum wage laws and union wage minima legally enforced nation-wide suggest a society unaware that, for most people in these times, having a job is basic to realising some important aspects of one's talents and personality and even just to staying healthy – which are about as fundamental a human right as there is. Our generally laissez-faire attitude toward any net wage subsidy to low-wage employees suggests a society that now rejects even the most minimalist notion of economic justice to low-wage workers – the claim this group might assert to the rent their inputs add to the wages and salaries of high earners.

These principles lead naturally to the position that the state should be spared the expense of providing wage subsidies to 'low-wage individuals' who happen to 'have alternative income sources, have assets (such as a house), be part of a family group that has sufficient total income' or have few or no children. This is, I suppose, the position behind America's Earned Income Tax Credit, which (in rough terms) rebates to workers with dependent children the payroll taxes they and their employers paid, and Britain's Family Credit, which helps out low-wage employees with dependent children. The position is wrongheaded on many counts.

- With regard to that minority of low-wage workers who in fact have dependent children, the child benefit certainly does not go very far, if anywhere, to create a gain from working. Such a worker gets the child credit if she works; but she also gets it, no doubt, if she does not work. There will presumably be some workers, therefore, who are induced by the 'income effect' of all this child support not to work – workers who would have been forced to work had there been no such free good made available, and whose wages could have been supplemented, thus reinforcing the employment effect, out of the savings on the child credit.

- The symbolism is misplaced since the tax credit or benefit will tend to be seen as a reward for having had (or having new) children, not for having a job – the reward for that they will gauge by the wage that single workers earn in the same job with the same paycheck; thus these child benefits will do relatively little to galvanise young men into leaving the underground economy for the world of legitimate jobs and do even less to induce young women into deferring children in order to gain job experience, with its option value.
- Insofar as the child credit/benefit does increase the supply of workers at a given wage (that is, paycheck), it drives down the wage of those workers who have until now opted for a job over children.
- There is no anti-child tilt to any of these replies. A generous wage subsidy scheme such as I am advocating would offer low-wage workers who desire to bring up children to do so out of their subsidies – some part of which would be financed from the revoked child credits, another part from the tax share of the additional rent to high earners resulting from the additional employment of low-wage workers, and another part from the savings to the government budget from reduced crime and social dysfunctionality generally. I am simply saying that measures to reduce unemployment and, more broadly, to increase the general orientation toward work instead of welfare should remain neutral with respect to individual desires to rear children.

Undergirding these points is my basic premise: society will continue to suffer a range of social pathologies as long as it fails to recognise and prize productive people's contribution to the business of society by means of rewards to employment perceived as tolerably just and thus nourishing self-respect. As soon as society throws off the utilitarian needs-based thinking, in which work is a source of disutility and people are simply pleasure machines, those pathologies – joblessness, depression, drugs, violence, crime and the rest – will recede considerably.

The other point by Jeff Frank that I want to contest is the one comparing the annual cost of the wage subsidy proposed here and the investment cost 'per job in regional investment programmes'. Frank argues that my $6000 figure per year as a way to pull the bottom annual full-time wage up to, say, $13,000 does not cost less than existing methods through development projects. It is not surprising to me that there is talk that governments can convert what would otherwise be, say, $7000 a year jobs into $13,000 jobs through one-off subsidies around $100,000 per job to private or state enterprises, essentially bribing them to add the requisite capital and make the necessary redesign so that the workers in question will have the marginal production (and average product after interest costs) to cover the higher wage. We already know from James Heckman's sensational calculation that restoring the relative wage of the bottom group in the USA to its level at the end of the 1970s would cost the Federal government something in the neighbourhood of a $1.7 trillion, the interest and amortisation on which is not much greater than my outlay of somewhat more than $110 billion per year.

The main advantage of the wage subsidy is that its application can begin almost at once for all low-wage workers – those who are full-time employees in the private sector in my version, though there will be a general effect on wages and the unemployment rate of the lowest paid workers. Its effects on wage rates and unemployment would be swift and sweeping. In contrast, the economic development approach would, even if totally successful, take years – no, decades – to pull up those $7000 wage rates to the $13,000 level. Development would not this year suddenly elevate this year's crop of 21-year-olds to $13,000 jobs, then next year do the same for that year's crop of 21-year-olds, and so forth. Demand could be raised only by degrees over a long haul. Thus the development approach might leave large numbers of older workers little helped before they reached retirement. Furthermore, some communities might for one reason or another miss out on the investment initiatives altogether, and so feel less of the effect on wages and unemployment than some other areas experience.

There are also some positive drawbacks to the development approach. The regional and other governmental departments may make a mistake in their vision of the industries in which the region can develop. Finally, I am not sure whether its governments could devise incentive-compatible agreements with firms that would ensure that the additional jobs at $13,000 would actually materialise or, once realised, be maintained indefinitely.

Dale Mortensen's comments include the one that seems to be at the front of most critics' minds. This is the objection that the wage-subsidy scheme, in pulling up wage rates at the bottom, the more so the closer they are to the bottom, would sharply reduce private rates of return to education and thus dampen the demand for the education that has historically helped the disadvantaged to move to better jobs and pay. Originality breaks out, though, with Mortensen's interesting thought that offsetting subsidies might be an appropriate accompaniment of the wage subsidies.

Of course, any kind of tax or subsidy has distortionary effects through its substitution effects on the behaviour of households and firms. Possibly the distortions in the form of reduced incentives to education are as important as any. However, we are not starting from a perfectly Pareto-optimal world into which a wage subsidy would introduce regrettable distortions. The whole configuration of distortions from corrective subsidies is to some considerable extent the counterpart of the 'distortions' caused by the market place in setting required wages above market-clearing levels (which are above the marginal social opportunity cost of the available labour) and then offering only jobs where the required wage is covered by the marginal *private* productivity for each grade of labour (which are below the corresponding marginal social product, which embraces the beneficial externalities that result when involuntary unemployment is reduced). If so, the wage subsidies are to a large extent simply eliminating distortions generated by imperfect markets, particularly the labour market.

One of these pre-existing distortions inherent in the market place, I will argue, is a tendency for *too much* education. The outsize joblessness at the low end of the wage scale sets a great many low-wage workers on a rat race to move from the bottom rungs of the scale to higher ones in order to have a better chance of getting a job. Let me sketch the argument. Assume for the moment that the force of inventive problems drives up the wage rates of low-wage workers no more (or not appreciably more) in proportionate terms than it does the wages of those higher up the scale. It is clear that when vertical supply curves are replaced as the supply-side relationship determining wage rates by an equilibrium wage-setting curve, with unemployment the horizontal distance between the two curves at the going wage, the positive-intercept feature of the wage curve tends to create a higher equilibrium unemployment rate for the workers facing a low demand price of labour (demand wage) than it does for the workers facing a higher demand price of labour. This will certainly be the case if there is a common wage curve for every kind, or grade, or worker, as in the bold modelling by Gilles Saint-Paul.[31] With this creation of a differential unemployment rate and, further, with all wages equiproportionately higher (by assumption) so that the absolute wage differential between one productivity category of labour input and another is actually increased, the profitability of extra education with which to escape the bottom rungs of the wage ladder is unambiguously increased. It is, I would guess, increased far beyond the equilibrium level in a full-information competitive model.

The only catch in the argument is the possibility that this process pushes up wage rates at the low end proportionately more – much more – than farther up the wage scale. But that possibility is by no means general, nor the presumption. Under perfect substitutability, in which three bottom guys then do work of two middle-level chaps, the wage ratios are constants, given the technology and the fiscal parameters. Under imperfect substitutability, the greater percentage cutback of employment at the low end will cause a greater percentage wage increase at that same end. But against this must be set another effect: it is not as if there always were quitting, shirking, absentee and other personnel problems, causing low demand for labour and thus low wage rates but no unemployment, and then one day employers discovered incentive pay as a way to reduce these personnel problems. Instead, we should imagine the economy in a perfectly competitive equilibrium, with no unemployment and no corrective subsidies, and then Eve eats the apple, ushering in an age of self-interested employee behaviour. In the new equilibrium (without corrective subsidies), the demand-price-of-labour schedules may be dragged down, as employers cannot eliminate all quitting, shirking, and so forth. It is quite possible that the demand-wage schedule for low-productivity workers is depressed proportionately more than that of high-productivity workers, since the latter have all sorts of inherent incentives to perform well to further their promotion and impress their boss into a salary raise or year-end bonus.

If this line of argument is right, workers are at present spurred by joblessness and, possibly on top of that, depressed wages at the low end, into investing in much more human capital than could be justified by the resulting productivity gains. (Moreover, if this extra education or skill depresses the wage rates of those who chose not to make the investment at the initial wage rates, those who previously could afford the luxury of not incurring the psychic cost of the extra time in education or vocational school might calculate they could no longer afford to skip it, thus causing a round of defensive investment in response to the primary round.) In that case, reduced government outlays subsidising advanced education and training might be another source of budgetary savings made possible by the wage subsidy. But perhaps I go too far! The truth may lie somewhere between my semi-jocular suggestion that subsidies to education could be reduced if wage subsidies were introduced and Professor Mortensen's sense that educational subsidies would have to be increased.

The last point in Mortensen's discussion is the contention that a hiring subsidy provides more bang for the buck than a reduction in the payroll tax costing more or less the same amount to the government's budget.

I would comment first that a reduction in the unemployment rate of disadvantaged workers – say, the jobless rate of young urban males with only a high school degree or less – from 25 per cent to 10 per cent, while something of a miracle, would not by itself reduce the general unemployment rate by more than a percentage point in Western countries since they do not represent more than a fifteenth of the labour force, if that. Of course, some of the improved job experience in youth would carry over to later ages, so that in steady state the general unemployment rate would be reduced somewhat more. (But these disadvantaged youth eventually do settle into some kind of job or leave the labour force to spend time in prison.) In any case, a reduction of the general unemployment rate by something around one-half a percentage point, which Mortensen calculates in his payroll tax example, seems like quite a lot to me. And, as he says, the scale of the wage subsidies I propose are somewhat larger than the payroll reduction he analyses.

Mortensen's claim is that a hiring subsidy costing the same in budgetary terms would do much more to reduce unemployment while raising wage rates very nearly as much at the same time. That is hard to understand, since the stimulus to demand presumably moves us up a wage curve, and the farther rightward we go (in the employment direction) the higher up we will also go. It must be that, in the Mortensen–Pissarides model, the shift from the lower payroll tax to the hiring subsidy shifts down the wage curve while shifting up the demand curve by enough to make the wage rise on balance. Perhaps the explanation is that a hiring/rehiring subsidy could reduce or eliminate firms' reasons to keep wages above the market-clearing level for the purpose of combating labour turnover; quitting would not matter any longer to a firm if the government picked up the tab for the firm-specific training of the replacement for each department employee. Thus the wage curve would be shifted down.

Subsidies to hiring would bring their own set of distortions, however. As just implied, subsidies that offset recruiting and training costs would lead firms to lower their guard against quitting by employees. This rise of the quit rate could result in a big rise in the budgetary cost of the subsidies programme. There is also a temptation to fraud, as is there in the case of wage subsidies. Firms would have incentives to funnel existing employees and newly hired ones to new corporate subsidiaries set up for the purpose of rehiring those employees in order to gain the subsidy money. There is also the possibility that two firms might collude to collect the subsidies by effectively trading their employees in order to record new hires. For me, an appeal of the wage-subsidy idea is that it is very 'up front'. The benefits are not front-loaded, the costs not back-loaded.

Let me conclude with a brief reflection on a question that often comes up in discussions of wage subsidies. With American friends I have sometimes heard the comment, 'Well, they are certainly needed in Europe, but not really here'. I suppose the thought is that Europe's unemployment rates are vastly higher than that in the USA, so the need for the unemployment reduction is greater there. From European friends I often hear the comment 'Such a scheme may be good for the USA and maybe for the UK, both countries where wage dispersion is wide, but not for continental Europe'.

I suppose that the main benefit of the wage subsidies in the USA will take the form of higher wage rates, with a less important effect on unemployment. The reason is that 'wage rigidity' is relatively small there, which means that the wage curve is relatively steep. And the main benefit of the wage subsidies on the European continent will take the form of lower unemployment rates – more workers demanded at those rigid real wage rates – with little improvement in wage rates. The reason, again, is that wage rigidity is relatively great in Europe, so the wage curve is relatively flat.

This split in the outcome – employment effects going mostly to the continent, wage effects going mostly to the other countries – seems all for the best. Each country or region draws from the subsidy scheme the thing that it most badly needs. If you give a nutritionally well rounded meal to a collection of undernourished persons who are quite different in the nature of their nutritional deficiencies, they will all benefit but in different ways, for different reasons. We would not want it any other way.

NOTES

This chapter was written during a year as Visiting Scholar at the Russell Sage Foundation, New York City. A large part of it is a heavy reworking of an earlier draft (Phelps, 1994c). A subsection on a scheme that simply exempts employees under a low-wage threshold from certain payroll taxes has been added.

1 These estimates, based on models of how structural shocks alter the natural rate, derive from Phelps (1994b). Some of the out-of-sample calculations are reported in Phelps and Zoega (1993). A very brief sketch of natural-rate theory, with references to some of the antecedent literature, can be found in section 1 below.

2 One can view the burden of payroll taxes and personal taxes on wage incomes either as reducing the net wage that employers can afford to pay without

reducing the net wage workers require *or* as raising the cost per worker that employers are required to pay without reducing the labour cost they can afford to pay. I generally take the former view, but these views are analytically equivalent. In any case, the rise of the wedge is not a 'supply-side' phenomenon any more than it is a 'demand-side' one. It is a shock of the 'third kind'.

3 Lacking unemployment rates classified by wage rate, we have to proxy by education. In Italy, for example, the unemployment rate of those whose education stopped in secondary school is more than twice that of workers who reached or graduated from university. See de Luca and Bruni (1993, table 23, p. 53). For this country, however, the unemployment rate of those whose education stopped in primary school was actually below the general unemployment rate.

4 For example, a six-point rise in the unemployment rate from, say, 3 per cent of the *total* labour force to 9 per cent might correspond to an increase of unemployment among *disadvantaged* workers from 12 per cent to 36 per cent – a 24 point increase. So large an increase might be devastating for the disadvantaged families affected. But the assumption of proportionality may exaggerate the incidence of increased joblessness on the disadvantaged. The unemployment rate among the less skilled might be substantial even when the unemployment rate of the more skilled is negligible if, as appears to be the case, the less educated need more training; then the former unemployment rate would tend on that account to rise less than proportionately with the general unemployment rate.

5 These two factors, which would account for a tendency for the relative net pay of low-wage workers to decline, could mask the presence at the same time of a relative increase in the labour cost required for cost-effective performance by low-wage workers.

6 Italy presents an exception at the lowest educational category to the observation of increased relative unemployment, and even the next to lowest category of worker shows little increase in relative unemployment rate. This anomaly may be linked with the operation of the underground economy.

7 It is not suggested that no country has ever done anything of this sort with the intention of pulling up the lowest wage rates and employment rates. In the heyday of Keynesianism there was a conscious effort in many countries to use public-sector employment to expand the employment opportunities of some people – not infrequently the least productive through jobs requiring little ability, skill and enthusiasm. As certain public enterprises grew to be quite bloated in some countries it was asserted in justification that a major cutback would have a permanent effect on the wage rates and employment frequency of the affected workers. But this method of stimulating the demand for the least productive workers has not been conceived as a means to an intentional and radical improvement in the rewards of low-wage workers in general. It could be said that public-sector employment has had the *latent* function of achieving an *incremental* improvement in the opportunities of various *subgroups* among the low-wage population (for the sake of political gain). Similarly, the Great Society programmes in training and schooling aimed at increasing the skills of the disadvantaged. But none of these programmes was ever tried on the heroic scale that might have made an appreciable difference in the relative earnings of the bottom decile of workers.

8 The substance of this section was first formulated in Phelps (1994a).

9 Perhaps the most familiar application is to the spread of knowledge. Society does not leave it entirely to the market place to determine how much knowledge persons acquire because it regards the benefit to the country of an additional spread of knowledge as exceeding the benefit to the recipients of the knowledge as measured by what they would be willing to pay for it. Various government subsidies to education, in supplementing the payments by the recipients, serve to bring the total payment for education more closely in line with the total benefit to society. In a sense, the subsidy corrects for a bias in the benefit of education as the recipient sees it. The size of the subsidy can be interpreted as a measure of society's estimate of the gap between the two benefits of additional education – the social and the private.

10 It may strike some as circuitous at best to cast the equity consideration into the externality cast, but it appears to be valid and perhaps useful to do so.

11 Rand (1964).

12 Rand does not pause to reflect on whether that arrangement is really a cost-effective arrangement, thus one that is Pareto-efficient. Perhaps the 'free riders', by paying a small share of the cost (a clear gain to the others) would gain on balance from the resulting incentives toward more frequent bus service.

13 Rawls (1971).

14 'Equilibrium' here means a state or path along which expectations are being confirmed.

15 See Phelps (1968); Stiglitz (1974, pp. 194–227); and Salop (1979). Two early models of employee shirking are Calvo (1979, pp. 117–25) and Solow (1979, pp. 79–82).

16 For the employee there is the moral hazard that the employer will defraud the employee of the deposit by portraying himself as unable to repay the deposit or by making false accusations of shirking by the employee. For the employer there is the hazard that the employee will allege that the firm abused him to induce him to quit in order to claim the deposit and the hazard that the employee will fight dismissal for a good cause even though it was true that the employee shirked.

17 This consideration is introduced in Phelps (1972). Some of the consequences of non-wage income sources for unemployment and wages in the context of a labour force that is homogeneous with respect to productivity are studied in Phelps (1994b).

18 The properties of the equilibrium *wage rate* of the disadvantaged are sensitive to particulars. It could be that the equilibrium wage of the disadvantaged is relatively more elevated – relatively higher as a ratio to productivity – despite their higher unemployment rate, which serves to curb their quitting and shirking to a degree. In special cases, however, the equilibrium wage of the disadvantaged is pushed back by the increased unemployment to the same level relative to productivity that the advantaged exhibit (so that both kinds of workers are competitively priced).

19 Operating in the reverse direction, at least over a small range of employees, is the point that the effort put forward by an employee in a managerial position impinges on the effectiveness of all the employees under her – her span of control – while in the great majority of cases the effort of a low-wage worker affects only her own effectiveness (not the incremental product resulting from

the addition or subtraction of other employees). This consideration would suggest that high-wage workers reaching managerial positions are subject to the greatest proportionate wage escalation, contrary to the argument above. Two qualifications suggest themselves, however. First, in a variety of cases, such as aircraft construction and maintenance, the most minor and detailed work may be more crucial for profitability than the work of a great many vice-presidents. Second, the argument just sketched would seem to apply primarily to the top managers, who are a minuscule fraction of the labour force, and not to middling supervisory personnel, who may play a routine coordinative role and receive rather little extra compensation.

20 For an example of recommendations calling for more flexibility in labour markets, see OECD (1994).
21 For such an argument, see Murray (1994, pp. 61–6).
22 This section borrows freely from Phelps (1990), now published in Papadimitriou (1994).
23 There would be a similar incentive to over-report the weeks worked of full-time employees who worked only a part of the year. That problem is not met by the proposal here to limit the subsidy to full-time jobs.
24 Drèze and Malinvaud (1993).
25 See Aliber (?1979).
26 See Jackman and Layard (1986) and Salop (1979, pp. 117–25).
27 Snower (1993).
28 Alternatively the legislation might say that the previous high-water mark of the workforce is the base for use in computing the net hiring. Then a firm having reached its highest level ever through its initial response to the subsidies would then never have the hope of receiving subsidies again. Thus employment would recede from the high-water mark, tending to fall back to the level it would otherwise have taken had the subsidy scheme not been introduced.
29 Heckman (1993).
30 A particular drawback of this scheme is that its costs would commence in full from the first day, while the benefit in reduced unemployment and a general elevation of wage rates at the bottom of the spectrum would take time to emerge fully.
31 See chapter 3 in this volume.

REFERENCES

Aliber, R.Z., ?1979. 'A proposal to reduce the waste of unemployment', Graduate School of Business, University of Chicago, undated

Calvo, G., 1979. 'Quasi-Walrasian theory of unemployment', *American Economic Review, Papers and Proceedings*, **69**, 102–7

de Luca, L. and M. Bruni, 1993. *Unemployment and Labour Market Flexibility: Italy*, Geneva: ILO

Drèze, J. and E. Malinvaud, 1993. 'Growth and employment: the scope of European initiative'; published as J.E. Drèze, E. Malinvaud *et al.*, *European Economic Review*, **38** (1994)

Gottschalk, P. and M. Joyce, 1992. 'Is earning inequality also rising in other industrialized countries?', Boston College, Department of Economics (October), mimeo

Heckman, J., 'Assessing Clinton's program on job training, workfare, and education in the workplace', *NBER Working Paper*, **4428**, Cambridge, MA: NBER

Jackman, R.A. and P.R.G. Layard, 1986. 'A wage-tax, worker-subsidy policy for reducing the "natural" rate of unemployment', chapter 7 in W. Beckerman (ed.), *Wage Rigidity and Unemployment*, London: Butterworth

Murray, C., 1994. 'Regaining lost ground', *City Journal*, **4** (Spring)

OECD, 1994. *The OECD Jobs Study: Facts, Analysis, Strategies*, Paris: OECD

Papadimitriou, D. (ed.), 1994. *Aspects of the Distribution of Wealth and Income*, New York: St Martin's Press

Phelps, E.S., 1968. 'Money-wage dynamics and labor-market equilibrium', *Journal of Political Economy*, **76**, Part 2, 678–711

1972. *Inflation Policy and Unemployment Theory*, New York: Norton

1990. 'Economic justice to the working poor through a wage subsidy', Jerome Levy Institute (November), mimeo

1994a. 'The case for low-wage employment subsidies', 3rd Annual Report of the International Panel on Economic Policy Evaluation, Paris: OECD

1994b. *Structural Slumps: The Modern Equilibrium Theory of Unemployment, Interest, and Assets*, Cambridge, MA: Harvard University Press

1994c. 'A program of low-wage employment credits', Russell Sage Foundation, *Working Paper*, 55 and Confindustria, *CSC Ricerche*, **93** (May)

Phelps, E.S. and G. Zoega, 1993. 'Do the main structural forces of the 1970s and 1980s account for the 1990s slump as well? An update of a postwar time-series cross-section study', *Rivista di Politica Economica*, **83**

Rand, A., 1964. *The Virtue of Selfishness*, New York: New American Library

Rawls, J., 1971 *A Theory of Justice*, Cambridge, MA: Harvard University Press

Salop, S., 1979. 'A model of the natural rate of unemployment', *American Economic Review*, **79**

Snower, D., 1993. 'Getting the benefit out of a job', *Financial Times* (23 February)

Solow, R.M., 1979. 'Another reason for wage stickiness', *Journal of Macroeconomics*, **1**

Stiglitz, J.E., 1974. 'Wage determination and unemployment in LDCs', *Quarterly Journal of Economics*, **88**

Discussion

JEFF FRANK

There are a number of conventional reasons for providing assistance to low-income individuals. Potential externalities are associated with high crime, poor health and cultural deprivation. In any case, there are equity arguments for redistribution. Phelps in chapter 7 introduces a third class of arguments. He claims, on the basis of an efficiency wage model, that significant labour market inefficiencies can be lessened by appropriate assistance to the low paid. This third rationale is important, not just in strengthening the case for assistance, but in indicating the appropriate methods.

Typically, if we are concerned about income distribution, we would introduce a benefits scheme rather than intervene in particular markets. Agricultural subsidies are the classic example of the problems associated with market intervention as a method of raising incomes. Phelps' particular focus is on the low paid in employment, as well as on the employed in this low-skills market. Schemes such as Family Credit in the UK have been introduced precisely to help out those in employment but on low wages. The advantage of a straightforward benefits scheme is that it can be targeted. Low-wage individuals may have alternative income sources, assets (such as a house), be part of a family group that has sufficient total income, and have differing needs, depending (for example) on the number of children. Since it is expensive in efficiency terms to raise revenues from taxation, targeting of benefits is important.

Wage subsidies for low-skilled jobs as proposed by Phelps would raise wages and employment even if the labour market was efficient. But in an efficiency wage labour market there may be an extra gain to the programme. Phelps' claim is that the market for the low skilled might be represented by an equilibrium such as *A* in figure D7.1. Each firm tries to pay wages above the average to ensure that workers do not 'shirk'. In the aggregate, each cannot pay above the average, but the wage is driven up to the point where unemployment provides the punishment to deter potential shirkers. Now suppose that there is a wage subsidy which shifts labour demand out. In a world where workers have no leisure value, the new equilibrium appears as *B*. Equilibrium unemployment goes down. Further, since there is no leisure value, unemployment is fully wasteful and the reduction is a clear efficiency gain.

For policy purposes, it is helpful to gauge the order of magnitude of the efficiency gain. We provide an approximate formula for the punishment suffered by a discovered shirker when she is sacked. She loses the wage W until such time as she is able to regain a new job. In a simple queuing model, the time needed to move through the unemployment queue takes the form $U/\delta N$, where δ is the exogenous rate at which job matches break up even if there is no shirking and N is employment. The punishment to shirking is then $WU/\delta N$. In any situation where shirking is avoided by efficiency wages, the equilibrium entails a shirking punishment equal to

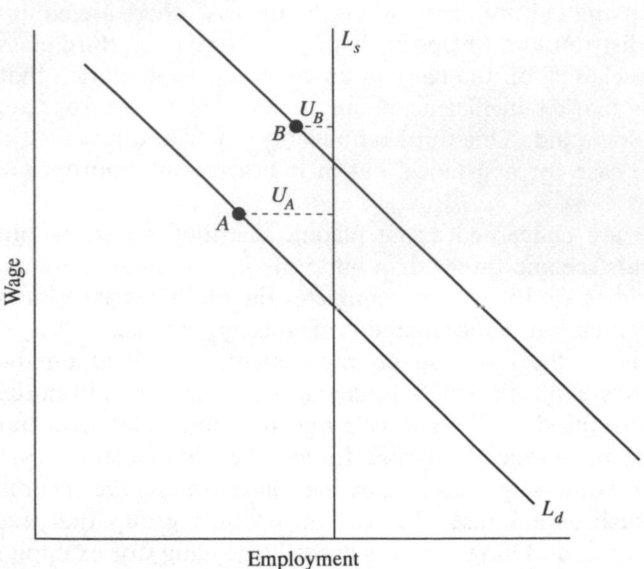

Figure D7.1 The low-wage equilibrium, *A*, and associated unemployment, U_A, and the high-wage equilibirum, *b*, after a wage subsidy is introduced.

the cost of the effort needed to avoid shirking. That is, $WU/\delta N$ is roughly constant across equilibria. Equilibrium *A* in figure D7.1 meets this with a low wage and high unemployment; equilibrium *B* with a high wage and low unemployment. Since we are considering low-skill workers, it might not be unreasonable to suppose that the equilibrium in the absence of policy might involve 20 per cent unemployment. It follows then that a large wage subsidy that leads to a doubling of the wage would, to maintain a constant $WU/\delta N$, lead to a rough halving of unemployment. The government would pay 50 per cent of the wage bill for a 10 per cent rise in employment – that is, there is an efficiency gain of roughly 20 per cent of the total expenditure.

Is that efficiency gain a worthwhile return on the government expenditure? In isolation, it is unlikely. There are efficiency losses involved in collecting taxes that are likely to exceed 20 per cent. But if the government is intending to redistribute income in any case, the efficiency gain of 20 per cent must be set against the targeting gains in more traditional in-work benefits programmes. In a labour market where the participants are relatively homogeneous and there may be a strong efficiency wage element – perhaps young male workers – there is a strong case for Phelps' approach. But if there is reason to believe that the participants are heterogeneous, targeting of in-work benefits may be more efficient.

In any case, it may be felt that the problem with the Phelps proposal is that it subsidises low-skill jobs: 'If you subsidise bad jobs, you will get a lot of them.' Firms will create bad jobs at the expense of good jobs and physical capital investment. Workers will have a disincentive to invest in human capital. Phelps proposes very large subsidies in the order of $6000 a year. This is the equivalent of very large capitalised sums of $60,000 at a real interest rate of 10 per cent, and $120,000 at a real interest rate of 5 per cent. These are the sort of sums that are often calculated as the cost per job in regional investment programmes. If we will be incurring this sort of cost, it seems better to pay it on a one-off basis in creating good jobs then in permanent subsidies to bad jobs.

Discussion

DALE T. MORTENSEN

Professor Phelps in chapter 7 provides strong and eloquent arguments supporting market intervention on behalf of low-wage workers. By encouraging the employment of low-income workers at higher wages, a wage subsidy would offset incentives to engage in negative social behaviour and would strengthen positive social values, the work ethic and respect for private property. A low-wage subsidy is needed to offset the recent rise in income inequality, whatever its source. Finally, a wage subsidy would reduce wasteful unemployment induced by imperfections associated with bargaining, rationing, and incentive wage policies.

The specifics of design that are discussed in chapter 7 seem to be sensible and useful. Phelps' efforts directed at proposing a programme that would minimise abuse by employers are of obvious practical importance. After restricting the subsidy to full-time workers only and then graduating it to reduce the incentive for fraud, Phelps uses US data for 1990 to obtain a cost estimate of $110 billion to bring hourly earnings up to $7 per hour for the lowest paid. However laudable and even though small relative to a $6 trillion economy, as he points out, this number is large in the current US political environment. Frankly, it would be difficult to imagine that such a programme would form a plank in either party's platform in the near future. However, if the US earnings distribution continues to widen and/or low-wage unemployment attains European levels, income redistribution of this form may well be on the agenda of the twenty-first century.

Phelps' proposal would cause some obvious distortions that he does not explicitly discuss. For example, a subsidy targeted at low hourly wage earners designed to bring wages up to at least $7 per hour will reduce private returns to education. Since private investment in education is a major component of the total in the USA and because available evidence suggests that it is quite sensitive to price signals, an offsetting increase in government subsidies to education may be necessary as well.

Phelps' recommendation that the subsidy be restricted to full-time employment also has its consequences. As I understand the scheme, an employer of someone who was earning $4 per hour would be paid $3.50 per hour and would be required to pay the worker $7.00 per hour under the scheme, i.e. the 50 cent difference is a bribe offered to induce the employer not to reclassify the worker as a $3 per hour type (and hence collect $1 per hour) when in fact she is worth $4. Now, however, the employer has an incentive to create one full-time job at the expense of two half-time jobs offered previously. The substitution of full-time for half-time jobs may be regarded as a good side-effect of the proposal by some, but would constitute a distortion if in fact the current composition of full- and part-time jobs offered reflects an equilibrium that appropriately accommodates existing taste and technology.

Phelps concludes chapter 7 by considering various modifications of his own proposal as well as alternative schemes suggested by others. In his response to the Jackman and Layard analysis of a wage subsidy, he states: 'In my view, it is important that the scheme adopted produce *both* more jobs and better pay for low-wage workers.' Yet, I am not really clear about how his own proposal is intended to accomplish this dual goal. For example, his ideal scheme seems to be equivalent to an earnings tax credit paid directly to the worker, i.e. a payment to each low-wage worker that would make up the difference between her 'market wage' and $7 per hour. Later the ideal is modified to incorporate a graduated subsidy to employers paid only to full-time workers. In any case, the calculations Phelps presents assume no employment effect.

Obviously, to obtain an employment effect some part of the subsidy must act to reduce employer cost in equilibrium. This fact raises the issue of subsidy incidence. The classic argument on this point is that a wage subsidy, say in the form of a reduced payroll tax, will have little employment effect because labour participation is nearly perfectly inelastic. However, given the model of Phelps' book, *Structural Slumps* (1994, see also chapter 5 in this volume), this result does not follow because the wage curve, which replaces the neoclassical labour supply curve in his analysis, is not vertical. Given the upward-sloping wage curve, both wage and employment increase in response to the shift out in demand induced by a wage subsidy, although of course the wage rate will not increase by the full amount of the subsidy. I presume that these were the positive effects that Phelps expects his proposal to have on both wage and employment.

The Mortensen and Pissarides (1994) equilibrium model of the natural rate has a very similar structure, in the sense that wage bargains are responsive to the unemployment rate and the two are jointly determined by combining this wage curve with a demand relation between employment and the wage. In Mortensen (1994), I conduct computational experiments with a version of the model calibrated to reflect conditions in the USA which yield results that compare the effects of different policies on unemployment and wage rates. The results of the experiment suggest that a reduction in the payroll tax has a rather small employment effect, particularly relative to a hiring subsidy of the same overall outlay. In particular, I calculate that a $1500 per year per employee reduction in the payroll tax (which would be less expensive but of the same order of magnitude as Phelps' programme if applicable to each of the 61 million full-time private employees) would reduce unemployment by only 44/100th of a point and would increase the equilibrium average wage earnings by $1300 per year. However, if the same total outlay were used to finance a hiring subsidy or new jobs tax credit designed to offset recruiting and training costs, the computed effect would be a 3-point reduction in unemployment and a $1400 increase in average earnings per worker per year. Hence, in the Mortensen–Pissarides model at least, a hiring subsidy provides a much bigger bang for the buck.

REFERENCES

Mortensen, D.T., 1994. 'Reducing supply-side disincentives to job creation', paper presented at the Annual Symposium of the Federal Reserve Bank of Kansas City, Jackson Hole, Wyoming (26–27 August)

Mortensen, D.T. and C.A. Pissarides, 1994. 'Job creation and job destruction in the theory of unemployment', *Review of Economic Studies*, **61**, 397–415

Phelps, E.S., 1994. *Structural Slumps: The Modern Equilibrium Theory of Unemployment, Interest, and Assets*, Cambridge, MA: Harvard University Press

8 Technological development, competition from low-wage economies and low-skilled unemployment

JACQUES H. DREZE and HENRI SNEESSENS

The economic position of the less skilled members of the workforce has deteriorated over the past 20 years, both in Western Europe and in the USA. In Europe, the deterioration manifests itself primarily through higher unemployment. In the USA, it manifests itself mainly through lower real and relative wages. The phenomenon has a cyclical aspect, associated with slow growth and recessions. There is, however, also mounting evidence of a structural trend, associated with technological development and competition from low-wage economies – a trend that is likely to gain rather than lose momentum over the coming years. The combination of uncertain growth perspectives and a lasting structural weakness exacerbates the conflict between equity and efficiency: how can we promote full employment without producing unsustainable income inequalities?

This chapter surveys some of the evidence and arguments. Section 1 reviews briefly the current situation, the weight of the evidence behind proposed explanations, and the theoretical case for international wage convergence. Section 2 discusses policy objectives and brings out the efficiency–equity dimension of the problem. Section 3 evaluates some policy alternatives and draws conclusions.

1 The weakened position of less-skilled workers

1.1 High unemployment and low wages

The simplest and most objective measure of skills is educational attainment. Table 8.1 records unemployment rates for five levels of education in 19 OECD countries in 1989. In every single country there is a marked decline in unemployment as education rises. For workers with

Table 8.1 *Unemployment rates, by level of educational attainment*[a]

Country	Pre-primary and primary	Lower-secondary	Upper-secondary	Higher education non-university	Higher education university	Total
USA	8.5	9.1	4.6	3.3	2.2	4.4
Japan	–	7.0	6.5	7.7	2.3	4.4
Germany	–	13.8	6.8	3.7	4.5	7.3
France	11.8	10.5	6.6	3.4	3.0	8.1
Italy	5.9	6.8	7.7	–	4.8	6.6
UK	–	10.0	5.6	2.7	2.4	6.4
Canada	10.3	9.8	6.8	5.0	3.6	6.7
Australia	8.1	7.0	4.2	4.6	3.7	5.4
Austria	–	3.6	2.4	–	1.1	2.7
Belgium	14.0	9.2	4.7	2.7	2.0	7.5
Denmark	–	12.1	7.1	4.0	3.4	8.3
Finland	–	4.1	3.1	1.6	1.7	3.0
Ireland	25.8	15.1	6.6	3.9	2.6	13.9
Netherlands	13.6	7.6	4.8	4.6	5.0	6.5
New Zealand	9.3	4.7	4.9	5.1	2.9	6.0
Portugal	6.0	5.8	6.4	6.0	6.1	6.0
Spain	12.7	15.6	13.1	–	10.7	12.9
Sweden	–	1.4	0.9	0.9	1.0	1.0
Switzerland	–	1.4	0.6	0.3	0.8	0.8
Simple average of above countries	10.9	8.4	5.7	3.9	3.4	6.3

[a] Adult population aged 25–64 in 1989, except Japan (1987), Denmark (1988), New Zealand (1990) and the Netherlands (1990).
Source: CERC (1991).

Table 8.2 *Unemployment rates, by skill, Britain and the USA, 1984 and 1987*

	Britain (1984)	USA (1987)
Professional and managerial	5.3	2.3
Clerical	8.0	4.3
Other non-manual	12.2	4.3
Skilled manual	12.6	6.1
Personal services	15.5	7.7
Other manual	15.5	9.4
All	10.8	6.2

Source: Layard, Nickell and Jackman (1991).

lower-secondary education, unemployment is 33 per cent above average, but two-and-a-half times as high as for workers with post-secondary education. Although comparative data are lacking, country studies confirm that unemployed workers are less educated than employed workers, and that a high proportion of unemployed workers have a low level of education (EC, 1992, p. 34). A study by OECD (1989), covering seven countries with comparable data, also found that the increase of unemployment between the early 1970s and late 1980s had generally been more pronounced for the least educated workers.

Education is not a perfect indicator of skills valued on the labour market.[1] We are not aware of a better proxy, however. In particular, we do not know whether skill differences *within* professional categories are more significant than skill differences *between* these categories. The data for the UK and the USA in table 8.2, borrowed from Layard, Nickell and Jackman (1991),[2] reveal that professional differences in unemployment rates are comparable to educational differences (as given in table 8.1) in the USA, and exceed those in the UK.

As for evolutions over time, figures 8.1 and 8.2, pertaining to France, reveal much stability in the professional *distribution* of unemployment. But the general progress in education implies a declining proportion of less educated workers in the labour force. Accordingly, the stable proportion of the less educated among the unemployed means a growing disparity between their fast-growing unemployment rate and the average rate (see figure 8.2). This evolution implies clearly that *employment prospects* for the unskilled have deteriorated, both absolutely and relative to the prospects for the skilled. From a normative (policy) viewpoint, it is clearly desirable on efficiency grounds to reduce overall (inefficient) unemployment. When distributive considerations suggest a special

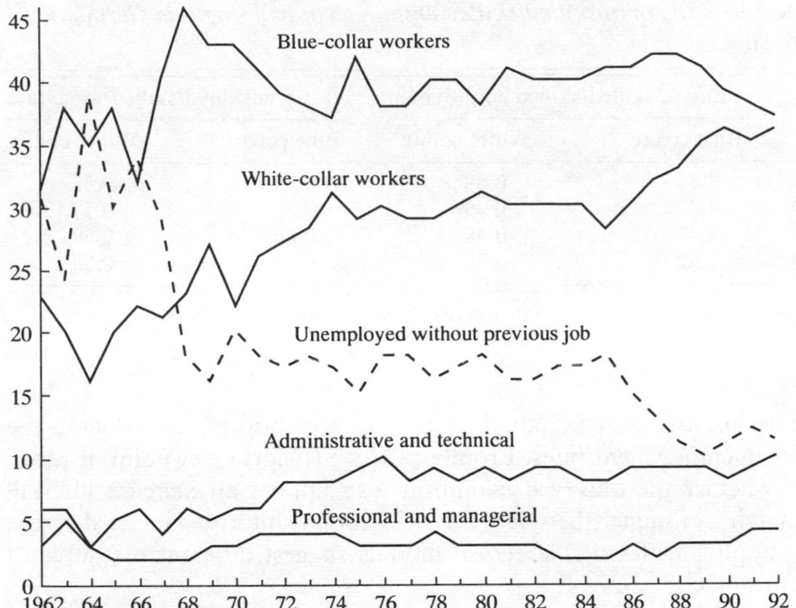

Figure 8.1 Structure of unemployment, by occupation, France, 1962–92, percentage of total unemployment
Source: Maillard and Sneessens (1994)

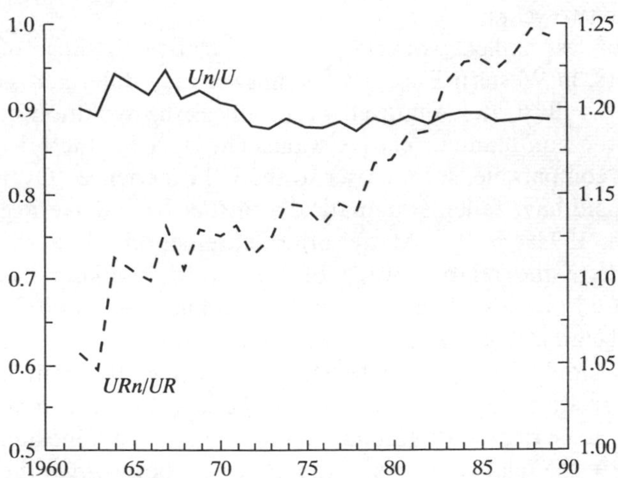

Figure 8.2 Low-skilled unemployment, in levels, (*UN*/*U*), and in rates, (*URn*/*UR*), France, 1960–90, proportion of total unemployment
Source: Maillard and Sneessens (1994)

Table 8.3 *Ratio of unskilled/skilled employment and wages in Germany, 1966–90*

	Ratio unskilled/skilled employment		Ratio unskilled/skilled wage rate	
	Blue-collar	White collar	Blue collar	White collar
1966	1.34	0.88	0.78	0.56
1970	1.42	0.75	0.78	0.57
1980	1.17	0.43	0.80	0.59
1990	1.02	0.38	0.82	0.58

Source: Statistisches Bundesamt, Fachserle 16, Löhne und Gehälter

concern for the least favoured, they also give priority to reducing the *higher* unemployment rates. From a positive (theory) viewpoint, it is not clear whether the observed evolution also implies an increase in 'skill mismatch' (mismatch between the skill composition of labour demand and supply). Different *theoretical* models suggest different measures of skill mismatch.[3]

In the USA, a reduced labour demand bears more on wages than on unemployment in the medium run. The weakened position of less skilled workers is illustrated by figure 8.3, which plots real wage distributions for adult men in 1979 and 1987, two years with identical median wages.[4] The proportion earning less than US $20,000 rose from 32 per cent to 38 per cent between the two years.

Have the wages of less skilled workers declined, relative to those of more skilled workers, in Western Europe? The answer may differ across countries, as figure 8.4 illustrates. Figure 8.4 reproduces the evolution of the manual versus the non-manual relative wage. The data for the UK, though not directly comparable, seem closer to the US experience: 'Over the 1980s, the low paid have fallen systematically further behind average earnings' (Atkinson, 1993a, p. 9).[5] At the other extreme, one finds the case of France, where the relative wage of less skilled workers has substantially increased (see also Sneessens and Shadman-Mehta, 1995). Germany seems to be an intermediate case, with a moderately decreasing relative wage. One should however be careful when using the manual versus non-manual relative wage as a measure of the less skilled relative wage. A closer look at German data (see table 8.3) suggests the opposite, i.e. a slight *increase* in the relative wages of the unskilled, both *within* the blue-collar and *within* the white-collar group. This happened in spite of a marked decline in the proportion of unskilled jobs within both groups, and of the rise in unskilled unemployment.

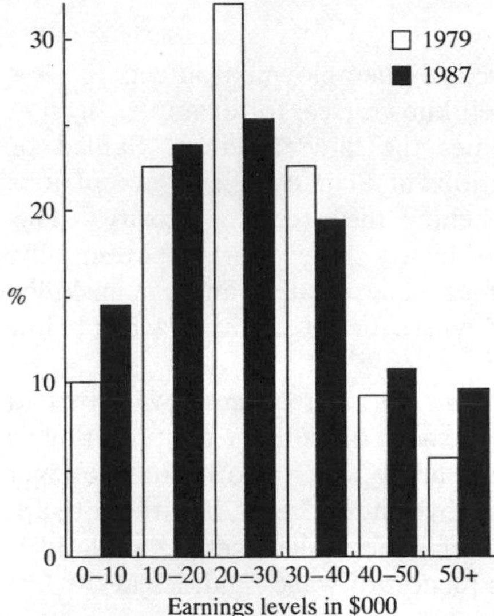

Figure 8.3 25–54-year-old working men, by wage and salary income, USA, 1979 and 1987
Source: Levy and Murnane (1992)

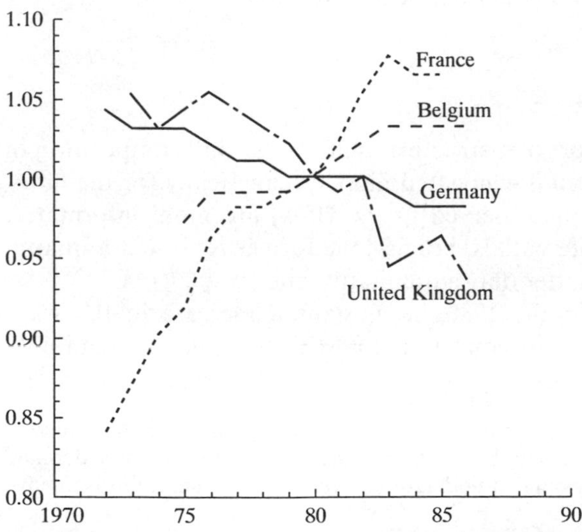

Figure 8.4 Relative wage of manual versus non-manual workers, 1970–90 (1980 = 1)
Source: EUROSTAT data

1.2 Cyclical element

The arguments to the effect that cyclical unemployment affects the less skilled workers more severely are well known (see, for example, Bean *et al.*, 1990). First and foremost comes the 'ladder' effect. Skilled or educated workers who do not find jobs at their own level accept jobs below qualification, for which somehow they receive priority.[6] This aggravates the difficulties encountered by less skilled workers: eventually, most of the unemployment becomes concentrated among unskilled workers, at the bottom of the ladder, where the possibility of work below qualification hardly exists.

The upgrading of labour qualifications during recessions was stressed for the USA by Okun (1981). An element of indirect confirmation is found in the EC (1991) employment survey which shows that younger workers, hired after the rise of unemployment in the 1970s, are more apt to work below qualifications than their older colleagues.[7] The 'ladder' effect stresses the employment consequences of wage rigidities at the low end of the wage scale – a feature to which we return below.

A second argument about cyclicality is related to labour hoarding:

> Labour hoarding matters because it is likely that in the case of significant recruiting and training costs for skilled labour, firms will be more likely to choose to hoard skilled labour than unskilled labour during temporary downturns in activity. (Bean *et al.*, 1990)

1.3 Structural trend

The arguments in support of a structural shift in the skill composition of labour demand have been documented most systematically for the USA. The wage differentials (as observed in the USA) are more informative than unemployment differentials, because the former represent a quantitative measure and the latter only a qualitative one.

The USA witnessed in the 1980s a substantial increase in the wage differentials associated with education (mostly the 'college premium'), accompanied by an *increase* in the proportion of more educated workers:

> The positive correlation of relative wages and quantity changes among demographic groups in the 1980s strongly suggests that relative demand shifts ... are necessary to understand recent wage structure movements. (Katz, 1992–3)

Three elements are invoked in explanation of the relative demand shifts:

(i) Skill-biased technical change, imputed to the spread of microcomputers and to the increased share of advanced technologies (high-tech) in the US capital stock.

(ii) The relative decline in the number of high-wage, blue-collar jobs in industry, reflecting the relative stagnation of output, and sustained growth of productivity, in that sector ('deindustrialisation').

(iii) The increased competition from low-wage economies, interpretable as an increased implicit supply of less educated workers ('out-sourcing').

Quantitative assessment of the three effects and of their relative importance is difficult, and complicated by the need to allow for supply factors and for deviations from competitive wages. The first explanation is usually assigned the highest weight (to some extent by default), followed by the other two in that order. For the last effect, a weight of 15 per cent is mentioned (Katz, 1992–3, p. 13). We now consider in more detail the issues of skill-biased technical change and increased foreign competition.

1.4 Skill-biased technical change and factor substitution

The evidence of skill-biased technical change remains fairly limited and circumstantial. In the USA, the starting observation is that skilled employment relative to unskilled employment has increased steadily after 1973. In the 1970s, however, this increase was associated with a relative (as well as an absolute) real wage decrease, while in the 1980s it was associated with a (relative) increase. If we assume full employment and perfect competition, this change must result from demand and/or supply shifts. The observed mix of employment and of real wage changes suggests that, at least in the 1980s, the supply shift must have been accompanied by an even stronger demand shift.

Various studies, based on detailed microdata bases, have tried to disentangle the various factors to be taken into account. The basic observation is that most of the wage premium for higher education accrues, *within* specific industries or sectors of the economy, in reward of a general, unexplained efficiency advantage (Bound and Johnson, 1992; Katz and Murphy, 1992). The identification of that advantage with technological development remain largely interpretative. Reference is made to studies reporting a *ceteris paribus* wage premium (17 per cent in 1984 and 19 per cent in 1989) for computer use (Krueger, 1993), as well as to a positive correlation between employment of highly educated workers and investment in computer technologies, intensive R&D, or high-tech capital intensity (Berman, Bound and Griliches, 1983; Berndt and Morrison, 1991). These illustrations are suggestive, but do not rule out alternative interpretations (for example, in terms of product mixes within these industries). A more recent study (Entorf and Kramarz, 1994) on somewhat richer French data, suggests that computer-based new technologies are used by abler workers, so that the wage premium obtained by the latter is not simply due to the fact that using new technologies increases their productivity.

Another source of information about demand for skills comes from the estimation of production functions. Bean and Pissarides (1990) constructed an econometric model with two kinds of labour (non-manual and manual), which they estimated on British manufacturing sectoral data over the period 1970–86. The authors obtain some evidence of non-neutral technological progress at the sectoral level, in favour of skilled labour. A similar finding is obtained on French data by Sneessens and Shadman-Mehta (1995). They distinguish two skill groups. A high-skill group consists of 'professional and managerial workers', a lower-skill group includes all white-collar employees and blue-collar workers. The authors estimate a trend rate of substitution of the more skilled for less skilled workers of some 4–5 per cent per year before 1974 and 2–3 per cent thereafter. That trend probably captures the three elements mentioned above to explain relative demand shifts. Such a trend is impressive, and it seems unlikely that the higher rate could have persisted. The decline after 1974, although at first glance contrary to the US evidence, is consistent with the lower rates of technological progress after 1974 found in many empirical studies in association with the slower growth of output and reduced investment rate (Drèze and Bean, 1990).

1.5 Foreign competition and factor-price equalisation

International trade theory offers a direct argument in support of the claim that increased competition from low-wage economies should affect negatively the market position of low-skilled workers, resulting in lower wages (or higher unemployment in case of downward wage rigidity). The argument comes from the factor-price equalisation theorems associated with the Heckscher–Ohlin model of trade.[8] These theorems state that, under certain conditions, *free trade in final* (e.g. consumer) *goods brings about international parity of factor prices* (e.g. wages).

The reasoning is straightforward. Assume that m goods are traded at competitive world prices p (a row vector), and produced through identical constant returns technologies, using m factors of production with input coefficients A (an m m matrix). Let factor prices in country c be w_c. Equilibrium requires

$$p \leq w_c A \tag{1}$$

with equality in case of positive production. If country c produces the m goods, so that (1) holds with equality, and the matrix A has full rank, then (1) can be inverted to yield

$$w_c = pA^{-1} \tag{2}$$

The factor prices are thus fully determined by the world prices of traded goods p, and should be identical in all countries producing the full set of these goods.

It is not easy to assess the relevance of the theorem, since the assumptions are relatively strict. For instance, the assumption of identical constant returns technologies is exceedingly unrealistic. Of course, there are extensions – but we do not wish to assess technicalities, only broad tendencies. On the one hand, it is clear that factor-price equalisation forces are at work in world trade. In spite of numerous and significant departures from the theoretically sufficient conditions, competitive pressures on goods markets must entail *some* tendency towards wage convergence. On the other hand, prevailing departures from wage convergence are glaring and suggest that the pressures towards equalisation remain largely ineffective. In particular, the wage disparities displayed in table 8.4 would seem to exceed by far what can be accounted for by tariffs, transportation and transaction costs, product differentiation, returns to scale and the like. At the same time, examples of relocation of activities to low-wage economies abound. It seems indeed hard to deny that low-skilled workers face increasing competition from low-wage economies, with negative implications for their wage and employment prospects. Of particular concern to Western European workers is the competition from Eastern Europe. The *ratio* of wage costs in the West and the East is alleged to exceed 10 or sometimes even 20. Distances being what they are, it should not take very long for Eastern competition to spread across manufacturing and many services.[9]

That increased competition from low-wage economies affects primarily the less skilled workers in Europe and the US is the commonly accepted premise – confirmed to some crude extent by the analysis of US data. But the confirmation remains crude. More detailed evidence, for specific skill groups, would be valuable.

Table 8.4 *Hourly wage costs for production workers in manufacturing, 1992*

Country or area	Index US = 100	$ US
USA	100	16.17
Canada	105	17.02
Australia	80	12.94
Hong Kong	24	3.89
Japan	100	16.16
Korea	30	4.93
New Zealand	49	7.91
Singapore	31	5.00
Taiwan	32	5.19
Belgium	136	22.01
Denmark	124	20.02
Finland	116	18.69
France	104	16.88
Germany	160	25.94
Ireland	82	13.32
Italy	120	19.41
Netherlands	128	20.72
Norway	143	23.20
Portugal	31	5.01
Spain	83	13.39
Sweden	150	24.23
Switzerland	144	23.26
UK	91	14.69
Trade-weighted measures		
All economies excluding the USA	96	15.46
Europe	126	20.40
Asian NIEs[a]	30	4.84

[a] Asian newly industrialising (Hong Kong, Korea, Singapore and Taiwan).
Source: US Bureau of Labour Statistics (March 1993).

2 Policy objectives

What conclusions should be drawn from the overview above? First, the position of less educated workers is undoubtedly weak on today's labour markets, both in the USA and in Europe. Second, that position is weaker today than 10–20 years ago, due to a combination of cyclical and structural forces. Third, there is a presumption that technological development and competition from low-wage economies have contributed to that deterioration. Fourth, in continental Europe, the resistance of relative wages of less skilled workers has been an aggravating factor.

Fifth, the competition from low-wage economies, including in particular Eastern Europe, is still far from having exerted its full effects. Sixth, the fragility of our knowledge on all these counts is both a cause of embarrassment and an invitation to prudence.

2.1 Jobs versus income

The situation thus summarised creates a difficult policy problem. Jobs and income are two dimensions of well-being. In much economic theorising, worker preferences are depicted as rising with income, but declining with hours worked. That approach fails to recognise that most individuals attach a positive value to having a regular job – even though a good number might prefer to work shorter hours.[10] There are two main reasons why a regular job is valued. The first is that work is a major avenue of social integration and personal fulfilment. The second is that a regular job, where the employment relationship is expected by both parties to have some stability, is the basis on which other durable relationships or living patterns are built – founding a family, owning a house, establishing community relationships or consumption patterns. For these reasons, it is natural to rank full employment as a major social objective.

Such a viewpoint is supported not only by welfarist or utilitarian approaches but also by theories of social choice and justice based on capabilities (Sen, 1985) or primary goods (Rawls, 1971). Sen emphasises 'the positive freedom to chose how to live one's own life'. Rawls emphasises, under the name of self-respect or self-esteem, 'having a rational plan of life, which calls upon a person's natural capabilities, and is confirmed and appreciated by others' (pp. 440 passim). A regular job is undoubtedly essential to these achievements.[11]

2.2 The policy dilemma

In our view, it must remain an important policy objective in its own right that the *least*-skilled or educated workers have access to regular jobs, susceptible of providing an adequate basis for freely planning their lives. It must also be a policy aim that these jobs provide an adequate income, which is equally essential to positive freedom. The policy dilemma is that if the position of less skilled workers is indeed weakened, and likely to remain weak for a number of years to come, it will be difficult to reconcile the goal of providing jobs to all with the goal of providing an adequate income to all. Market-clearing wages will not satisfy the income goal, wages yielding an adequate income will not be conducive to full employment. This conflict of goals between full employment and income protection is vividly illustrated by the contrast between the USA (with more employment at lower wages) and Western Europe (with higher wages but more unemployment).[12]

Reconciling full employment with 'adequate' incomes for less skilled workers leaves few options. The first is of course education and training to raise skill levels. From a long-run viewpoint this is undoubtedly the most constructive policy. Every effort should be made to pursue it effectively. This probably calls for devising a more effective training programme than straight schooling – since the target group consists mostly of workers who leave school early, in spite of the broad availability of public education. The success of the German and Austrian apprenticeship system remains a model worthy of understanding and emulation (Soskice, 1994). Also, due attention must be paid to the issue of working habits and discipline, which is distinct from that of technical skills.

There are, however, two limits to what can be accomplished through training. A long-run limit concerns the minority of workers with limited learning abilities. A short-run limit concerns the special problems associated with the current high level of unemployment. Training brings some of the unemployed to the head of the queue, but does not affect the length of the queue.[13] Except for isolated narrow qualifications, hardly accessible to the bulk of those presently unemployed, labour supply is not a constraining factor today. Measures addressed to labour demand, including reductions in labour costs, must be the order of the day.

The crux of the dilemma is thus how to reconcile *labour costs low enough to promote employment of low-skill workers* with *reasonable incomes for these workers* and *proper incentives towards economic efficiency* (incentives to work and incentives to acquire skills). The difference between the short run and the long run is the number of workers concerned, but not the nature of the dilemma. We should be prepared to face the dilemma squarely, and for many years to come.

It is obvious that the dilemma so defined is a matter of public policy. There are no private incentives to address the problem. Any solution involves an element of contemporaneous redistribution – even though, from a longer-run viewpoint (from the viewpoint of unborn members of a future generation, whose native skills are stochastic), redistribution may be interpreted as efficient risk-sharing.[14] What policies are conducive to 'reconcile labour costs low enough to promote employment of low-skilled workers with reasonable incomes for these workers and proper incentives towards economic efficiency'? We review two main policy alternatives. One involves minimum wages with appropriate labour taxes or subsidies, the other is based on flexible wages with appropriate income transfers. Prior to that review, we discuss briefly the related policy objective of a trade liberalisation.

2.3 *Free trade as a policy objective*

With reference to competition from low-wage economies, it must be recognised that our current practice includes definite elements of protectionism, especially with regard to immigration. The merits of free trade are not unequivocal or unchallenged.[15] It is natural to wonder whether economies with elaborate programmes of social protection can afford to face the competition from low-wage economies. Perhaps they should protect themselves from wage equalisation by restricting the imports of goods or services produced in low-wage economies.

The second-best argument in support of protectionism rests on the domestic distortion associated with downward wage rigidities (due to minimum wages or simply to unemployment benefits). In the presence of such a distortion, a tariff protection may Pareto-dominate free trade from a world viewpoint (Drèze, 1993b). However the tariff policy is superior only when world prices are not too far away from domestic prices under autarchy. And the Pareto-domination requires compensating transfers (aid).

Our purpose here is not to endorse the protectionist argument. It is rather to underscore the implications of domestic distortions and the desirability of avoiding them, if possible. It is also to list free trade as a potential policy objective in its own rights. As noted by Krugman (1993) and McCulloch (1993) in a recent overall assessment, it may well be that 'free trade is suboptimal in theory yet optimal in practice' (McCulloch, 1993, p. 371). A pressing issue for Western Europe today is the speed and extent of openness to the East – where disequilibrium is pervasive. Raising productivity and wages in Eastern Europe is the key dimension of convergence, and should be promoted (with the prudence suggested by the East German situation). Still, it is part of the overall picture that we are a long way from equilibrium at the world level, that we will face mounting competition from low-wage economies for many years to come, a competition particularly detrimental to low-skilled workers, and that we must aim for some kind of second-best outcome.

3 Policy alternatives

3.1 Minimum wages cum tax exemptions or subsidies

To set the stage, we present in table 8.5 some data on minimum wages in 10 Western European countries. A striking feature is the high ratio of minimum wages (where they exist) to median wages (namely, 60–70 per cent). We may add that the fraction of workers whose wages are directly tied to the minimum is of the order of 10 per cent (CERC, 1991). We also present in table 8.6 some data on social insurance contributions (SIC) and income taxes in nine European countries, the USA and Japan. According to table 8.6, the average wedge in Europe is close to 40 per cent, with 24 per cent coming from employer contributions (ESIC), 11 per cent from employee contributions and 15 per cent from income taxes (at mean earnings).

3.2 Reducing taxes on minimum wages

The first natural step towards reconciling low labour costs to employers with reasonable workers' incomes is to eliminate the wedge driven between them by SIC and income taxes. A policy initiative paper by Drèze and Malinvaud *et al.* (1994) suggests exempting minimum wages from ESIC in all European countries, with substitute resources allocated to social security from indirect taxation (with preference for an EU-level energy tax). The main suggestion is to scale the exemption so that it disappears around median or mean wages. This implies a reduction of labour taxes on all wages below the median, but an increase in marginal rates between the minimum and the median. (In countries without a well defined minimum wage, wages below two-thirds of the median should be fully exempted according to the proposal.)

We explain first the reasons for the specific modalities, then the overall logic. ESIC are singled out so as to reduce labour costs to employers without affecting take-home pay. The incentives to reduce labour costs exist in all EU countries, due to high unemployment concentrated among low-skilled workers. Whether take-home pay at minimum wages should be reviewed upwards or downwards is a matter to be considered country by country, given the marked differences in absolute levels revealed by table 8.5. There may also exist specific motivations, linked to the ratio of unemployment benefits to minimum wages and the need to maintain work incentives. The matter of income tax introduces the issues of comprehensiveness and progressivity. It is better kept separate, though in

Table 8.5 *Minimum wages in Western Europe, 1985–91, selected years*

Country	Year	System	Level (ECU per month)	Ratio to median wage (%)	Exceptions
Belgium	1988	Economy-wide at age 21	783	66	– 7.5% per year of age below 21
Germany		Negotiated at sectoral regional level			
Spain	1991	Economy-wide at age 18	399	54	–39% at age 17 –61% below age 17
France	1987	Economy-wide at age 18	556	61	Not applicable below age 18
Greece	1988	Economy-wide private sector public sector	 332 418	 67	Depends upon marital status and seniority
Ireland		No minimum wage			
Italy		Negotiated at sectoral level			
Netherlands	1988	Economy-wide at age 23	898	72	–10% per year of age below 23
Portugal	1985	Economy-wide at age 18	148	73	–25% below age 18 –17% for domestic services
UK		No minimum wage			

Source: CERC (1991).

Table 8.6 *Social insurance contributions and income tax at average earnings, blue-collar workers, 1991*

	SIC rates		Average income tax rate	Wedge as percentage of private cost
	Employer	Employee		
Belgium	41.9	12.1	11.6	46.2
Denmark	0.0	2.5	36.0	38.5
France	43.8	17.1	1.0	43.1
Germany	18.2	18.2	8.7	38.1
Ireland	12.2	7.8	16.4	32.4
Italy	50.1	9.0	14.2	48.9
Netherlands	10.8	10.7	32.5	48.8
Portugal	24.5	11.0	0.9	29.2
UK	10.4	7.6	15.5	30.3
Unweighted mean	23.5	10.7	15.2	39.5
USA	7.7	7.7	11.3	24.8
Japan	7.6	7.0	2.4	15.8

Source: OECD, *Economic Perspectives* (January 1993).

Denmark it would come into the picture if the wedge is to be reduced (ESIC is zero in Denmark).

Lower labour costs are clearly desirable at the low end of the wage scale. Where minimum wages are set by law, they may be kept at unchanged levels when ESIC are eliminated. At the upper end, it is likely that wages clear markets for specific skills, so that ESIC reductions would result in unnecessary wage increases. That is a good reason to scale the exemption down to zero around the centre of the wage distribution. In comparison to a flat exemption applicable to all wages, the loss of revenue is reduced by a factor of 3:1 (Drèze and Malinvaud *et al.*, 1994).

The rationale for exempting minimum wages from ESIC is twofold. First, if one wishes to reconcile lower labour costs with reasonable incomes, it does not make sense to aggravate the problem through mandatory contributions (taxation). Second, the deadweight cost of redistributive programmes is a reason to aim for uniformity, that is to 'equalise, as far as possible, the benefit levels in all social security systems between which individuals are likely to move' (Lindbeck *et al.*, 1994, proposal 50). This principle of uniformity would recommend that social security benefits of recipients of minimum wages be set at roughly the same levels as those of unemployed or non-working persons. In several countries, the current situation is close to that guideline. In such a case, the fact that a person takes up employment at minimum wages has zero marginal cost for the social security system. It is thus logical to finance minimum level benefits from general revenue, while putting the higher tiers on an actuarial basis.[16]

The benefits expected from the proposed measure depend upon the wage-elasticity of effective demand for low-paid labour. That elasticity is alleged to be higher at low wages than at high wages, in particular due to substitution between skills and with capital (see Hamermesh, 1986). By scaling the exemption down, substitution of high for low skill is further discouraged; by taxing energy, which is complementary to capital, substitution of capital for labour is discouraged.

The econometric simulations carried out at DGII of the European Commision (EC, 1993a), at Office Français des Conjonctures Economiques (Sterdyniak *et al.*, 1994) and by Sneessens and Shadman-Mehta (1995) concur in suggesting medium-term effects of the order of two percentage points of employment for ESIC exemptions on low-skilled wages amounting to one percentage point of GDP, *at unchanged budget deficits*. The Drèze and Malinvaud *et al.* proposal is thus at best a partial remedy to the current unemployment problem, but still a highly desirable one.[17] The only questionable aspect is the increased *marginal* rate of ESIC between minimum and median or mean wages. (By and large, marginal ESIC rates would be doubled over that range.) This should not affect individual incentives to acquire skills, since take-home pay is unaffected. But it might discourage firms from investing in worker skills in that range due to the increased relative costs of more skilled labour. Thus, correcting a short-run disequilibrium might have undesirable consequences in the longer run. The trend favouring more skilled labour is quite strong, however, and undoubtedly perceived by firms. Accordingly, this drawback is unlikely to be severe.

3.3 Minimum wages cum subsidies

A further avenue towards reconciling employment, incomes and incentives keeps minimum wages and unemployment benefits at a level deemed reasonable for income protection, but issues *employment subsidies* to firms using low-skilled labour. This is entirely analogous to the ESIC exemption proposal, carried into *negative contributions* (the subsidies). The exemption proposal is meant as a partial correction to the massive wasteful unemployment which prevails today. Employment subsidies could aim at restoring full labour-market efficiency. This raises the issue of how to define an efficient outcome in the presence of subsidies. The issue is illustrated in figure 8.5

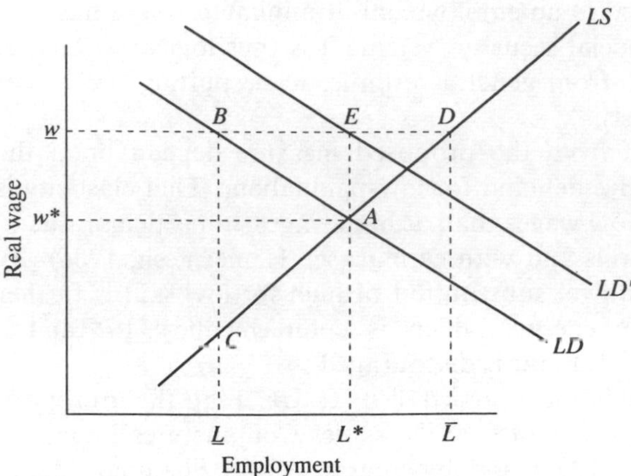

Figure 8.5 Labour market equilibrium with subsidies

In figure 8.5, labour demand is *LD*, labour supply is *LS*, and the competitive outcome (w^*, L^*) is at *A*. The figure is supposedly drawn for unskilled labour. The construction could be interpreted as keeping constant the wages for higher skills. Alternatively, and more meaningfully, it should be interpreted as incorporating implicitly the adjustments in wages and employment for higher skills that would naturally accompany changes in unskilled wages. In particular, if higher unskilled wages lead to higher wages and less employment at the next skill level, the additional unemployed of that next level enter the labour supply in the figure ('ladder' effect). The elasticity of 'effective' labour supply is thus a hybrid concept, combining the effect of wages on participation rates for low-skilled workers and the effect of low-skilled wages on unemployment at other skill levels. Similarly, but less importantly perhaps, labour demand should be interpreted as inclusive of skill-substitution effects, given the adjustment of other wages to unskilled wages.

Suppose now that w^* is lower than the wage level $\underline{w}$ deemed to provide a reasonable income to unskilled workers. Under a minimum wage equal to $\underline{w}$, the market outcome is at *B*, with employment $\underline{L}$ and wasteful employment $L^* - \underline{L}$.[18] Note however that measured unemployment at $\underline{w}$ will be $\bar{L} - \underline{L}$, since effective labour supply will correspond to point *D*.[19]

In order to bring about an efficient level of employment, an employment subsidy equal to $\underline{w} - w^*$ could be offered to firms, thereby raising their labour demand to *LD'*. The outcome will then be ($\underline{w}$, L^*) at point *E*. Note again that measured unemployment will remain positive, and equal to $\bar{L} - L^*$. A little calculation shows that

$$\frac{\bar{L} - L^*}{L} = \bar{u} \approx \frac{w - w^*}{w^*} \cdot \eta_{LS \cdot W}$$

and hence

$$\frac{w - w^*}{w^*} = \frac{\bar{u}}{\eta_{LS \cdot W}} \tag{3}$$

where $\eta_{LS \cdot W}$ denotes the wage elasticity of labour supply. In other words, the subsidy leading to an efficient employment level is a percentage of the market wage approximately equal to the ratio of measured unemployment to the elasticity of labour supply. We do not regard that elasticity as known or easy to estimate. One should also ask whether the unemployed at E are those workers whose reservation wage exceeds w^*; the answer is probably negative.

3.4 *Flexible wages cum transfers*

The alternative to ESIC exemptions and/or employment subsidies is to lower or eliminate minimum wages as well as unemployment benefits, and issue to workers a transfer independent of employment status.[20] The need to consider simultaneously wages and unemployment benefits is obvious: lower wages at unchanged benefits would destroy incentives to work, which are already minimal in some cases today.

We concentrate on the simplest proposal, which calls for letting wages adjust to clear the labour market, with no unemployment benefits, while issuing transfers independent of employment status. Such transfers are called 'social dividend', e.g. by Meade (1989) or 'participation income', e.g. by Atkinson (1993a). The simple idea is to reconcile market-clearing wages with income protection by issuing a transfer to all or most *citizens*, whether employed or not. Proponents of this idea typically advocate individual transfers, accruing in the same amount to all male and female adults, with lower amounts for children (and probably higher amounts for elderly or disabled individuals). The 'participation income' variant restricts benefits to members of the labour force (employed or unemployed) and specific groups such as workers enrolled in training programmes, persons doing voluntary work or caring for dependents and disabled persons. Whatever the variant, all other forms of social transfers (pensions, family allowances, sickness allowances, unemployment benefits) are discontinued. The transfers are financed from general revenues. The standard example is a proportional income tax on all income other than the social dividend, with abolition of all income tax allowances.

The first merit of this idea is to (hopefully) restore labour market efficiency at the low end of the wage scale, by letting wages fall to market-clearing levels and eliminating the so-called 'unemployment trap' – a term referring to situations where work is discouraged by the prospective loss of unemployment benefits or means-tested allowances. The second merit is to introduce simplification and uniformity in our social security systems, which have grown in complexity. The main drawback is a relatively high budgetary outlay, which means a high level of distortive taxes. In particular, higher income tax rates may interfere with labour market efficiency at higher wage levels.

As an illustration Atkinson (1993a) reports the possibility of funding a participation income of £936 per adult per year on a 'revenue-neutral' basis, and of £1976 per year if income tax rates were raised by 10 percentage points. (In these calculations, means-tested benefits are maintained, but the number of recipients falls by 10 per cent and 50 per cent respectively.)

One major issue raised by this approach is that of market-clearing wages. Would a (nearly) competitive outcome emerge on the market for low-skilled labour? This is of course a complex issue, which cannot be treated properly here. Serious doubts about the possibility of implementing market-clearing wages come from theories of wage formation that stress the exercise of market power by unions (see for example, the surveys of Oswald, 1985, or Pencavel, 1985) or insiders (see Lindbeck and Snower, 1988). The more specific insider–outsider theory links that market power to the costs faced by firms attempting to hire below prevailing or contractual wages.[21] It would be in the spirit of that theory to recognise that these costs are apt to be lower for less skilled workers (which may help explain the recourse to legal minimum wages, rather than contractual union wages, for low-skilled labour). On the other hand, there seems to exist a broad social consensus in favour of minimum wages, a consensus that might be mobilised in favour of the alternative based on a form of 'participation income'.

3.5 An earned-income credit

An intermediate programme consists of abandoning minimum wages, but keeping unemployment benefits, while issuing transfers to low-paid *employed* workers, thereby restoring incentives to work. The 'earned income credit' practised in the USA is an example (see International Revenue Service, 1993, section 35). The idea is to eliminate the 'unemployment trap' by making up, in totality or in part, the loss of benefits suffered by an unemployed who goes to work. The US earned income credit has a ceiling of US $1.511 per year. This may be compared to average benefits, assessed by Burtless (1987), at US $4.350 per recipient.[22] Also, the credit falls progressively from its maximum at the income level US $12.200 down to zero at income level US $23.050. An additional requirement for eligibility is a 'qualifying child'.

Under full replacement, the combination of unemployment benefits and an earned-income credit is comparable to a subsidy *per worker* independent of employment status. Compared to a participation income, it is limited to workers. The cost can also be reduced by eliminating the credit progressively as earned income rises.

3.6 The market for personal services

Thus far, we have concentrated on reducing labour costs as a way of promoting employment of low-skilled workers. Reduced labour costs may promote employment by slowing down capital–labour substitution or skill substitution. They may also promote employment through lower relative prices for goods with a high intensity of low-skilled labour. It must however be recognised that technological development and competition from low-wage economies narrow down the range of goods or services where employment prospects exist. One area is immune from competition from either machines or foreign workers, namely 'proximity services', which involve a *local personal* relationship. There seems to exist a domain of growing but imperfectly met needs, with an employment potential so far unrealised.

The following list of 'proximity services' appears in EC (1993b):

1 Assistance to elderly and disabled persons
2 Childcare
3 Assistance to young children
4 Assistance to school children
5 Personal and public safety
6 House improvements
7 Collective local transportation
8 Environmental protection
9 Cultural and recreational activities
10 Neighbourhood stores.

The list is quite heterogeneous. We quote it as suggestive of directions worth exploring.

The question of interest here is whether these directions hold promise for low-skilled jobs. Answers are mixed, and vary down the list. Still, if one considers why employment towards meeting these needs is not more developed, two reasons come up recurrently: demand insolvency at market prices, and limited supply through firms resorting to paid employment.

One suggestion towards addressing the *demand-solvency* aspect has received some attention in France and Belgium, namely 'service vouchers' (also mentioned in EC, 1993b). The underlying idea is to privilege personal services as an area of early implementation of some of the measures discussed above, by allowing households hiring labour to deduct from their own income tax the taxes applicable to their hirings (employee SIC and income tax of the worker).[23]

This may sound far-fetched, and quite remote from our subject. Perhaps it is not, experience will tell. We think, however, that in many cases (like items 5–8 on the above list) a more structured organisation of the *supply side* will be needed, to pull long-term unemployed and low-skilled workers into the production of proximity services. This element is important to translate measures of labour cost reduction into employment. Again, some suggestions exist – like the Belgian proposal to exempt non-profit organisations producing proximity services from ESIC on low-skilled labour (a proposal also mentioned in EC, 1993b).

4 Conclusion

Although the evidence remains in part circumstantial, we believe, together with a growing number of US labour economists and European policy advisers, that technological development and competition from low-wage economies confronts Western European countries with a difficult policy dilemma: is it possible to reconcile labour costs low enough to promote full employment of low-skilled workers with reasonable incomes for these workers and proper incentives for economic efficiency?

Constructive measures towards resolving that dilemma start with practical education and training, then go on to promote the demand and institutionalised supply of proximity services. Reliance on the price mechanism points towards measures reducing or eliminating the wedge between labour costs to employers and net marginal earnings of employees. A basic policy choice must be made between on the one hand the avenue of minimum wages, unemployment benefits and employment subsidies concentrated on the low end of the wage scale, and on the other the avenue of flexible wages, hence no durable unemployment benefits, but a 'participation income' issued on an individual basis to all adult members of the labour force. Although the second avenue has some merits, including its more 'individual' approach to social security, these hinge crucially on the prospects for implementing flexible wages. Union-wage and insider–outsider theories of wage determination cast doubts but would need to be verified specifically for low skill levels.

Short of making that basic policy choice, reductions or exemptions of employers' contributions to social security constitute a natural first step that deserves urgent attention from policy makers. Such measures are indispensable to the sustainability of free trade between countries with highly dissimilar levels of social protection.

NOTES

This chapter is reprinted with kind permission from *Swedish Economic Policy Review*, 1 (1994), pp. 185–214.

1 For instance, a paper by Hamermesh and Biddle (1993), based on North American data for 1971–81, reports that

> holding demographic and labour market characteristics constant, ... plain people earn less than people of average looks, who earn less than the good looking. Further, the penalty for plainness is slightly larger than the premium for beauty. The effects also are slightly larger for men than for women.

2 There are only two tables in that *magnum opus* involving educational or professional differences – but the significance of table 8.2 is highlighted by the fact that it is printed three times (pp. 45, 291, 330). Although the data in tables 8.1 and 8.2 do not cover identical years, they sustain unambiguously the comments in the text.

3 Thus, Layard, Nickell and Jackman (1991) would interpret the unchanged *distribution* as unchanged mismatch. Sneessens and Shadman-Mehta (1995) interpret the growing *disparity* as growing mismatch. The former authors start from a Cobb–Douglas matching function; the latter authors derive a CES employment function, by explicit aggregation over quantity-constrained firms.

4 US $27,778 and 27,898 respectively, at 1988 prices.

5 See also Atkinson (1993b) for a detailed documentation of increased income inequality in the UK since the mid-1970s.

6 It is reported by Bewley and Brainard (1993) that firms are reluctant to hire over-qualified workers, whose morale will be low if there are no prospects for upgrading. Still, the superior ability of the more skilled or educated workers to find *some* job is seldom disputed.

7 Unfortunately, no comparable data for a low-unemployment period are available; one cannot exclude that work below qualification disappears with seniority, irrespective of the unemployment situation.

8 Cf. Jones and Neary (1984), Ethier (1984) or Neary (1980) for surveys.

9 The data in table 8.4 are not available for Eastern Europe. However, Plan Econ Inc. in Washington publishes data for net monthly wages which, in 1992, stood

well below US $100 for Romania and Bulgaria, below $150 for the Czech Republic and Slovakia and below US $200 for Hungary and Poland.

10 Drèze (1986) spells this out.

11 Of course, it is equally essential to workers in low-wage countries.

12 See also the conclusion in Freeman (1993).

13 See Calmfors (1994) for a more extensive discussion.

14 See Drèze (1989) or Drèze and Gollier (1993) for an elaboration of that statement.

15 Maurice Allais has been a vocal critique of the GATT agreements; see his articles in *Le Figaro* (15–16 November 1993), and references given there.

16 'Actuarial' should be understood in terms of reinsurance prices, which allow for state-dependent corrections, rather than in strict probability terms. With that understanding, we agree with proposals 45–46 of Lindbeck *et al.* (1994).

17 If the low-skilled workers represent 30 per cent of the labour force, two percentage points of total employment represent 6.6 per cent of the low-skilled labour force. The simulations report a higher gain of low-skilled employment but some decline of skilled employment.

18 A rough measure of the waste is given by the triangle ABC. To a first approximation, the area of that triangle is

$$\frac{w^*}{2} * \left(\frac{L^* - \underline{L}}{L^*}\right)\left(\frac{1}{\eta_{LS \cdot W}} - \frac{1}{\eta_{LD \cdot W}}\right)$$

where $\eta_{LS \cdot W}$ is the wage elasticity of labour supply and $\eta_{LD \cdot W}$ the wage elasticity of labour demand.

19 A simple calculation, analogous to that underlying n. 18, shows that

$$\frac{\bar{L} - L^*}{\bar{L} - \underline{L}} \approx \frac{\eta_{LS \cdot W}}{\eta_{LS \cdot W} - \eta_{LD \cdot W}}.$$

This formula could be used to evaluate what fraction of measured unemployment is wasteful unemployment.

20 See Drèze (1993a) as well as Sneessens and Van der Linden (1994) for an earlier comparison of these alternatives.

21 Bewley and Brainard (1993) implicitly offer an 'upside-down' explanation, where the reluctance of firms is linked to the morale of new hires rather than to the activities of insiders.

22 These are US $ at 1980 prices.

23 The name 'service vouchers' arose from a specific proposal, whereby households could buy at Post Offices vouchers with which the services of unemployed workers could be hired: one page of the voucher would be used by the worker in payment of employee SIC and income tax, another page would be used by the hiring household to claim an income tax deduction.

REFERENCES

Allais, M., 1993. 'Le rapport de la Banque Mondiale et de l'OCDE sur le libre-échange: (1) Une gigantesque mystification, (2) Une erreur fondamentale', *Le Figaro* (15–16 November)

Atkinson, A.B., 1993. 'Beveridge, the national minimum and its future in a European context', London School of Economics, *STICHERD Discussion Paper*, **WSP/85**

1993b. 'What is happening to the distribution of income in the UK?', London School of Economics, *STICHERD Discussion Paper*, **WSP/87**

Bean, C.R. and C. Pissarides, 1990. 'Skill shortages and structural unemployment in Britain: a (mis-)matching approach', in F. Padoa Schioppa (ed.), *Mismatch and Labour Mobility*, Cambridge: Cambridge University Press

Bean, C.R., P. Bernholz, J.P. Danthine and E. Malinvaud, 1990. 'European labour markets: a long-run view', *CEPS Paper*, **46**

Berman, E., J. Bound and Z. Griliches, 1993. 'Changes in the demand for skilled labor within US manufacturing industries: evidence from the Annual Survey of Manufacturing', *NBER Working Paper*, **4255**, Cambridge, MA: NBER; *Quarterly Journal of Economics*, **109**, 367–97 (1994)

Berndt, E.R. and C. Morrison, 1991. *High-Tech Capital, Economic Performance and Labour Composition in US Manufacturing Industries: An Exploratory Analysis*, Cambridge, MA: MIT Press

Bewley, T. and W. Brainard, 1993. *A Depressed Labour Market, as Explained by Participants*, New Haven: Yale University Press

Bound, J. and G. Johnson, 1992. 'Changes in the structure of wages in the 1980s: an evaluation of alternative explanations', *American Economic Review*, **82**, 371–92

Burtless, G., 1987. 'Jobless pay and high European unemployment', chapter 3 in R.Z. Lawrence and C.L. Schultze (eds.), *Barriers to European Growth: A Transatlantic View*, Washington, DC: Brookings Institution, 105–61

Calmfors, L., 1994. 'Active labour market policy and unemployment – a framework for the analysis of crucial design features', *OECD Economic Studies*, **22**, 7–47

CERC, 1991. 'Les bas salaires dans le pays de la CEE', *La Documentation Française*, **101**, 3–86

Drèze, J.H., 1986. 'Work-sharing: some theory and recent European experience', *Economic Policy*, **3**, 561–619; reprinted as chapter 17 in J.H. Drèze, *Underemployment Equilibria*, Cambridge: Cambridge University Press (1991)

1989. 'Wages, employment and the equity–efficiency trade-off', *Recherches Economiques de Louvain*, **55**, 1–31; reprinted as chapter 12 in J.H. Drèze, *Underemployment Equilibria*, Cambridge: Cambridge University Press (1991)

1993a. 'Can varying social insurance contributions improve labour market efficiency?', chapter 8 in A.B. Atkinson (ed.), *The Economics of Partnership: A Third Way?*, London: Macmillan

1993b. 'Labour market policies and second-best tariffs: an illustration', CORE, Louvain-la-Neuve, mimeo

Drèze, J.H. and C.R. Bean (eds.), 1990. *Europe's Unemployment Problem*, Cambridge, MA: MIT Press

Drèze, J.H. and C. Gollier, 1993. 'Risk sharing on the labour market and second-best wage rigidities', *European Economic Review*, **37**, 1437–82

Drèze, J.H. and E. Malinvaud, with P. De Grauwe, L. Gevers, A. Italianer, O. Lefebvre, M. Marchand, H. Sneessens and P. Champsaur, J.M. Charpin, J.P. Fitoussi and G. Laroque, 1994. 'Growth and employment, the scope for a European initiative', *European Economy*, **1**, 75–106

EC, 1991. 'Evolution de l'emploi dans la communauté', *Economie Européene*, **47**

1992. 'L'emploi en Europe', Luxembourg: Office of Official Publications of the European Community

1993a. 'Taxation, employment and environmental fiscal reform for reducing unemployment', *DGII Document*, **II/645/93–EN**

1993b. 'Création d'emploi dans les services abrités par un abaissement du coût salarial', *DGV Social Papers*

Entorf, H. and F. Kramarz, 1994. 'The impact of new technologies on wages: lessons from matching panels on employees and their firms', *CREST Paper*, **9407**

Ethier, W.J., 1984. 'High dimensional issues in trade theory', chapter 3 in R.W. Jones and P.B. Kenen (eds.), *Handbook of International Economics*, Amsterdam: North-Holland

Freeman, R., 1993. 'Working under different rules', *NBER Reporter*, **93**, 1–7

Hamermesh, D.S., 1986. 'The demand for labour in the long run', in O.C. Ashenfalter and P.R.G. Layard (eds.), *Handbook of Labour Economics*, Amsterdam: North-Holland

Hamermesh, D.S. and J.E. Biddle, 1993. 'Beauty and the labour market', *NBER Working Paper*, **4518**, Cambridge, MA: NBER

International Revenue Service, 1993. 'Your federal income tax', Washington, DC: Department of the Treasury

Jones, R.W. and J.P. Neary, 1984. 'The positive theory of international trade', chapter 1 in R.W. Jones and P.B. Kenen (eds.), *Handbook of International Economics*, Amsterdam: North-Holland

Katz, L.F., 1992–3. 'Understanding recent changes in the wage structure', *NBER Reporter*, **10–15**

Katz, L.F. and K. Murphy, 1992. 'Changes in relative wages, 1963–1987: supply and demand factors', *Quarterly Journal of Economics*, **107**, 35–78

Krueger, A.B., 1993. 'How computers have changed the wage structure: evidence from micro data, 1984–89', *Quarterly Journal of Economics*, **108**, 33–60

Krugman, P., 1993. 'The narrow and broad arguments for free trade', *American Economic Review*, **82**, 362–6

Layard, P.R.G., S.J. Nickell and R.A. Jackman, 1991. *Unemployment: Macroeconomic Performance and the Labour Market*, Oxford: Oxford University Press

Levy, F. and R.J. Murnane, 1992. 'US earnings levels and earnings inequality: a review of recent trends and proposed explanations', *Journal of Economic Literature*, **30**, 1333–81

Lindbeck, A. and D. Snower, 1988. *The Insider–Outsider Theory of Employment and Unemployment*, Cambridge, MA: MIT Press

Lindbeck, A., P. Molander, T. Persson, O. Petersen, A. Sandmo, B. Swedenborg and N. Thygesen, 1994. *Turning Sweden Around*, Cambridge, MA: MIT Press

Maillard, B. and H. Sneessens, 1994. 'Caractéristiques de l'emploi et du chômage par PCS: France, 1962–1989', *Economie et Prévision*, 113/114, 113–26

McCulloch, R., 1993. 'The optimality of free trade: science or religion?', *American Economic Review*, **83**, 367–71

Meade, J.E., 1989. *Agathotopia: The Economics of Partnership*, Aberdeen: Aberdeen University Press

Neary, J.P., 1980. 'International factor mobility, minimum wage rates and factor price equilibrium: a synthesis', *IIES Seminar Paper*, **158**
OECD, 1989. *Employment Outlook*, Paris: OECD
1992. *Education at a Glance*, Paris: OECD
Okun, A., 1981. *Prices and Quantities: A Macroeconomic Analysis*, Oxford: Basil Blackwell
Oswald, A., 1985. 'The economic theory of trade unions: an introductory survey', *Scandinavian Journal of Economics*, **82**, 160–93
Pencavel, J., 1985. 'Wages and employment and trade unionism: microeconomic models and macroeconomic applications', *Scandinavian Journal of Economics*, **87**, 195–225
Rawls, J., 1971. *A Theory of Justice*, Cambridge, MA: Harvard University Press
Sen, A., 1985. *Commodities and Capabilities*, Amsterdam: North-Holland
Sneessens, H., 1994. 'How should we measure skill mismatch? An example', Département des Sciences Economiques, Louvain-la-Neuve
Sneessens, H. and F. Shadman-Mehta, 1995. 'Real wages, skill mismatch and unemployment persistence', *Annales d'Economie et Statistique*, **37/38**, 255–92
Sneessens, H. and B. Van der Linden, 1994. 'De l'optimalité des systèmes d'assurance chômage: quelques réflexions', *Recherches Economiques de Louvain*, **60**, 129–62
Sneessens, H., F. Shadman-Mehta and B. Maillard-Adamiak, 1993. 'Pénurie de main-d'oeuvre qualifiée et persistence du chômage', *Rapport en Commissariat général du Plan*, Paris
Soskice, D., 1994. 'Reconciling markets and institutions: the German apprenticeship system', in L.M. Lynch (ed.), *Training and the Private Sector: International Comparisons*, Chicago: University of Chicago Press
Sterdyniak, H., E. Fourmann, F. Lerais, M. Delessy and F. Busson, 1994. 'Lutter contre le chômage de masse en Europe', *Observations et Diagnostiques Economiques*, **48**, Paris: OFCE

Discussion

JOZEF KONINGS

Drèze and Sneessens' chapter 8 gives a survey of recent trends in unemployment and the evolution of relative wages. In particular, it stresses the high proportion of the low-skilled unemployed in Europe and the increasing wage dispersion in the USA. I will concentrate on two factors that have been explored in chapter 8, the role of technological development and the role of competition from low-wage countries, in my view the most relevant ones. Since the chapter is a survey study, my discussion can be seen as complementing some of the issues raised. I will start by addressing some of the issues on the relationship between technological development and the emergence of low-skilled unemployment; I will then make some remarks on the role of international trade and will conclude with complementing some of the policy options addressed by Drèze and Sneessens.

1 Technological progress and unemployment

The observation that the low skilled in particular find it harder to find a job and that wage differentials between low skilled and high skilled have increased (especially in the USA) suggests that there has been a relative demand shift in favour of high-skilled workers, as argued in the chapter. While the authors particularly stress the importance of low-skilled unemployed and build their discussion around this theme, it is the case that the unemployment rate for the high skilled has also increased, at least from the 1970s to the 1980s, as shown in table D8.1. This suggests that countries have been subject to adverse shocks that are neutral with regard to skill. The question is then to allocate the overall increase in unemployment between neutral and relative shocks. Drèze and Sneessens stress the importance of relative demand shifts in favour of the high skilled, quoting Bean and Pissarides (1990) and Sneessens and Shadman-Mehta (1995). Recent empirical work by Nickell and Bell (1995, 1996) indicates that the relative demand shift against the unskilled explains a modest but significant part of the large rise in unemployment in some European countries from the 1970s to the 1980s. Depending on the method used and the country under investigation, the relative demand shift can explain between 11 per cent and 32 per cent of the unemployment increase in European countries (Nickell and Bell, 1996).

Another point worth remarking is that the maintained assumption of the relative demand shift hypothesis is that technological progress is seen as a substitute for low-skilled labour. This need not be the case, as recent evidence using plant-level data for the UK and Australia shows. Blanchflower and Burgess (1996) show that the introduction of new technology raises employment growth by 2.5 per cent–3.5 per cent per annum on average, and this is irrespective of blue-collar or white-collar employment (I assume that blue-collar workers are more associated with low-skilled labour). Thus the next obvious candidate to explain the increase in (unskilled) unemployment over the 1970s and 1980s is international trade.

Table D8.1 *Male unemployment rates, by education percentages, 1971–82 to 1991–3*

Country and education	1971–82	1983–90	1991–3
Germany			
Total	3.1	5.6	4.1
High education	1.7	3.1	2.2
Low education	6.4	13.0	10.7
Italy			
Total	7.7	11.2	11.2
High education	12.7	13.1	12.5
Low education	4.6	7.3	7.5
Netherlands			
Total	6.3	10.0	6.8
High education	3.2	5.7	5.0
Low education	7.0	14.0	9.9
Spain			
Total	8.9	16.9	15.1
High education	6.2	9.9	9.0
Low education	10.6	19.6	20.0
Sweden			
Total	2.4	2.5	5.8
High education	1.0	1.1	2.8
Low education	2.9	3.3	6.9
UK			
Total	5.0	9.0	10.8
High education	2.4	4.4	6.2
Low education	7.5	15.9	17.1
Canada			
Total	6.8	9.1	11.5
High education	2.5	3.9	5.1
Low education	8.3	11.9	16.1
USA			
Total	4.9	6.2	6.0
High education	2.0	2.4	3.0
Low education	7.8	11.3	11.0

Source: Nickell and Bell (1996).

2 Globalisation and unemployment

Drèze and Sneessens refer to the Heckscher–Ohlin model of trade to offer a theoretical argument for the observed wage dispersion between skill groups and the increase in unskilled unemployed. They express the fear of increased competition from low-wage countries, especially from Eastern Europe. Globalisation can also contribute to the relative demand shift in favour of high-skilled jobs if firms respond to import competition from low-wage countries by moving low-skilled intensive activities abroad.

It is not obvious that international trade alone can be blamed for the current situation in Western labour markets. First, in the long run as tariffs, trade barriers and transportation costs fall one would expect wage convergence between countries. Second, despite the appealing logic of the Heckscher–Ohlin model, several points can be raised which may prove its predictions to be wrong. While the Heckscher–Ohlin framework typically deals with *inter-industry* trade, most international trade is *intra-industry*. Theoretical contributions to explain observed intra-industry trade patterns are based on increasing returns and product differentiation. The exploitation of increasing returns to scale which gives rise to North–North trade is one of the elements which can offset or reduce the negative impact of trade liberalisation on wage levels and employment (Helpman and Krugman, 1985). Third, there is no conclusive evidence about the effects of international trade on job creation and destruction (see Wes, 1995, for a survey). Presumably other factors interact in an intricate way with international trade. As suggested by Konings and Vandenbussche (1995) future research in this area will most probably focus more on the interactions between labour market and product market imperfections in the context of international trade. Konings and Vandenbussche (1995) distinguish between unionised and non-unionised manufacturing firms, and find only in unionised firms a negative effect of increased competition on both employment and wages.

3 Policy

In their policy recommendations Drèze and Sneessens favour a reduction in labour costs as a way of promoting employment of low-skilled workers. While this can be a useful measure in countries where labour demand wage elasticities are high (such as Belgium, where the long-run wage elasticity is estimated to be above 1, Konings and Roodhooft, 1996), it is not necessarily the perfect remedy for other countries with low wage elasticities. As Nickell and Bell (1996) point out 'relative wages in Germany appear to be comparatively rigid, whereas relative wages in the US and the UK are flexible, yet unskilled unemployment in Germany is lower than in the UK and much the same as in the US'.

More important is the capacity of an economy to react in a flexible way to shocks, both in product and in labour markets. Measures that increase job turnover will probably lower long-term unemployment, as shown in Garibaldi *et al.* (chapter 15 in this volume): an increase in job destruction will imply an increase in job creation in the steady state, allowing workers to exit the unemployment pool at a faster rate. Of course, this also implies that the length of a job is shorter, but the average unemployment duration will be as well.

REFERENCES

Bean, C.R. and C. Pissarides, 1990. 'Skill shortages and structural unemployment in Britain: a (mis-)matching approach', in F. Padoa Schioppa (ed.), *Mismatch and Labour Mobility*, Cambridge: Cambridge University Press

Blanchflower, D. and S. Burgess, 1996. 'New technology and jobs: comparative evidence from a two country study', London School of Economics, Centre for Economic Performance, *Discussion Paper*, **285**

Helpman, E. and P. Krugman, 1985. *Market Structure and Foreign Trade*, Cambridge, MA: MIT Press

Konings, J. and H. Vandenbussche, 1995. 'The effect of foreign competition on UK employment and wages: evidence from firm-level panel data', *Weltwirtschaftliches Archiv*, **131**, 655–72

Konings, J. and F. Roodhooft, 1996. 'How elastic is the demand for labour in Belgian companies?', Katholieke Universiteit Leuven, mimeo

Nickell, S.J. and B. Bell, 1995. 'The collapse in demand for the unskilled and unemployment in the OECD', *Oxford Review of Economic Policy*, **11**, 40

1996. 'Changes in the distribution of wages and unemployment in OECD countries', *American Economic Review, Papers and Proceedings*, **86**, 302–8

Sneessens, H. and F. Shadman-Mehta, 1995. 'Real wages, skill mismatch and unemployment persistence', *Annales d'Economie et Statistique*, **37/38**, 255–92

Wes, M., 1995. 'Globalisation and wages', London School of Economics, Centre for Economic Performance, *Working Paper*

9 Macroeconomic and policy implications of shifts in the relative demand for skills

OLIVIER J. BLANCHARD

'The aim of this chapter is to draw the macroeconomic and policy implications of widening wage inequality. This will be done under six areas of discussion, followed by conclusions.

1 The race between relative demand and relative supply

The first point I wish to make is not specifically about macroeconomic implications. It emerges from my reading of the body of research. What has happened is usually described as having come from an increase in relative demand for skills. It is in fact better described as a race, over the last 20 years, between increases in relative demand for skills and increases in relative supply. In the 1970s, relative supply won; in the 1980s, relative demand won. But, in both decades, the race has been rapid.

To make the point more precisely, let me rely on the work of Katz and Murphy. Katz and Murphy (1992) aggregate labour in two groups, high school (H) and college (C), and estimate the following relative demand relation, in inverse form, using data from 1963 to 1987:

$$\log(W_C/W_H) = -0.709 \ \log(C/H) + \text{constant} + 0.033 \text{ time.} \quad (1.1)$$

The relative wage depends on the relative supply of C and H – the coefficient implies a fairly high elasticity between the two, $\sigma = 1/0.709 = 1.4$ – and a time trend, which captures the shift in relative demand. The coefficient on time is the same throughout: contrary to common perceptions, Katz and Murphy find little evidence of acceleration of the shift in relative demand.

Now do the following computation. Suppose that there had been no change in relative supply, so that $\log(C/H)$ had remained constant. Then over those 24 years, the relative wage of college workers would have

Table 9.1 *Relative demand and supply shifts, 1963–71 to 1979–87, selected years*

	1963–71	1971–9	1979–87
Change in (W_C/W_H)			
due to increase in demand (est.)	26.4	26.4	26.4
due to increase in supply (est.)	−22.2	−28.9	−18.0
Net (est.)	4.2	−2.5	8.4
Net (actual)	7.7	−10.4	12.8

increased by 0.033 (24) = 79 per cent! The actual increase was only 10 per cent. The difference is accounted for by the increase in relative supply. Table 9.1 builds on Katz and Murphy to show the contribution of shifts in demand and supply to the evolution of the wage.

What is striking is how large the numbers in the first two lines of table 9.1 are, how large the shifts in relative demand and supply have consistently been. If one is an optimist, one can read table 9.1 as suggesting that it would not take much change in either the rate of change of supply or demand to re-establish balance. If one is a pessimist, one can read it as suggesting that things could easily get much worse, that wage inequality may easily deteriorate faster. But, in any case, the message of table 9.1, of rapid changes in both demand and supply, strikes me as important.

2 Unemployment

Let me now turn to macro-implications. The main macro-implication of the increase in net relative demand for skills is likely to be higher aggregate unemployment or, more generally, non-employment.

The reason is obvious. The labour supply of the unskilled is much more elastic than that of the skilled worker. Thus, the increase in the wage of skilled workers does not increase their labour supply very much, if at all. But the decrease in the wage of unskilled workers can lead to a large decrease in their labour supply.

How large has the effect been so far? The question has been looked at carefully by Juhn, Murphy and Topel in Juhn *et al.* (1991). Estimating labour supply elasticities of workers with different levels of wages, they found that they could explain all of the increase in non-employment of 2.3 per cent for prime-age males from the early 1970s to the late 1980s (of which 0.7 per cent took the form of higher unemployment).

In thinking about what happens in the future, the elasticities at the low end of the wage scale are critical. The elasticities estimated at the low end of the wage scale by Juhn *et al.* are large by the standards of the labour literature, of the order of 0.3. These may however be quite optimistic. Labour supply depends not only on the real wage, but on real wage relative to what is provided by the safety net. When getting close to the safety net, attachment to work is likely to be weak, the elasticity of labour supply like to be large. My sense is that, in the USA at this point, minimum wage or no minimum wage, labour supply is likely to be very elastic at $4–5 an hour.

What does this imply? One can use the estimates from Katz and Murphy to do a rough computation. Assume that relative demand is given by (1.1). Now assume that the elasticity of high-school labour is given by:

$$\log(H/\bar{H}) = \alpha \log(W_H/W_C) \tag{2.1}$$

where $\bar{H}$ is the number of H workers, and α is the elasticity with respect to the relative wage. Assume that the labour supply of C workers is inelastic, so that all C workers are employed, and $C = \bar{C}$. Finally assume that relative number of H workers relative to C workers continues to decrease at the same rate as in the last eight years, so that:

$$\Delta(\bar{H}/\bar{C}) = -2.4 \text{ per cent.} \tag{2.2}$$

Then a few simple steps give:

$$\Delta(H/\bar{H}) = -1.6 \text{ per cent } \frac{\alpha}{1 = 0.709\ \alpha} \tag{2.3}$$

If for example, the elasticity of supply of H workers is equal to 1 – rather than the 0.3 used by Juhn *et al.* – then the annual decrease in the employment rate of H workers is equal to 0.9 per cent. As H workers account for roughly 60 per cent of the labour force, this represents a decrease in the employment rate of about 0.5 per cent a year, a large number indeed. I believe the basic message of this computation to be right. At the current wages, the labour elasticity of low skill workers may be quite high. If there is no change in demand and supply trends, and no change in policy, we could well see a large decrease in employment rates in the future.

3 The USA versus Europe

The effects of the shift in relative demand on non-employment will obviously be worse if there is a binding minimum wage. But, in the USA, the wage at which labour supply becomes extremely elastic cannot be very far from the minimum wage. So it is not clear that this makes a large macro-difference.

The same is not true of Europe, where the minimum wage is a substantially higher percentage of the median wage. But here, I want to debunk a theme which is popular in the press, and has been endorsed by Krugman (1994). The theme is that the difference between unemployment rates in Europe and the USA comes from different responses to a similar relative demand shift. The USA, the argument goes, has chosen larger wage inequality, avoiding most of the increase in unemployment. Europe, instead, has limited the increase in wage dispersion, pricing a large number of workers out of the market as a result; the result has been high unemployment.

It is not hard to see why this idea might be popular. The increase in unemployment in Europe has indeed been much larger among the low skill than the high skill workers. Table 9.2, borrowed from Stephen Nickell and Brian Bell (1994), shows the basic evolutions for four European countries.

So why doubt the Krugman explanation?

I have no doubt that a higher relative minimum wage, combined with the shift of relative demand, has led to more unemployment of the unskilled in Europe. Even that proposition, however, is surprisingly hard to establish from a look at the cross-section of European experiences.

But the change in the distribution of unemployment rates in table 9.2 is also exactly what we would expect to happen in response to a shift in aggregate rather than relative demand for labour. It is well understood that in response to a neutral adverse shift in demand, various effects – 'ladder' effects, 'ranking' effects, the labour supply elasticities we discussed earlier – all lead the unemployment rate of low-skill workers to increase much more than the unemployment rate for high-skill workers. Back of the envelope computations I have done for a few countries suggest that the evolution of the distribution of rates is roughly what one would expect if the only shock had been an aggregate shock, and the elasticities of skill-specific unemployment rates had remained the same as in the past. A more careful computation by Nickell and Bell leads them to conclude that only about one-fifth of the increase in unemployment in the UK is due to the relative demand shift.

Table 9.2 *Evolution of unemployment rates, for high- and low-education workers, in four European countries, 1979–82 to 1993, selected years*

		1979–82	1993			1979–82	1991
France	Overall	5.2	9.4	UK	Overall	7.7	10.0
	High ed.	2.1	13.6		High ed.	3.9	5.7
	Low ed.	6.5	13.6		Low ed.	12.2	17.4
			1991				1993
Germany	Overall	3.8	5.4	Spain	Overall	11.7	17.9
	High ed.	1.6	2.4		High ed.	7.9	10.7
	Low ed.	4.5	6.2		Low ed.	13.5	24.0

Definitions: France: high – 2 years of university or more; low – primary school certificate or less. Germany: high – professional, technical and related, administrative workers; low – production and related workers, transport equipment operators and labourers. UK: high – passed A levels or more; low – no qualifications. Spain: high – university; low – primary education or less.
Source: Nickell and Bell (1994, table 2).

There is thus a trade-off between unemployment and wage dispersion. But it is not the one shown by a simple comparison of the USA and Europe.

4 The shape and size of transfers

If, either on income distribution grounds, or on grounds of externalities, one believes that something should be done to avoid either the increase in wage dispersion, or the increase in unemployment rates for the unskilled, what measures should one advocate?

No economist is likely to be in favour of a substantial increase in the minimum wage as a solution to the shift in relative demand. Most proposals, on both sides of the Atlantic, have focused on employment subsidies for the unskilled. Jacques Drèze *et al.* (1995) have argued for the elimination of payroll taxes for low wage workers. Phelps (1994) has argued for the introduction of a graduated subsidy, phased out at pre-subsidy hourly wages of $10 (see also chapter 7, in this volume).

How large might these subsidies be? This clearly depends on the goal, both in terms of wage inequality and of unemployment rates. A simple computation, once again, based on the Katz–Murphy relation, is instructive.

Suppose we wanted to re-establish the wage differential between *H* and *C* workers at its level of about 10 years ago. Based on table 9.1 (p. 283), this would require an increase in about 15 per cent in the wages of *H* workers. How large a subsidy it would require depends in turn on the elasticities of demand and supply. Take the elasticity of demand from the Katz–Murphy equation. Assume that the supply of C workers is inelastic. Assume that the supply of H workers is a function of the wage differential, with elasticity 0.2 – a number which appears roughly consistent with the average of the Juhn *et al.* estimates over the relevant range of wages. Then, the subsidy to firms should be equal to 15 per cent $(1 + 0.2\ 0.7) = 17$ per cent.

How large a subsidy does this represent in terms of the wage bill? From Bound and Johnson (1995), we know that H workers account for roughly 60 per cent of employment. Their wage is about 65 per cent of the wage of C workers. Thus, a subsidy equal to 15 per cent of their wage implies an increase in the wage bill of $(0.6 \times 0.65 \times 1.17 + 0.4 \times 1)/(0.6 \times 0.65 + 0.4 \times 1) - 1 = 8.3$ per cent of the wage bill, or about 4–5 per cent of GDP.

This is a very large sum indeed. But it is not very different from other estimates. Heckman (1994) has asked a closely related question, how much would have to be spent on training to go back to the 1979 differential, and estimates the cost to be about $160 billion on an annual basis, about 3 per cent of GDP. Phelps evaluates his scheme (under the assumption of zero labour supply elasticity) to be around $110 billion. And it only takes care of the widening to date. Under the assumptions that the shifts are the same in the future, the cost of maintaining the wage differential increases at a rate of about 0.4–0.5 per cent of GDP per year.

Is it likely that anything like this will be put in place? The answer must be ‘no’. The political mood is surely not propitious for the creation of new large transfer programmes. The main insight from the theory of political economy here is that the earlier such a system is put in place, the more likely it is to have political support. The earlier it is put in place, the more it looks like a social insurance programme, the less like a transfer programme. But it may already be too late: the winners and the losers are already fairly well identified.

5 Supply responses

The increase in net relative demand for skills lead to an increase in the returns to acquiring those skills. Can we expect the effect to be strong enough that increases in relative supply will catch up again with increases in relative demand, leading to little or no further wage dispersion?

The answer from current forecasts, as discussed in a paper by Levy (1995), is indeed for some supply response. The longer-run outcome depends on two factors. On the one hand, the return to education has increased; this should indeed lead to a positive supply response. On the other, the income of the currently unskilled has decreased. If credit markets are imperfect, so that borrowing against future earnings is difficult, or if primary and secondary education are largely locally financed, this makes it harder for the unskilled, or their children, to acquire education.

Which effect dominates has implications which go far beyond the sign of the supply response: if the sign is negative, wage and skill inequality are likely to be magnified over time. The issues here have been clarified in particular by the work of Benabou (1992). But, as far as I know, there is little evidence on the relative strengths of the effects. Whether an increase in wage inequality is likely to lead to more or less education in the USA today is still to be empirically settled.

Even if we do not have the answer, the analysis still has a clear implication. Reducing credit market imperfections, and allowing people to borrow against future earnings, is more desirable than before. There are good theoretical reasons to think that the government can play a role here, and some good empirical reasons to think that it can play more of a role than it has played in the past. If, in addition, a transfer programme is put in place to reduce wage dispersion, there is an additional argument for avoiding the distortion between unskilled work and education, thus for a subsidy for college education for poor students.

6 Technological progress

I see two interesting issues about technological progress in this context.

6.1 Skill-biased technological progress

The first is whether, assuming that a good part in the shift in relative demand has come from skill-biased technological progress, this bias will continue in the future. One can think of scenarios in which the future is different from the past. Krugman (1994) indicates that, maybe, the next step for computers is to replace skilled workers. He mentions lawyers and accountants. Or, maybe, computers become so user-friendly that they no longer require workers to have computer skills in order to use them. The problem here is that, as far as I know, these speculations fairly summarise the state of our knowledge: in short, we do not know.

A slightly more solid reason for believing that the future will be different from the past is based on the fact that technological progress is not exogenous. The shift in relative wages in the last decade has increased the return to developing techniques of production which use relatively more unskilled workers. Here, again, we do not know much, if anything. But, at least, the argument relies on a basic economic mechanism, a response to relative prices.

6.2 Higher productivity growth

The second is whether the increase in the relative supply of skilled workers – if it indeed it happens – will allow firms to adopt new and more sophisticated technologies faster and better, leading them to sustain higher productivity growth. If this were the case, I could end on a rather optimistic note. I could argue that skill-biased technological change may not only lead to an increase in the education of the US labour force, but may also hold the key to higher technological growth in the future.

Unfortunatley, there is little evidence to sustain this claim. In this case, we actually have the beginning of an answer from a paper by Kahn and Lim (1994). Kahn and Lim look at the relation between multifactor productivity (tfp) growth and the share of skilled labour, measured as the proportion of workers with 12 years or more of education. At first glance, their results look quite impressive. Their results imply the following relation across sectors:

$$\text{tfp growth} = -6.22 \text{ per cent} = 11.25 \text{ per cent} \tag{6.1}$$

where β is the share of skilled labour. The average share is 0.62, so that average tfp growth is 0.75 per cent per year. Taking the results as implying a causal relation between the share and productivity growth – rather than common factors, or omitted variables – the results are quite impressive. They imply, for example that, if the share of skilled labour in the USA was increased from 0.62 to 0.70, tfp growth would increase to 1.65 per cent. But, unfortunately, the results are largely driven by two sectors, both with low shares of skilled labour and low productivity – tobacco and petroleum. Both of them also suffer from notorious measurement problems. Thus, one cannot see the evidence as very conclusive.

7 Conclusions

What are the macro-implications of the increase in the relative demand for skills? Here are the conclusions of a neophyte:

- The trend increase in the net relative demand for skills, if it continues, has the potential to lead to substantially higher overall unemployment.
- If the trend continues, the size of the transfers needed to offset the increase in wage inequality is much too large to be politically feasible. Subsidies, such as cuts in payroll taxes for the unskilled, are desirable, but will have limited effects.
- A positive supply response, sufficient to eventually offset the trend in demand, cannot be taken for granted. Measures avoiding local finance effects of increased income inequality on primary and secondary education, and allowing for easier borrowing by poor students for higher education, seem essential.
- The induced increase in skills, if it indeed takes place, is good news for growth. There is however no evidence of further good news, in the form of an effect of an increase in the proportion of skilled workers on the rate of technological progress.

NOTES

This chapter was originally prepared for the New York Fed Conference on US Wage Trends (3–4 November 1994).

REFERENCES

Benabou, R., 1992. 'Heterogeneity, stratification and growth', Cambridge, MA, MIT, mimeo

Bound, J. and G. Johnson, 1995. 'What are the causes of rising wage inequality in the United States?', *Economic Policy Review*, **1-1**, Federal Reserve Bank of New York (January), 9–17

Drèze, J. *et al.*, 1995. 'Croissance et emploi: l'ambition d'une initiative européene', reprinted in J. Drèze, *Pour l'Emploi, la Croissance et l'Europe*, Brussels: de Boeck Editions

Heckman, J., 'Is job training oversold?', *Public Interest*, **115**, 91–115

Juhn, C., K. Murphy and R. Topel, 1991. 'Why has the natural rate increased over time?', *Brookings Papers on Economic Activity*, **2**, 75–142

Kahn, J. and J.-S. Lim, 1994. 'On the contribution of human capital to growth', University of Rochester, mimeo

Katz, L.F. and K.M. Murphy, 1992. 'Changes in relative wages, 1963–1987, supply and demand factors', *Quarterly Journal of Economics*, **107**, 35–78

Krugman, P., 1994. 'Past and prospective causes of high unemployment', Annual Symposium of the Federal Reserve Bank of Kansas City, Jackson Hole, Wyoming (26–27 August), mimeo

Levy, F., 1995. 'The future path and consequences of the earnings gap', *Economic Policy Review*, **1-1**, Federal Reserve Bank of New York (January), 35–41

Nickell, S.J. and B. Bell, 1994. 'Would cutting payroll taxes on the unskilled have

a significant effect on unemployment?, Oxford University (September), mimeo
Phelps, E.S., 1994. 'Wage subsidy programmes: alternative designs', chapter 7 in this volume

Discussion

GYLFI ZOEGA

Blanchard's chapter 9 argues that a fall in the relative demand for unskilled labour is partly to blame for the moderate rise in equilibrium unemployment in the USA and the much larger increase in most of the European countries. It finds proposals of wage subsidies and graduated payroll taxes too costly to be practical, and concludes that governments should limit themselves to reducing credit constraints to help unskilled workers to invest in skills and education. In light of the large changes in relative demand and supply of skilled and unskilled labour, large changes in the skill premium can be expected and have to be tolerated, at least in the short run.

I would like to offer three glimmers of hope in this otherwise gloomy picture. The first one is that some countries appear to have escaped the dreaded trade-off between rising earnings inequality and an increase in relative unemployment among unskilled workers. An explanation of this puzzle could provide a way out for the USA, the UK and other countries which apparently face the dilemma. Second, the proposed wage subsidies, although very costly themselves, may allow a reduction in many other spending programmes; the gross estimates exaggerate the net social cost. Finally, some recent proposals are not as costly as the general wage subsidy; some could even be implemented at close to zero cost.

Chapter 9 argues that a shift in the relative demand of skilled versus unskilled labour affects aggregate unemployment because of the convexity of the wage curve, representing real wage rigidity. With a constant-elasticity wage curve, a fall in the demand for labour affects employment more and real wages less than an increase of the same size. Therefore, a shift in demand away from unskilled workers to skilled workers would raise aggregate unemployment, assuming both groups find themselves on the same curve.

This analysis is consistent with that of Krugman (1994), who claims that in the face of a fall in the relative demand for unskilled labour, there arises a trade-off between increased wage dispersion and high unemployment differentials across skill levels.[1] The idea is that in Europe the welfare state makes the wage curve flatter. This makes unemployment respond more to shifts in relative demand in Europe while the dispersion of wages is more affected in the USA.

While the Blanchard–Krugman hypothesis is plausible on the surface, closer examination of the empirical evidence casts doubt on its general validity as an explanation of European unemployment. If both the USA and Europe faced the same fall in the relative demand for unskilled labour, they should have exploited the trade-off between wages and unemployment differently. Gottschalk (1993) found that the USA experienced a much larger increase in inequality of earnings – measured by the 90/10 wage ratio for prime-aged male heads of households – than Canada, France and the UK. Davis (1992) found a compression in the bottom half of the earnings distribution in France from the early 1970s to the late 1980s, and Nickell (1995) found a similar compression at the bottom of the German earnings distribution – both measured by the 50/10 log wage ratio. The implication is that the relative unemployment of the unskilled should have increased by more in France and Germany than in the United States. But, as shown in table D9.1 this is not borne out by the facts. Some countries on the European mainland have experienced almost constant unemployment ratios in spite of a falling wage dispersion at the bottom of the earnings distribution. This applies, most importantly, to Germany and France. So if Germany can do it, why can't the others?

The USA, the UK and Canada seem to have experienced a deterioration in both the relative wage and the unemployment rates of the least educated. France and Germany appear to have been spared both experiences. This may either imply that changes in relative labour demand have not been identical across the countries or that the response to these changes has differed markedly. But the difference in the response cannot be explained by different levels of real-wage rigidity – i.e. the welfare state.

If we assume that the shift in relative demand for skilled and unskilled labour is caused by technological progress, it becomes difficult to claim that countries should differ much in this regard. The question then arises how a country could escape the trade-off between unskilled unemployment and low unskilled wages. Nickell (1995) has floated the idea that guaranteeing a minimum level of abilities in the school system may make economies better able to deal with changes in technology. The rationale

Table D9.1 *Ratio of unemployment among the least educated to general unemployment, 1978–93*

		1978	1982	1990	1993
Canada (men only)	low	9.0	13.5	12.2	16.8
	total	7.5	11.0	8.1	11.8
	ratio	1.20	1.23	1.51	1.42
France (men only)	low	3.3	6.0	7.3[a]	NA
	total	3.6	6.8	8.1	
	ratio	0.92	0.88	0.90	
Germany (men only)	low	5.0	NA	13.09[b]	NA
	total	2.79		6.99[b]	
	ratio	1.79		1.87[b]	
Italy	low	6.8	8.5	9.9	10.3[c]
	total	7.2	9.0	11.0	1158
	ratio	0.94	0.94	0.90	0.90
UK (men only)	low	6.0	15.9	11.9	18.2
	total	4.5	12.1	7.4	12.0
	ratio	1.33	1.31	1.61	1.52
USA (men only)	low	7.1	12.7	9.6	14.1
	total	5.3	9.9	5.6	7.1
	ratio	1.34	1.28	1.71	1.99

Definitions: Canada: No more than 8 years of schooling; France: Holders of the BEPC degree; Germany: Lower secondary school or less; Italy: No more than 8 years of schooling; UK: No qualifications or low qualifications; USA: Less than 4 years of high school.

[a] 1988; [b] 1987; [c] 1992.

Data sources: Canada: *Statistics Canada*; France: Insee, Division 'Emploi'; Germany: OECD; Italy: Confindustria, Rome; UK: *Labour Force Survey*; USA: Bureau of Labor Statistics, *Current Population Survey*.

goes back to a paper by Nelson and Phelps (1966). The ability to learn is claimed to be a function of the level of education. The educated have 'learned how to learn', so to speak. If the least educated German and French workers are better trained than their US and UK counterparts, they may also be quicker to adapt to computer technology, operate new machinery or even to switch between industries. This would cause the relative demand for unskilled workers to fall less in the face of technological progress than in the UK and the USA.

Blanchard's policy conclusion that the aim of public policy should be to reduce credit market constraints could then be supplemented by proposing a reduction in the private cost of training brought about by higher standards of basic education. By making workers start out with a higher level of basic skills, they will be able to learn more easily and adapt to a rapidly changing environment.

My second point is the following. The general wage subsidy to disadvantaged workers proposed by Phelps (1994) could raise both relative wages and relative employment of unskilled workers. In so doing, it may make possible considerable savings in other public programmes. Although Phelps has estimated his programme to cost $110 billion annually, he claims that the programme would be largely self-financing. The savings would come out of some of the existing programmes, such as food-stamps, Medicaid and the administration of justice. He could for this reason claim that his proposal does not involve so much additional spending as a restructuring of current programmes to affect incentives to work. While a proposal to spend an additional $110 billion is unlikely to be passed as legislation, gradual changes in existing programmes along these lines may be politically feasible.

Finally, Snower (1993) and Layard and Jackman (1994) have come up with proposals aimed at reducing long-term unemployment in Europe. These programmes apparently do not require significant resources. Since most of the long-term unemployed happen to be unskilled, such programmes could be used to improve the lot of the less advantaged workers. The Snower proposal involves issuing vouchers which enable unemployed workers to subsidise their employment for a limited period of time by converting their unemployment benefits into hiring/training subsidies (see chapter 6 in this volume). By offering a larger voucher to the long-term unemployed, they could be brought back into productive employment. If the programme were to be implemented along these lines, it would be entirely self-financing and so presumably politically feasible. The Layard–Jackman proposal involves limiting the duration of unemployment benefits and forcing workers to receive training at the end of that period to help them adapt to changes in industry skill requirements and their own loss of productive capacity brought about by an unemployment spell (see chapter 7 in this volume). Such training programmes would not come free, but would probably be very inexpensive compared to Phelps' proposed general wage subsidy. But while these programmes may help reduce the unskilled unemployment rate and hence aggregate unemployment – they would not help lift the lowest wages.

NOTE

1 Although Krugman formulates his idea in terms of labour supply and for that reason talks about employment, not unemployment, his ideas could just as easily be expressed in terms of a wage curve which represents real wage supply.

REFERENCES

Davis, S.J., 1992. 'Cross-country patterns of change in relative wages', *NBER Macroeconomics Annual*, **7**, Cambridge: MA: NBER

Gottschalk, P., 1993. 'Changes in inequality of family income in seven industrialised countries', *American Economic Review*, **83**, 136–42

Jackman, R.A. and P.R.G. Layard, 1994. 'Preventing long-term unemployment: an economic analysis', London School of Economics, Centre for Economic Performance, mimeo

Krugman, P., 'Past and prospective causes of high unemployment', Annual Symposium of the Federal Reserve Bank of Kansas City, Jackson Hole, Wyoming (26–27 August), mimeo

Nelson, R.R. and E.S. Phelps, 1966. 'Investment in humans, technological diffusion, and economic growth', *American Economic Review*, **56**, 69–75

Nickell, S.J., 1995. 'The collapse in demand for the unskilled: what can be done?', paper prepared for the conference on 'Demand-side Strategies and Low-wage Labor Markets', New York (26–27 June)

Phelps, E.S., 1994. 'A program of low-wage employment tax credits', Russell Sage Foundation, *Working Paper*, **55** and Confindustria, CSC Ricerche, **93** (May)

Snower, D., 1993. 'Converting unemployment benefits into employment subsidies', *Discussion Paper*, **8/93**, Birkbeck College, London

10 Would cutting payroll taxes on the unskilled have a significant impact on unemployment?

STEPHEN J. NICKELL and BRIAN BELL

1 Introduction

> Reduce non-wage labour costs, especially in Europe, by reducing taxes on labour.

So says the 1994 *OECD Jobs Study* as one if its policy recommendations for the reduction of unemployment.[1] As a further recommendation, it adds

> Reduce direct taxes (social security and income taxes) on those with low earnings.

The idea here is to boost the relative demand for low-skill workers.

The first recommendation is one which is often made. Indeed, commentators point to the very high level of social security contributions faced by employers in many European countries (over 40 per cent in Belgium, France and Italy, for example) as being crucial to the allegedly poor state of the European labour market, including its high unemployment. However, a glance at Denmark, where employers pay no social security contributions, non-wage labour costs are negligible and unemployment is around the EU average quickly reveals the weakness of this view. Figure 10.1 shows why. Here we see average unit labour costs (i.e. labour costs incurred in producing $10 of value added) in 13 OECD countries where we have split these into wage costs and payroll taxes. Figure 10.1 shows clearly that there is no significant relationship between unit labour costs and payroll tax rates, the slope of a regression of the former on the latter being a mere 14 cents for every 10 percentage points of tax, with a *t*-static of 0.5. The reason is that, in the long run, payroll taxes tend to be shifted onto employees.

In fact, not only do non-wage labour costs tend to be borne by employees but so do income taxes and excise taxes. So shifting the tax

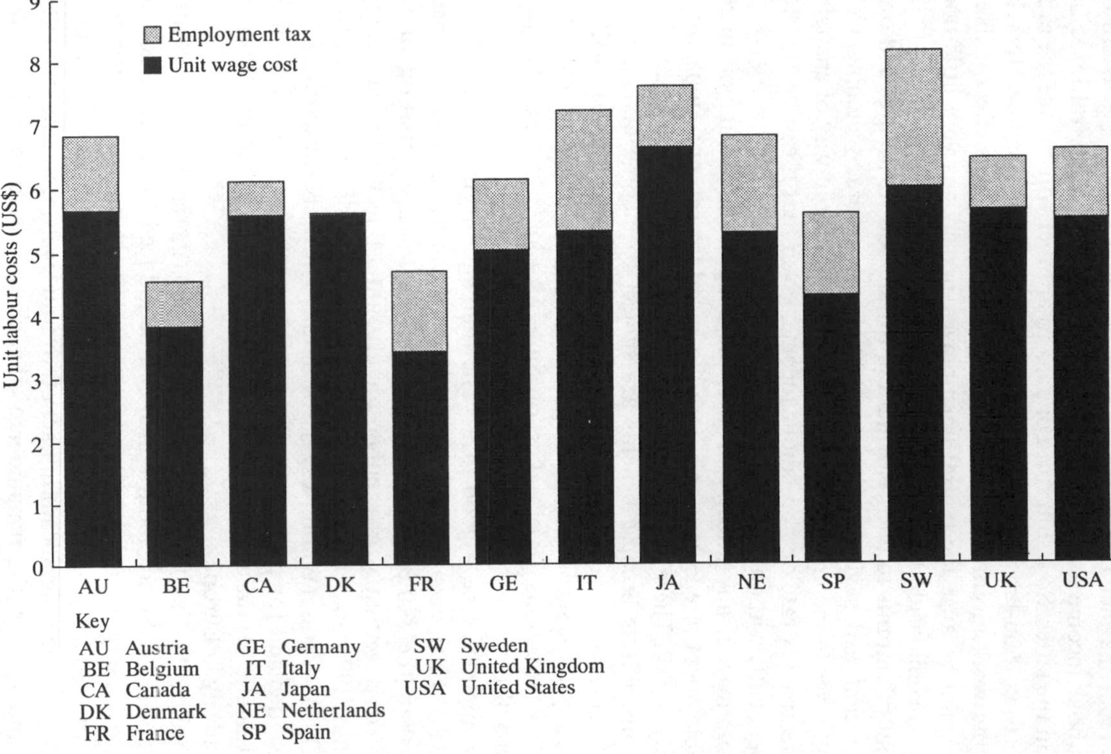

Figure 10.1 Comparison of unit wage levels and employment tax, OECD countries, 1980–90

burden from one type of tax to another is not going to have much impact on employment in the long run as the cross-section evidence[2] reported in OECD (1990, annex 6A) indicates. The only possible significant effect arises from the fact that income taxes and excise taxes tend to fall on non-labour income as well as labour income, whereas payroll taxes fall only on the latter. So a shift from one tax to another will change the ratio of post-tax non-labour income to post-tax labour income, thereby changing work incentives and hence unemployment. This effect is likely to be small because the typical unemployed person has very little non-labour income aside from benefits. Thus, for example, in 1987 over 50 per cent of entrants to unemployment in Britain had no savings and only 15 per cent had savings of over £1000. Furthermore, switching from payroll taxes to income taxes, say, is a very complicated way of changing the effective tax rate on non-labour income, given that it can be adjusted independently without any difficulty.

To summarise, any attempt to generate a significant reduction in the unemployment rate by cutting across-the-board tax rates on employment is likely to fail. There may be some short-run real wage resistance effects and some effects because benefits are subject to income taxes but not payroll taxes. But the former will not last and the latter will be small. So let us turn to the second recommendation quoted at the outset, namely to focus tax reductions (or subsidies) on those with low earnings – basically the unskilled.

Why might this be a good idea? The following arguments have been proposed. First, because the unskilled have much higher unemployment rates than the skilled.[3] Second, because the relative situation of the unskilled is getting worse, either on account of technological change (Machin, 1994 or Berman *et al.*, 1994), or because of competition from the Third World (Wood, 1994), or both. Third, because the falling relative demand for the unskilled is an important part of the reason for the dramatic rise in unemployment in the OECD over the last 20 years, particularly in Europe.

According to the first two arguments, any increase in the relative demand for unskilled labour which can be induced by selective tax cuts would certainly improve the lot of the unskilled and reduce their high levels of unemployment. According to the third argument, it might do more by having a significant impact on overall levels of unemployment.

Our intention in the remainder of this chapter is to investigate these arguments. In section 2 we look briefly at why the unemployment rate of the unskilled might be higher than that of the skilled, and how we might expect their relative unemployment rates to respond both to relative demand shocks and to more neutral shocks. In section 3, we examine the facts – namely what has happened to relative unemployment (and non-employment) rates, and wage rates throughout the OECD. Then, in the final section 4 we discuss the implications of these facts for the proposed policy measures.

2 The determinants of unemployment rates by skill

Why might the unskilled have higher rates of unemployment? There are a number of straightforward reasons. First, there is the obvious fact that the skilled can do many of the unskilled jobs and during recessions firms can make use of this fact to 'hoard' skilled workers for the usual reasons. The second related reason is that the unskilled have higher turnover rates because their lack of human capital, particularly of the specific type, greatly weakens their attachment to firms. As a consequence, they have much higher entry rates into unemployment. Third, their low wages ensure that their unemployment benefit replacement rates tend to be higher than for skilled workers, reducing their incentives to work. Finally, any tendency for there to be a floor on wages will raise the unemployment of the unskilled relative to the skilled both by reducing the relative demand for the unskilled and by raising the relative supply, since the incentive to acquire skills is reduced. Such floors on wages may arise because of minimum wage laws, the activities of unions, the ready availability of a given level of benefits or simply because some employers may find it distasteful, or indeed unprofitable, to pay very poor wages.

2.1 A simple model of sectoral unemployment

To illustrate one or two further points let us provide a simple model which follows that set out in Layard *et al.* (1991, pp. 301–6). Suppose output (Y) is produced by a CES production function of the form

$$Y^{\rho} = \phi \Sigma \alpha_i N_i^{\rho} \qquad (\rho \leq 1, \Sigma \alpha_i = 1) \tag{1}$$

where $1-\rho = 1/\sigma$, σ being the elasticity of substitution. N_i is the ith type of labour and the α_i parameters reflect productivity. Assuming competition in the product market, labour demand is given by

$$W_i = \alpha_i \phi (N_i/Y)^{-1/\sigma} = \alpha_i((1 - u_i(L_i/L)^{-1/\sigma} X \quad (i = 1 \dots n) \tag{2}$$

where W_i is the real wage, L_i is the labour force in the ith sector, L is the total labour force, u_i is the unemployment rate among type i workers and $X = \phi(Y/L)^{1/\sigma}$, an aggregate productivity factor.

Suppose wages in each sector are determined by a standard wage equation of the form

$$W_i = \gamma_i f(u_i)X \quad (f' < 0) \tag{3}$$

which may contain elements of labour supply, efficiency wages or union bargaining.

These equations immediately reveal the short-run level of unemployment for each group of workers (i.e. for L_i/L given). Eliminating W_i yields

$$u_i = g(\underset{+}{\gamma_i/\alpha_i}, \underset{+}{L_i/L}) \tag{4}$$

so unemployment is increasing in wage pressure γ_i, relative to productivity, α_i and in the relative size of the group. Wages are given by

$$W_i = w(\underset{+}{\alpha_i}, \underset{+}{\gamma_i}, \underset{-}{L_i/L}, \underset{+}{X}) \tag{5}$$

This short-run equilibrium is illustrated in figure 10.2.

In the longer run, the size of each group (L_i/L) is not given because migration occurs. Such migration will tend to equalise expected rewards in each sector. $W_i(1-u_i)$, relative to the (flow) cost of belonging to the sector, $(1+c_i)$, say. So groups in which $W_i(1-u_i)/(1+c_i)$ is low will experience outmigration and vice versa.

2.2 *The impact of relative and neutral shocks*

Consider first, the impact of a rise in the relative demand for skilled workers. Suppose, in the context of the model, there are two types of workers with (1) having α_s, α_u as the productivity coefficients of skilled and unskilled workers respectively. Then we want to know the consequences of a rise in α_s and a fall in α_u. In the short run, it is immediately clear that skilled unemployment will fall and wages will rise. The opposite will happen to the unskilled. In the longer run, however, the unskilled may respond to the additional incentive to acquire the training necessary to become skilled (the rise in u_u/u_s and the fall in W_u/W_s). As a consequence both relative wages and relative unemployment rates will start to move back towards their original positions. However, given all the practical constraints which operate in this process of adjustment, it is likely to take a very long time.

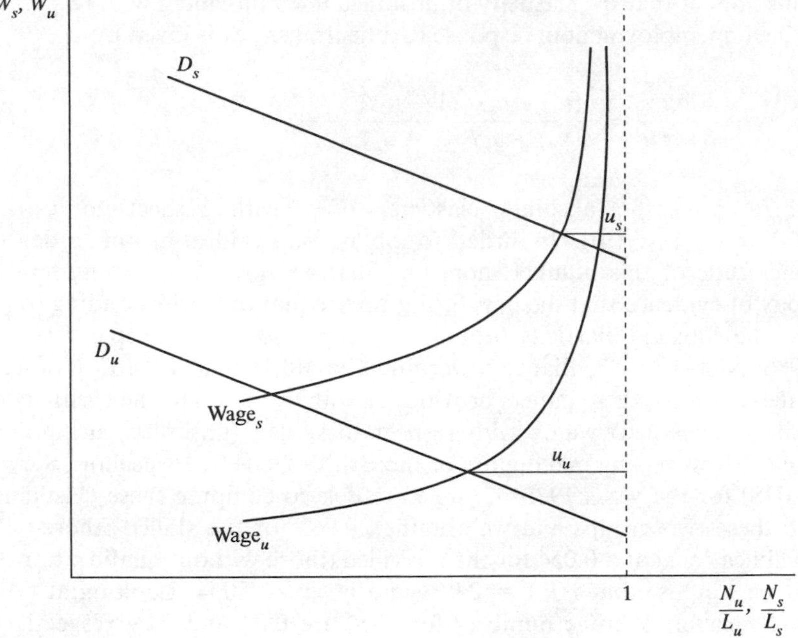

Figure 10.2 The skilled and the unskilled labour markets

Now let us consider the consequences of a neutral shock. Although there is no explicit role for aggregate demand shocks in this model, such shocks are equivalent to equiproportional changes in the wage equation parameters γ_i. Note that we can introduce nominal inertia in the wage equation by temporarily fixing the nominal wage and letting the output price change, thereby generating equiproportional shifts in W_i. Of course, neutral wage shocks are also captured by equiproportional shifts in γ_i. So in response to these shocks, we find from (3) that

$$\frac{W_u}{W_s}\frac{f(u_s)}{f(u_u)} = \frac{\gamma_u}{\gamma_s} = \text{constant} \tag{6}$$

and keeping the shares L_i/L ($i = u,s$) constant, we can use (2) to eliminate W_u/W_s and obtain

$$\frac{(1-u_s)^{1/\sigma}f(u_s)}{(1-u_u)^{1/\sigma}f(u_u)} = \frac{\alpha_s\gamma_u(L_u/L)^{1/\sigma}}{\alpha_u\gamma_s(L_s/L)^{1/\sigma}} = \text{constant.}$$

This implies that the elasticity of unskilled unemployment with respect to skilled unemployment in response to a neutral shock is given by

$$\frac{\partial \log u_u}{\partial \log u_s} = \frac{\eta(u_s) + u_s/\sigma(1 - u_s s)}{\eta(u_u) + u_u/\sigma(1 - u_u)} \tag{7}$$

where η is the absolute elasticity of f with respect to u (i.e. $\eta(u) = -uf'(u)/f(u)$). In order to obtain some idea of the order of magnitude of this number, note first that we now have a considerable body of evidence that the best-fitting wage equation corresponding to (3) has the constant elasticity (double log) form (see, for example, Oswald, 1986; Nickell, 1987; Blanchflower and Oswald, 1994a, 1994b). Unfortunately, none of these papers provides us with estimates of the elasticity of skilled (unskilled) wages with respect to skilled (unskilled) unemployment. However, by making use of the British General Household Survey (GHS) for the years 1978–92, we were able to compute these elasticities for these two groups and we obtained 0.062 for the skilled (those with qualifications) and 0.054 for the unskilled (those without qualifications).[4] So we suppose that $\eta(u_s) = 0.062$ and $\eta(u_u) = 0.054$. Looking at table 10.2, sensible average numbers for u_s,u_u are 0.03 and 0.09 respectively and we set the elasticity of substitution between skilled and unskilled labour at $\sigma = 3.0$ (this is the average substitution elasticity between blue- and white-collar workers in aggregate manufacturing in table 3.7 of Hamermesh, 1993. The formula above then yields

$$\partial \log u_u / \partial \log u_s = 0.83 \tag{8}$$

This tells us that if we have a neutral adverse shock, we may expect the unskilled unemployment *rate* to rise by around four-fifths of the skilled unemployment *rate*.[5] This shift is illustrated in figure 10.3. Since the question of how skilled and unskilled unemployment rates move in response to neutral shocks is such a vital one, we pursue this further by looking briefly at the structure of unemployment by skill in practice.

Two facts are particularly relevant. First, it appears that the variation in unemployment rates across skill levels is mainly due to variations in entry rates as opposed to mean durations (see table 10.1). Second, the *secular* trends in unemployment over the last two decades correspond, in most countries, to relatively stable inflow rates and sharply increasing durations. This suggests that neutral shocks will, in the long run, tend to raise unemployment durations across the board and unemployment rates across skill groups will rise near to equiproportionately.

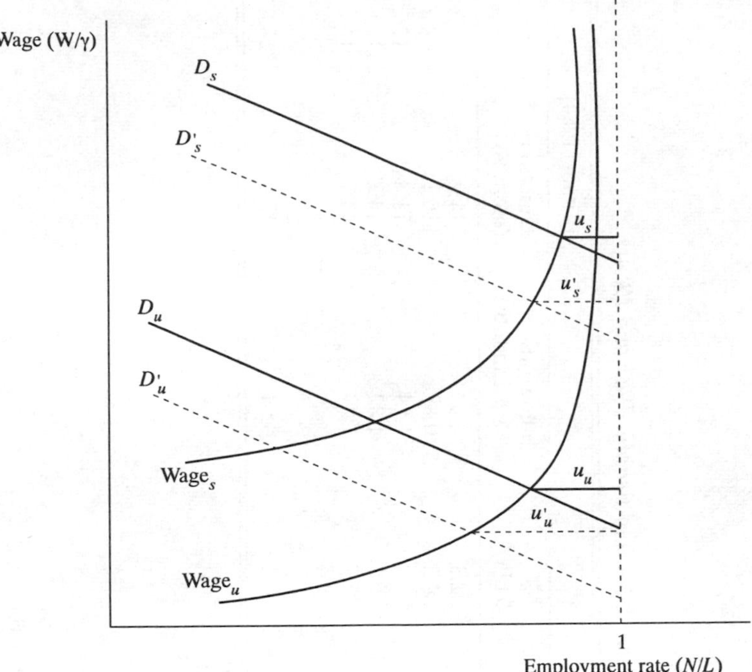

Figure 10.3 Unemployment responses to an adverse neutral demand shift
Note: For purposes of clarification, figure 10.3 is drawn so that the shock shifts the demand curve; thus we have w_i/γ_i on the vertical axis

To summarise, therefore, we can expect changes in the relative demand for skills to shift relative unemployment rates in the short term and indeed in the longer term if skill supplies do not adjust. Relative wage rates will tend to shift in the opposite direction, and, in so far as there are rigidities which limit relative wage adjustments, the impact on relative unemployment rates will be even bigger. Neutral shocks will tend to move unskilled rates by somewhat less than skilled rates. As a consequence, if falls in the relative demand for skills are important in practice, we should expect to see a rise in the unskilled unemployment rate and a fall in the skilled unemployment rate, with these changes being superimposed on the rises in both rates generated by adverse neutral shocks of the kind described above. So if we see a rise in the unskilled rate which is proportionately *greater* than the rise in the skilled rate, this implies that the relative decline in the demand for unskilled workers has

Table 10.1 *Unemployment, by occupation: inflow and duration, USA and Britain, 1987 and 1984*

	US (1987)			Britain (1984)		
	Inflow rate (% per month)	Duration (months)	*u* (%)	Inflow rate (% per month)	Duration (months)	*u* (%)
Professional and mangerial	0.74	3.0	2.3	0.50	11.2	5.3
Clerical	1.58	2.6	4.3	0.88	10.1	8.0
Other non-manual				1.14	11.8	12.2
Skilled manual	1.97	2.9	6.1	1.02	14.2	12.6
Personal service	2.96	2.4	7.7	1.32	14.1	15.5
Other manual	2.84	3.0	9.4			
All	2.23	2.6	6.2	0.94	12.8	10.8

Source: (Layard *et al.*, 1991, chapter 6, table 3, p. 291).

played a significant role. So in section 3 we shall look at relative unemployment rates across the OECD to see what has happened.

3 Unemployment and wages by skill

Our aim in this section is to try and elicit just how important the decline in the relative demand for the unskilled has been in explaining the increase in OECD unemployment in the last two decades. Recall that we are looking for an increase in the relative unemployment rate of the unskilled and a fall in their relative wages. Furthermore, if this is to have been a significant factor in the overall increase in the unemployment rate, then we must expect most of the increase in unemployment to be concentrated among the unskilled, as Juhn *et al.* (1991) argue has occurred in the USA.

3.1 Relative unemployment rates

The data on which we focus are the unemployment rates for men in different education groups. We concentrate on men because measured women's unemployment often depends crucially on unemployment benefit and other rules which change from time to time, thereby corrupting intertemporal comparisons. Sometimes we have to replace the education grouping by an occupational breakdown because the former is unavailable. However, the occupational breakdown is less satisfactory because the notion of an occupational unemployment rate is less clear-cut. The numerator of such a rate refers to those unemployed whose last job was in relevant occupation group. But these individuals are not restricted to searching for work within this group and may well search in other groups, particularly at a lower level. Consequently, the allocation of unemployed individuals across occupation groups is, to some degree, arbitrary. This problem does not, of course, occur with education groupings.

Our basic unemployment data are presented in table 10.2 and figure 10.4, with the relevant wage data appearing in tables 10.3 and 10.4. The following broad-brush facts emerge clearly. First, for most countries where the data are available, the relative unemployment rate of the low-education group has risen from the 1970s to the 1980s. Second, during the recent recession, the relative unemployment rate of the low-education group has fallen substantially in the vast majority of countries. Third, only in Britain and the USA have there been dramatic falls in the relative wages of the unskilled during the 1980s, although there has been a significant small decline in Germany. In some other countries there have

Table 10.2 *Male unemployment rates, by education or occupation,*[1] *1971–4 to 1993, selected years*

		1971–4	1975–8	1979–82	1983–6	1987–90	1991	1992	1993
FR	Total			5.2[a]	6.7[b]	7.2	7.0	7.9	9.4
	High ed.			2.1[a]	2.5[b]	2.6	2.8	3.9	5.9
	Low ed.			6.5[a]	9.0[b]	10.8	10.6	12.1	13.6
	Ratio			3.1	3.6	4.1	3.8	3.1	2.3
GE	Total		3.1	3.8	7.6	6.8	5.4		
	High occ.		1.6[e]	1.6	3.0	2.9	2.4		
	Low occ.		3.1[c]	4.5	8.8	7.6	6.2		
	Ratio		1.9[c]	2.8	2.9	2.6	2.6		
IT	Total			1.8[d]		4.7[e]			
	High ed.			3.4[d]		4.6[e]			
	Low ed.			1.6[d]		4.7[e]			
	Ratio			0.47[d]		1.02[e]			
	Total				7.1	7.9	7.5	8.1	
	High ed.				8.5	8.4	8.1	8.6	
	Low ed.				4.4	5.9	5.4	5.6	
	Ratio				0.52	0.70	0.67	0.64	
	Total (M + F)		7.2	8.2	10.5	11.8	10.9	11.5	
	High ed.		12.3	12.2	13.1	13.1	12.2	12.8	
	Low ed.		4.4	4.8	6.4	8.1	8.1	7.3	7.7
	Ratio		0.36	0.39	0.49	0.62	0.60	0.60	
NE	Total		4.4[f]	5.4[g]	11.7[h]				
	High ed.		2.1[f]	2.4[g]	4.6[h]				
	Low ed.		4.7[f]	6.8[g]	16.9[h]				
	Ratio		2.2[f]	2.8[g]	3.7[h]				

	Total (M + F)		5.5[f]	7.1[g]	13.2[h]	6.9[i]	6.5	6.5	7.5
	High ed.		2.9[f]	3.4[g]	6.2[h]	5.2[i]	4.6	6.1	5.4
	Low ed.		5.7[f]	8.3[g]	18.0[h]	9.9[i]	9.5	9.3	10.9
	Ratio		2.0[f]	2.4[g]	2.9[h]	1.9[i]	2.1	1.8	2.0
SP	Total		6.1	11.7	18.5	15.3	12.8	14.5	17.9
	High ed.		4.5[j]	7.9	11.0	8.8	7.3	8.9	10.7
	Low ed.		7.7[j]	13.5	21.4	17.7	16.7	19.2	24.0
	Ratio		1.7[j]	1.7	1.9	2.0	2.3	2.2	2.2
UK									
	Total	2.9[k]	4.4	7.7	10.5	7.5	10.0	11.5	
	High ed.	1.4[k]	2.0	3.9	4.7	4.0	5.7	6.6	
	Low ed.	4.0[k]	6.4	12.2	18.2	13.5	17.4	16.9	
	Ratio	2.9[k]	3.2	3.1	3.9	3.4	3.1	2.6	
AL	Total			6.8	9.8	7.9	9.5	11.5	12.1
	High ed.			3.5	4.4	3.9	4.8	5.9	6.2
	Low ed.			8.3	12.2	10.0	11.7	14.2	14.8
	Ratio			2.4	2.8	2.6	2.4	2.4	2.4
NZ	Total					5.4	8.4	10.6	10.1
	High ed.					2.2	4.8	6.6	6.5
	Low ed.					8.8	14.2	17.6	17.0
	Ratio					4.0	3.0	2.7	2.6
CA	Total		6.9	6.6[l]	10.3[m]	7.8	10.8	12.0	11.7
	High ed.		2.6	2.4[l]	4.3[m]	3.4	4.5	5.6	5.3
	Low ed.		8.2	8.3[l]	12.5[m]	11.3	15.4	16.3	16.6
	Ratio		3.2	3.5[l]	2.9[m]	3.3	3.4	2.9	3.1
USA	Total	3.6	5.5	5.7	7.3	5.0	5.8		
	High ed.	1.7	2.2	2.1	2.7	2.1	2.8		
	Low ed.	5.3	8.6	9.	12.8	9.8	11.0		
	Ratio	3.1	3.9	4.5	4.7	4.7	3.9		

Table 10.2 *Continued*

		1971–4	1975–8	1979–82	1983–6	1987–90	1991	1992	1993
JA	Total	1.4[n]		2.4[o]		3.0[p]		2.1	
	High ed.	1.2[n]		1.6[o]		1.4[p]		1.2	
	Low ed.	1.6[n]		2.9[o]		4.1[p]		2.6	
	Ratio	1.3[n]		1.8[o]		2.9[p]		2.2	
AU	High occ.				1.1	1.0	1.3		
	Low occ.				4.9	3.9	3.7		
	Ratio				4.5	3.9	2.8		
FN	Total				6.6[q]	4.6	9.3	15.5	
	High ed.				1.6[q]	1.2	3.1	6.3	
	Low ed.				8.8[q]	5.9	11.2	18.4	
	Ratio				5.5[q]	4.9	3.6	2.9	
NW	Total	1.2[r]	1.9	2.1	2.7	3.9	5.5	5.9	
	High ed.	1.0[r]	0.8	0.9	0.8	1.5	2.3	2.8	
	Low ed.	1.9[r]	2.2	2.9	3.8	6.0	8.8	8.9	
	Ratio	1.9[r]	2.8	3.2	4.8	4.0	3.8	3.2	
SW	Total	2.8	1.9	2.4	3.1	1.8	3.1	5.6	8.8
	High ed.	1.3	0.8	0.9	1.1	1.0	1.5	2.8	4.2
	Low ed.	3.2	2.4	3.1	4.1	2.4	3.9	6.5	10.4
	Ratio	2.5	4.0	3.4	3.7	2.4	2.6	2.3	2.5

[1] For notes, see appendix, pp. 323–4.

Table 10.3 *Earnings differentials, by education, males, early 1970s–late 1980s*

	Ratio of high- to low-education groups		
	Early 1970s	Early 1980s	Late 1980s
FR		1.66	1.63
GE		1.36	1.42
IT	1.96	1.60	1.61
NE		1.50	1.22
UK	1.64	1.53	1.65
AL	1.89	1.54	1.58
CA	1.65	1.40	1.42
USA	1.49	1.37	1.51
JA	1.33	1.26	1.26
SW	1.40	1.16	1.19

Source: OECD Employment Outlook (1993, Table 5.6), Davis (1992).

been slight shifts in relative wages over this period, and there are no countries where the relative wages of the less educated have risen in this period except the Netherlands. Overall, therefore, there is some evidence that from the 1970s to the 1980s, the fall in the relative demand for unskilled workers has had the expected impact on unemployment rates. However, there seems to be no evidence that the unemployment rate effects are any more severe in countries where the wage effects are minimal or perverse (i.e. where there is apparent wage rigidity).

3.2 *The impact of unskilled unemployment to the overall unemployment rate*

The next step is to see the extent to which overall increases in unemployment are concentrated on the unskilled or low educated. Here we focus on the change from the early (if available) or mid-1970s to the middle or late 1980s. We can divide the countries where the data are available into two groups. In the first group, most of the unemployment increase is concentrated on the unskilled. In the second group, the rise in unemployment has involved a substantial increase in high-education unemployment as well as in low-education employment. The key results are in table 10.5. The first group of countries consists of the USA, Japan, Norway and Sweden and what they have in common is that the total rise in unemployment to be accounted for is small in terms of percentage points (successively 1.4, 1.6, 2.7, 0.6). The second group of countries contains Germany, Netherlands, Spain, the UK and Canada. In this

Table 10.4 *Earnings dispersion for males, 1973–91*

		1973	1975	1979–81	1985–6	1987–8	1989–90	1991
FR	D9/D5	2.00	2.09	2.05	2.10*	2.09	2.11	2.11
	D1/D5	0.62	0.61	0.63	0.64*	0.66	0.66	0.66
	D9/D1	3.23	3.43	3.25	3.28*	3.17	3.20	3.20
GE	D9/D5			1.47	1.65*	1.65	1.65	1.65
	D1/D5			0.67	0.69*	0.71	0.72	0.71
	D9/D1			2.19	2.39*	2.32	2.29	2.32
IT	D9/D5			1.44	1.51	1.56		
	D1/D5			0.69	0.73	0.75		
	D9/D1			2.09	2.07	2.08		
UK	D9/D5	1.70	1.66	1.72	1.85*	1.91	1.96	1.99
	D1/D5	0.68	0.70	0..68	0.63*	0.62	0.61	0.59
	D9/D1	2.50	2.37	2.53	2.94*	3.08	3.21	3.37
AL	D9/D5		1.50	1.50	1.56	1.55	1.55	1.59
	D1/D5		0.75	0.74	0.72	0.71	0.70	0.70
	D9/D1		2.00	2.03	2.17	2.18	2.21	2.27
CA	D9/D5	1.67		1.67	1.68	1.71	1.75	
	D1/D5	0.52		0.48	0.42	0.45	0.44	
	D9/D1	3.21		3.48	4.00	3.80	3.98	
USA	D9/D5		1.93	1.95	2.09	2.10	2.14	
	D1/D5		0.41	0.41	0.38	0.38	0.38	
	D9/D1		4.71	4.76	5.50	5.53	5.63	
JA	D9/D5			1.63		1.67	1.73	
	D1/D5			0.63		0.61	0.61	
	D9/D1			2.59		2.74	2.84	
SW	D9/D5	1.57		1.68!	1.50	1.56		1.57
	D1/D5	0.76		0.78	0.76	0.76		0.73
	D9/D1	2.07		2.15	1.97	2.05		2.15

Notes: D9, D5, D1 are upper limits of the deciles of the earnings distribution.
* implies change in measurement, so not comparable to previous numbers
Source: Employment Outlook (1993, Table 5.2).

group, the total rise in unemployment to be accounted for is more substantial in terms of percentage points (successively 3.7, 7.3, 9.2, 4.6, 3.9) and, in each case, the proportionate rise in high-education unemployment is also significant although generally somewhat smaller than the proportionate rise in low-education unemployment. So we can conclude that, when looking at the rise in unemployment from the 1970s to the 1908s, there is a group of countries (two non-EU European, two non-European) where the rise in unemployment is small and mostly due to the rise in low-skill unemployment. Then there is a larger group of

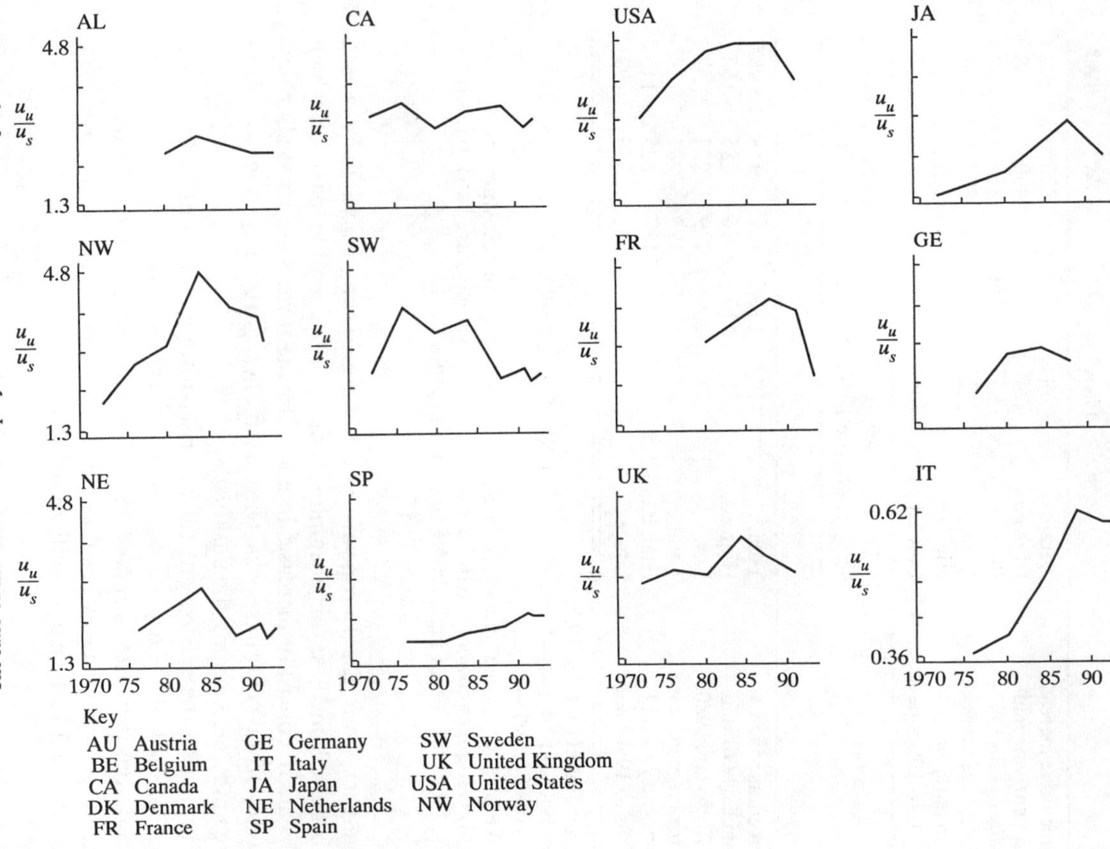

Figure 10.4 Unemployment ratios, 1970–90

Table 10.5 *Percentage increases in male unemployment from the 1970s*

		Countries where most of the increase to the 1980s is among the unskilled			
		USA[a]	JA[a]	NW[a]	SW[b]
Percentage increase from early or mid-1970s to late 1980s	Total	39	114	225	22
	High ed.	24	17	−50	−8
	Low ed.	85	156	216	59
Percentage increase from early or mid-1970s to 1990s peak	Total	61	50	392	214
	High ed.	65	0	180	223
	Low ed.	108	63	378	225

		Countries where a significant part of the increase to the 1980s is among the unskilled				
		GE[c]	NE[d]	SP[c]	UK[a]	CA[d]
Percentage increase from early or mid-1970s to late 1980s	Total	119	116	151	158	49
	High ed.	81	119	96	185	65
	Low ed.	145	260	129	237	52
Percentage increase from early or mid-1970s to 1990s peak	Total			193	281	74
	High ed.			137	625	115
	Low ed.			212	336	99

Notes: Based on table 10.2.
[a] = 1987–90/1971–4; [b] = 1983–6/1971–4; [c] = 1987–90/1975–8;
[d] = 1983–6/1975–8.

We only go to the mid-1980s in SW because since unemployment in the late 1980s is so much lower than in the early 1970s, the numbers are hard to interpret. Late 1980s figures for males in NE are not available.

countries (four EU European, one non-European) where there was a substantial increase in unemployment, a considerable part of which appears to consist of increases in unemployment rates across skill groups arising from neutral shocks with a smaller part being due to excess unemployment among the unskilled.

Turning to the subsequent further rise in unemployment in the sharp recession of the early 1990s, in all countries except Japan we see substantial increases in *skilled* unemployment (often relative to unskilled unemployment), suggesting that this latest episode was neutral or even biased towards the higher skill group.

3.3 *Unemployment versus non-employment*

It may be that we are getting a false impression by focusing on unemployment rates, because it is possible that the unskilled have been leaving the labour force in increasing numbers because of their inability to find work. Thus, the hypothesis is that if we look at non-employment rates (i.e. include non-participants who are neither employed nor looking for work and add them to the unemployed job-seekers) we shall find a different picture with bigger increases in the relative non-employment rates of the unskilled from the 1970s to the 1980s.

In table 10.6, we present the data for the UK and the USA, including unemployment rates for comparison purposes and restricting ourselves to the over-25s to remove problems with changes in higher education. The upshot is plain from the numbers in table 10.6. The *pattern* of non-employment rates is very similar to the *pattern* of unemployment rates. In particular, in the UK, we see that the high-education non-employment rate more than doubles from the early 1970s to the late 1980s. Just to check that it is not simply due to an increase in early retirement by those on occupational pensions, we repeat the exercise in table 10.7 for the UK under-55s. While the numbers are lower, the pattern remains the same with the percentage of skilled non-employed rising by a factor of over two and a half from the early 1970s to the mid- to late 1980s.

As an aside, it is interesting to ask why we have all these new prime-age male non-participants. In fact, the biggest category of increase in both the UK and USA is in the number of men suffering from illness or disability (see Yellen, 1991, Table 1, for the USA). In table 10.8a, we set out the number of male disability pensioners of working age over the last two decades in the UK, and we see a continuing increase which over the whole 20-year period represents over 4 per cent of the labour force. Furthermore, there is no evidence that the increase has been particularly rapid during recessions, indeed the small boom of the late 1970s and the large boom of the late 1980s show some of the biggest increases. In table 10.8b, we use an alternative data source (GHS) which uses self-reported information and confirms the overall picture. Why there has been this increase is not clear, but one element is, presumably, that it has become easier to obtain invalidity benefit. This, at any event, is the implication of the UK National Audit Office Report (1989) on the subject.[6]

Returning to our main theme we may, in summary, conclude that there is no evidence that looking at non-employment as opposed to unemployment has any impact on the conclusions of section 2.[7] In particular, it remains true that in those countries where unemployment increased significantly in the 1980s, a substantial part of that increase was due to neutral shocks across skill groups and could not, therefore, be attributed to the fall in the relative demand for unskilled workers. However, it is difficult to say *precisely* how much of the rise can be so attributed, but we can try and obtain some rough orders of magnitude.

Table 10.6 *UK and US male unemployment and non-employment rates, by education, 1971–92*

	Age 25–64: UK						
	1971–4	1975–8	1979–82	1983–6	1987–90	1991	1992
Unemployment							
Total	2.7	3.8	6.9	9.6	7.0	9.0	10.3
High ed.	0.8	1.6	2.9	3.6	3.1	4.7	5.8
Low ed.	3.6	5.0	9.8	15.4	12.1	15.2	15.7
Ratio	4.5	3.1	3.4	4.3	3.9	3.2	2.7
Non-employment							
Total	7.9	9.7	14.8	19.9	18.3	20.9	22.6
High ed.	4.0	5.1	6.8	9.1	8.7	11.5	13.4
Low ed.	9.8	12.6	20.3	29.7	29.5	32.7	34.7
Ratio	2.5	2.5	3.0	3.3	3.4	2.8	2.6
	Age 25–64: US						
	1971–4	1975–8	1979–82	1983–6	1987–90	1991	
Unemployment							
Total	3.6	5.5	5.7	7.3	5.1	5.8	
High ed.	1.7	2.2	2.1	2.7	2.1	2.8	
Low ed.	5.3	8.6	9.4	12.8	9.8	11.0	
Ratio	3.1	3.9	4.5	4.7	4.7	3.9	
Non-employment							
Total	11.3	15.1	15.6	17.8	15.6	16.3	
High ed.	5.6	6.7	6.7	8.0	7.6	8.3	
Low ed.	18.0	25.8	28.3	34.0	31.0	32.4	
Ratio	3.2	3.9	4.3	4.3	4.1	3.0	

Sources: UK: General Household Survey data tapes. USA: As in appendix, p. 000–000.

Table 10.7 *UK male unemployment and non-employment rates, by education, 1971–92*

	Age 25–55						
	1971–4	1975–8	1979–82	1983–6	1987–90	1991	1992
Unemployment							
Total	2.4	3.7	6.7	9.1	6.6	8.5	10.2
High ed.	0.8	1.5	2.6	3.4	2.9	4.4	5.7
Low ed.	3.4	5.3	10.1	15.6	12.3	15.2	15.7
Ratio	4.3	3.5	3.9	4.6	4.2	3.5	2.8
Non-employment							
Total	4.4	6.0	9.7	12.9	11.2	13.9	15.7
High ed.	2.0	3.2	4.4	5.6	5.1	7.5	9.3
Low ed.	5.7	8.3	14.1	21.3	20.3	23.5	25.1
Ratio	2.9	2.6	3.2	3.8	4.0	3.1	2.7

Source: General Household Survey data tapes.

Table 10.8 *Long-term disability, 1972–82*

(a)	Males aged 20–64 in receipt of invalidity benefit (000)				
1972	322	1980	522	1988	781
1973	341	1981	538	1989	818
1974	349	1982	578	1990	852
1975	352	1983	617	1991	891
1976	437	1984	664	1992	963
1977	452	1985	701		
1978	488	1986	722		
1979	529	1987	746		

Source: *UK Social Security Statistics* (annual), table D1.22 (also includes those in receipt of Severe Disability Allowance, known as Non-Contributory Invalidity Pension prior to November 1984; this started in 1976, hence the jump in the series between 1975 and 1976).

(b)	Proportion of males in the population who are unable to work because of long-term sickness or disability				
	Age 25–64	Age 25–55		Age 25–64	Age 25–55
1973	2.1	1.0	1983	4.5	2.2
1974	2.5	1.1	1984	3.9	1.9
1975	2.3	0.9	1985	4.8	2.3
1976	2.4	0.9	1986	4.6	2.4
1977	2.4	1.0	1987	4.4	2.0
1978	2.5	1.2	1988	4.6	2.3
1979	3.1	1.3	1989	4.9	3.1
1980	3.5	1.6	1990	5.2	2.9
1981	3.3	1.7	1991	4.9	2.6
1982	4.2	2.1	1992	5.9	3.5

Source: General Household Survey data tapes.

3.4 *How much of the rise in unemployment is due to the fall in unskilled demand?*

It is clear that in the first group of countries displayed in table 10.5, most of the unemployment increase from the 1970s to the 1980s is due to a fall in the demand for unskilled workers. The second group is more interesting, however, because the overall rise in unemployment is substantial in terms of percentage points. Taking the average over all five countries, we find that over the periods specified in table 10.5, the skilled unemployment rate rose from 2.44 to 4.96 per cent (103.3 per cent), the unskilled unemployment rate rose from 5.54 to 14.22 per cent (156.7 per cent) and the total unemployment rate rose from 4.68 to 10.42 per cent

(122.6 per cent). In order to allocate these changes between relative demand shifts and neutral shocks, we may first note from (1), (2) and (3) that a relative demand shift corresponds to $d\alpha_s = -d\alpha_u = d\alpha > 0$ and a neutral shock has the form $d \ln \gamma_s = d \ln \gamma_u = d \ln \gamma > 0$. But we must also take account of the shifts in the supplies of skilled and unskilled workers over the relevant period. So taking differentials of (2) and (3) and solving out, we find that the relative demand shift, $d\alpha$, satisfies[8]

$$d\alpha = \frac{\alpha_u \alpha_s}{\alpha_u + \alpha_s}\left[\varphi(u_u)du_u - \varphi(u_s)du_s + \frac{1}{\sigma}dln\left[\frac{L_s}{L}\right] - \frac{1}{\sigma}dln\left[\frac{L_u}{L}\right]\right] \quad (9)$$

where $\phi(u) = 1/\sigma(1-u) + \eta(u)/u$. Having computed $d\alpha$, we can then work out the unemployment changes which would have come about as a consequence of the relative demand shift alone. Setting $d \ln \gamma_i = 0$ in the differentials of (2) and (3) yields

$$\varphi(u_u)du_u = \frac{1}{\sigma}dln\left[\frac{L_u}{l}\right] + \frac{d\alpha}{\alpha_u},\ \varphi(u_s)du_s = \frac{1}{\sigma}dln\left[\frac{L_s}{L}\right] - \frac{d\alpha}{\alpha_s}. \quad (10)$$

In order to obtain numerical estimates, we require some parameter values. In section 2, p. 0, we have already provided estimates of $\eta(u_s) = 0.062$, $\eta(u_u) = 0.054$, $\sigma = 3.0$. The average values of unemployment given above are $u_s = 0.037$ and $u_u = 0.099$. Our data also reveal that over the relevant period, the average shares of skilled and unskilled are 14.5 per cent and 37.3 per cent respectively. Furthermore, the proportional changes in these shares are 0.65 and −0.66 respectively. Finally, from (2), we have the $\alpha_u/\alpha i_s = (W_u/W_s)((1-u_u)L_u/(1-u_s)L_s)^{1/\sigma}$. Assuming $W_u/W_s \simeq 0.66$ from table 10.3 and using information on unemployment and skill shares, we calculate that $\alpha u/\alpha_s = 0.8845$. Using (9) and (10) then reveals that the relative demand shock alone raises unskilled unemployment by 2.95 percentage points and reduces skilled unemployment by 0.07 percentage points. Since the unskilled represents 37.3 per cent of the labour force and the skilled represent 14.5 per cent (with the middle group remaining unaffected by the relative demand shift), this reflects an overall unemployment increase which is about 19 per cent of the total increase of 5.74 percentage points. The remaining 81 per cent is, therefore, down to neutral shocks.

To summarise, it seems likely that for the second group of countries in table 10.5, somewhere around 10–25 per cent of the increase in unemployment from the 1970s to the 1980s could have arisen from the collapse in demand for the unskilled. Since this is obviously a rough and ready guesstimate, in section 3.5 we consider this question for Britain in more detail.

3.5 The impact of the decline in demand for unskilled workers on long-run unemployment in Britain

The main problems with attempting to measure the effect of the collapse in demand for the unskilled on overall unemployment is finding variables which accurately capture changes in the excess demand for labour by skill. In Britain, the CBI collects, from a large number of companies, answers to the questions: (i) Is a shortage of skilled labour likely to limit your output over the next four months? and (ii) Is a shortage of other labour likely to limit your output over the next four months? As a measure of the *relative* excess demand for *skilled* labour (*Skill*), we simply take the percentage of firms saying 'yes' to (i) divided by the percentage saying 'yes' to (ii). In table 10.9, we report this variable and the aggregate level of unemployment, for comparison.

Three points are clear. First, while the skill variable fluctuates a lot, its level has risen substantially over the last three decades, particularly from the boom years before the first oil shock to the boom years of the late 1980s. Second, relative skill shortages tend to hit their cyclical peak when the economy is emerging from a slump (i.e. the late 1970s and mid-1980s), for the demand for skilled labour then appears to pick up sharply whereas that for unskilled labour appears to be more sluggish. Third, in the recession of the early 1990s and its aftermath, skill shortages seem less severe than in the early 1980s, confirming the general pattern we observed in relative unemployment rates. As a consequence of these points, we might expect some positive long-run relationship between unemployment and relative skill shortages, but the short-run dynamics are likely to be complicated.

In order to investigate the contribution of relative skill shortages to the shifts in long-run equilibrium unemployment, we simply investigate the long-run empirical relationship between unemployment and the supply-side variables which we would expect to influence it over the longer term. As well as the skill variable, we follow the analysis in Layard *et al.* (1991, chapter 9) by considering a terms of trade variable (TT = log real import prices weighted by the import share), union power variable (UP = log union/non-union wage mark-up), the benefit replacement ratio (RR = log benefits to net income ratio), the tax wedge ($T - t_1 + t_2 + t_3$, t_1 = payroll tax rate, t_2 = income tax rate, t_3 = excise tax rate), an index of employment turbulence (IT).[9] Note that if taxes tend to be borne by labour in the long run, as we suggested in our Introduction, we should

Table 10.9 *Relative skill shortages and unemployment, 1963–92*

	Skill	u (%)		Skill	u (%)
1963–6	2.54	2.63	1979–82	4.30	8.13
1967–70	3.42	3.03	1983–6	8.93	11.63
1971–4	3.85	3.55	1987–90	6.45	7.98
1975–8	5.48	5.55	1991–4	4.51	9.67

Sources: CBI, *Industrial Trends Survey*; Layard *et al.* (1991, Table A3); *OECD Employment Outlook* (1994).
Unemployment is the OECD standardised rate.

find that the tax wedge, T, has no significant long-run effect on unemployment.

In order to investigate the long-run effects of these variables on unemployment, we focus simply on long-run cointegrating relationships. Of the above variables, all are $I(1)$ (including log unemployment) with the exception of industrial turbulence (IT) which, not surprisingly, is stationary.[10] Of course, the existence of an apparent unit root in some of these series is a 'local' result. For example, unemployment appears to have a unit root over this particular period despite the fact that it certainly does not have a unit root over the long haul. Thus, during the period 1850–1990 it exhibits no trend whatever. This is not to say that it is stationary, for it exhibits apparent mean shifts from time to time.

We use two methods to compute a long-run relationship between log u and the supply-side variables. First we use the standard Johansen (1988) multivariate procedure and second we estimate an unrestricted dynamic regression with log u as the dependent variable (five lags on all variables) and take the long-run solution. The former method enables us to investigate the extent of cointegration whereas the latter is a simple method which eliminates the substantial small sample biases inherent in the static regression method recommended in the original presentation by Engle and Granger (1987) (see Banerjee *et al.*, 1986, 1993 for a discussion of these).

The Johansen cointegrating vector (the eingenvalue tests reveal there is only one), normalised on log u, gives

$$\log u = 26.7TT + 0.059Skill + 0.76 + 8.95RR \\ + 2.14UP(+\text{ constant}) \quad 1964(4) - 1992(4)$$

and the long-run solution of general dynamic model is

$$\log u = -35.7 + \underset{(4.51)}{17.99TT} + \underset{(0.042)}{0.108\,Skill} + \underset{(1.39)}{1.60T}$$
$$+\underset{(1.73)}{4.88RR} + \underset{(1.26)}{1.94UP} + \underset{(0.22)}{0.22IT} \quad 1964(4)\text{–}1992(4)$$

(standard errors in parentheses).

Several points are worth nothing. First, the tax-wedge effect is not significantly different from zero, which is consistent with the hypothesis that these taxes fall on labour in the long run. Second, (log) unemployment is cointegrated with the available supply-side variables, confirming the results reported in Nickell (1988). Of course, unemployment will also be cointegrated with a set of demand variables more or less by definition (combine demand) = output, and the production function). We make this remark because it is sometimes mistakenly supposed that this fact is evidence against the natural rate hypothesis.[11] Third, the skill effect is both statistically and numerically significant.

So what is the overall contribution of the change in relative skill demand to the rise in unemployment in the long term? The answer is that the *Skill* variable contributes 0.42 percentage points to the 2.25 percentage point increase in *u* from the 1960s to the 1970s (19 per cent) and 1.42 percentage points to the 6.6 percentage point increase in *u* from the 1970s to the 1980s (21.5 per cent). So our estimate is that in Britain, the decline in the relative demand for unskilled workers has contributed around 20 per cent of the long-run increase in unemployment up to the 1980s. This looks quite consistent with the numbers for Britain reported in table 10.5 and the overall estimates presented in the previous section.

Having ascertained the facts to the best of our ability, it simply remains for us to discuss the policy of cutting payroll taxes on the unskilled or, equivalently, subsidising their employment. This is the topic of the final section 4.

4 Should payroll taxes on the unskilled be cut?

Here, we shall address a number of questions. First, what are the aims of cutting payroll taxes on, or providing job subsidies for, the unskilled? Second, are these aims going to be fulfilled? Finally, is this policy going to have a significant impact on overall unemployment? Before plunging in, two points are worth noting. First, even if unemployment rises solely as a result of neutral shocks, the position of the unskilled is seriously worsened because their absolute rise in unemployment is so great. Second, we should point out that much of our discussion here is based on already published work, notably Layard *et al.* (1991, chapter 6) and, more especially, the analysis in Wood (1994, chapter 10) which could hardly be bettered.

The basic idea behind cutting payroll taxes or providing job subsidies for the unskilled is to raise the demand for unskilled labour. This will, potentially, reduce unskilled unemployment, raise unskilled take-home pay and contribute towards an overall reduction in unemployment. If this can be achieved, it is good on efficiency grounds (although, of course, taxes have to rise elsewhere, generating efficiency costs) and, furthermore, it is good on social grounds. There are strong social reasons for raising both living standards and employment opportunities among the unskilled in a world where, for example, one quarter of *prime*-age men in this category are currently not working (see table 10.7) compared with around 5 per cent a mere 20 years ago. The social problem exacerbated by this level of non-employment are numerous and very costly, so they provide an independent reason for trying to generate more unskilled jobs.

So is cutting payroll taxes or providing job subsidies for the unskilled going to work? Given the following two propositions, the outlook does not, at first sight, look very hopeful.

(i) If there are no barriers to the acquisition of training, shifts in the demand for unskilled relative to skilled workers may have little long-run impact on relative unemployment rates because changes in unemployment rates and wages will tend to be offset by 'migration' from the unskilled to the skilled.
(ii) In the long run, if wages are flexible, payroll taxes are borne by labour. So labour costs and employment are unaffected although take-home pay will change.

The first proposition (see section 2) seems to suggest that there is not much point in doing anything. Indeed cutting payroll taxes on the unskilled may mean fewer people training for skilled work with wages and unemployment rates little affected. But, we may safely argue that barriers to the acquisition of training are extensive enough to ensure that (i) simply does not apply. However, then we run into (ii) (see Introduction) which indicates that payroll tax cuts will not influence unemployment other than via the roundabout route of raising take-home pay and hence reducing the benefit replacement rate or, more generally, the ratio of non-labour income to labour income (post-tax). The argument we must make here is that wages at the low end are not flexible because of the wage floor generated by minimum wage laws, unions or the benefit system. This fact ensures that payroll taxes are not wholly borne by labour at the bottom end of the pay distribution. Thus, when payroll taxes are imposed, wages at the bottom end cannot fail because of the minimum wage, say, and unemployment goes up instead. This ensures that moving in the opposite direction with payroll tax cuts and job subsidies may have a significant long-run employment effect as well as some positive impact on take-home pay.[12] The overall effect will, however, reduce the incentive for the unskilled to acquire training.

Finally, what role should this policy play in a concerted effort to cut overall unemployment? At the outset, it is worth noting that it is not possible for us to give a full answer to this question, because we are not in a position to compare this policy with other ways of spending the money either on the unskilled (e.g. subsidised training, public-sector job creation) or more generally (e.g. reforming the benefit system, active labour market policy). However, several points can be made. First, even if we could completely reverse the impact of the decline in the relative demand for the unskilled, we would only reduce *overall* unemployment by a relatively small, albeit significant, amount. This is because the majority of the increase in unemployment has been the consequence of factors which have operated neutrally with regard to skill (in those countries where unemployment has risen substantially). Second, we must be careful not to reduce significantly the incentive to acquire skills. This may require some additional policy on the training front. Third, the social problems which have arisen not only from the collapse in the relative demand for the unskilled but also from the substantial rise in overall unemployment remain a crucial issue, particularly as they seem to be getting worse. These require special attention based on an analysis which goes far beyond just unemployment questions.

Overall, therefore, we can argue that cuts in payroll taxes or job subsidies for the unskilled cannot be expected to play a major role in reversing the inexorable rise in aggregate unemployment. But they could make a contribution. Finally, however, it is worth emphasising that the parlous position of the unskilled in an era of high unemployment is producing a slew of social problems which are becoming one of the most intractable issues facing the developed world. This makes an overall reduction in unemployment and, thereby, an improvement in the position of the unskilled, a matter of urgency.

Appendix: notes to table 10.2

FR: France. *Source*: *Enquête sur L'Emploi, INSEE* (annual publication).

Low education: no certification or only primary school certificate. High education: two years' university education or further education college degree or university degree.

[a] = 1982 only; [b] = 1983, 1986 only.

Data refer to males, aged 15 +.

GE: (West) Germany. *Source*: *ILO Yearbook of Labour Statistics* (various issues, tables 3C, 10C).

Low occupation: production and related workers, transport equipment operators and labourers.

High occupation: professional, technical and related, administrative and managerial workers.

[c] - 1976–8 only.

Data refer to males.

IT: Italy. *Source*: First set, *Rilevazione delle forze di lavor*, reported in an as yet unpublished OECD table (our thanks to John Martin). Remaining sets, *Annuario Statistico Italiano*, ISTAT (our thanks to Barbara Petrongolo and Marco Manacorda).

Low education: lower secondary or less.

High education: upper secondary or higher,

[d] = 1980 only; [e] = 1989 only.

Data refer to males, aged 25–64 except for (M + F) which refers to males and females.

NE: Netherlands. *Source*: Dutch Central Bureau of Statistics, provided for us by Jan van Ours and Erik Brouwer.

Low education: basic education or completed junior secondary school or junior vocational training.

High education: completed vocational college or university education.

[f] = 1985, 1977; [g] = 1979, 1981; [h] = 1983, 1985; [i] = 1990.

Data in the first set refer to males, aged 15–64; in the second set (M + F) to males and females, aged 15–64.

SP: Spain. *Source*: Spanish Labour Force Survey from the Bank of Spain data base (our thanks to Juan Dolado).

Low education: illiterate and without studies or primary.

High education: superior (essentially university).

[j] = 1976–8.

Data refer to males, aged 16–64.

UK: United Kingdom. *Source*: General Household Survey data tapes.

Low education: no qualifications.

High education: passed A levels (18+ examination) or professional qualification or university degree.

[k] = 1973–4.

Data refer to males, aged 16–64.

AL: Australia. *Source*: *The Labour Force: Educational Attainment, Australia*, Australian Bureau of Statistics.

Low education: did not attend highest level of secondary school.

High education: university degree.

Data refer to males, aged 15–69.

NZ: New Zealand. *Source*: Statistics New Zealand (our thanks to Giles Hancock).
Low education: no qualification.
High education: school or post-school qualification.
Data refer to males, aged 16–64.

CA: Canada. *Source*: *The Labour Force*, Statistics Canada (various issues).
Low education: up to level 8.
High education: university degree.
^{l} = 1979, ^{m} = 1984–6.
Data refer to males, aged 15+.

USA: United States. *Source*: *Handbook of Labor Statistics*, Bureau of Labor Statistics (1989, Table 67); *Statistical Abstract of the United States* (1993, Table 654).
Low education: less than 4 years of high school.
High education: 4 or more years of college.
Data refer to males, aged 25–64.

JA: Japan. *Source*: *Employment Status Survey* (our thanks to Toshiaki Tachibanaki).
Low education: junior high school.
High education: university.
^{n} = 1971, 1974; ^{o} = 1979, 1982; ^{p} = 1987.
Data refer to males, aged 16–64.

AU: Austria. *Source*: as Germany.
Low and High occupation as Germany.
Data refer to males.

FN: Finland. *Source*: *Työvoiman Koulutus ja Ammatit*, 1984–1992/1993, Statistics Finland.
Low education: basic education only.
High education: higher education both lower and upper levels.
^{q} = 1984–6.
Data refer to males, aged 15–74.

NW: Norway. *Source*: *Labour Market Statistics*, Statistik Sentrallyra.
Low education: primary level.
High education: university level.
^{r} = 1972–4.
Data refer to males *and* females, aged 16–74.

SW: Sweden. *Source*: *Swedish Labour Force Surveys* (our thanks to Bertil Holmlund).
Low education: pre-upper secondary school up to 10 years.
High education: post-upper secondary education.
Pro-rata adjustments as follows: post-1986, change in measurement reduced aggregate unemployed by 16 per cent, post-1982, change in measurement increased aggregate unemployed by 9 per cent.
Data refer to males, aged 16–64.

NOTES

We are extremely grateful to Erik Brouwer, Juan Dolado, Bertil Holmlund, John Martin, Barbara Petrongolo, Toshiaki Tachibanaki, Jan van Ours, Jane

Roberts and Giles Hancock (Statistics New Zealand) for help with the data and to Bob Gordon, Olivier Blanchard, Edmond Malinvaud, Derek Morris, Dennis Snower, Richard Layard and Patrick Minford for helpful comments. We must also thank Andrew Glyn, Richard Freeman and particularly Adrian Wood for stimulating our interest in this area. Indeed, this chapter can be viewed as an appendix to Wood's brilliant book, *North–South Trade, Employment and Inequality* (Wood, 1994). Finally, we are grateful to the ESRC for providing research funding under the auspices of the Centre for Economic Performance and to the ESRC Data Archive for use of the General Household Survey. Material from the General Household Survey made available through the ESRC Data Archive has been used by permission of the Controller of H.M. Stationary Office.

1 See OECD (1994, 46).

2 There is also a lot of time-series evidence on the question of the incidence of various taxes. Indeed every time-series wage equation in existence contains explicit or implicit estimates of the incidence of both employment and excise tax rates. In fact many wage equations imply very large effects of taxes on labour costs simply because relevant tax effects are omitted entirely. However, from those studies which take tax effects seriously, the evidence is very mixed. For example, Knoester and van der Windt (1987) report large long-run effects of employee taxes on labour costs for 10 OECD countries. Furthermore, Calmfors (1990, Table 3) reports long-run payroll tax effects in all Nordic countries except Finland. However, Bean *et al.* (1986) only find significant tax effects in five out of 15 OECD countries.

There are three basic problems. First, the time-series results in this area tend to be very fragile. Second, short time series find it very hard to discriminate between fairly long-lasting temporary effects and permanent long-run effects. And finally, many macro-models are constructed with little care or thought given to tax effects and how they feed through into the long-run real equilibrium of the economy.

The consequence of this last point is that if one feeds various tax changes into macro models, one often finds that they have dramatic long-run effects on employment and output, not via their aggregate demand effects but because of their impact on wages. Generally, these effects should not be taken seriously because of the strong cross-section evidence that the pattern of employment, income and excise taxes does not make a significant difference to employment rates in the long run.

3 This is not true in countries without unemployment benefit systems. In many such countries, measured unemployment rates are higher for the well educated, essentially because the uneducated cannot afford to be unemployed (see, for example, Bhalotra, 1993, for India, and table 10.2, p. 000, for Italy).

4 The elasticities were computed as follows. First we split the male sample into two groups, those without qualifications and those with qualifications. Then, within each sample we ran a cross-section regression for each year (1978–92) explaining ln wages by age, age^2, SIC code, part-time dummy, race dummy, marital status dummy and 11 region dummies. We then took the fitted value for a standardised individual for each region. Using these standardised wages for each region along with the regional unemployment rates for the two education groups, we ran separate ln wage, ln unemployment pooled regressions over the period 1978–92 with time dummies and region dummies.

The reported elasticities are the absolute coefficients on ln unemployment in the two regressions.

5 It is natural to ask how a shock which leads initially to equiproportional rises in wage rates and equiproportional falls in *employment* rates (and hence equal *percentage point* rises in unemployment rates), can lead eventually to rises in unemployment which are getting on for *equiproportional*. What happens is that the initial rise in skilled unemployment is *proportionally* much greater than the initial rise in unskilled unemployment. The constant elasticity form of the wage equation then induces a much greater second-round fall in skilled wages relative to unskilled wages and hence a much larger second-round rise in skilled employment relative to unskilled employment, particularly as demand is highly elastic. The final outcome is then as described in (8).

6 See, in particular, some of the comments in National Audit Office (1989, pp. 2, 3).

7 Another point worth raising is the possibility that we might get a different picture if we focused not on the unemployment rate of particular education or skill groups, but on certain percentiles of the skill distribution. The argument for doing this is that because of the overall increase in skill levels, the high-education groups have, on average, become bigger and less 'skilled', and the low-education groups have become smaller and less 'skilled', thereby raising unemployment rates in both groups. Looking carefully at the available data indicates that taking account of this does not appear to change the overall pattern of our findings.

8 Eliminating W_i between (2), (3) and taking differentials yields

$$(1/\sigma(1-u_u)+\eta(u_u)/u_u)du_u = d\alpha/\alpha_u + d\ln\gamma + \frac{1}{\sigma}d\ln(L_u/L)$$
$$(1/\sigma(1-u_s)+\eta(u_s)/u_s)du_s = -d\alpha/\alpha_s + d\ln\gamma + 1/\sigma d\ln(L_s/L).$$

Eliminating $d\ln\gamma$ gives (9) in the text and setting $d\ln\gamma = 0$ gives (10).

9 $TT = s\ln(P_m/P^*)$, s = imports/GDP (*ETAS*). P_m = import price index for the UK (*ETAS*), P^* = unit value index of world manufacturing exports from *UN Monthly Bulletin of Statistics* converted from dollars to pounds using the exchange rate (*ETAS*). *UP* = log (union/non-union mark-up). This is estimated using the method described in Layard *et al.* (1978). *RR* = benefit replacement ratio from social security statistics, table H3.10, using a weighted average of different family types. $T = t_1 + t_2 + t_3$. t_1 = employment 'tax' borne by the firm = ln (total labour costs per unit of output/wages and salaries per unit of output); t_2 = direct tax rate = $(DT + SS)/HCR$, DT = direct taxes on household income, SS = households' contributions to social security schemes, HCR = households' current receipts *less* employer contributions to social security schemes from *OECD National Accounts*; t_3 = indirect tax rate = ln (GDP deflator at market prices/GDP deflator at factor cost). *IT* = industrial turbulence = absolute annual change in the proportion of employees in production industries (*BLSHA*, *YB*, *DEG*). *BLSHA* = *British Labour Statistics, Historical Abstract*, *DEG* = *Department of Employment Gazette*, *ETAS* = *Economic Trends Annual Supplement*, *YB* = *British Labour Statistics Year Book* (published annually from 1969 to 1976).

10 The data are quarterly from 1963 to 1992. Unit root tests are as follows: variable (*DF*, *ADF*(4)), log u (−0.71, −1.31), Δ log u (−5.39*, −3.97*), *TT*

(−0.93, 0.22), ΔT (−13.6*, −4.7*), *UP* (−1.26, −1.46), ΔUP (−4.06*, −3.58*), *RR* (−0.16, −1.93), ΔRR (−3.32*, −2.66), *T* (−2.34, −2.33), ΔT (−13.5*, −4.2*), *OIL* (−1.19, −1.48), ΔOIL (−8.84*, −4.66*), *IT* (−3.01*, −3.41*), *Skill* (−1.49, −3.32*), $\Delta Skill$ (−4.81*, −5.71*). *DF* is the Dickey–Fuller *t*-statistic with a constant in the model. *ADF* ($) is the Augmented *DF* *t*-statistic with a constant and four lags. * means significant at the 5 per cent level.

11 Consider the simple log-linear natural rate model:

(i) $y = m - p$	demand	(y = output, m = money stock, p = prices)
(ii) $y = a_1 n$	production	(n = employment)
(iii) $\bar{y} = a_1 l$	full utilisation output	($\bar{y}$ = full utilisation output, l = labour force)
(iv) $p = w + \beta_0 + \beta_1(y - \bar{y}) - \beta_2(p - p^e) + z_p$	prices	(w = wages, z_p = exogenous shifts in price behaviour)
(v) $w = p + \gamma_0 - \gamma_1 \log u - \gamma_2(p - p^e) + z_w$	wages	(z_w = exogenous wage pressure)

(ii), (iii) imply $y - \bar{y} = -a_1 u (u = 1 - n)$ and hence unemployment will be cointegrated with demand. However (ii), (iii), (iv) and (v) imply that $\beta_1 a_1 u + \gamma_1 \log u = (\beta_0 + \gamma_0) + (z_p + z_w) + (\beta_2 + \gamma_2)(p - p^e)$. Since $(p - p^e)$ is $I(0)$ and in practice, β_1 tends to be very small (and UK wage equations tend to be based on log u), this equation implies that log u will be cointegrated with the supply-side variables z_p,z_w.

12 Note that with a pay floor, payroll tax cuts have different effects from income tax cuts which have no effect on labour costs and hence on employment. With flexible pay, of course, payroll tax cuts have exactly the same effect as income tax cuts.

REFERENCES

Banerjee, A., J. Dolado, D.F. Hendry and G.W. Smith, 1986. 'Exploring equilibrium relationships in econometrics through static models: some Monte Carlo evidence', *Oxford Bulletin of Economics and Statistics*, **48**, 253–77

Banerjee, A., J. Dolado, J.W. Galbraith and D.F. Hendry, 1993. *Cointegration, Error-Correction and the Econometric Analysis of Non-Stationary Data*, Oxford: Oxford University Press

Bean, C.R., P.R.G. Layard and S.J. Nickell, 1986. 'The rise in unemployment: a multi-country study', *Economica*, **53**, S1–S22

Berman, E., J. Bound and Z. Griliches, 1994. 'Changes in the demand for skilled labor within US manufacturing: evidence from the Annual Survey of Manufacturing', *Quarterly Journal of Economics*, **109**, 367–97

Bhalotra, S., 1993. 'Differentials in urban unemployment rates across Indian states', Wolfson College, Oxford, mimeo

Blanchflower, D.G. and A.J. Oswald, 1994a. *The Wage Curve*, Cambridge, MA: MIT Press

1994b. 'An introduction to the wage curve', *Journal of Economic Perspectives*, **9(3)**, 153–68

Calmfors, L. (ed.), 1990. *Wage Formation and Macroeconomic Policy in the Nordic Countries*, Oxford: Oxford University Press

Davis, S.J., 1992. 'Cross-country patterns of change in relative wages', *NBER Working Paper*, **4085**, Cambridge, MA: NBER; *NBER Macroeconomics Annual*, 7 (1992)

Engle, R.F. and C.W.J. Granger, 1987. 'Cointegration and error correction: representation, estimation and testing', *Econometrica*, **55**, 251–76

Hamermesh, D., 1993. *Labour Demand*, Princeton: Princeton University Press

Johansen, S., 1988. 'Statistical analysis of cointegration vectors', *Journal of Economic Dynamics and Control*, **12**, 231–54

Juhn, C., K.M. Murphy and R.H. Topel, 1991. 'Why has the natural rate of unemployment increased over time?', *Brookings Papers on Economic Activity*, **2**, 75–142

Knoester, A. and N. van der Windt, 1987. 'Real wages and taxation in ten OECD countries', *Oxford Bulletin of Economics and Statistics*, **49**, 151–69

Layard, P.R.G., D. Metcalf and S.J. Nickell, 1978. 'The effect of collective bargaining on relative and absolute wages', *British Journal of Industrial Relations*, **16**, 287–302

Layard, P.R.G., S.J. Nickell and R.A. Jackman, 1991. *Unemployment: Macroeconomic Performance and the Labour Market*, Oxford: Oxford University Press

Machin, S., 1994. 'Changes in relative demand for skills in the UK labor market', in A. Booth and D. Snower (eds.), *Acquiring Skills: Market Failures, their Symptoms and Policy Responses*, Cambridge: Cambridge University Press

National Audit Office, 1989. *Invalidity Benefit: Report by the Comptroller and Auditor General*, London: HMSO

Nickell, S.J., 1987. 'Why is wage inflation in Britain so high?', *Oxford Bulletin of Economics and Statistics*, **49**, 103–28

1988. 'The NAIRU: some theory and statistical facts', in R. Cross (ed.), *Unemployment, Hysteresis and the Natural Rate Hypothesis*, Oxford: Basil Blackwell

OECD, 1990. *Employment Outlook*, Paris; OECD

1994. *The OECD Jobs Study: Facts, Analysis, Strategy*, Paris: OECD

Oswald, A.J., 1986. 'Wage determination and recession: a report on recent work', *British Journal of Industrial Relations*, **24**, 181–94

Wood, A., 1994. *North–South Trade, Employment and Inequality: Changing Fortunes in a Skill-Driven World*, Oxford: Clarendon Press

Yellen, J.L., 1991. 'Discussion of Juhn *et al.*', *Brookings Papers on Economic Activity*, **2**, 127–33

Discussion

ROBERT J. GORDON

Nickell and Bell's chapter 10 provides valuable insights on a theme that keeps recurring in economic debates in the world at large: 'can a shift in the *relative* demand for labour in favour of skilled workers and against unskilled workers explain an increase in the *aggregate* rate of unemployment?' As Krugman (1994) and others have previously argued, the answer is clearly 'yes' if a wage floor (e.g. minimum wage) prevents the wage rate for unskilled workers from dropping, leading to extra unskilled unemployment that becomes part of aggregate unemployment. The difficulties, as we shall see below, are in finding the quantitative counterpart of the relative demand shift in microeconomic data, and in attributing to that demand shift more than a small part of the overall rise in unemployment that has plagued Europe since the early 1980s.

The title of chapter 10 proclaims that it is about payroll taxes, but it is not, at least after the first page. Any link between the payroll tax and unemployment is dismissed by 'a glance at Denmark' and by figure 10.1, which shows no significant relationship between unit labour costs and payroll tax rates. But figure 10.1 is not convincing, because there are many causes of the cross-country variation in unit labour costs displayed there. A role for the payroll tax that is not evident in the simple bivariate regression reported by the authors might emerge in a full-blown multiple regression study. However, there are two more direct reasons – that the authors should have cited – why the payroll tax is borne by workers. First, any factor of production bears a tax imposed on it if it is supplied inelastically, as is the supply of prime-age male workers. Second, long-run data exhibit constancy in the share of compensation in national income, where 'compensation' is defined to include payroll tax revenue collected from both employers and employees. Thus an increase in the payroll tax must reduce the after-tax wage rate if the share of before-tax compensation is to remain constant.

Most of chapter 10 is not about payroll taxes, but rather about skill differentials and their impact on aggregate unemployment. Before looking at the facts and results, what do we expect from basic economic theory? Consider a world with two kinds of workers in an equilibrium where skilled workers earn a wage that exceeds that of the unskilled workers by the amount of a 'training cost' factor (*TC*). A shift in demand toward skilled workers will initially raise the wage of skilled workers and reduce the wage of unskilled workers. But now the wage differential exceeds *TC*, inducing a supply adjustment that raises the supply of skilled workers, reduces the supply of unskilled workers, and re-establishes the initial wage differential equal to *TC*. If there is a wage floor for unskilled workers at the initial equilibrium unskilled wage, the initial response will be an increase in the unemployment of unskilled workers. But the wage differential (caused by the increase in the skilled wage) still is sufficiently above *TC* to induce the same supply shift that would occur in the absence of the wage floor. As a result, any tendency of a demand shift to raise the unemployment of unskilled workers, and hence the aggregate unemployment rate, is strictly temporary.

There are many reasons why this theoretical scenario does not occur in the real world. There are formidable barriers that prevent unskilled workers from transforming themselves into skilled workers and paying the cost out of their *future* wages. Basic education may be lacking to undergo training; imperfect capital markets prevent unskilled workers from borrowing against future earnings; and also technological developments – including personal computers – may have raised the magnitude of *TC*.

A real strength of chapter 10 is its compendium of cross-country data on relative unemployment rates and on earnings differentials by skill. Table 10.2 on relative unemployment rates displays a mixed picture. There was a secular increase (between the late 1970s and early 1990s) in the relative unemployment rate of the 'low' (education or occupation) group only in Germany, Italy, Spain and Japan. In many of the other countries the relative unemployment rate stayed flat, fell, or was 'hump-shaped' (rising and then falling).

Perhaps more surprising is table 10.3, which shows no increase in the USA between the early 1970s and late 1980s in the earnings ratio of high- to low-education groups. This finding, and the fact that the value of the ratio is in the middle of the array of countries rather than at the top, together contradict the standard impression that the skill differential in the USA is both high and rising. In fact, not a single country displays a rising earnings differential by education in table 10.3, and there are large declines in Italy, the Netherlands, Australia, Canada and Sweden.

Table 10.4 is much more compatible with standard views of the US experience. The D9/D1 earning ratio is much higher for the USA than for any other country, and its increase has been notable. An even greater proportional increase between the first observation and the last took place in the UK. Little, if any, increase in inequality was observed in France, Germany, Italy and Sweden.

Comparing tables 10.3 and 10.4, the former seems to be an anomaly. While chapter 10 makes no attempt to explain how its results could be consistent with those of other tables, one might speculate that the reasons for increasing wage inequality have little to do with the returns to education *per se*. Instead, the 'super-star' phenomenon which has raised the earnings of movie stars, media idols, and professionals with a global reach, has occurred for those with high and low educational attainments alike.

Chapter 10's most original contribution is its estimate that roughly one-fifth of the increase in British unemployment between the 1970s and 1980s was due to a decline in the relative demand for unskilled workers. This result is obtained in two ways. First, in table 10.5 a simple examination is made of the relative increase over time in the unemployment rates of the skilled and unskilled. Second, a regression analysis is made of the long-run change in the UK unemployment rate (table 10.6). The similarity of results by the two unrelated methods, based on different definitions of skill, is convincing.

Despite its earlier denial of any effect of payroll taxes on unemployment, chapter 10 winds up by recommending a policy which attempts to reduce unskilled unemployment by cutting payroll taxes on the unskilled or by introducing wage subsidies for the unskilled. How is this inconsistency reconciled? The key insight is evident in our basic economic model outlined above. With a wage floor (due to minimum wages, unions, or benefit levels) that applies to the wage defined net of payroll tax, an increase in the payroll tax will reduce the demand for unskilled labour and a reduction in the payroll tax will raise the demand for unskilled labour.

A free-market American economist might scoff at the second-best nature of the policy recommendation. If the problem is the wage floor, get rid of the wage floor. Such economists were at the forefront of the opposition of an increase in the US minimum wage during the Congressional debate of 1996. But the authors resist this approach, because their humanitarian streak balks at any approach that would further reduce the well-being of the low-skilled. They would maintain the wage floor but reduce the payroll tax on the unskilled. I would heartily endorse their proposal, but take it one step further. Why not abolish the payroll tax and replace it by higher taxes on consumption? This would simultaneously help the unskilled, if the Nickell–Bell analysis is correct, and would stimulate saving, investment and economic growth. In a volume such as this, a reminder is sometimes needed that we care not just about the aggregate unemployment rate and the distribution of unemployment and earnings across skill groups, but also about the rate at which the rising tide lifts the average standard of living.

REFERENCES

Krugman, P., 1994. 'Past and prospective causes of high unemployment', Annual Symposium of the Federal Reserve Bank of Kansas City, Jackson Hole, Wyoming (26–27 August), mimeo

11 Preventing long-term unemployment: an economic analysis

RICHARD LAYARD

1 Introduction and review

The EU has set the target of halving unemployment by the year 2000 (CEU, 1993). How can thus be done without increasing inflation? The strategy must be to reduce those kinds of unemployment which do little to restrain inflation. The most obvious such category is long-term unemployment.

1.1 Effects of long-term unemployment

Let us examine the evidence. In wage equations long-term unemployment is usually found to have a very small (or zero) effect in reducing wage pressure.[1] The reasons for this are obvious: long-term unemployed people are not good fillers of vacancies. This can be seen from data on exit rates from unemployment: exit rates decline sharply as duration increases. Equally, aggregate time series show that, for a given level of unemployment, vacancies increase the higher the proportion of unemployed who are long-term unemployed.

If long-term unemployment is an optional extra, depending on social institutions, it is not surprising that there are striking differences in its prevalence across countries. As table 11.1 shows, in the 1980s the majority of countries had between 3 and 6 per cent of the labour force in short-term unemployment (of under a year). But there were huge differences in long-term unemployment. It was under 1 per cent in the USA, Japan, Canada and Sweden and over 8 per cent in Spain, Belgium and Ireland.

Clearly some short-term unemployment is necessary in any economy, to avoid the inflationary pressure which would develop in an over-tight labour market. But long-term unemployment is not needed for this purpose.

Table 11.1 *Short- and long-term unemployment as a percentage of the labour force, 1980s average*

	Long-term	Short-term	Total
Australia	1.9	5.5	7.4
Belgium	8.0	3.0	11.1
Canada	0.8	8.4	9.2
Denmark	2.4	5.6	8.0
Finland	0.7	4.1	4.8
France	3.9	5.0	9.0
Germany	3.0	3.6	6.7
Greece	2.9	3.6	6.6
Ireland	8.1	6.1	14.2
Italy	6.4	3.4	9.9
Japan	0.4	2.0	2.4
Netherlands	4.7	5.0	9.7
NZ	0.4	4.1	4.5
Norway	0.2	2.5	2.7
Portugal	2.5	4.7	7.3
Spain	10.1	7.4	17.5
Sweden	0.2	2.2	2.4
UK	4.2	5.2	9.5
USA	0.6	6.5	7.1

Sources: OECD, *Employment Outlook*, OECD, *Labour Force Survey*.

1.2 Causes of long-term unemployment

So how can it be prevented? To consider this we need to know under what conditions it occurs. Figure 11.1 provides a striking clue. It shows on the vertical axis the maximum duration of benefit in each country and on the horizontal axis the percentage of unemployed people in long-term unemployment (over a year). In countries like the USA, Japan, Canada and Sweden benefits run out within a year and so unemployment lasting more than a year is rare. By contrast in the main EU countries benefits have typically been available indefinitely or for a long period, and long-term unemployment is high.

The relationship shown in figure 11.1 is of course a partial correlation. But if one allows for multiple causation, the effect of benefit duration upon the aggregate unemployment rate remains strong and clear.[2]

The effect of unemployment benefit availability upon unemployment is not surprising. Unemployment benefits are a subsidy to idleness, and it should not be surprising if they lead to an increase in idleness. In principle, of course, the benefits are meant to protect individuals against

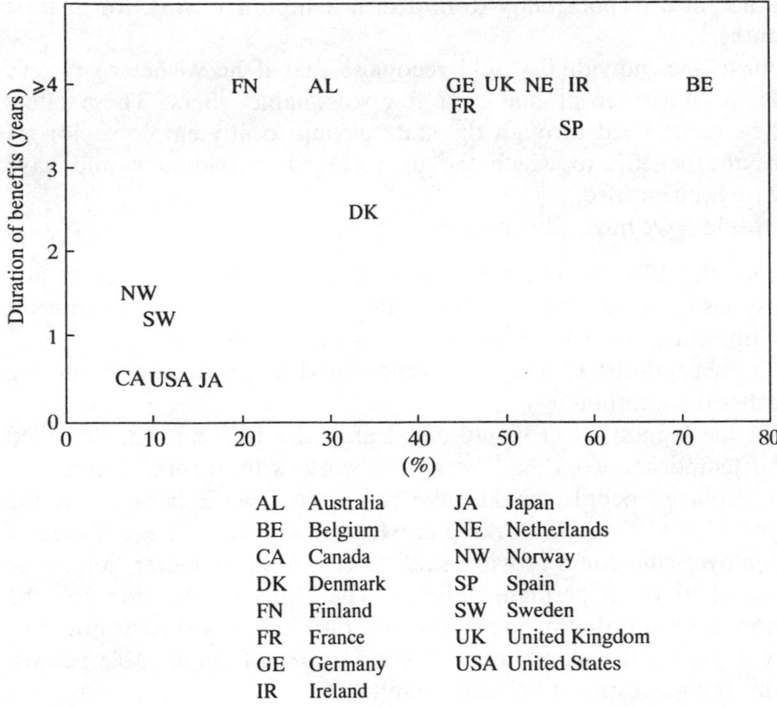

Figure 11.1 Percentage of unemployed people out of work over 12 months, by maximum duration of benefits, 1984

an exogenous misfortune and there is meant to be a test of willingness to work. But in practice it is impossible to operate a 'work test' without offering actual work. So after a period of disheartening job search, unemployed individuals often adjust to unemployment as a different life-style.

1.3 Preventing long-term unemployment

What should we do about the situation? One possibility would be to reduce the duration of benefits to, say, one year and put nothing else in its place. This would be the American-style solution. But we know this only works because people thrown onto the labour market accept an ever-widening inequality of wages. A much better approach would be to help people to become more employable so that they would justify a better wage. This leads to our central proposal. After 12 months the state should stop paying people for doing nothing. But at the same time it should accept a responsibility to find them temporary work for at least six months.[3]

In return, the individual would recognise that if he wishes to receive income, he must accept one of a few reasonable offers. These offers would be guaranteed through the state paying to any employer for six months the benefits to which the unemployed individual would have otherwise been entitled.

This would have huge advantages:

(i) After the 12th month, it would relieve the public finances of any responsibility for people who are already in work. It is very difficult to prevent fraud without being able to offer full-time work.[4]

(ii) Between months 12 and 18, people would be producing something rather than nothing.

(iii) But the biggest effect would come after the 18th month. Provided the temporary work had been real work with regular employers, unemployed people would have re-acquired work habits plus the ability to prove their working capacity. They would have a regular employer who could provide a reference – or (even better) retain the individual on a permanent basis. The main justification for the proposal is not that it employs people on a subsidised basis but that, by doing so, it restores them to the universe of employable people. This is an investment in human capital.

That is the central objective of the exercise. Job creation schemes in the past have often failed because the jobs have been marginal and have failed to make the individual more employable thereafter. The job subsidy should therefore be available to any employer (private or public). There should also be the fewest possible restrictions on the kind of work that can be done. Clearly, no employer should be allowed to employ subsidised workers if he is at the same time dismissing regular workers. But there should be no condition (as there was in the UK's former Community Programme) that the work done should be work that would not otherwise be done for the next two years. Such a requirement is a formula for ineffectiveness.

The reason why job creation schemes have so often had these disastrous limiting conditions is the fear of substitution and displacement. This fear is understandable but misplaced.

1.4 Substitution and displacement

Most opposition to active labour market measures is based on fears of displacement and substitution. In their extreme form these derive from the 'lump-of-labour fallacy': there are only so many jobs so, if we enable *X* to get one of them, some other person goes without work. This is a complete fallacy.

However it is easy to see how it arises. In the most immediate sense, the proposition is true. If an employer has a vacancy and, due to a job subsidy, *X* gets it rather than *Y*, *Y* remains temporarily unemployed. But by definition *Y* is inherently employable. If he does not get this job, he will offer himself for others. Employers will find there are more employable people in the market and that they can more easily fill their vacancies. This increases downwards pressure on wages, making possible a higher level of employment at the same level of inflationary pressure.

On average over the cycle the level of unemployment is determined at the level needed to hold inflation stable. Active labour market policy increases the number of employable workers, and thus reduces the unemployment needed to control inflation. Equally, in the short run a government that has a given inflation target (or exchange rate target) will allow more economic expansion if it finds that inflationary pressures are less than would otherwise be expected.

Many people find it difficult to believe that (inflationary pressure equal) jobs automatically expand in relation to the employable labour force. So we devote the whole of section 2 of the chapter to that issue.

1.5 Benefits and costs

We can now proceed to sum up the effects of the scheme and its impact on human welfare. In a formal sense, it would abolish long-term unemployment. However this is to over-claim since someone who reverts to unemployment after 18 months (after his temporary job) is not really short-term unemployed, even though this would be his classification in the statistics. So let us consider the impacts on the flow of a cohort entering unemployment.

During the first 12 months, some people may, it is true, delay taking a job because their potential employer has an incentive to wait for the subsidy. But more people will take a job who would not otherwise have done so because they would not like to end up on the programme. The hope is that a completely new climate would develop in which neither individuals nor the Employment Service accept the idea that someone should reach the humiliating position of being confronted with temporary work as the only possible source of income. In Sweden in the 1980s typically about 3 per cent of the workforce reached the 14th month of unemployment (when benefit ran out): in Britain the figure was about five times larger.

Going on, between the 12th and 18th months all the cohort is now employed. After the 18th month the proportion employed should be very much higher than it would have been, due to the employability of those concerned.

Thus it is reasonable to suppose that unemployment would fall by roughly the same size as the stock of long-term unemployed, leading to a substantial increase in production. Suppose average European unemployment fell to 5 per cent compared with a counterfactual rate of, say, 9 per cent. Output would be at a minimum 2 per cent higher.

This is the *social gain* (not to mention an additional non-income-related gain in psychic well-being among those affected). What is the *social cost*? Very little. The Employment Service would need more administrative staff, but this is a tiny cost compared with the gain.[5] (The typical EU country spends only 0.1 per cent of GNP on its Employment Service.)

The balance is also favourable if we focus exclusively on the *benefits and costs to the public finances*:

(i) After the 12th month the taxpayers stop supporting those who are already fraudulently in work.

(ii) Between the 12th and 18th month, the taxpayers keep paying benefit but now it goes to employers not workers. However an employer who would anyway have hired somebody unemployed between 12 and 18 months will of course claim the subsidy, so that there would on this account be some deadweight – i.e. extra expenditure.

(iii) After the 18th month, there will be major savings on benefits and extra taxes received. On any reasonable estimate the total of all these will be a positive saving to the government, and a saving higher than the extra cost of the Employment Service.

1.6 Carrot and stick

Why does this analysis seem so much more cost-effective than most existing active labour market policy? Because it is much more drastic. *Job subsidies without compulsion to accept an offer can easily be ineffective.*

Consider for example the proposal put forward by Snower (chapter 6 in this volume) which has inspired a recent British government initiative. The idea here is to make possible the conversion of a person's unemployment benefit into an employment subsidy, but not to make it mandatory. While the social net benefits should be positive, they may well be small. Major falls in unemployment are unlikely down this route. What is needed is a shift of regime.[6] No one would now design a system like the existing one. But it requires courage and commitment to change it. One thing, however, is sure. Unless it is changed, we shall be almost as far from the EU's target early next century as we are now.

In the rest of the chapter, we first discuss the issue of substitution and displacement (section 2). We then in section 3 review the effects of existing work-based policies in Sweden and the USA as a basis for evaluation of our own proposal.

2 Substitution and displacement

Programmes to help unemployed people have always been subject to two types of criticism. First, they may help people to do things they would have done anyway. Such expenditure is called 'deadweight' since it has no effect but involves a public outlay. The social cost of this public outlay is the excess burden of the tax that financed the outlay. While this can be an important issue, it is not the main criticism.

The second and more serious objection is that, if unemployed workers get jobs they would not otherwise have got, this may not increase total employment but simply deprive other workers of jobs. This can happen either if each firm employs the same number of people as before but just *substitutes* one lot of workers for another, or if some firms expand employment and output but *displace* employment in other firms.

2.1 No job fund

Such arguments taken to the limit are based on the idea that the total number of jobs is somehow fixed, presumably by the level of aggregate demand. But there is no reason to suppose that demand is ever the main constraint in an economy. The monetary and fiscal authorities can always generate more demand. The constraint is the inflation constraint.

This is illustrated by the Phillips curve A_0A_0 in figure 11.2. When the employment rate is about $(1-u^*)$ inflation tends to rise, and vice versa. Most governments and electorates seem to have some kind of inflation objective. Given this objective, the level of employment depends on u^*. Only policies which alter u^* will change the actual level of unemployment. But, conversely, if a policy reduces u^*, it *will* reduce u. This is illustrated by the new inflation constraint A_1A_1. There is no fixed number of jobs to be done. Given the inflation target, the number of jobs is fixed entirely on the supply side of the economy.

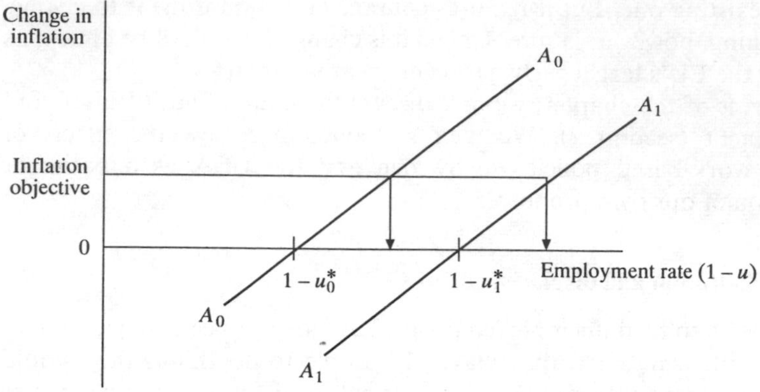

Figure 11.2 The inflation constraint

2.2 *Employability*

The main thing that determines the number of jobs is the number of 'employable' people in the economy. Economists generally take for granted the idea that, *ceteris paribus*, the number of jobs rises in proportion to the labour force, so we will for the moment take that as read. The more difficult issue is the notion of 'employability'. People clearly differ along a wide spectrum of employability. Near one end is *A*: a skilled worker who is willing to take any job and searches every day. Near the other is *B*: unskilled worker with an excessive reservation wage who only samples the job market once a month. If there are vacancies, *A* will probably be hired soon and *B* after a longer spell of unemployment.

More specifically, we can denote the 'employability' of an individual c_i, and the average employability of all unemployed people c. Then the total number of unemployed people hired in a given period (H) will depend on the number of vacancies (V) and on the number of unemployed people (U) weighted by their average employability (c).[7] Hence

$$H = f(V, cU) \quad (f_1, f_2 > 0). \tag{1}$$

Thus our concept of 'employability' refers to the capacity to fill vacancies.

How, then, does the employability of the unemployed affect the number of jobs (for a given inflation path)? The path of inflation is given by the wage–price spiral, which we shall depict in the simplest possible form.

Prices (p) are a mark-up on expected wages (w^e) so that, using small letters for logarithms:

$$p - w^e = \beta_0. \tag{2}$$

Wages (w) are a mark-up on expected prices (p^e), and this mark-up is affected by 'inflationary pressure', denoted by Φ and defined below. Thus

$$w - p^e = y_0 + \phi. \tag{3}$$

Substituting expected prices from (2) we have

$$w - w^e = \beta_0 + y_0 + \phi.$$

If price inflation is perceived as a random walk, then when $w = w^e$-inflation is stable; when $w > w^e$-inflation falls.

Thus the key determinant of the inflation path is Φ. Evidence suggests strongly that inflationary pressure increases with the chances of finding work for an unemployed person of given employability i.e. $\left(\frac{H}{cU}\right)$.[8] Thus

$$w - w^e = \beta_0 + y_0 + y_1 \frac{H}{cU}.$$

If unemployment is constant, hires equal separations, i.e. employment (N) times the separation rate (s). So

$$w = w^e = \beta_0 + y_0 + y_1 \frac{s}{cU/N}.$$

Hence for a given inflation path, unemployment is inversely proportional to average employability (c).[9]

The basic concept of this chapter is that cU is a constant. More generally, if U_i is the number of unemployed of type i, $\Sigma c_i U_i$=constant. Going on, we could for simplicity assume that there are only two types of unemployment, short-term and long-term, and that long-term unemployment causes people to be less employable ($c_L < c_S$).[10] It follows that

$$c_s U_s + c_L U_L = \text{constant}.$$

From this position we can immediately understand the effect of measures to increase the employability of the long-term unemployed (i.e.

to raise c_i). It will be clearest if we simply compare the equilibrium positions before and after c_L is reduced. After c_L has fallen, this is what we observe:

(i) The inflow into unemployment (*sN*) is unchanged (and so therefore is the outflow *H*).[11]

(ii) The exit rate from unemployment for a person with given employability is unchanged, since

$$\frac{H}{c_i U_i} = \frac{H}{cU}.$$

Therefore the exit rate from short-term unemployment is unchanged.

(iii) Since (a) the entry to short-term unemployment is unchanged and (b) the exit rate is unchanged, the stock of short-term unemployment is unchanged. Therefore $c_s U_s$ is unchanged.

(iv) It follows that U_L is lower by the same proportion that c_L is higher. Since the outflow from long-term unemployment is given by

$$\frac{H_L}{c_L U_L} = \frac{H}{cU},$$

it follows that the long-term unemployed are filling exactly the same number of vacancies per period as before. *They do not prevent a single extra short-term unemployed person from being hired.* What happens is that there are fewer long-term employed but they are being hired at a faster rate. The position is illustrated in figure 11.3.

Thus there is no substitution or displacement whatever in aggregate terms. Because long-term unemployed are more employable, their numbers fall. Total hirings of long-term unemployed have not increased.

In the transition from one equilibrium to another the hirings of long-term unemployed people do, of course, increase. But so, of course, do total hirings, which is the method by which employment increases and unemployment falls.

2.3 The proposed scheme

The preceding analysis does not of course reflect in detail our proposed scheme. In figure 11.3, we assume that all who complete short-term unemployment enter long-term unemployment, but that people are

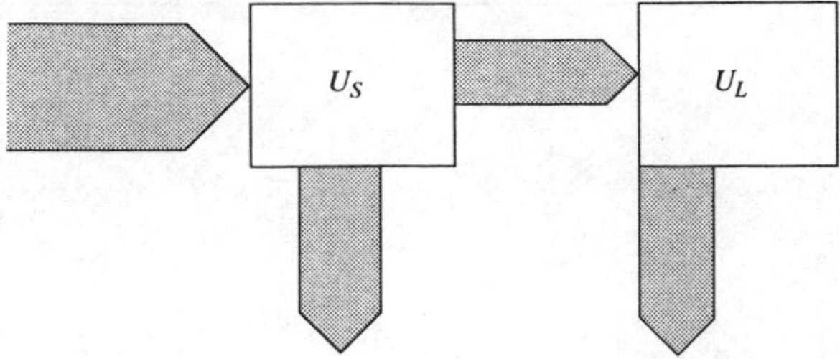

Figure 11.3 Stocks and flows

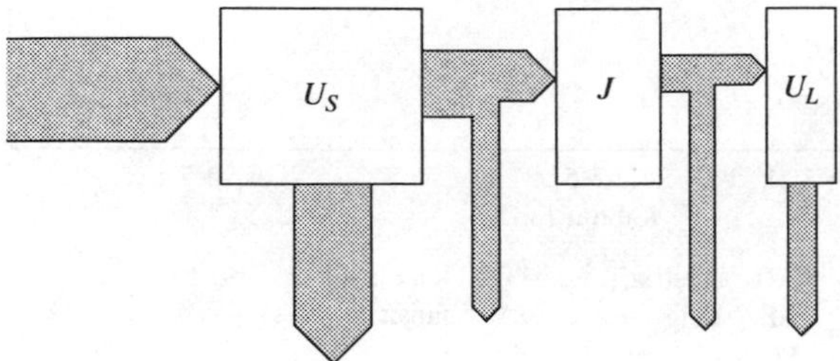

Figure 11.4 The Layard scheme

helped to leave at double the previous rate. We can now depict our own scheme more exactly in figure 11.4. In between short-term unemployment and long-term unemployment there is a six-month period of temporary work. This leads to two extra flows. Some people who complete short-term unemployment do not take temporary jobs (J). And some who take temporary jobs never re-enter unemployment at the 18th month. Total unemployment falls by the fall in U_L.

2.4 People cause jobs

Finally we revert to the question of whether in given institutional conditions the labour force determines the number of jobs (taking the cycle as a whole). Economists take this for granted, but rarely bother to document it. This is done in figure 11.5. As the graph shows, there is nothing special about the USA or Japan as creators of jobs, as is constantly alleged. They just happen to be good creators of people.[12]

To ram home the point, figure 11.6 shows that the same applies to 'jobs for men' and 'jobs for women'. These do not go their own merry way. They respond with remarkable precision to the ratios of men and women

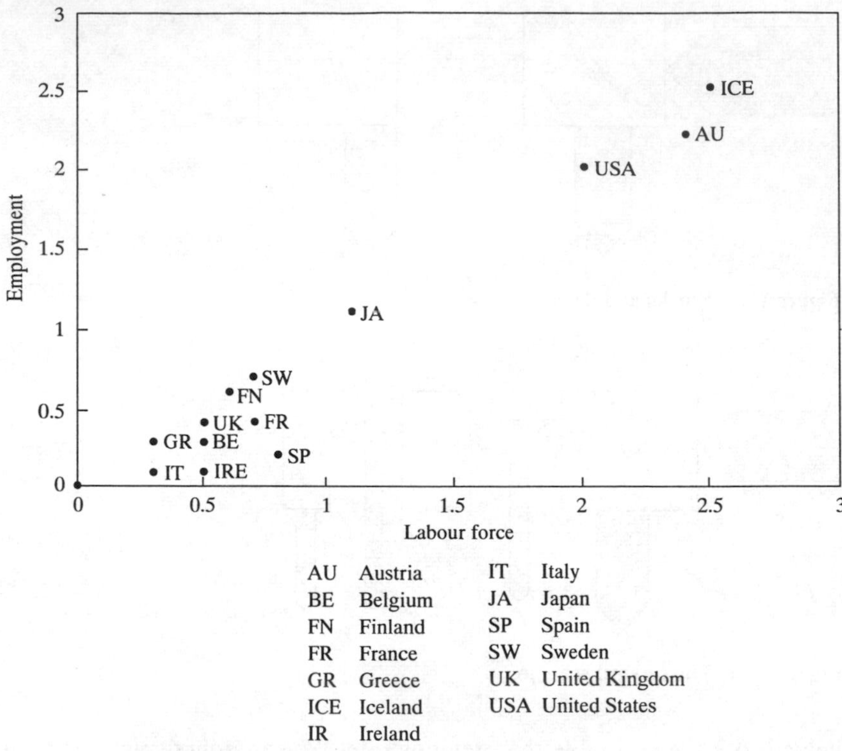

Figure 11.5 Percentage growth in the labour force and in employment, 1960–89, annual average percentage change
Source: OECD.

in the labour force. In almost every country the proportion of men aged 16–64 wanting to work has fallen and the proportion of women wanting to work has risen. This is the overwhelming source of the fall in the male–female ratio in employment, which has tended to occur within nearly all industries.

3 Relevant experience

What empirical evidence is there that could throw light on the feasibility of our proposal or its effects? We are aware of only two main types of evidence that really help.

First there is cross-sectional evidence of decadal unemployment rates across countries having different ways of treating unemployed people (see figure 11.7). In Layard *et al.* (1994) we estimated such a regression,

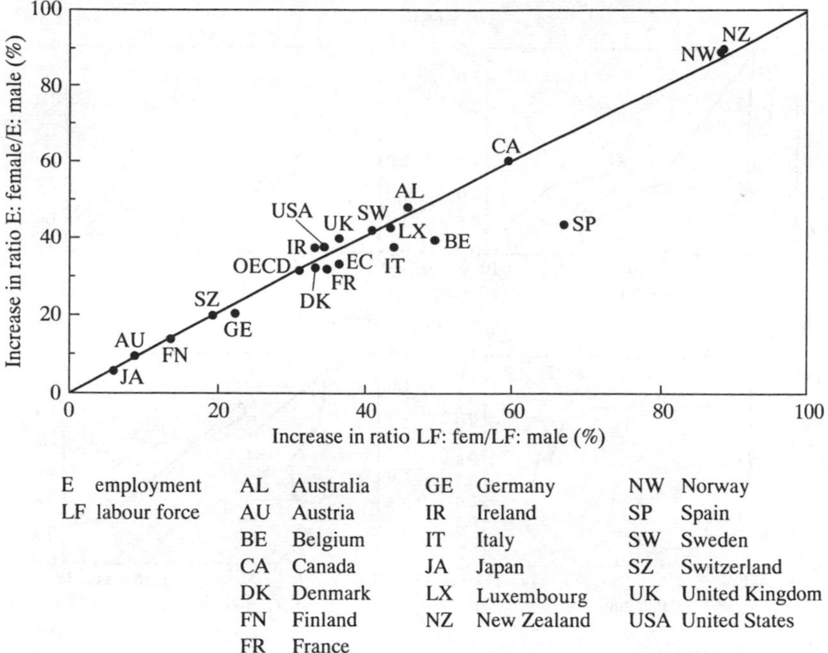

E	employment	AL	Australia	GE	Germany	NW	Norway
LF	labour force	AU	Austria	IR	Ireland	SP	Spain
		BE	Belgium	IT	Italy	SW	Sweden
		CA	Canada	JA	Japan	SZ	Switzerland
		DK	Denmark	LX	Luxembourg	UK	United Kingdom
		FN	Finland	NZ	New Zealand	USA	United States
		FR	France				

Figure 11.6 Change in relative labour force, and change in relative employment, by sex, 1970–90

which showed that unemployment increases with the duration of unemployment benefit and falls with expenditure on active labour market policy (per unemployed person). Only with these variables is it possible to explain the extraordinarily low rate of unemployment in Sweden throughout the 1970s and 1980s (around 2 per cent on average). Sweden operated and still operates essentially the system we have been advocating.

Second, there are the randomised experiments with 'conditionality' for recipients of AFDC in the USA (Gueron, 1990). These show that AFDC recipients who are exposed to work requirements subsequently became more likely to be in work, and had higher earnings and lower AFDC receipts – adding up to higher total incomes.

Our proposal is, we believe, immune to the criticisms of many training programmes offered to unemployed people. These often show a poor rate of return, especially when those retrained had little previous skill or where the quality of training was poor. For most people whose previous work experience was semi- or unskilled the best way to become employable is to work. We believe that only a regime change which makes this the normal course of affairs can make major inroads on European unemployment.

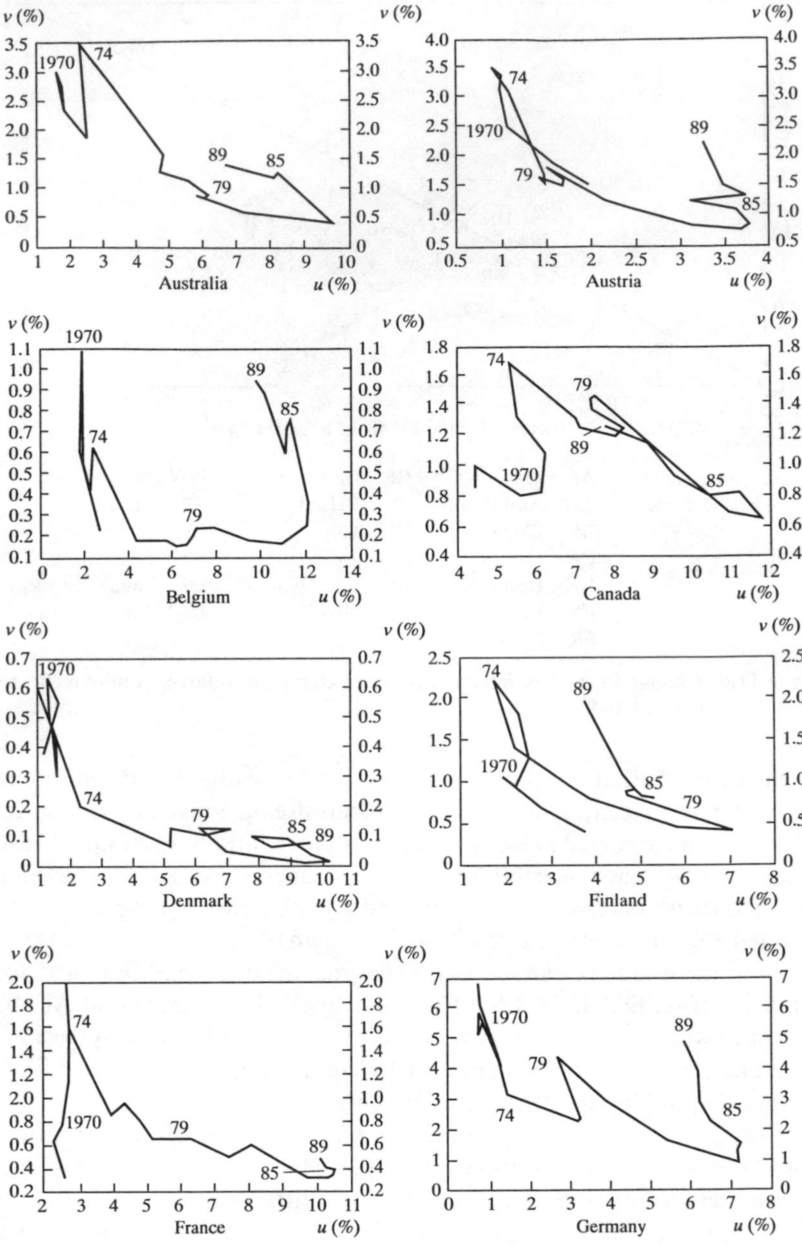
v (%)
3.5 3.0 2.5 2.0 1.5 1.0 0.5 0
1970
74
89
85
79
1 2 3 4 5 6 7 8 9 10
Australia
u (%)
v (%)
4.0 3.5 3.0 2.5 2.0 1.5 1.0 0.5
74
1970
79
89
85
0.5 1 1.5 2 2.5 3 3.5 4
Austria
u (%)
v (%)
1.1 1.0 0.9 0.8 0.7 0.6 0.5 0.4 0.3 0.2 0.1
1970
89
85
74
79
0 2 4 6 8 10 12 14
Belgium
u (%)
v (%)
1.8 1.6 1.4 1.2 1.0 0.8 0.6 0.4
74
79
89
1970
85
4 5 6 7 8 9 10 11 12
Canada
u (%)
v (%)
0.7 0.6 0.5 0.4 0.3 0.2 0.1 0
1970
74
79
85
89
1 2 3 4 5 6 7 8 9 10 11
Denmark
u (%)
v (%)
2.5 2.0 1.5 1.0 0.5 0
74
89
1970
85
79
1 2 3 4 5 6 7 8
Finland
u (%)
v (%)
2.0 1.8 1.6 1.4 1.2 2.0 0.8 0.6 0.4 0.2
74
1970
79
89
85
2 3 4 5 6 7 8 9 10 11
France
u (%)
v (%)
7 6 5 4 3 2 1 0
1970
89
79
74
85
0 1 2 3 4 5 6 7 8
Germany
u (%)

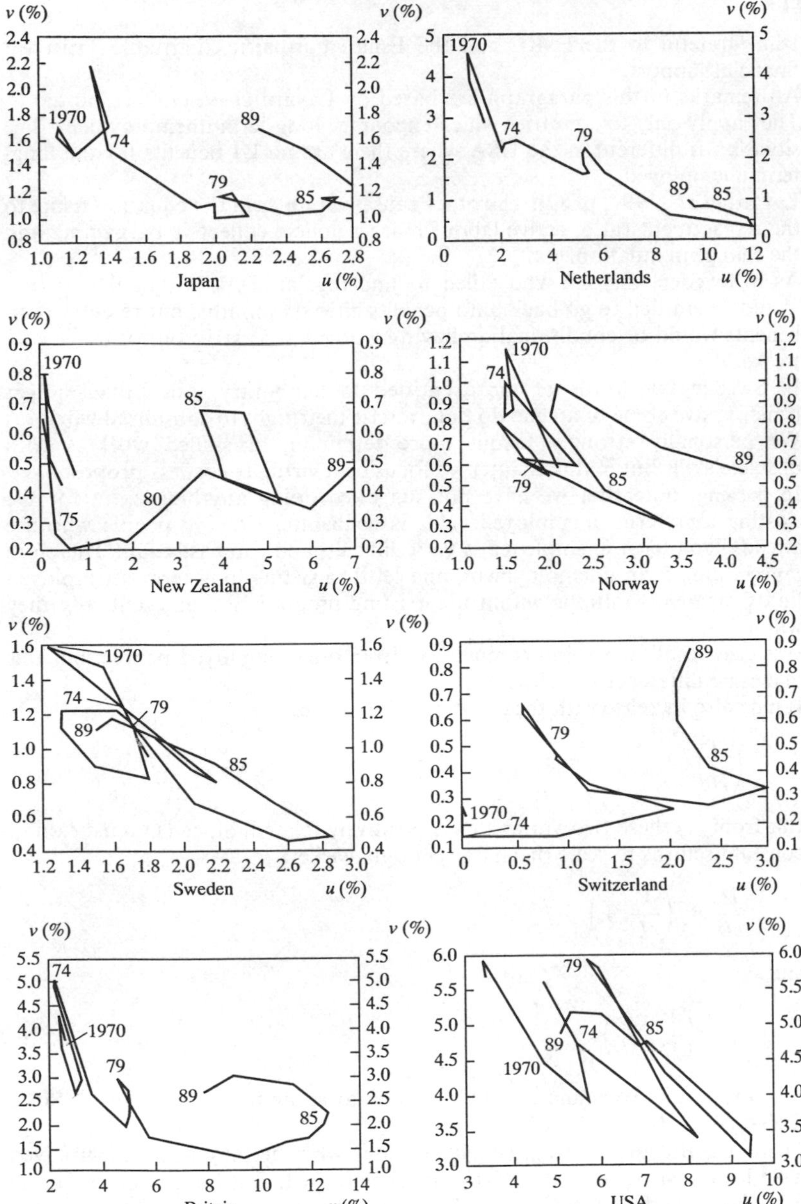

Figure 11.7 Vacancy rates, v, and unemployment rates, u, 1970–85

NOTES

I am grateful to the ESRC and the Esmée Fairbairn Charitable Trust for financial support.

1 All remarks in this paragraph are based on Layard *et al.* (1991, chapter 4). They apply only to countries which encourage long-term unemployment. The situation is different in the USA where there are no UI benefits for the long-term unemployed.

2 Layard *et al.* (1994, p. 82). The other causal variables in the equation relate to the replacement ratio, active labour market policy, collective bargaining and the change in inflation.

3 As in Sweden, anyone who failed to find regular work within that period would be entitled to go back onto benefits after six months; but re-entry onto benefits would be conditional on having worked at least 15 out of the last 52 weeks.

4 In Sweden two-thirds of those entitled to temporary jobs because their benefits have come to an end do not exercise their right to subsidised work.

5 We personally strongly favour more retraining of skilled workers with obsolete skills but in this chapter we focus on a virtually costless proposal.

6 In passing, note that we have not suggested doing anything extra for the existing long-term unemployed. This is deliberate. Helping people who are already long-term unemployed is very difficult, and can easily fail. Therefore *prevent* long-term unemployment, and let the existing long-term unemployed find their own solutions within the existing programmes, as eventually they will.

7 It is easy to allow for job competition from other employed people, but this makes no difference of substance.

8 It may also increase with the duration of vacancies

$$\left(\frac{H}{H}\right).$$

But from (1) these two variables are positively related. Since (1) must exhibit constant returns to scale (in a large enough market),

$$\frac{H}{cU}=f\left(\frac{V}{cU},1\right)$$

and

$$1=f\left(\frac{V}{H},\frac{cU}{H}\right).$$

9 In a more fully dynamic context we need to allow for changes in U. Since $\Delta U = sN - H$, $H/cU = (s-(\Delta U)/N)/cU/N$.

10 There are also of course selectivity reasons why the long-term unemployed have lower exit rates than short-term unemployed. But Layard *et al.* (1991) provides powerful evidence that the long-term unemployed also *cause* lower employability.

11 If s is constant, there is a second-order rise in sN and H, due to the rise in N.

12 If the population of working age is used on the horizontal axis, the diagram still works well.

REFERENCES

CEU, 1993. *Growth, Competitiveness, Employment. The Challenges and Ways Forward into the 21st Century*, Brussels: Commission of the European Communities

Gueron, J.M., 1990. 'Work and welfare: lessons on employment programs', *Journal of Economic Perspectives*, **4**, 79–98

Layard, P.R.G., S.J. Nickell and R.A. Jackman, 1991. *Unemployment: Macroeconomic Performance and the Labour Market*, Oxford: Oxford University Press

1994. *The Unemployment Crisis*, Oxford: Oxford University Press

Discussion

GUILLERMO DE LA DEHESA

Richard Layard's chapter 11 is very stimulating, and contains an interesting policy proposal to prevent long-term unemployment. His 'compulsory job scheme' seems to have more advantages than similar previous schemes. It is neither a pure benefit transfer system (BTP), since work is compulsory, nor a workfare scheme, since the work is not for a benefit but for a regular wage (see also chapter 6 and 7 in this volume). It has also the advantage of avoiding cheating by the would-be long-term unemployed, given that they have to choose between taking a temporary job for six months or losing the unemployment benefit and keeping only their non-market activity income. Therefore, only in the case that the non-market income is much larger than the after-tax compulsory job wage they will choose the first option, but in both cases the free-riding of unemployment benefits will be excluded. Finally, it encourages the potential long-term unemployed to try to find a job before ending up at the compulsory temporary job offered by the proposed scheme.

Nevertheless, I see a series of practical shortcomings in the scheme that could easily be avoided. The first one is that the scheme supposes that it is possible to get a job precisely on day 360 of the unemployment benefit period. Even if the job is compulsory it takes some weeks to find a simple job that does not entail functional or geographical mobility, and even longer if it implies mobility. Therefore, either the time schedule of the scheme should be made longer or the unemployed should be approached, in order to find a job, at least three months before the unemployment benefit ends and the compulsory work starts.

The second drawback under this scheme relates to the exclusive position of the state Employment Service to find the jobs for the unemployed. Why the state employment offices only? In many European countries most of the jobs for the unemployed are found by private employment agencies, not by the state services. Both private and public agencies should be used to make the scheme work better.

The third problem is that, in the proposed scheme, the state or the state-owned companies may become the employer in the last instance or the residual employer of last resort. If a European government decides to go ahead with this scheme, it will have an incentive to use the state administration or the state-owned companies as the residual employer to avoid any failure of the scheme and make it appear a success. The unemployed will also prefer to work for the state than for the private sector, given that the chances of finding a more secure and stable job are larger in the former. In the end, the scheme could become a traditional 'active employment policy' that uses the state sector as an employer to reduce unemployment, as in the Swedish case.

The fourth comment relates to the decision of applying the scheme to prevent future long-term unemployment instead of reducing the present long-term unemployed. The only reason for this appears to be that the scheme will be more successful when being applied to short-term than to long-term unemployed since, by definition, the short-term unemployed are more employable than the long-term unemployed. But maybe this scheme, or a similar one, could also be applied to the present long-term unemployed to make them more employable? The risk with this proposal is that those short-term unemployed who are less employable will have to wait for the full 12 months because the potential employer will have an incentive to wait for the subsidy. On the other hand, the more employable of short-term unemployed will have an incentive to find a job before the 12 months' deadline to avoid being forced to take a temporary job. If such is the case, it will perhaps be more efficient to impose some kind of training on the short-term unemployed in the first 12 months, not only in order to avoid cheating with non-market activities but also to make them employable.

Regarding training, Layard is very reluctant to impose any requirement or condition on the employer. I think that to improve the scheme some 'on-the-job' training should be imposed on the employer or, at least, some motivation created by transferring to him or her part of the unemployment benefit as a wage subsidy and part as a training subsidy. Such training subsidy will make more probable the future renewal of the six-month job contract than no training subsidy at all, given that the trained worker tends to be more productive for the employer.

In sum, some improvements could be introduced to make the scheme more efficient. First, within the first period of 12 months that the unemployed receives the unemployment benefit, some kind of compulsory training should be introduced (at least during the first nine months), in order to help discourage parallel non-market activities. Second, during the last three months of the 12-month period, the unemployed should be approached to accept the six-month job (in the private sector, preferably), so as to be able to start work on day 360. Third, 'on-the-job training' should be encouraged and given an incentive through the allocation of a training subsidy as a percentage of the total unemployment benefit transferred to the employer. Fourth, it might be wise to try to start implementing this scheme also with the present long-term unemployed, who have a smaller chance of finding a job, than the young short-term unemployed who, by definition, are more employable. Another possibility is to use this compulsory job scheme for the short-term unemployed and a kind of 'Dennis Snower pure transfer scheme' for the long-term unemployed.

Discussion

PATRICK MINFORD

The idea of workfare is familiar as a method of putting additional pressure on the long-term unemployed to take jobs: the method offers training or a low-level public service job as a condition for continued receipt of benefit at the existing wage level. It works directly on the labour supply of the unemployed at the existing wage level. It specifically does not include the general run of jobs: it would undermine the incentive for the unemployed to take these jobs on unsubsidised terms if it did so. Layard's Workfare Scheme in chapter 11 differs from the usual scheme, first by including all jobs. Hence it amounts to a general temporary (six-month) job subsidy conditional on the worker having been unemployed for 12 months: Layard sees it as working on the demand for labour as well as on the supply. The scheme differs secondly in that no one would

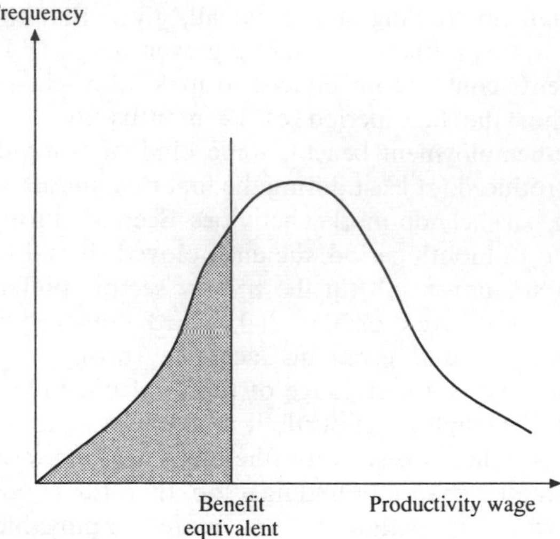

Figure D11.1 The unemployment trap (shaded area)

get benefits for longer than 12 months: it would be comprehensive across all the long-term unemployed whereas the usual workfare scheme leaves open the possibility of not having a place on the scheme or of taking a place, failing to get a job afterwards, and so continuing as unemployed. Layard's scheme is therefore comprehensive on the supply side and significant on the demand side.

Layard's model envisages two sorts of worker, the normal one with short spells of search between jobs, and the low-productivity worker who compares a low wage net of tax with an indefinite unemployment benefit. If the utility of the job falls below that of the benefit, the workers will remain unemployed, and if it does so indefinitely, unemployed indefinitely. I am content with this model, indeed have pressed its merits for a long time: it is consistent with a wide variety of time-series and cross-section evidence. It is illustrated by figure D11.1. Layard adds the hysteresis element that such indefinite inactivity will tend to lead to a decline in skills and motivation, lowering productivity and reinforcing the problem. With this element I have more difficulty: a rational individual should control such forces, becoming optimally 'lazier' when there is no economic return to work but reverting to active type when the return reappears. The evidence of the recent UK boom supports this: long-term unemployment dropped from 1.3 million to 0.5 million in 1990. I have also for long been in favour of the normal workfare scheme. But when it comes to Layard's, I have considerable doubts. The problem

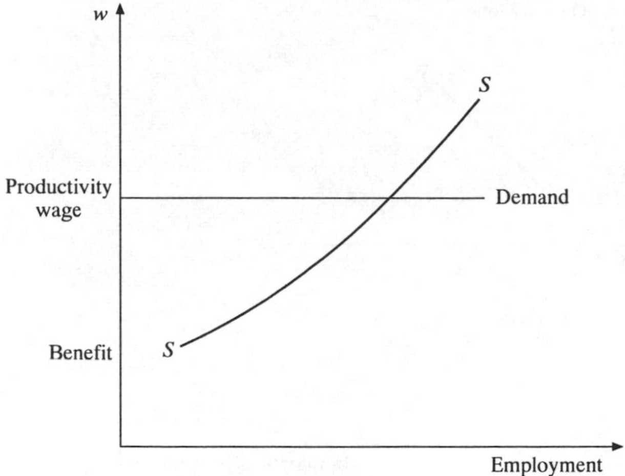

Figure D11.2 The low-wage job market before Layard's scheme

lies in the effects of the huge incentives offered to create and participate in scheme jobs.

To put the incentive in context, a firm hiring a low-wage worker can collect for six months a benefit that is more or less the same as the gross wage it is already paying: effectively a 100 per cent subsidy. Layard is concerned to repudiate the 'lump-of-labour' fallacy by stressing that this subsidy will be large enough to shift the general equilibrium labour market result towards more employment and less unemployment by lowering the net wage paid by employers of low-wage workers and increasing labour supply by preventing long-term unemployment. But this is not the issue.

The issue is rather the effect on the labour supply of the normal workers with short unemployment spells. Let us make the most favourable possible assumption from the job creation viewpoint: that this is a small open economy able to sell as much as it can produce on world markets at going prices and that there are competitive markets with constant returns to scale. Then the gross wages firm will pay are given by international prices and the technology: the subsidy to scheme jobs means that they will pay a gross wage higher by the extent of the subsidy. The level of employment then depends entirely on labour supply, demand being infinitely elastic.

Figures D11.2 and D11.3 show the situation in the low-wage job markets before and after the scheme. The scheme raises the wage offered to the 12-months' employed by the full amount of the subsidy. Let us

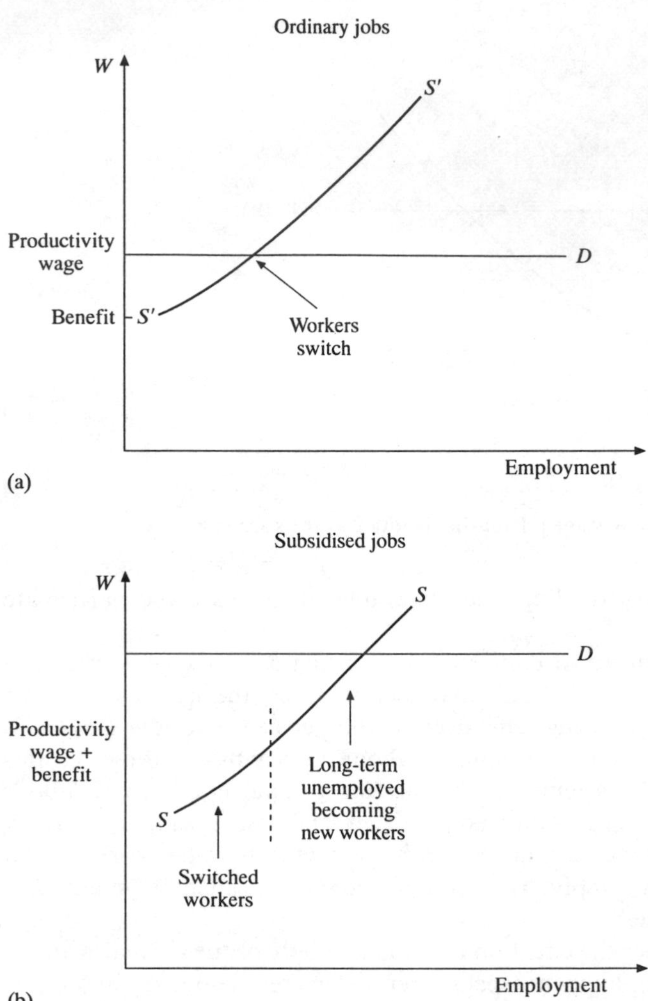

Figure D11.3 The low-wage job market after Layard's scheme

assume – as we must – that all the existing long-term unemployed now get a scheme job after 12 months of unemployment. This is the bonus Layard offers us. But what of 'substitute' and 'deadweight'? This of course comes, given our assumption, from substitution by people in existing low-wage jobs with average spells of unemployment: to qualify for a scheme job for six months they must be unemployed for 12 months. One can then work out that one scheme job requires the pattern of

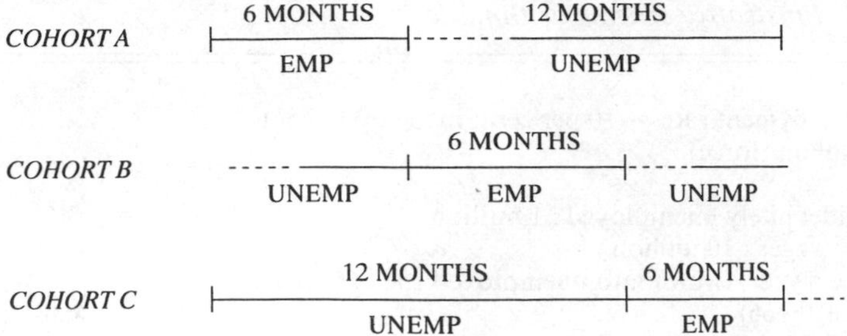

Comment: The pattern shown above requires 3 equal cohorts of N to provide N jobs (Average unemployment rate among $3N$ workers = 66%, made up of 1-year unemployment spell, 2/3 turnover rate p.a.).

Figure D11.4 The pattern of work among Layard scheme workers on scheme jobs

unemployment and working shown in figure D11.4. The average unemployment rate among scheme workers will be 66 per cent – one-year unemployment spells with a 66 per cent turnover rate. Given that a low-wage worker would get benefits close to net-of-tax wages and could on the scheme roughly double gross wages, there is presumably a high monetary return to switching: the costs would be those of personal reorganisation (to enjoy longer spells of leisure) and of stigma attached to long unemployment, but against this there would be some psychic return from more leisure. It might be that workers would opt for a period of time on a scheme job before returning to normal employment. We do not know but in finance it would be normal to assume such an arbitrage opportunity would be totally exploited – 100 per cent switching from existing low-wage jobs onto the scheme. The scheme seems wide open to large-scale substitution.

To illustrate the dangers, table D11.1 shows some hypothetical arithmetic based on 1 million scheme jobs being created by switching. The arithmetic may or may not be exaggerated – we do not know, but the result is cautionary: in it, unemployment rises and there is a huge fiscal cost.

Layard does not address this concern in chapter 11. Yet it is the danger that will most worry policy makers, since bitter experience of other temporary schemes has shown significant deadweight. This particularly ambitious scheme is so open to being overwhelmed by deadweight that it would be impossible to embrace it without strong evidence of factors limiting the sort of arbitrage sketched out in Table D11.1.

Table D11.1 *Illustrative scheme arithmetic*

Pre-scheme			
Suppose unemployment rate = 10 per cent, made up of (out of 28 million labour force).			
			%
Long-term (indefinitely unemployed : 1 million		=	3.6
Others on low wages : 10 million			
Lose jobs once a year, two-month unemployed spell (36 per cent of labour force 0.166)		=	6.0
Rest (high-skill, etc.)		=	0.4
			10.0
(Implied low-wage employment = 8.3 million)			
Post-scheme			
Suppose all long-term unemployed in trap (1 million) induced to take scheme job			
Suppose 1 million existing low-wage jobs switch (3 million workers)			
Then			*Overall unemployment* %
1 million	(14.3 of labour force) @ unemployment rate 66%		
3 million	(one-year spell, 2/3 turnover rate)		9.4
7 million	Other low-wage workers		4.1
(25 per cent of labour force turnover rate of 1.0 p.a., two-month spell)			
Rest			0.4
		Unemployed	13.9
(Implied number of low-wage jobs 7.1 million)			
Cost of scheme			
			$ billion
Induced unemployment benefits			8.5
Wage subsidy			15.6
		(3.2 per cent of GDP)	24.1
(Assuming benefit of £150 p.w.)			

Part Four

Labour market regulations

12 An analysis of firing costs and their implications for unemployment policy

ALISON L. BOOTH

1 Introduction

Mandatory firing costs were introduced in many European countries from the late 1950s through to the early 1970s.[1] Although employment protection regulations in European countries were introduced at different times and for a variety of reasons, they have much in common, for example statutory pre-notification periods, consultation requirements, and minimum amounts for redundancy pay (Buechtemann, 1992). These restrictions on firing have been blamed by some commentators for the high levels of European unemployment since the first oil price shock of 1973. The fact that employment in the USA has been relatively less protected by state regulation, and US unemployment since 1973 has been lower than in Europe, has reinforced the popular view that firing costs contribute to the high levels of European unemployment. A purpose of this chapter is therefore to examine the question of whether or not firing costs, both bargained and state-mandated, increase unemployment.

A number of recent empirical and theoretical studies have invested the extent to which European unemployment and unemployment persistence can be explained by employment protection provisions. With the exception of Lazear (1990), these studies suggest that firing costs cannot be blamed for increasing European unemployment, although they are likely to have reduced employment variation (see, for example, Nickell, 1978; Bertola, 1990, 1992; Bentolila and Bertola, 1990).[2] A conclusion is that firing costs affect employment dynamics more than the average level of employment. The fact that unemployment has been found to be more persistent in countries characterised by high job security provisions is argued by Bertola (1990, 1992) to reflect the stabilising effects of mandatory firing costs on aggregate employment. Since firing costs reduce the variance of employment over the business cycle, in a way that is spelt out in section 2 of this chapter, those workers who are laid off are likely to face a lower re-employment probability.

In most of the literature on firing costs, wage determination has been assumed exogenous, and the models have focused primarily on modelling labour demand in a dynamic framework. Where wages have been determined within the model, workers have been assumed to be risk-neutral (see, for example, Bertola, 1990 and Burda, 1992). An objective of this chapter is therefore to model both labour demand and labour supply in a model that captures elements of the real world that are missing from models focusing only on labour demand. In particular, the model aims to capture the fact that redundancy payments are only made to workers with some minimum period of continuous service with the firm. For this reason, it makes sense to think of redundancy pay in terms of some longer-term contractual relationship – explicit or implicit – between workers and firms. The model also allows for workers to be risk-averse, and the redundancy payment or firing cost can therefore be regarded as a means of providing to the worker some form of insurance against random fluctuations in product demand in the industry in which the individual is working.[3] Since typically most of workers' incomes derive from employment, and it is difficult for workers to diversify across jobs, it seems plausible to assume that workers are risk-averse rather than risk-neutral.

In this chapter, we examine the relationship between a particular form of conditional firing cost – redundancy pay – and unemployment, in a simple two-period model with uncertainty, in which risk-averse workers bargain with risk-neutral firms about redundancy pay and wages. The firm is free to determine employment unilaterally. We then compare the unemployment implications of the optimal redundancy payment with unemployment when there is statutory redundancy pay. While the analysis is partial equilibrium and cannot claim to describe the whole economy, it does nonetheless offer interesting insights about the relationship between employment, unemployment and firing costs in unionised sectors of an economy. There is evidence that in some sectors firms and workers bargain over the amount of non-statutory pay. For example, in many US and UK collective agreements, workers and firms bargain about both wages and the size of redundancy payments. By the mid-1960s, 25 per cent of all US wage earners were eligible for severance pay and 43 per cent were employed in firms having formalised dismissal rules (Jacoby, 1990, p. 172; Buechtemann, 1992, p. 44). In the USA, 39.2 per cent of union workers covered by major collective bargaining contracts in 1980 were covered by severance payment clauses (Pencavel, 1991, p. 64). Coverage varies substantially across sectors; for example 53.6 per cent of union workers in manufacturing were covered, compared with 27 per cent in non-manufacturing. In Britain, there are many instances of extra-statutory redundancy payment schemes typically negotiated by firms and unions, and sometimes by firms and individuals. The 1990 *Workplace Industrial Relations Survey* reveals that 51 per cent of workplaces bargaining with a union over wages also bargain over the size of non-manual non-statutory redundancy pay, while 42 per cent bargain over the size of manual redundancy pay (Millward *et al.*, 1992, pp. 251–2).

The principal results of the analysis in this chapter are as follows. First, the introduction of mandatory firing costs is unlikely to affect employment but is likely to increase the incidence of temporary employment contracts in sectors of the economy that may be characterised by a simple spot labour market. Secondly, the variance of labour demand will be reduced over the business cycle in sectors of the economy where there is a continuing employment relationship. Thirdly, bargaining over the level of firing costs is found to stabilise employment over the business cycle. Fourthly, in unionised sectors of the economy, or in sectors where workers have some bargaining power, the introduction of either mandated or negotiated firing costs may increase average employment. These findings suggest that eliminating mandatory firing costs or removing firing costs from the bargaining agenda is unlikely to reduce unemployment in European countries. Finally, we find that, if the level of mandated redundancy pay is greater than the level that would have been negotiated by voluntary bargaining between unions and friends, then bargained wages will increase and firms' profits will decline. This is likely to affect long-run investment.[4]

The remainder of this chapter is set out as follows. Section 2 considers the competitive labour market paradigm – a simple spot market for labour – and examines the impact of mandated firing costs on employment. Section 3 considers labour demand with longer-term contracts, and shows that firing costs reduce labour demand fluctuations in the face of anticipated fluctuations in product demand. An implication is that state-mandated redundancy pay lowers the variance of output and employment in sectors of the economy where it is in employers' interests to have long-term labour contracts. This finding suggests that risk-averse workers will prefer a contract with redundancy pay, since it irons out fluctuations in employment across time. We therefore consider in section 4 the nature of equilibrium employment in a labour market with contracts. The behaviour of risk-averse workers is explicitly incorporated into the model. The employment (and unemployment) predictions of this model are compared with other union models in section 5. To examine the impact of state-mandated redundancy pay, we initially suppose for expositional ease that the optimal level of redundancy pay is determined by the firm and workers. We then examine the impact of mandated redundancy pay. The optimal employment outcome is then compared with the outcome under state intervention, in section 6. The final section 7 summarises and makes some suggestions for future research. In particular, it is suggested that the case for statutory central determination of an appropriate economy-wide level of redundancy pay remains to be established.

Throughout the chapter it is assumed that firms bear the cost of redundancy payments, and that redundancy payments are only made to workers after a period of continuous service with the firm. This mirrors the situation for statutory redundancy pay in Britain and many European countries.[5] It is also assumed that workers receive all of any redundancy payment made by firms to workers.[6]

2 A competitive spot labour market

In this section, we consider the impact on employment of state-mandated redundancy pay in a perfectly competitive *spot* labour market. Assume all workers are identical, and there are no hiring costs. In each period, perfectly competitive firms hire workers at random from the pool of available workers, at the exogenously given market wage rate w. At the end of each period, workers return to the labour pool, and the whole process is repeated at the start of the next period. Some workers may get hired by one firm in two consecutive periods simply through the laws of probability, but there is no advantage to firms from implementing long-term contracts.

Now suppose that the state introduces a mandatory redundancy pay scheme. Following the institutional model for the UK and many other European countries, assume that the firm has to make a redundancy payment of an amount set by the state, to workers made involuntarily redundant after a minimum period of continuous service with the firm. Assume this minimum is one period. The implication of such a scheme is that firms will ensure that they do not hire workers for more than one consecutive period, in order to avoid the firing cost. A mechanism for achieving this might be a temporary employment contract, stipulating a maximum period of employment of just less than one period.

In summary, the implications of the introduction of state-mandated redundancy pay in a competitive spot labour market are as follows. First, in sectors of the economy where there are no gains to the firm from long-term contracts, there is likely to be an increase in temporary contracts following the introduction of statutory severance pay schemes. Secondly, demand shocks in this sector of the economy are immediately translated into employment and output fluctuations, and state-mandated redundancy pay has no impact on this outcome. However the spot labour market is a plausible characterisation of the labour market only where there are no gains to the firm from having longer-term contracts. We now consider labour demand under longer-term contracts; this is relevant to analysis of redundancy payments since these are based on length of service with a particular firm.

3 Labour demand in a competitive labour market with contracts

This section considers labour demand in a simple two-period model, in which the firm is free to determine *ex post* employment and dismissals unilaterally, given exogenously determined levels of w and r. The purpose of the section is to show the well-known result that firing costs are associated with reductions in the variance of labour demand across the business cycle (see, for example, Nickell, 1978). This result will then be used in the following sections where the supply behaviour of workers is explicitly incorporated into the analysis.

Consider a sector of the economy consisting of a number of perfectly competitive firms employing identical workers for up to two periods. In period 1, the firm makes its decision about how many workers to hire, taking into account known labour demand in period 1 and uncertain labour demand in period 2. Since period 2 demand is unknown *ex ante*, the firm making hiring decisions in period 1 takes into account the fact that it may have to make some workers redundant in the future. Workers made redundant receive a redundancy payment r, of an amount determined by the state but paid for by the firm. Since workers are assumed identical, second-period layoffs are random.

Agents' *ex ante* uncertainty about period 2 product demand (affecting period 2 labour demand) is captured by the assumption that the firm's period 2 output price θ_1 fluctuates across the υ possible states of nature. The probability of each price occurring is given by

$$\tau_i, i = 1, \ldots, \upsilon, \text{and} \sum_{i=1}^{\upsilon} \tau_i = 1.$$

The firm determines *ex post* employment and dismissals unilaterally, for given levels of w and r. Denote the number of workers hired in the initial period by m, and denote actual *ex post* employment in period 2 by

n_i, $i = 1, \ldots, v$. Assume $n_i \leq m$ in order to focus attention on redundancy. This requires that the state of nature in the first period is at its highest level so that employment is at a maximum.[7] If there is a bad state of nature or 'slump' in period 2, $(m - n_i)$ incumbent workers will be dismissed, and receive a redundancy payment r.

3.1 Labour demand

For a given level of wages, the firm's first-period certain profits are given by

$$\hat{\Pi}_i = (m) - wm \tag{1}$$

where $f(m)$ is the firm's production function, $f(0) = 0$, $f'(m) > 0$, and $f''(m) < 0$. The firm's output price, known with certainty in period 1, is given by θ. *Ex ante*, for the same given level of wages, period 2 *expected* profits are given by

$$E\hat{\Pi}_2 = \delta \sum_{i=1}^{v} \tau_i \{\theta_i f(n_i) - wn_i - r[m - n_i]\} \quad n_i \leq m \tag{2}$$

where $f(n_i)$ is the firm's period 2 production function, $f(0) = 0$, $f'(n_i) > 0$; $f''(n_i) < 0$. Output price θ_i is assumed to vary across states in period 2, and δ represents the firm's discount factor, $0 \leq \delta \leq 1$.

Proposition 1
Firing costs are associated with reduced labour demand in a 'boom' and increased labour demand in a 'slump', relative to the situation with no redundancy pay.

Proof of Proposition 1
The firm's problem in the initial period is to choose m (for a *given* w and r) to maximise *ex ante* profits given by

$$\begin{aligned} \max_m \; E\Pi &= \hat{\Pi}_1 + E\hat{\Pi}_2 \\ &= \theta f(m) - wm + \delta \left\{ \sum_{i=1}^{\theta} \tau_i \{\theta_i f(n_i) - wn_i - r[m - n_i]\} \right\} \\ & n_i \leq m. \end{aligned} \tag{3}$$

The first-order condition from (3) is

$$\theta f'(m) = w + \delta r. \tag{4}$$

Thus with redundancy payments in a competitive labour market with contracts, fewer workers are hired in the first period as compared with the usual labour demand function defined through $\theta f'(m) = w$. As $\delta \rightarrow 0$, period 1 employment $m \rightarrow m^*$, where m^* satisfies $\theta f'(m^*) = w$.

Now consider employment determination in period 2. At the start of period 2, the firm has an inherited workforce of m workers. For $n_i \leq m$, some workers must be laid off. The firm determines *ex post* employment n_i (once the state of nature is revealed) by maximisation of period 2 profits given by (2), yielding

$$\theta_i f'(n_i) = w - r. \tag{5}$$

As illustrated in figure 12.1, with firing costs the change in employment between period 1 and period 2 is shown by the horizontal distance $\Delta n(r > 0)$, since employment in period 1 is given from (4) while employment in period 2 is given by (5). This outcome can be compared to the change in employment in a model *without* redundancy pay, illustrated as $\Delta n(r = 0)$ in figure 12.1. Thus the variation in labour demand in a two-period model with redundancy pay is less than that of a two-period model with no redundancy pay. Notice also that the more myopic the firm ($\delta \rightarrow 0$), the closer will period 1 employment with redundancy pay be to m^*.[8]

This simple analysis has shown that firing costs are associated with reduced labour demand in a 'boom', and increased labour demand in a 'slump', relative to the situation with no firing costs. While the firing cost or redundancy pay stops workers losing their jobs, it discourages new hires.[9] An implication is that the introduction of experience-linked state-mandated redundancy pay will lower the variance of output and employment in sectors of the economy where it is in employers' interests to have long-term employment contracts. If we label such sectors as 'primary sectors', and denote sectors characterised by spot labour contracts as 'secondary sectors', then inter-sectoral empirical work should show that the introduction of state-mandated severance pay is associated with lower employment and output fluctuations in the primary sector than in the secondary sector. To the extent that long-term contracts emerge where there are specific training investments, this reduced variance in employment may prevent the loss of firm-specific human capital.

The finding that redundancy pay lowers the variance of employment suggests that, when we come to consider the behaviour of workers, risk-

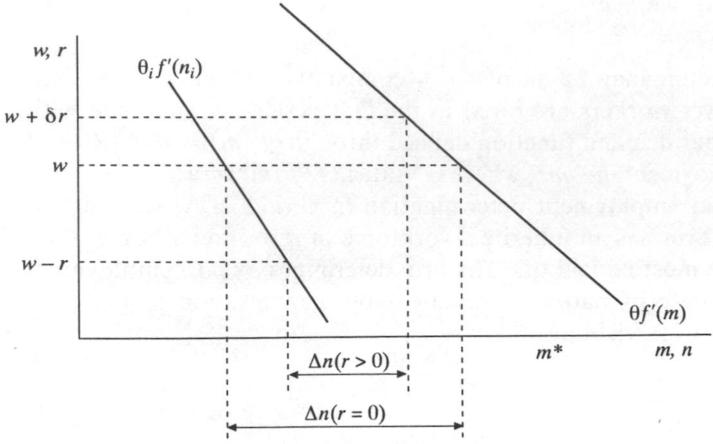

Figure 12.1 Labour demand variations with and without redundancy pay for a fixed wage rate, *w*

averse workers will prefer a contract with redundancy pay, since redundancy pay irons out employment fluctuations across time. Risk-neutral employers may be prepared to offer a contract with insurance against employment fluctuations. The model in section 4 therefore considers the behaviour of both firms and workers when it is in the interests of both parties to have long-term employment contracts.

4 Equilibrium employment with long-term contracts and voluntary redundancy pay

We now incorporate the supply behaviour of risk-averse workers into the two-period model. Since typically most of workers' incomes derives from employment, and it is difficult for workers to diversify across jobs, it seems plausible to assume that workers are risk-averse rather than risk-neutral. In contrast, firms comprise many shareholders who are able to diversify their portfolio of shares. Hence it is reasonable to assume that firms are risk-neutral.

We initially suppose that $r \geq 0$ (applicable only to layoffs in period 2) is determined optimally by the firm and the workforce at the start of period 2 before the realisation of the state of demand. In section 5, the outcome of this model is compared with orthodox union models. In section 6, we then examine the impact of government intervention through setting $r - \bar{r}$, where $\bar{r}$ denotes the state-mandated level of redundancy pay.

Continuing contracts involving more than one period of employment generally exist because the long-term contract generates some surplus to the firm. Therefore even in the absence of trade unions, the worker may be in a position to extract some of this surplus, since she can impose a cost on the firm by threatening to quit. This gives the worker some bargaining power. It might therefore be expected that, with long-term employment contracts, workers and the firm bargain over the share of any surplus even in a perfectly competitive labour market. While in what follows we refer to workers being in a union, the model is also applicable to any situation where non-union workers have some bargaining power.

The structure of the model is that, at the start of period 2 before the state of the world is known, the firm and the workforce together bargain over period 2 wages and the level of redundancy payments should any layoffs be necessary. After the realisation of the demand state, the firm then determines period 2 *ex post* employment unilaterally.[10] The outcome of the period 2 bargain is then inserted into the period 1 bargain, which is over period 1 wages alone. Redundancy payments are not made in period 1, since the workforce is eligible for payments only after one period of continuous experience with the firm, and anyway no one is laid off in period 1. Both parties perfectly anticipate the outcome of the period 2 bargain, and incorporate this into their period 1 maximand.

As noted in the Introduction, this pattern of bargaining over wages and redundancy pay reflects the structure of many collective bargaining arrangements in the UK. Pay bargaining and bargaining over the size of redundancy pay in the UK may occur at the establishment level, the organisation level, or the industry level (see Millward *et al.*, 1992). While there are no systematic data for the UK about whether or not pay and firing costs are negotiated simultaneously, bargaining over redundancy pay typically follows a formula related to pay. Therefore, if it were the case that pay awards were negotiated more frequently than redundancy pay, then redundancy pay would still alter every time pay altered since typically firing costs amounts are indexed on pay in a fashion that is determined by bargaining.[11]

We now consider the second stage of the model.

4.1 The period 2 outcome

At the start of period 2, there exists a pool of m identical incumbent workers, who have signed a contract with the firm before output in period 2 is known. The size of the pool of workers is determined in period 1. The m workers each have a continuous twice differentiable strictly concave (indirect) utility of income function, denoted by $u(w_2)$ when employed, and by $u(r+\beta)$ when involuntarily laid off, where β denotes unemployment benefits, and $r \geq 0$.[12] To ensure that labour is supplied, $w_2 > \beta$. The utilitarian union objective function can be written as

$$E\hat{v}_2 = \sum_{i-1}^{v} \tau_i\{n_i.u(w_2) + (m - n_i).u(r + \beta\} \tag{6}$$

The firm and the union through the generalised Nash bargaining process, determine w_2 and r by maximisation of the product of each party's gains from reaching a bargain, weighted by their respective bargaining strengths. The firm is free to make layoff decisions unilaterally, for given bargained levels of w_2 and r. Employment is determined from (5) above. This 'right-to-manage' model is widely used in the literature, on the grounds that it reflects actual bargaining situations.

4.2 *Equilibrium in the model*

At the start of period 2, workers and the firm bargain over any surplus in order to determine optimal w_2 and r. The firm then determines *ex post* employment (and therefore dismissals, $(m-n_i)$) once w_2 and r are set. We focus on $n_i < m$; this assumption can be rationalised by regarding the inherited workforce as being set in the best possible state of nature. Define a status quo or fallback position for each agent if no bargain is reached. For the firm, the status quo position is zero; if it does not reach a bargain with the striking unionised workforce, it does not have to pay these striking workers a redundancy payment. If it does not reach a bargain with incumbents, it cannot obtain any other workers. Therefore the firm's net gain from reaching a bargain in period 2 is simply its expected profits function, given below:

$$E\Pi_2 = \sum_{i=1}^{v} \tau_i\{\theta_i f[n_i(w_2, r)] - wn_i(w_2, r) - r[m - n_i(w_2, r]\}. \tag{7}$$

The status quo position for a representative worker is $u(\beta)$, since that is what an incumbent receives if no bargain is reached. (Redundancy pay does not appear in the threat point for the union, since, if negotiations break down, workers are not entitled to a redundancy payment, which is received *only* if workers are made involuntarily redundant.) But if there is a bargain, union utility is given by $E\hat{v}_2$ in (7). The *net* gain to the union can thus be written as Ev, defined as

$$Ev_2 \equiv E\hat{v}_2 - mu(\beta) = \sum_{i=1}^{v} \tau_i\{n_i(w_2, r).u(w_2) + [(m - n_i(w_2, r)].u(r + \beta)\} - mu(\beta). \tag{8}$$

The generalised Nash bargain is given by

$$\max_{w_2, r} \ B_2(w_2, r) = Ev_2^{\alpha} \ E\Pi_2^{1-\alpha} \tag{9}$$

where Ev_2 and $E\Pi_2$ are given by (8) and (7) respectively, and $0 \leq \alpha \leq 1$ is the bargaining strength of the union. As noted, the threat points for both parties are independent of r and w_2.

Proposition 2

(i) *Ex post* period 2 employment in a labour market where the firm unilaterally sets w_2, r and n is determined such that $\theta_i f'(n_i) = \beta$.

(ii) *Ex post* period 2 employment in a unionised labour market (where the union and the firm bargain at the start of the period about wages and redundancy pay) is also given by $\theta_i f'(n_i) = \beta$.

Proof of Proposition 2

This is given in the appendix, p. 379.

Proposition 2(ii) shows that, where incumbent workers and firms bargain over wages and redundancy pay, the outcome is efficient, in the sense that the wage corresponding to the *ex post* level of employment is equal to the opportunity cost of labour.[13] In the conventional right-to-manage union model where unions and firms bargain *only* over wages (and not redundancy pay), there is no mechanism for *ex post* redistribution; while the outcome is on the labour demand curve, efficiency is 'constrained' in the sense that the surplus is not maximised. However, Proposition 2(ii) shows that, with an *ex post* redistribution scheme involving redundancy pay, period 2 employment will be characterised by 'full efficiency' where the bargaining surplus is maximised.[14] The intuition underlying this result is that w_2 and r are set to maximise the bargaining surplus; if this were not the case, there would remain *ex post* gains to be exploited. The equality of *ex post* marginal productivity to the opportunity cost of labour guarantees maximisation of the bargaining surplus. The union and the firm share the maximised surplus: the lower is the relative power of the union, then the smaller its share of the surplus in the form of wages and severance pay. But employment remains unaffected by the union's relative bargaining power. These arguments are summarised in Proposition 3.

Proposition 3
In the right-to-manage bargaining model with redundancy pay on the bargaining agenda, an increase in union power α increases optimal w_2^* and r^*, but leaves *ex post* employment unaffected.

Proof of Proposition 3
This is given in the appendix, p. 380.

An implication of Proposition 3 is that as α approaches zero, we approach the perfectly competitive situation, where the share of the surplus going to workers is zero. This can be seen by setting $\alpha = 0$ in (9) and observing that, if the firm is free to determine wages, firing costs and employment unilaterally, it will always set 'effective' wages at the competitive level, given by $w_2 - r = \beta$ (Intuitively, this is because the firm shifts to a lower iso-expected-profits curve in (w,n) space, representing higher profits, as (w_2-r) declines.) This proves Proposition 2(i).

The bargaining model presented in this section has both efficiency and distributional implications. Period 2 labour allocation is efficient: the union and firm set wages and redundancy pay so that social surplus is maximised. This efficiency has been achieved through the introduction of an extra instrument onto the bargaining agenda – the firing cost. Distribution among incumbent workers is also affected, in the sense that workers' incomes are now invariant to their employment status.

It must be emphasised that the model has for simplicity assumed that in the second period the firm will never hire more workers; that is, the firm has hired its workforce in period 1 in the best possible state of the world, which will not get better in period 2. This assumption was made for tractability.[15] If this assumption were relaxed to allow the firm to hire new workers in period 2 in addition to retaining all its insiders, then the instrument of redundancy pay could not be used in period 2 to achieve efficient employment. We hope in future work to explore these issues.

4.3 *The period 1 outcome*

It is straightforward to show that period 1 employment, m, will be inefficient. This is because, in the initial period when m is determined, the firm and workforce cannot use the instrument of redundancy pay, which is available only for workers with continuous experience with the firm (that is, only in period 2).

Proposition 4
In the right-to-manage model with redundancy pay on the bargaining agenda, period 1 employment will be inefficient.

Proof:
See Appendix, p. 382.

4.4 *Summary of the conclusions of the two-period model with bargaining over wages and redundancy pay*

The simple two-period model with firing costs has several interesting predictions. First, there is inefficient employment in period 1, a standard result in any right-to-manage model of worker–firm bargaining over wages. But *ex post* employment in period 2 is efficient. This result is not found in the two-period union model without redundancy pay, as we shall see below. Secondly, with redundancy pay on the bargaining agenda, there is less cyclical fluctuation in employment.

An obvious question arising from this analysis is whether average employment in the bargaining model with endogenous firing costs is greater than that in orthodox models of the trade union with no firing costs. If this is the case, employment should be higher in unionised sectors of the economy where redundancy pay is negotiated than in unionised sectors where it is not. This issue is addressed in section 5.

5 A comparison of the unemployment predictions of the two-period redundancy pay model with other union models

To facilitate the comparison of the unemployment implications of the two-period redundancy pay model with other union models in the literature, the monopoly union framework will be used. (The monopoly union model is a special case of the generalised Nash framework employed above, where $\alpha = 1$.) In this section three models will be compared. First, we shall examine the *hiring-hall* (*HH*) *model*. This is the orthodox single-period union model with no redundancy pay, which is applicable to a union 'hiring hall' where each period workers are hired at random and return to the hiring hall at the end of the period. Secondly, we shall examine a two-period insider–outsider model of the form examined above, but *without* redundancy pay – what will be termed the *IO model*. Finally, we shall return to the insider–outsider model with redundancy pay that has been developed in this chapter, which we term the *IOR model.* In order to compare precisely the wage and employment predictions of each model, constant elasticity functional forms are used for individual worker utility and for the firm's labour demand function.[16] Worker utility is given by

$$u(w) = \frac{1}{\sigma} w^{\sigma} \qquad \sigma < 1; \quad u' > 0; \; u'' < 0 \tag{10}$$

where the degree of relative risk-aversion is $(1 - \sigma = -[u''(w)w]/u'(w)$. The marginal revenue product of labour is

$$n(w; \theta) = \theta w^{-e} \qquad e > 1; n' < 0, \; n'' > 0 \tag{11a}$$

for the HH and IO models, and for the IOR model period 1 labour demand is given by

$$\begin{aligned} m(w_1; \theta, \delta, r) = \theta(w_1 + \delta r)^{-e} \; e > 1; \; \partial m/\partial w_1 < 0; \\ \partial_2 m/\partial w_1^2 > 0; \; \partial m/\partial r < 0; \\ \partial m^2/\partial r^2 > 0; \; \partial^2 m/\partial w \partial r > 0. \end{aligned} \tag{11b}$$

Proposition 5
In a unionised economy, the presence of firing costs on the bargaining agenda increases period 2 employment and reduces period 1 wages. The effect on period 1 employment is ambiguous.

Proof of Proposition 5
This is given in the appendix (p. 382), and the principal results are illustrated in table 12.1 and figure 12.2. Table 12.1 shows the equilibrium period 1 monopoly union wage rate for each model (using the specific functional forms of (10), (11a) and (11b)), and the corresponding equilibrium level of employment, obtained from inserting the optimal wage rate into the appropriate labour demand equation. It is assumed that Θ is fixed across periods 1 and 2, in order to focus attention on illustrating the deadweight losses associated with union wage determination under the three union regimes.

Inspection of period 1 wage rates for each of the three models in table 12.1 shows that wages are highest in the HH model, and lowest in the IOR model. Where unions are forward-looking (that is, in the IO and

Table 12.1 *Equilibrium period 1 wages w^*_1 and employment levels m^* for the three models*

Wage level w_1^*	Employment level m^*
HH model	
$\left[\frac{e}{(e-\sigma)}\right]^{1/\sigma}.\beta$	$\theta\left\{\left[\frac{e}{(e-\sigma)}\right]^{1/\sigma}.\beta\right\}^{-e}$
IO model	
$\left[\frac{e(1-\delta)}{(e-\sigma)}\right]^{1/\sigma}.\beta$	$\theta\left\{\left[\frac{e}{(e-\sigma)}\right]^{1/\sigma}.[\beta\sigma-\delta\beta^{\sigma}]^{1/\sigma}\right\}^{-e}$
IOR model	
$\left[\frac{e}{e-\sigma}\right]^{1/\sigma}[\beta^{\sigma}-\delta(r+\beta)^{\sigma}]^{1/\sigma}$	$\theta\left\{\left[\frac{e}{e-\sigma}\right]^{1/\sigma}.[\beta^{\sigma}-\delta(r+\beta)^{\sigma}]^{1/\sigma}+\delta r\right\}^{-e}$

IOR models), the greater is the discount factor δ, the lower the period 1 wage. Intuitively, this is because the union is taking into account future utility of its membership. Note that the presence of redundancy pay on the bargaining agenda induces the union to set an even lower period 1 wage (compare the IO and IOR wage results).

Inspection of the period 1 employment levels for each of the three models in table 12.1 shows that $m^{*IO} > m^{*HH}$ unambiguously. But it is not clear from inspection of m^{*IO} and m^{*IOR} which is the larger.[17] However, since in the IOR model period 2 employment is characterised by the equality of marginal productivity to the opportunity cost of labour (from Proposition 2), there is no deadweight loss in period 2. In summary, the model produces no clear-cut results as to whether period 1 employment is higher or lower with redundancy pay on the bargaining agenda and with a forward-looking union. However period 2 employment is unambiguously larger in the model with redundancy pay. It therefore remains an empirical issue to determine whether *average* employment across the business cycle is greater or lower with firing costs.

Figure 12.2a illustrates period 1 wages and employment. The triangles illustrate deadweight losses associated with union wage-setting. Thus in the HH model, the deadweight loss associated with the union-set wage rate of w^{*HH} is given by the triangle *ABC*. Notice that the labour demand curve for the IOR model differs from that of the IO and HH models, from (11a) and (11b). In figure 12a, triangle *DEC* is greater than *FGC''*. However, the deadweight loss from the IOR model includes, in

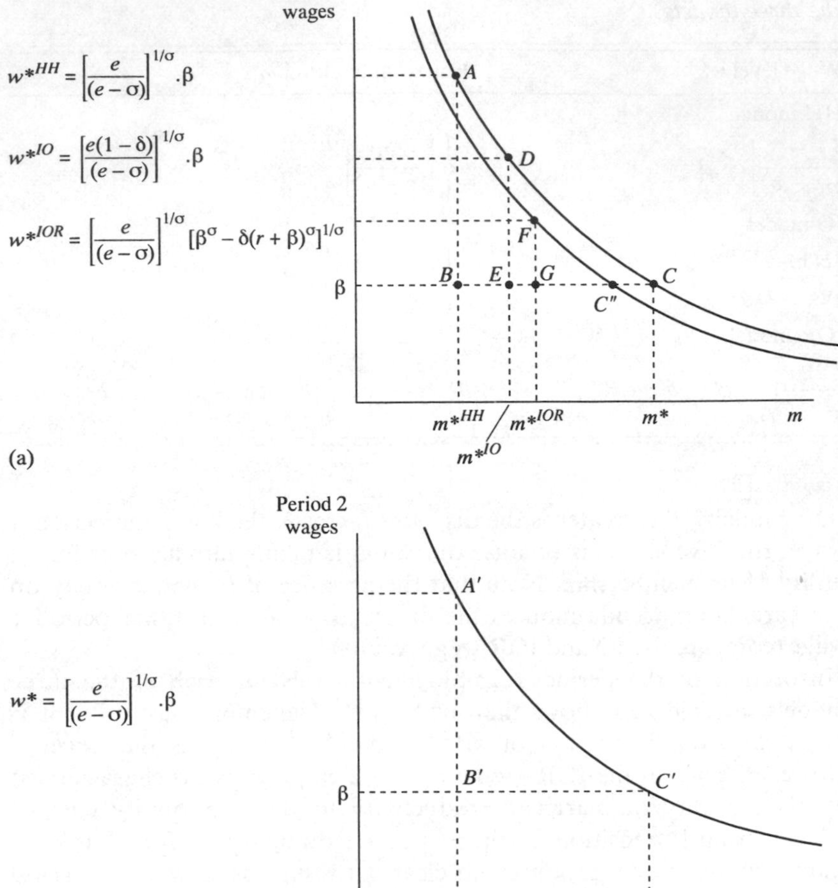

Figure 12.2 A comparison of welfare losses of three union models

(a) Period 1 employment, m
(b) Period 2 employment, n
Deadweight loss, HH model $= ABC + A'B'C'$
Deadweight loss, IO model $= DEC + A'B'C'$
Deadweight loss, IOR model $= FGC + \text{zero}$

addition to the triangle FGC'', the area between the two demand curves above the horizontal line denoting the opportunity cost of labour β. Period 2 wages and employment are shown in figure 12.2b. (Note that in figure 12.2 the demand parameter θ is assumed fixed across both time periods.) In figure 12.2b, the deadweight loss $A'B'C'$ associated with the HH and IO models is identical, since period 2 wage rates are identical in these models. But there is no deadweight loss in period 2 in the IOR model, since period 2 employment is determined by the equality of marginal productivity to the opportunity cost of labour β.

This comparison illustrates an important result of the IOR model, that firing costs bargained over by the union and the firm have a stabilising impact on employment. This outcome can also be compared with the predictions of the fixed-wage and fixed-firing costs model of Bentolila and Bertola (1990). But the crucial point of difference between the two approaches is that the result in this chapter derives from a model in which wages and firing costs are determined by a bargaining process, in which employment stabilisation is desired by risk-averse workers.

6 The unemployment implications of statutory redundancy pay

We now consider the implications of *statutory* firing costs on unemployment. In section 2 it was argued that, in the competitive spot labour market, there is likely to be an increase in temporary contracts following the introduction of statutory redundancy pay. Demand shocks in a spot labour market are immediately translated into employment and output fluctuations, and state-mandated redundancy pay has no impact on this outcome. It was also argued that the spot labour market is a plausible characterisation of the labour market only where there are no gains to the firm from having longer-term contracts, and that in longer-term employment relationships, bargaining models of wage determination are more appropriate. We shall examine, in section 6.1 below, the impact of mandated redundancy pay on the outcome of the bargaining model developed in section 4. It will be demonstrated that the imposition of statutory redundancy pay will not affect employment in such a situation, but will reduce profits if statutory firing costs are too high. Then we shall examine, in section 6.2, the employment implications of imposing mandated redundancy pay in a unionised economy with no redundancy pay.

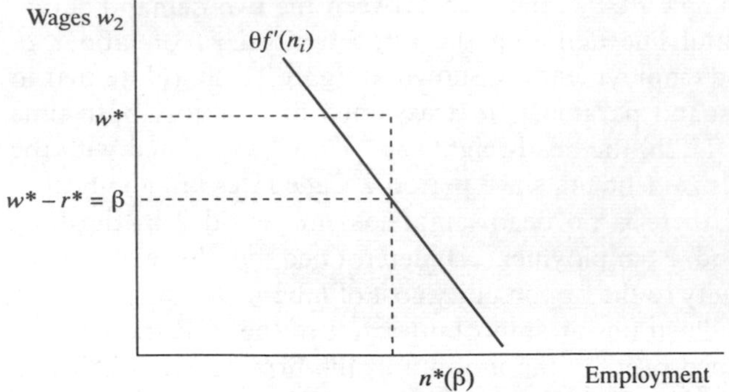

Figure 12.3 Imposition of mandated redundancy pay

6.1 *The bargaining model with state-mandated firing costs*

We now examine the period 2 unemployment implications of the bargaining model (with optimally-set redundancy pay) when the state intervenes to impose a level of redundancy payment.

Proposition 6

In labour markets where the workforce has some bargaining power and redundancy payments are on the bargaining agenda, the imposition of mandated redundancy pay $\bar{r}$ will result in an efficiency loss unless $\bar{r} \leq r^*$. If $\bar{r} > r^*$, *ex post* employment is unaffected in the neighbourhood of the equilibrium, but profits are reduced.

The implications of state-mandated redundancy pay can be seen by inspection of figure 12.3. Denote by $\bar{r}$ the state-mandated level of redundancy pay, and let r^* be the efficient level of redundancy pay. There are three possible cases: $\bar{r} < r^*$, $\bar{r} = r^*$, and $\bar{r} > r^*$.

Case (i): $\bar{r} < r^*$

If the firm and union can effectively negotiate to 'top up' the state-given level of severance pay, *ex post* employment should continue to be efficient. If the redundancy payment cannot be topped up, then *ex post* unemployment will result.

Case (ii): $\bar{r} < r^*$

Here *ex post* employment will be at its efficient level.

Case (iii): $\bar{r} < r^*$
Here the state-mandated redundancy pay has the effect of reducing the firm's share of any surplus. To see this, recall from the proof of Proposition 2 (ii) that

$$w_2 = r + \beta. \tag{12}$$

To determine the sign of dw_2^*/dr, notice that the constraint must still hold for small perturbations about the optimum. Therefore from (12) $dw_2^*/dr > 0$. Note further that, since *ex post* employment is determined so that marginal productivity is equal to the opportunity cost of labour (that is, where $\theta_i f'(n_i) = \beta$), a small increase in r above its optimum does not affect *ex post* employment. Therefore an exogenously-imposed increase in r above the optimum of r^* is associated with an increase in w_2^*, and thus the impact of this change is equivalent to an increase in union power. As a result, the firm's share of any surplus declines. ∎

6.2 The orthodox union model with state-mandated firing costs

Since only a part of the unionised sector in Britain bargains over the size of redundancy payments, it is worth considering the impact of state-mandated redundancy pay $\bar{r}$ on the standard union model with *no* bargaining over redundancy pay. In this situation, because $\bar{r}$ is imposed on the union and firm, $\bar{r}$ enters the generalised Nash bargain in a similar fashion to the model with bargaining over redundancy, given by (9). The difference between the two models lies in the fact that the redundancy payment is now exogenously given. Although there is a payment, the union–firm pair cannot use this as an instrument with which to achieve period 2 efficiency. We can write the (only) first-order condition from maximisation of the modified (9) with respect to w_2 as

$$\left\{ \sum_{i=1}^{v} \tau_i n_i u'(w_2) + \frac{[u(w_2) - u(\bar{r} + \beta)]}{n_i \theta_i f''(n_i)} \right\} \Big/ \left\{ \sum_{i=1}^{v} \tau_i n_i \right\} = \frac{(1-\alpha)Ev}{\alpha E\Pi} \tag{13}$$

Inspection of (13) and comparison with our earlier results (in Proposition 2) reveals that *ex post* employment is fully efficient only if, by chance, the state sets $\bar{r}$ such that $w_2 = \bar{r} + \beta$. If this is the case, then the mandated redundancy payment mimics the union model with bargaining over w_2 and r, and the same efficiency result holds. (Recall that in these models a necessary and sufficient condition for full efficiency is the equality of marginal productivity with the opportunity cost of labour.) However if, as seems more plausible, $w_2 > \bar{r} + \beta$ or $w_2 < \bar{r} + \beta$, then *ex post* employment will be inefficient, although it will be greater than in the case where $r = 0$.

7 Conclusion

It is in the nature of firing costs that workers are eligible only after an initial period of continuous service with a single firm. In a competitive spot labour market where there are no advantages to long-term employment relationships, the introduction of mandated redundancy pay will have no other impact on the labour market than that of increasing the incidence of short-term employment contracts. However, in a two-period model in which it is in firms' interests to have continuing employment relationships, firing costs will reduce the variance of labour demand across the business cycle. An implication of this result is that risk-averse workers may prefer a contract with redundancy pay, since it stabilises employment over time, and risk-neutral firms may be willing to offer such a contract. This chapter develops a simple model in which wages and firing costs are determined as part of a bargaining process. A striking result of this model is that the wage corresponding to the level of *ex post* employment is equal to the opportunity cost of labour (a necessary and sufficient condition for the bargaining surplus to be maximised). Thus firing costs bargained over by the union and the firm have a stabilising impact on employment in bad times and reduce hiring in good times. In this framework, *mandated* firing costs will not affect employment but may increase wages and reduce profits, if the mandated redundancy pay is higher than the negotiated amount would be. An implication is that the determination of the level of firing costs is best left to individual or collective bargaining.

Of course, there are other reasons for state-mandated redundancy pay that are not captured by the model in this chapter. These reasons relate predominantly to market failure. For example, statutory redundancy pay might protect workers against firm bankruptcy should an unanticipated demand shock drive the firm out of business and prevent the firm paying the bargained firing cost. Here the notion that statutory firing costs may provide a second-best solution relates to the missing-markets view whereby firms are unable to insure against bankruptcy due to moral hazard. A related argument arises because of the fact that in the model redundancy pay is a form of insurance that is conditional on the mode of worker separation, about which there may be asymmetric information. Such conditional insurance may therefore require intervention by a third party to intervene in disputes.

There are also other hypotheses aiming to explain the existence of statutory firing costs. For example, it has been argued that firing costs reduce the moral hazard problems associated with state unemployment benefit systems, since they prevent firms laying off workers too readily to take advantage of statutory unemployment insurance (Buechtemann, 1992). Another hypothesis is that mandated firing costs give workers some bargaining power, and therefore redress the perceived imbalance between capital and labour. Saint-Paul (chapter 3 in this volume) views the introduction of firing costs in terms of political economy, involving a redistribution between skilled and unskilled labour, or between employed and unemployed workers. Bentolila and Bertola (1990, 399) suggest that, where demand fluctuations arise because of Keynesian coordination failures rather than through the operation of competitive markets, firing costs might improve workers' welfare due to an aggregate demand externality. Finally, Booth and Zoega (1994) formally investigate the possibility that mandated firing costs might be a second-best response to market failures arising through the combination of quitting externalities, irreversible investments in human capital, and repeated demand shocks. All of these hypotheses warrant further investigation.

The principal finding of this chapter for unemployment policy is that redundancy pay is unlikely to cause unemployment to increase, and therefore attempting to legislate against redundancy pay is not a policy option in the fight to reduce unemployment. However, the analysis also suggests that levels of redundancy pay might best be determined by bargaining rather than being imposed centrally. While there are market failure arguments for mandatory redundancy pay, they represent an undeveloped research area. The case for statutory central determination of an appropriate economy-wide level of redundancy pay remains to be established.

Appendix

Proof of Proposition 2 (ii)

The first-order conditions of (9) are given by the following, where the period 2 subscripts have been omitted for expositional ease:

$$B_w : \frac{Ev_w}{E\Pi_w} = -\frac{(1-\alpha)Ev}{\alpha E\Pi} \tag{A1}$$

$$B_r : \frac{Ev_r}{E\Pi_r} = -\frac{(1-\alpha)Ev}{\alpha E\Pi}. \tag{A2}$$

Equate (A1) to (A2) and rearrange to obtain the equilibrium condition

$$\frac{E\Pi_w}{E\Pi_r} = \frac{Ev_w}{Ev_r} \tag{A3}$$

Partial differentiation of (7) and (8) in the text with respect to w_2 and r respectively produces

$$E\Pi_w = \sum_{i=1}^{v} \tau_i \left\{ -n_i + \frac{\partial n_i}{\partial w_2} [\theta_i f'[n_i(w_2, r)] - w_2 + r] \right\} \tag{A4}$$

$$E\Pi_r = \sum_{i=1}^{v} \tau_i \left\{ -(m - n_i) + \frac{\partial n_i}{\partial r} [\theta_i f'[n_i(w_2, r)] - w_2 + r] \right\} \tag{A5}$$

$$Ev_w = \sum_{i=1}^{v} \tau_i \left\{ n_i u'(w_2) + \frac{\partial n_i}{\partial w_2} [u(w_2) - u(r + \beta)] \right\} \tag{A6}$$

$$Ev_r = \sum_{i-1}^{v} \tau_i \left\{ (m - n_i) u'(r + \beta) + \frac{\partial n_i}{\partial r} [u(w_2) - u(r + \beta)] \right\}. \tag{A7}$$

From (5), period 2 labour demand can be written as $n_i = n((w_2 - r)/\theta_i)$. From differentiation of (5),$\partial n_i / \partial w_2 = 1/\theta_i f''(n_i)$ and $\partial n_i / \partial r = -1/\theta_i f''(n_i)$. Thus

$$\partial n_i / \partial w_2 = -(\partial n / \partial r) \quad \forall \ \theta_i. \tag{A8}$$

Insert (A4)–(A7) into (A3), and use the result in (A8) to obtain

$$\frac{\sum_{i=1}^{v} \tau_i n_i}{\sum_{i=1}^{v} \tau_i (m - n_i)} == \frac{\sum_{i=1}^{v} \tau_i \{ n_i u'(w_2) - \frac{\partial n_i}{\partial r} [u(w_2) - u(r + \beta)] \}}{\sum_{i=1}^{v} \tau_i \{ (m - n_i) u'(r + \beta) + \frac{\partial n_i}{\partial r} [u(w_2) - u(r + \beta)] \}}. \tag{A9}$$

By inspection, $w_2 = r + \beta$ solves the expression in (A9). Workers' incomes are invariant to their employment status. Since from (5) $\theta_i f'(n_i) = w_2 - r$, then it is also the case that $\theta_i f'(n_i) = \beta$.■

Proof of Proposition 3

From the Proof of Proposition 2, we know that $w_2 = r + \beta$. This suggests that the bargaining problem can be reduced to a bargain over w_2, subject to the constraint that

$$r = w = \beta \tag{A10}$$

The generalised Nash bargain of (9) can now be rewritten (dropping the period 2 subscript) as:

$$\max_w \tilde{B}(w) = E\tilde{v}^{\alpha} E\tilde{\Pi}^{1-\alpha} \tag{A11}$$

where, using (A10), $E\tilde{v}$ and $E\tilde{\Pi}^{1-\alpha}$ are given by

$$\begin{aligned} E\tilde{v} &= \sum_{i=1}^{v} \tau_i\{n_i u(w) + [m - n_i].u(w)\}/m - u(\beta) \\ &= [u(w) - u(\beta)] \end{aligned} \tag{A12}$$

and

$$E\tilde{\Pi} = \sum_{i=1}^{v} \tau_i\{f[n_i(\beta/\theta_i)] - wm + [m - n_i(\beta/\theta_i)].\beta\}. \tag{A13}$$

The first-order condition from maximisation of (A11) is

$$\tilde{B}_w = \frac{\alpha E v_w}{E\tilde{v}} + \frac{(1 - \alpha E\tilde{\pi}_w}{E\tilde{\Pi}} = 0. \tag{A14}$$

Total differentiation of (A14) with respect to w and α and rearrangement yields:

$$dw^*/d\alpha == \tilde{B}_{w\alpha}/\tilde{B}_{ww}. \tag{A15}$$

For the generalised Nash maximand to be concave, $\tilde{B}_{ww} < 0$. Therefore

$$\text{sign}\ \{dw^*/d\alpha\} = \text{sign}\{\tilde{B}_{w\alpha}\}. \tag{A16}$$

Differentiation of (A14) with respect to α yields

$$\tilde{B}_{w\alpha} = E\tilde{v}_w/E\tilde{v} - E\tilde{\Pi}_w/E\tilde{\Pi} \quad > 0. \tag{A17}$$

From differentiation with respect to w of (A12) and (A13) respectively, $E\tilde{v}_w = u'(w) > 0$ and $E\tilde{\Pi}_w = -m < 0$. Hence $\tilde{B}_{w\alpha} > 0$.

To determine the sign of $dr^*/d\alpha$, return to the constraint (A10), which must still hold for perturbations about the optimum. Therefore

$$dw/d\alpha = dr/d\alpha \tag{A18}$$

and since $dw/d\alpha > 0$, $dr/d\alpha > 0$ also.

Finally, note that since *ex post* employment is determined so that marginal productivity is equal to the opportunity cost of labour (that is, where $\theta_i f'(n_i) = \beta$, union power does not affect *ex post* employment.■

Proof of Proposition 4

In period 1, firms and workers together bargain over the period 1 wage denoted by w_1, while the firm unilaterally determines the number of workers to hire, m. The expected gain to the firm from reaching a bargain over w_1 are given by 3, reproduced here for convenience:

$$E\Pi - \theta f(m) - w_1 m + \delta\left\{\sum_{i=1}^{v} \tau_i\{\theta_i f(n_i) - w_2 n_i - r[m - n_i]\}\right\} \quad n_i \leq m. \tag{3}$$

The utilitarian union's utility gain from reaching a bargain over w_1 (assuming the union has the same discount factor as the firm) is

$$\begin{aligned} Ev(w_1) &= \left\{m(w_1)u(w_1) + [p - m(w_1)]u(\beta)] - pu(\beta)\right\} \\ &\quad + \delta\left\{\sum_{i=1}^{v} \tau_i\{n_i u(w_2) + [m(w_1) - n_i]u(r+\beta]\} - m(w_i)u(\beta)\right\} \\ &= m(w_1).[u(w_1) - u(\beta)] + \delta m(w_1)[u(r+\beta) - u(\beta)] \end{aligned} \tag{A19}$$

where the result from the period 2 bargain that $w_2 = r + \beta$ has been used to simplify the equation. The generalised Nash bargain over w_1 is given as

$$B(w_1) = Ev^{\alpha} E\Pi^{1-\alpha}. \tag{A20}$$

It is straightforward to show that, at the optimum,

$$\alpha\left\{\frac{m'(w_1)[u(w_1) - u(\beta)] + m(w_1)u'(w_1) + \delta m'(w_1)[u(r+\beta) - u(\beta)]}{Ev}\right\} = \frac{(1-\alpha)m}{E\Pi} \tag{A21}$$

This is clearly an inefficient outcome for period 1 employment.

Proof of Proposition 5

Here we consider each of the three models in turn – the HH model, the IO model, and the IOR model.

1 The hiring-hall (HH) model

In the union hiring-hall model, each period workers are selected at random from the pool of available workers in the sector, given by p. For each period, the objective function of the utilitarian union is given by

$$E\hat{v} = \sum_{i=1}^{v} \tau_i\{m(w).u(w) + [p - m(w).u(\beta)\} \quad m < p \tag{A22}$$

where m denotes employment. When the union executive sets wages w by maximisation of (A22) subject to the firm's labour demand curve, the first-order condition multiplied through by w and rearranged yields

$$\frac{u'(w).w}{[u(w) - u(\beta)]} = \frac{m'(w).w}{m(w)} = e \tag{A23}$$

where e denotes the wage elasticity of labour demand. Insertion of the constant elasticity specific functional forms of (10) and (11a) into this equation yields $e = w^{\sigma}.w/\{[w^{\sigma} - \beta^{\sigma}]/\sigma\}$ which can be rearranged to give

$$w^{*HH} = \left[\frac{e}{(e - \sigma)}\right]^{1/\sigma}.\beta \tag{A24}$$

where the superscripts HH denote 'hiring hall'. Union wages are increasing in alternative wages β, and declining with relative risk-aversion $(1-\sigma)$ or with the elasticity of labour demand e. This optimal wage level can be substituted into the labour demand schedule to give the associated level of employment, as shown by m^{*HH} in table 12.1 (p. 000).

2 The insider–outsider (IO) model

This model differs from the static hiring-hall model above, because now workers who are hired in the initial period stay with the firm to become insiders by the start of period 2. We initially examine wage determination in period 2, where n denotes period 2 employment and m is the inherited pool of incumbent workers.

Period 2

$$\max_{w_2} E\hat{v}_2 = \sum_{i=1}^{v} \tau_i\{n_i(w_2).u(w_2) + [m - n_i(w_2)].u(\beta)\} \quad n_i < m. \tag{A25}$$

The first-order condition is given by

$$n_i(w_2).u'(w_2) + n_i'(w_2) - u(\beta)] = 0 \tag{A26}$$

which yields an optimal period 2 wage rate identical to (A24) above (the hiring-hall model wage rate), on the assumption that the elasticity of labour demand does not change across periods.

Period 1

Now consider wage determination in period 1. The union's wage-setting behaviour in period 1 determines the size of current employment (and the next period's incumbents) denoted by m. This two-period behaviour is captured in the following period 1 union maximand

$$E\hat{v}_1 = m(w_1)u(w_1) + [p - m(w_1)]u(\beta) + \delta \sum_{i=1}^{v} \tau_i \{n_i u(w_2) + [m(w_1) - n_i]u(\beta)\}. \tag{A27}$$

When the union sets w_1 by maximisation of (A27) subject to the firm's period 1 labour demand curve, rearrangement of the first-order condition yields

$$\frac{u(w_1).w_1}{[u(w_1) - (1 - \delta)u(\beta)]} = -\frac{m'(w_1).w_1}{m(w_1)} = e. \tag{A28}$$

Insertion of constant elasticity specific functional forms into this equation yields equilibrium wages as

$$w_1^{*IO} = \left[\frac{e(1 - \delta)}{(e - \sigma)}\right]^{1/\sigma} .\beta \tag{A29}$$

If the union is myopic ($\delta = 0$), (A29) reduces to (A24). If the union is not myopic, then the period 1 optimal wage is negatively related to the discount factor δ. For $0 < \delta < 1$, the period 1 wage will be lower than the union wage in the HH model; therefore period 1 employment will be relatively higher. However, period 2 employment will be identical in the HH and IO models. The net result is that average employment is higher in the IO model than in the HH model.

3 *The insider–outsider model with endogenous redundancy pay (IOR)*

From Proposition 2, we know that, for the right-to-manage model, $w_2^* = r^* + \beta$. This result also holds for the monopoly union model. Now consider the determination of wages in period 1. The utilitarian monopoly union maximises its objective function subject to the labour demand curve, which from (4) is given by $m = m(w_1; r, \delta, \theta)$. The union maximand is therefore

$$E\hat{v}_1 = m(w_1)u(w_1) + [p - m(w_1)]u(\beta) + \delta \sum_{i=1}^{v} \tau_i \{n_i u(w_2) + [m(w_1) - n_i]u(r + \beta)\}. \tag{A30}$$

Redundancy pay appears in the last term on the RHS of (A30), since incumbent workers laid off in period 2 are entitled to a redundancy payment. Use the result from Proposition 2 in the text that $w_2^* = r^* + \beta$ to simplify (A30), giving

$$E\hat{v}_1 = m(w_1)u(w_1) + [p - m(w_1)]u(\beta) + (w_1).u(r+\beta). \tag{A31}$$

The first-order condition is

$$m'(w_1)u(w_1)[u(w_1) - u(\beta)] + m(w_1)u'(w_1) + \delta m'(w_1)u(r+\beta) = 0 \tag{A32}$$

which upon multiplication through by $(-w_1/m)$ and rearrangement yields

$$\frac{u(w_1).w_1}{u(w_1) - [u(\beta) - (r+\beta)]} = -\frac{m'(w_1).w_1}{m(w_1)} = e. \tag{A33}$$

Substitute into (A33) the constant elasticity-specific functional forms of (10) and (11b) to obtain

$$w_1^{*IOR} = \left[\frac{e}{e-\sigma}\right]^{1/\sigma} . \left[\beta^\sigma - \delta(r+\beta)^\sigma\right]^{1/\sigma}. \tag{A34}$$

If $r=0$, (A34) collapses to (A29), and if $r=\delta=0$, (A34) collapses to (A24). Inspection of (A24), (A29) and (A34) shows that $w_1^{*HH} > w_1^{*IO} > w_1^{*IOR}$. Equilibrium period 1 employment m is calculated by insertion of (A34) into (11b) for the IOR model, and insertion of (A24) and (A29) into (11a) for the HH and IO models respectively. This yields the values for period 1 employment given in table 12.1.

NOTES

I should like to thank Monojit Chatterji, Melvyn Coles, Juan Dolado, Jacques Drèze, Dennis Snower, Gilles Saint-Paul, Gylfi Zoega, and seminar participants at Birkbeck College, the Australian National University, and the CEPR Conference on Unemployment Policy (1994) for helpful comments on an earlier draft. Any errors are my responsibility. Part of this chapter was written during a visit to the Research School of Social Science at the Australian National University, whose hospitality is gratefully acknowledged.

1 Rudimentary employment security regulations were introduced in France and Germany in the 1920s, in conjunction with unemployment insurance systems. While these employment protection regimes initially only involved pre-notification periods, they were later expanded. In Portugal and Spain, relatively rigid employment security regulations were imposed during dictatorial regimes, while in Italy and Britain employment protection regulations emerged during the 1960s and 1970s. Statutory redundancy pay was introduced in Britain with the passage of the Redundancy Payments Act 1965, and re-enacted in the Employment Protection (Consolidation) Act 1978. See Buechtemann (1992) and chapters therein for a detailed discussion.

2 However, Bentolila and Saint-Paul (1994) find that a rise in firing costs reduces average steady-state labour demand when these costs are low, but increases such demand when they are high.

3 The model thus forms part of the small literature modelling why negotiated redundancy pay is observed in some circumstances in the absence of statutory provisions (see Lazear, 1979; Booth and Chatterji, 1989).

4 Redundancy pay may therefore have a longer-run effect on employment than is predicted by the model, which for tractability assumes a fixed level of capital and does not address investment. For reasons of tractability, hours are also assumed fixed in the model.

5 In Britain solvent firms finance the entire redundancy payment. If the firm has serious cash flow problems, workers can be paid direct from the National Insurance (NI) Fund, and the firm pays back the amount later. If the firm is insolvent, the payment is again made from the NI Fund, and the debt is recovered from the firm's assets. Originally, the financing of state-mandated redundancy payments was through a supplement to firms' national insurance contributions, paid into the Redundancy Fund, from which firms could claim a rebate when making payments to redundant workers. From 1982 a supplement to workers' national insurance contributions was also introduced. With the passage of the Wages Act 1986, rebates from the Redundancy Fund were abolished for all but the smallest firms. Under the provision of the Employment Act 1989, rebates were no longer available for any firms and the Redundancy Fund was subsumed within the NI Fund.

6 While this applies to most European countries, it does not apply to Spain, for example, where there is a wedge between what firms pay and what workers receive owing to complex bureaucratic procedures (see Bentolila and Dolado, 1994).

7 If $n_i > m$, the firm would hire new workers in period 2, which complicates the analysis without adding any extra insights about redundancy pay. We therefore restrict our attention here to $n_i \leq m$.

8 For more complex models of the dynamic impact of firing costs on labour demand, see Bentolila and Bertola (1990, Bentolila and Saint-Paul (1994).

9 Lazear (1990) notes that, if workers were to make a private transfer fee *ex ante* to the firm of an amount equal to the severance payment, this distortion could be overcome. But should this not be possible (and such payments are typically not observed), labour demand will not be at its efficient level. Lazear (1990) gives credit constraints as a reason why private transfer fees are not made.

10 When workers have no power in the bargain, the firm determines w, r and employment unilaterally, which is the perfectly competitive model.

11 Bargaining does *not* occur over the size of the unemployment benefit level, which is determined by the state in practice in the UK and many European countries, and which for this reason is treated as exogenous in the model developed in this chapter.

12 More completely, we can write that utility in work is denoted by $v(w,h)$, where w is the wage rate, h denotes hours of work, and $v_w > 0$ and $v_h < 0$ (where the subscripts denote the partial derivatives). But to keep the analysis simple, suppose that hours are unity if employed and zero otherwise. Thus a typical worker's utility can now be written as by $u(w) = v(w,1)$ when employed, and by $u(\beta) = v(\beta,0)$ when unemployed.

13 This result holds whether the problem is initially set up with w and r fixed across states as above, or with contingent w and r. The result also holds in both the 'efficient bargaining' union model, where the union bargains over

wages, redundancy pay and employment (see Booth, 1996), and in the implicit contract literature (see Rosen, 1985; Manning, 1991, for surveys).

14 If β were increasing in (w,n) space, the opportunity cost of labour would in general differ across states of nature, and the efficiency result in Proposition 2 would be unlikely to hold.

15 If $n_i > m$ the analysis becomes more complicated since there are now two terms to consider in expected period 2 profits and union utility – the outcome in the bad states and the outcome in the good states. Moreover, the kink point between these regimes is also a function of r, since the critical point is that level of Θ at which $m-n=0$.

16 Any iso-elastic increase in demand has no impact on wages, but causes employment to increase.

17 To calculate the optimal r^* to be inserted into period 1 equilibrium employment in table 12.1 for the IOR model, it is necessary to solve (6) simultaneously for r and w_2, with the explicit constant elasticity and relative risk-aversion functional forms. The first-order conditions obtained from this exercise are two polynomial equations, which are not possible to solve either numerically or analytically. Therefore the conclusion that we reach is that it remains an empirical issue to determine whether period 1 employment in the IOR model is greater than in the IO model.

REFERENCES

Bentolila, S. and G. Bertola, 1990. 'Firing costs and labour demand in Europe: how bad is Eurosclerosis?, *Review of Economic Studies*, **57**, 381–402

Bentolila, S. and J. Dolado, 1994. 'Labor flexibility and wages: lessons from Spain', *Economic Policy*, **18**, 53–100

Bentolila, S. and G. Saint-Paul, 1994. 'A model of labour demand with linear adjustment costs', *Labour Economics*, **1**, 303–26

Bertola, G., 1990. 'Job security, employment and wages', *European Economic Review*, **34**, 851–86

1992. 'Labor turnover costs and average labor demand', *Journal of Labor Economics*, **10**, 389–411

Booth, A.L., 1996. 'Layoffs with payoffs: a bargaining model of union wage and severance pay determination', *Economica*, forthcoming

Booth, A.L. and M. Chatterji, 1989. 'Redundancy payments and firm-specific training', *Economica*, **56**, 505–21

Booth, A.L. and G. Zoega, 1994. 'Quitting externalities, employment cyclicality and firing costs', CEPR, *Discussion Paper*, **1101**, London: CEPR

Buechtemann, C.F., 1992. 'Employment security and labor markets an introduction', in C.F. Buechtemann (ed.), *Employment Security and Labor Market Behavior: Interdisciplinary Approaches and International Evidence*, Ithaca: ILR Press, Cornell University

Burda, M., 1992. 'A note on firing costs and severance benefits in equilibrium unemployment', *Scandinavian Journal of Economics*, **94**, 479–89

Jacoby, S.N., 1992. 'The new institutionalism: what can we learn from the old?', in D.J.B. Mitchell and M.A. Zaida (eds.), *The Economics of Human Resource Management*, Cambridge, MA: Blackwell, 172–90

Lazear, E.P., 1979. 'Why is there mandatory retirement?', *Journal of Political Economy*, **87**, 1261–84

1990. 'Job security provisions and employment', *Quarterly Journal of Economics*, **55**, 699–726

Lindbeck, A. and D.J. Snower, 1987. 'Efficiency wages versus insiders and outsiders', *European Economic Review*, **31**, 407–16

Manning, A., 1991. 'Implicit contract theory', in D. Sapsford and Z. Tzannatos (eds.), *Current Issues in Labour Economics*, London: Macmillan

Millward, N., M. Stevens, D. Smart and W. Haes, 1992. *Workplace Industrial Relations in Transition*, Aldershot: Dartmouth

Nickell, S.J., 1978. 'Fixed costs, employment and labor demand over the cycle', *Economica*, **46**, 329–45

Pencavel, J., 1991. *Labor Markets under Trade Unionism*, Oxford: Basil Blackwell

Rosen, S., 1985. 'Implicit contracts: a survey', *Journal of Economic Literature*, **23**, 1144–75

Discussion

JUAN JOSE DOLADO

In Europe as a panacea for European unemployment, chapter 12 should be welcomed. In a very simple and pedagogical way, Alison Booth reminds us that once we depart from the standard, static, competitive analysis that usually underlies the calls for increased flexibility, there is room for bargained redundancy payments without negative effects on employment. The argument goes as follows. In more realistic environments in which agents have market power and there is uncertainty, risk-averse workers will prefer a contract with redundancy pay since it irons out fluctuations in employment across time. Likewise, risk-neutral firms, which benefit from long-term employment relationships, will be willing to bargain firing costs with the workers. The outcome of this model is that the wage corresponding to the level of *ex post* employment equals the opportunity cost of labour, namely, the bargaining surplus is maximised. The argument is clear-cut and I could not agree more. Indeed, although the author considers this result to be 'striking', it is not difficult to show that the argument is isomorphic to the standard one used in the 'implicit contract' theory, in the case where the firm is allowed to choose the wage of the attached worker both under employment and unemployment, so as to avoid 'over-employment' (see Akerlof and Mizayaki, 1980).

Let us start by clarifying why the result is not so 'striking'. Using the notation of chapter 12 for period 2, consider a firm offering an implicit contract in terms of $(n,\ w_n w_u)$ where w_n and w_u denote the wage while working and laid off, respectively. Then the firm maximises expected profits given by

$$\sum \tau_i\{\Theta f(n_i) - w_{ni}n_i - [m - n_i]w_{ui}\} \tag{1}$$

subject to

$$\sum \tau_i\{n_i u(w_{ni} + [m - n_i]u(w_{ui} + \beta)\} \geq \bar{u}. \tag{2}$$

It is easy to show that the first-order conditions of this problem are given by

$$w_n = w_u + \beta,\ \forall i \tag{3}$$

$$\Theta f'(n_i) = \beta \tag{4}$$

which happen to be identical to the results in Proposition 2 of the chapter, with r playing the role of w_u.

Notwithstanding my general agreement with the spirit of the chapter, there are certain parts where limitations of the analysis could lead to slightly misguided conclusions. Playing my role as 'devil's advocate', my remaining comments will focus on some of these shortcomings.

First, the model in this chapter is one where firms can only fire. Thus, under this assumption, the result in Proposition 1 is rather straightforward, i.e. if there are firing costs firms will lay off fewer workers than if they do not exist. In general, in linear adjustment cost models there are two trigger points which define an inaction range in labour demand. Naturally, the effects on both the firing trigger points, and hence on average labour demand, depend on the sluggishness of revenue shocks. If they are very persistent we get Bentolila and Bertola's (1990) results. However, if shocks are i.i.d., a paper by Bentolila and Saint-Paul (1994) shows that firing costs reduce average ready-state labour demand when these costs are low, but raise employment when they are high. Booth acknowledges this problem and conjectures that had the assumption been relaxed by allowing the firm in period 2 to hire new workers, then the instrument of redundancy pay could not be used to achieve efficient employment. Indeed, this can be easily seen by allowing for two possible regimes in period 2: a recession (with revenue shift Θ_R) with probability p, and an expansion (with revenue shift Θ_E) with probability $(1-p)$. Thus, expected net profit and utility in period 2 will be

$$\Pi = p[\Theta_R f(n) - wn - r(m-n)] + (1-p)[\Theta_E f(n) - wn] \tag{5}$$

$$V = p[nu(w) + (m-n)u(r+\beta)] + (1-p)[nu(w)] - mu(\beta). \tag{6}$$

Maximising the generalised Nash bargain with respect to (w, r) yields the condition

$$u(w) = pu(r+\beta) \tag{7}$$

which, given that $u(\cdot)$ is an increasing function, implies that $w > (r+\beta)$. Thus, the conjecture is right, though I presume that had there been hiring costs and had these been subject to negotiation, we could still achieve efficient employment

Secondly, if rather than assuming that what firms pay and what dismissed workers receive is the same amount of redundancy payment, r, we assume the existence of 'red tape' costs (say, delays in production changes, legal proceedings, notice periods and official approval, etc.), then the amount received by the worker will be ϕr $(\phi \leq 1)$. In such a case, the main result in Proposition 2 (formula A.9 in the appendix) turns out to be

$$x = \frac{u'(w_2)x + z[u(w_2) - u(R)]}{\phi u'(R) - z[u(w_2) - u(R)]} \tag{8}$$

where x and z are constants and $R = \beta + \phi r$. Note that if $\phi = 1$, we get $w_2 = R$, namely the result stated in the chapter. But, if $\phi < 1$ then, given the concavity of $u(\cdot)$, we get $w_2 > R$ and $\Theta_i f'(n_i) > \beta$, namely, employment will be lower. Furthermore, if redundancy payments depend on the worker's tenure such that she receives $\phi r + \gamma w_1$ (firms pay $r + \gamma w_1$), then I believe that it is possible to show in terms of the deadweight losses in period 1 and 2 that the joint inefficiency in both periods could be larger than if firing costs are not bargained or even in the 'hiring-hall' model.

Thirdly, as in most models of linear costs in the literature, capital is

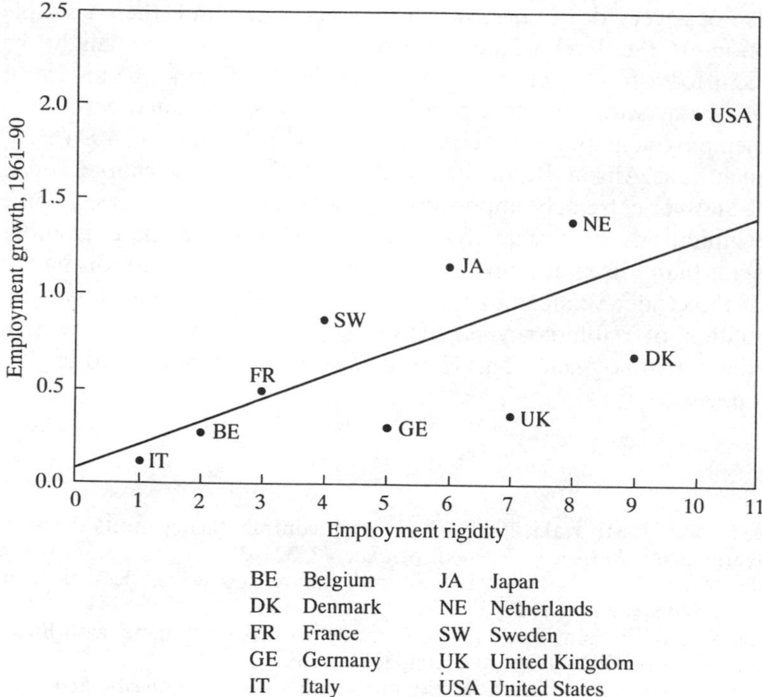

Figure D12.1 Employment rigidity versus employment growth

taken as given. It has been shown by Bertola (1991) that as r increases the value of the firm tends to decrease, shifting the labour demand schedule downwards and thus reducing employment. In this respect, firing costs might increase insiders' bargaining power (see Bentolila and Dolado, 1994) and, as shown in Proposition 3, this decreases firms' profits. Naturally, the follow-up to that proposition 'but leaves *ex post* employment unaffected' is only true if investment is not reduced, an unlikely event. Figure 12.1, by correlating Bertola's (1990) index of job security and average employment growth during 1960–90, but without conditioning on anything else, shows that such might be the case (see figure D12.1).

Finally, a word on hysteresis. The existence of a 'zone of inaction' in the presence of hiring and firing costs means that there is a payoff to waiting until things are less uncertain. All this means that the demand for labour might initially be rather slow to respond to business conditions or labour costs, but that if a large shake-out of labour does occur, as for instance in the wake of a very deep turndown in aggregate demand, then a simple restoration of the level of demand to the *statu quo ante* might be insufficient to restore employment to earlier levels. Again, on this front, there is circumstantial evidence that job security is associated with long-term unemployment and less job turnover (see Garibaldi *et al.*, 1994).

In conclusion, Alison Booth has written a stimulating chapter on a difficult and yet extremely important problem. I have emphasised some of the limitations of her analysis, but on the whole there is more agreement than disagreement. Labour economists need to dismantle some of the cruder versions of the conventional wisdom that advocates the abolition of redundancy payments as a necessary requirement in combating unemployment. This chapter moves one step forward in that direction.

REFERENCES

Akerlof, G. and H. Miyazaki, 1980. 'The implicit contract theory meets the wage bill argument', *Review of Economic Studies*, **47**, 321–38

Bentolila, S. and J. Dolado, 1994. 'Labor flexibility and wages: lessons from Spain', *Economic Policy*, **18**, 53–100

Bentolila, S. and G. Saint-Paul, 1994. 'A model of labour demand with linear adjustment costs', *Labour Economics*, **1**, 303–26

Bertola, G., 1990. 'Job security, employment and wages', *European Economic Review*, **34**, 851–86

1991. 'Flexibility, investment and growth', CEPR, *Discussion Paper*, **422**, London: CEPR

Garibaldi, P., J. Konings and C. Pissarides, 1994. 'Gross job reallocation and labour market policy', London School of Economics, Centre for Economic Performance, mimeo

Discussion

GILLES SAINT-PAUL

Chapter 12 by Alison Booth studies the case for redundancy payments in a bargaining model of employment and wage determination. The most interesting results of the chapter are that firing costs will endogenously arise as an outcome of bargaining between firms and workers, and that

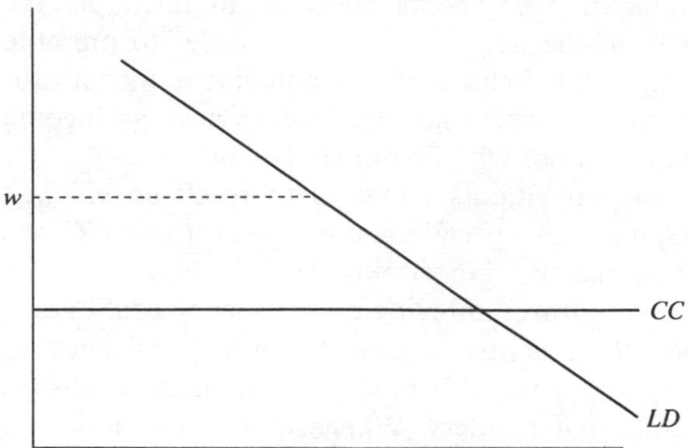

Figure D12.2 Booth's Proposition 2

the government's attempt to regulate such firing costs may have no effect on employment. The results are in sharp contrast with the 'conventional wisdom' that firing costs are bad altogether, and reduce employment, although such conventional wisdom is more widespread among non-economists than among economists.

I like the basic idea that firms will optimally provide employment protection to workers; I think the model provides a nice intuition for that result. However, the particular assumptions that are made tend to overstate the virtues of severance payments.

Let me focus on Proposition 2 in Booth's chapter. The logic of the argument is illustrated in figure D12.2. The flat line *CC* is the opportunity cost of labour, equal to β in chapter 12's model. The downward-sloping line *LD* is the marginal product of labour schedule. This schedule is shifted by some exogenous shock Θ. Before this shock is known, the firm and the worker negotiate over some fixed wage level w, and possibly a severance payment.

Efficiency requires that in all states of nature employment is determined by the intersection of the *CC* and *LD* schedules. If bargaining took place only over wages, this would require that w be equal to β, which is inconsistent with the workers having any amount of bargaining power. Bargaining over just wages then yields an inefficient outcome, with too low employment.

Suppose that, now, firms and workers bargain over some severance payment r. Then in each state of nature where the firms actually fire, the marginal cost of labour is equal to $w-r$. Clearly, setting $r=w-\beta$ allows us to reach the efficient level of employment in all these states of nature, while granting workers a positive share of the surplus.

In Booth's model, redundancy payments allow us to uncouple the marginal cost of labour from the negotiated wage in order to preserve efficiency. Furthermore, the great beauty of this outcome is that it also allows for full insurance, since workers who get laid off have an income equal to $\beta + r = w$, the same as those who do not get laid off.

The result that redundancy payments allow us to reach an efficient outcome hinges, however, on some special assumptions. First, if *CC* was upward-sloping rather than flat, the opportunity cost of labour would in general differ across states of nature, implying that efficiency could never be reached with just two instruments. Second, the firm is assumed to always be in the firing regime in Booth's model: employment is always less than some fixed number of insiders. Whenever the firm is hiring rather than firing, then the marginal cost of labour is equal to $w+h$, where h is the hiring cost, rather than $w-r$; redundancy payments can therefore not achieve efficiency in those states of nature; what would be required is a hiring subsidy equal to $w-\beta$.

Nevertheless, it is true that there are many models where the firm would like to grant some employment security to workers, possibly by writing a redundancy payment clause in the contract. This will be true in all models where the present discounted value of being employed must exceed that of being unemployed by some level; examples of such models include the dynamic efficiency wage model of Shapiro and Stiglitz (1984), or dynamic insider–outsider models such as that in Pissarides (1990). In these models, workers require some present discounted rent; the future differences between the wage and the opportunity cost of labour are more heavily discounted when the probability of losing one's job is higher; to maintain the present discounted rent constant, wages must then rise – and profits must fall. Firms would then make more profits when the probability of losing one's job is lower; they would therefore have an incentive to grant some employment security to their workers.

REFERENCES

Pissarides, C., 1990. *Equilibrium Unemployment Theory*, Oxford: Basil Blackwell

Shapiro, C. and J. Stiglitz, 1984. 'Equilibrium unemployment as a worker discipline device', *American Economic Review*, **74**, 433–44

13 Labour market regulation and unemployment

PAUL GREGG and ALAN MANNING

1 Introduction

There is understandable concern about the stubbornly high level of unemployment in OECD countries, and a strong desire to find policies that can reduce it. It is no longer fashionable to blame a shortfall in aggregate demand for this situation, as such an explanation is generally thought to be unable to address the progressive rise in unemployment over the last 25 years. Among economists, the most common current view has been to identify the problem as being on the supply side of the economy and in the labour market in particular. 'Interference' in the free workings of the labour market which keep real wage costs above market-clearing levels is seen as one of the main causes of unemployment. The proposed cure for unemployment generally involves removal of these interferences or what we will call labour market de-regulation.[1]

In this chapter we argue that this faith in the merits of labour market de-regulation is misplaced. We argue that economists have seriously over-emphasised the gains in terms of unemployment or more general measures of labour market efficiency to be obtained from de-regulation, and under-estimated the costs. If one asks someone who believes in the ability of labour market de-regulation to reduce unemployment about the source of their beliefs, they would probably cite various pieces of empirical evidence in support of their view. We consider this empirical evidence below and argue that it is much less persuasive than is commonly believed. We argue that the evidence is regarded as persuasive because of the touching faith that many economists have in the view that the de-regulation of the labour market moves it towards the perfectly competitive ideal in which everyone who wants a job can find one at a wage equal to the value of their contribution to society. We argue that a close examination of the behaviour of de-regulated labour markets suggests that they bear little relationship to the perfectly competitive model.

We do not want to argue that all labour market regulation is necessarily good for unemployment. But we do want to argue that the relationship between labour market regulation and unemployment is more complex than is generally suggested and that there are instances where increased de-regulation actually leads to increased unemployment or some other form of inefficiency in the operation of the labour market. Of course, the interesting question is then the optimal amount of labour market regulation: on this, we outline some general principles but have little to say about details.

The plan of this chapter is as follows. In section 2 we consider the broad framework of analysis which covers a range of economic opinion which places regulation as a key factor in rising unemployment. Section 3 considers the empirical evidence that is used to justify the case that labour market de-regulation leads to reduced unemployment and argues that it is much less persuasive than it might at first seem. We also consider some other pieces of evidence that are less rarely considered but also suggest that the link between regulation and unemployment may not be straightforward. We then try to provide some explanation for why de-regulation may not always reduce the unemployment problem, and we argue that the reason is that de-regulated labour markets contain important elements of monopsony, so that making jobs attractive to workers is at least as important as encouraging job creation by firms in determining the level of unemployment. Labour market regulation is necessary to give workers some countervailing power against employers. We conclude by considering what principles should determine the optimal amount and form of labour market regulation.

2 The conventional analysis of regulation in the labour market

The most important interferences in the workings of the labour market that are normally mentioned in discussions on unemployment are the following (some of which are of more importance in some countries and at some times more than others):

- Social security systems which provide a safety net for the living standards of those out of work and which reduce the gap in living standards between those in or out of work and are thought to reduce the incentives to find or keep jobs. Where the safety net is paid by taxes on wages it will also raise total labour costs.
- Minimum wages which are thought to price workers out of jobs if set at levels above those prevailing in an unregulated labour market.
- Employment protection legislation such as restrictions on the ability of

employers to hire and fire at will also raise labour costs and are thought to lead to reduced flexibility and possibly reduced employment.

- Trade unions which are thought to raise wages to levels which destroy jobs and perhaps to reduce productive efficiency through restrictive practices.

In this chapter, we will use the term 'labour market de-regulation' (or simply 'de-regulation') to refer to the type of policies which have as their aim the reform of social security system to make benefit provision less generous, the reduction or abolition of minimum wages, the removal of employment protection and reductions in the power of trade unions. Using a single term to refer to a collection of policies which, at least in some aspects, may have very different effects on the labour market, is potentially dangerous but we believe that the basic ideas behind all these policy recommendations is essentially the same and that they have enough in common to be usefully discussed in the same terms.

There are a number of different attitudes to the relationship between labour market regulation and the behaviour of OECD unemployment. According to one view (for example, the views of Minford and Riley, 1994, in the UK), the rise in OECD unemployment since the 1950s and 1960s is itself caused by the increased scope of labour market regulation that occurred in many countries in the 1960s and 1970s and in some cases continued into the 1980s. According to another view (the influential insider–outsider view popularised by Blanchard and Summers, 1986 and Lindbeck and Snower, 1989), it was labour market regulation combined with a number of adverse but temporary shocks like the oil price rises in the 1970s that caused unemployment to remain high long after the original impetus for the rise in unemployment had disappeared. A third view, becoming increasingly popular (for example, Juhn, Murphy and Topel, 1991), is that technological change that is biased in favour of skilled labour, perhaps combined with globalisation of the world economy, has led to a deterioration in the economic position of the unskilled in OECD countries and that labour market regulation has hindered the required adjustment in the wage structure, with the consequence of high unemployment concentrated on the less skilled.

But although these analyses differ in their views of the fundamental origins of the rise in unemployment, they all tend to emphasise that labour market de-regulation should be part of the solution. This type of analysis is well summarised by the OECD *Jobs Study* (OECD, 1994, p. 22) which concluded that

> wages have significant consequences for employment and unemployment. The process of wage determination is strongly influenced by labour market pressures, social perceptions, legislation and industrial relation systems.

This study represents the culmination of two years' intense effort. As would be expected from a mainstream transnational body it represents a synthesis of collective wisdom derived from the last five years or so of the analysis of the functioning of the labour market. The report is permeated with the notion of the 'flexible labour market', but 'flexibility' is a word open to numerous interpretations.

The OECD is clear about the flexibility it seeks as a result of policy reform – that wages should be highly sensitive to unemployment and that the unemployed should enter work frequently, so as to avoid a build-up of long-term unemployment. 'Wage flexibility' should mean that as unemployment rises, real wage costs should fall relative to productivity. This, it is argued, raises profitability, stimulates growth and encourages employment. Just as wages should be sensitive to unemployment at the aggregate level, they should also be sensitive to concentrations of unemployment in society, so that if unemployment is higher for young people their wages should fall relative to older workers. This would in turn induce employers to recruit young people. The second aspect of flexibility should be that the pool of the unemployed should turn over rapidly to avoid the development of a large stock of long-term unemployed. The long-term unemployed are envisaged as not only suffering greater deprivation but as losing usable skills and motivation, which becomes part of the structural unemployment problem.

From these notions of flexibility, the OECD suggests nine principles of policy which should, in their view, combine to ensure that employment grow in line with the population wanting to work with a reasonable level of unemployment:

- (i) Macroeconomic policy should be set to encourage sustainable growth.
- (ii) Technical development should be encouraged, as should its diffusion into the economy.
- (iii) Flexible working time, both in current hours and amount of life-time in the labour force, should be encouraged.
- (iv) A positive entrepreneurial climate to encourage business start-ups should be generated.
- (v) Wages and non-wage labour costs should be made more flexible across groups in the workforce, especially for the young.
- (vi) There should be reform of employment security provision.

(vii) Active labour market expenditure should be increased instead of passive benefit provision.
(viii) Workforce skills should be improved through education and training programmes.
(ix) Unemployment benefit systems (and tax) should be reformed to encourage positive incentives to go into work.

Many (but not all) of these proposals are designed to lessen the impact of the labour market regulations of the sort described earlier. A crude summary of the conventional view would be that it is necessary to reduce labour costs (broadly defined) to increase employment, and to the extent that this means reductions in wages paid to workers, the incentive to work can only be maintained by a reduction in welfare payments to the unemployed. The policy option advocated is not complete labour market de-regulation, but the case for retaining some regulation is normally in terms of equity rather than efficiency. So, for example, in its discussion of the role of minimum wages, the OECD study (p. 46) said that OECD countries should

> if it is judged desirable to maintain a legal minimum wage as part of an anti-poverty strategy, consider minimising its adverse employment effects.

It is taken for granted that minimum wages are bad for employment and only equity considerations may justify their retention.

3 Empirical evidence on the relationship between labour market de-regulation and unemployment

In this section, we review the empirical evidence for the case that labour market regulation can be held responsible for unemployment. This literature is voluminous, and a complete survey is impossible (see for example, Bean, 1994, for a survey of European experience), but what follows is, we believe, a fair representation of the work that has been done.

3.1 Time-series evidence

First, there is a considerable amount of econometric work on macroeconomic data designed to shed light on the determinants of unemployment (in Europe the so-called 'Chelwood Gate' conference papers being good examples – see Blanchard, 1990, for a summary). Typically these studies involve a regression of the unemployment rate on a set of variables thought to influence unemployment, or the estimation of a system of equations from which the determinants of unemployment can be inferred. The sort of variables thought to influence unemployment include some measures of labour market regulation and also some other variables thought to be relevant. These models are generally dynamic, so can be used to explain the behaviour of unemployment in both the short run and the long run. It may be invidious to single out individuals, but a good example of this sort of work is the book by Layard, Nickell and Jackman (1991) which ends up estimating an equation for the unemployment rate in 19 countries for the period 1956–88. The variables included as determinants of the unemployment rate are the duration and generosity of unemployment benefits (measured as the replacement ratio), some measure of collective bargaining structure and the proportion of employees with job tenure less than two years (which is designed to proxy job security legislation).

If one reads this sort of study, one often comes away with the impression that these models are really rather successful in explaining the changes in unemployment both across countries and over time. But appearances are deceptive. If one examines these models closely one generally finds that within them they contain a time trend, suitably chosen dummy variables or some variable that behaves something like them (but is itself implausible as an explanation of the rise in unemployment) that does a very large part of the work in explaining changes in unemployment over time. So, for example, Layard, Nickell and Jackman (1991) contains a dummy variable which implies that, for some reason, there was a permanent jump in the unemployment rate in 1970.

So these models do not provide a very coherent explanation of the time-series behaviour of the unemployment rate. The reason why these models are unable to explain the rise in unemployment in terms of increased labour market regulation is a simple one. From the late 1960s unemployment throughout the OECD has been on a rising trend. In the 1960s and 1970s labour market regulation was increased in most countries. So if one was writing about unemployment in the first half of the 1980s, it is not surprising that there seemed to be a connection between increased unemployment and increased labour market regulation. But this analysis was not ignored by policy makers, and from the early 1980s the labour market policies adopted in most countries (although some more than others) have ended to favour de-regulation; yet, unemployment continued to rise. A striking example of this is the UK, where the Conservative government that took power in 1979 pursued a very aggressive policy of labour market de-regulation. Yet at no point in the 1980s and 1990s has the unemployment rate been below the highest level experienced in the period from 1945 to 1979. Another good example is the USA, where the labour market has always been relatively unregulated and, if anything, has become less so. But there has still been a rise in unemployment which it has been thought necessary to explain, as is evidenced by the title of Juhn, Murphy and Topel (1991), 'Why has the natural rate of unemployment increased over time?'. Furthermore, since the 1979 oil price rise no serious external shock has hit the developed markets and if anything the shocks have been positive (e.g. the collapse of raw material prices).

In the mid-1980s, this realisation that economists were at a loss in explaining the rise in unemployment led to the popularity of insider–outsider and hysteresis models (Blanchard and Summers, 1986; Lindbeck and Snower, 1989) which emphasised the importance of unemployment persistence after temporary shocks. These ideas were attractive when they were invented in the mid-1980s as it was then relatively plausible to believe that the high unemployment was the result of a very slow adjustment after temporary shocks like the 1970s oil price shocks. But we are now in the mid-1990s and there has been no noticeable reduction in unemployment and there seems to be something permanent about it, so these models come to seem much less plausible. All the empirical studies which try to explain the rise in unemployment find that the rise is permanent, not just a very drawn-out response to some temporary shocks.

The inability of our econometric models to explain the rise in unemployment in terms of increased labour market regulation or any other commonly included shock-type variable has inevitably led to a search for a new 'answer'. A number of candidates are available. Phelps (1994) has argued that real interest rates are important (see also chapters 5 and 7 in this volume); elsewhere we have argued (Manning, 1991) that the rate of productivity growth may be important. But the most fashionable current explanation is that the labour market opportunities for the less skilled relative to the more skilled have been declining. This type of argument has its origins in the USA, where it seems to fit the data very well. For example, Juhn, Murphy and Topel (1991) document that the unemployment–population ratio for the top 60 per cent of prime-age men (in terms of predicted wages) hardly changed between 1967 and 1990 while the unemployment–population ratio for the bottom 10 per cent rose from something over 4 per cent to about 12 per cent. In terms of non-employment the changes are more dramatic, the rates for the bottom 10 per cent tripling to about 35 per cent. At the same time the real hourly wages of the bottom 10 per cent have fallen by 30 per cent since 1970 while the real hourly wages for the top 60 per cent are essentially constant. This evidence is very strongly indicative of a shift in demand against the less skilled. Why there has been a shift against the unskilled is less clear. The two most favoured explanations are competition with low-wage labour in developing countries and technical progress that is biased against the unskilled (the studies by Berman *et al.*, 1994 and Murphy and Welch, 1993, suggest that the former explanation cannot be the whole story). These are long-term trends rather than temporary shocks, and we would expect both these mechanisms to be at work in all industrialised countries.

The argument then continues that countries which have institutions which maintain the living standards of those at the bottom end of the wage distribution (like welfare states, minimum wages and trade unions) avoid the extreme falls in living standards for less able workers but at the cost of preventing relative wage adjustment and, as a consequence, high unemployment. So, while labour market regulation is not the fundamental cause of the labour market problems currently being experienced, it does determine the form that those problems take. Yet whilst the rise in unemployment in the USA has been entirely among the least able it has been in spite of the large falls in real wages that these individuals have had. If the European countries have not had enough real wage adjustment because of labour market regulation, then we would expect the divergence in unemployment rates to be much larger in Europe than in the USA. But there is little evidence that this is the case (see, for example, the evidence provided on a number of countries by Nickell and Bell, chapter 10 in this volume).

Take the example of the UK. While it is true that the absolute gap between the unemployment rates of the skilled and unskilled has widened, it is not true that the relative unemployment rates have widened. Figure 13.1 reports the results for the UK of the Juhn *et al.* (1991) decomposition in which the unemployment and non-employment rates of prime-aged men are computed for various deciles of the predicted wage distribution. Although there is a widening in the absolute unemployment differentials between the top and bottom of the earnings distribution there is no very obvious movement in the relative unemployment rates. One can debate whether it is the absolute or relative unemployment rates that are more relevant (see Layard *et al.*, 1991, chapter 6; Manning *et al.*, 1995), but the important point is that it does not matter which measure is used for the USA while it does for the UK. The relative deterioration in the employment prospects of the least skilled does not seem to be greater in the UK than the USA, which is a strong prediction of the theory that blames labour market regulation and skill-biased change for current labour market problems. Indeed, on the

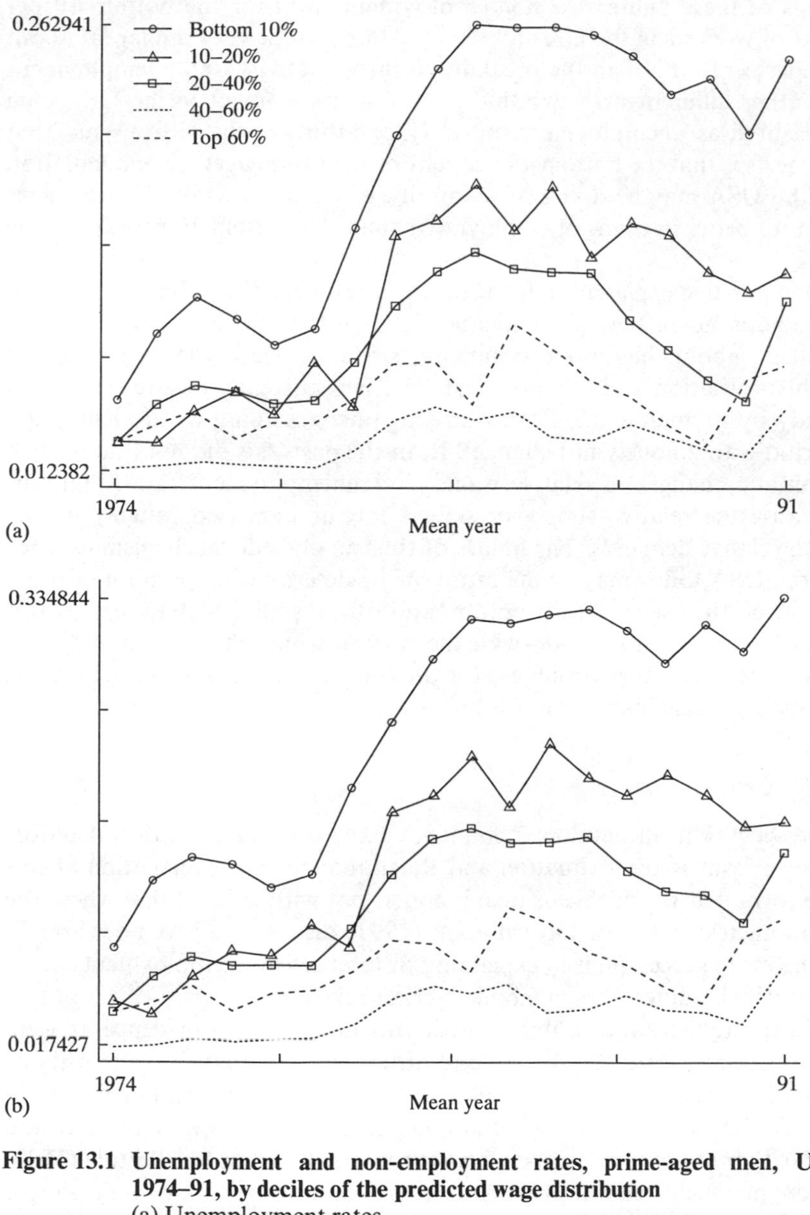

Figure 13.1 Unemployment and non-employment rates, prime-aged men, UK, 1974–91, by deciles of the predicted wage distribution
(a) Unemployment rates
(b) Non-employment rates
Source: Juhn *et al.* (1991)

basis of these figures the non-employment rates for the bottom 10 per cent of workers in the UK and the USA seem to be very similar (at about 35 per cent) although the breakdown into inactivity and unemployment is rather different with two-thirds of non-employment in the UK being measured as unemployment but only one-third in the USA. What that suggests is that the bottom 10 per cent of the prime-aged male population in the USA may be doing substantially worse in terms of relative wages and no better in terms of employment than the bottom 10 per cent in the UK.

One possible explanation for these findings is the following. Skill-biased change is not a new phenomenon. The shift towards the use of more skilled labour has been occurring since at least the beginning of industrialisation and it is not clear that it is currently at a faster rate (a study by Berman *et al.*, 1994, warns against assuming we are living in a period with uniquely fast change). If, in the past, this did not lead to such dramatic changes in relative wages and unemployment rates, that was because the relative supply of skilled labour increased roughly in line with relative demands. The failure of this supply-side mechanism to work in the USA today may be the cause of the deteriorating position of those who find themselves at the bottom end of the skill distribution, and this may have something to do with the way in which the education system and general social environment for the most disadvantaged in the USA is probably worse than it is in Europe.

3.2 Cross-section evidence

The view that all developed countries have been faced with a deteriorating labour market situation and that labour market regulation affects the form that the problems take is consistent with the fact that where the econometric model of Layard *et al.* (1991) discussed above does appear to be more successful is in explaining differences in unemployment across countries by differences in labour market regulation.

However, there are problems with this cross-section evidence as well. For example, Burda (1988), among others, reports that the generosity of unemployment benefits is correlated with unemployment, but the study in OECD (1991) finds no relationship. Lazear (1990) finds that job security provisions are associated with unemployment but Bertola (1990) finds no such relationship. And there seems to be no very simple relationship between the power of trade unions and unemployment, as is shown by Calmfors and Driffill (1988) and the papers that have followed from it.

To illustrate these types of problems table 13.1 presents single variable

Table 13.1 *Single variable correlations*

	Mean tenure	Bertola index	T U density	Coverage rate	Benefit duration	Replacement ratio	Minimum wage
Change in unemployment rate	−0.080	−0.281	−0.053	0.039	0.078	−0.054	0.111
	(0.534)	(0.296)	(0.037)	(0.024)	(0.035)	(0.034)	(0.050)
No. of countries	10	10	14	14	16	16	9
R^2	0.00	0.06	0.12	0.11	0.24	0.12	0.49
Unemployment rate in 1990	−0.438	−0.183	−0.059	−0.01	0.035	−0.068	0.015
	(0.333)	(0.244)	(0.023)	(0.024)	(0.040)	(0.028)	(0.032)
No. of countries	10	10	14	14	16	16	9
R^2	0.17	0.17	0.26	0.00	0.07	0.26	0.02
Long-term unemployment (%)	1.75	−4.40	−0.25	0.30	0.17	−0.22	0.82
	(2.54)	(1.69)	(0.21)	(0.17)	(0.34)	(0.30)	(0.32)
No. of countries	10	10	12	12	14	14	9
R^2	0.05	0.33	0.07	0.16	0.02	0.04	0.33
Male non-employment rate	−0.21	0.056	0.042	0.015	0.088	−0.059	−0.090
	(0.642)	(0.211)	(0.045)	(0.056)	(0.053)	(0.029)	(0.036)
No. of obs.	9	9	11	11	13	13	8
R^2	0.33	0.00	0.04	0.01	0.23	0.10	0.29
Changes in male non-employment rate	−0.660	−0.199	0.029	0.035	0.120	−0.061	−0.074
	(0.622)	(0.209)	(0.033)	(0.037)	(0.035)	(0.036)	(0.081)
No. of obs.	9	8	10	10	11	11	7
R^2	0.13	0.03	0.03	0.07	0.48	>0.14	0.12

regressions of a variety of measures of labour market performance on a variety of measures of labour market regulation based on the available data for 16 OECD countries (the data is presented in the appendix, p. 000). Although multivariate regressions would be desirable, the small sample sizes combined with the fact that few countries have a complete set of regulation variables makes this impossible. We start with three of the most common measures of labour market performance: the unemployment rate in 1990, the change in the unemployment rate (the difference between the 1985–9 average and the 1960–4 average), and the percentage of the unemployed who are classed as long-term unemployed (defined as being unemployed for a year or more). As measures of labour market regulation, we use benefit duration and the replacement ratio as measures of the generosity of the social security system, trade union density and the collective bargaining coverage rate as measures of the bargaining power of workers, the minimum wage relative to the average wage as a measure of the strength of minimum wage legislation and the average job tenure and the Bertola index of job security as measures of the strength of employment protection legislation (note that low values of the Bertola index mean high employment protection).

If the conventional analysis of labour market regulation is correct, we would expect to find labour market performance to be negatively correlated with benefit duration, replacement ratios, trade union density, coverage, the minimum wage, job tenure and positively correlated with the Bertola index. Yet, when one looks at the results in table 13.1, the most striking thing is that it is very rare to find any significant relationship at all. Those relationships that are significant at the 10 per cent level or less are summarised in table 13.2. Consistent with the conventional analysis is the relationship between the change in unemployment between the 'golden age' years and the 1980s and the minimum wage and benefit duration, and between the proportion of long-term unemployed and the Bertola index and the minimum wage. But against this needs to be set the fact that the replacement ratio is negatively correlated with both the level and change in unemployment, and the same is true of the relationship between trade union density and the level of unemployment. There is simply no strong evidence for the conventional view that regulation is associated with poor unemployment performance.

There are also reasons why one should be cautious even in interpreting these regressions, at comparing unemployment rates across countries is fraught with dangers. The unemployment rates that are most commonly used in comparisons across countries are the standardised ones produced by the OECD which are based on a common definition and so, in theory,

Table 13.2 *Significant relationships between regulation and performance*

	Consistent with conventional view	Not consistent with conventional view
Unemployment rate		Trade union density Replacement ratio
Change in unemployment rate	Benefit duration Minimum wage	Replacement ratio
Proportion long-term unemployed	Bertola index Minimum wage coverage rate	
Non-employment rate	Benefit duration	Mean job tenure Replacement ratio Minimum wage
Change in non-employment rate	Benefit duration	Replacement ratio

should be comparable. The standardisation is based on the ILO definition which counts someone as unemployed if they are not currently doing any paid work, if they have looked for a job in the recent past and if they are ready to start work within a specified time period. The problem is that whether someone is classed as 'unemployed' on this definition is not likely to be invariant to the system of unemployment insurance. For example, potential recipients of unemployment benefit or income support in the UK are only eligible if they are actively looking for work and ready to start work, i.e. if they can be classed as unemployed on the ILO definition. On the other hand, in countries with less extensive welfare states or in countries which do not tie benefit provision to a similar condition, there is no incentive for someone without a job to have themselves classed as unemployed on the ILO definition.

This means that we would like to have some measure of the lack of work which is not sensitive to the institutional details of labour market regulation. In recent years, there has been increasing attention paid to rates of non-employment, i.e. to include those classed as inactive with those conventionally measured as unemployed. Traditionally, those people without a job but classed as inactive have not been seen as a cause for concern as it has been assumed that their classification as inactive means that they do not want a job. While this may be true for some of those classed as inactive (and there is good evidence that unemployment and inactivity are different states), there are very good reasons for thinking that this is not true of all those classed as inactive. For example, many countries (the USA, the UK, the Netherlands and possibly others) have seen a large increase in the number of workers classed as inactive because of sickness. In the UK, the numbers of men on Sickness and Invalidity Benefits have doubled from about 600,000 in 1979 to 1.4 million in 1992 (see chapter 11 in this volume). In addition around 450,000 have been added to those claiming Income Support but unable to search for work due to illness. It is simply incredible to think that an epidemic has been sweeping these countries making millions too sick to work. A more plausible explanation is the following. In many countries there are monetary incentives to be classed as sick rather than unemployed as benefit provision tends to be more generous for the sick, does not suffer time limitations and requirements to seek work are less onerous. On the other hand, those classified as sick may have less access to state employment agencies. Given a choice, individuals may choose sickness benefit, particularly at times when jobs are scarce and, as a result, they are classed as inactive. But there is a strong suspicion that these are people who would be in work if the labour market was more favourable.

So, at least some of the inactive should almost certainly be classed together with the unemployed as a source for concern about labour market performance, and certainly when one is concerned about the social distress and benefit dependence associated with the absence of available employment. But once one does this, countries that appear to be successful on one measure of labour market performance may no longer appear to be so successful on another. For example, consider the figures in OECD (1993). If we consider men aged 25–54 (for the reason that we think their attachment to the labour market should be very strong) the average of the unemployment rate over the 1980s for the USA is 5.2 per cent, which is slightly lower than the reported (unweighted) average over most OECD countries of 5.3 per cent. But once one looks at non-employment rates the USA no longer appears so attractive as its average non-employment rate of 12.1 per cent is above the reported average of 11.2 per cent. One should not make too much of this comparison as one should not simply judge labour market performance by what it provides for prime-aged men, as some countries have institutions which effectively protect this group at the expense of women and/or young workers. But it does illustrate the point that comparisons of labour market performance across countries can be sensitive to the measures used.

To investigate whether there is any evidence for this, the last two rows of table 13.1 present regressions of the male non-employment rate and its change against the measures of labour market regulation discussed above. The relationships that are significant at the 10 per cent level or less are presented in table 13.2. The correlation between benefit duration and non-employment remains consistent with the conventional view.

But the main change from the results obtained using the unemployment rate is that the minimum wage is now no longer associated with poor labour market performance; indeed, it is significantly negatively related to the non-employment rate. This is consistent with recent microeconomic work in the USA and UK on the effects of minimum wages on employment. Studies in the USA by Card (1992a, 1992b), Card and Krueger (1994) and Katz and Krueger (1992) and studies in the UK by Machin and Manning (1994a) and Dickens *et al.* (1994) have all found zero or positive effects of minimum wages on employment. Our findings in table 13.1 are consistent with the view that a minimum wage raises employment but also attracts more workers into the labour market, possible because the labour market is offering better opportunities.

3.3 'Experimental evidence': labour market de-regulation in the UK

Another way of considering whether de-regulation improves labour market performance is to closely examine the experience of countries that have shifted policy explicitly to follow this route. In the 1980s and 1990s, the UK is probably the clearest example. Since 1979, welfare benefits have been made much less generous. This has been achieved by removing the link with past wages (abolishing the Earnings Related Supplement, see chapter 12 in this volume) and pegging benefits to prices rather than wages. Hence, average replacement rates have fallen from around 25 per cent in the 1970s to around 18 per cent currently (OECD *Jobs Study*, 1994). Trade union power and membership has been reduced. Membership has fallen from around 13 million in 1979 to 9 million in 1993. Coverage of bargaining over wages has ceased for about 10 per cent of those in work and the wage mark-up has probably fallen marginally (see Metcalf, 1994, for details and other supporting information). Job security provisions have been reduced or abolished. The qualifying period for employment protection against unfair dismissal (except discrimination) has risen progressively from six months to two years (five years for part-time workers). Finally, minimum wages disappeared (save in agriculture) in 1993 when the Wages Councils which set industry minima were abolished. Prior to abolition, their influence had also been reduced through the 1980s (see Dickens *et al.*, 1993).

On wages, these policies have had the desired effect. The UK has seen the most rapid increase in wage inequality or any OECD nation over the last 15 years (see, for example, Schmitt, 1993 or Gregg and Machin, 1994). But despite the flexibility in relative wages which is all or more than many advocates of the policy wanted, the predicted reduction in unemployment that was supposed to be associated with this wage flexibility has not happened. Blanchflower and Freeman (1995) found that the annual entry rate into work for unemployed men fell from 46 per cent in 1979 to 32 per cent in 1990 at the top of the last upswing. For women these numbers were the same, at 43 per cent in both periods. Furthermore, large numbers of people, especially less educated men, have become inactive. These men (and a smaller number of women) are not even bothering to search for work but are accepting semi-enforced retirement or long-term sickness (see Schmitt and Wadsworth, 1993). Blanchflower and Freeman sum it up (p. 75):

> the observed outcomes raise the disheartening possibility that the reforms in fact brought the UK a mixture of the worst of two possible worlds: the massive wage inequality of the decentralised US labour market together with high and lengthy spells of unemployment, European-style.

4 Why might labour market de-regulation not always reduce unemployment?

We have argued so far that the empirical evidence for the benefits of labour market de-regulation in reducing unemployment is not as persuasive as is sometimes made out. The reason that it is regarded as persuasive by many economists is that they have a strong *a priori* belief that regulation increases unemployment. The source of this belief is that the models that most economists use to analyse regulation and unemployment assume that de-regulation will move labour markets towards the perfectly competitive ideal in which all individuals can get a job if they want it at a wage equal to the value of the output they produce (their marginal product). This is not to say that these economists believe that unregulated labour markets will be market-clearing; most probably believe that there will be some involuntary unemployment in completely de-regulated labour markets (perhaps because of efficiency wage considerations or frictions in market operation). But the analysis suggests that regulation moves the economy even further from market-clearing.

But even though many economists would not profess to believe in the perfectly competitive model, its pernicious influence implicitly pervades much analysis. A good example is the literature on the effects of unemployment benefits on unemployment durations (see Devine and Kiefer, 1990 or Atkinson and Micklewright, 1991, for a summary of this literature). Commonly cited in support of the view that increasing unemployment benefits will inevitably increase unemployment is micro-economic evidence that is predominantly cross-sectional in nature. This evidence shows that, other things being equal, individuals who have higher receipts of unemployment benefits have, on average, longer spells of unemployment than those individuals who receive lower benefits. Can we conclude from this evidence that raising the general level of benefits will raise unemployment? This is a reasonable conclusion if one thinks of the labour market as basically competitive, as one could then argue that the distribution of wages reflects the distribution of marginal products, that the productivity of a worker is (at least to a first approximation) unaffected by the level of unemployment benefits and hence raising benefits must reduce the gap between income in work and income out of work, and that this will tend to raise unemployment.

But if the labour market is not basically competitive, this type of reasoning does not necessarily hold. We will give two examples. First, suppose, for the sake of argument, that the number of jobs is fixed independent of the level of benefits and that the unemployed compete among themselves for those jobs. It is plausible to believe that those individuals with lower benefits will be more desperate to find work, so will compete harder to get a job and hence will tend to have shorter spells of unemployment, thus explaining the cross-sectional evidence. What this implies is that an individual's spell of unemployment will be influenced by their search intensity relative to the average which will itself be influenced by their level of benefits relative to the average level. The size of the effect of the average level of benefits on an individual's unemployment duration is of crucial importance in determining the effect on unemployment of a general increase in unemployment benefits, yet cannot be identified from cross-sectional evidence alone. The assumption that the labour market is perfectly competitive allows one to assume that the effect of average benefits is zero, but that is no more than an assumption.

For a second example, consider the following argument. The theoretical search and matching models used to justify the empirical analysis of the effects of benefits on unemployment durations is a model of a labour market with frictions in which workers cannot move instantaneously to a job that pays their marginal product. The implications of these models are generally only discussed from the point of view of the behaviour of workers. But if one considers their implications for the behaviour of firms, one realises that labour market frictions give employers some monopsony power in setting wages. We would expect firms to use this market power to pay wages that are below marginal products and are, in part, determined by the wage that workers are prepared to work for (their reservation wage), which will be influenced by unemployment benefits. If we raise unemployment benefits this will raise the reservation wages of workers, which will tend to lead to a rise in wages but this will not necessarily led to a reduction in employment as firms were paying wages below marginal products.

What this type of analysis would suggest is that it is important to avoid a situation in labour markets where there is considerable heterogeneity in reservation wages of workers with similar productivity. For example, the current system in the UK provides very little in the way of welfare support for young people and individuals with a working partner. This only encourages firms to create low-paying jobs with the aim of employing these workers in them, but this has the effect of making those jobs unattractive to, for example, middle-aged workers who have recently lost their jobs or those in families dependent on means-tested welfare benefits. There is evidence for the UK that the vacancies open to those not in work are now dominated by part-time and temporary jobs. Further, there is strong evidence that those not in work but who have a working partner are much more able to take these jobs than those with no partner (e.g. single parents) or those families where all adults are not in work. What is more, this distinction has worsened considerably since 1979. Thus, the incentives for the unemployed to take available work are poor, mainly because of the collapse of vacancies for full-time work (see Gregg and Wadsworth, 1994). Consequently, on all these criteria the labour market appears to be functioning less well than before.

The main argument that we would advance here is that the conventional analysis of the labour market makes the mistake of assuming that the only important deviation from perfect competition is the monopoly power possessed by some groups of workers. It completely ignores monopoly power on the other side of the labour market, i.e. that possessed by employers. We would argue that the monopsony power of employers is important and becomes more important the greater the degree of labour market de-regulation.

Theoretical developments have almost universally been aimed at assessing the sources of monopoly power of workers, i.e. why workers can maintain wages above market-clearing levels. Jobs are then seen as being in short supply and the constraint on employment in the economy is the supply of jobs by employers. So most policy analysis focuses exclusively on the need to increase the incentives to employers to hire labour, even if that means making jobs less attractive to workers. The elements of de-regulation described above are all aimed at reducing possible sources of monopoly power of workers, even if they raise the monopsony power of employers.

A good example of this bias is the analysis of severance costs. There is a voluminous literature on how the presence of firing costs that must be paid by the firm acts as a disincentive to the hiring of workers, and how workers (known as 'insiders') may be able to exploit these turnover costs to raise wages and hence further hinder job creation. Yet one will look in vain for a single analysis of the quitting cost imposed on workers in all countries which is the result of entitlement to welfare benefits being reduced or withdrawn if a worker leaves a job voluntarily (in a number of countries including the USA there is complete disqualification). We might expect these quitting costs to make workers more cautious in taking jobs and they might enable employers to reduce wages as workers find it costly to quit. Atkinson and Micklewright (1991) state that 8–10 per cent of new claimants in the UK are disqualified for this reason and the data in Murphy and Topel (1987) would suggest that a similar proportion in the USA could be affected, so the proportion of workers involved is not negligible.

Most economists probably think that one can ignore monopsony in thinking about labour markets and hence that there are good reasons for holding the view that 'only firms matter' for job creation. In labour economics textbooks, the case of monopsony is generally treated as being synonymous with the company town and hence extremely rare. But labour markets will be to some extent monopsonistic as long as the labour supply to a firm is not perfectly elastic, i.e. as long as a firm that cuts wages by an infinitesimal amount does not find that all their workers instantaneously disappear. It seems impossible to claim that monopsony does not exist in this sense. A second reason why many economists are extremely sceptical about the relevance of monopsony is that they think that most unemployment is involuntary and that this is inconsistent with monopsony models in which employment is supply-determined. But the existence of monopsony power and involuntary unemployment are not incompatible. Monopsony power will exist whenever the supply of labour to a firm is not perfectly elastic. Involuntary unemployment will occur whenever the supply of workers who want to work in the firm is greater than the number of workers that the firm is prepared to hire. It is perfectly possible to have both these conditions satisfied, as is shown in more formal models by Manning (1994, 1995).

The existence of monopsony power in the labour market suggests that it should be possible to raise wages through appropriate labour market regulation without necessarily jeopardising employment. But if one wants to argue that certain labour market regulation can raise employment, one needs to argue that the supply of labour to the market as a whole is not inelastic, i.e. that increases in the attractiveness of jobs cause more workers to participate, unemployed workers to search harder, or increase the incentives for workers to invest in human capital, or some combination of these. While it would be commonly agreed that the labour supply of women is elastic, the conventional view has been that the labour supply of prime-aged men is virtually inelastic and hence one cannot expect to reduce their unemployment rates by appropriate labour market regulation. But recent evidence suggests that this might not be the case.

For the case of the USA, Juhn *et al.* (1991) have argued that the rising unemployment (or non-employment) rates and declining real wages for the less skilled over the period 1967–90 can be interpreted as a move down a labour supply curve that is not inelastic. This interpretation is not without its problems as it is not clear that it can explain the movements of wages and employment over the period 1945–67 when real wages for this type of worker rose substantially but employment rates were approximately constant, but it does suggest that employment outcomes for this group of workers are determined as much by supply as by demand. Of course, the authors interpret the demand curve facing these workers as being a competitive one, but if it came from a monopsonistic labour market one could then raise employment by appropriate labour market regulation.

To the extent that this is recognised in conventional thinking it is normally put in terms of the reservation wages of these workers being high in relation to the wages in the jobs open to them. In the conventional analysis of this situation, the reservation wage is thought to be strongly (if not exclusively) influenced by the level of welfare benefits and the wage available by their marginal product so that it is labour market regulation itself that is seen as making the supply curve elastic. The conclusion drawn is that to reduce unemployment for this group one needs to reduce their benefits or (perhaps more kindly) increase their marginal product through training programmes. A policy like a minimum wage can only price these workers out of jobs. But as Juhn *et al.* (1991) and Topel (1993) emphasise, most of these workers receive very little in the way of benefits (they rely instead on savings, loans, friends and families) so that one cannot really blame welfare systems for making the supply curve elastic.

The view that there are important frictions in the labour market and that this gives firms potential monopsony power seems very reasonable.

But the frictions which make job mobility costly for workers also tend to make it costly for firms to replace workers. This means that there are important elements of bilateral monopoly in the relationship between employer and worker. Monopsony will only be the outcome if the firm has unilateral power to set wages: one could argue that this is not the case, i.e. that workers are able to exercise their potential bargaining power even in de-regulated labour markets so that it is not *a priori* obvious that wages will be too low in these markets. We would not want to deny that some workers do manage to exploit the bargaining power that labour market frictions give to them. But we would argue that the ability of workers to do this is greater where that person has scarce skills, firm-specific information or their effort and cooperation are important to the functioning of the firm. Then the more educated, skilled and senior in the firm's hierarchy the person is, then the more individual power they possess. But these are not the workers on whom unemployment is concentrated, and we would argue that in de-regulated markets for unskilled labour it is a very close approximation to the truth to say that employers set wages: it is simply not accurate to think of workers in fast food restaurants and supermarkets as having substantial power to negotiate their wages. We would provide two pieces of casual evidence for the view that employers set wages in unregulated unskilled labour markets. First, we are all familiar with advertisements for job vacancies which provide information on the wage to be paid: any potential worker has obviously had no say in determining this wage. Yet we never see advertisements from unemployed workers advertising their labour at a fixed wage to potential employers. And the study of Machin and Manning (1994b) of the unregulated market for labour in UK residential homes for the elderly found that there is incredibly little wage dispersion within firms, with a third of firms having no wage dispersion at all. This simply could not be the outcome of bargaining of the employer with workers who are heterogeneous.

As legal regulation of minimum standards and most union organisation is about protecting or supporting the position of the economically vulnerable not reinforcing the position of the powerful groups (although there are exceptions), we would expect such regulation to be protecting groups which would otherwise have no bargaining power. The agenda of de-regulation outlined earlier in this chapter undermines the position of the weak but makes no assault on the sources of the bargaining power of more privileged workers. As such, it will serve to raise inequality in society, but not efficiency. Indeed, one often gets the impression that the only important aspects of monopoly power are among the disadvantaged. The popular 'insider–outsider' model with its assumptions that replacement of workers is costly and workers set wages seems most appropriate to the analysis of managerial labour markets, but is more commonly used to analyse unskilled labour markets.

So far, we have argued that de-regulated labour markets are not likely to be efficient. If one takes a historical view, one should not be surprised at this conclusion. The de-regulated labour markets of, say, late Victorian London, were not thought of by contemporaries as models of efficiency (although, disturbingly, they seem to satisfy many of the criteria laid down for a well functioning labour market by many modern commentators), and the origins of labour market regulation lay in widespread dissatisfaction with the operation of these labour markets. They were felt to provide only short-term menial jobs at low wages which gave workers little or no incentive to acquire skills and encouraged the entry of bad employers. However, one should not conclude from this that all labour market regulation (including the seemingly very restrictive job security provisions of some Southern European countries today) will lead to an improvement in labour market performance. Rather it is that there is some optimal level and form of regulation which strengthens the position of workers in the labour market. It is obviously of crucial importance to say something more precise about what this form may be. Doing this is made rather difficult because extraordinarily little attention has been paid by economists to this possibility and so there is little existing work to cite on the subject. So, we are unable to go much beyond suggesting some broad principles.

5 The optimal amount and form of labour market regulation

Let us start by considering a variety of existing models to consider what they say about the optimal amount of power that workers should have in wage-setting. For the moment, we will equate labour market regulation with policies to strengthen the power of labour relative to employers, although later we will try to take a more discriminating approach as different types of labour market regulation will generally have different effects. We assume (which, as we have argued above, seems reasonable for the labour market for less skilled workers) that, in an unregulated labour market, it is employers who set wages and workers have no bargaining power.

In the matching model of Pissarides (1990) it is the respective importance of unemployed workers and vacant jobs in determining the number of matches that determines the optimal amount of bargaining power that workers should have. In the simplest version of this model, which assumes a perfectly elastic supply of jobs and a totally inelastic supply of workers to the market, fixed search intensity and no investments in human capital, increases in worker bargaining power always increase unemployment although it is possible that unemployment can be inefficiently low (in this case the labour market is filled up with too many low-quality jobs which one can think of as a casual labour market). But in versions of the model where worker search intensity is a choice variable unemployment may not be monotonically related to worker bargaining power. In this framework, the view that all labour market de-regulation is good is (crudely) consistent with the view that only the behaviour of firms matters for job creation. However, there is no empirical evidence for this position; estimates of matching functions suggest that it is not just vacancies alone that determine the outflows from unemployment (see Blanchard and Diamond, 1990, for the USA and Pissarides, 1986, for the UK).

In the model of Lockwood (1986) the model of Pissarides is generalised to allow for (exogenously given) variation in worker quality. In this case, it is optimal to give workers all the bargaining power, as if firms extract any share of the rents they have a private incentive to try to find a high-quality worker, an activity that is socially wasteful. The model of Acemoglu (1994) modifies the matching model to allow both workers and firms to make investments in human and physical capital. Crudely, the efficient level of worker bargaining power is determined by the relative sensitivity of these investments to the expected rewards. In the models of Albrecht and Axell (1984) and Burdett and Mortensen (1989), which assume an inelastic supply of firms and an elastic supply of workers, it is optimal to give all the bargaining power to workers. Eckstein and Wolpin (1990) relax the assumption that jobs are inelastically supplied and find that the optimal power of labour is lower.

One could add almost endlessly to this list of studies. The important point is that the optimal bargaining power of workers in search and matching models is not zero, so that complete labour market de-regulation should not be expected to lead to efficiency. One might wonder whether any general principles emerge about the factors that are likely to determine the optimal amount of labour market regulation. Generally, increasing wages will increase the incentives of workers to undertake activities like job search, investment in human capital and make them more likely to accept jobs. On the other hand, it reduces incentives for firms to engage in recruitment, investment and makes them more wary in hiring workers. The optimal amount of labour market regulation will be higher the more important are the actions of workers relative to the actions of firms in determining labour market outcomes and the more sensitive are those actions to economic incentives.

This says nothing about the form that labour market regulation should take, as the different forms of intervention that we have discussed are likely to have different effects. For example, we would expect both the payment of unemployment benefits and minimum wages to raise wages for those in work, but they have opposite effects on the incentives of the unemployed to seek work which we would expect to be greater with minimum wages. On the other hand, minimum wages may be hard to enforce, while raising wages by universally raising welfare payments may be more self-enforcing, as no individual will have an incentive to work for low wages. On the other hand, benefits are often paid at very different rates to different groups which also have important consequences. We would also expect trade unions to have similar effects to minimum wages as they raise wages without reducing incentives for the unemployed to seek work and collective bargaining has the advantage that the negotiated wage can take into account local circumstances in a way which it is difficult for minimum wages to do. However, it may be very difficult to establish effective trade union organisation in some sectors so that some form of minimum wage legislation would be needed.

So the appropriate form of regulation is likely to depend on the particular circumstances of the labour market. Each aspect of regulation will have limits beyond which it no longer serves to counter monopsonistic power, and all policy needs to be geared to understanding these limits and how policy design can minimise any other costs. But equally there is a regulation agenda that can be used to limit the monopolistic power of elite workers, which limits the availability of such jobs and intensifies job competition in other sectors of the labour market. Controls which shareholders can use to control company directors are one obvious area, as is opening up professional closed shops in areas such as accountancy, the legal professions, etc. If skills are a source of limiting monopsony power then avoiding the presence of a large pool of low-skilled people with limited education again may help.

6 Conclusion

Because of their upbringing, in which perfectly competitive models are given exaggerated emphasis, economists are too easily persuaded that labour market regulation reduces the efficient workings of labour markets and can only be justified on equity grounds. What is staggering is that only sources of inefficiency which give market power to workers have received serious analysis. This strong *a priori* belief colours the reading and interpretation of empirical evidence and leads to one-sided policy analysis that emphasises only the need to increase the incentives for employers to hire workers while neglecting the need to make these jobs attractive to workers (except in so far as welfare benefits are thought to reduce the incentives to work). We have argued that totally deregulated labour markets are not likely to be efficient, primarily because they are likely to be monopsonistic in nature for those groups of workers who are most prone to unemployment. These workers are those who benefit most from such regulation. We believe that one can make a perfectly respectable economic case that some degree of labour market regulation is necessary for an efficient labour market. Working out the amount and form that this regulation should take then obviously becomes a crucial matter for economic research, but it is an issue that barely makes an appearance in most policy analyses at present.

Data appendix

Netherlands	Change in average unemployment rate: 1960/4–1985–9	Unemployment rate: 1990	Average unemployment rate: 1985–91	Percentage of unemployment with duration > 1 year	Male non-employment rate: 1992	Change in male non-employment rate: 1973–92
Australia	5.4	6.9	7.7	21.6	15.9	11.8
Austria	1.5	3.2	3.4	na	na	na
Belgium	7.8	7.2	8.3	69.9	na	na
Canada	2.3	8.1	8.9	5.7	18.1	10.2
Denmark	7.1	8.3	7.2	33.7	13.2	na
Finland	3.3	3.4	4.9	6.9	na	na
France	8.8	8.9	9.8	38.3	11.5	7.3
Germany	5.9	4.8	5.8	48.3	13.1	8.5
Greece	na	na	7.4	na	na	na
Italy	6.8	10.3	10.4	71.2	14.2	6.6
Japan	1.3	2.1	2.5	19.1	3.8	0.5
Netherlands	8.4	7.5	8.9	48.4	10.5	3.2
New Zealand	4.8	7.7	6.5	na	15	na
Norway	1.2	5.2	4.5	19.2	13.7	5.0
Spain	na	na	18.6	na	na	na
Sweden	0.6	1.5	2.1	4.8	12.2	6.6
UK	7.9	6.8	9.1	36	18.7	12.2
USA	0.5	5.4	6.1	5.6	13.8	5.4

Note: na Data not available.
Sources: Unemployment rates (levels and changes), non-employment rate (levels and changes), long-term employment: OECD, *Labour Force Statistics* (1971–1991); OECD, *Employment outlook*.

	Median job tenure: 1991	Bertola index (job security)	Trade union density	Trade union coverage	Max. benefit duration (months)	Initial replacement ratio: 1988	Min. wage as percentage of av. wage
Australia	3.5	na	40	80	Indef	43	35
Austria	na	na	46	98	Indef	41	na
Belgium	na	2	51	90	Indef	60	66
Canada	4.1	na	36	38	Indef	37	na
Denmark	na	9	na	na	Indef	35	69
Finland	5.2	na	72	95	Indef	26	na
France	7.5	3	10	92	Indef	26	61
Germany	7.5	5	32	90	Indef	52	69
Greece	na	na	na	na	na	50	na
Italy	na	1	na	na	6	15	50
Japan	8.5	6	25	23	6.9	48	na
Netherlands	3.1	8	26	71	36	70	72
New Zealand	na	na	45	67	Indef	40	na
Norway	6.5	na	56	75	18.5	62	na
Spain	na	na	na	na	na	50	na
Sweden	na	4	83	83	13.8	90	na
UK	4.4	7	39	47	Indef	26	52
USA	3	10	16	18	4.6	50	33

Notes: na Data not available. Indef Benefits are of potentially unlimited duration.
Sources: Median job tenure: OECD, *Employment outlook* (1989, 1992, 1993).
Job security provision: Bertola (1990).
Trade union density and coverage: OECD.
Replacement ratio and benefit duration: OECD.
Minimum wage: Freeman (1994).

NOTE

1 This is something of an ugly term, as not all the 'interferences' in the labour market that we will consider are naturally thought of as regulation, e.g. trade unions may emerge spontaneously without any government intervention. But it is very convenient to have a single term to describe a package of policies, and the term we use is quite common.

REFERENCES

Acemoglu, D., 1994. 'Search in the labour market, incomplete contracts and growth', Cambridge, MA: MIT, unpublished

Albrecht, J. and B. Axell, 1984. 'An equilibrium model of search unemployment', *Journal of Political Economy*, **92**, 824–40

Atkinson, A.B. and J. Micklewright, 1991. 'Unemployment compensation and labour market transitions: a critical review', *Journal of Economic Literature*, **29**, 1679–1727

Bean, C.R., 1994. 'European unemployment: a survey', *Journal of Economic Literature*, **32**, 573–619

Berman, E., J. Bound and Z. Griliches, 1994. 'Changes in the demand for skilled labor within US manufacturing industries: evidence from the Annual Survey of Manufacturing', *Quarterly Journal of Economics*, **109**, 367–97

Bertola, G., 1990. 'Job security, employment and wages', *European Economic Review*, **34**, 851–86

Blanchard, O., 1990. 'Unemployment: getting the questions right – and some of the answers', in J. Drèze and C. Bean (eds.), *Europe's Unemployment Problem*, Cambridge, MA: MIT Press

Blanchard, O. and P. Diamond, 1990. 'The aggregate matching function', in P. Diamond (ed.), *Growth, Productivity, Unemployment*, Cambridge, MA: MIT Press

Blanchard, O. and L. Summers, 1986. 'Hysteresis and the European unemployment problem', in S. Fischer (ed.), *NBER Economics Annual*, **1**, Cambridge, MA: MIT Press, 15–77

Blanchflower, D. and R. Freeman, 1993. 'Did the Thatcher reforms change British labour market performance?' in R. Barrell (ed.), *The UK Labour Market: Comparative Aspects and Institutional Developments*, Cambridge: Cambridge University Press

Burda, M., 1988. 'Wait unemployment in Europe', *Economic Policy*, **7**, 391–416

Burdett, K. and D.T. Mortensen, 1989. 'Equilibrium wage differentials and employer size', University of Essex, unpublished

Calmfors, L. and J. Driffill, 1988. 'Centralization of wage bargaining and macroeconomic performance', *Economic Policy*, **6**, 13–61

Card, D., 1992. 'Using regional variations in wages to measure the effects of the federal minimum wage', *Industrial and Labor Relations Review*, **46**, 22–37

1992b. 'Do minimum wages reduce employment? A case study of California, 1987–89', *Industrial and Labor Relations Review*, **46**, 38–54

Card, D. and A. Krueger, 1994. 'Minimum wages and employment: a case study of the fast food industry in New Jersey and Pennsylvania', *American Economic Review*, **84**, 772–93

Devine, T. and N. Kiefer, 1990. *Empirical Labor Economics: The Search Approach*, Ithaca: Cornell University Press

Dickens, R., S. Machin and A. Manning, 1993. 'The effect of the Wages Councils on employment', London School of Economics, unpublished

Eckstein, Z. and K. Wolpin, 1990. 'Estimating a market equilibrium search model from panel data on individuals', *Econometrica*, **58**, 783–808

Freeman, R., 1994. 'Minimum wages again!', *International Journal of Manpower*, **2**, 1–19

Gregg, P. and S. Machin, 1993. 'Is the rise in UK inequality different?', in R. Barrell (ed.), *The UK Labour Market: Comparative Aspects and Institutional Developments*, Cambridge: Cambridge University Press

Gregg, P. and J. Wadsworth, 1994. 'More work in fewer households?', NIESR, for the Joseph Rowntree Trust, mimeo

Juhn, C., K. Murphy and R. Topel, 1991. 'Why has the natural rate of unemployment increased over time?', *Brookings Papers on Economic Activity*, **2**, 75–142

Katz, L. and A. Krueger, 1992. 'The effect of the minimum wage in the fast food industry', *Industrial and Labor Relations Review*, **46**, 6–21

Katz, L. and K. Murphy, 1992. 'Changes in relative wages, 1963–1987: supply and demand factors', *Quarterly Journal of Economics*, **107**, 35–78

Layard, P.R.G., S.J. Nickell and R.A. Jackman, 1991. *Unemployment: Macroeconomic Performance and the Labour Market*, Oxford: Oxford University Press

Lazear, E., 1990. 'Job security provisions and employment', *Quarterly Journal of Economics*, **55**, 699–726

Lindbeck, A. and D.J. Snower, 1989. *The Insider–Outsider Theory of Employment and Unemployment*, Cambridge, MA: MIT Press

Lockwood, B., 1986. 'Transferable skills, job matching and the inefficiency of the "natural" rate of unemployment', *Economic Journal*, **96**, 961–74

Machin, S. and A. Manning, 1994. 'Minimum wages, wage dispersion and employment: evidence from UK Wages Councils', *Industrial and Labor Relations Review*, **47**, 319–29

1994b. 'The structure of wages in what should be a competitive labour market', London School of Economics, unpublished

Manning, A., 1991. 'Productivity growth, wage-setting and the equilibrium rate of unemployment', *Discussion Paper*, London School of Economics, Centre for Economic Performance

1994. 'Labour markets with company wage policies', London School of Economics, unpublished

1995. 'How do we know that real wages are too high?', *Quarterly Journal of Economics*, **60**

Manning, A., J. Wadsworth and D. Wilkinson, 1994. 'Making your mind up: mismatch in Britain', London School of Economics, unpublished

Metcalf, D., 1994. 'Transformation of British industrial relations?', in R. Barrell (ed.), *The UK Labour Market: Comparative Aspects and Institutional Developments*, Cambridge: Cambridge University Press

Minford, P. and J. Riley, 1994. 'The UK labour market: micro rigidities and macro obstacles', in R. Barrell (ed.), *The UK Labour Market: Comparative Aspects and Institutional Developments*, Cambridge: Cambridge University Press

Murphy, K. and R. Topel, 1987. 'The evolution of unemployment in the United States', *NBER Macroeconomic Annual 1987*, 11–57
Murphy, K. and F. Welch, 1993. 'Industrial change and the rising importance of skill', in S. Danziger and P. Gottschalk (eds.), *Uneven Tides: Rising Inequality in America*, New York: Russell Sage
OECD, 1989, 'Educational attainment of the labor force', *Employment Outlook*, Paris: OECD
1991. 'Unemployment benefit rules and labour market policy', *Employment Outlook*, , chapter 7, Paris: OECD
1993. *Employment Outlook*, , Paris: OECD
1994. *The OECD Jobs Study: Facts, Analysis, Strategies*, Paris: OECD
Phelps, E.S., 1994. *Structural Slumps: The Modern Equilibrium theory of Employment, Interest, and Assets*, Cambridge, MA: Harvard University Press
Pissarides, C., 1986. 'Unemployment and vacancies in Britain', *Economic Policy*, **3**, 499–559
1990. *Equilibrium Employment Theory*, Oxford: Basil Blackwell
Schmitt, J., 1993. 'The changing structure of male earnings in Britain, 1974–1988', *Discussion Paper*, London School of Economics, Centre for Economic Performance, **122** (March)
Schmitt, J. and J. Wadsworth, 1993. 'Why are two million men in Britain inactive?', London School of Economics, unpublished
Topel, R., 1993. 'What have we learned from empirical studies of unemployment and turnover?', *American Economic Review, Papers and Proceedings*, **83**, 110–15

Discussion

JUAN J. R. CALAZA

Gregg and Manning's chapter 13 runs contrary to the current intellectual fashion in economics which considers that labour market rigidity is largely responsible for the high level of unemployment seen at present in the majority of OECD countries. In other words, economists belonging to the dominant stream of thinking state that by decreasing labour market rigidity, unemployment will decrease as well.

Gregg and Manning's central message can be summarised in a few points: (i) perfect competition does not exist in the labour market and therefore the monopsony power of firms and 'aristocracy workers' ought to be compensated by an equivalent level of bargaining power of unskilled workers; (ii) to minimise unemployment one must adopt an optimal level of regulation; (iii) zero regulation does not necessarily result in zero unemployment. Personally, I believe that Gregg and Manning are right.

In the analytical framework of de-regulation, the labour market is considered to be more important than the goods and services markets in combating the unemployment problem. In Europe, this approach has been criticised several times by Blanchard, Drèze, Malinvaud, Morishima and Pasinetti, among others. Economists who start with the hypothesis that the goods and services markets are in equilibrium whilst the labour market is unbalanced, underestimate, to a certain extent, real interest rates, production capacity and demand, and will therefore naturally tend to focus their attention on the labour market, neglecting the others.

Even if it is no longer fashionable to blame a shortfall in aggregated demand for a high level of unemployment in OECD countries, one cannot forget that only countries that have a sustained demand on every front – foreign trade, accumulation of capital, household consumption – as Japan has, are able to attain and to maintain full employment. Certainly, as Pasinetti has suggested, Keynesian measures are not enough to counter-balance the problems of structural change. However, the over-estimated importance accorded to the labour market creates a bias in favour of certain economic policies which privilege firms rather than workers, even if these measures are taken with the aim of favouring the latter. This bias would be neither ethically nor economically dangerous if the result aimed for was achieved by drastically reducing unskilled unemployment. Personally, I doubt whether this would be the case for one elementary reason: a firm's goal is not to create employment but to obtain profits. Indeed, firms do not make profits by hiring the workforce but by producing goods and services. Thus, the goods and services markets logically dominate the labour market in order to create employment, even if the satisfactory functioning of the latter is a necessary condition for full employment.

Due to a number of facts supporting the argument that cyclical unemployment affects unskilled workers more than skilled ones, some economists (namely, labour economists) have taken advantage of this to reject macroeconomic theory as an analytical device in order to reduce unemployment. According to them, if one considers that the unemployment of less productive workers should be dealt with independently of global unemployment one is tacitly accepting that there is a discontinuity in the aggregated labour demand curve. This is so because macroeconomic variables such as the average wage, interest rates or overall demand for goods would have a negligible impact on the demand for unskilled workers. Therefore, following the approach of the labour economists – who for the moment seem to be gaining the upper hand over macroeconomists – only a flexible and fluid labour market can resolve the problems of structural change in the composition or employment. Furthermore, according to the OECD, as the workforce is very heterogeneous, wage variance has an important influence on the overall performance of the labour market. As a result, job perspectives for the young and the unskilled depend to a large extent on their relative wages, which in turn depend on the free movement of market forces. In spite of what certain analysts would have us believe, it cannot be taken for granted that wages are generally too high in Europe. There is no doubt that some wages may be too high with regard to productivity and, in that case, it would be advisable to reduce them, but only on condition that the overall macroeconomic wage is not affected. Otherwise, its repercussion on the demand for goods and services would prove disastrous for the general level of employment.

The crucial point is that one must not deny the importance of a microeconomic solution to unemployment – that is to say, an approach in which the different labour markets have a role to play via wage differentials – nor of the major macroeconomic role of the average wage. This is the reason why the focus of attack in the battle against unemployment of unskilled workers is shifting. Some labour economists accept that it is not the average wage that is called into question but only the wage of less-qualified labour, whose level remains inflexible due to the barrier of the minimum wage. Besides, the unskilled workers are the hardest hit by the competition threat posed by low-wage countries where labour is far less expensive.

In reality, the structural substitution of skilled workers for unskilled ones has many different explanations. However, I do not think that labour costs are the relevant cause. With regard to the industrial activity involved in international trade, labour is replaced by capital. The reasons for this are more technical than financial as the reliability and homogenisation of production is increased. For the past 10 years, labour costs in France have risen at a slower rate than capital costs. But this does not prevent machinery from replacing labour at an ever-increasing pace. Hence, as in some European countries the economic cycle are assymetric – the unskilled work destroyed during a slowdown is not compensated for by new creations when economic activity recovers – to increase the ability of employers to fire would be an additional cause of unemployment.

From another point of view, the freezing or eventual reduction of the minimum wage in order to reduce unemployment requires discussion. In France, experience exists on such things as monthly grants for the hiring of young people or certain types of contracts which may be concluded below the minimum wage. None of these attempts has resulted in a significant rise in the employment of the categories targeted. Where there has been employment it often has an evictionary effect, the less expensive job replacing the usual more costly jobs, instead of adding to them. The reduction in labour costs thus serves to improve the 'bottom line' of firms and not to increase employment or reduce prices. There are firms which receive subsidies for jobs which they would have created anyway. Or, when aid mechanisms are concentrated on certain groups, the beneficiaries may replace other workers. In France, numerous studies allow us to estimate that only 20 per cent–40 per cent of the subsidised jobs created are effective supplementary posts. In other words, the subsidy of five jobs is only certain to cause the creation of one effective new post: active labour market expenditure has only a limited effect as a spur to action. The defence of de-regulation and the use of *active* labour market expenditure instead of *passive* benefit provision often serves to mask the main problem: that of the reduction of the working week. In France, in 1993, the total cost of active measures, such as unemployment subsidy of hiring and professional training was 140 billion francs. But what was the impact of such *active* spending? According to the INSEE the actual creation of jobs in the private sector was 213,000 of which one must remove 58,000 posts due to the displacement effect and 108,000 by way of the windfall and deadweight effects. In consequence, the net effect was the creation of only 47,000 jobs.

I do not know whether Gregg and Manning share the preceding analysis but in any case they seem to have arrived at the same conclusions, namely that firms have a myopic macroeconomic approach to the problem and are unable by themselves to radically reduce unemployment of unskilled workers if one assumes the globalisation of the world economy. For instance, after the de-regulation of the monetary and financial markets, a causal relationship between profits and employment cannot be taken for granted. It is uncertain whether the profits obtained by the decrease in salaries would create new jobs as a result of new investments in Europe, in the same way as a cut in wages would not encourage demand by way of a reduction in prices. In fact, the possibility of investing profits in financial markets outside Europe offering high returns, today competes strongly with our own productive investment. For this and other reasons, the microeconomic hypothesis which assumes a clear negative correlation between employment and wage costs has an incomplete validity in the macroeconomic framework, as Malinvaud and Pasinetti have stressed many times.

In a different perspective where economies of scale are important, from a single firm's point of view the distribution of gains among its 'labour aristocracy' – the insiders, in modern parlance – may be more advantageous than the spreading of profits among all the impersonal consumers. Furthermore, Yash P. Mehra has shown, by the use of cointegration techniques, that wage and price series containing stochastic elements are related by way of Granger-causality, running from the *rate of change in prices to the rate of change in wages, but not vice versa, as suggested by the price mark-up view*. Thus, if these findings prove to be robust enough one may conclude that by fighting oligopolistic practice in the goods and services markets, wages will be contained as well. Now the conclusion is straightforward, as Gregg and Manning point out: *a regulation agenda can be used to limit the monopolistic power of elite workers*. Indeed by limiting the oligopolistic power of firms in the goods and services markets – an urgent measure that must be undertaken in Spain – low wages will have a stronger purchasing power, thereby decreasing eventual subsidies or compensations aimed at maintaining the Rawlsian standard of living in relation to the self-esteem of unskilled workers. That is to say, the success of the regulation measure in the labour market are conditioned – at least in part – by the fight against oligopolies in the goods and services markets, otherwise low wages would serve as a subsidy for the skilled workers coming from the unskilled workers.

The American case is often shown as a paradigmatic example of a good functioning of the labour market which enables the creation of many more jobs than in Europe. Nevertheless, things are not as simple as that. One cannot consider the US labour market for unskilled workers as representative of a capitalist economy but rather a 'servant' one. In a capitalist economy, production factors, namely capital and labour, are considered to be scarce. When a production factor has a price approaching zero it is thought to be a free disposal one. Labour has never been a free disposal factor in a mature economy but rather in systems where servitude is extended. The assumption made by Gregg and Manning which presumes that the monopoly power possessed by employers becomes more important the greater the degree of labour market de-regulation is confirmed in the USA. In the unskilled labour market, firms are easily able to impose monopsonistic wages, as those willing to work often do not even speak English. Even if 'firms' are very small – for example, a household demanding domestic services – they are strong enough to impose their conditions. Wages are so low that many of the young prefer to turn to crime rather than work. There are 1 million people in US prisons, in France the figure is twenty times less for a population only five times less, and the forecast for the next four years leads us to expect that prison population in the USA will double.

Certainly, social security systems may reduce the incentive to find or keep jobs, as relative wages which are too low do not stimulate some to search for a job, rather push them into crime. What may we conclude? In general, the question is in what manner *activity* levels (the employment–population ratio) are related to unemployment. At a first glance, in those countries where the activity level is very high (i.e. Switzerland, Japan, the USA) the unemployment rate is low compared with countries (i.e. France, Italy, Spain) where the activity level is low. Notwithstanding the most serious problem lies in the fact that European firms have adapted to unemployment and a large number of them benefit from it. The wage discipline imposed by a high level of unemployment allows firms to reduce labour costs without having to reduce prices: firms see their profits rise by the reduction of employment. This is why an article in the *New York Herald Tribune* (February 4–5) was called, not without irony, 'Markets gain on jobless rise'. It is this same logic which dictates that when the level of unemployment goes down, certain European central banks raise interest rates in order to avoid an eventual acceleration in inflation as result of increased demand for goods and services. For all these reasons I believe that Gregg and Manning's chapter, in attracting our attention to the dangers of indiscriminate de-regulation is to be warmly welcomed.

REFERENCES

Blanchard, O. *et al.*, 1994 *Pour l'Emploi et la Cohesion Sociale*, Paris: OECD

Drèze, J., 1995. *Pour l'Emploi et la Croissance en Europe*, Paris: de Boeck Editions

Malinvaud, E., 1994. *Diagnosing Unemployment*, Cambridge: Cambridge University Press

Mehra, Y.P., 1994. 'Wage growth and the inflation process: an empirical approach', in B. Bhaskara Rao (ed.), *Cointegration*, New York: St Martin's Press

Morishima, M., 1992. *Capital and Credit*, Cambridge: Cambridge University Press

Pasinetti, L.L., 1981. *Structural Change and Economic Growth*, Cambridge: Cambridge University Press

1993. *Structural Economic Dynamics*, Cambridge: Cambridge University Press

Part Five

Policy, job reallocation and the unemployment–productivity relation

14 Is there a trade-off between unemployment and productivity growth?

ROBERT J. GORDON

1 Introduction

1.1 *The transatlantic divide*

Over the past decade there has been a steady divergence in the interests of European and American macro and labour economists. Persistently high unemployment in Europe has held centre stage in the concerns of Europeans, and little consensus has emerged regarding the share of blame to be attributed to cyclical or structural factors, nor on the particular mix of structural factors to be held responsible. In the USA, by contrast, there is near total agreement that fluctuations in unemployment have been cyclical in nature, and that the underlying 'Non-Accelerating Inflation Rate of Unemployment' (NAIRU) has changed little over the past two decades. Since there are few puzzles in the behaviour of unemployment, American economists have increasingly shifted their emphasis toward the view that the central problems of the US economy are (i) slow growth in productivity and in real wages, and (ii) an increasing dispersion of the income distribution that has resulted in an absolute decline in real wages for workers below the 20th or even the 50th percentile (depending on the exact measure used).

This chapter explores the hypothesis that the divergence of emphasis across the Atlantic is misplaced, and that the apparently separate problems of high unemployment in Europe and low productivity growth in America may be interrelated. Is there a trade-off between low unemployment and high productivity growth? If so, what factors have caused Europe and America to move to different positions on the unemployment–productivity trade-off (UPT) schedule? What events and policies can cause this schedule to shift in a favourable or unfavourable direction? Are there policies that Europe could adopt that would reduce structural unemployment without eroding its advantage over the USA of faster productivity growth? In parallel, could the USA adopt policies that would boost productivity growth without creating extra structural unemployment?

Not only is there a transatlantic divide in the interests of European and American economists, but there is also an asymmetry in the degree to which they look to the other side of the Atlantic for solutions. While American economists have devoted little attention to European practices and institutions as providing lessons for the United States, in contrast many Europeans have pointed to the 'flexibility' of the US labour market as a likely source of the lower unemployment rate in the USA than in Europe, and as providing a desirable model for European reforms. However, the fact that buoyant US employment growth has been accompanied by growing income inequality has more recently caused European economists to draw back from unqualified admiration of US labour market institutions.[1] In Europe at present there is an active search for policies that might reduce unemployment without having adverse side-effects on productivity or the income distribution – these are policies that we shall describe as shifting the UPT schedule in a favourable direction.

1.2 Contribution of this chapter

This chapter provides a new perspective on alternative policies designed to reduce European unemployment. It introduces the idea of the UPT schedule and distinguishes between policies that move a country along a given schedule and those that shift the schedule. The productivity impact of alternative anti-unemployment policies therefore becomes a criterion, little discussed previously, for choosing among these policies. However, the chapter shows how misleading is the facile contrast of Europe following a path of high productivity growth, high unemployment, and relatively greater income equality, in contrast to the opposite path being pursued by the USA. Many structural shocks that initially create a positive trade-off between productivity and unemployment set in motion a dynamic path of adjustment involving capital accumulation or decumulation that in principle can eliminate the trade-off.

2 Basic analytics

Our theoretical discussion begins by setting out the UPT schedule. We then provide an interpretation of this schedule in terms of the standard labour market model so often used to analyse the persistence of European unemployment. That model then helps us to distinguish between factors that cause movements along the UPT schedule and those factors that cause the UPT schedule to shift its position.

2.1 *The UPT schedule*

The UPT schedule can be drawn in terms of levels or changes. Figure 14.1 illustrates the version expressed in terms of changes, plotting the change in output per hour on the vertical axis against the change in the unemployment rate on the horizontal axis. The 'change' version of the UPT schedule is intended to focus on developments over the length of one business cycle or longer, e.g. causes of changes in the unemployment rate over the 15-year period between 1979 and 1994. The point labelled 'USA' is plotted at zero on the horizontal axis, reflecting the fact that the USA had no change in its unemployment rate between 1979 and 1994, while the point labelled 'Europe' is plotted further to the right, reflecting the fact that the unemployment rate for the EC/EU more than doubled, from 5.7 per cent in 1979 to 11.8 per cent in 1994. In the vertical direction the change in productivity for Europe is greater than for the USA.

Why do we focus on the change version of the UPT schedule rather than the level? By most measures the *level* of labour productivity is still higher in the USA than in Europe, and so a plot of the level of productivity versus the level of unemployment for the USA and Europe would have a negative slope. The high level of productivity in the USA is assumed to reflect historical factors dating back before 1960, whereas we want to examine the consequences of more recent changes in structure and in policies on the evolution of productivity and the unemployment rate. The change version of the UPT schedule allows us to 'factor out' contributions to the high level of US productivity that predate the period of interest.

It is important to note that the vertical axis of the UPT diagram refers to the change in output per hour, not the change in multifactor productivity (hereafter MFP, that is output relative to both labour and capital inputs, not just labour input). We can establish some basic relationships starting with the definition that labour's income share (S) is equal to the real wage (W/P) divided by output per hour (Q/H). Using lower-case letters for logs, this definition implies that the growth rate of the real wage is equal to the growth rate of productivity plus the growth rate of labour's share:

$$(\Delta w - \Delta p) = (\Delta q - \Delta h) + \Delta s. \tag{1}$$

Using the same notation as in (1), and designating the change (or growth rate) of MFP as Δa, the growth rate of capital as Δk, and the elasticity

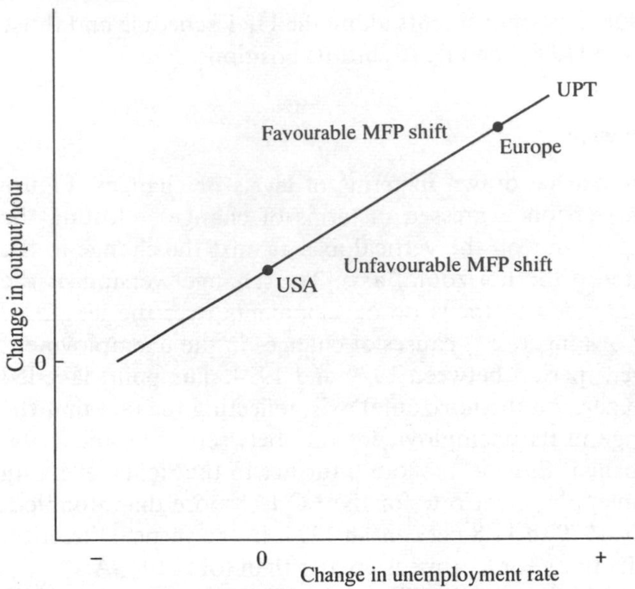

Figure 14.1 The UPT schedule

of output to a change in capital as $(1-\alpha)$, the change in output per hour is:

$$\Delta q - \Delta h = \Delta a + (1 - \alpha)(\Delta k - \Delta h). \quad (2)$$

(2) neatly separates factors that account for the positive slope of the UPT schedule from those that account for shifts in that schedule. Any positive change in Δa shifts the schedule up and a negative change shifts the schedule down. In contrast, any event (labelled below as a 'wage-setting shock') that causes an increase in $\Delta k - \Delta h$ by simultaneously raising unemployment while reducing employment (and hours), for a given growth rate of capital, causes the economy to move northeast along the UPT schedule from a point like that marked 'USA' to a point like that marked 'Europe'. Finally, for any given change in unemployment and employment, a downward shift in the growth rate of capital shifts the UPT schedule downward, just as does a reduction in Δa.

The initial focus in our analysis is on factors that cause movements along the UPT schedule, while subsequently we examine factors that cause adverse or favourable shifts in the schedule. The ultimate goal is to distinguish unemployment-reducing policies for Europe that tend to have an adverse impact on productivity (moving Europe southwest from its position in figure 14.1) from those that do not.

2.2 *The standard labour market model*

The relationship between unemployment and productivity is implicit in the standard labour market model so often used to discuss the persistence of European unemployment.[2] Figure 14.2 incorporates three relationships. First, the kinked line N^S is a labour-supply curve, relating the total labour force plotted horizontally to the level of the real wage plotted vertically. At the level of unemployment benefits $(W/P)_B$ the schedule is horizontal while at higher levels of the real wage the schedule is vertical, following the weight of evidence suggesting that this relationship is highly inelastic.

Second, the downward-sloping N^D curves represent the negative relationship between the level of employment and the real wage. In elementary textbooks, this relationship is interpreted as reflecting the price-taking, profit-maximising behaviour of firms operating in competitive labour markets. For such firms, employment is determined by setting the real wage equal to the marginal product of labour, which is assumed to be subject to diminishing returns with increased employment. Thus, for this analysis to be consistent with a production function exhibiting constant returns to scale, the quantity of other factors of production (especially capital, energy and materials) is held constant along any particular N^D curve. However, in much of the recent literature this graphical analysis has been shown to be consistent with imperfectly competitive product markets in which prices are set as a mark-up on marginal labour cost. In this case, any tendency for the mark-up to increase with the level of employment would increase the negative slope of the schedule. In the imperfectly competitive case these downward-sloping schedules reflect the joint outcome of pricing and employment decisions by firms and are sometimes called 'price-setting' schedules.

In contrast to the traditional textbook diagram, in which the upward-sloping lines are called labour supply schedules, in the recent literature these are called wage-setting schedules (W^S). Higher employment is postulated to elicit higher real wages as the outcome of bargaining between unions and employer associations and is also consistent with the efficiency wage model. As employment increases, the bargaining power of workers is postulated to increase.

In figure 14.2, the economy is initially in equilibrium at point A along curves ${N^D}_0$ and ${W^S}_0$, equilibrium employment is represented by E_0 and equilibrium unemployment (U_0) by N_0-E_0. In the competitive interpre-

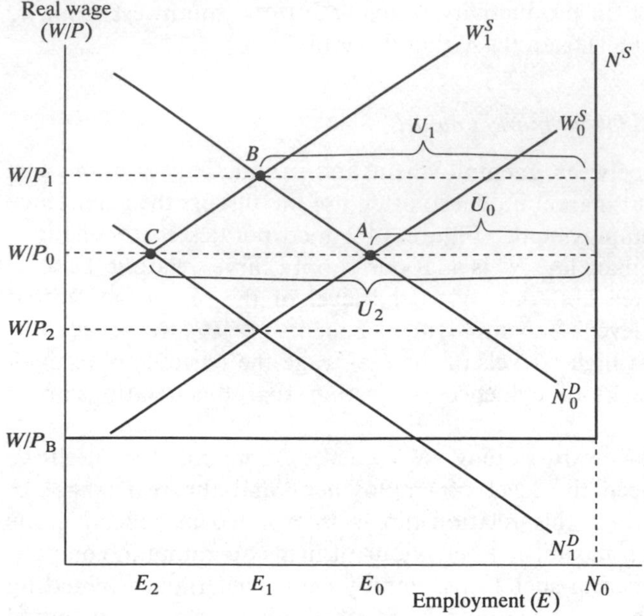

Figure 14.2 Unemployment and productivity in the standard labour market model

tation of the labour demand curve, the marginal product of labour is $(W/P)_0$, and in the special Cobb–Douglas case, the average product of labour is $(W/P)_0/s$, where s is labour's income share.

2.3 *Wage-setting shocks*

Now, let us examine two types of shocks and inquire into the circumstances in which an increase in unemployment could coincide with an increase in the level of productivity (which in our discussion of the labour market diagram refers to output per employee, since hours per employee are assumed fixed, as is MFP). First, consider a wage-setting shock that shifts the $W^S{}_0$ curve upwards to the position $W^S{}_1$. Such a shock might be caused by an autonomous increase in the bargaining power of trade unions, or any event (like the French general strike of spring 1968) in which a given group of workers band together and autonomously raises the wages that it requires to supply a particular amount of employment. The result of such a wage-setting shock is to move the economy from point A to point B, where the original labour demand curve $N^D{}_0$ intersects the new higher $W^S{}_1$ curve.

Such a wage-setting shock establishes a trade-off between higher unemployment and higher output per employee. At point *B* unemployment has risen from U_0 to U_1, while the marginal product of labour has risen from $(W/P)_0$ to $(W/P)_1$. In the Cobb–Douglas case, the average product of labour increases in proportion to the marginal product.

The economy, however, is unlikely to settle at point *B* for long. Compared to point *A*, at point *B* output and employment are lower, and the marginal product of capital has fallen because the fixed stock of capital is being combined with less labour input. The demand for capital will fall, and a period of disinvestment will occur that shifts the labour demand curve down and to the left to a position like ${N^D}_1$. If the higher wage-setting schedule remains in effect, then on standard assumptions about the structure of the model, the labour demand curve must shift downwards to the point at which the new wage-setting schedule intersects the original real wage $(W/P)_0$, as shown at point *C* in figure 14.2.[3]

Once the process of adjustment in capital input is completed, unemployment has grown from the initial level U_0 to the intermediate level U_1 to the final level U_2. However, at point *C* we do not observe a trade-off between unemployment and output per hour, since the marginal and average products of labour have returned to their initial values (the same as point *C* as at point *A*), while unemployment has increased greatly. However, this model does help capture a key feature of the European unemployment puzzle of the 1980s and 1990s – at point *C* there has been a substantial increase in the unemployment rate without any decline in the rate of capacity utilisation, which is assumed to be constant in the model. At point *C* Europe has 'disinvested' and substantially reduced the ratio of capital to the labour force, without reducing at all the ratio of capital input to labour input. Unemployment has occurred in an environment of disinvestment in which there is now insufficient capital fully to employ the labour force (N_0).

Indeed, a notable feature of the permanent rise in European unemployment in the 1980s is that this rise was not accompanied by a permanent drop in capacity utilisation. For instance, German unemployment was higher in 1990 than in 1979 but so was the rate of capacity utilisation. As shown by Franz and Gordon (1993), the mean utilization unemployment rate ('MURU') for Germany has increased almost as much as the actual unemployment rate, implying that there no longer exists sufficient productive capacity to provide jobs for enough people to attain the unemployment rates of the 1970s, much less the 1960s. Bean (1994, p. 613) shows that the same phenomenon has occurred for the EC/EU as a whole.

2.4 Energy price shocks

Most European discussions of the productivity–unemployment connection have in mind not wage-setting shocks but rather the effects of the oil shocks, and these can be illustrated in figure 14.3. An increase in the real price of oil shifts down the labour demand curve to schedule $N^D{}_1$, by reducing the quantity of energy and hence the marginal product of labour.[4] Starting from point *A*, the economy's equilibrium position shifts southwest to point *D*. As before, unemployment has increased and the marginal product of labour has fallen from $(W/P)_0$ to $(W/P)_2$ and (in the Cobb–Douglas case) the average product of labour falls in proportion.

Thus far we have learned that a shock that increases unemployment may either raise or lower productivity. An adverse productivity shock can create a negative correlation between the level of unemployment and the level of productivity, while a wage-setting shock can create a positive correlation between the level of unemployment and the level of productivity, at least over the period of time prior to the downward adjustment of the capital stock to the wage-setting shock.

How does the economy adjust to an energy price shock? Several possibilities are illustrated in figure 14.3, where points *A* and *C* represent the same situation as in figure 14.2. During the early 1980s the seminal work of Branson and Rotemberg (1980), Sachs (1979) and Bruno and Sachs (1985), emphasised the contrast between real wage rigidity in Europe and real wage flexibility in the USA. Taken literally, this dichotomy would imply that a given adverse energy price shock would shift Europe from point *A* to point *C*, as the result of a horizontal wage-setting curve. In contrast, the same shock would shift the USA from point *A* to point *H*, as the result of flexible wage-setting institutions that cause the wage-setting curve to shift down until it intersects the lower labour demand curve at the original level of employment.

Other possibilities are suggested by Elmeskov and MacFarlan (1993), who use the same diagram to interpret the concept of hysteresis. With full hysteresis, the equilibrium unemployment rate depends on the current unemployment rate. Following an energy price shock (or an adverse aggregate demand shock) that shifts the labour demand curve in figure 14.3 from $N^D{}_0$ to $N^D{}_1$ the economy moves from *A* to *D*, as before. But under full hysteresis there is a vertical long-run wage-setting schedule $W^{S'}$ which moves to the current level of employment. Under partial hysteresis or 'slow adjustment', the wage-setting schedule does not shift down all the way to point *H* but comes to rest at a schedule like $W^S{}_2$, and employment is prevented from rising above E_3. In short, points *C*, *D*, *G* and *H* (all of which lie along the lower labour demand curve $N^D{}_1$)

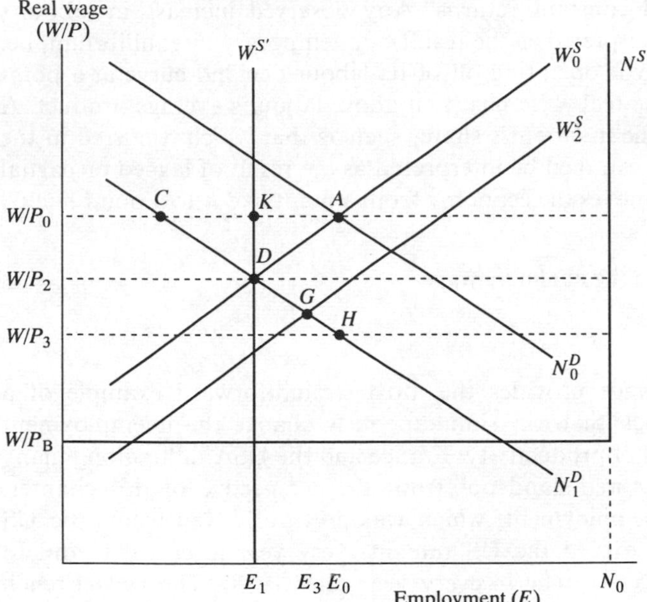

Figure 14.3 The effects of an oil shock on employment and the real wage

represent alternative responses to an adverse productivity shock under the extremes of real wage rigidity and full flexibility, and the intermediate cases of full and partial hysteresis.

We note that, while the *event* of an adverse energy price shock can create a negative correlation between unemployment and productivity, any *adjustment following the shock* along the labour demand curve (e.g. between points *C* and *H*) can create a positive correlation. In this sense any slow or gradual adjustment of wage-setting following a shock creates the same positive correlation between unemployment and productivity as occurs in figure 14.2 following a wage-setting shock.

Much of the literature in the early 1980s (e.g. Bruno and Sachs, 1985), emphasised that labour's share of national income had risen in Europe at the time of the first energy price shock, and took this as *prima facie* evidence that European unemployment was structural, caused by excessive real wage rigidity. As pointed out by Krugman (1987, pp. 60–5), Bean (1994, p. 577), and others, there is no such necessary link between real wage rigidity and labour's share. If the labour demand curve $N^D{}_1$ is derived from a Cobb–Douglas production function, then labour's share cannot change at all under the assumptions of perfect competition and constant returns. Any observed increase in labour's share must be interpreted as the result of a temporary disequilibrium, i.e. that the economy is operating off of its labour demand curve at a point like *K*, so that the real wage has risen above labour's average product. A subsequent decline in labour's share, such as that which occurred in the EC in the 1980s, can then be interpreted as the result of lagged or partial adjustment that moves the economy from a point like *K* to a point like *G*.

3 An example: the minimum wage

3.1 Data and theory

The minimum wage provides the most straightforward example of a wage-setting shock that can simultaneously change the unemployment rate and the level of productivity. France and the USA differ along many dimensions, but three stand out from the perspective of this chapter. First, French unemployment, which was previously well below the US rate, climbed to exceed the US rate in every year after 1983 (and to exceed the EC/EU average in every year after 1988). The 1994 French unemployment rate of 12.6 per cent exceeded by a wide margin the US rate of 6.1 per cent.[5] Second, French productivity growth exceeded that in the USA during the 1979–92 period, but by a much wider margin of 1.51 points per annum outside of manufacturing than the 0.25 margin of French superiority in manufacturing.[6] Third, the effective minimum wage (SMIC) continued its slow upward creep in France during the 1980s, as shown in figure 14.4, while in the USA the effective minimum wage had fallen from roughly the French level in the late 1960s to well under half of the French level after 1982.[7] Figure 14.4 under-states the importance of the SMIC, since the proportion of the French workforce covered by the SMIC is much higher than the equivalent proportion in the USA (Bazan and Martin, 1991, p. 214).

The labour market diagram in figure 14.5 provides an analysis of an increase in the French real minimum wage and a decrease in the US real minimum wage. Note that, to use the same labour market analysis provided in figures 14.2 and 14.3, we define the minimum wage in real terms, that is, divided by the product price deflator, in contrast to the data plotted in figure 14.4, which define the effective minimum wage in terms of the ratio of the statutory minimum wage to nominal labour compensation. Since real labour compensation for low-paid workers grew in France much faster than in the USA during this period, figure 14.4 understates the divergence between the two countries in the real minimum wage.

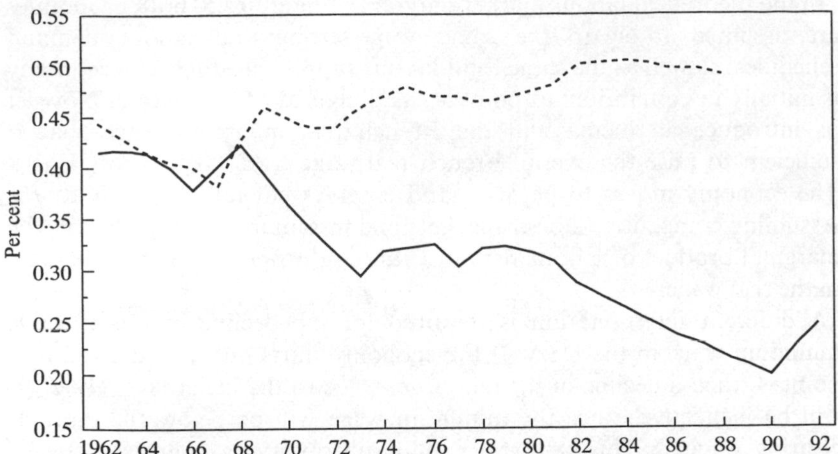

Figure 14.4 The minimum wage relative to average hourly compensation, 1962–92
Source: France: Bazan and Martin (1991, chart 2, p. 204); USA: Statutory minimum wage divided by average hourly compensation

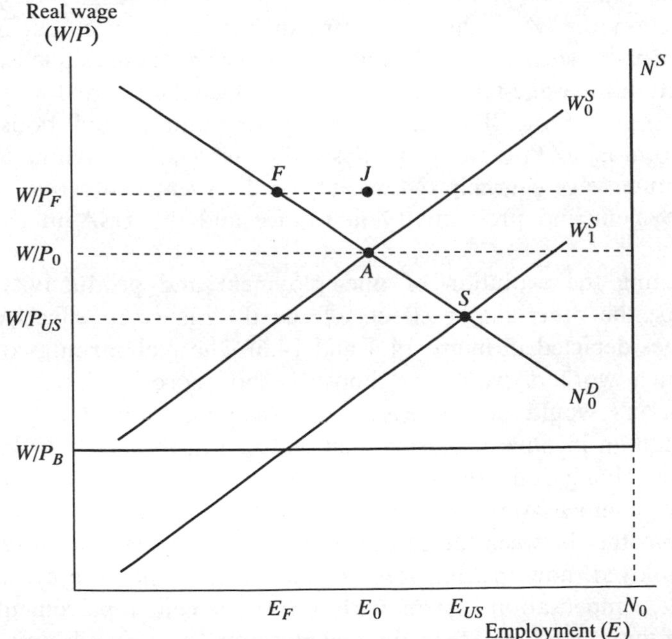

Figure 14.5 The effect of an increase in the real minimum wage in France and a decrease in the USA

In the theoretical labour market diagram of figure 14.5, both economies are assumed to share the same wage-setting and labour demand schedules, as well as the same total labour supply schedule. The economy is initially in equilibrium at point A, as in figures 14.2 and 14.3. Now let us introduce an increase in the French real minimum wage that is sufficient to raise the overall French real wage from $(W/P)_0$ to $(W/P)_F$. The economy moves to point F, and employment falls from E_0 to E_F. Assuming competitive labour markets and instantaneous adjustment, the marginal product of labour rises in France in proportion to the increase in the real wage.

A different interpretation is required for the decline in the effective minimum wage in the USA. If the economy starts out in equilibrium at point A, then a decline in the minimum wage to the lower level $(W/P)_{US}$ will be ineffective, since the minimum wage will be below the market-clearing wage. In this case, we would still observe a contrast between France and the USA represented by the difference between points F and A; in France productivity would grow and employment would shrink relative to the USA.

Another possibility is that the steady erosion of the real minimum wage in the USA has contributed to a downward shift in the wage-setting curve to a position like $W^S{}_1$ – this downward shift may have been partly due to other causes, such as the decline in US union density. Such a downward shift in the wage-setting curve would reduce the US real wage from $(W/P)_0$ to $(W/P)_{US}$, shift the economy to point S and boost employment from E_0 to E_{US}. In this analysis, the divergent behaviour of the real minimum wage can help to explain the divergent behaviour of both unemployment and productivity in France and the USA in the 1980s.

Beyond affecting the evolution of unemployment and productivity, what would be the other major effects of the divergence in effective minimum wages depicted in figure 14.4 and 14.5? The real earnings of low-paid French workers would be boosted and those of low-paid American workers would be depressed, thus helping to explain the contrast between an income dispersion that widened in the USA in the 1980s while remaining roughly constant in France. If there were no unemployment compensation system, there would be an increased dispersion in incomes between the employed French, now making more, and the unemployed, now making zero. But in the extreme case of an unemployment compensation system with a 100 per cent replacement ratio (ignoring taxes), an increase in the real minimum wage would raise the welfare not only of the employed but of the unemployed as well. The French government would be obliged to pay out extra unemployment compensation shown in figure 14.5 by the rectangle FJE_0E_F. This amount takes the form of a transfer to the current unemployed from some combination of current workers and future generations of taxpayers.[8]

If the labour demand curve in figure 14.5 had a unitary elasticity, then labour income (and labour's income share) would be the same at points *A* and *F*. With full-replacement unemployment compensation, the most obvious effect would be to create an increase in government transfer expenditures as a share of GDP, with possible side-effects in the form of higher taxes or a higher public debt–GDP ratio, which in the latter case might lead as well to higher real interest rates. Another effect, often discussed in connection with the hysteresis hypothesis, would be an erosion of the skills of the newly unemployed ($E_0 - E_F$). Ironically, measured national productivity could increase while the skills of the population deteriorate, because a decrease in the employment–population ratio would be accompanied by a decline in the skills of the unemployed.

3.2 *Literature on the effects of the minimum wage*

There is a contradiction between the analysis of figure 14.5 and the recent literature on the effects of the minimum wage. Studies like those of Bazan and Martin (1991) for France, Dickens *et al.* (1993) for the UK, and Card (1992), Card, Katz and Krueger (1993), Card and Krueger (1994), and Krueger (1994) for the USA, all seem to indicate that the minimum wage has small or negligible effects on employment. These results occur despite findings that minimum wages 'spill over' to other wages, for instance the finding by Bazan and Martin (1991) that a one percentage point increase in the real value of the SMIC increases the real value of real youth earnings by 0.4 of a percentage point.

There are at least two interpretations of the small measured employment effects of changes in the minimum wage. An equilibrium interpretation is that the labour demand curve in figure 14.5 is extremely steep, accounting for the absence of employment effects in the studies cited above. Under this interpretation an increase in the minimum wage is an excellent way to boost productivity with minimal employment effects. However, one doubts that the hypothesis of a near-vertical long-run labour demand curve can be supported, as this would conflict with a large production function literature supporting an elasticity of substitution in the range of 0.5 to 1.0 (Bean, 1994, p. 614), and with the long-run constancy of labour's share that is consistent with an elasticity of 1.0. Indeed, Bazan and Martin (1991, p. 215) 'believe it to be the case' that an increase in real youth labour costs have reduced youth employment, despite their inability to establish this response 'satisfactorily'.

An alternative view is that the short-run response is small while the long-run response is large, i.e. that the process of substitution caused by a significant increase in the minimum wage (or any other shock to the wage-setting curve) takes a significant time to occur. In this interpretation the labour demand curve gradually rotates through time, starting steep and becoming flatter, and this lagged adjustment process is inadequately captured in studies that focus on short-run responses.

The same problems may affect the studies of the US minimum wage by Card and his co-authors. These studies found no adverse employment effects following increases in the minimum wage above the Federal level in particular states of the USA. But there is a different problem as well. It is very likely that by 1990 the US minimum wage had dropped so low as to be ineffective, that is, to be below the market-clearing wage rate like point *A* in figure 14.5. The US studies cited here focused on increases in the minimum wage from a low level, and if at this level the minimum wage was ineffective, then it is no surprise that no employment effects could be found.

Finally, even when academic studies fail to provide convincing demonstrations of effects that seem theoretically plausible, anecdotal evidence seems compelling that the divergent evolution of the French and US minimum wages plotted in figure 14.4 has resulted in very different employment practices, particularly in the service sector. US supermarkets (often in some places, always in others) employ two people at each check-out lane, one to ring up the purchases and the other to place the purchases in bags. French supermarkets expect customers to bag their own groceries and sometimes to provide their own bags. Similarly, American restaurants, from the high-priced gourmet level down to the mid-level, employ 'bushboys' to set and clear tables (these are often recent legal or illegal immigrants) while 'waitpeople' take orders and serve food. In contrast, in much of Europe staffing levels in restaurants are noticeably lower, and waitpeople set and clear tables in addition to taking orders and serving food.

4 Mechanisms

As we have seen, a positive correlation between unemployment and the level of productivity can be generated by any factor that shifts the wage-setting curve, and this correlation can persist for as long as it takes for the capital stock to adjust. In this section we distinguish those variables that shift the wage-setting schedule and cause movements *along* the UPT schedule of figure 14.1 from those other factors that may cause changes in productivity or in unemployment without simultaneously changing both; these cause shifts in figure 14.1's UPT schedule.

4.1 Shifts in the UPT schedule

First we translate the preceding labour market analysis in terms of the UPT schedule, which reappears in figure 14.6. Recall from our discussion of figure 14.1 that movements in MFP and in capital relative to a fixed level of employment and unemployment cause shifts in the UPT schedule, while changes in employment and unemployment occurring with a fixed level of MFP and capital input cause movements along the UPT schedule.

The economy begins at point *A* in figure 14.6, the same situation of initial equilibrium as at point *A* of figure 14.2, where the initial unemployment rate is U_0. Next, an adverse wage-setting shock shifts the economy to point *B*, as in figure 14.2, with a higher marginal and average product of labour and a higher unemployment rate U_1. The initial UPT_0 schedule drawn between points *A* and *B* in figure 14.6 shows that over the period of time encompassed by situations *A* and *B*, the unemployment rate increases by the amount $U_1 - U_0$, while growth in productivity (output per employee) is boosted above whatever rate prevailed at point *A*.

In the long run there will be a period of disinvestment that, as shown in figure 14.2, reduces productivity and the real wage to the original level at point *C* while further boosting the unemployment rate from U_1 to U_2. The same situation is shown in figure 14.6 by the downward shift in the UPT schedule to UPT_1. A point like *C* depicts the cumulative change from the initial equilibrium situation at point *A*. There is a cumulative change in unemployment ($U_2 - U_0$), while productivity growth is unchanged from the initial situation at point *A*. Thus one conclusion from this analysis is that the process of capital accumulation implies that in the long run the UPT schedule becomes flat or even horizontal, as implied by the horizontal schedule UPT_{LR}.

The movements in figure 14.6 from point *A* to *B* to *C* are caused by a wage-setting shock followed by capital decumulation. Other factors that might shift the UPT schedule in an unfavourable (downward) direction include an adverse oil price shock, while better education or an exogenous improvement in the rate of innovation would shift the UPT schedule in a favourable (upward direction). Figure 14.6 suggest that we might fruitfully distinguish those causes of higher European unemployment that can be interpreted as initially causing a northeast movement

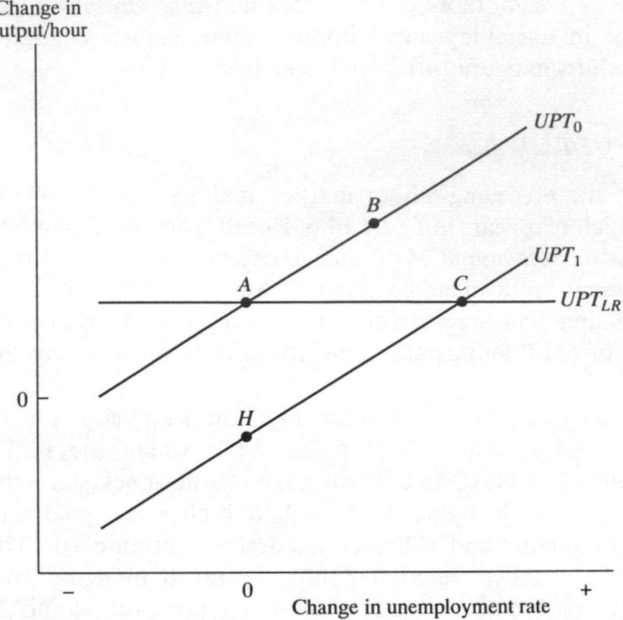

Figure 14.6 Movements along and shifts in the UPT schedule

along the UPT schedule from those that can be interpreted as causing shifts in that schedule. Similarly, we might investigate the suggested causes of slow productivity growth and increased inequality in the United States by applying the same distinction involving movements along versus shifts in the UPT schedule.

4.2 *Sources of upward shifts in the wage-setting schedule*

Bean (1994, pp. 579) interprets the wage-setting mechanism in terms of this equation:

$$w - p^e = -\gamma_1 U + (1 - \gamma_2)(w - p)_{-1} + Z_w\Gamma + \epsilon_w, \qquad (3)$$

where lower-case letters are logs, w is the log wage, p is the log price, U is the unemployment rate, and Z_w is a vector of variables 'that include the reservation wage and whatever factors are thought to influence the markup over the reservation wage'. Thus any element in Z_w may in principle be a source of a shift in the wage-setting schedule and at the same time a source of a movement along a given UPT schedule.

The typical European list of elements that would shift Z_w upward (drawn from Bean, 1994, pp. 587–96) includes the following.

(i) A *higher minimum wage*, as discussed previously.

(ii) An *increase in the level and/or coverage of unemployment benefits*, which raise the effective replacement ratio of the unemployment benefits system and hence the reservation wage.[9]

(iii) An *increase in the price wedge*. Since firms care about the product-price real wage and workers care about the consumption-price real wage, any increase in consumer prices relative to product prices would shift up the wage-setting schedule. An increase in this wedge occurred at the time of the first oil shock, which also marks the beginning of the productivity growth slowdown. An increase in the price wedge can also be caused by a decline in the terms of trade that raises import prices relative to the prices of domestic production.

(iv) An *increase in the tax wedge*. Since firms pay pre-tax wages but workers receive after-tax wages, any increase in payroll or income taxes can shift up the wage-setting schedule. Tax wedges in Europe range from 40 to 70 per cent, in contrast to a range of 20–25 per cent in the USA and Japan.[10]

(v) An *increase in worker militancy*. An increase in union power would shift up the wage-setting schedule, raising both unemployment and productivity. Trade union membership as a share of the labour force is only 15 per cent in the USA but is much higher in most European countries, in the 30–40 per cent range in Germany, Italy, and Britain, and 80 per cent in Sweden (France is an exception with a share below that of the USA). One problem with this explanation is that, while relatively high, the trade union membership share fell in most European countries in the 1980s (primarily as a result of the growing share of employment in the service sector).

4.3 *Factors which may shift the UPT schedule*

Numerous other factors have been cited as causes of high European unemployment, but these do not involve causation going initially from wage-setting behaviour to subsequent response by productivity and the unemployment rate. Hence they are best interpreted as factors causing an adverse (downward) shift in the UPT schedule of figure 14.6.

(vi) *Supply shock combined with real wage rigidity*. As in figure 14.3, an adverse supply shock (e.g. a higher real price of oil) can simultaneously cause unemployment to rise and productivity to fall, thus shifting the UPT schedule downward. The dichotomy between real wage rigidity and real-wage flexibility determines where the economy winds up on the lower UPT schedule, so that the position of Europe might be interpreted as similar to point *C* on the lower UPT schedule of figure 14.6, and that of the USA at a point like *H*.

(vii) *Mismatch*. A shift in technology may create unemployment if there are barriers to labour mobility across occupations, regions and industrial sectors. An increased pace of technological change or growing openness to foreign trade might increase structural unemployment without causing a change in productivity, either up or down. Thus mismatch can be interpreted as shifting the UPT schedule to the right, i.e. down.

(viii) *Labour market regulations*. Numerous forms of employment regulation lead to the general diagnosis that European labour markets are more 'rigid' than in the USA. The exhaustive analysis of Grubb and Wells (1993) includes among these regulations restrictions on employers' freedom to dismiss workers; limits on the use or the legal validity of fixed-term contracts; limits on the use of temporary work; restrictions on weekly hours of regular or overtime work; and limits on use of part-time work. Also included in this category is mandated severance pay. Here the important point is that when aggregate demand is high, such regulations can stabilise employment and reduce the incidence of temporary layoffs in response to mild recessions. But when a major decline in demand occurs, perhaps amplified by an upward shift in the wage-setting schedule for the reasons outlined above, such regulations can stabilise *unemployment* by raising the present discounted value of the cost to employers of hiring an extra worker in response to an upturn in demand.[11] Again, such regulations may increase unemployment without necessarily changing productivity and should be interpreted as causing a rightward shift in the UPT schedule.

(ix) *Product market regulations*. A particular form of regulation that potentially boosts both unemployment and productivity is the draconian type of shop-closing rules imposed in Germany and some other countries. A movement to Sunday and evening opening, underway currently in Britain, clearly creates jobs but reduces retailing productivity by spreading the same transactions over more labour hours. While such regulations push unemployment and productivity in the same direction as a wage-setting shock, there is no reason why the mix of unemployment and productivity responses should trace out a labour demand curve, and hence we treat such regulations as shifting the UPT schedule rather than causing a movement along it.

4.4 Sources of slow productivity growth and increasing inequality in the USA

Bean (1994) effectively criticises much of the research attributing the rise in European unemployment to particular items on the above list and concludes that there must be multiple causes, rather than a single cause. Can we identify some of the above items as promising explanations by comparing behaviour in the USA and Europe? While the replacement ratio of unemployment benefits (item (ii) on the above list) changed little in either the EC or in the USA between the late 1960s and late 1980s, the fraction of US employees eligible for benefits has fallen substantially. While the price wedge (iii) behaved similarly in the EC and USA, the tax wedge (iv) in the EC is both higher and increased more between the late 1960s and late 1980s (Bean, 1994, p. 586). The rigid real wage hypothesis (vi) seems consistent with the observed bulge in the EC labour share between 1974 and 1982. While there is no reason for mismatch (vii) to have difference between Europe and the USA, there is clearly a major difference between the USA and particular European countries in the extent of labour market and product market regulation (viii) and (ix).

Perhaps the leading candidate for causing divergent behaviour across the Atlantic is the marked decline in US union membership (v), from 26.2 per cent in 1977 to 15.8 per cent in 1993 (union members as a fraction of wage and salary workers). Together with the sharp reduction in the real minimum wage (i), this decline in union representation plausibly exerted downward pressure on the US wage-setting schedule throughout the 1970s and 1980s. The result was the well known dichotomy between rapid growth in US employment relative to Europe, but a less widely recognised implication is that some part of the continuing productivity growth divergence must have occurred as well.

In addition to unions and the minimum wage, any US list of factors causing depressed real wages and productivity must include immigration and imports. Annual *legal* immigration as a per cent of the population has steadily increased in each decade of the postwar period (Simon, 1991), although this percentage is still far below the records set during 1890–1914 (also a period of slow productivity growth). In addition, a large and undetermined amount of illegal immigration has added substantially to the supply of unskilled labour and plausibly added to downward pressure on the wage-setting schedule. Finally, Johnson and Stafford (1993) have argued convincingly that an increased supply of medium-technology goods from newly industrialising countries can cause an absolute decline in the real wage of an advanced country (or group of countries) that previously had a monopoly on the manufacturing of those goods. To the extent that the USA was more open to Asian imports than some European countries that imposed quantitative trade restrictions (notably France and Italy), imports of goods can put the same kind of downward pressure on the wage-setting schedule as imports of people, i.e. immigration.

5 Productivity growth differences across countries and sectors

The growth rates of output per hour and of MFP for seven countries, nine sectors, and three alternative aggregates (private, private non-farm, and private non-farm, non-manufacturing, non-mining – PNFNMNM) are provided in tables available from the author. Also available are tables showing *levels* of output per hour for each sector in 1992, converted into dollars at OECD 1992 exchange rates.

5.1 Means and variances of output per hour growth rates

Some of the main features of the data are summarised in table 14.1, which displays in the top frame unweighted means and variances across the nine sectors for each of the seven countries, and in the bottom frame unweighted means and variances across the seven countries for each of the nine sectors. The averages show the now familiar post-1973 slowdown and indicate that post-1973 productivity growth for all countries averaged together was about the same in 1973–9 as in 1973–92. This would appear to rule out the energy price shocks as a major causative factor.

Every country experienced a post-1973 slowdown, but some (USA, Canada and Japan) did better during 1979–92 than 1973–9, while the four European countries all experienced slower productivity growth after 1979 than during 1973–9. The bottom section of table 14.2 (p. 000) shows that every sector experienced a post-1973 slowdown. In agriculture, mining and construction, productivity growth was more rapid after 1979 than during 1973–9, while for manufacturing and trade there was no difference, and for transport/communication, FIRE, and services, there was a further slowdown after 1979.

Table 14.1 *Growth rates of output per hour, mean and variance by country and sector*

Country	1960–73	1973–9	1979–92
United States	2.15 (3.99)	−0.95 (13.83)	2.01 (3.93)
Canada	3.53 (3.14)	0.77 (10.14	1.64 (1.17)
Japan	8.47 (5.68)	2.68 (6.14)	3.17 (0.91)
France	4.64 (4.13)	3.68 (2.08)	3.14 (2.86)
Germany	4.97 (2.01)	4.23 (3.18)	2.36 (2.05)
Italy	6.38 (2.05)	1.91 (3.09)	1.87 (3.38)
UK	4.02 (5.67)	3.32 (23.59)	2.91 (9.27)
Average	4.88 (3.81)	2.23 (9.57)	2.44 (3.37)

Sector	1960–73	1973–9	1979–92
Agriculture	6.59 (3.87)	2.59 (7.77)	4.49 (2.09)
Mining	5.67 (17.07)	1.83 (97.82)	3.55 (6.64)
Manufacturing	5.93 (5.57)	2.89 (5.48)	2.82 (0.98)
Utilities	6.08 (1.30)	3.25 (5.65)	2.45 (3.48)
Construction	3.49 (10.74)	0.74 (2.01)	1.67 (0.84)
Trade	4.35 (5.02)	1.92 (2.03)	2.09 (0.89)
Transport/ communication	5.15 (1.18)	2.91 (3.61)	2.93 (3.21)
FIRE[a]	2.40 (5.94)	2.22 (1.60)	1.09 (0.94)
Services	3.52 (7.03)	1.42 (2.32)	0.62 (3.17)
Average	4.80 (6.30)	2.20 (14.25)	2.41 (2.37)
Av. excluding mining	4.69 (4.95)	2.24 (3.80)	2.27 (1.84)

Note: [a] Fire, Insurance and Real Estate.

Is productivity growth more variable across countries or across sectors? The variances across countries within given sectors are averaged with and without mining, because of the huge variance of mining (including oil production) productivity during the oil shock period, 1973–9. Comparing the first (1960–73) and last (1979–92) periods, the variance across sectors for given countries was smaller than the variance across countries for given sectors in the earlier period, whereas the reverse was true in the latter period. The relatively low cross-country within-sector variance during 1979–92 suggests that technological convergence may have played a role in causing rapid productivity growth outside the USA prior to 1973 or 1979, followed by more modest rates as individual sectors neared the frontier achieved by American technology.

5.2 What did capital contribute to the productivity slowdown?

Our theoretical analysis treats MFP growth as exogenous. The growth rate of output per hour relative to MFP growth can be affected by wage-setting shocks that boost real wages and productivity, or by subsequent disinvestment that reduces real wages and productivity.

The relation between growth in output per hour and in MFP is defined in (2) above, which is repeated here:

$$\Delta q - \Delta h = \Delta a + (1 - \alpha)(\Delta k - \Delta h). \tag{4}$$

Thus the growth rate of output per hour ($\Delta q - \Delta h$) is simply the growth rate of MFP (Δa) plus the contribution of the growth in capital per hour [$(1 - \alpha)(\Delta k - \Delta h)$].

Table 14.2 decomposes the observed growth rate of output per hour for the non-farm business sector in the G-7 countries between the separate contributions of capital and MFP. For most countries all three columns reveal a slowdown in growth rates between the first period (1960–73) and the final period (1979–92), but there are some anomalies. Between the first and last periods the capital contribution actually accelerates in both the USA and Canada, and consequently the slowdown in MFP growth is greater than in the growth rate of output per hour. Table 14.2 also reveals that for 1979–92 the excess of growth in output per hour for Europe versus the USA is more than explained by MFP growth. Because the 1979–92 contribution of capital in France and Germany is only slightly more than in the USA, capital contributes almost nothing to explaining the excess of growth in output per hour for these two countries over that in the USA. Because the 1979–92 contribution of capital in Italy and the UK is much less than in the USA, capital makes a *negative* contribution to the explanation for those two countries.

The contribution of capital growth to the slowdown in growth in output per hour is exhibited in table 14.3 not just for non-farm private business, but also for manufacturing and a large 'residual' sector, private non-farm, non-manufacturing, non-mining (PNFNMNM). Here we note that the contribution of capital to the slowdown in all three sectors is negative for both the USA and Canada, while it is positive in the four European countries (except for manufacturing in Italy, where there is a negative contribution of capital to the slowdown in growth of output per hour, and for UK manufacturing, where there is no slowdown in the growth of output per hour, but rather an acceleration).

There is some support in tables 14.2 and 14.3 for the relationships

Table 14.2 *Growth rates of output per hour, the contribution of capital, and multi-factor productivity, non-farm private business sector, 1960–92*

	Output per hour			Contribution of capital			Multi-factor productivity		
	1960–73	1973–9	1979–92	1960–73	1973–9	1979–92	1960–73	1973–9	1979–92
USA	1.92	0.46	1.20	0.57	0.60	0.82	1.35	−0.14	−0.38
Canada	3.02	1.27	1.41	0.72	0.91	1.45	2.30	0.36	−0.04
Japan	8.23	3.08	3.22	–	1.79	1.59	–	1.29	1.63
France	4.90	3.94	2.55	1.26	1.55	0.98	3.64	2.39	1.57
Germany	5.33	4.38	2.36	1.90	1.69	0.92	3.43	2.69	1.44
Italy	6.71	1.99	1.90	1.15	−0.64	0.19	5.56	2.63	1.71
UK	3.53	2.20	1.27	1.21	1.04	0.05	2.32	1.16	1.22

Table 14.3 *The contribution of capital and of MFP to slowdown in growth rate of output per hour, 1979–92 as compared to 1960–73, by major sector*

	Private non-farm business			Manufacturing			Private NFNMNM[a]		
	Slowdown	% Share capital	% Share MFP	Slowdown	% Share capital	% Share MFP	Slowdown	% Share capital	% Share MFP
USA	−0.72	−35	135	−0.78	−40	140	−0.71	−24	124
Canada	−1.61	−45	145	−2.03	−49	149	−1.03	−61	161
France	−2.35	12	88	−4.05	4	96	−1.52	26	74
Germany	−2.97	33	67	−3.83	24	76	−2.32	54	46
Italy	−4.81	20	80	−3.02	−11	110	−5.49	27	73
UK	−2.26	51	49	0.66	88	12	−2.07	51	49

Note: [a] Non-farm, non-mining, non-manufacturing.

suggested in this chapter. For the aggregate economy (the non-farm economy displayed in table 14.2 and the first three columns of table 14.3), there was a very substantial slowdown in the contribution of capital in Europe but not in the USA. This supports the emphasis placed above on the role of wage-setting shocks in setting into motion a process of capital decumulation, while also causing an increase in unemployment. A notable exception is provided by Canada, where the contribution of capital accelerated rather than slowed down, while Canadian unemployment increased between 1960–73 and 1979–92 almost as much as in the four large European economies.

5.3 Productivity growth regressions

This chapter has examined the dynamic interaction of unemployment and productivity. It has shown that the correlation between unemployment and productivity can be positive, zero, or negative, and the same carries over to the correlation between the *change* in unemployment and the *growth rate* of productivity.

However, the above analysis makes a definite prediction about at least one correlation, that there should be a negative correlation between the change in unemployment and the change in capital per member of the labour force. To the extent that increased unemployment is initially caused by a positive wage-setting shock, we should observe a decline in capital relative to the labour force (or relative to the initial level of employment).

To examine these interrelations, we run a set of regression equations in which the dependent variables are alternatively growth in output per hour, growth in capital per member of the labour force, and growth in MFP. Each variable is measured as the growth rate for a particular country and sector over the three time intervals shown in tables 14.2 and 14.3, that is, 1960–73, 1973–9, and 1979–92. The explanatory variables are a set of dummy variables for country effects, sector effects, time effects, as well as two economic variables. First, in common with numerous recent studies of the convergence process, we include the level of productivity in a given country sector relative to that for the USA in the same sector at the beginning of a particular interval. The coefficient on this relative level variable should be negative, indicating that country sectors with a low initial *level* of productivity grow relatively rapidly. Second, we include the change in a country's unemployment rate over each time interval, since our analysis above relates the level of the unemployment rate to the level of productivity, or the change in the unemployment rate to the growth rate of productivity.

Thus the regression equation is:

$$(\Delta q - \Delta h)_{ikt} = \alpha_0 + \alpha_1 \Delta U_{kt} + \alpha_2 \frac{(Q/H)_{ikt}}{(Q/H)_{itUS}} + \Sigma\beta_k DC_k + \Sigma\gamma_i DS_i + \Sigma_t DT_t + \epsilon_{ikt}. \quad (5)$$

Here DC is a set of country dummies (with the USA taken as the base), DS is a set of sector dummies (with manufacturing taken as the base), and DT is a set of time interval dummies (with 1960–73 taken as the base).

The results are presented in table 14.4. The equation explaining the growth rate of output per hour is presented three times in columns (1)–(3). The first two columns differ only in that (1) excludes the country sector level effect. Inclusion of this effect in (2) substantially reduces the size of the country dummies, indicating that part of the more rapid productivity growth in the European countries relative to the USA can be attributed to the convergence effect. Inclusion of this effect in (2) has no impact on the unemployment change coefficient, which is negative but insignificant in both columns (1) and (2). Exclusion of this variable in column (3) further reduces the size of the country effects, indicating that the high values of the country effects in columns (1) and (2) are in part offsetting the negative coefficient on the change in unemployment for the European countries. Several sector dummies are highly significant, indicating that across all countries productivity growth is significantly slower in construction and FIRE than in manufacturing (the base sector). Interestingly, exclusion of the unemployment variable in column (3) yields a highly significant slowdown coefficient on the 1979–92 time effect; in columns (1) and (2) the productivity slowdown is spuriously explained by the increase in unemployment.

In column (4) the dependent variable is capital per potential hour, where 'potential hours' is defined as the hours that would have been worked if a country had the unemployment rate at the beginning of the period rather than at the end of the period. Here the country-sector productivity level effect is again highly significant, and the change in the unemployment rate has the expected negative sign at a significance level of 5 per cent.[12] Country-specific dummy variables for the four European countries are positive and significant, indicating that a substantial part of the productivity growth advantage of several European countries is explained by their more rapid rate of capital accumulation (holding constant the change in their unemployment rates). The pattern of sector-specific dummy coefficients is somewhat different, with mining experien-

Table 14.4 *Regression equations explaining growth rates by country and sector, three intervals, 1960–92*

	Output per hour			Capital per potential hour	Multi-factor productivity
	(1)	(2)	(3)	(4)	(5)
Constant	2.55**	4.77**	5.12**	4.93**	4.33**
Productivity level relative to USA	–	−2.45**	−2.48**	−2.63**	−2.36**
Change in unemployment	−0.46	−0.43	–	−0.56*	–
Canada	1.37*	0.35	−0.06	0.27	−0.48
France	3.81**	2.34**	1.35	2.45**	0.68
Germany	3.35**	2.34**	1.68**	2.29**	0.91
Italy	2.48**	2.79**	2.28**	1.97**	2.10**
UK	3.55**	2.36**	1.43*	1.78*	0.75
Agriculture	1.53*	0.87	0.86	0.96	−1.74**
Mining	−0.64	−0.68	−0.68	2.28**	−1.63**
Utilities	0.42	0.36	0.36	−0.93	−0.43
Construction	−1.87**	−2.13**	−2.13**	−0.38	−2.07**
Transport/ communication	0.11	0.17	0.16	−1.47	0.56
Trade	−0.11	−0.90	−0.89	−0.30	−1.02
FIRE	−1.99**	−2.13**	−2.14**	−2.77**	−2.16**
Services	−1.76**	−1.30	−1.29	−0.32	−1.67**
1973–9	−1.41**	−1.12*	−1.65**	0.10	−1.33**
1979–92	−0.74	−0.23	−1.28**	0.13	−0.82*
$\bar{R}^2$	0.34	0.39	0.39	0.43	0.37
SEE	2.30	2.20	2.21	2.19	1.90

Notes: * Indicates that coefficient is significant at 5 per cent level; ** at 1 per cent level.

cing unusually rapid capital accumulation and FIRE experiencing unusually slow capital accumulation. Somewhat unexpectedly, there are no time-specific slowdown effects, indicating that whatever slowdown in capital accumulation has occurred is entirely explained by the country sector productivity level variable and by the change in unemployment.

Finally, column (5) presents the same regression with the change in MFP as dependent variable. Here the country-specific effect is significant only for Italy. Thus it appears that most of the productivity advantage of France, Germany, and the UK over the USA, so evident in column (1), can be explained by convergence and capital accumulation. Significantly negative sector-specific effects are now present for MFP growth in agriculture, mining, construction, FIRE, and services (again, relative to manufacturing). The time-specific dummy coefficients indicate that between two-thirds and three-quarters of the productivity slowdown in column (3) can be attributed to a slowdown in MFP growth, and the rest can be attributed to a slowdown in capital accumulation associated with higher unemployment.

To summarise, we find that much of the productivity growth advantage of Europe countries over the USA is explained by convergence and more rapid capital accumulation. Only for Italy does more rapid growth in MFP explain a significant part of the productivity growth differential. The element of our theoretical analysis that is validated by the regression results concerns the growth of capital per potential hour, which seems to have decelerated more in countries with larger increases in unemployment. The theoretical analysis showed that productivity could be either positively or negatively correlated with unemployment in a world exposed to a mixture of wage-setting shocks and oil price shocks, and so it is not surprising that the regressions do not identify a significant correlation between productivity (output per hour or MFP) and unemployment.

6 Conclusions

The point of departure for this chapter is the divergence between the concerns of European and American economists. The persistence of high unemployment dominates European policy discussions, whereas American economists are increasingly concerned with the slow growth rate of real wages and a large increase in the dispersion of incomes. This chapter argues that these phenomena may be more closely related than is commonly recognised. The many factors that are believed to have contributed to European unemployment by shifting upward the European wage-setting schedule may also have increased the growth rate of European productivity relative to that in the USA.

However plausible the notion that wage-setting shocks can create a positive correlation between unemployment and productivity, that relation is likely soon to be eroded by changes in the rate of capital accumulation. We find that countries with the greatest increases in unemployment had the largest slowdowns in the growth rate of capital per potential labour hour, a correlation that is consistent with the important role that capital accumulation plays in our analysis. Europe entered the 1990s with much higher unemployment in the USA but with approximately the same rate of capacity utilisation, indicating that there was no longer sufficient capital to equip all the employees who would be at work at the unemployment rates of the late 1970s.

The raw numbers show substantially more rapid growth in output per hour in the four large European countries than in the USA. Our empirical analysis shows that none of this is related to the large increase in unemployment in Europe between the 1960s and the 1980s. Instead, faster productivity growth in Europe mainly reflects the convergence effect, i.e. that Europe started at a lower level of productivity and gradually converged toward the US level, and the impact of more rapid capital accumulation. The fact that European productivity growth slowed down more than that in the USA is attributed both to the gradual weakening of the convergence effect and also to the negative impact of wage-setting shocks which both increased the unemployment rate and reduced the growth rate of capital per potential labour hour.

The policy implications of this analysis apply both to the European and US settings. In Europe there is an increasing call for eliminating regulations and for more labour market flexibility. Yet there has thus far been little discussion of the fact that different types of reforms may help reduce structural unemployment but may have different effects on productivity. Proposed structural reforms to make European labour markets more 'flexible' – such as reducing the real minimum wage, reducing unemployment compensation, reducing the price and tax wedges, and weakening the power of labour unions – can all be interpreted as attempts to shift down the wage-setting schedule. In the language of this chapter, they cause a country to move southwest along the UPT schedule, thus imposing a cost of reduced productivity that offsets some of the benefits of reduced unemployment. Some or all of this productivity cost may be offset in the medium run by more rapid capital accumulation, as the improved environment for profitability creates a stimulus for investment.

Rather than working indirectly through the wage-setting schedule, policy makers would be better advised to adopt policies that reduce unemployment directly, especially policies to reduce mismatch and improve the efficiency of labour markets by better training or fewer employment regulations. Reform of product market regulations, such as a liberalisation of German shop-closing hours, might reduce measured productivity while improving consumer welfare through extra convenience that is omitted from GDP.

Policy implications for the USA can be developed from the same analysis. Attention should be directed to policies that shift the UPT schedule upwards, e.g. by reducing mismatch and eliminating unnecessary regulations. Placing upward pressure on the US wage-setting schedule by boosting the real minimum wage, and policies that attempt to reverse the decline in union penetration, would move the USA northeast along the UPT schedule. Some or all of the short-run productivity benefit might be offset in the medium run by slower capital accumulation, as the deteriorating environment for profitability squeezes investment. Policies that attempt to exploit the UPT trade-off seem likely to boost unemployment without creating any lasting benefit in the form of faster productivity growth.

NOTES

This research was supported by the National Science Foundation. David Rose and Gareth Siegel provided outstanding help with the data and tables. Bart van Ark, Eric J. Bartlesman and Charles Bean provided essential data on hours per employee. Charles Bean and Dennis Snower provided important comments on an earlier draft. Because of the chapter's length, it is not possible to include here either appendix tables or the explanation of data sources. These are readily available from the author.

1 Saint-Paul (1994) is a particularly articulate and convincing example.

2 This section provides a bare-bones graphical discussion of a model developed in more detail by Alogoskoufis and Manning (1988), Blanchard (1990), Bean (1994) and Layard *et al.* (1991).

3 Consider a Cobb–Douglas production function $Y = AH^{\alpha}K^{1-\alpha}$, the same as (2) in the text (where the latter is converted into logs). The marginal product of labour and the real wage are equal to $\alpha Y/H$ and the marginal product of capital is equal to $(1-\alpha)Y/K$. Designating the initial equilibrium situation at point A with asterisks, the wage-setting curve is $w = \alpha(1+\lambda)(Y^*/H^*)(H/H^*)^{\lambda}$, where at point A the 'wage push' parameter (λ) is initially set at zero. A hypothetical 'wage push' of 3 per cent ($\lambda = 0.03$) pushes the economy from point A to point B, and assuming $\alpha = 0.75$ and $\lambda = 0.5$, we can calculate that there will follow at point B an increase in the real wage of 1 per cent and a decline in labour input of 3.9 per cent. Once we allow subsequent disinvestment that decreases the capital stock, and if the capital stock continues to adjust until the marginal product of capital is equal to a fixed supply price of capital, then output, labour input, and capital input must all decline in proportion, so that the Y/H and Y/K ratios return to their original values. With the assumed parameters of the wage setting curve, this requires a decline in output and factor inputs of 5.8 per cent at point C.

4 If MFP is defined as output relative to the weighted inputs of not just labour and capital but also energy, then MFP remains constant and the entire cause of the downward shift of the schedule $N^D{}_1$ is the reduced quantity of energy. However, if as in the empirical research in this chapter, MFP is calculated relative to the weighted inputs of just labour and capital input, then MFP is lower along schedule $N^D{}_1$ than along schedule $N^D{}_0$.

5 These comparisons refer to the official US 1994 unemployment rate and the projection of the French 1994 unemployment rate, *OECD Economic Outlook* (December 1994, annex table 54, p. A58).

6 The French and US output per hour growth rates for 1979–92 are, respectively, 2.14 and 0.63 per cent per year in private non-farm, non-manufacturing, non-mining, and 2.85 and 2.50 per cent per year in manufacturing.

7 Note that the data in figure 14.4 use the Bazan and Martin (1991) data for France but not for the USA. The denominator for the US minimum wage used by Bazan and Martin, that is, average hourly earnings for non-farm private production workers, is well known to be biased downward quite severely as a measure of the growth of nominal compensation (see Bosworth and Perry, 1994). In figure 14.4 we use as a denominator average hourly compensation.

8 Saint-Paul (1994, p. 3) argues that

> an increase in the minimum wage may well have adverse impacts on inequality. This is because while it redistributes income from the skilled to the unskilled workers, by creating unemployment it also redistributes income from the poorest to the lower-middle class.

This argument appears to neglect the unemployment compensation received by those who lose their jobs as a result of a higher minimum wage.

9 See Lindbeck (1994b, p. 1)

> It is a commonplace that very generous unemployment benefits with long, or even unlimited duration and with lax work tests contribute to unemployment persistence.

10 Lindbeck (1994b, p. 9).

11 See Lindbeck (1994a, pp. 2–3).

12 If the growth rate of capital per potential hour is replaced by the growth rate of capital per actual hour, the coefficient on the change in unemployment declines from −0.56 to −0.47, and the significance level changes from 5 per cent to about 9 per cent.

REFERENCES

Alogoskoufis, G.S. and A. Manning, 1988. 'On the persistence of unemployment', *Economic Policy*, **7**, 427–69

Baily, M. and R.J. Gordon, 1988. 'The productivity slowdown, measurement issues, and the explosion of computer power', *Brookings Papers on Economic Activity*, **9**, 348–420

Baumol, W.J., S.A.B. Blackman and E.N. Wolff, 1989. *Productivity and American Leadership: The Long View*, Cambridge, MA: MIT Press

Bazan, B. and J.P. Martin, 1991. 'The impact of the minimum wage on earnings and employment in France, *OECD Economic Studies*, **16**, 199–221

Bean, C.R., 1994. 'European unemployment: a survey', *Journal of Economic Literature*, **32**, 573–619

Bernard, A. and C.I. Jones, 1994. 'Comparing apples to oranges: productivity convergence and measurement across industries and countries' CEPR (Stanford), *Discussion Paper*, **389**

Blanchard, O., 1990. 'Unemployment: getting the questions right – and some of the answers', in J.H. Drèze and C.R. Bean (eds.), *Europe's Unemployment Problem*, Cambridge, MA: MIT Press

Bosworth, B. and G.L. Perry, 1994. 'Productivity and real wages: is there a puzzle?', *Brookings Papers on Economic Activity*, **25**, 317–44

Branson, W. and J.J. Rotemberg, 1980. 'International adjustment with wage rigidity', *European Economic Review*, **13**, 317–44

Bruno, M. and J.D. Sachs, 1985. *Economics of World Stagflation*, Cambridge, MA: Harvard University Press

Card, D., 1992. 'Do minimum wages reduce employment? A case study of California, 1987–89', *Industrial and Labor Relations Review*, **46**, 38–54

Card, D. and A. Krueger, 1994. 'Minimum wages and employment: a case study of the fast food industry in New Jersey and Pennsylvania', *American Economic Review*, **84**, 772–93

Card, D., L.F. Katz and A.B. Krueger, 1993. 'An evaluation of recent evidence on the employment effects of minimum and subminimum wages', *NBER Working Paper*, **4528**, Cambridge, MA: NBER

Crafts, N., 1992. 'Productivity growth reconsidered', *Economic Policy*, **15**, 387–426

Dickens, R., S. Machin and A. Manning, 1993. 'The effects of minimum wages on employment: theory and evidence from the UK', *Discussion Paper*, London School of Economics, Centre for Economic Performance

Elemeskov, J. and M. MacFarlan, 1993. 'Unemployment persistence', *OECD Economic Studies*, **21**, 57–88

Franz, W. and R.J. Gordon, 1993. 'Wage and price dynamics in Germany and America: differences and common themes', *European Economic Review*, **37**, 719–54

Freeman, R.B., 1994. 'How labor fares in advanced economies', in R.B. Freeman (ed.), *Working Under Different Rules*, New York: Russell Sage Foundation

Gordon, R.J., 1993. 'The jobless recovery: does it signal a new era of productivity-led growth?', *Brookings Papers on Economic Activity*, **24**, 271–316

Gordon, R.J. and N.M. Baily, 1991. 'Measurement issues and the productivity slowdown in five major industrial countries', in G. Bell (ed.), *Technology and Productivity: The Challenge for Economic Policy*, Paris: OECD, 187–206

Grubb, D. and W. Wells, 1993. 'Employment regulation and patterns of work in EC countries', *OECD Economic Studies*, **21**, Paris: OECD, 7–58

Johnson, G.E. and F.P. Stafford, 1993. 'International competition and real wages', *American Economic Review, Papers and Proceedings*, **83**, 127–30

Krueger, A.B., 1994. 'The effect of the minimum wage when it really bites: a reexamination of the evidence from Puerto Rico', *NBER Working Paper*, **4757**, Cambridge, MA: NBER

Krugman, P., 1987. 'Slow growth in Europe: conceptual issues', in R.Z. Lawrence and C.L. Schultze, *Barriers to European Growth: A Transatlantic View*, Washington, DC: The Brookings Institution, 48–75

Layard, P.R.G., S.J. Nickell and R.A. Jackman, 1991. *Unemployment: Macroeconomic Performance and the Labour Market*, Oxford: Oxford University Press

Lindbeck, A., 1994. 'The welfare state and the employment problem', *Seminar Paper*, **561**, Institute for International Economic Studies, Stockholm

1994b. 'The unemployment problem', *Seminar Paper*, **575**, Institute for International Economic Studies, Stockholm

Sachs, J.D., 1979. 'Wages, profits, and macroeconomic adjustment: a comparative study', *Brookings Papers on Economic Activity*, **10**, 269–319

Saint-Paul, G., 1994. 'Searching for the virtues of the European model', CEPR, *Working Paper*, **950**, London: CEPR

Simon, J., 1991. 'The case for greatly increased immigration', *The Public Interest*, **102**, 89–103

Discussion

CHARLES R. BEAN

Richard Gordon's chapter 14 represents an innovative attempt to bring the productivity dimension into discussion of the causes of high unemployment in Europe. According to Gordon, low productivity growth and stable unemployment in the USA and high productivity growth and rising unemployment in Europe are intimately related phenomena, something that has not been properly recognised. In fact I am not sure this is the case, as many of those who defend the European model of labour market organisation with heavy regulation, generous welfare states, etc. would argue that the deregulated Anglo–US model delivers lower unemployment only by generating low productivity 'McJobs' in hamburger flipping and the like.

Furthermore, as Gordon's contribution highlights, whether there is indeed a trade-off between unemployment and productivity is actually quite a complex question. The analysis, in essence, represents a re-working of the standard 'battle-of-the-mark-ups' model, as in figure 14.2, with productivity rather than the real wage on the vertical axis, and unemployment rather than employment on the horizontal axis. In figure 14.2 the price-setting relationship is downward-sloping in the short to medium run if capital is fixed because of the diminishing marginal product of labour. (The mark-up of prices over marginal cost must also not be too anti-cyclical.) This immediately transfers into an upward-sloping unemployment–productivity trade-off (UPT). However, if the production function exhibits constant returns to scale and capital is variable, then the price-setting relationship is flat, and so is the UPT. The level of real wages and productivity is pegged down by the cost of capital, which would be determined by the rate of time preference in a closed economy or the world rate of interest in a small open economy subject to perfect international capital mobility. This dynamic adjustment of the UPT as capital accumulation/decumulation occurs – portrayed in figure 14.6 – makes the use of the UPT tricky as a diagnostic tool. The fact that the long-run UPT is flat also qualifies the suggestion towards the end of the chapter that policies which shift the wage-setting schedule down are best avoided because of their adverse effect on productivity; this is only a transitory phenomenon with productivity ultimately unaffected, but both employment and output higher.

Gordon's analysis concerns the relationship between the *level* of unemployment and the *level* of productivity (or alternatively between the *change* in unemployment and productivity *growth*). It is worth noting that there is another strand of literature that concerns the relationship between the *level* of unemployment and productivity *growth*. The causal relationship here can run in both directions. Consider first the effect of productivity growth on unemployment. There are three possible mechanisms here. First, rapid productivity growth raises the marginal profitability of opening up new job slots, raises vacancies, and lowers equilibrium unemployment (the so-called 'capitalisation effect'). Second, in a bargaining context rapid productivity growth also raises future wages and thus makes workers less inclined to press for higher wages today (in case they jeopardise their employment status). Third, if productivity growth occurs through Schumpeterian 'creative destruction', then faster productivity growth raises the rate of job destruction and the rate of inflow into unemployment, so tending to raise equilibrium unemployment. The net effect of these three forces is therefore ambiguous, although Alogoskoufis *et al.* (1995) argue that the evidence suggests that the first two effects dominate the latter. Since the reduction in the rate of productivity growth was greater in Europe than the USA, this may help to explain why unemployment also rose more in Europe.

In order to generate causality running from the level of unemployment to productivity growth one needs to introduce endogenous growth mechanisms into the picture. An obvious one is learning-by-doing effects, which will not take place if workers are out of a job. More generally, unemployment and productivity growth may be jointly determined by labour market features. Thus Bean and Pissarides (1993) show in an overlapping-generations framework with an endogenous growth technology that an upward shift in the wage-setting schedule not only raises the level of equilibrium unemployment, but also raises productivity growth because it redistributes income towards the workers who are also the savers in their economy. Alternatively high wages (caused, for example, by a high minimum wage or high union power) may induce a bias in technical progress towards labour-saving innovation. Note that this last mechanism, although apparently similar to the standard substitution of capital for labour, is subtly different in the capital–labour substitution will be reversed if wages fall back, but the production function will be permanently affected by biased technical change.

Let me finish with a remark concerning policy choices. Gordon argues that in Europe attention should be directed towards those policies that lower unemployment without lowering productivity, i.e. that *shift* the UPT rather than seeking to move along it. Acceptable policies under this banner include reducing mismatch and deregulation of labour and product markets; deemed less appropriate are policies that shift the wage-setting schedule, such as lowering benefits or reducing union power. However, from a welfare angle what matters is output *per capita* of the population, not of the employed labour force. Distributional effects aside, *anything* that reduces unemployment will be welfare-improving provided labour's marginal product exceeds the social opportunity cost of working.

REFERENCES

Alogoskoufis, G., C.R. Bean, G. Bertola, D. Cohen, J. Dolado and G. Saint-Paul, 1995. *Unemployment: Choices for Europe (Monitoring European Integration)*, **5**, London: CEPR

Bean, C.R. and C.A. Pissarides, 1993. 'Unemployment, consumption and growth', *European Economic Review*, **37**, 837–54

15 Gross job reallocation and labour market policy

PIETRO GARIBALDI, JOZEF KONINGS and CHRISTOPHER PISSARIDES

The popularity of the notion of 'labour market flexibility' in the policy debate in Europe and the interest in sectoral reallocations as a source of the business cycle in the USA, have led to the accumulation of statistical information on job reallocations in several OECD countries. The manufacturing data gathered by Davis and Haltiwanger (1992) in the USA have been particularly influential. Davis and Haltiwanger found that a large number of jobs close down each quarter and an equally large number open up, apparently for specific reasons unrelated to sector or economy-wide performance. When the OECD (1994) compiled comparable data for several of its members, it found that the US experience was by no means exceptional, though it also found that job reallocations elsewhere were on average not as frequent.

Concurrently with the collection of data for the OECD, a number of authors have developed theoretical models to explain the processes of job creation and job destruction. A natural way to think about job creation is in terms of the matching of job-seekers with hiring firms, along the lines of the equilibrium search literature. The search literature, however, had only a rudimentary discussion of job destruction and several suggestions have been put forward about the factors underlying the destruction process. In the analysis of Mortensen and Pissarides (1994) jobs differ according to productivity and job destruction takes place when the productivity of a job, following a shock, drops below a reservation value. Thus job destruction in this model follows the same principles as job creation in more conventional matching models when there are productivity differentials that are specific to the match. In both cases jobs are independent 'islands' that are subjected to both idiosyncratic and common shocks, and the key variable that determines whether they are active or not is a unique reservation productivity (for other approaches to job creation and job destruction, see Davis and Haltiwanger, 1992; Bertola and Caballero, 1994).

Our interest in this chapter is to draw together the international data compiled by the OECD (1994) with a view to understanding the relation between unemployment and job reallocation and the role of labour market policy in the determination of job reallocations. Of course, we have no strong theoretical reasons for supposing that more job reallocation is better than less, or vice versa. We also do not have evidence yet of a firm relationship between overall unemployment and job reallocation. But we present evidence that low job reallocation is associated with more long-term unemployment. Since the latter is bad, in terms of the loss of skill of the unemployed and the disenfranchisement of those who suffer it, the supposition is that policies that restrict job reallocation are not good for the ability of the market to turn over its unemployment stock quickly.

In section 1 we give some definitions and briefly describe the job reallocation data. In section 2 we discuss the relation between unemployment and job reallocation in the context of the flow approach to labour markets. Finally, in section 3, we look at the relation between labour market policy and job reallocations, with the help of simple charts for 10 OECD countries with comparable data.

1 Preliminaries

Gross job reallocation is normally defined as the sum of the absolute value of the change in employment in each unit in the sample (normally an establishment but sometimes a company) expressed as a proportion of total employment. More specifically, the job creation rate (*JC*) is defined as the sum of all increases in employment expressed as a proportion of total employment, and job destruction (*JD*) as the sum of all decreases in employment, again expressed as a proportion of total employment.

Note that because in each case we are dividing by total employment, not just employment in either expanding or contracting establishments, the figure obtained for *JC* is not the average expansion rate of expanding establishments and the one for *JD* is not the average contraction rate of contracting establishments. If, say, exactly half of establishments expanded, then to find the average expansion rate, *JC* has to be doubled.

The difference between *JC* and *JD* gives the rate of net employment change. Their sum gives the gross job reallocation rate. Because of our definitions, the gross reallocation rate is the average change (positive or negative) experienced by the typical establishment in the sample, expressed as a proportion of mean employment for each establishment. To express it as a proportion of beginning-of-period employment, one can use the transformation $2(JC+JD)/(2-JC-\mathrm{JD})$, so if, say, gross reallocation on our definition was 0.2, using beginning-of-period employment would make it 0.22.

Our analysis in this chapter compares average job reallocation rates for the OECD countries that have comparable data in order to say something about the role of labour market policy. Since job reallocation rates are highly sensitive to the phase of the cycle that the economy is in, for the comparison to be meaningful the economies have to be either in about the same phase of the cycle over the same period or the period has to be long enough to average across cycles. Our sample period is for 1982–9, when the economies covered were coming out of recession and productivity growth was positive. The only exception amongst the OECD countries with comparable data was New Zealand, which experienced a deep recession with large negative productivity growth during this period. For this reason, we decided to drop New Zealand from the sample. We also decided to make no effort to bring Japan into the sample (the only major OECD economy left out), because with its peculiar job tenure arrangements it would be difficult to compare its job reallocation rate with that of other OECD countries.

Table 15.1 gives the job reallocation rates for the 10 countries in our sample. It also splits job reallocation according to whether the reallocation of jobs was due to contraction or expansion of existing establishments (continuing establishments) or to new entry or exit. The reason for the split is partly that much of what we shall have to say about policy relates more to large established units than to small new ones and partly that data for what official statistical tables call 'entry' and 'exit' are likely to be less reliable than data for continuing establishments. Another reason that one might want to split the sample is that the theory of job creation and job destruction as it applies to continuing establishments is often different from the one that applies to entry and exit.

Table 15.1 shows that gross job reallocation rates across the 10 OECD countries ranges from a low of about 14 per cent for Belgium to a high of nearly 30 per cent for Denmark. When entry and exit are removed the range drops to about 9 per cent for the UK and Belgium to 20 per cent for Canada. The new entry and exit figures show some peculiarities, with France having approximately twice as high a figure as the rest of the sample, with the exception of Sweden and Denmark. In contrast, when only continuing establishments are considered, France and Germany have a broadly similar figure, which is between the figure for the low-reallocation countries of Europe (the UK and Belgium) and the high-reallocation countries of North America. The North American countries do emerge as countries with more reallocation, as conventional wisdom would lead us to believe, but not by much when compared, for example to Sweden (which might have a high reallocation rate because of its limited-duration job subsidisation programmes).

Table 15.1 *Job reallocation in OECD countries, 1982–9*

Country	Total job reallocation	Continuing establish.	Entry/ exit
Belgium	14.4	8.9	5.5
Canada	26.3	20	6.3
Finland	22.4	15.1	7.3
France	27.1	12.9	14.2
Germany	16.5	12.1	4.4
Italy	23.4	15.7	7.7
Sweden	29.1	17.6	11.5
UK	15.3	8.7	6.6
USA	23.3	18.9	5.7
Denmark	29.8	18.7	11.1

Sources: OECD (1994); Davis and Haltiwanger (1992); Leonard and Van Audenrode (1994).

If there are large net changes in employment in the sample, the conventional definition of gross job reallocation can give rise to some peculiarities. For example, imagine a situation where no establishment in the sample expands but all establishments contract by 5 per cent. Then, the gross job reallocation rate will be 5 per cent, though there has been no job reallocation within the sample. Contrast this with a situation where 3 per cent of workers leave from half the establishments and get jobs in the other half. In the latter case the gross job reallocation rate will be 3 per cent, lower than in the former cases, though in the latter there has been a genuine reallocation of 3 per cent of the jobs.

For this reason, a more satisfactory definition of job reallocation is what is often called the 'excess' job reallocation, defined as the average of gross reallocation *minus* net employment change for each year in the sample (or, alternatively, as twice the average of either JC or JD, whichever is the smaller in each year). Unfortunately we do not have enough data for the countries in our sample to compute the net reallocation rate for all of them. For the five countries for which we have data, the relation between gross and excess reallocation turns out to be linear with positive intercept and slope less than one, and correlation coefficient 0.97. Table 15.2 gives the gross and excess reallocation rates for the five countries. We do not, however, have any priors on what that relation should be or why it turned out to be almost exactly linear in our subsample. For this reason we did not make any attempt to use the estimated relation to derive a transformation for all the countries in the sample, restricting ourselves to the use of the gross reallocation rate.

Table 15.2 *Gross and excess job reallocation*

Country	Source	*JR*	Excess
Germany	Boeri and Cramer (1993)	15.94	14.23
UK	Konings (1993)	7.18	2.81
USA	Davis and Haltiwanger (1992)	20.43	15.62
Canada	Baldwin *et al.* (1994)	20.52	17.77
Italy	Contini and Revelli (1993)	23.06	21.96

2 Unemployment and job reallocation

A number of different and often contradictory views about the relation between job reallocation and unemployment have been expressed. The current interest in job reallocation has been partly stimulated by the interest in the 'sectoral shifts hypothesis', especially in the USA. This is the view, first put forward by Lilien (1982), that the business cycle in the USA is largely driven by reallocation shocks – that is, shocks that shift real demand from some sectors of the economy to other sectors and which on aggregate might be neutral. A faster pace of reallocation, according to this view, requires more inter-sectoral labour mobility: if there is inertia to mobility, unemployment results in the contracting sectors that might last sufficiently long to mirror the cyclical persistence of unemployment in the real economy.

Although intense testing of this view has rejected it as the dominant explanation of the business cycle, even in the USA where unemployment persistence is a lot less than it is in Europe, if there is any truth in this hypothesis we should expect to observe a positive association between unemployment and gross job reallocation. For if the pace of allocative shocks is faster, gross job reallocation rates should be higher at the same time that unemployment is higher.

Contrary to this view, it is often stated that large rates of job reallocation indicate a 'flexible' labour market that is better able to adapt to new conditions. By implication, the allocation of resources in a labour market that has more job reallocation should be better and so unemployment should be less.

Unfortunately, neither economic theory nor empirical work is yet in a position to shed light on the relation between gross job reallocation and the allocation of resources in the labour market. For example, one question to which we do not have an answer is whether individuals participating in a market with more job reallocation should expect to find a better quality match during their job search. Future work will undoubtedly shed light on this and other related questions. But in the absence of a theoretical framework that could shed light on the welfare implications of more or less job reallocation, it is difficult to evaluate the welfare effects of policy measures that influence job reallocation.

For this reason, we follow here a different route. We outline first a way of thinking about unemployment, derived from the flow approach to the labour market, that shows that there should not necessarily be a relation between gross reallocation and unemployment, though it is unlikely that there should be no relation between gross job reallocation on the one hand and either unemployment or its duration on the other. We then look at our cross-section of OECD countries and discover that there is a relation between the duration of unemployment and gross job reallocation. We draw some tentative conclusions about the process of job search in the labour market and the contribution of job reallocation to it, before we proceed to evaluate the effects of policy measures on job reallocation.

Looking at employment flows first, we follow the empirical literature and define the rate of job creation (*JC*) and the rate of job destruction (*JD*) during a year by

$$JC = (\text{no. of jobs created/total employment})$$
$$JD = (\text{no. of jobs destroyed})/\text{total employment})$$

If there is an exogenous rate of labour force growth of n, employment flows in the steady state have to satisfy,

$$JC - JD = n.$$

Gross job reallocation is conventionally defined as $JR = JR + JD$.

Let us now look at unemployment flows. In the steady state, the mean duration of unemployment is defined as

$$D = (\text{Total unemployment})/(\text{Outflow from unemployment}).$$

If the rate of unemployment is to remain constant during periods of population growth, the number of unemployed workers has to grow at rate n. Writing total unemployment as U, we therefore have,

$$\text{Unemployment inflow} - \text{Unemployment outflow} - nU.$$

The unemployment inflow is made up of workers who lost their jobs because of job destruction and of some other workers, mainly those quitting their jobs to enter unemployment and new labour force entrants. We can therefore write the above formula for unemployment equilibrium in the form,

$$\text{Job destruction} + \text{Other inflow} - \text{Outflow} = nU.$$

Straightforward manipulation of this formula gives,

$$JD + (\text{Other inflow})/(\text{Employment}) - u/(1-u)D = nu/(1-u)$$

where u is the rate of unemployment. Since from the definition of job reallocation we know that $JD=(JR-n)/2$, we can write the above formula in the form,

$$JR = 2u'/D + \text{other terms}$$

where u' is the ratio of unemployment to employment and the other terms depend on the rate of labour force growth and the other inflow into unemployment as a proportion of employment.

This formula shows that there is an equilibrium relation between the rate of unemployment, the gross job reallocation rate and the mean duration of unemployment but that this relation depends also on other factors. As an example of what might cause differences in job reallocation rates across countries, suppose that two countries have the same unemployment rate, say 8 per cent, but one has population growth rate of 2.5 per cent and the other 1.5 per cent. Then, the formula above says that job reallocation in the country with the faster growth should be 2.35 percentage points higher than in the country with the lower growth. Country differences in the flow into unemployment other than those caused by job destruction can also produce differences in job reallocation rates at given rate and duration of unemployment. Since (in the absence of reliable data) such differences are likely to be larger than differences in population growth rates, we would expect this factor to be a more important cause of distortion in the relation between unemployment, its duration and the job reallocation rate.

Having noted that, however, it would be surprising if there were no relation between the three variables in what is essentially a formula between five variables, one of which (the labour force growth rate) is not likely to differ much across the OECD. In an international cross-section, we might well find that all three are related, or that the two are related and the third is following its own path. But complete independence between unemployment, its duration and the job reallocation rate is highly unlikely.

In figure 15.1 we plotted the gross job reallocation rates against an OECD-adjusted definition of unemployment for the 10 countries in our sample. There is a small negative correlation, derived from the negative association between gross job reallocation in continuing establishments and unemployment.

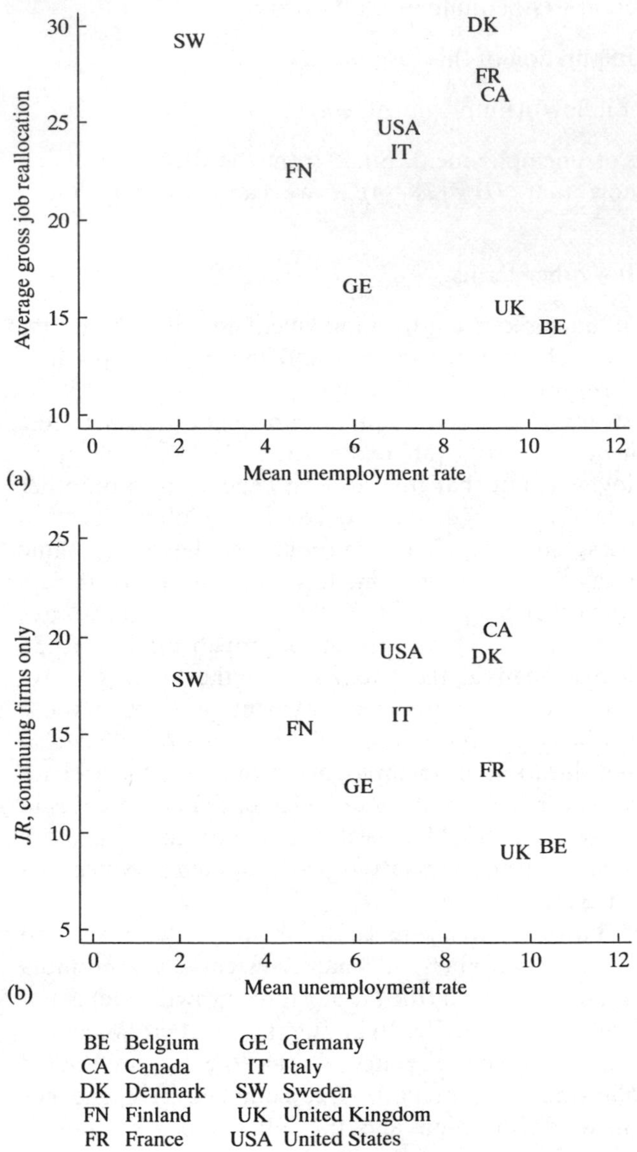

Figure 15.1 Job reallocation and unemployment

There is, however, a stronger correlation between gross job reallocation and the duration of unemployment. Figure 15.2 shows that countries with less job reallocation have more long-term unemployment. The relation is again stronger for the job reallocation that is due to continuing establishments than for the whole economy. As in the case of total unemployment, there is virtually no relation between entry and exit and the gross job reallocation.

Thus, in our decomposition shown in the formula above, the correlation appears to be mainly between the gross reallocation rate and the duration of unemployment, with very little correlation between the gross reallocation rate and unemployment. Of course, the formula above does not suggest any explanation for the observed relations. A possible explanation for the correlation between gross job reallocation and long-term unemployment runs along the following lines.

We think of the process that allocates workers to jobs as taking place in a large hiring hall (see also chapter 12 in this volume). Workers search for jobs with given intensity, they are prepared to accept jobs on the basis of a variety of reservation wages and firms choose which workers to hire on the basis of the expected productivity of the match and the wage rate. If the job reallocation rate is small, not many new jobs and also not many previously employed workers enter the hiring hall. The unemployed workers have fewer jobs to search but there is also less competition for them, because of the smaller inflow of workers into the hall. Our finding suggests that the unemployed are less likely to find a job when the inflow of both job vacancies and job-seekers is down. In the absence of the active job matching induced by large job reallocation rates, the unemployed are more likely to enter long-term unemployment.

If this way of looking at the matching process is correct, doubts can be cast on the 'insider–outsider' explanation of the persistence of unemployment and on the view that the unemployed cannot compete for jobs with employed or newly-unemployed job-seekers. Insider–outsider theory in this context would imply that the already unemployed are not active participants in a matching round generated by the entry of new jobs and new workers. This does not appear to be the case. The competition theory (Burgess, 1991) claims that the outflow from unemployment is virtually independent of the number of job vacancies in the market, which is also inconsistent with the view expressed above.

The process described is, however, consistent with a purely random matching game when the number of job vacancies is less than the number of job-seekers (or when there are increasing returns to scale in matching) and even more so with the matching ideas put forward by Coles (1992). In his model pre-existing unemployed benefit more from newly created

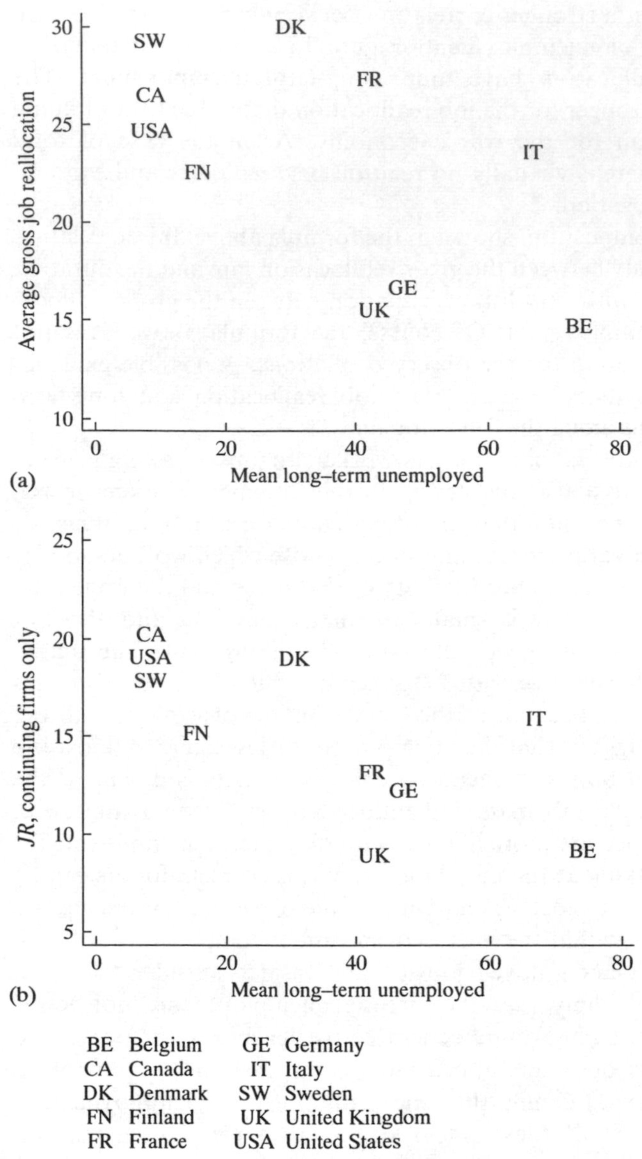

Figure 15.2 Job reallocation and long-term unemployment

job vacancies than from ones that already existed, because they had searched some or all of the already existing ones in the past without success.

Since long-term unemployment is wasteful in terms of the loss of skill and the disenfranchisement of those who suffer it, the lower long-term unemployment associated with higher turnover is one beneficial effect that we can identify at this level of analysis.

Another way of looking at the theoretical relations behind the correlations found between unemployment, its duration and job reallocations is to think of the job reallocation rate as largely determined by vector of variables X, the unemployment rate as largely determined by another vector Y, and the duration of unemployment determined by both X and Y. Such a formulation justifies the observed correlation between the job reallocation rate and long-term unemployment reported here, the correlation between the rate of unemployment and long-term unemployment previously found by several studies and also the absence of a close correlation between unemployment and gross job reallocation.

The analysis in section 3 identifies policy variables that belong to the set X, that is, variables that might explain the co-movement between job reallocation and long-term unemployment for a given rate of unemployment.

3 Job reallocation and labour market policy

We look at three kinds of labour market policy and, rather briefly, at what might be described as industrial policy. The labour market policies that we look at are direct restrictions on the firm's ability to fire employees, 'passive' policy, which we measure by income support for the unemployed, and 'active' policy, which we measure by the amount of money spent per unemployed worker on measures designed to speed the transition from unemployment to employment. Industrial policy refers to subsidisation of industrial production or employment.

3.1 Employment protection legislation

We refer to restrictions on the firm's ability to dismiss employees as employment protection legislation. Our measure of such legislation derives from the OECD, where an index is constructed showing the sum of weeks' notice and weeks' compensation that has to be given to dismissed employees. In our sample and for the period of our analysis this index ranged from virtually zero for the USA to 7 for Belgium and Italy.

The obvious link between employment protection legislation and the gross job reallocation rate is that restrictions on dismissals impose a shadow price on the firm, leading to a drop in dismissals. Because the entry into unemployment is as a consequence reduced, there is less exit, that is, less job creation. Alternatively, looking at it from the firm's point of view, a shadow price on dismissals should lead to higher labour costs and so lower demand for labour. Either way, employment protection legislation should lead to less job reallocation. This link, which has featured in the labour demand literature several times (see, for example, the survey by Nickell, 1986), has also been explored more recently in models with explicit job creation and job destruction processes by Millar and Mortensen (1994) and Garibaldi (1994).

The negative correlation between employment protection legislation and job reallocation is clearly visible in our sample, especially when entry and exit of firms is excluded from the sample (figure 15.3). Since restrictions on dismissals apply mainly to large firms, the fact that there is no relation whatsoever between entry and exit on the one hand and employment protection legislation on the other (not shown in the figures 15.3a and 15.3b) is not surprising. The simple correlation coefficient between the gross job reallocation rate of continuing establishments and the OECD index of employment protection legislation is −0.57.

3.2 Passive policy measures

Next we consider the relation between unemployment compensation, the main determinant of the generosity of passive policy measure, and gross job reallocation. In the model of Mortensen and Pissarides (1994) more generous unemployment compensation reduces the cost of unemployment and raises the wages of labour. The implication on impact is that there is less job creation and more job destruction, with the Beveridge curve shifting out. But the economy eventually settles down to a higher-unemployment equilibrium, where job creation and job destruction are equal to each other. Whether they equalise at higher rates or lower ones, when compared with the previous steady state, is not possible to say without knowledge of parameter values (although it should be noted that in simpler versions of the model, when the wage rate is independent of the rate of unemployment, higher unemployment benefit always leads to a higher job destruction rate in the steady state and so to more reallocation). So, although the generosity of the unemployment insurance system unambiguously raises unemployment, it can either reduce or lower gross job reallocation.

In figure 15.4 we plot gross job reallocation against the summary index

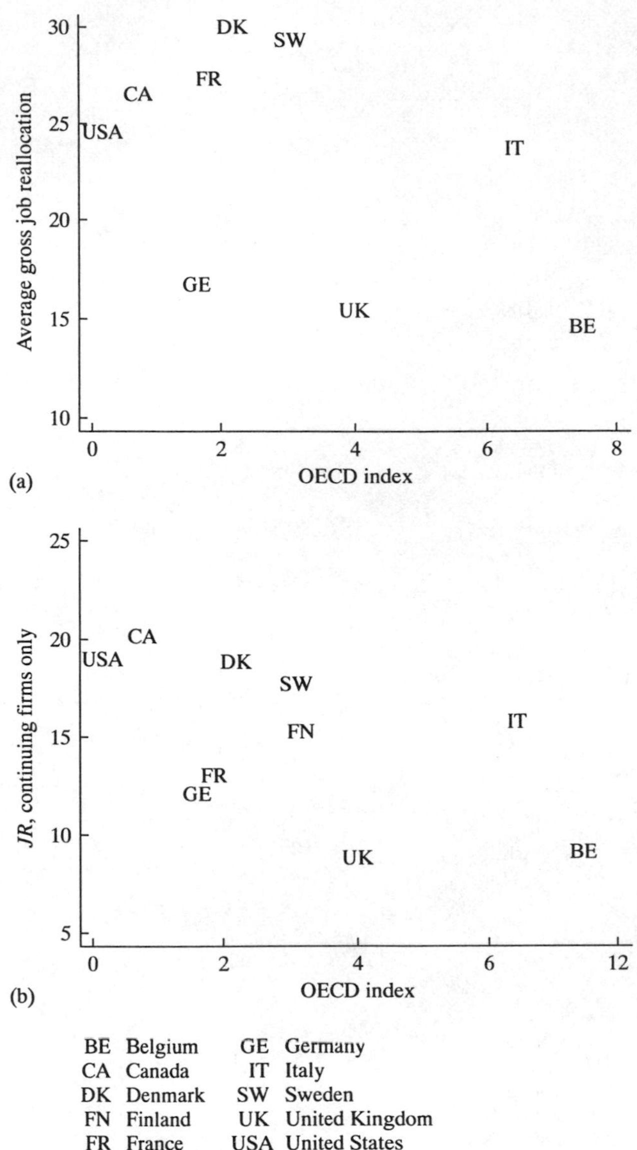

Figure 15.3 Job reallocation and employment protection legislation

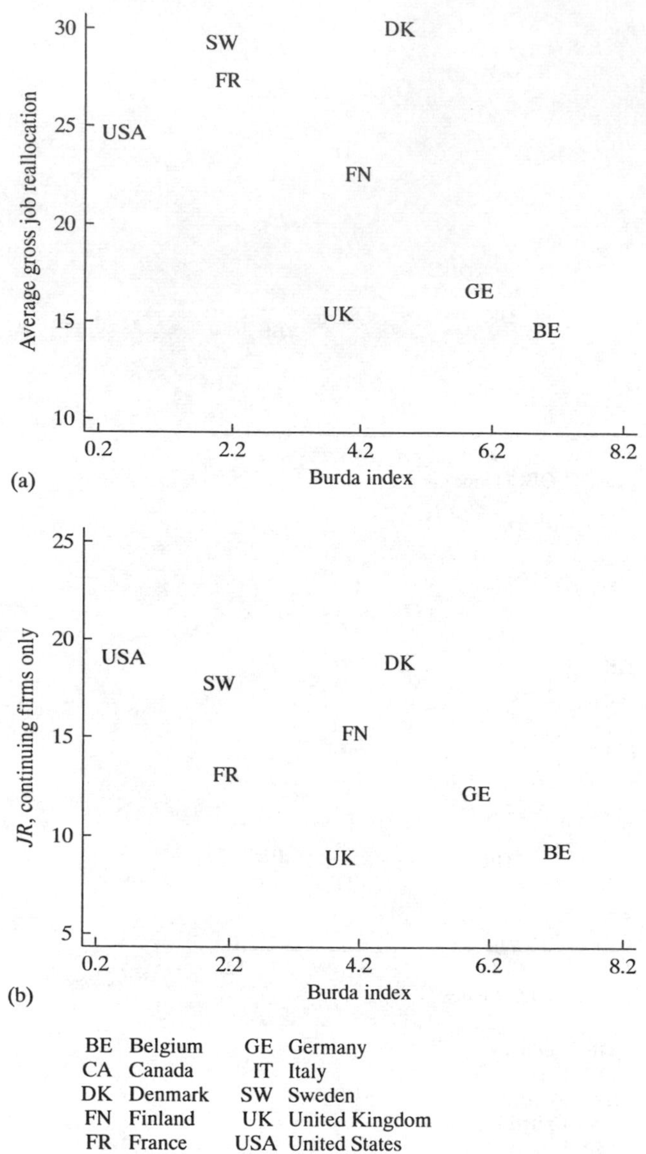

Figure 15.4 Job reallocation and unemployment insurance: 1

for the generosity of the unemployment insurance system in the OECD constructed by Michael Burda (1988). There is a clear negative relation, with the simple correlation coefficient a strong 0.6. Interestingly, even new entry and exit are negatively related to the generosity index, though with a smaller correlation coefficient of 0.39. On closer examination of the relation between gross job reallocation and the two main components of the generosity index, the level of unemployment benefit and the duration of benefit entitlement, an interesting contrast emerges. The relation between the level of benefit and job reallocation is positive, but that between job reallocation and the duration of benefit is strongly negative. Figure 15.5 shows the two relations for continuing establishments.

Our models of job creation and job destruction are not yet in a position to tell us why there is this contrast between the level of benefits on the one hand and their duration on the other. Simulations with the level of benefits in the Mortensen–Pissarides model shows that the economy settles at slightly higher job turnover rate when the level of benefits is increased indefinitely. The analysis of limited duration benefit is a lot more complicated because we lose the stationarity of the optimal strategies. In partial models of search, the prospect of benefit exhaustion leads to a decline in the reservation wage during search and therefore to an increased probability that the worker will be willing to accept a job quickly. Since the jobs that are likely to be accepted in this rather desperate state are not likely to be good long-term jobs, we would expect job destruction to be more frequent. Put differently, in countries where workers know that the state will support them indefinitely they spend more time looking for regular stable jobs; if support is expected to run out they would be prepared to take irregular jobs on a short-term basis. When employers realise the attitude they are more likely to bring on to the market the irregular short-term jobs in the latter case than in the former.

3.3 Active policy measures

Much has been written recently on the advantages of active versus passive labour market policies (OECD, 1993, 1994). Active measures include the subsidisation of employment, the subsidisation of training, the running of a state Employment Service and the provision of help to unemployed job-seekers, in the form, for example, of guidance how to fill in job application forms. Thus, spending on active measures either make the unemployed more employable or they help their job-seeking activities. Passive measures simply provide income support.

There is some evidence that active measures reduce overall unemploy-

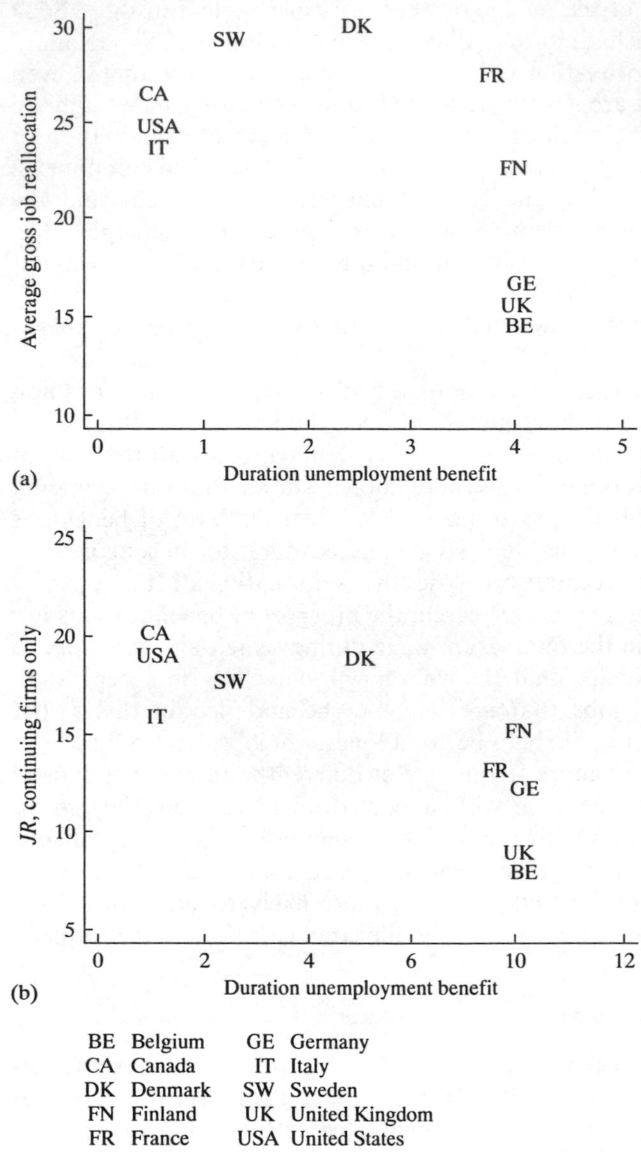

Figure 15.5 Job reallocation and unemployment insurance: 2

ment but the evidence with regard to job reallocations is mixed. One of the difficulties in making international comparisons of the effects of active labour market policies is how to deal with Sweden. Because Sweden spends far more on active labour market policies than other OECD countries do, any international comparison involving a small number of countries is bound to be dominated by Sweden. If we are not careful in drawing inferences from the comparison we might end up building an argument entirely on the comparison of two points, one for Sweden and one for the rest of the OECD.

This problem shows up in our comparisons too. In figure 15.6 we plot average job reallocation rates against two measures of active policies, the average spending per unemployed worker as a proportion of output per head and the ratio of active to passive spending. Because Sweden is way above all other countries on both measures and because it has a high job reallocation rate, the correlation coefficients between each of our measures and the job reallocation rate are both positive and equal to 0.25. But if Sweden is excluded from the comparison it is clear from figures 15.6a and 15.6b that the relation between active policy and job reallocations is, if anything, negative, though weak.

In view of this, we cannot infer anything about the relation between job reallocation and active measures from our small sample. Indeed, one is likely to learn more about the contribution of active policy to job reallocation from a detailed study of Swedish labour markets than from an international comparison. For example, job reallocation rates are likely to be positively affected by active measures if the jobs that are subsidised to hire unemployed workers are not regular long-term jobs, or if workers are dismissed when the subsidy ends. But they might reduce job reallocations if the subsidisation stops firms from closing down jobs that are hit by negative shocks.

3.4 Industrial policy

Finally, we examine the role of subsidies to industry. Our source for the data is the statistical office of the EU, so we have data only for the member countries in our sample and for the USA. It has been argued by Leonard and van Audenrode (1993) that subsidies to industry slow down the process of job renewal by supporting ailing plants. This should imply strong negative correlation between job reallocation and industrial subsidies, at least for continuing plants. There is some evidence for this in our sample for continuing plants, with a correlation coefficient between the two for the seven countries of −0.25 (figure 15.7). But the relation is lost when we consider total reallocation (since only established ailing

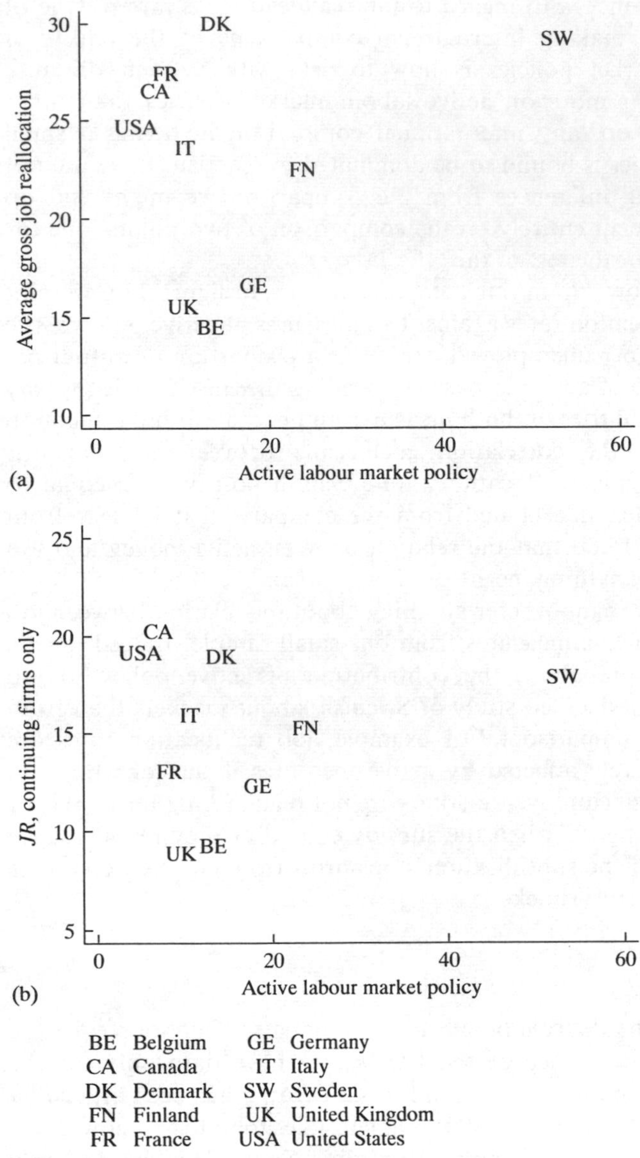

Figure 15.6 Job reallocation and active labour market policy

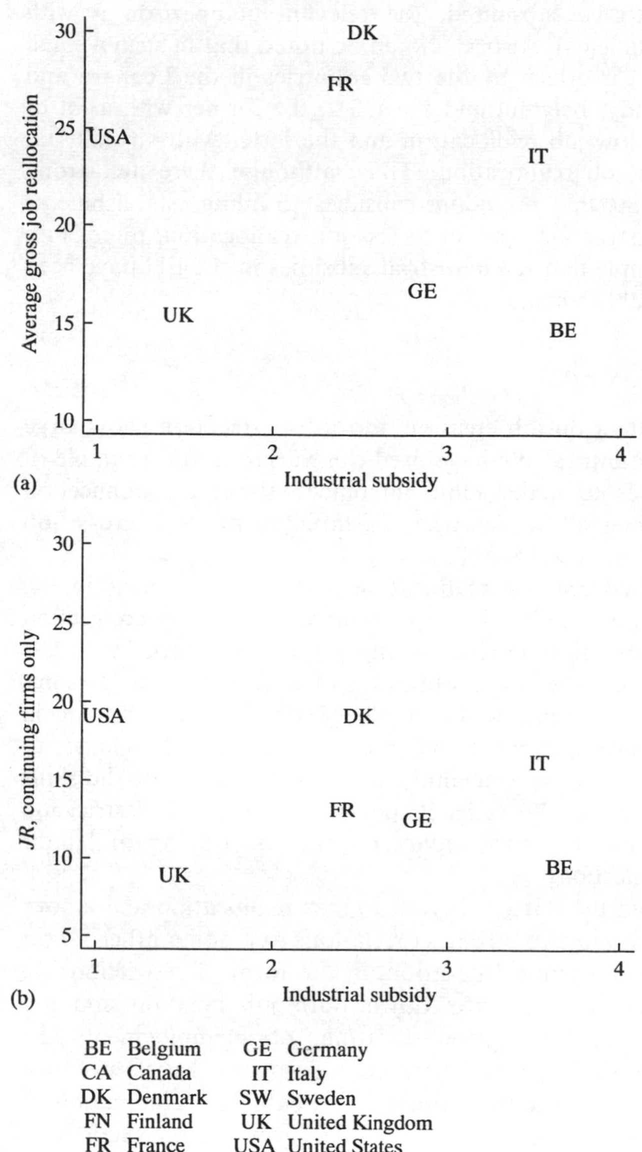

Figure 15.7 Job reallocation and industrial subsidy

plants are likely to be subsidised, the relevant comparison is with continuing establishments). Also, it should be noted that in such a small sample, the relation is driven by the two countries in the Leonard and van Audenrode study, Belgium and the USA, the former with a lot of subsidies and very low job reallocation and the latter with virtually no subsidies and high job reallocation. Thus, although there are strong theoretical arguments that providing subsidies to ailing establishments leads to less job destruction, and so to less job reallocation, there is no evidence in our sample that the industrial subsidies in the EU have been directed at such establishments.

4 Conclusions

The international data on job creation and job destruction show large variations across countries. We have used this variation for a sample of 10 OECD countries to make some inferences about the connection between gross job reallocation and unemployment and gross job reallocation and labour market policy.

The connection between job reallocation and unemployment in the international domain is rather loose, but there is a strong connection between reallocation and long-term unemployment. Countries with less job reallocation experience longer durations of unemployment, presumably because in those countries the employed do not easily relinquish their jobs to enter unemployment and give the unemployed a chance to replace them. Since long-term unemployment is not good for the skills and the morale of those who suffer it, policy measures that restrict job reallocation will have negative impact on the functioning of labour markets in this connection.

When we examined the relation between gross reallocation and labour market policy we found two strong correlations and some other looser ones. Employment protection legislation, in the form of restrictions on the dismissal of employees, slows down both job creation and job destruction, and so leads to longer durations of unemployment. The indefinite availability of unemployment compensation also slows down the reallocation of jobs. The mechanism is probably the elimination of low-productivity jobs that the long-term availability of income support is likely to bring about.

In contrast, the level of unemployment benefit seems to exert a mild positive influence on job reallocation, though not a very important one. Spending on active labour market policies, perhaps surprisingly, does not appear to exert a significant influence on job turnover, though it should be pointed out that when using OECD data to say something about active policy conclusions are dependent on how one treats Sweden, because of its far higher spending on these measures. As it turns out, Sweden has a high job reallocation rate but our summary data cannot identify active policy spending as the reason.

Finally, industrial subsidies appear to have a mild negative effect on job reallocation, though a warning should be sounded here, too. We have data for this comparison for only seven of our countries and the comparison is dominated by the experience of two countries, the USA with no subsidies and high turnover and Belgium with a lot of subsidies and low turnover.

Appendix: definitions and sources

Cross-country comparisons

Job reallocation

Data come from OECD, *Employment Outlook* (1994, chapter 3). They are drawn from national, primarily administrative sources that differ in their methods of collection, in their employment coverage and sectoral classification. The information refers to establishments except for Canada, Italy and the UK, where data refer to firms. An attempt was made by the OECD to standardise as much as possible. For the USA we used the manufacturing rates computed by Davis and Haltiwanger (1990), adjusted to make them comparable to rates for the entire economy. The transformation was based on a comparison between Canadian job flows for the overall economy (OECD, 1993) with Canadian flows for the manufacturing sector only (Baldwin *et al.*, 1994). This led to multiplying the job flow rate for manufacturing by 1.2. We did not use the US figures in OECD (1994) because they are based on a much smaller data set with two-year frequency. The two-year frequency biased the picture in favour of entry and exit.

Other variables

- Unemployment: OECD (1992) standardised series in Layard *et al.* (1991).
- Active labour market policies: OECD (1992, table 2.B.1) and own calculation. Percentage of GDP spent on active labour market policies divided by the unemployment rate. Data refer to annual averages between 1980 and 1990.
- Employment protection legislation; sum of required severance payments and maximum period of notice to be given to dismissed employees: OECD (1993).
- Long-term unemployment; unemployment of more than one year duration over total unemployment. Data refer to annual averages between 1980 and 1990: OECD (1993).
- Subsidies: Subsidies to firms as a percentage of value added (Leonard and Van Audenrode, 1994).
- Duration of unemployment benefits: Layard *et al.* (1991).
- Replacement ratio: Layard *et al.* (1991).

Time series

Table 15.2 is based on a time series for each country. The sources are:

- UK: Konings (1993). Sample of 993 big firms for UK manufacturing sector between 1973 and 1986.
- USA: Davis and Haltiwanger (1990). Sample of 70 per cent of US establishments in the manufacturing sector. Data collected by the Bureau of Census between 1973 and 1986.
- Italy: Contini *et al.* (1992). Sample of 80 per cent of Italian firms between 1980 and 1988. Data collected by the Italian social security system INPS.
- Canada: Baldwin *et al.* (1994). Annual census of the Canadian manufacturing sector (1972–1986).

REFERENCES

Baldwin, J., T. Dunne and J. Haltiwanger, 1994. 'A comparison of job creation and job destruction in Canada and the United States', *NBER Working Paper*, **4726**, Cambridge, MA: NBER

Bertola, G. and R.J. Caballero, 1994. 'Cross-sectional efficiency and labour hoarding in a matching model of unemployment', *Review of Economic Studies*, **61**, 435–56

Boeri, T. and U. Cramer, 1993. 'Why are establishments so heterogeneous?', mimeo

Burda, M., 1988. 'Wait unemployment in Europe', *Economic Policy*, **7**, 391–426

Burgess, S.M., 1991. 'A model of competition between employed and unemployed job seekers: an application to the unemployment outflow rate in Britain', University of Bristol, *Discussion Paper* **90/260**

Coles, M.G., 1992. 'Understanding the matching function: the role of newspapers and job agencies', University of Essex, mimeo

Contini, B. and R. Revelli, 1993. 'Job creation and labour mobility: the vacancy-chain model and some empirical findings', *R & P Working Paper*, **8/R & P**, Turin

Contini, B., S. Gavosto, R. Revelli and S. Sestito, 1992. 'Creazione e distruzione di lavoro in Italia', *Temi di discussion Banca d'Italia*, **177**

Davis, S.J. and J. Haltiwanger, 1990. 'Gross job creation and destruction: microeconomic evidence and macroeconomic implications', *NBER Macroeconomic Annual*, **5**, 123–68

1992. 'Gross job creation, gross job destruction and employment reallocation', *Quarterly Journal of Economics*, **3**, 819–63

Davis, J., J. Haltiwanger and S. Schuh, 1993. 'Small business and job creation: dissecting the myth and reassessing the facts', *NBER Working Paper*, **4492**, Cambridge, MA: NBER

Garibaldi, P., 1994. 'Is job reallocation counter cyclical when firing is costly and takes time', *Working Paper*, , Centre for Economic Performance, LSE

Konings, J., 1993. 'Gross job creation and gross job destruction in the UK manufacturing sector', *Discussion Paper*, **176**, Centre for Economic Performance, LSE

Layard, P.R.G., S.J. Nickell and R.A. Jackman, 1991. *Unemployment: Macroeconomic Performance and the Labour Market*, Oxford: Oxford University Press

Leonard, J. and M. Van Audenrode, 1993. 'Corporatism run amok: job stability and industrial policy in Belgium and the United States', *Economic Policy*, **17**, 355–400

Lilien, D., 1982. 'Sectoral shocks and cyclical unemployment', *Journal of Political Economy*, **90**, 777–93

Millar, S.P. and D.T. Mortensen, 1994. 'The unemployment and welfare effects of labor market policy: a comparison of the US and UK', Northwestern University, mimeo

Mortensen, D.T. and C. Pissarides, 1994. 'Job creation and job destruction in the theory of unemployment', *Review of Economic Studies*, **61**, 397–416

Nickell, S.J., 1986. 'Dynamic models of labor demand', in O. Ashenfalter and P.R.G. Layard (eds.), *Handbook of Labour Economics*, Amsterdam: North-Holland

OECD, 1992. *Employment Outlook*, Paris: OECD

1993. *Employment Outlook*, Paris: OECD

1994. *Employment Outlook*, Paris: OECD

Discussion

BRIAN BELL

The relationship between gross job reallocation and labour market variables is an important one, that both theory and empirical work must address. Chapter 15 by Garibaldi, Konings and Pissarides represents a first stab at the empirical side. In this Discussion, I begin with a consideration of the relevance of cross-country differences in gross job reallocation. I then discuss the comparability of the data for the 10 countries considered and finally assess the validity of the empirical results presented in the chapter.

1 Do cross-country variations in gross job reallocation tell us anything?

At first glance, the gross job reallocation rates reported in chapter 15 would surprise most labour economists. If it is supposed that high levels of reallocation signify a flexible labour market, then apparently Sweden and France have some of the most flexible labour markets in the OECD, and even Italy has broadly similar results to the USA.[1] This suggests that such a simple interpretation cannot be given to reallocation rates.

The authors acknowledge that there are 'no strong theoretical reasons for supposing that more job reallocation is better than less'. Indeed, the only reason suggested for favouring high levels of job reallocation is that it appears to be negatively correlated with long-term unemployment. In light of this the authors suggest that 'policy measures that restrict job reallocation will have negative impact on the functioning of labour markets'. Surely, however, policy makers are likely to be interested in more general measures of economic welfare. Most importantly, chapter 15 shows no relationship between reallocation rates and the total unemployment rate.

I now outline one simple reason why cross-country reallocation rates may not be as informative about the labour market as is first thought. Consider a world in which the only type of shocks that occur are industry-specific, i.e. they affect the same industry in each country in the same way. Further suppose that labour market structures are identical in all economies and that all labour markets are perfectly flexible. However, due to historical and comparative advantage reasons, the shares of employment in different industries differ across countries. Then equilibrium will be characterised by differing gross job reallocation rates provided the industry-specific shocks are not drawn from identical distributions. Since I assume that labour markets have exactly the same characteristics in all countries, it follows that one cannot, *a priori*, assume that differing gross job reallocation tells us anything about labour markets in different countries. It may simply reflect differing industrial mixes.

I make this point not because I think it is necessarily an accurate description of the world, but rather to warn against making rash judgements about labour markets from reallocation rates. Furthermore, the evidence in table II of Davis and Haltiwanger (1992) shows that job reallocation rates vary quite significantly across two-digit industries in the USA. For example the average job reallocation rate varies between 14.0 per cent in Tobacco to 28.8 per cent in Lumber and Wood Products. Hence there may well be something in the industrial mix story. I conducted a simple experiment to investigate this issue for the UK. I matched the two-digit industries in Davis and Haltiwanger (1992) as closely as possible to two-digit industries in the UK. I then calculated the employment shares for the UK and applied them to the US reallocation rates. The implied total job reallocation rate in manufacturing for the UK would then be 19.9 per cent which is only marginally below the figure for the USA (20.5 per cent). This experiment does not, however, provide proof against an industrial mix story, since we do not have an establishment-level job reallocation rate for the UK, and the rate reported in the chapter (15.3 per cent) is likely to be biased downward because it is a firm-level measure. Furthermore it may be argued that the UK and USA are the most similar countries in the OECD in terms of industrial mix, and the explanation may be more successful in other countries.

2 Is the data what we think it is?

OECD (1994, p. 104) advises that, when using this data, 'cross-country comparisons must be made with great care'. I highlight two concerns with the data used in chapter 15.

First, it is unclear whether the data for Canada, Italy and the UK can be compared with the other countries in the sample. Data for these three countries are derived from firm-level sources, while data for the remaining countries are from establishment-level sources. Though firm-level reallocation rates are biased downwards by omitting within-firm reallocation across establishments, we have little idea as to the extent of the bias or whether the bias is similar across countries. Konings (1993) suggests that the bias is not insignificant for the UK, though the establishment-level data he had access to was far from ideal.

Secondly, the distinction between reallocation caused by continuing establishments and by births/deaths is important. Garibaldi *et al.* concentrate on continuing firms' reallocation, arguing that 'the theory of job creation and job destruction as it applies to continuing establishments is often different from the one that applies to entry and exit'. While this is true, there is a more pressing empirical justification for concentrating on continuing establishments only. OECD (1994) point out that definitions of birth and death vary widely across countries. For example, births can appear for any of three reasons: (i) the creation of a new business from scratch, (ii) the take-over of an existing business by an entrepreneur, and (iii) the reallocation of an existing business into another area or industry. Presumably economists wish to concentrate on (i) but different countries have different definitions.[2] Similar problems affect the definition of deaths.

This is not to say that we should ignore the role of births and deaths in the process of job reallocation. For the USA, Davis and Haltiwanger (1992) show that 20 per cent (25 per cent) of job creation (destruction) occurs because of births (deaths). Indeed in France, openings and closures exceed the continuing establishments in job creation/destruction rates (OECD, 1994, p. 106).[3] However, given the problems outlined in this section, Garibaldi *et al.* are surely right to concentrate on continuing establishments only.

3 Are the empirical results significant and robust?

All the results reported in chapter 15 are based upon bivariate correlations between reallocation rates and alternative policy measures. A simple analogy to the empirical growth literature suggests the danger of such analysis. Levine and Renelt (1992) have shown that many results from cross-country regressions of growth are not robust to changes in the conditioning set of variables in the regression. Of course, bivariate correlations have no conditioning set, and so the results are likely to be even more fragile.

To test the robustness of the results, I performed a set of simple regressions. First I estimated bivariate regressions of the relationships reported in the chapter and recorded the significance of the correlation. I then ran regressions in which I included a single conditioning variable and tested whether the coefficient on the policy variable of interest remains significant (and of the same sign). So, for example, to test the robustness of the employment protection (EPL) effect, I ran regressions that include EPL and total unemployment as independent regressors, EPL and the Burda index, etc. I only include one conditioning variable because we begin with only 10 degrees of freedom.[4] There are seven independent variables (Unemployment rate (*UR*), Proportion of Long-Term Unemployment (*LTU*), Employment Protection Legislation (*EPL*), the Burda measure (*Burda*), Benefit Duration (*BD*), Active Labour Market Policies (*LMP*), and Industrial Subsidies (*IS*)). Bivariate results are in table D15.1 and multivariate results in table D15.2.

The signs on the coefficients in table D15.1 are consistent with those reported in chapter 15 but the *t*-statistics show that only two correlations are significant, namely the long-term unemployment and benefit duration effect. Hence most of the effects highlighted in the paper have no significant statistical foundation. Table D15.2 confirms this impression. Though the signs are in general consistent with Garibaldi *et al.*, once again only the duration effects are shown to be robust to the inclusion of conditioning variables. Interestingly, when both *BD* and *LTU* were

Table D15.1 *Bivariate results for job reallocation*

Variable	Coefficient	*t*-statistic
UR	−0.55	1.0
LTU	−0.13	2.5
EPL	−0.60	1.0
Burda	−1.11	1.8
BD	−1.98	3.7
LMP	0.04	0.4
IS	−1.10	0.6

Note: The results report cross-country regressions using gross job reallocation rates for continuing establishments as the dependent variables. All data is from Garibaldi *et al.*'s chapter 15.

Table D15.2 *Multivariate results for job reallocation*

Variable of interest	No. of times coefficient has same signs as table D14.	No. of times coefficient is 5% significant	Highest *t*-statistic
UR	6 of 6	0 of 6	1.3
LTU	6 of 6	3 of 6	2.4
EPL	5 of 6	0 of 6	1.5
Burda	5 of 6	0 of 6	1.6
BD	6 of 6	4 of 6	4.4
LMP	3 of 6	0 of 6	0.8
IS	4 of 6	0 of 6	1.9

included together both proved statistically significant (*t*-statistics of 3.4 and 2.3 respectively), which may indicate separate effects.

It follows therefore that policy makers would be unwise to base policy changes on their effects on reallocation rates since most of the results are not robust.

4 Should we be concentrating separately on job creation and job destruction rates?

Use of the gross job reallocation rates tells us nothing about whether the effect of a policy is operating on the creation or destruction of jobs. A simple example of this is given by considering the effects of employment protection legislation. Chapter 15 finds that more strict employment protection legislation results in lower job reallocation. However, two

Table D15.3 *Job creation and destruction regressions*

Variable	Job creation coefficient (*t*-statistic)	Job destruction coefficient (*t*-statistic)
EPL	0.03 (0.1)	0.31 (0.6)
Burda	0.03 (0.1)	−0.39 (0.5)
BD	−0.91 (3.1)	−0.81 (1.7)
LMP	−0.02 (0.3)	0.07 (1.3)
IS	1.4 (0.9)	2.07 (1.6)

Note: The dependent variables are job creation and destruction rates for continuing establishments only.

separate effects are at work here. Employment protection may be expected to reduce the job destruction rate for obvious reasons but may also reduce the job creation rate since employers will be more wary about taking workers on, knowing that they will face financial penalties if they subsequently have to make workers redundant. Of course in equilibrium, the job creation and destruction rates should be the same, but even over the relatively long period of 1973–86, Davis and Haltiwanger (1992) finds the rates to be different.

I now report regression results for each of the policy variables on job creation and job destruction rates. I follow Garibaldi *et al.* in focusing on continuing establishments only, and report only simple bivariate results. Results are presented in table D15.3, though we do not have data for the USA or Belgium. Again, the only statistically significant relationships are for benefit duration with roughly equal effects on creation and destruction.

In conclusion, theory does not at present provide much guidance as to whether higher rates of job reallocation are good or bad. In this chapter, the authors have boldly assessed the empirical evidence that exists. Their results suggest no clear pattern between reallocation, unemployment and labour market policy. Given this, policy makers are surely better advised to concentrate on results relating policy measures to unemployment directly. At the same time, the authors have provided a challenge to both theorists and empiricists to explain their observations.

NOTES

1 Though note that if only continuing establishments are considered, the USA has the second highest reallocation rate after Canada.

2 Even worse, since the data in chapter 15 refer exclusively to the 1980s, privatisation would be counted as a birth according to OECD (1994, p. 130).

Clearly this is nonsensical, and is as far from reallocation in the terms in which we think of it as it is possible to be.

3 These results for France are highly suspicious, but I have no idea whether they accurately reflect the state of affairs.

4 Indeed all the results in these comments and in chapter 15 must be treated with extreme caution given the small power that tests will have with so few observations.

REFERENCES

Davis, S.J. and J. Haltiwanger, 1992. 'Gross job creation, gross job destruction, and employment reallocation', *Quarterly Journal of Economics*, **107**, 819–63

Konings, J., 1993. 'Gross job creation and gross job destruction in the UK manufacturing sector', *Discussion Paper*, **176**, London School of Economics, Centre for Economic Performance

Levine, R. and R. Renelt, 1992. 'A sensitivity analysis of cross-country growth regressions', *American Economic Review*, **82**, 942–63

OECD, 1994. *Employment Outlook* 55 (June), Paris: OECD

Discussion

ANA L. REVENGA

In recent years, interest in employment reallocation has grown, motivated both by policy concerns over job creation and by the availability of new data. Much of this recent literature, however, has been country-specific, and has focused primarily on the issue of whether job reallocation is driven by structural or cyclical forces. In chapter 15, Pissarides *et al.* break away from this single-country focus, and attempt to do some comparative analysis. They carry out a brave exercise of trying to extract conclusions from 10 data points. Their attempt to do cross-country work should be applauded; unfortunately, one ultimately learns very little from this exercise. Let me elaborate why.

I would like to make two basic points. The first relates to the quality of the data used, the second to the adequacy of the empirical framework.

1 Comparability of the data

Chapter 15 relies exclusively on the comparison of job reallocation rates across several OECD countries. Looking at the data used to calculate these rates, it becomes obvious that there are many potential comparability problems. For one thing, the samples vary significantly across countries, which matters because of the extreme cyclical sensitivity of job reallocation rates. For example, whereas for some countries the sample corresponds to the expansionary 1984–9 period, for others (Belgium) it refers to the recessionary 1980–3. Yet for others, e.g. Finland, it corresponds to 1986–9. Periodicity of the data also varies: sometimes they are annual, at other times biannual. In the case of most countries, the data are establishment-based. But for Canada, Italy and the UK, they are firm-based. In the case of the USA, moreover, the original data pertained just to manufacturing, and have been adjusted to reflect totals for the whole economy using patterns for job flows for Canada. The point of all this is that the standard errors associated with the calculation of job reallocation rates for each of the countries are probably quite large, large enough to make comparisons that rely exclusively on the relative ranks of job reallocation rates across countries suspect.

If one examines table 15.1, in fact, it becomes clear that the range of job reallocation rates across countries is fairly narrow: they range from a low of 14.4 per cent for Belgium to a high of 29.8 per cent for Denmark. Those rates for continuing establishments range from 8.7 per cent to 20 per cent. My guess is that, if one took into account the standard errors resulting from comparability problems in the data, one would not be able to reject the hypothesis that job reallocation rates are roughly similar across countries, and lie somewhere in the range of 15–25 per cent.

Roberts (1996) calculated similar job reallocation rates for several semi-industrialised countries, namely Colombia, Chile and Morocco. His estimates range from 26–30 per cent for total job reallocation, and from 13–21 per cent for job reallocation within continuing firms. Interestingly, these estimates fall right within the range calculated for the OECD. All of this suggests that job turnover rates do not vary much across countries regardless of large differences in variables like economic structure and institutions. Alternatively, it could suggest that job turnover rates do not mean very much.

2 Confused causality

The authors' stated intention at the outset of chapter 15 is to obtain some new insights on the impact of labour policies on unemployment.

They do this by looking at the effect of policies on job reallocation, and then exploring the link between job reallocation and unemployment. The causality is apparently straightforward: if lower job reallocation is associated with higher unemployment and/or longer duration, then policies which contribute to lowering job reallocation will clearly tend to increase unemployment and/or lengthen duration. The policy variables are, in some sense, the 'exogenous' variables, while job reallocation rates and unemployment are endogenous.

Conceptually, this is a nice setup. The problem is that, empirically, the causality is not all that clear. And the way the analysis is carried out, on the basis of two-way correlations, does not contribute to clarify this causality or the relationships between the 'exogenous' policy variables and the endogenous job reallocation and unemployment outcomes.

As the authors themselves acknowledge, the analysis may simply pick up the influence of policy variables that simultaneously affect job reallocation and unemployment duration without there being a direct link between the former and the latter. Alternatively, the correlations could be spurious, reflecting the effects of other, unmodelled variables. For example, employment protection legislation appears to be associated with lower job reallocation (a fairly intuitive proposition). Does this mean that employment protection legislation is also associated with longer unemployment duration? We don't know. First, that relationship is never tested directly. Second, even if we were to find such a relationship, we do not know whether changes in job reallocation rates constitute the channel through which the effects of employment protection policies are felt; nor does chapter 15 provide a framework for exploring that issue. Moreover, could it not be that employment protection legislation is correlated with other factors that affect both job reallocation and unemployment duration, so that what we pick up are the effects of yet a different policy variable? As long as the analysis remains at the two-way correlation level, these questions are impossible to resolve.

Of course, with 10 data points, it is difficult to carry out any multivariate analysis. However, the authors could have been a bit more creative in their use of the data by exploiting, for example, the time dimension of the sample. They also could have structured the experiment more carefully, by examining the relationship between the relevant policy variable and the two outcome variables first independently, and then jointly.

A final problem with this analysis is that policies are not necessarily exogenous, so it becomes very hard to interpret the association between policies and turnover. For example, take the case of unemployment insurance (UI): does the USA have higher job reallocation rates because of its less generous UI? Or is it that high job creation rates make UI less necessary? Again, the direction of causality is not clear.

3 Conclusions

What comes across most strongly from this exercise is that job reallocation rates are quite similar across countries. The number of job positions being created and destroyed in Europe and the USA are just not that different. Yet we know that Europe and the USA differ dramatically in their rates of inflows and outflows from unemployment. This suggests that in trying to understand differences in unemployment behaviour and the impact of policies, we need to focus on worker flows and what determines their move in and out of unemployment, rather than on job creation and job destruction rates.

REFERENCES

Roberts, M.J., 1996. 'Employment flows and product turnover in three developing countries', forthcoming in M.J. Roberts and J.R. Tybout (eds.), *Industrial Evolution in Developing Countries: Micro Patterns of Turnover, Productivity and Market Structure*, Oxford: Oxford University Press

Part Six

Comparing unemployment policies

16 Unemployment in the OECD and its remedies

PATRICK MINFORD

There is evidence today of dramatic changes in the labour market as a result of competition between low-wage 'emerging-market' economies and the rich OECD countries. In previous work I and others (for example, Bean, Layard and Nickell, 1986; Davis and Minford, 1986; Layard and Nickell, 1985; Minford, 1983; and see Layard, Nickell and Jackman, 1991, for other relevant work) have explored how far one can account for changing unemployment in the OECD through general equilibrium models of the open economy. These models have used conventional 'elasticities' equations for the current account, assuming that the prevailing competition facing OECD countries was imperfect competition in manufactures from other OECD countries.

Such models have given fairly plausible results to date. The story they have told has also been qualitatively persuasive. In summary, it has identified the basic cause of high unemployment as long-duration unemployment benefits or equivalent social support. Given such a source of 'real wage rigidity' all sorts of developments whose effect would under flexible wages be to lower real wages have the effect of causing unemployment. It is possible to estimate the 'natural rate' of unemployment within such models, as the equilibrium once macroeconomic shocks to demand have died away. Theories of 'efficiency wages' are really, for all the claims one finds for them as a 'general' theory of unemployment (e.g. Phelps, 1994), merely one special development of the sort just described: if the 'outsiders' do not exhibit real wage rigidity then the fall in outsider real wages would displace downwards the comparator for insiders and the whole wage structure would be flexible. Thus unions, insiders or other sources of employee wage premia can all contribute to the explanation of unemployment within this framework of real wage rigidity created by social support.

This model remains adequate as a representation of the supply of labour. But if the nature of competition in the goods market is changing because of low-wage countries then some adaptation of the model is in order. That is what this chapter attempts. The trade interpretation of increasing wage dispersion offered in this chapter suggests that the problem for social policy is likely to get steadily worse without action (whereas the alternative technological interpretation suggests that there need be no worsening, indeed a reversal would be as likely – of course to the extent that technology is driven by emerging markets competition this would not be an 'alternative' at all).

1 Trade, development and global competition

The rapid growth first of Japan, then of the 'Little Dragons', and now most recently of the other 'emerging markets' (of Asia, Latin America and Eastern Europe), seems to suggest there may be some elixir that could suddenly turn previously torpid or declining economies into growth miracles. The most recent effort to produce evidence for it is Dollar (1992) and in the theory of growth Parente and Prescott (1993, 1994) have developed a formal framework in which what they call 'business capital', their name for the formula, is the key input into the growth process. The elixir could also be called 'open economy capitalism'; the adoption of secure property rights, not merely for home nationals but also for foreigners. The latter is a vital component because of the role played by foreign investment and technology transmission in the traded sector (perhaps also, but to a far more modest extent, the non-traded sector). The purpose of our model is to link the processes of growth, convergence and trade into a single theory, no component of which should prove unfamiliar but whose linkage has not hitherto to my knowledge been made.

The large and rapidly expanding literature of endogenous growth and convergence (for example, Romer, 1986; Lucas, 1988; Barro, 1991; Rebelo, 1991) has paid little attention to the role of trade and comparative advantage; the same was true of an earlier postwar literature (Solow, 1956; Denison, 1967, 1974). Yet it is in the traded sector of developing countries that growth tends first to manifest itself, through it too that technology is mostly transferred; also through it is exerted one of the major forces of convergence, that of wage equalisation. It therefore seems worthwhile to examine how far trade theory can add to the insights already achieved in this area.

This chapter sets out a particular model of two linked open economies, 'North' and 'South', and examines the nature of ultimate convergence and what the key elements are determining its pace. The theory on which it is based is that of Heckscher, Ohlin and Samuelson (hereafter HOS; Heckscher, 1991; Ohlin, 1933; Samuelson, 1948), with some suitable modifications to be discussed. There are many other trade theories: for example industrial oligopoly, intra-industry, product cycle, as well as the Ricardian (with no explicit production function) theory. However the relative attraction of HOS in the context of growth is that it is focused on the production function and its factor inputs. The dynamics by which factor and product properties evolve need to be captured by other theories; but these can be, as it were, bolted on to HOS.

The key assumption in HOS of constant returns to scale needs to be defended, especially as it is rejected in the industrial oligopoly approach. Again the latter may perhaps be thought of as a theory of first-mover advantage, giving insight into the dynamics of industrial competition. Yet ultimately constant returns to scale must prevail because increasing returns must be exploited by expanding firm size (if necessary, at the international level) while decreasing returns are eliminated through competitive entry by new firms. In such a world where constant returns have been produced, first-mover advantage ceases to be relevant if it can be challenged by new entrants. Thus the USA may have been the first successfully to establish a huge firm in aircraft production but that cannot prevent a firm in other countries challenging it, and perhaps ultimately displacing it, on cost grounds. HOS theory examines such industrial patterns purely on a cost basis without considerations of corporate history. It seems hard to argue with such a position from a long-term perspective: once a world-wide industry has exploited its increasing returns, then if its firms, however new, are cheaper in country *X* they will surely displace those of country *Y*, however long established.

The other key assumption of HOS, that factors of production can be distinguished by broad type, is self-evident. But as has long been recognised by HOS theorists (Jones, 1967) if less in application, it is important to distinguish mobile from immobile factors of production; only the latter play the usual HOS role of determining comparative advantage. Mobile factors accommodate to that pattern. Thus for example if capital is mobile at a price set internationally, its quantity will not help to determine comparative advantage (most empirical studies have dubiously proceeded as if capital was immobile: see Minford, 1989; Wood, 1994).

The model in this chapter builds onto these two basic HOS assumptions four main elements:

(i) A division of factors of production into mobile and immobile, mainly based on the degree of international market integration.
(ii) A non-traded goods sector, familiar from open economy macroeconomics.
(iii) The assumption that technology is superior in the North (where it

will generally have been created) and that it is transferred to the South in a catching-up process, that responds both to the physical ease of transfer and to the legal and physical environment of the South.

(iv) Assumptions about the supply of factors that give them non-zero elasticity explain both employment and skill formation. Some of them are quite rudimentary (and ad hoc), based on ideas from other areas of study; all invite much further research.

The rest of this chapter sets out the model (sections), whose equations are in the appendix on p. 528, and its broad implications – briefly, as a fuller account is contained in Minford, Riley and Nowell (1994); it then reviews some simulations from a calibrated version of the model (sections 3–4). Finally we discuss the implications for policy (sections 5–6).

2 The model

We distinguish five factors of production: capital, raw materials, land, unskilled ('raw') labour, and skill or human capital (embodied in labour).

Land is of course immobile. Labour we also treat as immobile, mainly for reasons of politics. Wages being generally higher in the North, because of its superior technology, migration would be from the South to North, probably in large quantities if permitted. Northern citizens, however, dislike this prospect and migration is restricted, except for small number of workers needed for specific reasons.

Raw materials are a traded good, and so treated as mobile. So is capital: most capital goods are tradeable, and finance is provided in a highly integrated world capital market, which is well known to generate near equality between long-term real borrowing rates. Of our five factors therefore three only are immobile: labour, human capital and land. These then become the key determinants of comparative advantage and development.

We identify three traded industries: agriculture (and other primary production), manufactures (other than those with 'complex', hard-top-transfer technology), and services (where we also include complex manufactures). These industries are respectively intensive in land, unskilled labour and skilled labour. The non-traded industry is considered fairly intensive in both unskilled labour and land.

With three immobile factors and three traded goods, our 3×3 system determines the absolute level of wages, returns to human capital and land rents given world prices of traded goods: these relative factor prices then fix factor shares in the three traded industries, whose size in turn depends on the amounts of the three factors available to the traded sector.

To determine these amounts we note that domestic goods prices are fixed by the costs of the three factors, given constant returns of scale and competition here as elsewhere. (Needless to say, unskilled wages in particular must be identical in the traded and non-traded sectors, implying that any international pressure lowering them in the traded sector is transmitted automatically into the non-traded sector.) Hence prices of domestic relative to traded goods are given by world prices and technology; by implication, any exogenous rise in demand for domestic goods is satisfied by a supply shift into domestic goods at constant prices – infinite supply elasticity. We therefore determine the amounts of the immobile factors available to traded goods industries simply by subtracting from their total supplies the requirements of domestic industry demand (figure 16.1).

It follows that total supply is strictly limited by immobile factor supplies, while its composition depends partly on the size of domestic goods demand and partly on the relative supplies of immobile factors left over after the satisfaction of this demand. We may now ask how total demand is determined.

Total supply and its composition will create a demand for capital goods: investment demand. The flow of real income from supply over time will create a dynamic problem of intertemporal utility maximisation for consumers. Government demands and tax rates, treated here as exogenous, modify this problem: but the government's intertemporal budget ensures that the present value of taxes equals that of government spending. The consumers' transversality condition ensures that their present value of consumption equals that of their net income (i.e., that of total income *less* government spending); they then set an optimal rate of consumption which if we treat households as infinitely-lived will obey the permanent income hypothesis. It follows that a 'young' LDC will, both in anticipation of rising income and in response to the high investment needs of growth, have demand typically well in excess of supply: the counterpart will be capital inflows on the balance of payments, its net demand on the international capital market. The model of the DC is under the assumption of no agricultural protection no different in specification: only its technology is superior.

Having sketched in the demand and productive conditions in both North and South, we now turn to the supply of immobile factors, hitherto held fixed, and to the transfer of technology.

Land we take as given in supply. But as we have already explained, since it is used in the non-traded sector, its supply to the traded sector is

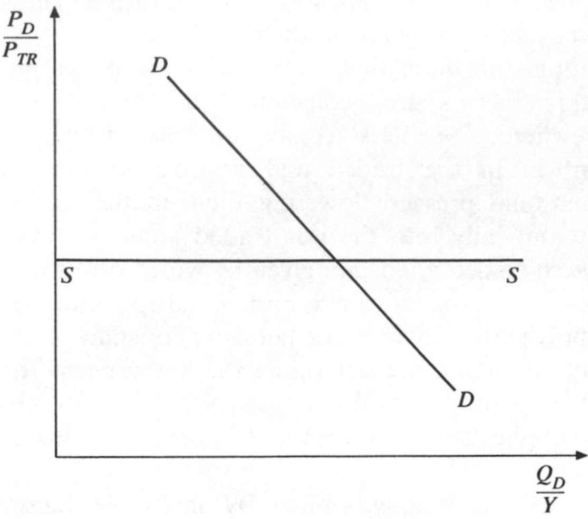

Figure 16.1 The supply and demand for non-traded (domestic) goods

constrained by its use in the non-traded sector. Hence there is a 'supply curve' of land to the traded sector, unlike the usual HOS setup.

Human capital is plainly the result of investment in education and training (in its widest sense). We assume that this investment is affected by the country's structure of marginal tax rates: the incentive to upgrade human capital depends on its returns, and the steeper the marginal tax rates schedule the less will be post-tax pay differentials and the less therefore the return to this investment.

The supply of raw labour is assumed to depend on the marginal tax rate on participation and the supply of hours by low-paid workers: this rate is overwhelmingly determined by the social security system, its benefits and conditionality. We summarise this for participation by the ratio of unemployment benefit to (unskilled) wages and the severity of 'work-testing' conditions (checking on the genuineness of search); and for the supply of hours by the net benefit withdrawal rate (the rate of 'negative income tax') for in-work benefits and the degree of monitoring of need for these (i.e. monitoring not related purely to actual means, but rather evaluating potential means).

Though we have not formally modelled unemployment, we identify it with the gap between the 'population' of unskilled workers and their employment level; we assume that there is only a minimal ('frictional') unemployment rate among skilled workers because their wages are well above benefit levels, and that their unemployment rate varies little. Such an implicit model is essentially the same as that of Minford (1983).

We abstract in this study from the rate of population growth itself by expressing the theory entirely in *per capita* terms. Our concern here is with living standards not with the size of nations.

Finally we consider technology, which we represent for simplicity as a factor-neutral multiplicative term in our constant-returns production functions. Under HOS theory if these terms were identical across nations there would be immediate factor-price equalisation.

We do not observe such rapid convergence. Accordingly we assume here that we do not have the same technology across nations: again this does not violate our perceptions of the real world – for whatever reason the schools, hospitals, factories and financial intermediaries (to take a few examples at random) of Bangladesh do not use the same advanced technologies of their equivalents in New England.

The basic reason for this we suggest is that technology is invented in one place (usually in a DC) and then must be transferred, mainly through inward investment though also by licensing and technical assistance, to local investors. Either way, it requires investment (either physical or equivalent investment in the licence contract) by foreign companies with the prospect of returns through outward transfer of profits. Our assumption is that these returns depend on a framework of property rights which provide foreign investors with some guarantees against expropriation. The speed of technology transfer we assume thus depends on the strength of property rights (for foreigners in particular), besides the technology of transfer itself (as set by computer power and transport costs). Hence the level of an LDC's technology term depends on the integral over time of these rights. (One could add that infrastructure capital spending in an LDC must also play a role both in raising the profitability of such technical transfer and in affecting the technological level of existing private capital in the LDC.)

This idea has similarity to that of Parente and Prescott's (1993, 1994) concept of 'business capital'. They enter this term directly as a factor input in the production function and proxy it by the level of the aggregate tax rate, this being the stimulus to entrepreneurship and business formation. In effect we have divided their notion into two parts: the effect of marginal tax rates on the supplies of labour and human capital, and the effect of property rights guaranteeing the appropriation of contracted returns. (We do not concern ourselves with taxes on capital because their incidence does not fall on capital owners in conditions of complete capital mobility: the issue is one of time-inconsistency, whether they can be sure to get their returns at all.)

There is also a relation here to work on 'self-enforcing' contracts between investors and (unreliable) LDCs – see Worrall, 1990; Thomas and Worrall, 1994). Plainly, there must be some such contract for any country with a given degree of unreliability. Our point could be put in those terms by relating the inefficiency of the contract (as compared with one written without concern for self-enforcement) to the poorness of property rights.

3 Simulation of the North–South model

To explore the nature of the future developments that may face the OECD it is helpful to simulate the model we have described above. The general nature of these results will be no surprise given the model's parentage. But it is impossible to work out the detailed implications of such a complex general equilibrium system even qualitatively, let alone quantitatively, without simulation; remembering the huge non-linearities in it we can see that the sort of shocks of interest that displace the model hugely away from its base trajectory cannot be assessed even by comparative statics of a linearised model (even this would be a computer task for such a large model).

The shock that is of primary interest is that of progressive technology transfer to the manufacturing sector of the South. We have chosen a growth rate of productivity in this Southern sector of 2.3 per cent a year: this generates about 4 per cent per year wage growth (relative to world manufacturing prices) for their unskilled workers. This seems a reasonably realistic order of magnitude to use as a benchmark for these countries as a group: the wage growth (deflated by dollar prices) among manufacturing workers of nine newly industrialising countries reviewed by the Bureau of Labor Statistics (Mexico, Hong Kong, Korea, Singapore, Taiwan, Pakistan, India, Sri Lanka, Israel) has been about 5 per cent p.a., unweighted, from 1975 to 1992 (or the nearest available year).

The mechanism underlying the results can be quickly summarised in familiar HOS terms. The rise in Southern productivity in manufacturing raises the relative reward to the (immobile) factor in which manufacturing is intensive – unskilled labour. The supply of this factor rises in the South, and via the Rybcynski theorem the expansion of manufacturing is accompanied by a contraction in the Southern supply of traded services and agriculture. The additional income in the South is spent broadly across all traded goods as against the additional Southern supply of manufacturing and contraction in that of services and agriculture. This raises world prices of services and agriculture, improving the terms of trade of the North and so its welfare. This fall in manufacturing's relative price however causes, via the Stolpher–Samuelson theorem, a fall in the real wages of the factor, unskilled labour, in which manufacturing is intensive, and a rise in the rewards of the factors, skill and land, in which it is not intensive. Overall both North and South gain from the rise in the South's productivity by more than the crude addition to world disposable income that this represents – in other words there are gains from trade. But there is a strong distributional effect in the North against unskilled labour.

It is worth pointing out, though it is obvious enough, that there may well be many other supply shocks hitting the world economy. These would overlay the effect here. I mention this because a Brookings study (Lawrence and Slaughter, 1993) concluded that such forces as shown in this simulation could not have been of any significance in the USA because the precise pattern of trends depicted here cannot be found in the US data. In the absence of a fairly complete analysis of other shocks, however, this conclusion is unsound – we discuss both it and other similarly sceptical US studies below.

Turning to the detailed results one can see that the stylised HOS story set out above is basically matched by the computer model. The orders of magnitude are of some interest and do not seem wholly implausible. Within the OECD the rewards to skill and land grow respectively by 2.6 and 2.8 per cent p.a. and unskilled wages fall by 1 per cent p.a. relative to the numeraire, manufacturing prices. In real terms (i.e. relative to the consumer price deflator, which rises by 1 per cent p.a.) figures are all reduced by 1 per cent p.a.: hence real wages fall by 2 per cent p.a., a pretty serious development. As a result there is a contraction of unskilled labour supply by 0.5 per cent p.a., 11 per cent overall in the 23 years; this is assumed to produce an increase in unemployment among unskilled workers, though some of them would retrain. In that period both human capital and land in use rise by 50 per cent; unemployment of skilled labour is assumed to be the minimal required for frictional reasons and so is assumed to be unaffected. Real disposable income rises by 1.9 per cent p.a.

In the South unskilled wages relative to manufacturing prices rise by 4 per cent p.a., and relative to a general basket by 2.5 per cent p.a. (the overall deflator rises by 1.5 per cent p.a.). There are also rises in the rewards of skill and land, by about one-third of this rate. The supply of unskilled labour rises by 56 per cent over the 23 years (2 per cent p.a.) and there are contractions in the supplies of both skill and land in use by 1.1 per cent p.a. or 20 per cent over the 23-year period – remember this is before other shocks and policy changes in these countries. Real disposable income rises by 2.8 per cent p.a. or 90 per cent over the whole period.

The weighted average growth in real disposable income across the world economy is 2 per cent p.a. against the direct effect of the productivity shock at 0.35 per cent p.a. The reason for this huge trade gain multiplier is that additional supplies of factors are released as well as the gains from exchange and specialisation.

4 A preliminary test of the emerging market hypothesis

A number of US authors (Borjas *et al.*, 1992; Bound and Johnson, 1992; Katz, 1992; Katz and Murphy, 1992; Krueger, 1991; Lawrence and Slaughter, 1993) have to varying degrees rejected the idea that the productivity growth in emerging markets has been the main cause of declines in the relative wages of unskilled OECD workers: the 'emerging market' hypothesis (in the US it is known, with a curl of the lip, as the 'Perot hypothesis'). The causal chain goes, as we have seen, through a rise in the relative prices of skill-intensive goods and services to the fall in the relative wage of Western unskilled workers. This terms of trade effect is both sufficient and necessary for the emerging markets to be the cause of the unskilled wage fall. Sufficient, because as we have seen in this model the Stolper–Samuelson theorem ensures that terms of trade movement powerfully drives wages. Necessary, because without terms of trade movement the fall in Western unskilled wages must be due to some other cause: presumably general technological change biased against unskilled labour. Lawrence and Slaughter look at this chain and find little evidence in US data of this terms of trade movement. Other authors look at the labour market itself, and explanations of relative wage movements in terms of shifts in supply and demand factors. Katz and Murphy, in fact, attribute a high proportion of wage movements to shifts in industry composition (away from unskilled labour-intensive products) as well as a little to rises in imports associated with the trade deficits of the 1980s; the former should, as they recognise, be included in trade-led change because changing comparative advantage must presumably explain changing industrial composition. Bound and Johnson, however, attribute hardly anything to these sources; while Borjas *et al.* attribute 15 per cent on the basis of a calculation of the factor content (skilled and unskilled labour) of US trade deficits, and the effect this would have in increasing the 'effective' relative supply of unskilled labour on the US market.

Lawrence and Slaughter have also made play with changes in factor use in the USA: that the increasing relative price of skilled labour should have driven down its factor share, had technology changes been unbiased in the West. They find again little evidence of change in skilled labour's share, and so conclude that there must have been a pro-skill bias in technology change. The main other evidence of this bias is also indirect, obtained as the residual once other explanations have been exhausted. Such is found pre-eminently by Bound and Johnson who attribute virtually the whole explanation to technical change. Some play is made with the unexplained relative wage movements *within* industries: it is argued that this in particular cannot be attributed to trade since this would affect primarily whole industries. The only direct evidence is found by Krueger from microdata where computers' introduction is found to be associated with an increase in the use of skilled, college-educated labour. Putting this together with the absence of a terms of trade effect they conclude overall that the source of the rise in skilled wages is technological.

A thorough critique of what is by now a large and growing US literature would have been too much for this chapter, which in any case focuses on world-wide, not specifically US, trends. I have not attempted it (but see Wood, 1994, for some comments and tests that give some support to the hypothesis). But one may point to a variety of apparent problems with these US studies.

Let us begin with the studies that focus on the labour market. Katz and Murphy state candidly that their work is 'partial equilibrium' and this is a fair comment on the whole of this part of the literature (i.e. all except Lawrence and Slaughter and to some extent Borjas *et al.*). All use in somewhat differing ways simple supply and demand models for different groups of workers differentiated by skill. Taking the supply of each group as exogenous, they then estimate relative wage reduced-form equations whose arguments are relative supplies, relative demands and technical change as the residual (specific and general change are distinguished with 'general' being found by averaging assumptions). Katz and Murphy estimate demand by weighting together industry demands using input–output: Bound and Johnson go further and estimate industry relative wage effects based on the wages they normally pay (so a contraction in a high-paying industry would tend to lower wages in a group intensively used by that industry). In both studies, the large rise in the relative supply of college graduates in the 1980s significantly depresses their relative wages, creating much more for these demand and technical factors to explain. In principle, Bound and Johnson apply this methodology in the most general way. They note that their equation encompasses the four candidate explanations of rising wage inequality: trade, union decline, supply and technology. The flavour of their results is shown by their decomposition of the 0.163 log rise (18 per cent) in the college versus high school wage premium from 1979 to 1988: 0.036 is 'rents' (union and other monopoly power), −0.10 is supply, 0.013 is demand, the other 0.215 is technical change (of which only 0.019 is specific).

One could scrutinise this and other decompositions in terms of this methodology and note the ways in which the trade explanation may have been short-changed. Two points are worth noting. First there is the discrepancy between the Katz–Murphy and Bound–Johnson results on demand owing to different methods of attribution. The latter pair may seem more thorough in producing weighted industry wage effects, but they do this at the expense of introducing wages into the explanation: a quantity-based demand measure has the advantage of being free of endogenous variable bias. Secondly the industrial breakdown is extremely broad, particularly in manufactures. Katz–Murphy at least break this down into low-tech, basic and high-tech, Bound–Johnson only into durable and non-durable. This means that within-industry changes are likely to be highly trade-dependent; there is for example movement 'up the value added chain' within each such narrowly-defined industries as knitted clothing.

However there is a far deeper problem with this whole manner of testing the trade hypothesis, as the model of this chapter shows. The general equilibrium causation described here is from world prices to relative wages; from relative wages and other factor prices to relative factor supplies; and from relative factor supplies to relative quantities produced. This causal ordering basically comes from the constant-returns-to-scale assumption of HOS combined with the assumption of market-clearing. Another way of putting the point is that HOS produces a set of strong identifying restrictions which deny those (exogenous supplies of factors and industry quantities, implying that we are estimating demand-for-labour equations) implicitly used in this labour literature. The brutal truth is that this literature is simply beside the point. (This is not to say that it is irrelevant *per se* – it may well test a variety of other interesting hypotheses – merely that it does not test the trade hypothesis, at least in the form set out here.)

The study of Borjas *et al.* lies midway between this labour market approach and a fully-fledged test of the HOS hypothesis. Borjas *et al.* use HOS in terms of the factor content of US international trade. They argue that imports compete with US production while exports are an additional demand for it. Hence the labour content of net exports can be converted into a derived net demand for US labour, which can be entered into the sort of labour market model just considered. They find this explains 15 per cent of the relative wage behaviour. However their approach is vulnerable to the same criticism that it does not test the HOS causal process. The factor content of imports works to drive up the (world) terms of trade for the skilled labour-intensive products in which the US has a comparative advantage: these price changes in turn drive up the profitability of these products and so the relative wages of skilled labour. but of course it is not just the factor supply to US trade that does this but rather that to the whole world market: so the HOS factor content idea is fair enough but would need to be applied at a global level – a difficult task. It is easier to test the hypothesis at the price–wage stage.

This leaves Lawrence and Slaughter, who have noted these difficulties and have properly confronted the trade hypothesis from the general equilibrium viewpoint (i.e. within its own terms). Their results are exclusively for the USA but as a Northern country *par excellence* its behaviour should be consistent with it. Their methods are straightforward. They review the same facts on relative wages (I ignore their points about average wages which are irrelevant to the hypothesis here): they gather data on the terms of trade between unskilled labour-intensive manufactures and the rest, and they look also at changes in factor intensity within US manufacturing.

As they point out, HOS requires that the terms of trade improve for skilled labour-intensive products and that this causes further a substitution in all industries away from skilled labour. They check US manufacturing behaviour in the 1980s for these two facts. They define skilled labour as non-production, unskilled as production workers. Using the Bureau of Labor Statistics international price data, they find that in both exportable and importable industries prices weighted by shares of non-production employment grew less rapidly than prices weighted by shares of production employment – the opposite of HOS. As for factor intensity, they find that at SIC 2, 3 and 4 levels within the NBER Trade and Immigration data base there was in the vast majority of industries rising skilled labour intensity, in spite of generally rising skilled relative wages – again the opposite of HOS. Finally they find in the same data base that industries weighted by non-production employment shares had faster productivity growth than when weighted by production employment, and this more than offset their tendency to enjoy falling relative prices – suggesting that technological change was the force driving up skilled labour demand and wages. If correct, the Lawrence–Slaughter view would not contradict our model, but it would imply that the dominant US shock was to the technology parameters of the US price–cost equations. It would in principle be possible for a strong emerging market effect to be supplemented by such a technology shock; but the world terms of trade of unskilled-intensive manufactures should at least decline if so, and this should show up equally in the US terms of trade. Therefore the Lawrence–Slaughter facts are a serious challenge for the hypothesis. As we shall see, their terms of trade facts diverge hugely, not merely from HOS but also from international data. Beginning therefore with their price data, we may ask how far they control for quality and composition drift: it is highly likely that the composition of US exports of unskilled labour-intensive products would have moved under competitive pressure rapidly up the value added chain.

The method of generating terms of trade data also does not correspond to HOS. What we want is a separation of industries into skilled and unskilled labour-intensive, and the relative prices of these two. What we get is the same prices used twice, but with different weights. Suppose that the US production structure was changing rapidly in the direction of skill-intensive industries whose prices were rising rapidly: their base-period weights would be low.

It is possible that problems arise with the use of non-production labour as the measure of skill. For example the USA has a comparative advantage in sophisticated transport equipment (aeroplanes, etc.): the skilled labour used in this industry is very largely production workers. In computing skill content (Minford, 1989) I used the average wage of workers employed: it is by no means clear that the implied ordering of industries is the same as using the share of non-production workers. It is also odd to look separately at exportable and importable industries: it is differences between these two groups that contribute the terms of trade changes! Indeed earlier Lawrence and Slaughter indicate that aggregate terms of trade improvement contributed an additional 2 per cent to US living standards over the 1980s: this covers more than manufactures but it still sits oddly with the later data. In short, we may reasonably ask for some more straightforward measures of the relevant terms of trade, to set beside the international facts, to which I now turn.

We do appear to have reasonable data on international prices. The unit value indices gathered by the UN are base-weighted and highly disaggregated. They, too, do not control for quality change; but because they are world prices the bias from this source should be less (in US goods we would expect to see products where low-wage competition is great go rapidly upmarket, as for example into fashion clothing; worldwide 'clothing' is subject to less drastic change). They also have the major advantage that we can select the products corresponding to the theoretical categories of our model and establish 'world' price series for them.

It therefore seems logical to start our empirical search with some basic international price data. In earlier work (Minford, 1989) I found uncontroversially that skill-intensive manufactures largely coincided with machinery and transport equipment, MTE. The UN usefully provides a price index for this, based on four large exporters (the USA, Japan, Germany and Sweden).

Further, as our theory suggests, traded services are skill-intensive. Indeed the category was named 'services'. However this is intended to include other skill-intensive products. Thus we aggregate traded services and MTE into our 'services' model category. Services price data is the US CPI for services. We weight the two series by their share in export value added (not recorded exports: goods exports are gross product while services are net value added): sources for this are national accounts data for manufacturing and balance of payments data for services credits.

For our unskilled-intensive category of 'manufactures' we use the UN series for the prices of LDC manufactured exports.

The result is shown in figure 16.2. It reveals a large and impressive shift in the terms of trade in favour of skill-intensive product over the past twenty years.

For the record figure 16.3 shows the ratio of the straightforward UN manufactured export price series for DCs and LDCs. This reveals a terms of trade shift within manufactures in favour of developed countries that is of a similar order to the adjusted measure above. As MTE and service prices have moved similarly (being driven by common western factor prices and technology), this is not surprising.

This preliminary empirical attempt suggests that the North–South simulation may well be telling the key story. The relevant terms of trade have been declining steadily while relative wages have been falling steadily. What remains to be fitted into the picture is just what has been happening to technology and factor shares in industry; here, too, we must carefully consider the Lawrence–Slaughter data.

Lawrence and Slaughter's key facts are reproduced in their figure 7, our figure 16.4. This displays relative wage and factor intensity changes over the 1980s. We criticised above the use of non-production workers in ranking skill intensity of US manufacturing industries. Let us nevertheless suppose for purposes of argument that within any given industry *changes* in skilled employment and wages are reasonably correlated with *changes* in non-production employment and wages. Notice that in panel C, the disaggregated 4-digit SIC level, there is a clear negative relationship between relative wage change and relative non-production worker intensity. This at least is consistent with the view that, holding technology constant, the terms of trade-driven rise in relative wages caused factor substitution generally.

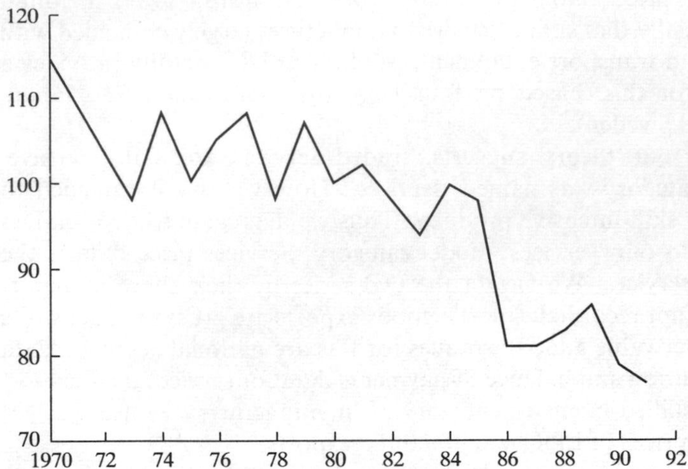

Figure 16.2 The ratio of DCs' manufacturing export prices ($) to DCs' export prices of machinery and transport equipment and of services ($), 1970–92
Source: *UN International Trade Statistics Yearbook*, various issues. For services, the source is the *UK Pink Book*, export of services price index converted into dollars. The weights are based on shares of non-oil exports and exports of services in UK trade of these, respectively 0.73 and 0.27

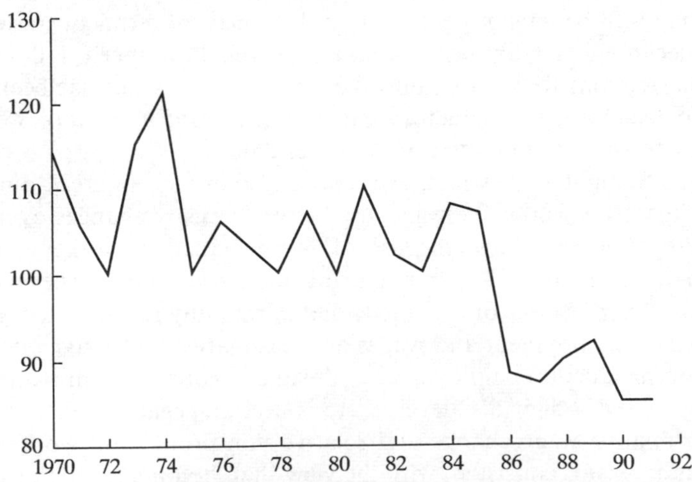

Figure 16.3 The ratio of LDCs' to DCs' manufacturing export prices ($), 1970–92
Source: *UN International Trade Statistics Yearbook*, various issues

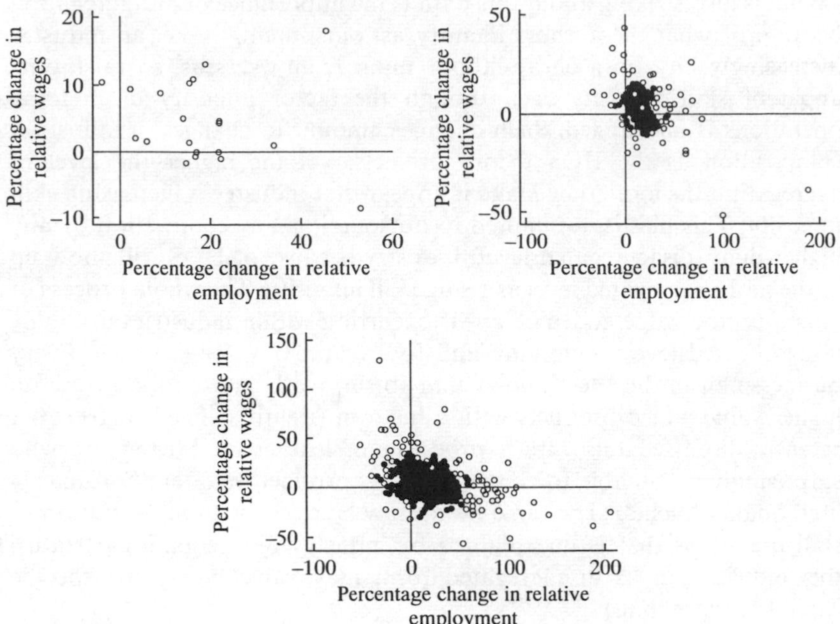

Figure 16.4 Percentage changes in the 1980s in the relative wages and relative employment of non-production and product in labour in manufacturing
A 2-digit SIC industries
B 3-digit SIC industries
C 4-digit SIC industries
Source: Employment and wage data: NBER, Trade and Immigration data base; the graphs are reproduced from Lawrence and Slaughter (1993)

However the authors in effect note the unconditional average rise in non-production worker intensity: most industries had rising intensity. They also stress that only 10 per cent of industries were in the upper-left quadrant where both relative wages rose and intensity fell. But both these points are odd. Nothing in HOS says that industries' wage experience must be uniform, given regional aggregation, for example (or measurement of skills). Presumably what is at issue is whether in addition to the effect of the general rise in relative wages on factor intensity there is an effect of rising relative productivity. The authors state that regressions are unnecessary for their tests: but in this case surely they are necessary. Certainly an eyeball check on the 4-digit data suggests a positive but not obviously large intercept for the independent rise in non-production worker intensity.

What is also striking about this data is the importance of disaggregation because of what the authors identify as 'outsourcing' – i.e. an industry increasingly buys in a cheap-labour input from overseas, so raising its apparent skill intensity even though the factor intensity of ongoing operations is unchanged. Such changes amount to changes in industrial composition as the HOS theory predicts: yet the higher the level of aggregation the more they make it appear that industry is increasing skill intensity. This bias is not limited to outsourcing: any contraction by any higher-digit (disaggregated level) industry because of HOS will show up at the more aggregated level as rising skill intensity. The whole process of 'going up the value added chain' is occurring within industries at highly disaggregated levels – clothing and footwear types, for example. Every businessman in the West knows that to survive he must concentrate on higher value-added products within his own (tightly-defined) market – I recently discussed this with a producer of leather on Merseyside who surprisingly is still able to compete in this product in an extraordinarily high quality 'niche'. (The same point may be relevant to the variation of skill premiums that is unexplained by industry or occupational status: the 'industry' in its disaggregated form may value highly the specific capital of those in it.)

Since disaggregation to the 4-digit level so reduces the intercept we are entitled to wonder whether as the level of disaggregation tended to infinity it would not eliminate it altogether.

In short, the technological evidence in the Lawrence–Slaughter paper is not clearly inconsistent with the emerging markets hypothesis. Those 4-digit industries facing rises in their relative wages of non-production labour tended to use less of it and it is not clear that there is any significant independent upward drift in their relative use, such as would arise from relative productivity shift.

We are left with Lawrence–Slaughter's direct evidence on total factor productivity in the two sectors. Here again the authors use the technique of weighting exportables and importables by production and non-production employment; as for prices this technique appears to be inferior to a partitioning of products by skill intensity, the focus of HOS. However, as noted above, there is no reason to exclude the existence of an overlapping technology shock. The emerging market hypothesis asserts the presence of one major shock, it does not deny the possibility of others also.

5 Implications for the OECD natural rate of unemployment

The HOS model set out here has strong implications for income distribution in OECD countries. Given that social support in these countries stresses the importance of an income 'safety net', the form that this safety net takes will greatly affect unemployment rates among low-wage workers according to the theory of labour supply with which we began and which is preserved in this HOS framework. Let us remind ourselves of the 'unemployment trap' model which underpins the labour supply curve with real wage rigidity. Figure 16.5, panel (a), shows how for a given population distribution over marginal value product a certain minimum support level may work to affect labour supply and unemployment.

Low-wage competition has the effect of concentrating large numbers of people at low levels of marginal value product. The distribution could tend to the bimodal illustrated in panel (b). The effects of unconditional income support on low-wage work could be quite literally to destroy it, creating a huge fiscal burden and massive (even 100 per cent) low-wage worker unemployment. The seriousness of this can be seen from the fact that in the UK, a fairly typical OECD economy, no less than 50 per cent of the workforce are manual workers, half of whom have 'skills' of questionable value in today's world. If one goes on to question the value of the skills of many non-manual workers, the percentage of workers at risk escalates. Those who reject low-wage competition in favour of skill-biased technological change in the North as the reason for increasing wage dispersion are of course still faced with the same current policy issue. However, because the nature of technological change is of its essence unpredictable, even if past dispersion was due to it, there could be no presumption that increased dispersion would result from it in the future. Accordingly the prospective policy problem is different: on the interpretation of this chapter there will be a relentless steady trend similar to that of the past as technical transfer spreads across the vast populations of the emerging markets, whereas on the technological interpretation there might be such a continuation of past trends or indeed there could be a reversal (as the new technology, for example, displaced high-level skills and required complementary unskilled activities). A policy of 'wait and see' would be far more attractive on the latter view.

The process of low-wage competition identified in this chapter creates most serious and obvious problems for social policy, to which I now turn.

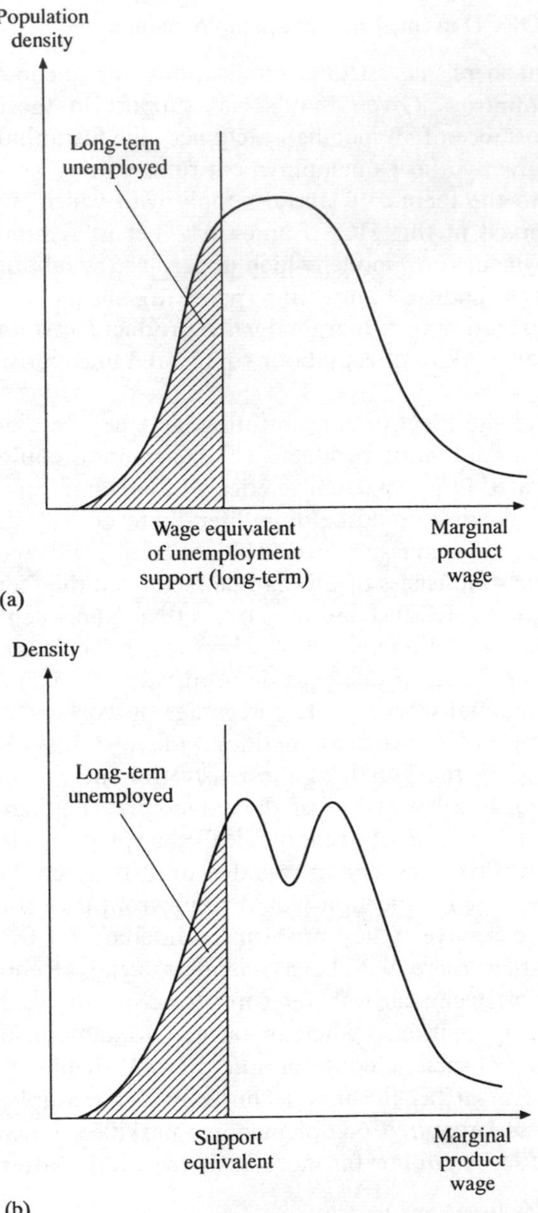

Figure 16.5 The wage distribution before and after low-wage competition
(a) The usual distribution
(b) The distribution after low-wage competition

6 The social problem of low-wage competition

Three main approaches are put forward for income support.

One is *negative income tax* (NIT). This is pretty much what we do now in the UK (since Sir Norman Fowler's reforms of social security in 1987). In this system help is given to many poor families whose breadwinners may be the wife working part-time with the husband in casual work, or both working part-time, or one working full-time at low wages. Judging from our experience to date, this system does a fairly good job in keeping the social peace. The problem with it is that to prevent it becoming hugely expensive it has to be means-tested rigorously and benefits withdrawn gradually as incomes rise. This withdrawal rate runs at 70 per cent or more (100 per cent for part-timers) under our present system, and it is of course an equivalent marginal tax rate for these families.

A second approach is the *basic income guarantee* (BIG), whereby the marginal tax rate is brought down to the normal rate by giving a 'basic income' which is not means-tested or withdrawn. Any income other than this state transfer is taxed in a normal way. The difficulty with BIG is that the huge expense of giving this universal flat-rate benefit raises the marginal tax rate on the average family. Hence while the marginal tax rate for the poor family is lowered as compared with NIT, that for the average family is raised. Since the latter is both far more numerous and more productive, this is a poor result overall from the viewpoint of incentives and efficiency. The comparison is illustrated in figure 16.6.

Hence to this point we appear to be stuck with NIT, at some optimal withdrawal rate, as the least bad approach. The optimal rate is the best point on the implicit trade-off just described between lowering the withdrawal rate for the poor and raising the marginal tax rate for the rest as you do so (because more receive benefit and so face the poverty withdrawal rate, and also the cost goes up, raising the average tax rate). Optimality can be judged by overall efficiency. I made a rough effort at this calculation for the UK in Minford (1990) and concluded that the post-Fowler rates were then about right: some quarter of a million households in work faced high withdrawal rates (the 'poverty trap') but this could be expected to fall as real wages grew provided real benefits were kept constant. I have seen no attempt to update that sort of calculation, and it may well still be about right for households in work.

We should, however, note that unemployment benefits can also create a dependency trap. Clearly an assumption of the NIT system is that there is tight monitoring of job search with benefit withdrawal as the sanction for refusal to take available jobs. The idea then is to push people into the job market and support them there through in-work NIT.

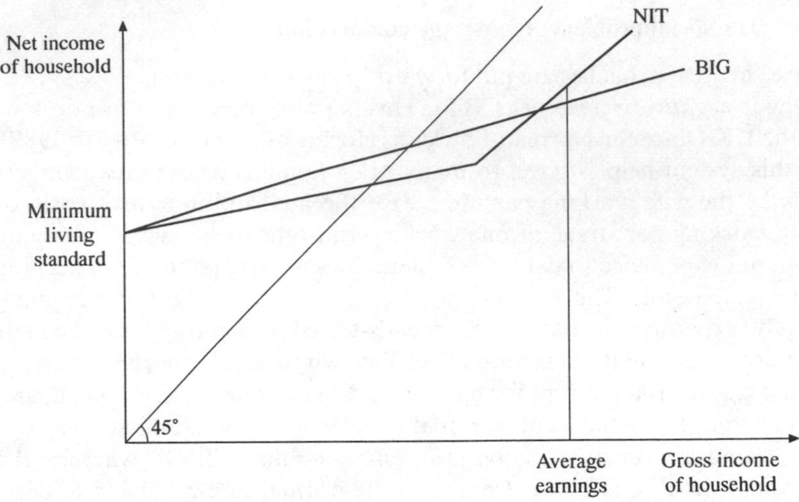

Figure 16.6 BIG and NIT illustrated

A third approach is *low-wage job subsidies*. These might seem to be analytically the same as in-work NIT. It is of course irrelevant to their incidence whether they are paid to employer or employee. But the crucial difference is that job subsidies are attached to particular jobs rather than to people with low household incomes. This means that from the viewpoint of income distribution – poverty support – they are less well targeted. This creates the problem that they do not achieve their social objective. At the same time, precisely because they are not related to household income, they do not create labour supply disincentives in terms of hours with a given job. They still create a distortion between types of job: jobs just outside the subsidy net will lose supply because given the fixed gross wage cost they will pay less (net) to workers than jobs just inside. The distortion could be minimised by tapering the job subsidy as the wage rate rises; but this makes it similar to NIT in its disincentive effects on taking a better-paid job. (In this model neither NIT nor job subsidies affect the gross wage cost to employers: all the incidence is on the net income of the employee and the effect on jobs then comes through employees' labour supply.) It also has, like the NIT, a positive effect on unskilled labour supply and so unemployment; but not so positive as the NIT which is more closely targeted on poor households with high replacement ratios. However, it damages training incentives and reduces human capital; this may be less of a problem with NIT because it is still less well correlated with low wages (some on NIT may not have low wages but low hours, while many on low wages do not qualify for NIT).

More recently there has been a revival of interest in a fourth approach: income support systems modelled on *charity*, like that of the Victorians. In these, welfare assistance is put on a selective basis, decentralised in the hands of local agencies whose job is to use judgement about need: this is related not so much to actual income as potential income and unavoidable commitments or circumstances. Incentives can then be maintained, help targeted on those in need, and costs kept down. This approach in effect extends monitoring from job search – the 'worktesting' that underlies NIT as a way of getting people back to work without forcing down their income – to efforts to improve in-work circumstances. This is a harder task than checking on search, but some progress in it should be feasible.

In the UK we will undoubtedly be investigating how far we can move away from a general NIT system towards more such selectivity ('targeted NIT'), given the cost even of the benefit system we have and the prospect that the low-wage competition we are facing will increase the scope of the problem.

7 Policies to deal with the low-wage dilemma

If we leave BIG on one side then we could categorise the welfare effects of the three main policies – low-wage subsidies, NIT and targeted NIT – as follows. NIT is distributed according to household income at a point in time. This is not particularly well correlated with low wages at a point in time, because of the number of earners in a household (many low-waged women are second earners while low-waged young people may also be supplementary earners, in fact even if not *de jure*). Hence NIT should not have such a pronounced effect on the relative (life-time) earnings of skilled workers relative to low-waged workers and accordingly should not affect the incentive to train so badly. At the same time, it is better targeted on income distribution. Since it is related well to household income it improves the incentive for those with high unemployment benefits to leave unemployment and take a job: low-wage subsidies do this less well because they are less well related to household income.

The drawback of NIT is that it creates a poverty trap for those on low household incomes in work, damaging their incentive to supply more effort either by working more hours or by taking a better-paid job. This drawback is still present under wage subsidies which reduce the relative rewards of better-paid jobs, though it does not apply to hours.

It is this drawback that could be improved by targeted NIT where the additional monitoring of *potential* income could improve these incentives.

There is a further dimension that is important once one recognises political pressures: the (political) 'shock-proofness' of the system, by which I mean its capacity to become more supportive if the environment turns out more hostile (with large drops in the lowest real wages) or to wither away if there is little problem (if trickle down turned into a downpour). The dilemma is related to an ongoing process, not a one-off shock: and we do not know whether it will intensify, be offset by other developments, and much else. In this dimension low-wage subsidies which require a large political effort to instal appear quite inflexible. NIT, whether targeted or not, is related to changes in low incomes by construction and therefore has 'shock-proofness' built in.

We may also consider the properties of other policies that have been urged to address the dilemma: minimum wages, protective subsidies to manufacturing and wage subsidies given exclusively to the long-term unemployed.

The minimum wage has the attraction for politicians that it has no explicit direct fiscal cost: more precisely, its cost is borne not by a general income tax but as a tax on employers. But, of course, this very feature makes it damaging to jobs. Within the model developed here, since employers could not pay an 'effective' minimum wage (i.e. one set above the market-clearing rate) and survive, the jobs affected would simply disappear; there would therefore be a fiscal burden in unemployment benefits and lost tax revenue. Furthermore those whose wages were forced up to the minimum would never enjoy it because they would become unemployed. Therefore their incomes would be depressed, assuming replacement ratios of less than unity. Training incentives would be unaffected (in fact would be increased) as would in-work incentives since low-wage jobs below the minimum would simply be eliminated: forced to choose between the dole, rather than the low-wage job, and the better job presumably incentives to take the better job are enhanced. Indeed this is often given as one motive for a minimum wage: that it would force the economy towards higher-wage jobs – this is the Germanic philosophy, as evidenced by the high-wage development strategy being pursued in East Germany.

Protection is the same in principle as low-wage subsidies in this model. Through the Stolper–Samuelson mechanism there is a one-to-one correspondence between subsidising 'manufactures' and unskilled labour; the same discussion therefore applies. Incidentally, it highlights the questionable nature of low-wage subsidies under international trading regulations such as GATT.

Two schemes suggested for subsidising the unemployed (Snower, 1994; Layard, 1994; see chapters 6 and 11 in this volume) share the characteristic that to qualify someone must have been unemployed for a certain length of time. In Layard it is 12 months and in Snower the subsidy is an increasing function of time unemployed. In both the subsidy is temporary (six months in Layard). The problem with both is the additional incentive for those with lower unemployment spells or in work to become unemployed, and for longer, in order to attract the subsidy; in the Layard scheme the large subsidy (equal to the whole benefit package and available for any job) constitutes a substantial incentive. Shower argues that this incentive can be held down by lowering the subsidy and letting it increase only slowly as unemployment duration rises; but if the scheme is to have any impact on employment the subsidy cannot be of trivial size, and if it is to be prevented from becoming general it must be withheld from the short-term unemployed. This suggests a subsidy growing from zero for the short-term unemployed to something of the Layard size after 12 months: essentially a more complex version of their scheme. Far from being trivial, as some have suggested because they would be restricted to a limited number of workers, these programmes would offer a substantial arbitrage opportunity in the labour market: in the model here the wage on 'scheme' jobs (i.e. with subsidy) would rise in equilibrium to the productivity wage *plus* the subsidy and in equilibrium unskilled workers would raise their unemployment spells to qualify for this scheme wage until the marginal disutility of the longer spell equalled the extra reward (both put on a 'permanent' – i.e. discounted life-time – basis); given unemployment benefits not too far below unskilled wages, this switch could be substantial among low-spell workers and the result could be more, not less, unemployment among unskilled workers. This result is somewhat reminiscent of the large-scale interwar 'OMO' unemployment noted by Benjamin and Kochin (1979) where workers shared jobs, each working half the week and receiving benefits (= a wage subsidies) in the other half. In other dimensions these unemployment-related subsidies are similar to general low-wage subsidies.

The preceding discussion permits us to rank these policies (for a given fiscal cost, which we will presume to be met by a general, and far from costless, income tax) in terms of their effectiveness in meeting objectives and their damaging side-effects. Table 16.1 shows such a ranking: it should be taken in the spirit of a summary of the discussion.

Table 16.1 *The low-wage dilemma*

Ranking the schemes (each assumed to have equal fiscal cost, paid for out of general income tax)

Effects on:	Unemployment	In-work incentives	Training	Poverty	Shock-proof?
Low-wage subsidies	+	–	– – –	+	No
NIT	+ +	– –	– –	+ +	Yes
Targeted NIT	+ + +	0	–	+ + +	Yes
Minimum wage	– – –	+	+	– –	Yes
Protection	+	–	– – –	+	No (yes if quota)
Vouchers for long-term unemployed	–	–	–	+	Yes

Scale: + – + + + : modestly–extremely helpful
– – – – – : modestly–extremely damaging
0 : neutral effect.

What emerges is that NIT, 'targeted' as effectively as possible (which among other things reduces its fiscal cost), has the best overall features of these various suggestions for dealing with the West's low-wage dilemma. It has high effectiveness on unemployment because it is limited to poor households (in the 'unemployment trap') for whom the incentive to work is least. By targeting, its effects on in-work, incentives can be minimised. It has maximum effectiveness in relieving poverty because it goes only to 'poor' households. it will also wither away or be boosted according the quantitative intensity of the dilemma. Finally, its effect in diminishing the rewards to training will be limited by the fact that many in low-wage jobs will not receive any help, being members of better-off households.

8 Conclusions

The growing threat of low-wage competition to the living standards of unskilled workers in rich countries is likely to put strain on those countries' commitment to free trade. It is important for their overall welfare as well as that of the DC, that this commitment is maintained: both global and rich country welfare is maximised by free trade in our model.

How, then, to relieve the strain under free trade? We have seen that a system of income supplementation for those in work (Negative Income Tax or NIT) offers a way forward, and that incentive problems created by it (the 'poverty trap') could be minimised by a targeted system administered locally with discretion – the Victorian model. Britain is increasingly experimenting with such systems in different benefit areas (e.g. the social fund and sickness benefit) and the same principle is used in monitoring unemployment benefits.

In moving forward much will depend on how fast these low-wage trends develop. British experience suggests that people will tolerate a system that does not drive household incomes below some basic subsistence level, much as defined in the price-indexed official income support levels. It may well be that while low wages in Britain do not grow much in real terms (as has happened in the last two decades), they do not fall either. In that case, we could manage without any significant increase in the cost of social benefits. But the situation on mainland Europe with its higher wage costs may well be much more difficult.

Appendix: the equations of the North–South model

The model's intention and basic construction is explained in the text: here, we provide a bare description of the equations.

The model consists of three blocks of equations: two 'country' blocks for the North and the South respectively, and a world block.

Each country block consists of equations:

(1)–(4): price = cost in each sector. The production function assumed throughout is Cobb–Douglas. The capital cost is given by the price of manufactures times the long-run cost of capital.
(5)–(8): demand for labour, human capital, land and physical capital.
(9)–(11): supplies of immobile factors: labour, human capital and land.
(12): demand for domestic (non-traded) goods/services.
(13): total output (GDP) identity.
(14): (South) capital inflow (current balance) given by the GNP identity: total demand *less* GNP (GDP *minus* foreign debt service).
(15): (South) total demand given by demand for capital *plus* consumption expenditure (by government and households).
(16): (South) consumption function.
(17): (South) GNP *per capita* identity.

These equations are formally identical for the North, except that:

(14): (North) foreign capital inflow is equal to the negative of the capital inflow into the South (the world currents balance constraint).
(15): (North) total demand given by the GNP identity.
(16): (North) consumption given by the total demand identity.
(17): (North) GNP *per capita* identity.
(18): (North) the world real interest rate is solved out to satisfy the North's consumption function, given consumption from (16) (in effect this equation therefore sets real interest rates so that world demand equals world supply).

The world block of equations fixes world prices (the price of manufactures is the numeraire and is set at 1.0, (3):)

(1)–(2): world demand = supply for traded agriculture and services.
(4): price of traded goods identity.
(5): world demand for traded goods = total world demand *less* total world demand for domestic goods (identity).

South

Prices

$$p_M = w^{0.5} * h^{0.1} * 1^{0.1} * (p_M * r)^{0.3} * \pi_M^{-1} \tag{1}$$

$$p_S = w^{0.5} * h^{0.5} * 1^{0.1} * (p_M * r)^{0.3} * \pi_s^{-1} \tag{2}$$

$$p_A = w^{0.1} * h^{0.1} * 1^{0.5} * (p_M * r)^{0.3} * \pi_A^{-1} * PA \tag{3}$$

$$p_D = (1.0/\pi_D) * w^{0.3} * h^{0.1} * 1^{0.4} * (p_M * r)^{0.2} \tag{4}$$

Factor demands

$$N = w^{-1} * (0.3 * p_D * y_D + 0.5 * p_M * y_M + 0.1 * p_S * y_S + 0.1 * p_A * y_A) \tag{5}$$

$$H = h^{-1} * (0.1 * p_D * y_D + 0.1 * p_M * y_M + 0.5 * p_S * y_S + 0.1 * p_A * y_A) \tag{6}$$

$$L = 1^{-1} * (0.4 * p_D * y_D + 0.1 * p_M * y_M + 0.1 * p_S * y_S + 0.5 * p_A * y_A) \tag{7}$$

$$K = 0.2 * [(1.0/p_M * r) * (0.2 * p_D * y_D + 0.3 * p_M * y_M + 0.3 * p_S * y_S + 0.3 * p_A * y_A)] + (1.0 - 0.2) * k_{-1} \tag{8}$$

Factor supplies

$$N = 43.0987 * (w/b)^{0.5} * POP^{0.5} * G^{0.5} \tag{9}$$

$$H = 94.8683 * (h/w)^{0.5} * G^{0.5} \tag{10}$$

$$L = 10.0 * (1/w)^{0.5} * POP^{0.5} \tag{11}$$

Expenditure equations and identities

$$y_D = 0.2766 * E^{1.0} * (p_D/p_T)^{-0.5} \tag{12}$$

$$y = y_D + y_M + y_S + y_A \tag{13}$$

$$K_F = K_{F,-1} + E - y + r_{-1} * K_{F,-1} \tag{14}$$

$$E = C + \Delta K \tag{15}$$

$$C = 0.2 * (0.9 * (y - r_{-1} * K_{F,-1}) - 120.0 * r_{-1} + (1.0 - 0.2) * C_{-1} \quad (16)$$

$$yPC = (p_D * y_D + p_M * y_M + p_S * y_S + p_A * y_A)/(p_D^{0.6} * p_T^{0.4}) - r_{-1} * K_{F,-1})/POP \quad (17)$$

World

Traded goods market-clearing

$$p_s = p_T + (0.2 * E_T - \Sigma y_s)/75.0 \quad (1)$$

$$p_A = p_T + (0.4 * E_T - \Sigma y_A)/100.0 \quad (2)$$

Identities

$$p_M = 1.0 \quad (3)$$

$$p_T = p + M^{0.4} * p_S^{0.2} * p_A^{0.4} \quad (4)$$

$$E_T = \Sigma E - \Sigma y_D \quad (5)$$

Equations for the North are identical apart from constants and (14)–(18) which are:

$$K_F = K_{F,-1} - \Delta K_{F,[SOUTH]} \quad (14)$$

$$E = y - r_{-1} * K_{F,-1} + \Delta K_F \quad (15)$$

$$C = E - \Delta K \quad (16)$$

$$yPC = ((p_D * y_D + p_M * y_M + p_S * y_S + p_A * y_A)/(p_d^{0.6} * p_T^{0.4}) - r_{-1} * K_{F,-1})/POP \quad (17)$$

$$r = (C - (1.0 - 0.2) * C_{-1} - 0.2 * 0.9 * (y - r_{-1} * K_{F,-1}))/(-120.0 * 0.2) \quad (18)$$

Notation

Subscripts

D Domestic or non-traded
M Manufacturing
S Services (traded)
A Agriculture (traded)
T Traded
F Foreign (thus K_F = capital borrowed from abroad)

Variables from North and South

p Price
y Output (GDP)
yPC *Per capita* GDP
N (Unskilled) labour
H Skilled labour or human capital
L Land
K Capital (physical)
w Wages (of unskilled labour)
h Skilled wages or rent on human capital
r real rate of return on physical capital
E Expenditure
l Rent on land
π Aggregate factor productivity
PA Tariff (or equivalent) protection for agriculture
b Rate of unemployment benefit
POP Working population
G Government expenditure/GDP

NOTE

This chapter draws heavily on the analysis of Minford, Riley and Nowell (1994). I am grateful to participants at this conference for their comments, particularly to my discussants Jonathan Haskel and Stephen Nickell.

REFERENCES

Barro, R.J., 1991. 'Economic growth in a cross-section of countries', *Quarterly Journal of Economics*, **106**, 407–44

Bean, C.R., P.R.G. Layard and S.J. Nickell, 1986. 'The rise in unemployment: a multi-country study', *Economica*, **53**, S1–S22

Benjamin, D. and L. Kochin, 1979. 'Searching for an explanation of unemployment in inter-war Britain', *Journal of Political Economy*, **87**, 441–70

Borjas, G., R. Freeman and L. Katz, 1992. 'On the labour market effects of immigration and trade', in G.J. Borjas and R. Freeman (eds.), *Immigration and the Workforce*, Chicago: University of Chicago Press

Bound, J. and G. Johnson, 1992. 'Changes in the structure of wages in the 1980s: an evaluation of alternative explanations', *American Economic Review*, **82**, 371–92

Davis, J. and P. Minford (1986). 'Germany and the European disease', *Recherches Economiques de Louvain*, **52**, 373–98

Denison, E.F., 1967. *Why Growth Rates Differ: Postwar Experience in Nine Western Countries*, Washington, DC: Brookings Institution

1974. *Accounting for the United States Economic Growth, 1929–1969*, Washington, DC: Brookings Institution

Dollar, D., 1992. 'Outward-oriented developing countries really do grow more rapidly: evidence from 95 LDCs, 1976–85', *Economic Development and Cultural Change, 1992*, **40**, 523–44

Friedman, M., 1968. 'The role of monetary policy', *American Economic Review*, **58**, 1–17

Hayek, F.A., 1945. 'The use of knowledge in society', *American Economic Review*, **35**, 519–30; reprinted in F. Hayek, *Individualism and Economic Order*, Chicago: University of Chicago Press (1949)

Heckscher, E., 1919. 'The effect of foreign trade on the distribution of income', *Economisk Tidskrift*, **21**, 497–512; reprinted as chapter 13 in *AEA Readings in the Theory of International Trade*, Blakiston, Philadelphia (1949), 272–300

IMF, 1993. *World Economic Outlook* (May), Appendix, Washington, DC: IMF, 197

Jones, R.W., 1967. 'International capital movements and the theory of tariffs and trade', *Quarterly Journal of Economics*, **81**, 1–38

Katz, L. and K. Murphy, 1992. 'Changes in relative wages, 1963–1987: supply and demand factors', *Quarterly Journal of Economics*, **107**, 35–78

Krueger, A.B., 1991. 'How computers have changed the wage standard: evidence from microdata 1984–89', *NBER Working Paper*, **3858**, Cambridge, MA: NBER; *Quarterly Journal of Economics*, **108**, 33–60 (1993)

Lawrence, R.Z. and M.J. Slaughter, 1993. 'International trade and American wages in the 1980s: giant sucking sound or small hiccup?', *Brookings Papers on Microeconomics*, **2**, 161–226

Layard, P.R.G. and S.J. Nickell, 1985. 'The causes of British unemployment', *National Institute Economic Review*, **111**, 62–85

Layard, P.R.G., S.J. Nickell and R.A. Jackman, 1991. *Unemployment: Macroeconomic Performance and the Labour Market*, Oxford: Oxford University Press

Lucas, R.E., Jr., 1988. 'On the mechanics of an economic development', *Journal of Monetary Economics*, **22**, 3–42

Minford, P., 1983. 'Labour market equilibrium in an open economy', *Oxford Economic Papers*, **35**, S207–44

1989. 'A labour-based theory of international trade', in J. Black and A.I. Bean (eds.), *Causes and Changes in the Structure of International Trade 1960–85*, London: Macmillan, 196–240

1990. 'The poverty line after the Fowler reforms', in A. Bowen and K. Mayhew (eds.), *Improving the Incentives for the Low-Paid*, London: Macmillan for NEDO

Minford, P., J. Riley and E. Nowell, 1994. 'The elixir of growth: trade, non-traded goods and development', University of Liverpool/CEPR, *Discussion Paper*, **1165**

Ohlin, B., 1933. *Interregional and International Trade*, Cambridge, MA: Harvard University Press

Parente, S.L. and E.C. Prescott, 1993. 'Changes in the wealth of nations', *Federal Reserve Bank of Minneapolis Quarterly Review* (Spring), 3–16

1994. 'Barriers to technology adoption and development', *Journal of Political Economy*, **102**, 298–321

Phelps, E.S., 1994. *Structural Slumps: The Modern Equilibrium Theory of Unemployment, Interest, and Assets*, Cambridge, MA: Harvard University Press

Rebelo, S., 1991. 'Long-run policy analysis and long-run growth', *Journal of Political Economy*, **99**, 500–21

Romer, P.M., 1986. 'Increasing returns and long-run growth', *Journal of Political Economy*, **94**, 1002–37

Rybczynski, T.M., 1955. 'Factor endowments and relative commodity prices', *Economica*, **22**, 336–41

Samuelson, P.A., 1948. 'International trade and the equalisation of factor prices', *Economic Journal*, **58**, 163–84

Snower, D.J., 1994. 'The simple economics of benefit transfers', chapter 6 in this volume

Solow, R.M., 1956. 'A contribution to the theory of economic growth', *Quarterly Journal of Economics*, **70**, 65–94

Stolper, W. and P.A. Samuelson, 1941. 'Protection and real wages', *Review of Economic Studies*, **9**, 58–73

Summers, R. and A. Heston, 1988. 'A new set of international comparisons of real product and price levels estimates from 130 countries, 1950–1985', *The Review of Income and Wealth*, **34**, 1–25

1991. 'The Penn World Tables (Mark 5): an expanded set of international comparisons, 1950–88', *Quarterly Journal of Economics*, **106**, 327–68

Thomas, J. and T. Worrall, 1994. 'Foreign direct investment and the risk of expropriation', *Review of Economic Studies*, **61**, 81–108

Wood, A., 1994. 'North–South Trade, Employment and Inequality: Changing Fortunes in a Skill-Driven World, Oxford: Clarendon Press

Worrall, T., 1990. 'Debt with potential repudiation', *European Economic Review*, **34**, 1099–1109

Discussion

JONATHAN HASKEL

In many recent models of unemployment the role of trade is peripheral. In Layard *et al.* (1991), for example (hereafter LNJ), unemployment is the outcome of the interaction between labour demand (or price-setting) and a wage-setting mechanism. Trade shocks might shift labour demand, or wage-setting if the consumer/producer price wedge is altered. The results reported by LNJ generally assign trade a small role in explaining the rise in unemployment in the OECD (see, e.g. p. 433).

By contrast, Minford seeks to place trade centre-stage in explaining OECD unemployment and wage inequality. The thrust of Minford's argument, which uses the Heckscher–Ohlin–Samuelson (HOS) model, can be seen as follows. There are two countries, the UK, whose population is predominantly skilled, and China, predominantly unskilled. Manufactured goods, whose production is unskilled labour-intensive, are traded freely. Complex/high-tech goods, which are skilled labour-intensive, are non-traded. Minford considers the shock of main interest to be a progressive transfer of technology from the UK to Chinese manufacturing. Such a productivity increase lowers the relative price of manufactured goods in China. This worsens the terms of trade for manufactured goods in the UK, and so causes the UK to shift production towards skill-intensive goods. In turn, this raises the relative demand for skilled worker and so their relative wage (a Stolper-Samuelson-type effect). The rise in the relative skilled wage causes their relative employment to fall in all industries; the skilled workers required in the expanded skill-intensive sector are provided by economising on their use when they become relatively more expensive.

Because this argument predicts an increase in the skilled–unskilled wage differential it has been considered widely in the literature as an explanation of rising wage inequality in developed countries (see, e.g., Krugman, 1994; Lawrence and Slaughter, 1993, hereafter LS; and Wood, 1995). Minford adds an extra ingredient, however. He assumes that the social security system provides a floor to the wage of the unskilled. As Chinese manufacturing becomes increasingly cheaper, then, the warranted real wage of the unskilled gets closer and closer to the wage floor, and unemployment results. Minford argues that this risk is quantitatively important. He claims that half of manual workers 'have "skills" of questionable value in today's world'. On this basis he further argues that '[t]he effects of unconditional income support on low-wage work could be quite literally to destroy it, creating ... massive (even 100 per cent) low-wage worker unemployment'.

Such characteristically apocalyptic logic makes Patrick Minford's chapter 16 an attractive and entertaining read. I shall, however, argue that his conclusions are over-stated. Since Minford's chapter divides into arguments concerning the emerging markets hypothesis and those concerning policies, I shall discuss each in turn.

1 The emerging markets hypothesis

1.1 Factor price convergence

An obvious route by which trade would affect Northern labour markets is via factor-price equalisation (Samuelson, 1948, 1949). Minford rules this case out, however, because in his model the North and South have different technologies. Although manufactured goods are freely traded, 'complex' goods are not. So technology can only be transferred by the North building/licensing production in the South. However Northern firms are deterred from doing so owing to contractual/political uncertainty which might lead to *ex post* appropriation of sunk investments. (Note that this story contrasts with Wood, 1994, who rejects factor-price equalisation because although all countries have access to the same technology the South has fewer skilled workers and so cannot exploit a given technology as readily.) Minford then ignores changes in political and contractual circumstances and assumes an uninterrupted transfer of technology to the South. The upshot of this is factor-price convergence; real unskilled wages in the North fall by 2 per cent p.a. whilst those in the South rise by 4 per cent p.a. Also wage inequality in the North rises: skilled wages rise by 3.6 per cent p.a. relative to the unskilled.

Whatever the theoretical arguments, Minford's numbers seem too large. In the UK between 1975 and 1990 the 10th percentile of the earnings distribution rose by 0.5 per cent p.a. in real terms and the gap between the 90th and 10th decile rose by 2.5 per cent p.a. Admittedly the USA has seen real wage declines at the bottom of the distribution, but the UK and US experience are relatively extreme in the OECD (Katz *et al.*, 1993). Furthermore the 90/10 differential surely over-states the effect that Minford is trying to model.

1.2 Relative prices

As Minford discusses at some length, a key mechanism in the HOS model is that the terms of trade in skilled labour-intensive products should improve for the North. That is, since manufacturing prices fall in the unskilled-intensive South, the price of unskilled-intensive goods should *fall* relative to the price of skilled-intensive goods. Unfortunately for the model, however, LS' calculations for the USA show precisely the opposite: the price of unskilled-intensive goods has *risen* relative to that of skilled-intensive goods (see their figures 8 and 9). LS therefore argue that international price movements cannot have been the major factor affecting US wages. Instead, they suggest that skill-biased technological change has been more important. Since relative price changes are critical to Minford's model, and since he restricts technical progress to be unbiased, this argument is potentially highly damaging to the analysis.

Fortunately for chapter 16, however, more recent research on price movements has returned different results. Sachs and Shatz (1949) make a number of adjustments to LS' work, such as excluding computers, and conclude that prices in the least skill-intensive decile relative to the most skill-intensive decile did indeed fall, as HOS requires. Minford's own calculations support this, as do Leamer's (1995) calculations for textiles and apparel. It would therefore appear that direct calculations of price movements are not robust enough to test the HOS predictions. At least two reasons have been suggested why this may be so. First, Richardson (1995) argues that price movements can go either way depending on what sectors are defined as exportable and importable. Second, Wood (1995) argues that the heterogeneity of goods within sectors obscures calculations, especially since the manufacturing process might be split up into different stages in different countries. Minford's reported data, which are based on machinery and transport equipment, may well therefore be vulnerable to this criticism.

1.3 Relative wages and employment

A second key prediction of the HOS model concerns relative wages and employment. Recall that if trade shifts Northern demand to the skilled sector these skilled workers must come from somewhere. Absent a strong supply response, the HOS mechanism is that the increased price of skilled labour causes a fall in the relative employment of the skilled in all sectors, until that fall is just enough to equal the rise in demand due to the shift between sectors. Hence if the HOS model is correct, all sectors should have experienced a rise in the relative wage of the skilled and a fall in their relative employment.

LS' results seem to contradict this prediction. At the two-, three- and four-digit classification less than 10 per cent of US industries had rising relative wages and falling relative employment (see LS' n. 52). LS' graphs are reproduced in chapter 15, and on the basis of some eyeball econometrics on figure 16.4c, Minford argues (a) there is a 'clear' negative relation between changes in relative wages and intensity and (b) there is only a small intercept (I assume on the x axis) which implies the absence of significant biased technological change that would be expected to raise non-productive skill intensity autonomously.

I doubt that many would be persuaded by this somewhat informal econometric procedure. Indeed Minford himself does not appear to be convinced, for he accepts that a technology shock might be important, and calls for further analysis. In the light of this suggestion figure D16.1 reproduces LS' graph of the proportional change in non-manual/manual relative wages and employment, 1980–9, for the UK (LS' data was not readily available to me). The data consists of 80 three-digit industries, and are described more fully in Haskel (1996).

Interestingly the data look quite similar to the US results, namely a cluster in the positive orthant. To add some precision to the discussion we follow Haskel (1996) and suppose that each firm has a CES production function

$$Y = [(A_s N_s)^{-p} + (A_u N_u)^{-p}]^{-1/p} Z$$

where A_j, $j = s,u$, is the level of Harrod-neutral labour-augmenting technology, N_j is employment, the subscripts s and u denote skilled and unskilled and Z is any other input. Assuming the firm faces wages W_s and W_u we can write the first-order conditions for the profit maximising choices of N_s and N_u in change in logs form as

$$\Delta(n_s - n_s) = \alpha\Delta(a_s - a_u) - \beta\Delta(w_s - w_u)$$

where lower case letters denote logs.

So, Minford's argument can be restated as follows. Trade-induced increases in relative wages, $\Delta(w_s - w_u)$ should, *ceteris paribus*, lower relative employment so that the bulk of points are in the top left-hand quadrant of figure D16.1. Alternately, biased technical progress, $\Delta(a_s - a_u)$ should raise relative employment, which, *ceteris paribus*, would

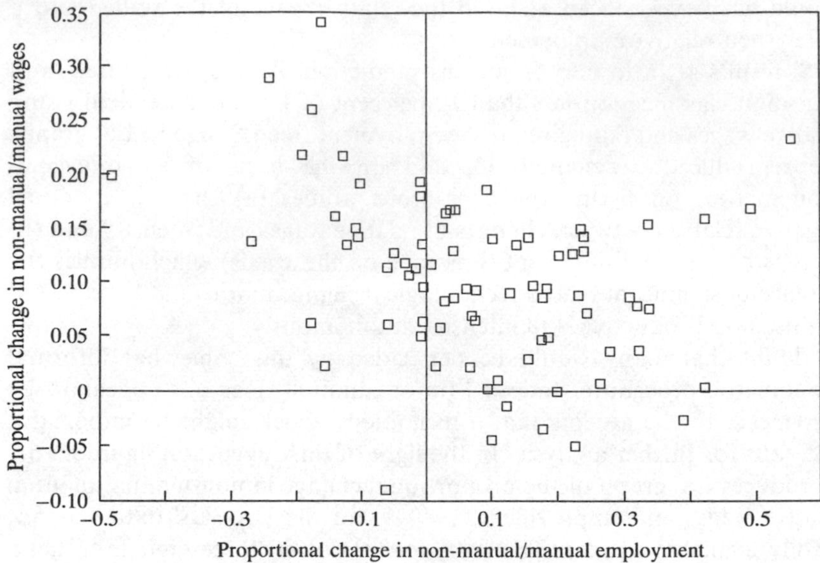

Figure D16.1 Changes in non-manual/manual relative wages and employment, 1980–1

show up either as a significant intercept on the *x* axis of figure D16.1 or in the regression of

$$\Delta(n_s - n_u) \text{ on } \Delta(w_s - w_u).$$

What does the UK data suggest? First, 37 per cent of employment is in the top left-hand quadrant, so the evidence in favour of the HOS mechanism as the predominant force moving relative employment is not overwhelming. Second, a heteroscedastic-robust regression gives

$$\Delta(n_s - n_u) = 0.15 - 0.75\Delta(w_s w_U),$$

with absolute *t*-statistics of 5.22 and 2.55 respectively. So the increase in $(w_s - w_u)$ has tended to reduce $(n_s - n_u)$ as theory would predict. The average rise in $(w_s - w_u)$ is 10 per cent; the regression predicts a 7.5 per cent fall in $(n_s - n_u)$. In fact $(n_s - n_u)$ has risen on average by 8.1 per cent, and the significant intercept in the regression suggests that biased technical progress accounts for this rise. So, at least on UK data, the assertion that technology is insignificant is incorrect. Admittedly the *a* constant is a crude measure of biased technical progress, but replacing it by a measure of average computer introduction over the period (for more on this variable, see Haskel, 1996) gave

$$\Delta(n_s - n_u) = 0.79\Delta COMPUTER - 0.65\Delta(w_s - w_u),$$

with absolute t-statistics of 5.75 and 2.60 respectively and an implied effect from $\Delta COMPUTER$ of 14.4 per cent. Again there seems to be an important biased technical progress effect.

Of course, one might criticise this exercise as excessively simple, ignoring as it does other influences, identification, etc. But the results, namely that the technical progress effect is quantitatively important, carry over to a more thorough analysis (Haskel, 1996). Since the Minford model does not even admit a biased technical progress effect it appears to omit a major factor acting on the relative employment of the skilled and unskilled at least in the UK. This makes me doubt the predictions of the model.

2 Policy implications

Having identified competition from low-wage countries and benefit-induced real wage floors as the key driving force behind unemployment, Minford turns to an analysis of policy. Reviewing negative income taxes (NIT), a basic income guarantee (BIG), low-wage job subsidies and subsidising the long-term unemployed, Minford argues in favour of a NIT. This argument is not based on the trade model but rather on some standard microanalysis of labour supply. The extra twist added by Minford is to advocate the use of decentralised targeting whereby local agencies assess 'need', as in the Victorian welfare system. Finally, Minford dismisses minimum wages (since there are no jobs for a wage above that determined by international trade) and protectionism.

Let me confine my comments to the sense in which such policy measures relate to Minford's model (the arguments over welfare benefits and labour supply are well rehearsed in the literature – see, e.g., Atkinson and Micklewright, 1991; and Layard's chapter 11 and Snower's chapter 6 in this volume). First, if the model is right, then (at convergence) a minimum wage above foreign levels would have a huge negative elasticity on employment. Even in open sectors such as textiles, we don't seem to see this (at least in the UK data, see Dickens *et al.*, 1995): another reason why, in my view, Minford's conclusions are over-stated. Secondly, an important efficiency argument supporting targeting the long-term unemployed is that they are ineffective in holding down wage pressure. In Minford's model, the main determinant of wage pressure is wages in the South. Since his model does not admit a key reason for targeting the long-term unemployed, then it is hardly surprising that Minford comes down against it.

Finally, Minford's faith in Victorian-style local welfare targeting of life-time needs seems misplaced to me. How are such 'needs' to be assessed? Who is to perform the assessment? Unequal treatment across people and localities would surely switch incentives away from job-seeking towards corruption and rent-seeking behaviour. Delegating benefit provision to local worthies may satisfy a nostalgic desire for a return to glories of a bygone age, but can hardly be said to have a firm economic rationale.

REFERENCES

Atkinson, A.B. and J. Micklewright, 1991. 'Unemployment compensation and labor market transitions: a critical review', *Journal of Economic Literature*, **29**, 1679–1727

Dickens, R., 1995. 'The evolution of male wages in Great Britain, 1975–1990', London School of Economics, Centre for Economic Performance, mimeo

Dickens, R., S. Machin and A. Manning, 1995. 'The effects of minimum wages on employment: theory and evidence from Britain', London School of Economics, Centre for Economic Performance, mimeo

Freeman, R., 1995. 'Are your wages set in Beijing?', *Journal of Economic Perspectives*, **9**, 15–32

Haskel, J., 1996. 'The decline in unskilled employment in UK manufacturing over the 1980s', Discussion Paper, **1356**, London School of Economics, Centre for Economic Performance

Katz, L., G. Loveman and D. Blanchflower, 1993. 'A comparison of changes in the structure of wages in four different OECD countries', in R. Freeman and L. Katz (eds.), *Changes and Differences in Wage Structures*, Chicago: University of Chicago Press

Krugman, P., 1994. 'Past and prospective causes of high unemployment' Annual Symposium of the Federal Reserve Bank of Kansas City, Jackson Hole, Wyoming (26–27 August), mimeo

Lawrence, R. and M. Slaughter, 1993. 'International trade and American wages in the 1980s: giant sucking sound or small hiccup?', *Brookings Papers on Microeconomics*, **2**, 161–226

Layard, P.R.G., S.J. Nickell and R.A. Jackman, 1991. *Unemployment: Macroeconomic Performance and the Labour Market*, Oxford: Oxford University Press

Leamer, E.E., 1995. 'A trade economist's view of US wages and "globalization"', mimeo

Richardson, J., 1995. 'Income inequality and trade: how to think, what to conclude', *Journal of Economic Perspectives*, **9**, 33–57

Sachs, J. and H.J. Shatz, 1994. 'Trade and jobs in US manufacturing', *Brookings Papers on Microeconomics*, **1**, 1–84

Samuelson, P.A., 1948. 'International trade and the equalisation of factor prices', *Economic Journal*, **58**, 163–84
1949. 'International factor-price equalisation once again', *Economic Journal*, **59**, 181097
Wood, A., 1994. *North–South Trade, Employment and Inequality. Changing Fortunes in a Skill-Driven World.* Oxford: Clarendon Press
1995. 'How trade hurt unskilled workers', *Journal of Economic Perspectives*, **9**, 57–80

Discussion

STEPHEN J. NICKELL

1 Introduction

The rapid decline in demand for unskilled workers in the OECD countries is causing serious problems, particularly in those parts of the world where the rate of decline in demand is significantly outpacing the rate of decline in supply. Minford's chapter is concerned with both the causes and consequences of this demand collapse. Section 2 presents a crudely calibrated world general equilibrium model with two countries (North, South), four goods, three of which are traded, and five factors, two being mobile. This model is simulated in order to investigate the implications of improvements in the technology of the South. The main focus is on the consequence for the wages of the skilled and unskilled in the North.

Sections 3–4 look at the 'trade versus technology' literature. This literature is concerned with the relative importance of trade globalisation and skill-biased technical change in causing the decline in unskilled demand. Minford comes out strongly in favour of trade globalisation as the key driving force. Finally, sections 5–6, there is an extensive analysis of the best welfare policy to cope with the problems of low pay and poverty induced by the decline in unskilled wages or employment.

2 Trade versus technology and the Minford model

The key problem with which Minford is concerned is the quantitative importance of 'North–South' trade developments in explaining the collapse in demand for unskilled workers in the North and the consequent worsening of their pay and employment prospects.

The basic structure of the simulation model is that of a two-country world with four goods (agriculture, manufactures, services, domestic) where the first three are traded. 'Services' consists of traded services and high-tech manufactures whereas 'manufactures' essentially refers to low-tech manufactures. Then there are five factors (unskilled labour, skilled labour, land, capital and materials), the first three of which are immobile. Using a constant returns assumption plus no specialisation immediately implies that the internationally determined prices of the three traded goods suffice to determine the relative prices of the three immobile factors even when differences in the 'level of technology' rule out full factor price equalisation.

The model is roughly calibrated and is then used to investigate the consequences of a 2.3 per cent p.a. growth in manufacturing productivity in the South. The result is that unskilled wages fall by over 3 per cent p.a. relative to skilled wages in the North and decline absolutely by 2 per cent p.a. This is an enormous impact, somewhat out of line with much of the substantial literature devoted to this subject.

Various points are worth noting. First, the structure of the model implies that relative pay across skill groups is independent of domestic shifts in supply. This is inconsistent with the substantial body of evidence showing that, for example, the rapid increase in the supply of college graduates in the USA in the 1970s generated a substantial reduction in the education premium. This suggests that a more realistic model might have the North specialising in high-tech manufactures. For example, in the USA, it is well known that only a tiny proportion of the unskilled produce traded manufactures. Of course, once we have specialisation, this will tend to reduce the extent to which relative factor prices depend on internationally determined goods prices.

Second, I could find no information on the actual volume of trade generated by the simulation model. This is vital because a persuasive model has to be consistent with the very small volume of trade between North and South. As Krugman notes:

> At the very least, this approach lays down a challenge to economists who claim that trade has had very large effects on wages: can they produce a general equilibrium model of the OECD, with plausible factor shares and elasticities of substitution, that is consistent both with

> their assertions and with the limited actual volume of trade? If they cannot, they have not made their case (Krugman, 1995b, p. 26–7)

Third, the implication of the model is that the wages of the skilled rise relative to the unskilled and, as a consequence, the relative employment of the unskilled rises in the non-traded sector. Yet, in an analysis of 402 UK establishments across all sectors, Machin (1995) reports that the proportion of skilled workers increases in more or less all establishments whether they are in the traded or the non-traded sectors. This fact is inconsistent with a pure trade story.

Overall, therefore, the evidence provided by Minford is not adequate to disturb the consensus view (see, e.g., Krugman, 1995) that trade has caused a significant but relatively small fraction of the shift in demand against the unskilled.

3 Solving the low-pay problem

Whether the decline in demand for the unskilled is generated by trade or technology, the fundamental problem remains unchanged. If the supply of unskilled workers declines more slowly, then the market-clearing wage for the unskilled will decline and may fall below the poverty line. Of course, in the long run, one solution is to provide a good enough education and training system so that the supply of unskilled workers is very low. Meanwhile, however, something must be done.

Minford discusses a number of possibilities but essentially they boil down to two. The first is job subsidies along with minimum wages. The second is some type of negative income tax system (NIT). Minford argues in favour of the latter, basically because it is better focused. There are many individuals in low-paid employment who are not poor, their spouses being relatively well paid. So raising their pay by job subsidies will not contribute to the alleviation of poverty. However, the main disadvantage of the NIT system is that it typically generates a very high marginal tax rate for low-paid workers (if it is not to cost a great deal). So a considerable proportion of the population becomes entangled with the benefit system, with very strong incentives to take undeclared employment.

The current system in Britain provides a good example. A couple with two children under 11 who pay £60 per week in rent are potentially entitled to Housing Benefit and Family Credit. Under the current rules, if the husband works 40 hours per week for £250, the weekly disposable income of the family after housing costs is £145.03. If he reduces his hours to 20 per week and earns £125, the family disposable income is

£130.10. The incentive to work 20 hours per week instead of 40 and either go fishing or do some undeclared work for the other 20, is quite a powerful one. And the total cost to the Exchequer of this shift is around £110 per week. (These figures are based on 1994–5 rules when median manual male weekly earnings were £262. The Family Credit system is currently being extended to childless households.) So while, in principle, the NIT system is better targeted, in practice there is a danger that, as in the above example, the incentive to become 'poor' under such a system may be quite substantial.

In fact, Minford is aware of this problem, and suggests that it can be avoided by using a 'targeted' NIT where there is monitoring of potential income by local agencies. Quite how they are to undertake this task is not clear. Overall, therefore, the superiority of the NIT system over the job subsidy/minimum wage system is not as clear-cut as Minford makes out.

Finally, I should add that despite my critical remarks, I found the chapter most stimulating. In particular, it reveals that there is probably no short cut to elucidating the impact of trade on relative wages. The framework set out by Minford in section 2 of the chapter is clearly a major step in the right direction.

REFERENCES

Krugman, P., 1995a. 'Growing world trade: causes and consequences', *Brookings Papers on Economic Activity*, **1**

1995b. 'Technology, trade and factor prices', *NBER Working Paper*, **5355**, Cambridge, MA: NBER

Machin, S., 1996. 'Changes in the relative demand for skills in the UK labor market', in A.J. Booth and D.J. Snower (eds.), *Acquiring Skills: Market Failures, their Symptoms and Policy Responses*, Cambridge: Cambridge University Press

17 The unemployment and welfare effects of labour market policy: a comparison of the USA and the UK

STEPHEN P. MILLARD and
DALE T. MORTENSEN

A presumption that natural rates of unemployment are excessive is common, particularly in the economies of Europe. Two culprits are typically identified in the literature, labour market policies intended to compensate for lost earnings and excessive market power in the hands of employed worker 'insiders'. According to Layard, Nickell and Jackman (1991), 91 per cent of the variation in unemployment rate averages over the 1983–8 time period across the principal 19 OECD industrial countries can be explained by variation in the liberality of unemployment insurance (UI) benefits, the extent of collective bargaining coverage, the degree of coordination in the wage determination process, and emphasis on active labour market policies. Although the authors recognise that unemployment rate differentials do not necessarily reflect differences in economic welfare, they argue that the effects of UI and labour bargaining powers are likely to yield 'too much' unemployment, particularly in Europe. Hence, their recommendations for the UK include a limitation on the duration of UI benefits, a strong 'willingness to work' test as a condition for the receipt of benefits, and an active labour market policy focused on those expected to have long unemployment spells. Active policies include adult training, recruiting subsidies, public employment as the 'employer of last resort' and wage subsidies.

The purpose of this chapter is to conduct computational experiments that reveal the quantitative implications of a particular labour market equilibrium model, that developed by Mortensen and Pissarides (1994), for the unemployment and welfare effects of existing labour market policy and possibly policy reforms. In particular, we study an extension of their model that incorporates a payroll tax, unemployment insurance policy, a firing penalty, severance pay and a hiring subsidy. First, the model is calibrated to be consistent with information about structural parameters, policy parameters and average rates of flow into and out of unemployment in the USA experienced over the 1983–92 time period. Following Layard *et al.* (1991), we then recalibrate the model for the UK by supposing that the differences in the average unemployment spell lengths and unemployment frequencies over the 1983–92 period by the two countries are due primarily to observable differences in government policies that impinge on the labour market and to known but less quantifiable differences in the market power of workers in the two economies. Finally, we evaluate the quantitative effects of policy reforms of the kind suggested by Layard *et al.* (1991) and others on both the duration and incidence of unemployment and on the level of economic welfare as measured by net output or consumption per participating worker.

The calibration exercise suggests that differences in policy parameters and greater UK worker power in the determination of wage rates are plausible explanations for the differences in unemployment spell duration and unemployment incidence. Indeed, the model attributes about two-thirds of the longer duration of unemployment in the UK and approximately one-third of the larger incidence of unemployment experienced in the USA to differences in labour market policies. Most of the remainder can be explained by greater worker bargaining power in the UK. Both the total contribution of labour market policy to unemployment and the welfare cost of policy measured in terms of aggregate net output per participating worker forgone are much larger in the UK than for the USA. Indeed, were unemployment insurance, payroll taxes and redundancy pay all eliminated in both countries the calibrated model suggests that the unemployment rate would fall to around 3.5 per cent of the participating labour force in both countries. However, the increase in aggregate net output per worker would be almost 5.5 per cent in the UK but less than 1 per cent in the USA. Finally, alternative reform experiments suggest that a combination of limiting the maximum UI benefit period, reducing redundancy pay and subsidising new hiring would be an effective way of both decreasing unemployment and increasing economic welfare.

1 A simple model of job creation and job destruction

The analysis that follows is based on the model of job creation and job destruction developed by Mortensen and Pissarides (1994) extended to account for labour market policy. In this framework, job creation is the outcome of a two-sided matching process in which workers and employers engage in search and recruiting activity. An essential implication of the existence of friction in the job–worker matching process is that wages are determined by some form of bargaining in which the outside option of being unemployed plays the role of determining the sensitivity of the wage to 'supply and demand' conditions and rentsharing makes the wage paid by an employer sensitive to that firm's labour productivity. These features, together with forward-looking decisions by employer and worker participants, determine the natural rate of unemployment.

In the model, job creation is viewed as a decision by an employer to seek a new worker for the purpose of engaging in productive activity that can be expected to generate future profit. Job destruction is reflected in a separate decision to terminate an existing employment relationship because the expected profitability of productive activity no longer justifies its continuation. Because the model permits heterogeneity in job–worker match productivity, job creation and job destruction take place at the same time in the aggregate as documented by the empirical work of Davis and Haltiwanger (1990, 1992). Furthermore, unemployment in the model reflects the process of reallocating labour from less to more productive economic activities. Mortensen (1994) has shown that this model contains propagation mechanisms capable of capturing the salient features of worker and job flow responses to movements in the value of labour product over the business cycle. As the model recognises both imperfect competition in wage determination and friction in the process that reallocates workers from less to more productive jobs, it implies a reduced-form relationship between unemployment and labour market policy parameters as well as parameters that reflect the relative market power of workers and employers in the wage bargaining process of the type estimated by Layard *et al.* (1991).

The essential equations of the model are derived in mathematical appendix 1 (p. 567). In order to gain an insight into how labour market policy and wage formation institutions are likely to affect unemployment in the model, the basic properties are sketched below. Fortunately, the essence of the model can be represented intuitively with the aid of two curves that resemble demand and supply relationships (see figure 17.1, p. 551).

Productive activity is the purpose of job–worker matches, which are formally indistinguishable from an establishment or a firm in the model. Although all workers are identical, the relative value of the product of a specific match changes from time to time without warning, an assumption which reflects the unforseen nature of shocks to taste and technology that affect the competitiveness of any existing producing firm. When new matches form, the best current information about which activities are most likely to be profitable in the future is used to determine what will be produced. These assumptions generally imply that new matches are more productive than old and that every job will eventually become unprofitable. Formally, the idiosyncratic shock to productivity implicit in this specification is modelled by supposing that new values arrive with frequency λ and are distributed according to the cumulative distribution function $F(x)$, i.e. idiosyncratic match productivity is a Markov jump process. Hence, the rate at which existing employment relationships are destroyed, equivalently *unemployment incidence or frequency*, is $\text{Inc} = \delta + \gamma F(R)$ where R represents the *reservation productivity* of a marginal match and δ is a parameter reflecting other exogenous reasons for job–worker separation. The reservation productivity is the endogenous value of match productivity below which expected future profitability no longer justifies continuation of the employment relationship.

An employer's intention to form a match is signalled by posting a job vacancy. The total cost of recruiting new workers is proportional to the number of vacancies posted. The rate at which vacancies are filled depends on the number of vacancies and the number of workers seeking employment through a relation which has become known as the *matching function*. Analogous to a production function, a matching function is a relationship between the search and recruiting inputs provided by workers and employers respectively and a resulting flow of new matches, the output. Under familiar regularity conditions and a constant returns to scale assumption, the rate at which unemployed workers are matched with vacant jobs, the *unemployment hazard*, is an increasing and concave function of the ratio of vacant jobs to searching workers denoted as $m(\theta)$ where θ represents the vacancy: searching worker ratio. The endogenous variable θ is a measure of *market tightness* and $\text{Dur} = 1/m(\theta)$ is the average *duration of a completed unemployment spell*. In the model, market tightness is determined by a free-entry condition which requires that the expected present value of future profits attributable to filling the marginal vacancy equal the cost of recruiting and training a worker.

Unemployment in the model outlined above, although a consequence of the transaction friction embodied in the matching function, reflects a continual process by which workers are reallocated from less to more productive activity. The dynamics of unemployment are easily expressed in terms of the notation introduced above. Letting the unit interval represent the available labour force, the flow into unemployment is the product of the employment hazard and the fraction employed, i.e. $(\delta + \gamma F(R))(1 - un)$ where un is the fraction unemployed. The flow out of unemployment is the product of the unemployment hazard and the fraction unemployed, i.e., $m(\theta)un$. Hence, the *steady-state unemployment rate*, that which equates the two flows, is approximately equal to the product of the incidence of unemployment and the duration of an unemployment spell. Formally,

$$\frac{un}{1-un}=\frac{\delta+\gamma F(R)}{m(\theta)}=\text{dur}\times\text{inc} \tag{1}$$

Because neither worker nor employer can instantaneously or costlessly find an alternative match partner in the market modelled, a match surplus expressed as a net capital value of continuing the match to its parties exists. In this context, wage determination is a bilateral bargaining problem which determines how this surplus is divided between employer and worker. A particular solution to the bargaining problem is not specified in the Mortensen–Pissarides model simply because wage determination institutions vary so much from one industry to another and across countries. Wages can be determined in a highly non-centralised way by bargaining between individual worker and employer pairs as is common the USA. Bargains between employer and union associations at various levels, the plant, the industry or even the nation, are common in many other industrialised economies and some manufacturing industries in the USA. In a few countries such as Australia and New Zealand, the public at large as well as representatives of labour and management are included in the bargaining process. One can expect the extent and use of worker market power to differ across these alternative institutional settings. In the formal model, the workers' share of match surplus, denoted by β, is regarded as a parameter with value reflecting the extent and use of worker bargaining power.

Under the assumption that the wage adjusts to assure the worker the fixed share β of match surplus, a layoff occurs if and only if the total surplus falls below zero as a consequence of an idiosyncratic shock to productivity. In the environment under study, the surplus value of a match equals the expected present value of the sum of the future incomes of worker and employer were they to continue the match *less* the capital value of separation. The latter is the sum of the present value of future worker and employer incomes were they to separate *plus* the expected present value of UI benefits received by the worker during her subsequent unemployment spell *plus* severance or redundancy pay received from her employer *less* the lump sum firing cost that the employer has to bear. Firing costs include those associated with any procedural or legal process that might be required of the employer in order to lay off a worker, redundancy pay, and the addition to UI taxes attributable to employer experience rating, a feature of the unemployment insurance system in the

USA. Note that redundancy pay nets out in the calculation of the net surplus value of a match to the extent that it is a transfer from employer to worker. In the case of a fully experience-rated tax, the unemployment benefit acts just like severance pay. However, because the wage paid reflects the 'threats' in the wage bargaining problem, which equal the capital value of unemployed search *plus* redundancy pay in the worker's case and the negative of total firing costs in the employer's, an increase in either redundancy pay or the unemployment benefit adversely affect equilibrium market tightness θ by increasing the wage that a worker will receive prior to separation.

The two endogenous variables, R and θ, are somewhat analogous to 'price' and 'quantity' respectively in the standard supply and demand framework. The equilibrium pair of values is determined by two relationships that are respectively downward- and upward-sloping as illustrated in figure 17.1 (for the details of the mathematics, see appendix 1). Specifically, employers post vacancies in numbers that equate the cost of recruiting with the expected future profits attributable to hiring a worker net of any cost of training the worker. As profitability declines with reservation productivity, this job creation condition implies the downward-sloping relation between market tightness and reservation productivity labelled *CC* in figure 17.1. Reservation productivity is determined primarily by the value of unemployed search to the worker which increases with market tightness. Hence, reservation productivity increases with market tightness. This positive relationship between R and Θ is illustrated by the curve labelled *DD* in figure 17.1. The equilibrium pair of values, that consistent with both requirements labelled (R^*,θ^*) in 17.1, lies at the sole intersection of the two curves. The labels remind the reader that the curve *CC* represents the job creation decision while *DD* reflects job destruction.

2 The qualitative effects of labour policy and wage formation institutions

Specific labour market policies and wage formation institutions affect the position of one or both of the curves in figure 17.1. Hence, hypothetical changes in either shift the curves and the associated equilibrium reservation productivity and market tightness pair. For example, an increase in the liberality of UI benefits due either to an increase in the replacement ratio or the length of the benefit period, increases the relative value of the unemployment option to workers. As a consequence, an increase in UI benefits induce an upward shift in the job destruction relation, *DD* in figure 17.1. Because the job creation condition *CC* is not

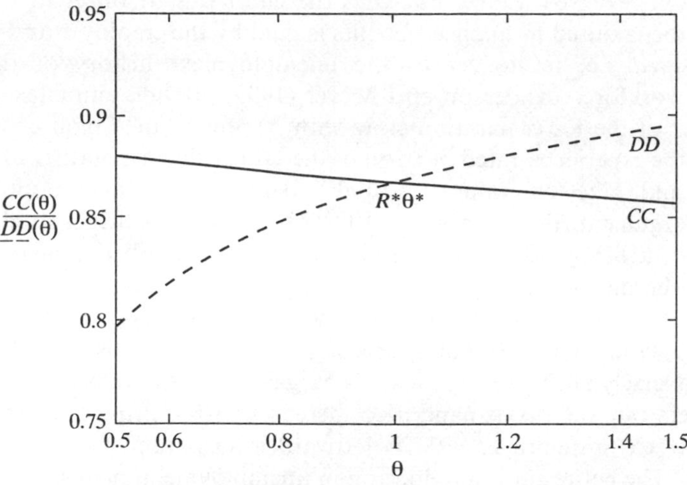

Figure 17.1 Equilibrium reservation productivity and market tightness

directly affected, at least when the benefit increase is assumed to have no effect on taxes, the equilibrium reservation productivity rises. As the increase in R induces a movement up along the CC curve in figure 17.1, the equilibrium rate of job creation as reflected in market tightness, Θ, is adversely affected. Hence, unemployment rises because both its incidence and the duration increase.

The adverse effect of UI benefit levels on the average duration of an unemployment spell are well documented in the literature, much of which is summarised in Layard *et al.* (1991) and in Devine and Kiefer (1991). Although estimates of the elasticity of the mean duration of an unemployment spell with respect to the UI benefit range between 0.03 and 1.44, they tend to cluster around 0.5. In their cross-country study, Layard *et al.* report an estimate of the marginal effect on the average unemployment rate of 0.17 per one percentage point increase in the UI replacement ratio. Although many authors attribute the effect of UI benefits on unemployment duration to the diminished incentive to search when benefits are paid conditional on remaining unemployed, the Mortensen–Pissarides model implies that the cause is distortion induced by UI benefits on the relative value of employment to workers. Brechling (1981) and Katz and Meyer (1990) provide evidence that supports the prediction that unemployment incidence as well as duration increases with UI benefit levels.

Feldstein (1976) argues that more liberal UI benefits encourage layoffs for the reason reviewed above, but that the effect can be offset to the extent that the tax used to finance benefits is paid by the employer and is *experience-rated*, i.e. set to reflect the unemployment history of the employer's workforce. Anderson and Meyer (1993) provide estimates of the elasticity of the job separation flow with respect to the layoff costs induced by the experience-rated portion of the UI tax that are statistically significant and take on values around −0.09, results that support Feldstein's argument. In the version of the Mortensen–Pissarides model studied here, a firing tax of this kind does affect the job destruction decision in the direction suggested by these empirical findings. Specifically, an increase in the degree of experience rating shifts down the job destruction relation, curve *DD* in figure 17.1. However, because a higher firing tax adversely affects the employer's bargaining position as well, the wage workers can and do demand also increases with a firing tax. As a consequence, *CC* in figure 17.1 shifts leftward in response to any firing tax increase. The net result is a reduction in unemployment incidence but an ambiguous effect on duration.

An increase in worker bargaining power, reflected in the share of match surplus received by the workers, has the same effect on the job destruction relation *DD* as an increase in the UI benefit, i.e. *DD* shifts up in response to the associated increase induced in the value of search for alternative employment. However, an increase in the workers' share also decreases future profitability given reservation productivity, so that *CC* shifts to the left. For both reasons, equilibrium market tightness falls but the effect on the equilibrium reservation productivity is ambiguous. In other words, the theory suggests that unemployment spell durations are longer in economies in which workers receive a larger share of match surplus, although the sign of difference in spell frequencies is unclear.

Layard *et al.* (1991) find that unemployment rates are positively associated with collective bargaining coverage across OECD countries, but are lower in those that have more coordinated and centralised wage determination processes. In interpreting their results, they argue that the market power of currently employed workers increases with the extent of collective bargaining coverage, holding the degree of coordination constant. However, more coordinated and centralised wage determination mechanisms take greater account of the equilibrium effects of higher wages on job creation because the participants in the process either represent unemployed as well as employed workers or employers and the general public. To the extent that workers' share in the model increases with collective bargaining coverage and decreases with the degree of coordination in the wage determination process, their reasoning and results are consistent with the Mortensen–Pissarides model.

Employment protection policy is represented in the formal model as either a financial penalty or tax imposed on the employer for terminating a job or as a severance transfer from employer to worker. The implied effects of a pure firing penalty are those discussed above for the case of an experience-rated UI tax. Unlike a firing tax, a severance payment has no direct effect on the job destruction decision because the productivity contingent wage is set to ensure that separation occurs only when in the interest of both parties. Nevertheless, redundancy pay does adversely affect the employer's 'threat' in the wage bargain and consequently increases the wage the employer will pay in every period prior to separation. As a consequence, an employer's incentive to post a vacancy is adversely affected by severance transfer.

Contrary to our result, Lazear (1990) has shown that a severance transfer has no effects in what he calls a 'frictionless' equilibrium in which workers are able to 'buy' jobs by offering to compensate employers up front for any future redundancy pay obligation imposed by policy. However, in the search equilibrium framework of Diamond (1982), Mortensen (1982) and Pissarides (1990) the kind of *ex ante* competition that might yield this result is simply not present. Burda (1992) also finds that a transfer has no effect. However, his conclusion is the consequence of two differences between the formulation he studies and ours. First, he assumes that the threat point in the bargaining over the gross value of a match is the value of search to the worker and the value of posting a vacancy to the employer *prior* to their meeting rather than the respective values of separation *after* the formation of a match as we do. Second, he assumes that separation is exogenous. As it turns out, the endogenous separation rate, unemployment incidence, would be directly affected by redundancy pay in our model if Burda's wage rule were adopted. Indeed, inefficient incidence would occur because his wage rule does not account for the transfer that is about to take place as a consequence of the separation. Although it does distort the job creation decision, our bargaining outcome rule is jointly efficient in this sense which is the reason for viewing its implications as worthy of study.

In terms of figure 17.1 an increase in redundancy pay leaves *DD* unchanged but shifts the *CC* curve to the left. As a consequence, unemployment duration and incidence both fall, with the net effect on the equilibrium unemployment rate left ambiguous. Not surprisingly, then, the empirical evidence on the association with unemployment is mixed. Lazear (1990) found that increasing severance pay by one month reduces employment per head about 0.4 per cent and reduces labour force participation rate by 0.3 per cent. As a consequence, the unemployment rate rises by 0.1 per cent. The results of Bentolila and Bertola

(1990) suggest that increases in firing costs decrease unemployment. Abraham and Houseman (1993) find that unemployment is reduced by employment protection policy but also recommend a hiring subsidy to ameliorate the adverse effects on job creation.

A hiring subsidy is incorporated in the model as a payment to the employer per new worker hired. In the context of the Mortensen–Pissarides model, a hiring subsidy can be regarded as any government action that reduces the private costs of either recruiting or training workers. The direct effect on job creation of a hiring subsidy is a shift in the job creation curve, *CC*, everywhere to the right in figure 17.1. Because this shift induces movement up along the job destruction condition *DD*, the net effect is an increase in market tightness and an increase in reservation productivity. Because the effects of a hiring subsidy on unemployment duration and incidence tend to offset one another, again the net qualitative effect on the equilibrium unemployment rate is ambiguous. Indeed, the positive 'displacement effect' on job destruction was used as an argument against the New Job Credit of 1977 in the USA. However, in the Mortensen–Pissarides model the consequence of displacement is greater productivity as less productive jobs are replaced by more productive ones at a higher rate. Hamermesh (1993) argues for such subsidies as a means of offsetting the disincentive effects of other labour market policies. Layard *et al.* (1991) provide evidence that active labour market policy, which includes subsidies to recruiting and training, reduces unemployment, although admittedly their characterisation of cross-country differences is crude.

Although any increase in a payroll tax, such as that used to finance social security in the USA and most European countries, is shifted to workers to some extent by a decrease in the wage, the incidence of the tax is shared between worker and employer given a bargaining model of wage determination even when worker participation is perfectly inelastic. By implication, the wage plus tax bill increases with the payroll tax rate which in turn implies that *DD* shifts up in figure 17.1 in response to an increase in the tax rate. Because expected future profitability also falls with the tax, *CC* shifts down. Hence, the qualitative effects of a payroll tax are similar to those of an increase in the workers' share parameter. Empirical evidence on the effects of a payroll tax is hard to find. Hamermesh (1993) follows much of the literature by arguing for a small employment effect, mainly on the grounds that labour force participation is highly inelastic. However, Phelps (1994) argues that one might expect large effects to the extent that wages are determined by 'efficiency' considerations.

3 Accounting for the UK–US unemployment rate differential

In this section, we calibrate versions of the Mortensen–Pissarides model for the USA and the UK to be consistent with observed differentials in the two major components of unemployment, the average duration of an unemployment spell and the incidence of unemployment, experienced in the two countries over the 10-year period 1983–92. The purpose is to ascertain whether known qualitative differences in labour market policy and wage setting institutions are reasonable quantitative explanations for unemployment duration and frequency differentials and to determine which – policy or institutions – is the more important explanation in the context of the model.

The procedure underlying the experiment conducted in this section is as follows. First, reasonable values of structural and policy parameters for both the US and the UK versions of the model are assigned based on empirical evidence where possible. Next for the USA, two parameters for which there is no direct evidence, the forgone value of leisure b and a measure of dispersion in the idiosyncratic shock denoted as γ, are chosen to match the average duration of unemployment and incidence of unemployment experienced over the 1983–92 period. Under the assumption that these and other non-policy structural parameter values are the same for the UK, the worker's share parameter and the value of leisure parameter are chosen to match average unemployment duration and incidence experience for the UK over the same period. A minimum requirement for consistency with prior expectation is that the calibrated value of the UK worker share exceeds that assumed for the USA.

A real rate of interest r of 1 per cent per quarter and an exogenous rate at which workers quit to unemployment δ of 1.5 per cent per quarter are values consistent with available empirical information. The elasticity of the matching function with respect to vacancies $\eta = \theta m'(\theta)/m(\theta)$ used is the estimate 0.6 obtained by Blanchard and Diamond (1989) for the USA. Although Pissarides' (1986) point estimate for the UK is lower, a value of 0.6 cannot be rejccted. This value is also the estimate obtained for the Netherlands by Van Ours (1991).

As earnings turn out to average about 85 per cent of maximal output per worker in the model, the fact that average US wages plus benefits equal $31,200 per year in 1990 (see *Statistical Abstract of the United States, 1993*, table 666) implies maximal worker output per quarter in 1990 dollars equal to $9070. Survey information reported in Hamermesh (1993) suggests that the average recruiting and training cost per worker was about $300 and $2500 respectively in 1990. Letting output per quarter in the most productive job serve as numeraire, these figures imply a training cost parameter $k = \$2500/9070 = 0.276$ and a recruiting cost parameter that solves $cm(\theta)/(\theta) = \$3000/\$9070 = 0.33$ per worker hired. Although maximal value of output per worker may differ in the UK, we assume that the same relative costs of recruiting and training prevail.

Although regression coefficients closely related to workers' share β are positive and highly statistically significant in the empirical wage equation literature, the typical point estimate is quite small (see Blanchflower, Oswald and Sanfrey, 1993). However, Abowd and Lemieux (1993) argue that these estimates are badly biased downward. Their regression coefficient, obtained using Canadian manufacturing data and an instrument variable approach, suggest a workers' share of about 30 per cent. Although non-cooperative bargaining theory implies a 50 per cent share and insider–outsider arguments suggest even larger values for the share, $\beta = 0.3$ is assumed in the US case for the purpose of the calculations that follow. The fact that uncoordinated collective bargaining is much more pervasive in the UK suggests a higher value for workers' share there. The value actually used is backed out of the model in a manner outlined below.

The policy parameters of the model include the social security or payroll tax rate paid by both worker and employer denoted as π, the UI benefit replacement ratio ρ, the maximum UI benefit period τ, a parameter ϵ representing the degree to which the UI tax is experience rated, a redundancy pay parameter Φ, and a hiring subsidy Ψ. For the purpose of the calibration, these parameters are set at values that approximate current US and UK policy. Specifically, the value $\pi = 0.075$ reflects the fact that employers and workers together pay 15 per cent of labour earnings as social security taxes in the USA. The comparable rate paid by both worker and employer in the UK is $\pi = 0.09$ for a total of 18 per cent.

The mandated benefit replacement ratio is 50 per cent of prior earnings and the maximum duration of benefits is six months in the USA. However, the actual fraction of laid off workers who receive UI benefits is much lower because not all qualify, primarily on the basis of insufficient prior employment, and because not all those who do qualify claim benefits. In our model, the estimates of the fraction eligible for UI, fractions ineligible by reason and take up rates for the 1977–87 period reported by Blank and Card (1991, table I) suggest that roughly 50 per cent of laid off workers in our model either would not qualify or would not apply. Hence, when appropriately interpreted as the product of the replacement ratio and probability of receipt of benefits, one obtains the parameter value $p = 0.5 \times 0.5 = 0.25$ for the USA. In the UK, the fraction of the unemployed who receive benefits, 73 per cent, is higher but the replacement ratio is lower, 36 per cent, according to Layard *et al.* (1991). Hence, the product for the UK $\rho = 0.26$, is virtually identical. As the period of the model is one quarter, $\tau = 2$ in the case of the USA six-month limitation and $\tau = \infty$ in the case of the UK indefinite benefit period. Anderson and Meyer (1993) estimate that a typical employer can expect to pay 60 cents of each additional dollar of UI benefits received by an employee in the form of higher future UI taxes. In other words, the average degree to which the UI tax is experience rated is reflected in the parameter value $\epsilon = 0.6$ for the US case and $\epsilon = 0$ for the UK.

For the purpose of the exercise, the only firing penalty included for the USA is that associated with the experience rating of the UI tax. Severance pay is assumed nil. Although existing estimates of the redundancy pay received by workers in the UK range up to three months of wage earnings, a value of one month's wage ($\phi = 0.27$) is assumed here. Finally, the hiring subsidy assumed is zero for both countries even though both do spend small amounts on training and job search assistance.

The arrival rate of the idiosyncratic productivity shock, λ, is assumed to equal 0.1 per quarter, a number close to that found consistent with US job and worker flow behaviour in Mortensen (1994). Direct observation provides little information about the value of leisure, b, and the parameter, γ, reflecting the dispersion of the productivity shock. Given the other parameter values, these were set in the US case so that the steady-state implications of the model match recent US unemployment experience in the 1983–92 time period. In particular, they are chosen so that the model's average completed duration of an unemployment spell is one quarter and its expected unemployment incidence is 7 per cent per quarter. The baseline structural and policy parameter values for the USA are summarised in the second column of table 17.1 in panels A and panel B respectively.

Although admittedly the empirical basis for these parameters choices is meagre, existing evidence on the association between policy and behaviour provides a reliability check. As noted above, econometric estimates of the elasticity of unemployment spell duration and the replacement ratio centre around 0.5. For US parameters, the model implies a slightly higher elasticity of 0.54. The estimate of the effect of the replacement ratio on the unemployment rate in the Layard *et al.* (1991) cross-country study is 0.17 while our model implies that this effect is 0.125 evaluated at US parameter values. Finally, the Anderson and Meyer (1993) estimate of the job separation elasticity with respect to the degree to which the UI tax is experience-rated is –0.09, very close to the theoretical value of –0.084 implied by our model. This consistency of the

Table 17.1 *Baseline parameter values and unemployment experience: the USA and the UK*

A Structural parameters (1)	USA (2)	UK (3)
Interest rate: r	0.010 per qr	0.010 per qr
E to U transition rate: δ	0.014 per qr	0.014 per qr
Recruiting cost: c	0.330 per qr	0.330 per qr
Training cost: k	0.275 per worker	0.275 per worker
Product shock arrival rate: λ	0.100 per qr	0.100 per qr
Min productivity: λ	0.713 per qr	0.713 per qr
Matching elasticity: η	0.600 per qr	0.600
Worker's share: β	0.300	0.584
Value of leisure: b	0.285 per qr	0.235 per qr
B Policy parameters	**USA**	**UK**
Payroll tax: π	0.075	0.09
U1 replacement ratio: ρ	0.25	0.26
U1 benefit period: τ	2 qrs	∞
U1 experience rate: ϵ	0.60	0.0
Severance pay: θ	0.0	0.27
Hiring subsidy: ψ	0.0	0.0
C Differentials	**US policy parameters**	**UK policy parameters**
US unemployment rate	6.5%	14.3%
Average duration	3.0 months	7.4 months
Expected incidence	3.0 months	6.8% per qr
UK unemployment rate	5.4%	9.2%
Average duration	4.2 months	9.0 months
Expected incidence	4.1% per qr	3.2% per qr

model with evidence on the actual effects of labour market policy supports the view that the quantitative results presented below are meaningful.

In the UK case, all structural parameters other than the worker's share β and the value of leisure b are assumed the same as those for the USA. These are chosen so that the steady-state implications of the model with UK policy parameters match UK unemployment duration and incidence experience over the 1983–92 time period, namely an average duration of unemployment equal to 3 quarters and an unemployment incidence of 3.2 per cent per quarter. The implied UK value of leisure is quite close to that for the USA while the value of workers' share is substantially higher, a fact consistent with the higher collective bargaining coverage in the UK. The baseline structural and policy parameter values for the UK are reported in column (3) of table 17.1, in panels A and B respectively.

A brief account of the extent to which differentials in the unemployment rate, duration, and incidence can be explained by differences only in labour market policy is indicated in panel C of table 17.1. The actual values of all three averages for the USA and the UK are those reported on the diagonal in columns (2) and (3) of panel C respectively. The hypothetical values of each implied by the model when evaluated at the values of the other country's policy parameters are reported in the opposite column. In other words, at UK policy parameter values, the US equilibrium steady-state unemployment rate would have been 14.3 per cent while the UK unemployment rate given US parameters would be 5.4 per cent. As the actual US and UK unemployment rates were 6.5 per cent and 9.2 per cent respectively, labour market policy over-explains the difference. After decomposing the effects into those on unemployment duration and incidence, the reason is clear. Policy differences have relatively little effect on the unemployment frequency differential but UK policy induces a duration of unemployment which is twice that associated with US policy parameters in both countries. As a consequence, the model suggests that the much smaller unemployment incidence in the UK relative to the USA can be attributed to the larger worker share.

4 The effects of individual labour market policies

In this section, we report the marginal effects of each policy – the payroll tax, unemployment insurance and employment protection on the duration, incidence, and rate of unemployment and on consumption per worker. Aggregate consumption per participating worker, the most comprehensive measure of economic welfare provided by the model is equal to market output *plus* the value of leisure of those not employed *minus* the cost of recruiting and training new hires (see mathematical appendix 2, p. 569, for formal definitions of these concepts). Although aggregate consumption per worker is a more appropriate measure of economic welfare than unemployment, it should be remembered that the model assumes risk-neutral agents. Consequently, welfare losses attributed to the existence of the unemployment insurance and employment protection measures are upper bounds to the extent that these policies actually provided valued insurance. Similarly, the welfare cost of the payroll tax is a measure of its deadweight loss, which does not account for the value of any government service, e.g. medical and old age assistance, that it might finance. Still, estimates of these deadweight losses are important and new.

Results for the USA are reported in panel A of table 17.2 and for the UK in panel B of table 17.2. For each entry in the table, the change is in the variable labelled at the top of the column induced by the elimination of the policy specified at the far left of the row. Finally, the total effects of eliminating all three forms of labour market intervention in the two countries are reported in the last row of each panel.

The model suggests that labour market policy is responsible for a large fraction of unemployment in both countries, 3 points of the 6.5 per cent unemployment rate in the USA and nearly 6 points of the 9.2 per cent rate in the UK. Obviously, the effect of policy is larger in the UK than in the USA. Indeed, the last rows of the two panels imply that the unemployment rates in the two countries would be approximately the same, about 3.5 per cent of the labour force, in the absence of any labour market policy. In this sense, policy differences explain the entire difference in the two country's unemployment rates. Most of the effect of existing labour market policy in both countries is on the average duration of an unemployment spell rather than unemployment incidence. Hence, the UK has a larger unemployment rate than the USA because its policy combination has a bigger impact on unemployment duration. Finally, the loss in consumption per work in the USA attributable to labour market policy measures is not insignificant, about 8/10th of a percentage point, but it is modest relative to the 5.4 per cent loss in consumption per participant that the model attributes to labour policy in the UK.

In both countries, all three forms of policy add to unemployment but the unemployment insurance programme is the largest single contributor, accounting alone for 2.3 of the 6.5 percentage points rate in the USA and 4.6 points of the 9.2 percentage point rate in the UK. The payroll tax is the second most important policy factor in both countries, responsible for well over 1 percentage point in the US unemployment rate and over 2 points in the UK rate. However, the deadweight loss of the payroll tax, over 2 per cent of consumption per participating worker, is virtually the same as the cost of UI in the UK. Furthermore, redundancy pay, the principal form of employment protection in the UK is the most costly of the policies accounting alone for almost 75 per cent of the deadweight loss of labour market policy even though it has the smallest effect on the unemployment rate. The only form of employment protection in the USA, the experience-rated portion of the UI tax, also contributes positively to unemployment because, as in the UK, its adverse effect on job creation more than offsets the reduction in unemployment incidence. Finally, note that the collective effect of all policies together is subadditive, i.e. the effect of the entire policy combination on either

Table 17.2 *The marginal effects of specific labour market policies*

Policy	Δun rate (%)	Δdur (months)	Δinc (%/qr)	$\Delta C/C$ (%)
A USA				
No payroll tax	−1.27	−0.60	−0.06	0.49
No UI	−2.29	−1.09	−0.06	0.75
No protection	−0.25	−0.33	0.53	0.24
No policy	−2.94	−1.37	−0.16	0.79
B UK				
No payroll tax	−2.05	−2.84	0.37	2.08
No UI	−4.55	−3.49	−0.72	2.04
No protection	−2.13	−4.74	1.97	4.06
No policy	−5.77	−6.69	1.23	5.40

unemployment or consumption per participant is much less than the sum of the marginal impacts of the individual policies.

5 The effects of labour policy reforms

Layard *et al.* (1991) recommend a limitation on the maximum period of UI benefits and an active labour market policy as ways of reducing unemployment in the UK. Snower (1994) proposes a scheme that would essentially finance a subsidy to hire a new worker from what would otherwise be paid to the worker as UI benefits were she to continue unemployed (see chapter 6 in this volume). Phelps (1994) strongly recommends a wage subsidy, possibly in the form of a payroll tax reduction, as a means of both increasing employment and the earnings of low-wage workers (see chapter 7 in this volume). The analysis of the impacts of the various labour market policies in section 4 suggests that any of these reforms could have a desirable impact. However, the relative magnitudes of the effects of these proposals on unemployment, consumption and tax revenue need to be ascertained. The presentation of the results of an analysis of the model for this purpose is contained in this section.

The cumulative effects on the steady-state unemployment rate, duration and incidence, and on steady-state consumption per participant and government revenue per participant of combinations of the policy reforms for the UK are presented in Tables 17.3A, B and C. In table 17.3A, the marginal effects of limiting the maximum UI benefit period to six months and of eliminating the redundancy transfer from worker to employer altogether are reported (first and second rows of table 17.3A).

Table 17.3 *The cumulative effects of UK labour policy reforms*

A UI benefit period and redundancy pay

	Δun (%)	Δdur (months)	Δinc (%/qr)	$\Delta C/C$ (%)
Limit maximum UI Benefit period ($\tau = 2$)	−2.52	−1.95	−0.33	1.30
No redundancy pay ($\phi = 0$)	−2.13	4.74	1.97	4.06
Limit UI period and no redundancy pay	−3.01	−4.74	1.76	4.42

B The wage subsidy case

	Δun (%)	Δdur (months)	Δinc (%/qr)	$\Delta C/C$ (%)
Reduce payroll tax ($\pi = 0.04$)	−1.25	−1.78	−0.21	1.26
Reduce payroll tax and limit UI period ($\tau = 2$)	−2.93	−2.98	−0.05	2.06
Reduce payroll tax and no redundancy ($\phi = 0$)	−3.22	−5.44	1.98	4.76
All of the above ($\pi = 0.04$, $\tau = 2$ and $\phi = 0$)	−3.74	−5.67	1.83	4.93

C The hiring subsidy case

	Δun (%)	Δdur (months)	Δinc (%/qr)	$\Delta C/C$ (%)
Subsidise new hires ($\psi = 0.04$)	2.72	−3.49	−3.99	2.02
Subsidise hires and limit UI period ($\tau = 2$)	0.90	−4.25	3.72	3.20
Subsidise hires and no redundancy pay ($\phi = 0$)	−3.75	−6.89	4.84&	6.06
(*Psi* = 0.04, $\tau = 2$ and $\phi = 0$)	−3.88	−6.93	4.78	6.11

In the third row, the cumulative effects of both limiting the UI benefit period and eliminating severance pay are reported. The results in table 17.3B focus on the effects of a wage subsidy in the form of a payroll tax reduction, both alone, and in combination with other reforms, while those of table 17.3C reflect the analogous effects of a hiring subsidy. The sizes of the wage and hiring subsidies considered are set so that results are comparable in the sense that the revenue costs of the two policies are approximately the same. The impact of each policy reform and the cumulative impact of every combination on government revenue are reflected in the last column of all three tables. Specifically, the number reported there is the change in the difference between the payroll tax and UI tax collected and the total of UI benefits paid out and any hiring subsidies, all expressed as a percentage of the total aggregate wage bill.

In a head to head contest, imposing a maximum benefit period of six months has a somewhat larger impact on the steady state unemployment rate than does the elimination of the assumed one month's wage redundancy payment, a reduction of 2.5 per cent compared with 2.1 per cent according to table 17.3A. However, the welfare gain of the latter, 4 per cent of consumption per participant, is over three times that attributable to limiting the maximum benefit period. The reasons for these quantitative differences in effects are reflected in the differential impact that the two policies have on unemployment duration and incidence. Imposing a benefit period limit affects both unemployment and consumption per participant primarily by shortening the expected duration of an unemployment spell by almost two months. The reservation level of idiosyncratic productivity and consequently average productivity per employed worker, is affected hardly at all. The elimination of redundancy payments shortens unemployment duration by much more, almost five months, but also increases incidence significantly, by almost 2 per cent per quarter. Because the latter effect offsets the former in large measure, the impact on unemployment is slightly smaller than that of the UI benefit-period limitation. However, because the increase in incidence reflects an increase in reservation productivity, consumption per participant increases by more than that attributable to the six-month UI benefit-period limit because employment increases by roughly the same amount but the productivity of those employed rises significantly in response to the elimination of redundancy pay. The results in the third row of figure 17.3A imply that a combination of both limiting the maximum UI benefit period and eliminating severance pay decreases unemployment by only half a point relative to the effect of the period limit alone, but increases consumption per participant by over 3 per cent.

The first row of table 17.3B provides experimental evidence drawn from the model on the effects of a 5 percentage point reduction in the payroll tax paid by both the worker and employer in every match. Relative to either a six-month limitation on UI benefits or the elimination of redundancy pay in the UK, a large cut in the payroll tax of 10 percentage points has small effects. The unemployment rate falls by 1.25 points, only half of the decrease that the model attributes to a benefit-period limit and substantially less than that resulting from the elimination of redundancy pay according to the results reported in table 17.3A. Although the net effect of the cut on consumption per participant is about the same as that obtained from the benefit-period limit, again the increase in consumption per participating worker resulting from the elimination of redundancy is roughly three times larger. In combination with either the benefit-period limit or the elimination of redundancy, a payroll tax rate cut of the magnitude considered reduces the unemployment rate by somewhat less than a point at the margin and adds only 7/10th of a percentage point to the gain in consumption per worker relative to that which either contribute alone, conclusions that are obtained by comparing results appropriately across tables 17.3A and 17.3B. Finally, were both the UI benefit limit in place and the redundancy transfer abolished, then the payroll tax would only reduce the unemployment rate by 7/10 of a point and increase consumption per participant by about 2/10th of a percent. The results of the experiment provide little support for such a cut in payroll taxes on efficiency grounds, at least as an add-on to the other reforms suggested.

The effects of a hiring subsidy comparable in terms of revenue requirement to the payroll tax rate cut, both alone and in combination with other reforms, are reported in table 17.3C. The first point to note is that a subsidy were it instituted alone would *increase* unemployment. Because the impact on incidence is proportionately larger than the decrease in duration induced by the subsidy, the former offsets the latter, resulting in an increase in the unemployment rate of almost 3 points. Still the increased productivity of those employed is more than enough to offset the decrease in employment and, as a consequence, consumption per participant increases by 2 per cent. By way of comparison, note that one could finance the hiring subsidy programme with a 5 point *increase* in the payroll tax paid by both worker and by employer at a consumption cost per participant of only 1.26 per cent, which would yield a net increase in consumption per participant overall of 0.74 per cent, provided that the effects reported in the fourth column of the first row of table 17.3B are symmetric with respect to sign. Still, unemployment would increase substantially overall were this joint policy adopted.

Although the results in the second row of table 17.3C imply that a subsidy in combination with a UI benefit-period limit would still increase unemployment, a hiring subsidy in combination with the elimination of redundancy pay has a huge impact on both unemployment and economic welfare. In particular, the unemployment rate would be reduced by 3.75 points while consumption per participant would be increased by 6 per cent as a consequence of both the increase in employment and productivity induced by the combination. Note that the marginal effects of adding the hiring subsidy given no redundancy pay obtained by comparing the results in the second row of table 17.3A with the third row of table 17.3C include a more than 1.6 point decrease in the unemployment rate, a two-month reduction in the average spell of unemployment, and a 2 per cent increase in consumption per labour force participant. Were this combination financed by a payroll tax *increase*, the implicit deadweight loss reflected in the results reported in the first row of table 17.3B suggest that unemployment would fall by at least 2.5 points and consumption per participant would rise by almost 5 per cent. Although the last row of table 17.3C implies that adding a UI unemployment benefit duration limit to this reform package would decrease unemployment, increase consumption and decrease the revenue requirement by even more, the marginal effects in all three dimensions are trivial.

6 Conclusions and suggestions for future research

In this chapter, we calibrate a variant of the Mortensen–Pissarides (1994) model to be consistent with information about structural parameters, policy parameters, and the average rates of flow into and out of unemployment experienced in the USA. We then recalibrate the model for the UK by supposing that the differences in the average unemployment spell lengths and unemployment frequencies over the 1983–92 period experienced by the two countries are due to observable differences in government policies that impinge on the labour market, to differences in the market power of workers in the two economies as reflected in the workers' share of future match surplus parameters, and to differences in the value of leisure forgone when employed. Finally, we evaluate the quantitative effects of policy reforms on both the duration and incidence of unemployment and on the level of economic welfare as measured by consumption per participating worker.

Over the 10-year period of comparison, 1983–92, the unemployment rates in the USA and UK averaged 6.5 per cent and 9.2 per cent of the respective country's participating labour force. The higher unemployment rate in the UK was the consequence of a much longer unemployment spell duration over this period, nine months as compared with three months in the USA. Indeed, during the period of comparison, the USA experienced an unemployment incidence of 7 per cent per quarter, over twice the 3.2 per cent per quarter rate experienced in the UK. According to the model, about two-thirds of the difference between the durations of the typical unemployment spell in the two countries and about one-third of the difference in the two country's unemployment frequencies, are explained by policy differences, in particular, the existence of a large redundancy payment in the UK and the limit on the duration of unemployment benefits in the USA. Most of the remainder in each case can be attributed to the inferred larger worker share of match surplus in the UK.

Given the calibrated model, we conduct counterfactual experiments that reveal what the unemployment rate, duration, and incidence as well as aggregate steady-state consumption per participant would be if any one of the policies were eliminated. In this way, we determine the quantitative implications of the model for the marginal contributions of each to the existing values of these aggregate statistics. The results of this experiment suggest that the payroll tax, the UI system and redundancy pay are respectively responsible for about 2, 4.5 and 2 points of the 9.2 per cent unemployment rate. Indeed, the elimination of the payroll tax, UI system and redundancy pay would increase consumption per participant by 2 per cent, 2 percent and 4 per cent respectively. As the elimination of all three policies together would reduce the unemployment rate only to 5.8 points and increase consumption per worker by 5.4 per cent, it is clear that the model embodies non-linearities in its implicit relationship between these policies and our outcome measures. Still, all three policies have large effects both at the margin and in combination with one or more of the other two.

The model implies that all forms of existing labour market intervention, the UI system, the payroll tax and employment protection policy, have large unintended effects on unemployment and economic efficiency. Reforms of these policies considered here, a maximum UI benefit period, the elimination of redundancy pay, a wage subsidy, and a new jobs subsidy, alone and in combination can reverse these effects to a substantial extent, but not without costs of their own. In particular, the elimination of either the UI system or the existing redundancy payment would increase efficiency at the expense of worker income security. Indeed, as all agents in the model are assumed to be risk-neutral, primarily for reasons of tractability, there is no account taken in the efficiency calculus of the insurance value of either UI or the redundancy transfer. Hence, the gains in consumption per participant reported above are upper bounds on the possible returns to reforms of these policies. Although a generalisation of the approach that takes account of risk-aversion is obviously needed to obtain a more realistic picture of the costs and benefits of these programmes, the magnitudes of the effects suggested by the model raise serious questions about the viability of these policies as currently designed.

Mathematical appendix 1: the model

The specific formulae of the model underlying the calculations reported in the text are derived in this section. There are three critical assumptions: first, entry by potential employers drives the expected capitalised stream of profit attributable to posting a new job vacancy to zero. Second, job destruction is efficient in the sense it takes place if and only if the sum of the expected capital values of separation to the two parties involved exceeds the sum of the values of continuation. Third, the wage rate underlying all value calculations is efficient in the sense that job destruction takes place if and only if both worker and employer prefer separation.

Let $J(x)$ represent the expected present value of future cash flow accruing to a job–worker match of productivity, x. Let c represent the cost of recruiting per vacancy per time period, k denote the match-specific cost of training a worker once hired, and Ψ be the government subsidy per new job created. Given that the flow rate at which vacancies and workers are matched is determined by an increasing, concave and linear homogeneous function of the numbers of vacancies and unemployed workers, the rate at which workers find employment is an increasing concave function of the vacancy:unemployment ratio, denoted as $m(\Theta)$. Free entry determines the equilibrium vacancy:unemployment ratio as that which equalises the cost of recruiting and training per worker hired to the employer's value of the currently most productive job type, which is indexed by $x=1$. In mathematical terms, this assumption implies that 'market tightness', represented by the vacancy:unemployment ratio θ, is determined by

$$c\theta = m(\theta)[J(1) - k + \psi] \tag{A1.1}$$

The wage paid in a match of productivity x is denoted as $w(x)$, a function to be determined. Both employer and worker contribute to a payroll tax at the rate π so that the employer's gross wage cost is $(1+\pi)w(x)$, the worker's net after-tax wage is $(1-\pi)w(x)$, and the total tax paid by the pair equals $2\pi w(x)$ given a match of productivity x. Future income is discounted at an exogenous rate r by all market participants and exogenous turnover occurs at rate δ. The productivity of any existing job is subject to uncertainty. Specifically, new values arrive at Poisson rate λ and are random draws from the distribution $F(z)$, a specification known to all participants. When a new value arrives which is less than the reservation productivity R, the employer pays out T equal to a lump sum firing tax or penalty *plus* any redundancy payment to the worker. Because an existing job has no value as a vacancy, the expected present value of match continuation given idiosyncratic productivity x to the employer, $J(x)$, satisfies the following asset pricing (Bellman) equation

$$\begin{aligned} rJ(x) = x - (1+\pi)w(x) - \delta J(x) + \gamma[\int_R^1 J(z)dF(z) \\ - F(R)T - J(x)]. \end{aligned} \tag{A1.2}$$

Analogously, the value of continuing to the worker, $W(x)$, is such that

$$rW(x) = (1-\pi)w(x) - \delta[W(x) - U] + \gamma[\int_R^1 W(z)dF(z) + F(R)[U+B] - W(x)] \tag{A1.3}$$

where U is the value of unemployed search and B is the expected present value of the worker's unemployment insurance (UI) benefit over a subsequent spell of unemployment *plus* any redundancy transfer received when a layoff occurs.

As reflected in (A1.2) and (A1.3), the employer must pay T but the worker receives $U+B$ in the event of a layoff. As separation is in the joint interest of both if and only if $U+B-T>J(x)+W(x)$, reservation productivity solves

$$S(R) = 0, \text{ where } S(x) = J(x) + W(x) - [U + B - T] \tag{A1.4}$$

represents the surplus value of continuing the match to the pair. (A1.2), (A1.3) and (A1.4) and a bit of algebra yield

$$(r+\delta+\gamma)S(x) = x - (r+\delta)[B-T] - 2\pi W(x) - rU + \gamma\int_R^1 S(z)dF(z), \tag{A1.5}$$

the functional equation that the surplus value function must solve.

To guarantee that job destruction, which occurs when productivity falls below the reservation value, is in the interest of both parties, we suppose that bilateral bargaining divides the surplus value of continuing, as determined by (A1.5), between the worker and employer. Letting β represent the worker's share, i.e.

$$\beta[J(x) + T] = (1 - \beta[W(x) - U - B], \tag{A1.6}$$

the wage rule that supports this division is

$$w(x)\frac{\beta[x+(r+\delta)T] + (1-\beta[rU+(r+\delta)B]}{\beta(1+\pi)+(1-\beta)(1-\pi)} \tag{A1.7}$$

by virtue of (A1.2)–(A1.6).

The fact that (A1.7) is linear in x implies that the function $S(x)$, which solves (A1.5), is also linear in x. Indeed, as $S'(x)=1-2\beta\pi w'(x)$ (A1.4), (A1.5) and (A1.7) imply

$$S(x) = \frac{(1-\pi)(x-R)}{(1-\pi+2\beta\pi)(r+\delta+\gamma)} \tag{A1.8}$$

where the reservation productivity is determined by

$$R+\frac{(1-\pi)\gamma}{(1-\pi-2\beta\pi)(r+\delta+\gamma)}\int_r^1(z-R)dF(z)$$
$$=rU+2\pi w(R)+(r+\delta)[B-T] \tag{A1.9}$$

The permanent income attributable to unemployed search, rU, is the sum of the value of leisure forgone when employed, b, *plus* the expected capital gain attributable to search, the product of the unemployment hazard $m(\theta)$ and the capital gain realised when employed in a vacant job. Therefore,

$$rU=b+m(\theta)[W(1)-U]$$
$$=b+m(\theta)\left[B+\frac{\beta(1-\pi)(1-R)}{(1-\pi+2\beta\pi)(r+\delta+\gamma)}\right] \tag{A1.10}$$

where the second equality follows by virtue of the bargaining outcome rule (A1.6) and the linear representation of surplus value (A1.8). Finally, these same two equations imply that the free entry condition (A1.1) can be rewritten as follows:

$$\frac{c\theta}{m(\theta)}=\frac{(1-\beta)(1-\pi)(1-R)}{(1-\pi+2\beta\pi)(r+\delta+\gamma)}-T+\psi-k. \tag{A1.11}$$

A labour market equilibrium is a triple (R,θ,rU) that solves equations (A1.9)–(A1.11). It is a simple matter to verify that a unique equilibrium exits if the value of leisure, b, is less than output in the most productive job $x=1$.

Mathematical appendix 2: functional forms and parameters

In both the USA and the UK, the unemployment benefit flow received by the worker depends on the wage paid during the previous spell of unemployment. Formally, after a job that had paid wage w the benefit flow received is ρw where ρ is the mandated replacement ratio. Given a maximum benefit period equal to τ, which is typically six months in the USA and effectively infinite in the UK, and the fact that the benefit ends if either the worker finds another job or the benefit period is exceeded by the subsequent length of the unemployment spell, the expected present value of the UI benefit stream during the spell *plus* any lump sum redundancy payment received by the worker at the beginning of the spell equal to ϕ is

$$B=\rho w(R)\frac{[1-e^{-\tau[r+m(\theta)]}]}{r+m(\theta)}+\phi \tag{A2.1}$$

Given that the UI tax paid is experience-rated as in the USA, the expected tax paid by an employer for laying off a worker plus any redundancy payment made at the job destruction date is

$$T = \varepsilon \rho w(R) \frac{[1 - e^{-\tau[r+m(\theta)]}]}{r + m(\theta)} + \phi \tag{A2.2}$$

where ϵ is the experience-rating parameter.

The particular forms of the unemployment hazard and the distribution of idiosyncratic productivity innovations functions used in the calculations are as follows

$$m(\theta) = \theta^{\eta} \tag{A2.3}$$

and

$$F(x) = \frac{x - \gamma}{1 - \gamma} \forall x \in [\gamma, 1] \tag{A2.4}$$

Given equations (A2.2) through (A2.4), one can compute the equilibrium reservation productivity and market tightness pair (R,Θ) using (A1.9)–(A1.11) for any specification of the parameters, such as the baseline values in table 17.1 (p. 000).

The dynamic laws of motion for the associated equilibrium level of market employment, represented by N, and the employment density over match productivity, denoted as $n(x)$, are represented by the differential equations

$$\dot{N} = m(\theta)(1 - N) - (\delta + \lambda F(R))N \tag{A2.5}$$

and

$$\dot{n}(x) = \lambda F'(x)N - (\delta + \lambda)n(x) \forall x < 1. \tag{A2.6}$$

Of course, the unemployment rate denoted as *un* in the text equals $1 - N^*$ where N^* is the steady-state solution to (A2.5). Letting $n(x)$ be the steady-state solution to (A2.6) enables us to calculate steady-state output and consumption, net output per participant, market *plus* home production *less* recruiting and training costs as

$$Y = \dot{N} + \int_R^1 (x - 1)n(x)dx \tag{A2.7}$$

$$C = Y + b(1 - N) - (c\theta + km(\theta)](1 - N). \tag{A2.8}$$

The steady-state effects of policy on unemployment, consumption and government transfers are obtained by computing the changes in these variables.

NOTE

The authors acknowledge the financial support of the National Science Foundation (NSF award no. SBR9308872, D.T. Mortensen principal investigator). The chapter was originally prepared for presentation at the CEPR Conference (Vigo, 24–27 September 1994). We appreciate the constructive suggestions of our discussants, Giuseppe Bertola and Michael Burda, and our colleagues in this project. Of course, the opinions expressed and any errors are our own responsibility.

REFERENCES

Abowd, J. and T. Lemieux, 1993. 'The effects of product market competition on collective bargaining agreements: the case of foreign competition in Canada', *Quarterly Journal of Economics*, **108**

Abraham, K.G. and S.N. Houseman, 1993. *Job Security in America*, Washington, CD: Brookings Institution

Anderson, P.M. and B.D. Meyer, 1993. 'The effects of unemployment insurance taxes and benefits on layoffs using firm and individual data, *Working Paper*, Northwestern University

Bentolila, S. and G. Bertola, 1990. 'Firing costs and labour demand in Europe: how bad is Eurosclerosis?', *Review of Economic Studies*, **57**, 381–402

Blanchard, O. and P. Diamond, 1989. 'The Beveridge curve', *Brookings Papers on Economic Activity*, **1**, 1–60

Blanchflower, O., P. Oswald and P. Sanfrey, 1993. 'Wages, profits and rent sharing', London School of Economics, Centre for Economic Performance, mimeo

Blank, R. and D. Card, 1991. 'Recent trends in insured and uninsured employment: is there an explanation?', *Quarterly Journal of Economics*, **106**, 1157–90

Burda, M.C., 1992. 'A note on firing costs and severance benefits in equilibrium unemployment', *Scandinavian Journal of Economics*, **94**, 479–89

Burdett, K. and R. Wright, 1990. 'Optimal firm size, taxes, and unemployment', *Journal of Public Economics*, **39**, 275–88

Brechling, F., 1981. 'Layoffs and unemployment insurance', in S. Rosen (ed.), *Studies in Labor Markets*, Chicago: Chicago University Press

Davis, S.J. and J. Haltiwanger, 1990. 'Gross job creation and destruction: microeconomic evidence and macroeconomic implications', *NBER Macroeconomics Annual*, Cambridge: MA, NBER

1992. 'Gross job creation, gross job destruction and employment reallocation, *Quarterly Journal of Economics*, **107**, 819–63

Devine, T.J. and N.M. Kiefer, 1991. *Empirical Labour Economics: The Search Approach*, Oxford: Oxford University Press

Diamond, P.A., 1982. 'Wage determination and efficiency in search equilibrium', *Review of Economic Studies*, **49**, 217–27

Feldstein, M.S., 1976. 'Temporary layoffs in the theory of unemployment', *Journal of Political Economy*, **84**, 837–57

Hamermesh, D.S., 1993. *Labor Demand*, Princeton: Princeton University Press

Katz, L.F. and B.D. Meyer, 1990. 'Unemployment insurance, recall expectations and unemployment outcomes', *Quarterly Journal of Economics*, **105**, 993–1002

Layard, P.R.G., S.J. Nickell and R.A. Jackman, 1991. *Unemployment: Macroeconomic Performance and the Labour Market*, Oxford: Oxford University Press

Lazear, E.P., 1990. 'Job security provisions and unemployment', *Quarterly Journal of Economics*, **55**, 699–726

Mortensen, D.T., 1982. 'The matching process as a noncooperative game', in J.J. McCall (ed.), *The Economics of Information and Uncertainty*, Chicago: University of Chicago Press

1994. 'The cyclical behavior of job and worker flows', *Journal of Economic Dynamics and Control*, **18**, 1121–42

Mortensen, D.T. and C.A. Pissarides, 1994. 'Job creation and job destruction in the theory of unemployment', *Review of Economic Studies*, **66**, 397–415

Phelps, E.S., 1994. 'Wage subsidy programs: alternative designs', chapter 7 in this volume

Pissarides, C.A., 1986. 'Unemployment and vacancies in Britain', *Economic Policy*, **3**, 499–559

1990. *Equlibrium Employment Theory*, Oxford: Basil Blackwell

Snower, D.J., 1994. 'The simple economics of benefit transfers', chapter 6 in this volume.

Van Ours, J.C., 1991. 'The efficiency of the Dutch labour market in matching unemployment and vacancies', *De Economist*, **139**

Discussion

GIUSEPPE BERTOLA

Chapter 17 is part of a recent and fast-growing literature based on the Mortensen and Pissarides (hereafter MP) extension of standard matching models. Since separations and hires occur simultaneously in reality, models of the labour market should allow for events affecting individual job–worker pairs rather than the aggregate economy. In previous models, the probability that such 'idiosyncratic' events would lead to match dissolution was taken to be exogenous, and no explanation could be provided for the variable intensity of labour reallocation over time and across labour markets; in the MP model, conversely, a realistic stochastic process for an individual job's productivity lets separation be the endogenous consequence of economic decisions, and gives the labour market some freedom of choice in determining the intensity of labour reallocation.

I was asked by Dennis Snower to discuss this growing literature's seminal paper, now published as Mortensen and Pissarides (1994). I am indeed very pleased to see that seminal idea followed up very much along the lines I thought would be fruitful. When extended to allow for realistic labour market institutions, the MP model provides a very elegant setting for addressing a number of important questions, and chapter 17 proves intriguing answers to some of them.

In chapter 17 and in other papers, Millard and Mortensen analyse the determinants of observed labour market outcomes across different institutional environments. They add to the basic framework a number of parameters representing real-life policy and institutions, and use US and UK evidence to carefully calibrate their effect on equilibrium unemployment and relocation intensity. Like all calibrations, this is a difficult exercise. In practice, the intensity of technological shocks at the level of individual matches is kept constant across policy experiments and, while the exercise is meaningful when the economies considered are as similar as the US and UK ones, the results have to be taken with a grain of salt. In particular, it should be noted that much more information is in principle available, about real-life labour and product markets than what is actually used to calibrate the model's parameters: if we do want to think of the USA and the UK, there are obvious differences in industry structure, firms' size distribution, and labour force composition. It would be nice to be able to use this information, along with that on labour reallocation, to calibrate all and not just some of the model's structural parameters, and perhaps even to test the model.

Chapter 17 uses the calibrated model to evaluate the effects of policy experiments. Here, too, the model provides very reasonable and interesting answers. If unemployment insurance and job security were reduced or eliminated, the model's labour market would generate more numerous and more productive jobs – i.e. its efficiency would be enhanced. This, of course, is qualitatively reasonable and unsurprising; still, it is quite interesting to find that efficiency-enhancing effects of labour market reform are quantitatively so important in a realistically calibrated model, and one would want to pursue the result further – for example, one might want to use such results as inputs to politico–economic stories focused on distributional conflicts, to try and explain why some countries' institutions are so much more strongly inefficiency-biased than others.

As usual, however, elegance and tractability have to be traded off against realism in model specification, and when looking further into structural calibration and policy issues one begins to encounter the limitations of the MP framework of analysis. It would be difficult, in fact, to let the model speak to many distinctive features of real-life economies, because the MP economy does not feature well-defined 'firms'. The demand side of the product market is populated by an unstructured constellation of production sites unrelated to each other rather than by firms (or sectors) whose overall level of employment matters for each job's productivity. For an abstract study of Diamond–Mortensen search externalities, of course, it is quite convenient and useful to model each job as a separate (stochastic) object; yet, the resulting model cannot really relate to industrial structure or size distribution data.

The particular nature of the labour market's demand side would also make it difficult to address the distributional side of real-life policy issues. In other models, one might try and interpret labour market institutions in terms of conflicts between 'workers' and a 'capitalist' class: with (stochastic) constant-returns production and free entry; conversely, there is really no factor of production other than labour, and 'firms' have no value. Perhaps more importantly, a model where workers are risk-neutral does provide a lucid analysis of many real-life policies' effects on productive efficiency, but is admittedly inadequate to address the insurance-provision role of job security and unemployment benefits in a world where individuals are risk-averse and labour income risk is imperfectly (if at all) insurable in existing markets. If models of this type could be extended to allow for risk-averse behaviour on the workers' part, the assumption of contingent renegotiation of wage rates should probably also be relaxed. In the model, in fact, the notion of 'job security' is rather different from its real-life counterpart: when wages are flexible, workers are exposed to product market shocks; real-life labour contracts try and address risk-sharing problems by specifying wages which react stickily (if at all) to changes in a firm's fortunes, at the cost of inefficient labour allocation and structural mismatches between labour supply and labour demand. The risk-neutrality assumed by matching models (for very good tractability reasons) prevents them from addressing such issues, and leads them to focus on possibly inefficient surplus-sharing rules in settings where wages are set by decentralised negotiations rather than centralised auction markets.

In summary, chapter 17 offers a very nice, compact, and quite realistic toolkit to describe the endogenous effect of institutions on labour market flows and unemployment. Yet, it is very important to understand exactly how this model (like all models) simplifies reality before drawing policy implications from the results. Efficiency considerations are important, but distributional issues are paramount, and models with linear utility and constant returns to labour cannot address the latter. A paper by

Bertola and Caballero (1994) does try and introduce decreasing returns to scale at the firm level, and a growing literature studies the equilibrium implications of uninsurable uncertainty. While we wait for further work in those areas to bear fruit, the relevant issues should be kept in mind.

REFERENCES

Bertola, G. and R.J. Caballero, 1994. 'Cross-sectional efficiency and labour hoarding in a matching model of unemployment', *Review of Economic Studies*, **61**, 435–57

Diamond, P.A., 1982. 'Wage determination and efficiency in search equilibrium' *Review of Economic Studies*, **49**, 217–27

Mortensen, D.T., 1982. 'The matching process as a noncooperative game', in J.J. McCall (ed.), *The Economics of Information and Uncertainty*, Chicago: University of Chicago Press

Mortensen, D.T. and C.A. Pissarides, 1994. 'Job creation and job destruction in the theory of unemployment', *Review of Economic Studies*, **66**, 397–415

Discussion

MICHAEL BURDA

Using the general equilibrium, job creation/destruction model of Mortensen and Pissarides (1994) (henceforth MP), Millard and Mortensen in chapter 17 (henceforth MM) pose the interesting question: to what extent are differences in US and UK unemployment rates due to differences in labour market policies and institutions? The gross flow approach, especially as elucidated in the MP model as well as Pissarides (1990), stresses the dynamics of labour markets at the expense of neglecting other, static aspects. In an economy with two states of labour force participation, the equilibrium unemployment rate is roughly equal to the product of an incidence rate and an average expected duration. Active labour market policies affect equilibrium unemployment by changing incidence, duration, or both. In addition to studying the effects on unemployment and output, MM have tried to ask the harder welfare (here: consumption) question in the context of their model, which is not necessarily a monotone decreasing function of the unemployment rate.

The equilibrium approach employed in chapter 17 has several advantage. First is the well known absence of $50 bills lying round on the sidewalk. Even though there are frictions built into the model, agents are free to do the best they can under the circumstances to deal with them and exploit available profit opportunities. Second, the model explicitly analyses flows of jobs (and thereby workers) in the labour market. Job creation and destruction have efficiency implications in the MP model, which can be affected by policy. Third, the model takes an all-encompassing view of wage determination, via a Nash bargain which splits gains from matching. Finally, and most importantly, it admits a positive social value of unemployment.

The MP model represents yet another set of lenses through which we can study complex processes in labour markets; chapter 17 is a useful complement to, but by no means a substitute for, other modes of labour market policy analysis. One of the most striking results of the chapter, I found, is that severance pay in the MP economy entails higher efficiency and welfare costs than unemployment benefits. The MP model predicts a productivity effect for severance pay which works through the job destruction margin; this effect is less relevant for unemployment benefits, which have primary impact on wage-setting. According to MM, there are large welfare gains from the elimination of redundancy pay, although it accounts for little of the UK–US unemployment differential in the end. Perhaps surprisingly, MM find that apart from severance benefits there is little welfare gain from adopting US-style institutions (although the average unemployment rate would be unambiguously lower). The model attributes current long durations and low unemployment incidence in the UK compared with the USA to a function of labour market policy; in fact, it 'over-predicts' these differences.

The first set of concerns I have involves choice of parameter values, which puzzled me in two respects. First, the parameter β, summarising the power of workers in bargaining, has no simple mapping to reality, but rather represents the subjective estimate of the authors. They associate higher values of this parameter with worker insider power and the 'lack of coordination' in collective bargaining, presumably invoking arguments found in Calmfors and Driffill (1988). That the USA is much less coordinated than the UK would imply a *high* value in the former; yet the discussion based on US unionisation rates implied a *lower* value. I am not sure where this leaves us in the end, since variation of this parameter has large effects on incidence, duration and unemployment in equilibrium

The second key parameter is the layoff penalty ϕ, which drives most of the interesting welfare results. The authors' model makes the interesting contribution that, unlike Lazear (1990) and Burda (1992), severance payments received by the employee longer cancel out. In reality, however the assumed differences between the USA and the UK may be exaggerated. Emerson (1988) reports that only 23 per cent of UK firms surveyed considered redundancy payments a barrier to additional employment; when compared with other EU countries surveyed, these numbers are modest indeed: 78 per cent for Italy, 63 per cent for Belgium, and 46 per cent for Germany. In fact, the UK was the lowest of all countries surveyed. How important can firing costs be here? This is especially true in light of the fact that severance benefits are often observed in excess of the legal minimum; in the USA, 'golden parachutes' are indeed paid voluntarily to many workers in the absence of mandatory rules, or are stipulated in collectively negotiated contracts.

A second set of concerns arises with model's ability to capture long-term developments in the labour market. While the model can be calibrated to account for observed cross-country differences in unemployment, how well can it account for unemployment and its breakdown (incidence versus duration) in the UK and the USA over time? Can it explain why labour markets were so tight in the UK with low unemployment incidence and duration in the 1960s, while the USA had tight labour markets but higher incidence and unemployment rates at the same time? What was the proximate cause of the rise in UK unemployment since the 1970s? If the answer is a shift in the distribution of match productivity, then why did this occur in the UK and not the USA?

Finally, chapter 17 neglects a broader set of labour market policies currently under discussion in OECD countries. For instance, direct job creation programmes are often mentioned in the UK, especially when combined with a simultaneous reduction of the jobless benefit; they represent another way of directly increasing the supply of vacancies and circumventing the matching process. It would be interesting to study the effect of such a policy on equilibrium unemployment. One might also consider measures which improve the matching process; even if these measures cannot be specified, one could ask: what is the welfare implication of a 1 per cent improvement in matching efficiency? It should be mentioned that MM assume the matching process to be the same in the USA and the UK, although search intensity, and thereby the efficiency of the matching process, is likely to depend on benefit levels. Yet another undiscussed policy area is minimum wages and wage councils guidelines which, when binding, may 'freeze out' low-productivity matches independent of worker power.

Beyond this, a number of other aspects of labour markets are simply not susceptible to analysis in the MP model. In its current form, the MP model cannot answer questions concerning (i) effects of aggregate demand on the labour market, (ii) dynamic interactions of worker and job flows, (iii) insider–outsider phenomena, (iv) hysteresis stemming from the deterioration of skills and labour force attachment, (v) dynamics of non-participation and thereby the ultimate incidence of labour taxes (labour force participation is exogenous), (vi) the evolution of the capital stock, (vii) ranking and other forms of heterogeneity among workers associated with long-term unemployment, and (viii) issues of tastes and risk aversion. For this reason, we should be somewhat suspicious of the welfare exercises in the chapter, even if we like the model, as I do. This is my reaction to the finding that hiring subsidies increase incidence and raise unemployment – even though the logic is plausible, how robust is that result to wage rigidities and other institutional influences on wage formation?

Finally, it is worth noting that the model leaves open the question of why policy parameters currently observed were chosen. If they are purposefully chosen, presumably on the basis of tastes for leisure or risk-aversion in the respective populations, wouldn't a change in these policies be welfare-*reducing*? It is not a cheap shot to ask where the institutions come from, and since policies are different in different countries, whether they should not be valued differently. Either they are a response to tastes and preferences, in which case they should be left alone, or they are in place to correct some market failure, i.e. the lack of an efficient capital or insurance market. In either case estimates of 'welfare effects' in chapter 17 are likely to be biased.

REFERENCES

Burda, M., 1992. 'A note on firing costs and severance benefits in equilibrium unemployment', *Scandinavian Journal of Economics*, **94**, 479–89

Calmfors, L. and J. Driffill, 1988. 'Centralization of wage bargaining and macroeconomic performance', *Economic Policy*, **6**, 13–61

Emerson, M., 1988. 'Regulation or deregulation of the labour market: policy regimes for the recruitment and dismissal of employees in the industrialized countries', *European Economic Review*, **12**, 777–817

Lazear, E., 1990. 'Job security provisions and unemployment', *Quarterly Journal of Economics*, **55**, 699–726

Mortensen, D.T. and C.A. Pissarides, 1994. 'Job creation and job destruction in the theory of unemployment; *Review of Economic Studies*, **66**, 397–415

Pissarides, C.A., 1990. *Equilibrium Unemployment Theory*, Oxford: Basil Blackwell

Index